£9
ma
20/08

Published in honour of Seán McGrail

CONNECTED BY THE SEA

*Proceedings of the Tenth International Symposium
on Boat and Ship Archaeology
Roskilde 2003*

Edited by Lucy Blue, Fred Hocker
and Anton Englert

ISBSA 10

Hosted by
The Viking Ship Museum, Roskilde
The National Museum of Denmark Centre for Maritime Archaeology
The National Museum of Denmark Institute of Maritime Archaeology
The Centre for Maritime Archaeology, University of Southampton

With support from
The National Research Foundation of Denmark
The National Humanities Research Council of Denmark
Queen Margrethe's Fund

Oxbow Books

Published by
Oxbow Books, Park End Place, Oxford OX1 1HN

© Oxbow Books and the authors 2006

ISBN 978 1 84217 228 5   1 84217 228 X

A CIP record for this book is available from the British Library

Cover: Photograph by Werner Karrasch, Viking Ship Museum

This book is available direct from
Oxbow Books, Park End Place, Oxford, OX1 1HN
(Phone: 01865-241249; Fax: 01865-794449)

and

The David Brown Book Company
PO Box 511, Oakville, CT 06779, USA
(Phone: 860-945-9329; Fax: 860-945-9468)

and

via our website
www.oxbowbooks.com

Printed in Great Britain by
Short Run Press, Exeter

Contents

List of Contributors

JONATHAN ADAMS
Centre for Maritime Archaeology, School of Humanities,
University of Southampton, Southampton,
SO17 1BJ, United Kingdom
Email: jjra@soton.ac.uk

JOHN ATKIN
University of Michel de Montaigne-Bordeaux III,
19, avenue du Prince Noir, 33750 Camarsac, France
john.atkin@etu.u-bordeaux3.fr

JENS AUER
104 Lower Road, Salisbury, Wiltshire,
SP2 9NL, United Kingdom
j.auer@wessexarch.co.uk

LAWRENCE E. BABITS
Maritime Studies, East Carolina University,
Greenville, NC 27858, USA

KROUM N. BATCHVAROV
INA Research Associate, 4200 Scotland, Apt 58,
Houston, TX 77007, USA
batchvarov@neo.tamu.edu

TOMASZ BEDNARZ
Polish Maritime Museum in Gdańsk,
ul. Ołwianka 9-13, 80-751 Gdańsk, Poland
t.bednarz@cmm.pl

CARLO BELTRAME
Università Ca' Foscari Venezia, Università degli studi
della Tuscia Viterbo,
Dorsoduro, 269 30123 Venezia, Italy
archeonautica@libero.it

SWARUP BHATTACHARYYA
18-D, Bagbazar Street, Kolkata 700003, India
saranga_nao@yahoo.com

LUCY BLUE
Centre for Maritime Archaeology,
School of Humanities,
University of Southampton, Southampton,
SO17 1BJ, United Kingdom
lkb@soton.ac.uk

RONALD BOCKIUS
Römisch-Germanisches Zentralmuseum,
Forschungsbereich Antike Schiffahrt, Mainz, Germany

GIULIA BOETTO
Centre Camille Jullian UMR 6573 CNRS - Université
de Provence, Maison Méditerranéenne des Sciences de
l'Homme, 5, rue du Château de l'Horloge BP 647,
F-13094 Aix-en-Provence, France
gibo23@libero.it

MAURO BONDIOLI
Via Strada Vecchia, 68/1 42011 Bagnolo in Piano (RE),
Italy

CLAIRE CALCAGNO
79 Sturges Road,
Medford,
MA 02155, USA
clairec@mit.edu

FRANK CANTELAS
Maritime Studies, East Carolina University,
Greenville, NC 27858, USA

FILIPE CASTRO
Nautical Archaeology Program,
Department of Anthropology, Texas A&M University,
College Station, TX 77843-4352 USA
fvcastro@tamu.edu

CARL OLOF CEDERLUND
Södertörns högskola (University college),
Box 4101, 141 89 Huddinge, Sweden
carl-olof.cederlund@sh.se

JOHN COLES
Fursdon Mill Cottage, Thorverton, Devon,
EX5 5JS, United Kingdom
jmcoles@btinternet.com

OLE CRUMLIN-PEDERSEN
Former Head of Institute and Centre for Maritime
Archaeology, Danish National Museum, Roskilde,
The Viking Ship Museum, Roskilde Box 298,
DK-4000 Roskilde, Denmark
ocp@vikingeskibsmuseet.dk

AOIFE DALY
Nationalmuseet, Forsknings- & Formidlingsafdelingen
Dansk Middelalder & Renæssance, Frederiksholms Kanal
12, DK - 1220 Copenhagen K, Denmark
aoife.daly@natmus.dk

ROBERT DOMZAL
Polish Maritime Museum, Gdańsk, Poland

MARION DELHAYE

ANTON ENGLERT
Viking Ship Museum, Vindeboder 12
DK-4000 Roskilde, Denmark
ae@vikingeskibsmuseet.dk

MIRAN ERIČ
Institute for the Protection of Cultural Heritage of Slovenia,
Cankarjeva 4, SI-1000 Ljubljana, Slovenia
miran.eric@guest.arnes.si

VALERIE FENWICK
4 Nightingale Mews, Royal Victoria Country Park,
Netley Abbey., SO31 5GB, United Kingdom
vierrafirma@aol.com

THOMAS FINDERUP
Viking Ship Museum, Vindeboder 12
DK-4000 Roskilde, Denmark

ANDREJ GASPARI
Institute for the Mediterranean Heritage,
Science and Research Centre of Koper,
University of Primorska, Garibaldijeva 18,
SI - 6000 Koper, Slovenia
andrej.gaspari@siol.net

EDWIN AND JOYCE GIFFORD
Little Pundells, Brockishill Road, Bartley,
Southampton, SO40 2LN, United Kingdom
joycegiff@waitrose.com

MORTEN GØTHCHE
Viking Ship Museum, Vindeboder 12,
DK-4000 Roskilde, Denmark
mg@vikingeskibsmuseet.dk

MATTHEW HARPSTER
Dibner Institute, MIT,
Cambridge, MA USA

DAVID HINTON
Archaeology, School of Humanities,
Avenue Campus, University of Southampton,
Southampton, United Kingdom
dah5@soton.ac.uk

FRED HOCKER
National Maritime Museums of Sweden,
Box 27131, S-102 52, Stockholm, Sweden
fred.hocker@maritima.se

ANDRÉ F.L. VAN HOLK
Nieuw Land Erfgoed Centrum (NLE), Oostvaardersdijk
01-13, 8242 PA Lelystad, The Netherlands
a.vanholk@nieuwlanderfgoedcentrum.nl

AB HOVING
Rijksmuseum, P.O.Box 74888,
1070 DN Amsterdam, The Netherlands
a.hoving@rijksmuseum.nl

GEORGE INDRUSZEWSKI
Vikingeskibsmuseet, Vindeboder 12,
DK-4000 Roskilde, Denmark
gi@vikingeskibsmuseet.dk

YAACOV KAHANOV
Recanati Institute for Maritime Studies,
University of Haifa, Israel
yak@research.haifa.ac.il

SVEN KALMRING
Stiftung Schleswig-Holsteinische Landesmuseen Schloß
Gottorf, Archäologisches Landesmuseum,
Forschungsprojekt Haithabu, Schloß Gottorf
D-24837 Schleswig, Germany
ESF.Haithabu@t-online.de

INESE KARKLINA
University of Latvia, Kundzinsala 13. line 9-2
LV1005 Riga, Latvia
inesekarklina@inbox.lv

BRAD LOEWEN

OLE MAGNUS
Rebslageriet, Borupvej 51,
8543 Hornslet, Denmark
rebslaaeriet@mail.tele.dk

CHRISTINA MARANGOU
Neophytou Douca 6, Athens 106 74, Greece
christina.marangou@eudoramail.com

SABRINA MARLIER
Centre Camille Jullian (CNRS-Université de Provence),
Maison Méditerranéenne des Sciences de l'Homme,
5 rue du Château de l'Horloge,
BP 647, 13094 Aix-en-Provence Cedex 2, France
marliersab_archeonavale@yahoo.fr

List of Contributors

SEÁN MCGRAIL
Centre for Maritime Archaeology, School of Humanities,
University of Southampton,
Southampton, SO17 1BJ, United Kingdom

KEITH MEVERDEN
Maritime Studies, East Carolina University,
Greenville, NC 27858, USA

HADAS MOR
Department of Maritime Civilizations,
University of Haifa, Israel

SØREN NIELSEN
Head of the boatyard, The Viking Ship Museum,
Vindeboder 12, 4000 Roskilde, Denmark
sn@vikingeskibsmuseet.dk

MARCUS NILSSON
Virtual Maritime Institute,
Polgatan 8.F, S-21611 Limhamn, Sweden
mln1318@linuxmail.org

WALDEMAR OSSOWSKI
Polish Maritime Museum,
ul. Ołowianka 9-13, 80-751 Gdańsk, Poland

A.J. PARKER
University of Bristol, 10 Montrose Avenue,
Redland, Bristol, BS6 6EQ, United Kingdom
A.J.Parker@bristol.ac.uk

PATRICE POMEY
Directeur de recherche au CNRS, Directeur du Centre
Camille Jullian, Archéologie méditerranéenne et
africaine, Centre Camille Jullian (UMR 6573),
Université de Provence-CNRS,
Maison Méditerranéenne des Sciences de l'Homme,
5, rue du Château de l'Horloge, 13090,
Aix-en-Provence, France
pomey@mmsh.univ-aix.fr

CHRISTIAN RADTKE
Archäologisches Landesmuseum in der Stiftung,
Schleswig-Holsteinische Landesmuseen Schloß Gottorf,
D 24837 Schleswig, Germany
bibliothek.alm@t-online.de

EDOARDO RICCARDI
Subacquea Navale Marittime,
Via A. Faggi 13, 17028 Bergeggi, Savona, Italy

ERIC RIETH
CNRS (LAMOP-UMR 8589),
Musée national de la Marine, Palais de Chaillot,
75116 Paris, France
e.rieth.cnrs@libertysurf.fr

PATRICIA SIBELLA
University of Michel de Montaigne-Bordeaux III,
Centre Camille Jullian, Aix-en-Provence, France.
psibella@hotmail.com

MARIJA ŠMALCELJ
Department of Archaeology,
Faculty of Philosophy, University of Zagreb,
Ivana Lucica 3, 10000 Zagreb, Croatia
marija.smalcelj@zg.hinet.hr

PETR SOROKIN
The Institute of the History of Material Culture,
Russian Academy of Science/191186, Dvorzovaja nab.18.,
St. Petersburg, Russia
Petrarh@PS2333.spb.edu

BÉATRICE SZEPERTYSKI
Laboratoire d'Analyses et d'Expertises en Archéologie et
Oeuvres d'Art, 10, rue Sainte Thérèse
33000 Bordeaux, France

ULRIKE TEIGELAKE
Landschaftsverband Rheinland,
Archäologischer Park/Regionalmuseum Xanten,
Trajanstr. 4, 46509 Xanten, Germany
uteigelake@freenet.de

KATRIN THIER
OED, Oxford University Press, Great Clarendon Street,
Oxford, OX2 6DP, United Kingdom
katrin.thier@oup.com

DANIEL VERMONDEN
Centre d'Anthropologie Culturelle, Institut de
Sociologie, Université Libre de Bruxelles (ULB),
Avenue Jeanne 44, CP 124, B-1050 Bruxelles, Belgium
Daniel.Vermonden@ulb.ac.be

TIMM WESKI
München, Germany

JAMES WHARRAM
James Wharram Designs, Greenbank Road,
Devoran, Truro, Cornwall TR3 6PJ, United Kingdom
wharram@wharram.com

TOMASZ WAZNY
Academy of Fine Arts, Laboratory of Dendrochronology,
ul. Wybrzeże Kościuszkowskie 37,
PL-00379 Warszawa, Poland
twazny@mercury.ci.uw.edu.pl

STÉPHANIE WICHA
Centre Camille Jullian, (UMR 6573, CNRS et Université
de Provence) Maison Méditerranéenne des Sciences de
l'Homme, 5 rue du Château de l'Horloge, B.P.647, 13094
Aix en Provence cedex 2, France
Institut Méditerranéen d'Ecologie et de Paléoécologie
(UMR 6116 CNRS- Aix Marseille) Faculté des Sciences
et Techniques de St Jérôme, avenue Escadrille Normandie
Niemen, 13397 Marseille, France
Wichafr@yahoo.fr

Preface

The 10th International Symposium of Boat and Ship Archaeology was held in Roskilde, Denmark 21–25 September, 2003 and was attended by more than 200 participants from 26 countries. The host institutions were the Viking Ship Museum in Roskilde, the National Museum of Denmark's Institute of Maritime Archaeology (NMU) and the Centre for Maritime Archaeology of the University of Southampton. In addition, the National Museum's Centre for Maritime Archaeology (NMF) took a leading role in the organisation of the symposium and was the initial administrative home. Unfortunately, NMF closed its doors just three weeks before the symposium began, in accordance with the grant from the National Research Foundation under which it had been founded in 1993, but is still listed here as one of the official sponsors.

The theme of the meeting was "Connected by the Sea," to emphasise the role of the sea, seafaring and watercraft as bridges rather than barriers between cultures. The administrative reality of cultural heritage management in recent decades is that maritime archaeology tends to take place within national borders, with a national focus. Yet the very premise of seafaring is the desire to travel beyond the horizon, to establish contact with other places and cultures. The history of maritime endeavour thus cannot be understood if examined on the basis of modern national boundaries, and the conference theme was chosen in order to encourage the maritime archaeological community to think in international terms. A grant was sought and received from the Danish Humanities Research Council (SHF) in order to provide assistance to scholars attending from countries that are generally perceived as less traditional bases of maritime archaeology than western Europe, the Mediterranean and North America. And a key theme of the meeting was long-distance seafaring and the connections between cultures.

The theme of connection was also explored in the context of the coastal zone, where the land meets the sea. As the purpose of maritime travel is to reach a particular destination, seafaring is oriented around the land as much as it is the sea. An entire day of the symposium was focused on this theme, particularly in relation to the development of shipbuilding, as well as coastal seafaring. A third aspect of the main theme was the role of maritime archaeology as a connection between different research disciplines. This field has, since its beginnings, attracted a wide range of specialists in maritime engineering, navigation, as well as craftsmen, in addition to traditional academic archaeologists. There is thus a long history of interdisciplinary study, with a particular emphasis at previous ISBSA's on the theory and practice of experimental archaeology. As Roskilde has been the home of a long-term program of sailing replica building and testing, it was only natural that one day of formal sessions should be devoted to this topic. In addition, one day was spent on the practical exploration of the Roskilde approach to experimental archaeology. Participants divided up into groups to try their hands at splitting oak logs into planks, testing Viking woodworking tools, hand-laying bast rope, and sailing the Viking Ship Museum's fleet of reconstructions and traditional small craft. Many of the most spirited discussions of the entire week arose on the water or in the boatyard, and several of the presentations made by Roskilde's craftsmen-researchers have been developed into papers for publication in this volume.

During the planning for this symposium, it was thought appropriate to recognise the longevity of the ISBSA and its continuing relevance to the field of maritime archaeology. This was the 10th meeting, at regular three-year intervals, since the initial one-off symposium held at the National Maritime Museum in Greenwich, England in 1976. This meeting had been conceived by the museum's director, Basil Greenhill, and the organisation and publication were entrusted to the head of the underwater archaeology unit, Seán McGrail. Professor McGrail has continued to be active in the organisation and publication of subsequent meetings, and it was the desire of the organising committee to commemorate his dedication to the symposia on the occasion of the 10th meeting. Thus it was decided that the publication of the proceedings would also be a *Festschrift* for Seán, and he was asked to give a plenary lecture during one evening. In typical McGrail fashion, he used this occasion to challenge us all to do a better job of publishing the results of experimental archaeology! This lecture appears in this volume as well, even if it is not traditional to include a paper by the honouree in a *Festschrift*. It was also decided to invite papers in honour of Seán from several of his colleagues who were not able to attend the meeting but who have worked in the areas in which he has concentrated his own research.

All of this material, along with several poster presentations that the organising committee thought deserved publication, makes for a very large book, one of the heaviest ISBSA publications to date. It is our hope that it will be used as much as previous proceedings, most of which end up quite dog-eared and festooned with bookmarks, rather than simply act as bookshelf ballast.

Acknowledgments

Although the symposium was primarily funded by the sponsoring institutions from their operating funds and by the participants' fees, grants were most gratefully received from the Danish Humanities Research Council and from Queen Margrethe's Fund. The organising committee in Roskilde had the assistance and advice of several previous ISBSA organisers, Patrice Pomey (Tatihou 1994), Jerzy Litwin (Gdańsk 1997) and Carlo Beltrame (Venice 2000). Their participation was most welcome. Many of the technical and administrative staff of the Viking Ship Museum, NMU and NMF committed untold hours to the answering of queries, booking of accommodation, organisation of transport, and the multitude of other tasks that have to be done in order for a conference to function. We are extremely grateful to those whose labour behind the scenes made the conference function, even when electrical power failed over most of Denmark just before one of the afternoon sessions commenced! Oxbow Books, who have published several other ISBSA proceedings, have been unfailingly helpful and generous in agreeing to fund the printing and distribution of this volume. Finally, Lucy Blue and Fred Hocker are very grateful to Anton Englert, who repeatedly tried to downplay his role in the editing and production of this volume, but without whom it would not have seen the light of day.

Keynote address:
An international forum for nautical research 1976–2003

Ole Crumlin-Pedersen

Recently, when sorting out some of my papers I came across the file of the first *International Symposium on Boat and Ship Archaeology*, held at Greenwich in 1976 (Fig. 1.1). This cast my mind back to those formative years in the 1970's when research in maritime archaeology in northern Europe became truly internationalised for the first time.

The key person leading this international development was Basil Greenhill, who in 1967, at the age of 47, had been appointed director of the National Maritime Museum in Greenwich, having completed a diplomatic career that had taken him to Pakistan, Afghanistan, Japan and Canada. One might think this was a strange choice but Mr. Greenhill was already an esteemed maritime historian, having published the two volumes on *The Merchant Schooners* in 1951 and 1957 which were later printed in three new editions as the standard work on the subject (Greenhill 1968). In 1967 *Westcountrymen in Prince Edward's Isle* came out (Greenhill and Giffard 1967, 3rd edition in 2003), in 1971 his book on *Boats and Boatmen of East Pakistan* followed, and in 1976 the *Archaeology of the Boat*, published very appropriately in the year of the first ISBSA meeting and later in a revised new edition (Greenhill 1976, 1995).

Basil Greenhill had considerable talents as an organiser, both within the museum and in establishing international contacts, such as the formation in 1972 of

Fig. 1.1. Group photograph of (most of) the participants in ISBSA 1, outside the Queen's House, National Maritime Museum, Greenwich in September 1976. Photo National Maritime Museum, Greenwich.

the International Congress of Maritime Museums. In the course of a few years he had transformed the museum from what has been described as "a dusty shrine to Admiral Horatio Nelson" into a more dynamic and wide-ranging institution dealing with a much broader range of maritime matters than ever previously imagined.

An interest in the history of boats and ships had followed Basil Greenhill ever since, at the age of 16, he was given the chance to join *Viking*, one of the last surviving large cargo-carrying, square-riggers, sailing from the Severn to her home port, Mariehamn in the Åland Islands, calling at Elsinore in Denmark en route. This early experience from his first visits to foreign countries obviously had a strong influence on him, since Denmark and Finland were amongst the first places he visited after his appointment as museum director, and he subsequently maintained strong links with both countries.

From Denmark, Basil Greenhill brought back to Greenwich some of the inspiration that was to materialise in the 'Department of the Archaeology of the Ship', that was established in the museum in 1973. By 1976 the department had developed into a regular research unit, the Archaeological Research Centre (ARC), under the direction Seán McGrail, and employed a staff of scholars including maritime historians, archaeologists, anthropologists and conservation specialists to deal with the challenges of the archaeology of the boat.

The archaeology of the boat was a subject that had already been brought into focus in 1970 when a well preserved 10th-century vessel was found at Graveney in the Thames Marshes and excavated by local archaeologists (Fenwick 1978). On this occasion a link was established between the archaeologists of the British Museum, who at that time had little knowledge about boats, and the staff of the Maritime Museum at Greenwich, who had limited archaeological experience. The find was eventually taken to Greenwich for conservation, and research into the vessel was undertaken by Eric McKee. A member of the British Museum staff who had been involved with the re-excavation of the Sutton Hoo ship burial (Bruce-Mitford 1975) assisted with editing the final publication (Fenwick 1978). The remarkably successful ARC unit remained functioning for ten years until, regrettably, in 1986, the entire unit was dismantled by Basil Greenhill's successor.

However, another incident provided further impetus for Basil Greenhill to pursue his interest in maritime archaeology; the discovery by Ted Wright of the remains of a number of Bronze Age boats buried in the Humber mudflats at North Ferriby (Wright 1990). Wright is reported as having suggested to Greenhill that Greenwich Museum should assemble the ship and boat archaeologists of the world and host a seminar on the North Ferriby and other early boat finds. Seán McGrail subsequently expanded the theme of the seminar to encompass a general focus on sources and techniques in boat archaeology (McGrail 1977). However, without Basil Greenhill's sincere interest in the subject and his organisational talents, the seminar would probably have never taken place. Basil Greenhill maintained an interest in the subject until his death in 2003, issuing with Sam Manning *The Evolution of the Wooden Ship* in 1988, as well as writing and editing numerous other books on maritime subjects. As late as 2000, he contributed to the scholarly discussion on European medieval ships and their possible connections to traditional boat types in the Indian subcontinent (Greenhill 2000).

Immediately following the symposium in September 1976, a hand-picked selection of the participants met in Basil Greenhill's office to discuss any further steps to be taken. It was generally agreed that such symposia should continue to be held at regular three yearly intervals. It was also suggested that a permanent organisational structure should be set up to support these meetings that would also aim to establish a common terminology and a database with information about all relevant finds. It was suggested that such a structure would require a financial basis for a semi-permanent staff with secretariat and a governing body with a president. I was, however, opposed to this proposed structure, fearing that it would soon divert the initiative away from active researchers to museum personnel wanting to promote their museums without themselves being engaged in research. By keeping the organisation of future meetings in the hands of active researchers, the initiative would live as long as there was a need for it – and it would die out once the interest or relevance faded. In the end, this less traditional approach was finally accepted, and a model established which has functioned until today. A working group is selected to organise the next symposium having the new host as chairman and three or four of the previous ISBSA hosts as advisors in the selection of themes and the practicalities of the meeting itself, including the publication of the proceedings (McGrail 2000).

This model has functioned well over the years, with Seán McGrail having edited many of the proceedings commencing with the first symposium published in the Archaeological Series of the National Maritime Museum

and the British Archaeological Reports series (McGrail 1977). The second meeting took place in 1979 in the newly established Deutsches Schiffahrtsmuseum in Bremerhaven, Germany. It was hosted by Detlev Ellmers and had medieval ships and harbours as the main theme since the Bremen cog was then being re-assembled in the museum (McGrail 1979).

The third meeting was held 1982 in Stockholm, Sweden, where Carl Olof Cederlund organised the themes around post-Medieval ships, since the *Vasa* and other large and well preserved Renaissance and later ships served as the focal point of Swedish maritime archaeology (Cederlund 1985). At the fourth meeting in 1985, focus moved away from Northern Europe to the Atlantic seaboard where Octavio Lixa Filgueiras in Lisbon, Portugal, invited his international colleagues to discuss local boats from Iberia and around the world (Filgueiras 1988).

At the fifth session of ISBSA in 1988, Reinder Reinders in Amsterdam, the Netherlands, took up the theme of the carvel construction techniques from antiquity to modern times with an approach inspired by Olof Hasslöf's distinction between shell- and skeleton-based design (Hasslöf 1972; Reinders and Paul 1991). For the sixth seminar in 1991, held at the Viking Ship Museum in Roskilde, Denmark, the interaction between different shipbuilding traditions was the main theme (Westerdahl 1994). The idea of holding the seminar outside the big cities as was the case with ISBSA 6, was also adopted by Patrice Pomey and Eric Rieth for ISBSA 7, held in 1994 on the small island of Tatihou, off the coast of Normandy in France. The publication edited by the organisers was delayed due to factors beyond their control, but finally came out in 1999 (Pomey and Rieth 1999).

As there was a strong interest in engaging our Eastern European colleagues as much as possible in the symposia, the invitation from Jerzy Litwin to hold the eighth ISBSA in Gdańsk, Poland, in 1997, was gladly accepted. Here the obvious theme was the interaction between river navigation, coastal and deep-sea seafaring (Litwin 2000). Since the Mediterranean and extra-European regions had also been poorly represented during the early meetings of ISBSA, there was a need to widen the field of contact, and the first move into the Mediterranean came with the acceptance of Carlo Beltrame's invitation for ISBSA 9 to take place in 2000 in Venice with its famous Arsenal and with ships and shipyards as a main theme (Beltrame 2003).

Set against this background, the choice of Roskilde to act once again as host for the tenth session of ISBSA in 2003 may seem to counteract attempts to widen the scope of the institution. However, the fact that scholars from as many as 28 different countries are attending the present symposium is a strong indication that the most important criteria for participants to travel from all over the world is not the location but the potential of the host country to provide a stimulating basis for discussions and workshop activities (Fig. 1.2). In our case, we feel that the collaborative efforts of the Viking Ship Museum, the National

Museum of Denmark and the University of Southampton in hosting this meeting has a great deal to offer, not least the results of intense international research in maritime archaeology that has been undertaken at these institutions over the last ten tears.

Just as the Archaeological Research Centre at Greenwich was only funded for ten years, the Centre for Maritime Archaeology of the National Museum of Denmark, situated here in Roskilde with close links to the Viking Ship Museum, has now been closed down after ten golden years. The last issue in the series of newsletters published by the Centre presents the history and achievements of the Centre in widening the approach to maritime archaeology over the ten years since 1993 (Crumlin-Pedersen 2003), which now includes many aspects of life in the past that were influenced by the interaction between man and the sea, but which were previously only seen from a landlubber's perspective.

In contrast to the situation at Greenwich however, and in spite of severe budget cuts and a reduced staff, maritime archaeology has a future in Roskilde. This has been demonstrated during this seminar in the efforts of the new generation at the Viking Ship Museum. The aims are to carry on and further develop the work which has been on going since the museum opened in 1969 (Damgård-Sørensen and Bill 2003). Thus, the present meeting is not the funeral feast for the Centre that is now closing but a demonstration of a strong will to find new ways in the years ahead to pursue the archaeological study of the interaction of man with the sea in the past, a theme for which Denmark has huge potential and consequently therefore a strong research obligation.

Fig. 1.2. Group photograph of (most of) the participants in ISBSA 10, in front of the Skuldelev 2 longship reconstruction at the Viking Ship Museum's boatyard in Roskilde, September 2003. Photo Werner Karrasch, Viking Ship Museum.

References

Beltrame, C. (ed), 2003, *Boats, Ships and Shipyards: proceedings of the Ninth International Symposium on Boat and Ship Archaeology, Venice 2000*. Oxbow Books. Oxford.

Bruce-Mitford, R.L.S., 1975, *The Sutton Hoo Ship-Burial vol. I. Excavations, Background, the Ship, Dating and Inventory*. British Museum. London.

Cederlund, C.O. (ed), 1985, *Postmedieval Boat and Ship Archaeology*. BAR International Series 256. Oxford.

Crumlin-Pedersen, O., 2003, Ten golden years for maritime archaeology in Denmark, 1993–2003. *Maritime Archaeology Newsletter from Roskilde*, 20: 4–43.

Damgård-Sørensen, T., and Bill, J., 2003, Maritime Archaeology in Roskilde – a glimpse into the future. *Maritime Archaeology Newsletter from Roskilde*, 20: 48–51.

Fenwick, V. (ed.) 1978, *The Graveney Boat*. BAR British Series 53. Oxford

Filgueiras, O.L. (ed), 1988, *Local Boats*. BAR International Series 438, I–II. Oxford.

Greenhill, B., 1968, *The Merchant Schooners I–II*. David and Charles. Newton Abbot Devon.

Greenhill, B., 1995, *The Archaeology of Boats and Ships. An Introduction*. Conway Maritime. London.

Greenhill, B., 1976, *Archaeology of the Boat: a new introductory study*. A. and C. Black. London.

Greenhill, B., 1988, *The Evolution of the Wooden Ship*. Batsford. London.

Greenhill, B., 2000, The Mysterious Hulk. *The Mariner's Mirror* 86.1: 3–18.

Greenhill, B., and Giffard, A., 1967, *Westcountrymen in Prince Edward's Isle*. University of Toronto Press. Canada.

Hasslöf, O., 1972, Main Principles in the Technology of Ship-Building. In O. Hasslöf, H. Henningsen and A.E. Christensen (eds), *Ships and Shipyards, Sailors and Fishermen. Introduction to Maritime Ethnology*, 27–72. Copenhagen University Press. Copenhagen.

Litwin, J. (ed), 2000, *Down the River to the Sea: proceedings of the Eighth International Symposium on Boat and Ship Archaeology*. *Gdansk 1997*. Polish Maritime Museum. Gdansk.

McGrail, S., 2000, The ISBSA: past, present and future. In J. Litwin (ed), *Down the River to the Sea: proceedings of the Eighth International Symposium on Boat and Ship Archaeology*, 269–272. Polish Maritime Museum. Gdansk.

McGrail, S. (ed), 1977, *Sources and Techniques in Boat Archaeology: papers based on those presented to a symposium at Greenwich in September 1976, together with edited discussion*. BAR Supplementary Series 29. Oxford.

McGrail, S. (ed), 1979, *The Archaeology of Medieval Ships and Harbours in Northern Europe: papers based on those presented to an International Symposium on Boat and Ship Archaeology at Bremerhaven in 1979*. BAR International Series 66. Oxford.

Pomey, P., and Rieth, E. (eds), 1999, *Construction navale, maritime et fluviale. Approches archéologique, historique et ethnologique*. Archaeonautica 14. CNRS éditions. Paris.

Reinders, R., and Paul, K. (eds), 1991, *Carvel Construction Technique*. Oxbow Monograph 12. Oxford.

Westerdahl, C. (ed), 1994, *Crossroads in Ancient Shipbuilding: proceedings of the sixth International Symposium on Boat and Ship Archaeology, Roskilde, 1991*. Oxbow Monograph 40. Oxford.

Wright, E.V., 1990, *The Ferriby Boats: Seacraft of the Bronze Age*. Routledge. London.

Walking on water:
Maritime archaeology by air, land and sea

Jonathan Adams

The tenth International Symposium on Boat and Ship Archaeology was obviously going to be a special event and so when invitations went out to potential hosts, it was no surprise that several institutions put themselves forward. This tenth triennial event would mark nearly three decades of research into all aspects of ancient watercraft and seafaring, core concerns of 'maritime archaeology', a field that in a growing number of countries around the world is becoming one of the most dynamic in the discipline. Over that period ISBSA has, in a real sense, both contributed to the development of maritime archaeology and manifested its output. An indication of its long term consistency is the way each of the volumes of proceedings have passed out of print and remain high on many students' lists of library reading.

At the University of Southampton we wanted to host ISBSA 10 for a very specific reason. Seán McGrail has been formally associated with the university since 1990. He had also been a key figure in the organisation and publishing of the very first ISBSA when it was held at the National Maritime Museum, Greenwich in 1976. What better way of celebrating the tenth symposium than by returning to some of the themes that drove that first meeting, particularly as many of them have subsequently remained or resurfaced as key concerns. In the event we became co-organisers with the Viking Ship Museum at Roskilde and the National Museum of Denmark's Centre for Maritime Archaeology. Roskilde was the obvious venue, a place that was inextricably linked to the subject's development and the home of Ole Crumlin-Pedersen, one of Seán's oldest friends and collaborators. How appropriate too, to use the symposium as a way of generating a hefty *Festschrift* for Seán in tribute to his inestimable role in the subject's development, a contribution that has been made in every facet, whether through carrying out and publishing research, education, heritage management or professional advice.

By way of illustrating the nature of that contribution, a brief look backwards is instructive, for Seán's arrival in archaeology coincided with the period when the British Isles began to tentatively investigate maritime archaeological sites both coastal and underwater. Compared to many of our neighbours, we were rather slow on the uptake. Ole Crumlin-Pedersen and Olaf Olsen's work on the Viking ships discovered at Skuldelev in Denmark and the rediscovery, salvage and excavation of *Vasa* in Stockholm harbour (Cederlund forthcoming), both had begun in the 1950s. By the time the excavation phase of these projects was completed, George Bass had carried out his groundbreaking excavation at Gelidonya in 1960, the Bremen cog had been recovered and Ulrich Ruoff had taken archaeology under water into the Swiss lakes. There are many other examples but Britain largely missed this burst of activity, the work of Joan du Plat Taylor and Honor Frost notwithstanding. The first projects that were set to have a long term influence in Britain cluster around the late 1960s and early 1970s. Ironically, this was just at the time when the New Archaeology was beginning to affect the cosy world of what it disparagingly called 'traditional archaeology'. Maybe this is one reason why British archaeology in general did not take too much notice of what was beginning to go on under water. Another reason was that many people carrying out investigations under water were not archaeologists by training and this contributed to a certain degree of development in isolation. Seán McGrail was to be one of the first who championed the potential synergy between maritime source material and archaeology at large. So while the likes of Muckelroy, Parker and Rule blazed a trail under water, McGrail did the same above it, emphasising a broader approach, as demonstrated by his definition of the subject (McGrail 1984a: 12) as compared to Muckelroy's (1978: 4).

But before attempting to place McGrail in the context of a developing maritime archaeology, we need to go even further back. It might surprise many who have only known him as the eminent professor of maritime archaeology and author of hundreds of publications, to learn that archaeology is his second career. His first, between 1946 and 1968, was in the Royal Navy, from 1951 onwards as

Jonathan Adams

Fig. 2.1. Fairey Firefly FR Mk.5 VT488, Lieutenant McGrail's mount during the Korean War, with nose art on the panel just behind the exhaust (after Harrison 1998: 129).

a pilot in the Fleet Air Arm. I have known Seán since 1977 and until recently I knew very little of his former existence. I knew he was a Master Mariner and that he'd been to sea in 'grey boats'. I also knew he'd been a pilot but not of what or where. I found out when I was visiting Fred and Emma Hocker's house in Roskilde. Fred, a connoisseur, not just of boats but of all technology, showed me into his beautifully equipped workshop and there on a table was a book about aircraft. It was open at a page showing a Fairey Firefly FR (fighter-reconnaissance) Mk. 5 in Korean War markings. The caption read: "Lieutenant J.F.K. 'Seán' McGrail … carried out many of 118 operational sorties against Korean targets (between 12 November 1952 and May 1953) in VT488 205/R from the deck of HMS *Glory*" (Fig. 02.1; Harrison 1998: 129). This was only one part of a flying career that included no less than 500 deck landings and 300 catapult launches. I had never heard Seán talk about this, not because he wouldn't if asked, but because it is unlikely to be pertinent to discussions centred on maritime archaeology. If it isn't germane to the issue he's the last person to throw in anecdotes simply for effect. However, there is an aspect in which this particular plane and others that he flew are relevant to his subsequent research interests and to our field in general. It is often acknowledged that boats are among the most symbolically laden of all artefacts (Crumlin-Pedersen and Munch Thye 1995). They typically last for a human lifespan, they are gendered, they are given names and in some societies are even afforded mortuary rites at the end of their use life (Adams 2003: 30). No wonder then that they are so often adorned in various ways, not in the sense of 'pretty' decoration but as a means of signifying and projecting aspects of identity, status, association and meaning. McGrail's Firefly carried similar messages, in the aerial equivalent of the oculus, his plane was decorated with 'nose art', one of the few British aircraft in that theatre to be so. The image was even painted on a removable panel so that it could be transferred to another aircraft (Harrison 1998: 129).

Following operational flying he spent periods as an instructor, an examiner and also took command of a squadron. In 1968, armed with his Board of Trade

certificate 'Master Mariner (Foreign Going)', he left the navy and headed for academia. Out of uniform, his progress was characterised by the same sense of purpose. Winning a scholarship, he predictably gained his BA in mathematics, history and econometrics with first-class honours. He was part way through his MSc in statistics when he was snapped up by the *National Maritime Museum* at Greenwich to fill a newly created post of Assistant Keeper (archaeology). The museum director at this time was the late Basil Greenhill, and in Seán he recognised someone who could help deliver his vision of a dynamic national museum that wasn't simply a repository of archives and dusty objects but an active research centre and a world class centre of excellence. Within a year Seán had become head of the Museum's newly created Department of Archaeology of Ships. In 1976 he became the museum's Chief Archaeologist and head of its Archaeological Research Centre. This was the year of the first ISBSA held at Greenwich, in which Seán was so central (Crumlin-Pedersen this volume). Its proceedings were published the following year, edited by Seán as *Sources and Techniques in Boat Archaeology* (BAR S29. Oxford). Never content with doing one thing at a time he had started a PhD at the Institute of Archaeology in London. This was published as *Logboats of England and Wales* in 1978, the same year as Keith Muckelroy's seminal *Maritime Archaeology*. Soon afterwards Muckelroy also went to work at Greenwich in the ARC under Seán, a partnership that would surely have been highly significant for maritime archaeology had it not been so tragically cut short when Keith was drowned in 1980. Indeed the ARC itself was not to last. The retirement of Basil Greenhill and changes in museum policy shifted the trajectory of the whole discipline. In 1986 Seán became Professor of Maritime Archaeology at the Institute of Archaeology in Oxford, where among his flock of bright young PhD students was Lucy Blue. His interest, indeed his passion for education in maritime archaeology has been a constant thread right through his work.

He 'retired' from Oxford in 1993 but by then he had already become Visiting Professor at Southampton, a post through which he still contributes regularly to postgraduate teaching in the Centre for Maritime Archaeology (CMA). In fact the creation of the CMA at Southampton is something that Seán had promoted for many years. At Southampton he found a department of archaeology keen to embed maritime archaeology in its undergraduate syllabus in response to growing student interest. He taught the first complete course in maritime archaeology at Southampton in 1991. I started teaching another a year later. It was the success of these two courses that convinced the Department to launch a Masters programme in 1995 and in 1997 to launch the CMA. Seán has therefore been something of a father figure for maritime archaeology at Southampton just as he has been in Britain as a whole.

But to return to his archaeological context so to speak: The cathartic crisis of identity induced by the New

Archaeology in the late 1960s – early 1970s was referred to by David Clarke as archaeology's 'loss of innocence' (Clarke 1973: 6), the very period when Seán was getting to grips with the discipline. One of the most substantive publications of this era was Clarke's 'Analytical Archaeology' published in 1968, the same year that Seán swapped naval life for civvy street. With his mathematical acumen and his navigator's mind set, it is not surprising that this book made a deep impression. Archaeology was donning the white coat of the natural sciences and Seán had the skills to explore that approach. I believe he'd agree that his advocacy of rigorous method in the pursuit of quantifiable data is at least partly informed by the approaches of Clarke and others at that time (Adams 2003: 13). This fed through into his recording and reconstruction of ancient watercraft and of course his use of experimental archaeology (Fig. 2.2). Here then is the germ of the McGrail 'floating hypothesis' (McGrail 1992), complemented by his ethnographic application (McGrail 1984b; McGrail *et al* 2003; Blue *et al* 1997). Just how far the elastic of inference can be stretched using experimental and ethnographic analogy were principal themes of ISBSA 1 and therefore explicitly of ISBSA 10.

It is this potent combination of experiment and ethnography that prevent McGrail being simplistically pigeonholed. No one who has worked with, been mentored or taught by Seán, was ever left in any doubt about the McGrail approach to study: rigour! Yet this has never been in an unthinking, procedural sense, rather that there must be a quantifiable chain of reasoning between the data, their analysis and subsequent conclusions. On the basis of the data he is quite happy to discuss the possible symbolic significance of the Hasholme logboat or its relations to social status and power, as well as calculating its stability and capacity. He would of course point out that in the case of the latter we can arrive at definitive conclusions about performance while the metaphysical aspects remain rather more diffuse. Perhaps this is why he has been such a good mentor and educator, never

discouraging interpretation but always advocating firm anchorage in the data. So, while in the 1990s McGrail's approaches appeared to be a little at odds with the increasingly post-processual thrust of much maritime archaeological work, things are now less polarised. Just as archaeological thinking in general has seen a gradual shift to the centre ground, so maritime archaeology acknowledges the importance of those aspects imported into the field by McGrail and Muckelroy in the 1970s and 80s. Maritime archaeology now relies on scientific analysis of the post-depositional processes of site evolution, yet admits no contradiction in seeking to understand the symbolic, as well as the functional meanings of 'active' material culture in pre-depositional and depositional contexts (Adams 2002: 330).

I cannot end without providing an insight into Seán's own development as a scholar. For although David Clarke made such a strong impression on him since he has become an academic, his predisposition for scientific enquiry is evident much earlier. It dates to 1956 when Seán was Air Warfare Instructor of 824 squadron. They flew Fairey Gannets, and were embarked in HMS *Ark Royal*, in Gibraltar. The Gannet, although one of the ugliest and most improbable looking aircraft to ever take off from a carrier, was said to be so versatile that it could be loaded 'with everything but the kitchen sink'. Never one to accept theory unchallenged, Seán decided that this particular hypothesis ought to be tested. Accompanied by the chief armourer, he scoured Gibraltar dockyard, found and 'liberated' a pusser's kitchen sink. At 14.20 on the 25th March, accompanied by his observer and a representative from Fairey Aviation, Seán flew the Gannet suitably 'armed' on the last sortie of the commission. The sink was loaded 'bung up and bilge free', suspended by wire strops and with two sonobuoy parachutes attached (Fig. 2.3). They flew alongside the *Ark* and dropped an antisubmarine flare, a marker marine, a non-serviceable, nondirectional sonobuoy, a 25lb practice bomb, an 82lb breakup bomb, a smoke-flame float, and finally, the kitchen

Fig. 2.2. *A guiding hand on the 'tiller' – a habitual role for the Professor. Seán acting as Trierarch aboard Olympias.*

Fig. 2.3. *Experimental technology: The Kitchen Sink Mk 1 before being loaded. Seán McGrail second from Right (Photo S. McGrail).*

sink. Needless to say, a full report was written and submitted, anticipating the timely manner in which his archaeological publications have appeared. Ballistics of the sink were said to be 'not unlike those of a brick-built chicken house'. Underwater trajectory was impossible to ascertain 'owing to marked disintegration on impact' (McGrail 2005: 23).

In 2003, we instituted the now annual *Land and Sea* conference at Southampton, an explicit attempt to promote integrative approaches across maritime archaeology and beyond. In reviewing the career of Seán McGrail, perhaps we ought to re-name it *Air, Land and Sea*, for the remit of the maritime archaeology he has helped to build clearly encompasses it all.

References

Adams, J., 2002, Maritime Archaeology, in C. Orser (ed), *Encyclopedia of Historical Archaeology*, 328–330. London: Routledge.

Adams, J., 2003, *Ships, Innovation and Social Change*. Stockholm: University of Stockholm.

Blue, L., Kentley, E., McGrail, S. and Mishra, U., 1997, The Patia Fishing Boat of Orissa: A Case Study in Ethnoarchaeology. *South Asian Studies* 13: 198–207.

Cederlund, C. O., forthcoming, Vasa I: *The archaeology of a Swedish warship of 1628*. Stockholm.

Clarke, D. L., 1968, *Analytical Archaeology*. London: Methuen and Co.

Clarke, D. L., 1973, Archaeology: the loss of innocence. *Antiquity* 47: 6–18

Crumlin-Pedersen, O. and Munch Thye, B., (eds), 1995, *The Ship as Symbol in Prehistoric and Medieval Scandinavia*. Copenhagen: National Museum of Denmark.

Harrison, W., 1998, Fairey Firefly variants. *Wings of Fame* 12: 112–141.

McGrail, S., (ed) 1984a, *Aspects of Maritime Archaeology and Ethnology*. Greenwich: NMM

McGrail, S., 1984b, Boat Ethnography and Maritime Archaeology. *International Journal of Nautical Archaeology* 13.2: 149–150

McGrail, S., 1992, Replicas, reconstructions and floating hypotheses. *International Journal of Nautical Archaeology* 21.4: 353–5.

McGrail, S., Blue, L., Kentley, E., and Palmer, C., (eds), 2003, *Boats of South Asia*. Studies in South Asia Series. RoutledgeCurzon: London.

McGrail, S., 2005, The Fairey Gannet: 'everything and the kitchen sink'. *Jabberwock* 53: 22–23. The Society of Friends of the Fleet Air Arm.

Muckelroy, K., 1978, *Maritime Archaeology*. Cambridge: Cambridge University Press.

1 Experimental archaeology and ships – principles, problems and examples

Ole Crumlin-Pedersen

In the pursuit of an understanding of the past, Experimental Archaeology can offer a methodology that may provide further insight into the subjects being studied, primarily with regard to aspects of technology, the consumption of resources and cultural interaction. This is not least the case when studying the remains of ancient ships in context, seeing the construction, maintenance, and use of the vessels as reflections of maritime aspects of the past, since these vessels were some of the most complex and challenging structures built and used by early man.

At the same time, Experimental Ship Archaeology is a problematic field since a research oriented approach to these projects is often overruled by other, conflicting aims. In recent years, full-scale reproductions of several ships of the past have been built around the world, claiming to provide important contributions to our understanding of the past. In some of these cases, however, the use of the terms 'experimental' and 'replica' is just a cover-up for raising money for a project whose aims have little relevance to scholarly study. Frequently, entrepreneurship rather than scholarship determines the objectives and sets the scene. Therefore, the present symposium has set aside two full days for papers, discussions, and practical demonstrations relating to issues of Experimental Archaeology. However, the discussion will no doubt still remain unresolved and continue to present a topic for discussion by new generations of maritime archaeologists in the years to come.

In order to demonstrate the range of aims that Experimental Archaeological projects pursue, fourteen vessels that were constructed in modern times with the declared intention to represent important examples of ship and boat building of the past, have been selected, listed and classified (Table 1.1). Most of these examples are generally well-known and some of them represent excellent scholarship and authentic craftsmanship. For others of these vessels, however, the construction is based on such insubstantial evidence that there is hardly anything to 'replicate' in the true sense of the word. The list might have been much longer, but these examples may suffice to illustrate the confusing and sometimes conflicting motives behind these prestigious and expensive projects.

Among these fourteen projects a mixture of at least nine different motives have been identified (Table 1.2). The first two are related to what we may call individual or national **self-promotion** through the use of famous ship types, voyages, or epochs in order to justify the endeavour. The next two are for **profit**, primarily geared towards the tourist and charter business. Motives five and six relate to **social activities**, either officially organised for the un-employed, or non-profit challenges taken up by private groups in order to promote community activity. **Educational and museological** aims are behind motive number seven, while the eighth motive group may be considered part of the protection or re-vitalisation of the physical **heritage**. Finally, the ninth is **research-**related in that it sees the project primarily as an important element in the scholarly analysis of a ship find or an ancient boat type.

For each of these fourteen vessels, two or more of these aims have been identified from the published evidence. In Table 1.1, the major aims are listed in priority sequence for each project. This is of course a subjective evaluation of the projects by the present author but this classification may still open up discussion on the different objectives behind the construction of these vessels.

For researchers and museum staff concerned with scholarly studies of maritime aspects of the past, as well as with the problems of protection of the maritime heritage, focus should be on those projects that have given priority to aims 9, 8 and 7. For those projects where 'fame' or 'business' are the primary objectives, scholarly research is often neglected or given a subordinate role, generally leading to weak academic analysis.

It is a fact, however, that most replica project managers have to play several cards in order to assemble the necessary resources and to get the project-organisation established to deal with the full range of problems, from the initial enquiry that helps determine the selection of

Table 1.1. Examples of 'replicas', 1893–2004 (Crumlin-Pedersen).

Name of 'replica' (country)	Based on evidence from	Date of original/ launch of 'replica'	Primary aims in priority sequence	Primary contributions to scholarly studies	Comments on use	Present condition	References
Viking (Norway)	Gokstad ship	c.895/ 1893	1, 2, 9	Viking seamanship and transatlantic navigation	One voyage	Preserved in Chicago	Andersen 1895; Christensen 1986
Kon-Tiki (Norway)	Iconography	/ 1947	9, 8	Oceanic raft navigation	One voyage	Museum exhibit in Oslo	Heyerdahl 1948
Hugin (Denmark)	Gokstad ship	c.895/ 1949	3, 2	None	One voyage	Preserved at Ramsgate	Vadstrup 1993
Imme Gram (Denmark)	Ladby ship	c.925/ 1963	6, 8, 9	'Grass-root' interest in ancient boat building	In continuous use with repairs	Owned by private group	Vadstrup 1993
Faering (England)	Gokstad small boat	c.900/ 1973	7, 9	Rowing trials procedure	A few trials trips	Museum exhibit at Greenwich	McGrail 1974; McKee 1974
Brendan (Ireland)	Text and local traditions	c.800/ 1976	1, 8, 9	Atlantic hide-boat seafaring	Voyaging in two years	?	Severin 1978
Saga Siglar (Norway)	Skuldelev 1 ship	c.1030/ 1983	1, 4, 9	Ocean seafaring	Sailed 1983-92 (aux. engine)	Wrecked in 1992, lost	Thoreth 1988; Crumlin-Pedersen 1989
Roar Ege (Denmark)	Skuldelev 3 ship	c.1040/ 1984	9, 8, 7	Focus on construction and sea trials	In continuous use with repairs	Owned and used by museum	Andersen & Andersen 1989; Andersen et al. 1997
Olympia (Greece)	Text, relief and boat shed	5th c.BC/ 1987	9, 2	Manual propulsion technique and speed	Three seasons of sea trials	Laid up in Piraeus	Shaw ed.1993
Hansekogge (Germany)	Bremen cog	1380/ 1989	5, 2, 9, 4	Handling medieval cogs under sail	Engine fitted after first seasons	Charter vessel based in Kiel	Baykowski 1991
Agnete (Denmark)	Gedesby ship	c.1300/ 1995	7, 8, 9	Handling medieval small cargo vessel	In continuous use	Owned and used by Medieval Centre	Bill forthcoming
Altaripa (Switzerland)	Bevaix barge	2nd c.AD/ 1997	9, 8, 7	High quality recording of construction process	Moored next to museum	Owned by museum at Neuchâtel	Arnold 1999
Tilia Alsie (Denmark)	Hjortspring boat	c. 350 BC/ 1999	9, 6, 7	Construction and use of early vessels	Sea trials and occasional use	Owned by the group of builders	Crumlin-Pedersen & Trakadas eds 2003
Havhingsten (Denmark)	Skuldelev 2 ship	1042/ 2004	9, 8, 7, 2, 3	Construction and use of longships	Launched in 2004, sea trials	Owned and used by museum	Crumlin-Pedersen & Damgård-Sørensen 2000; Nielsen 2001

In order to:
1. be the first person to re-enact a famous voyage (*fame*)
2. cherish a famous epoch or ship type of the past (*fame*)
3. promote local business and/or tourism (*business*)
4. earn a living in charter business (*business*)
5. provide job-training opportunities for unemployed (*social activity*)
6. provide a non-profit challenge for volunteers (*social activity*)
7. provide for museological activities (*education and visualisation*)
8. maintain or re-vitalise ancient manual skills (*heritage protection*)
9. improve the scholarly analysis of an ancient boat or ship type (*research*)

Table 1.2. Reasons for building a 'replica' (Crumlin-Pedersen).

materials, to the actual construction and sea trials and, finally, publication and long-term maintenance. Therefore, a project cannot be dismissed as not having scholarly objectives simply because there are elements of 'business' or 'prestige' involved, as long as these aims are not given priority over the research aims.

But even in cases where original archaeological, iconographic or textual evidence – or a combination of these – is at hand to inform the replica builder, there are frequently large lacunae in the sources on the nature of the rigging and equipment, and even of important parts of the hull. In the worst case, inadequate scholarship at the research phase, poor craftsmanship during construction, and incompetent seamanship due to lack of relevant experience, can lead to false conclusions on the nature and seaworthiness of ancient vessels.

The challenge of reproducing and testing an ancient seagoing vessel calls for a coordinated effort based on the professional aptitude of the archaeologist, historian and naval architect, combined with those of the boat builder, sailor, and navigator. This approach is necessary since the methodology involved in the replication process must involve the application of academic scholarship in combination with experienced and exploration-minded craftsmanship and seamanship. Only then can one expect to be able to appreciate building techniques and elements of seamanship that are now obsolete but which were highly functional within the technological options at the time after having been developed and handed down through the generations.

But even then there is a tendency to see the construction of a ship in the past as little more than a technological problem, separate from the vessel's complex role in contemporary society. Modern day social and mental constructs and limited relevant knowledge and skills, will inevitably impede our ability to replicate ancient vessels.

The complex context including rituals, initialisation processes and beliefs relating to the construction phases, choice of colour and decoration of the vessels, will invariably allude us. Such aspects are examples of what is lost to the modern observer. Secular symbolism also played an important role in many vessels, as reflected, for instance, in the motto of the *Vasa* exhibition in Stockholm: *The Power and the Glory*, being a clear reflection of the immense symbolic importance attributed to this royal ship by the king of Sweden in the early seventeenth century (Kvarning and Ohrelius 1998).

Therefore, one must not, in the study of the remains of an ancient vessel, neglect the wide range of links, beyond the purely functional, that probably existed between the vessel in question and the society that built it. These aspects may not materialise clearly in an initial study of the archaeological remains of a vessel but become more evident once the construction process is being replicated. Consequently, these aspects should be kept in mind in order for the study of the vessel to provide insight into the society that had the vessel built – exploiting the potentials of the find to illuminate several facets of life in a maritime community of the past in the course of the modern experimental process.

Even when not taking this wider perspective into full consideration, a ship-archaeological find may have much to offer. As stated by Dick Steffy (1994: 5), a vessel of the past carried much more than its cargo of goods and people, since it carried an immense cargo of knowledge. Therefore, one needs excellent recording and research procedures in order to exploit such monuments of technology as primary sources in the study of past societies.

When taking up the challenge of making a full-size reconstruction of an ancient vessel (whether the actual vessel is a clay pot or a ship) one is faced with a series of questions that would not usually concern scholars describing an archaeological find, thus demanding further rigour with respect to the recording and research methods. Reproducing the vessel forces the investigator to deal with problems of selection and processing of materials, with design and production procedures, as well as with aspects of its use.

The replication process of a boat or ship is far too complex to be reduced to a simple hypothesis-and-test-procedure, as recently claimed by some British scholars based on the standards of experiments in physics; there are simply too many variables at play simultaneously (Coates et al 1995; Crumlin-Pedersen 1995). The strength of single elements, such as individual fastenings, ropes, etc., may be tested following standard procedures (for example Valbjørn et al 2003: 95). However, no computer models currently exist that can truthfully simulate the behaviour at sea of an ancient sailing vessel, under various weather conditions, without allowing for extensive approximations and modifications that will require correlation with the results of full-scale trials for scaling. In effect we are not yet able to assess this in a comprehensive manner.

Ole Crumlin-Pedersen

This calls for an effort combining naval architectural calculations, testing in tanks and wind tunnels, and fully documented sea trials using high-quality replica vessels with fully competent crews. The outcome of the replica experiment should be judged primarily by the ability of the ship or boat to perform as a fully functional, complex unit, complying to contemporary safety standards, sailing in an environment equivalent to that which it would have encountered in antiquity.

An additional, but no less important, outcome of the experiment is the resulting increase in our knowledge relating to all aspects of the multifaceted interaction between man and the environment in the past. In this way, such a project serves as an eye-opener and training ground for future generations of archaeologists who, like most archaeologists of today, would otherwise be unfamiliar with the basics of wood working and boat building as well as with ancient seafaring and seamanship.

A fine example of a replication process was the construction of *Altaripa*, a replica of the 20 m long barge from the 2nd century AD found in Lake Neuchâtel in Switzerland (Arnold 1999). Here, the selection of the timber for planks and frames, and the reduction from 110 tons of raw materials to the weight of 7 tons for the finished vessel, was carefully recorded. Tool marks were

compared with the original timbers and rigorously documented and the working hours spent during all phases of the process were also recorded. Most recently, sailing trials have been undertaken and documented in a video.

Similarly, the Danish Hjortspring group ('Hjortspringbådens Laug', 'The Guild of the Hjortspring Boat') noted that they needed 12 tons of wood to build their 19 m long replica of the 4th century BC war canoe which was launched in 1999 with a hull weight of only half a ton upon completion (Fig. 1.1) (Valbjørn et al 2003). Here, extensive sea trials were carried out by a specialist team of paddlers, rigorously documented in the publication and evaluated in relation to the functionality of the original boat (Vinner 2003; Haupt and Fenger 2003). At the same time, the general archaeological context of the vessel as part of a large and unique offering of the spoils of war (Kaul 2003a), and the relation between the boat and numerous Bronze Age and Early Iron Age rock carvings in Scandinavia and the British Bronze Age boat finds, was assessed (Kaul 2003b; Crumlin-Pedersen 2003). These two examples demonstrate the potential of experimental ship and boat archaeology, when research aims are prioritised and a strict methodology is followed.

In planning and executing the whole range of activities relating to the Hjortspring project, a total of 26 major

Fig. 1.1. The lines and details of the Hjortspring replica Tilia *being recorded after the first sea trials. Photo by Werner Karrasch, Viking Ship Museum.*

phases or separate elements were identified (Table 1.3). Various branches of the National Museum in Copenhagen where the boat is on display, and in Brede, undertook the critical analysis of the conservation and restoration, as well as the reanalysis of the wood species and evidence for dating, while the Viking Ship Museum and the Centre for Maritime Archaeology in Roskilde undertook the ship-archaeological analysis, documentation of the replica, and the planning and execution of the sea trials.

The main part of the experimental project, however, was undertaken by the 'Hjortspring Guild'. This quality-minded organisation of 50–100 volunteers represent a broad range of occupations that brought both technical and administrative skills to the project, however, none of the team had a background in archaeology or boat building. The 'Hjortspring Guild' is based on the small island of Als off the Baltic coast of southern Jutland where the boat itself was excavated between 1921–22. The aim of the Guild was to replicate the boat at full scale as a locally based community activity that might provide a useful input to scholarly studies of this important find.

The 'Hjortspring Guild' established an informal but efficient internal organisation with working groups to deal with the many different aspects of the project, such as establishing a boatyard site, building a scale model, studying the original find, including objects in the museum's store rooms, searching for contemporary tools, making copies of these finds and developing the appropriate tool handles for the wood carving techniques, tracking down linden trees large enough for the boat – they had to go to Poland to find these – and conducting experiments with sewn fastenings.

To begin with the task seemed too large and complex to be achieved by many of the participants but then it was decided to construct two full-scale sections of the boat in order to train the volunteers in the manual skills required and investigate some of the technical problems they might encounter. Having done so, spirits rose again and the building of the complete replica commenced. Except for the felling and transportation of the trees that utilised modern equipment, all work was carried out using hand tools: axes, adzes and planes – without the use of saws.

Table 1.3. Methodological elements of the Hjortspring project (Crumlin-Pedersen).

Action		Executed by
1	Scrutiny of 1921-22 excavation and 1937 publication to check reconstruction	NMI
2	Analysis of effect of conservation on shrinkage of wood	NMC
3	Analysis of wood species for elements of the find	NMA
4	Supplementary excavation for un-treated dating samples	NMI
5	Natural science dating	NMA
6	Formation of building group with aims and internal organisation	HG
7	Building site identified and acquired	HG
8	Scale-model 1:10 of boat built	HG
9	Recording of original details and equipment in the National Museum	HG
10	Search for evidence on contemporary tools	HG
11	Search for wood	HG
12	Details of assembly studied and tested	HG
13	Studies of wood carving techniques, development of tool handles	HG
14	Construction of midship and stem sections as full-scale trials pieces	HG
15	Construction of boat, replicating using moulds and modern glue	HG
16	Calculation of hydrostatics and stresses	HG
17	Initial sea trials	HG
18	Recording of shape and flexibility	NMF
19	Sea trials, organisation and recording	VM
20	Archaeological and ethnographic studies of paddling techniques	NMF
21	Archaeological context of the find re-evaluated	NMP
22	Iconographic sources related to the boat	NMP
23	Boat type related to other early North European boat finds	NMF
24	Alternative interpretation of origin of the boat type	NMF
25	Publication in scholarly and popular monographs and articles	Jointly
26	Long-term maintenance and use	HG

Codes:
HG: Hjortspringbådens Laug, Als
NMA: National Museum unit for Archaeometry, Copenhagen
NMC: National Museum, Conservation Dep., Brede
NMF: Centre for Maritime Archaeology, Roskilde
NMI: Institute for Maritime Archaeology, Roskilde
NMP: National Museum unit for Prehistory, Copenhagen
VM: Viking Ship Museum; Roskilde

Ole Crumlin-Pedersen

Modern-type transverse interior moulds were used in order to ensure a proper replication of the shape of the boat, and since some of the planks were not wide enough, modern glue was used in a few cases. During the lengthy construction period, calculations were undertaken of the hydrostatics and the anticipated stresses and strains on the hull when sailing in calm waters as well as in 'standard waves'.

Then the Roskilde team came into action again, documenting the shape of the replica and testing its flexibility. After launching the boat, sea trials were undertaken during three seasons 1999–2001, the last two years with a team of 20 experienced sportsmen paddling the boat to a sprint speed of 7.6 knots and an average cruising speed of 4.7 knots. The boat was even tested in a strong wind of up to 16 m/sec and waves up to 1 m high (Fig. 1.2). In these extreme conditions, the hull twisted considerably but no damage occurred to the structure of the vessel.

For the publication (Crumlin-Pedersen and Trakadas 2003), a team of twelve authors described all these efforts and results, plus several aspects of the archaeological context. In the end, the results of studies into the boat itself and observations made during the construction phase of the replica lead to modifications to the excavator's 1937-reconstruction, giving a more pronounced longitudinal curvature of the bottom of the boat.

The 'Hjortspring Guild' will now care for the long-term maintenance and use of the boat, and members of the group are now providing assistance to the neighbouring Nydam Society, who in a similar fashion, want to build a replica of the 4th century AD oak boat from Nydam. The Nydam Society has already constructed a midship section of the boat, and thus within the next few years one may see another first class reconstruction of a classic boat find, each made by a talented and devoted community group, meeting the requirements of a proper experimental archaeological project.

As demonstrated in this volume, the Roskilde Viking Ship Museum is strongly engaged in experimental testing of ships and boats of the past. In contrast to short-term replica projects elsewhere, this museum aims at building up and maintaining experience in all aspects of Viking-Age and medieval boat building and seamanship, and has been doing so for over twenty years.

Several of the members of the group of builders of the museum's first proper replica, *Roar Ege*, in 1982–84 (Andersen et al 1997; Juel 2005), by 2003 held prominent positions in the museum, such as the head of research Jan Bill, the master boatbuilder Søren Nielsen, assisted by Tom Nicolaisen, the coordinator of the boat service Poul Nygaard, the head of the archaeological documentation workshop Ivan Hansen, and Vibeke Bischoff as model

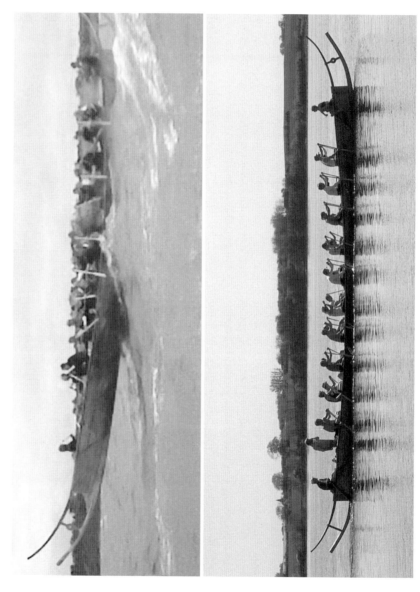

Fig. 1.2. Tilia undergoing trials at sea, in calm weather in 2001, and in heavy seas in 2000. Photos by M. Johansen and N. Haupt, Viking Ship Museum.

builder and graphics specialist. In addition, Erik Andersen, Max Vinner and the present author, all former members of the steering group of that project, are still active in the museum.

The presentation of the broad range of experimental archaeology projects carried out at Roskilde since 1982 particularly with respect to the five Skuldelev ships, as well as to other ancient vessels, will probably explain why the final publication of the Skuldelev ships has yet to be concluded. The first part of this publication on the archaeology and history of the ships was published in 2002 in the 'Ships and Boats of the North' series (Crumlin-Pedersen and Olsen 2002). It is to be followed by a volume that outlines the thinking behind the establishment of both models and plans that has brought about the comprehensive reconstructions of the five ships as fully functional units. This work was based on the evidence of the ships themselves, comparison with parallel finds and from studies of traditional practices in relevant areas. The third and final volume, reporting on all aspects of the experimental work relating to the ships, will appear after the launch in 2004 and the subsequent sea trials, of the longship under construction in Roskilde by 2003 as the last of the five Skuldelev ships to be reconstructed and tested.

References

Andersen, B., and Andersen, E., 1989, *Råsejlet – Dragens vinge*. Vikingeskibshallen, Roskilde.

Andersen, E., et al. 1997, *Roar Ege – Skuldelev 3 skibet som arkæologisk eksperiment*. Vikingeskibshallen, Roskilde.

Andersen, M., 1895, *Vikingefærden: en illustreret beskrivelse af "Vikings" reise i 1893*. Eget forlag. Kristiania.

Arnold, B., 1999, *Altaripa – archéologie expérimentale et architecture navale gallo-romaine*. Archéologie Neuchâteloise 25. Neuchâtel.

Baykowski, U., 1991, *Die Kieler Hansekogge*. Kiel.

Bill, J., forthcoming, *From Nordic to North European. Coastal Seafaring and Changes in Danish Shipbuilding AD 900–1600*. Ships and Boats of the North. Roskilde.

Christensen, A.E. 1986, "Viking", a Gokstad Ship Replica from 1893. In O. Crumlin-Pedersen and M. Vinner (eds), *Sailing into the Past. Proceedings of the International Seminar on Replicas of Ancient and Medieval Vessels, Roskilde, 1984*, 68–77. Vikingeskibshallen, Roskilde.

Coates, J., McGrail, S., Brown, D., Gifford, E., Grainge, G., Greenhill, B., Marsden, P., Rankov, B., Tipping, C. and Wright, E., 1995, Experimental Boat and Ship Archaeology: Principles and Methods. *International Journal of Nautical Archaeology* 24.4: 293–301.

Crumlin-Pedersen, O., 1986, Aspects of Viking-Age Shipbuilding in the Light of the Construction and Trials of the Skuldelev Ship-Replicas Saga Siglar and Roar Ege. *Journal of Danish Archaeology* 5: 209–228.

Crumlin-Pedersen, O., 1995, Experimental archaeology and ships – bridging the arts and the sciences. *International Journal of Nautical Archaeology* 24.4: 303–306.

Crumlin-Pedersen, O. 1996, Problems of Reconstruction and the

Estimation of Performance. In R. Gardiner (ed), *The Earliest Ships: the evolution of boats into ships*, 110–119. Conway's History of Ships. Conway Maritime Press. London.

Crumlin-Pedersen, O. 2003, The Hjortspring boat in a ship-archaeological context. In O. Crumlin-Pedersen and A. Trakadas (eds), *Hjortspring. A Pre-Roman Iron-Age Warship in Context*, 209–233. Ships and Boats of the North 5. Vikingeskibshallen, Roskilde.

Crumlin-Pedersen, O. and Damgård-Sørensen, T., 2000, A thoroughbred on the sea (1). The Irish longship rides again. *Maritime Archaeology Newsletter from Roskilde, Denmark*, 15: 1–36.

Crumlin-Pedersen, O. and Olsen, O., (eds) 2002, *The Skuldelev Ships I. Topography, Archaeology, History, Conservation and Display*. Ships and Boats of the North 4.1. Vikingeskibshallen. Roskilde.

Haupt, N. and Fenger, N.P., 2003, The paddles. In O. Crumlin-Pedersen and A. Trakadas (eds), *Hjortspring. A Pre-Roman Iron-Age Warship in Context*, 119–132. Ships and Boats of the North 5. Vikingeskibshallen. Roskilde.

Juel, H., 2005, *Roar's Circle*. Lutterworth Press, London.

Kaul, F., 2003a, The Hjortspring find. In O. Crumlin-Pedersen and A. Trakadas (eds), *Hjortspring. A Pre-Roman Iron-Age Warship in Context*, 141–186. Ships and Boats of the North 5. Vikingeskibshallen. Roskilde.

Kaul, F. 2003b, The Hjortspring boat and ship iconography of the Bronze Age and Early Pre-Roman Iron Age. In O. Crumlin-Pedersen and A. Trakadas (eds), *Hjortspring. A Pre-Roman Iron-Age Warship in Context*, 187–208. Ships and Boats of the North 5. Vikingeskibshallen. Roskilde.

Kvarning, L.-A. and Ohrelius, B., 1998, *The Vasa: the royal ship*. Atlantis. Stockholm.

McGrail, S., 1974, *The Building and Trials of the Replica of an Ancient Boat: The Gokstad Faering. Part I. Building the Replica*. Maritime Monographs and Reports 11. National Maritime Museum. London.

McKee, E., 1974, *The Building and Trials of the Replica of an Ancient Boat: The Gokstad Faering, Part II. The Sea Trials*. Maritime Monographs and Reports 11. National Maritime Museum. London.

Nielsen, S., 2001. A thoroughbred on the sea (2). *Maritime Archaeology Newsletter from Roskilde, Denmark*, 16: 11–15.

Severin, T., 1978, *The Brendan Voyage*. Arena. London.

Shaw, T., (ed) 1993, *The Trireme Project*. Oxbow Monographs 31. Oxford.

Steffy, J.R., 1994, *Wooden Ship Building and the Interpretation of Shipwrecks*. Texas A and M University Press. College Station. Texas.

Thorseth, R., 1988, *Saga Siglar. Århundrets seilas Jorda rundt*. Nordvest. Ålesund.

Vadstrup, S., 1993, *I vikingernes kølvand. Erfaringer og forsøg med danske, svenske og norske kopier af vikingeskibe 1892–1992*. Vikingeskibshallen. Roskilde.

Valbjørn, K.V., et al. 2003, Building and testing a Hjortspring boat. In O. Crumlin-Pedersen and A. Trakadas (eds), *Hjortspring. A Pre-Roman Iron-Age Warship in Context*, 54–102. Ships and Boats of the North 5. Vikingeskibshallen. Roskilde.

Vinner, M., 2003, Sea trials. In O. Crumlin-Pedersen and A. Trakadas (eds), *Hjortspring. A Pre-Roman Iron-Age Warship in Context*, 103–118. Ships and Boats of the North 5. Vikingeskibshallen. Roskilde.

2 Experimental boat archaeology: Has it a future?

Seán McGrail

In the autumn of 1972 Basil Greenhill, Director of the National Maritime Museum, arranged for a 'replica' of the 9th-century, 4-oared, Gokstad *faering* to be built at Greenwich. Although this appears to have been the first serious attempt to undertake experimental boat archaeology in Britain, at that time we at Greenwich had never heard of archaeological experiments. The idea that the building and trials of the Greenwich *faering* may have been such, only came later when the work was being written up for publication and we came upon a paper by John Coles (1966) on "Experimental Archaeology". Without the benefit of this revelation, no hypotheses had been formulated in the Greenwich experiment, and there were no research aims: master boatbuilder Harold Kimber just did what Arne-Emil Christensen's plans of the *faering* told him he had to do. Apart from Egon Hansen's work at Moesgard, the *Imme Gramme* 'replica' of the Ladby ship (Crumlin-Pedersen 1966, 1970) and Paul Johnstone's inconclusive Bronze Age boat experiment (1972, 1973), there appeared to be no projects to learn from, and nobody, not even in Denmark, seemed to have published anything on the theory of building 'replica' boats, explaining what might be gained by undertaking such a project.

Nothing was learnt about Viking Age boatmanship from this Greenwich experiment that could not have been learnt in an hour's discussion with Christensen. Nevertheless, experience was gained in the practical aspects of this type of research, even though an international 'jury' examined the Greenwich *faering* and ruled that it was not authentic. This was mainly because Harold Kimber decided, not unnaturally, that this boat would be a credit to his skills as a boatbuilder, and built her strong and sturdy, with planks and timbers of un-Viking-like scantlings although the shape was accurate.

The Plymouth Sound trials of the Greenwich *faering* were masterminded by Commander Eric McKee in mid-1973, and the National Maritime Museum subsequently published a two-part monograph (McGrail and McKee 1974). Dr. Greenhill then suggested that a 'replica' of the tenth-century Graveney boat (Fenwick 1978) should be built, thereby forcing us to consider the broader aspects

of experimental research, including its theoretical basis: in fact, so much time was spent sitting on one's arse theorising that we never actually got around to building this 'replica'.

Two years later, in September 1976, the first International Symposium on Boat and Ship Archaeology (ISBSA) conference was held at Greenwich (McGrail 1977). There was a session on 'Experimental Archaeology' and another on 'Hypothetical Reconstruction'. John Coles spoke on 'Theory and Principles' and concluded that experimenters needed a set of rules; Eric McKee and John Coles gave papers on reconstruction from the boat-builder's and from the naval architect's viewpoint; Tim Severin told us about his experimental hide boat *Brendan*, then over-wintering in Iceland; and the present author spoke about our work at Greenwich.

Subsequently, after publishing a survey of major themes in Experimental Archaeology (1979), John Coles moved into Wetlands Archaeology and later into Rock Art. Although nowadays almost every archaeological report includes some hypothetical reconstruction – of a Megalithic monument, an Iron Age house, a corn dryer, or even a human face – after the mid-1980s, land-based experimental archaeology seems not to have been pursued as an academic topic, except at the experimental establishments at Lejre in Denmark and Butser in southern England. Experimental Boat Archaeology, on the other hand, was pursued with vigour, if not always with scholarly rigour, and several high profile projects were greeted with enthusiasm by media and public alike.

Tim Severin completed his Atlantic crossing and went on to build and sail several other 'replicas' (1978, 1982, 1985, 1987, 1994). John Coates, working with Professor John Morrison, moved to centre stage with a project to reconstruct and build a 5th-century BC Athenian trireme (Morrison and Coates 1986). Ole Crumlin-Pedersen, who had spoken at ISBSA 1 on 'Some principles for the recording and presentation of ancient boat structures', also moved centre stage with his Skuldelev experimental research (1986 A, B and C).

Two Types of Experiment

The Skuldelev reconstructions, on the one hand, and the trireme reconstruction, on the other, became standard bearers for two different approaches to archaeological experiment: that is, the 'specific' approach and the 'representative' approach (McGrail 1992). The Trireme Project is an example of a representative experiment in which the reconstruction is a synthesis of the characteristic features of an identified class of vessel, mainly based on documentary and iconographic evidence: the vessel built is intended to be a typical example of that class. The Skuldelev reconstructions, on the other hand, are specific, each being based primarily on excavated evidence of one particular vessel.

Both approaches are valid ways of attempting to find out more about the past. Both require high quality evidence, and the rigorously-argued interpretation of that evidence; then the logically-developed formulation of a reconstruction; followed by authentic building of a full-scale model and scientifically-based trials. Both types of approach use all forms of evidence available: excavated, textual, iconographic, ethnographic, environmental, and the natural physical laws. Which approach is used in a particular case depends on whether the primary basis for the vessel is excavated evidence or textual-iconographic.

Representative experiments

Tim Severin's several 'replica' vessels were all of the representative type, as were those of Thor Heyerdahl (1978). So were the 1992 reconstructions of the ships in Columbus' 1492 fleet, although their creators may have thought otherwise. An experimental project dealing with Palaeolithic seafaring in eastern Indonesia is currently being undertaken by Robert Bednarik, an Australian Rock Art specialist (1997, 1998, 2003). If this is a serious experiment, it can only be representative, since environmental and artifactual evidence from 800,000BC is minimal.

Another project involving the reconstruction of a representative boat deals with the peopling of the South Pacific islands between c. 1500 BC and 1000 AD. Geoffrey Irwin (1992) has investigated such oceanic voyages using computer simulations. To achieve this, not only do the climate and sea levels have to be reconstructed, but also the navigational abilities of the crew and the performance of their boats. It is difficult to see how the latter can be done with any confidence since the excavated evidence for Oceanic boats is negligible; European observations of Oceanic boats are no earlier than the 16th century AD; and the earliest petroglyphs are from the 18th century (McGrail 2001: 317–319). Voyaging by computer has potential within experimental archaeology, but this is unlikely to be realised until more evidence for early boats is excavated.

Ole Crumlin-Pedersen's assessment of representative experiments is that they have helped our "understanding of the potentials of unfamiliar materials or building techniques" (1996: 110–111). This is truly a minimalist view. David Brown, the naval architect, is more hopeful (1998). He has likened such experiments to a technique known in industry and in the military as 'reverse engineering'. In its naval application this involves 'recreating' a ship depicted in a blurred photograph, using the natural physical laws and a knowledge of the ship owner's capabilities in design, building and operations. Since the end of the 'cold war' it has been shown that such Western 'recreations' of Soviet warships were usually close approximations of the original. In theory and in analogous practice, therefore, the best of representative archaeological experiments should result in a vessel which is probably as near the original in shape, in structure and in performance, as it is possible to get with the incomplete information at present available. When modified as proposed in post-trials evaluations (Morrison et al 2000: 245–6, 273–5) the Trireme ship reconstruction is probably in that category.

Interpretations of iconography

Other attempts have been made to formulate reconstructions based on representations of ancient boats: in the absence of supporting excavated or textual evidence these have not been impressive. As an example we may take the sailing vessel depicted on Middle Bronze Age frescos from the Cycladic island Thera/Santorini (Johnston 1997; Wachsmann 1998: 83–122; McGrail 2001: 113–122). Four authors who have published reconstructions of a Thera sailing vessel evidently based them on the same evidence (Gillmer 1978, 1985; Toby 1986; Giesecke 1983; Gifford 1997), yet their reconstructions differ significantly (McGrail 2001: Table 4.2), not only in overall measurements, for example, lengths vary from 15 to 17.6 m; but also in their shape ratios, for example, length/breadth ratios vary from 6.49 to 15.45. Sail areas also vary from 45 m^2 to 183/204 m^2. Performance estimates correspondingly range widely. Which then is the 'correct' reconstruction?

The only way to resolve this conundrum would be to assess each reconstruction against the original evidence: that is, the actual frescos and site documentation. In fact, the widely published illustration of a key element in any reconstruction, the sailing ship on the south frieze, West House, Room 5 (Basch 1987, fig. 267; Morgan 1988: fig.70; Throckmorton 1987: fig. 41; Wachsmann 1998: fig. 6.19), has itself already been reconstructed. This precisely what was excavated? Can any of the four published reconstructions be valid?

A general criticism of this type of project is to question whether the impossible is being attempted in trying to produce three-dimensional scale drawings from a two-dimensional fresco of an unknown scale, without excavated or textual controls.

Seán McGrail

Specific experiments

Many 'specific' experiments have been undertaken: in addition to the Skuldelev vessels, those most widely known in Europe include the Kyrenia ship (Katzev 1989; 1990; Steffy 1994: 45–59); the prehistoric Hjortspring boat (Crumlin-Pedersen and Trakadas 2003); and the medieval Bremen Cog reconstructions (Hoheisel 1994; Baykowski 1994; Brandt and Hochkisch 1995). A major defect of specific experiments is that, generally speaking, external criticism appears not to have been sought during the early stages of a project. Furthermore, few have so far been published comprehensively: the Hjortspring project may well be the first.

There are also half-scale models of specific reconstructions such as those of the medieval Sutton Hoo and Graveney vessels (Gifford and Gifford 1996) and prehistoric Ferriby Boat 1 (Gifford and Gifford 2004). Are these a valid alternative to a full-scale model? There is something to be said for them as a relatively inexpensive step towards building and testing a full-scale model, and valuable practical experience can be gained when using unfamiliar materials and exotic building techniques. However, the Reynolds number of a half-scale model will usually be too small for the effect of oars to be studied, and the complex interaction between sails and hull can only be satisfactorily evaluated after full-scale trials have been undertaken (Brown 1998). The knowledge gained about the past from half-scale models is limited when compared with what might be obtained from the building and trials of a full-scale reconstruction; not least, facts about the boat's use by full-scale human beings.

The National Trust for England has recently proposed building a full-scale model of the Early Medieval ship excavated within mound 1 at Sutton Hoo: this would be based on the existing half-scale model (Gifford 1996), itself derived (with additions) from measured drawings published by Dr. Bruce-Mitford (1975) in volume 1 of his *magnum opus* on the Sutton Hoo excavations. These two drawings (fig. 324 "the lines of the Sutton Hoo ship" and fig. 325 "the archaeological reconstruction") were not mentioned by Rupert Bruce-Mitford in his text, nor elsewhere as far as can be ascertained, and precisely how they were derived from the excavated evidence has never been explained.

Rather than accepting without question that these two drawings are definitive, the National Trust would be best advised to follow the methods used by the Viking Ship Museum at Roskilde in their recent re-assessment of the evidence for the Danish medieval burial ship from Ladby (Sørensen 2001). The context and the excavated evidence for the Sutton Hoo ship (first excavated in 1939) is so remarkably similar to that at Ladby (first excavated in 1934–6) that it is very likely that the innovative Danish research methods will be equally useful at Sutton Hoo, including the ingenuous way the position of the Ladby nails was displayed in a three-dimensional small-scale model and in a computer model, so that the original lines of the vessel could be determined as a step towards reconstruction of the hull shape (Bischoff 2003).

Experimental boat archaeology and gains in knowledge of the past

We may ask whether knowledge of the past has been increased by this plethora of representative and specific experiments. In a paper given at Roskilde twenty years ago it was concluded that:

"The results from boat replica experiments to-date are generally disappointing when measured by their contribution to knowledge of ancient technology and seafaring, rather than by gains in self-education, social benefit or national prestige" (McGrail 1986:12).

Although something has been learnt from a number of recent experiments, by and large that conclusion still holds; this assessment receives support from the discussion in Ole Crumlin-Pedersen's paper in the present volume.

How can this situation be improved, especially in respect of 'specific' experiments? Analysis of a range of boat archaeological experiments (especially those undertaken at Roskilde) suggests ways in which future experimenters could ensure that their projects would yield information about ancient nautical technology and seafaring. Crucial to success is the way the project takes shape in its early stages, well before any commitment is made to build a full-scale model. Undertaking such an experiment pre-supposes that those involved not only have a detailed knowledge of the full range of evidence specific to their particular project, but also have familiarised themselves with the principles and methods of experimental boat archaeology, and have learnt from the successes and failures of earlier experimenters.

The first essential act is to prepare a comprehensive project design that must include an exposition of the project's experimental philosophy, especially on the approach to reconstruction, and a clear statement of aims and the means of attaining those aims (McGrail 1986, 1992). The over-riding archaeological/historical aim of a project will determine how authentic a reconstruction must be: restricted aims may be satisfied by a limited, but appropriate, degree of authenticity. For example, if the aim is merely to investigate load/draft relationships and the manoeuvring ability of an ancient logboat, it could suffice to use a ballasted GRP boat, providing its shape and mass distribution were authentic. On the other hand, when comprehensive information about the building, the uses and the performance of an excavated boat is needed, authenticity will be required in all aspects of the experiment. This paper is focused on projects with comprehensive aims, but much of the discussion is also applicable to projects with limited ambitions.

The research design, having been subjected to internal criticism, must be promulgated for widespread evaluation. Many experimenters in the past have been in too great a haste to go into the forest and get the timber: only after the research design has been accepted by peer review, should an experiment begin.

A scholarly and rigorous project is most likely to ensue if the research is tackled in four distinct phases:

A. Determine precisely what was excavated by assessing or re-assessing the excavated evidence, the site and the research archives, and any published reports.

B. Using small-scale models of every plank and timber, and all other relevant evidence, encapsulate the Phase A evidence for the boat in an 'as-found/torso' model. This would be the boat as excavated, but with displaced timbers re-instated; fragmented timbers made whole; distorted, compressed and shrunken timbers rectified, and the vessel rotated to its probable attitude when afloat. When it is impossible to model planks and timbers, as in the Sutton Hoo project, alternative ways to determine the 'as-found/torso' hull shape must be found, as, for example, in the Ladby project.

C. If sufficient evidence exists, the Phase B scale model (or a scale drawing) is used as the basis for the reconstruction of the hull, the propulsion outfit, and the steering arrangements.

D. An agreed reconstruction drawing or model from Phase C may be used as a basis for building a full-scale model which should then be tested in a rigorous trials programme.

At the end of each of the first three phases (A, B and C) the evidence considered, the research undertaken, the drawings and/or models compiled, the conclusions drawn, and the intentions for the next phase should all be

published for criticism and subsequent modification as necessary, before proceeding to the next phase. A full-scale model should not be built until the fourth phase, and then only if earlier phases had shown that this was justified by the evidence and in relation to the project's aims.

Phases A, B, and C of this process may be illustrated by reference to the Romano-Celtic Barland's Farm boat (Figs 2.1, 2.2 and 2.3). This boat was excavated from the northern shores of the Severn Estuary in late-1993 (Nayling and McGrail 2004). The published reconstruction of the boat is not to be taken as a blueprint for a full-scale 'replica': rather it is a first approximation. It is hoped that this reconstruction, the evidence on which it is based, and the manner in which it was produced, will be widely criticised. The aim then would be to revise the reconstruction in the light of that criticism, and submit a new hypothesis for evaluation.

The Barland's Farm boat was dismantled on site, each plank and element of framing timber being lifted for individual documentation. The medieval ship excavated in 2003 from a waterfront site in Newport, Gwent was similarly dismantled; it would be possible, therefore to build an 'as-found/torso' model of this ship if the timbers were to be individually recorded. The medieval boat from Magor Pill, Gwent (Nayling 1998) was recovered as a

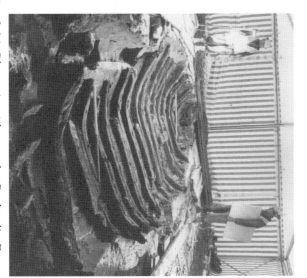

Fig. 2.1A Phase A evidence: the Barland's Farm boat during excavation. (Glamorgan-Gwent Archaeological Trust)

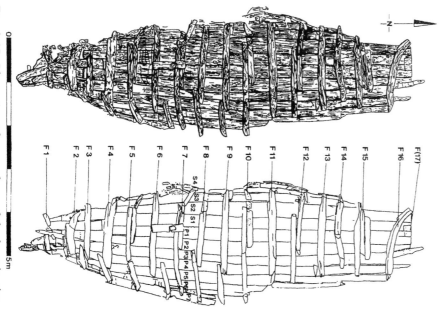

Fig. 2.1B Phase A evidence: plans of the boat in situ – photogrammetry to the left, field drawing to the right. (Glamorgan-Gwent Archaeological Trust)

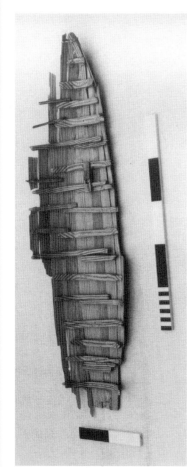

Fig. 2.2A Phase B 'as-found/torso', 1:10 scale model of the Barland's Farm boat remains derived from measured drawings of every plank and framing timber, and other Phase A evidence. (Seán McGrail)

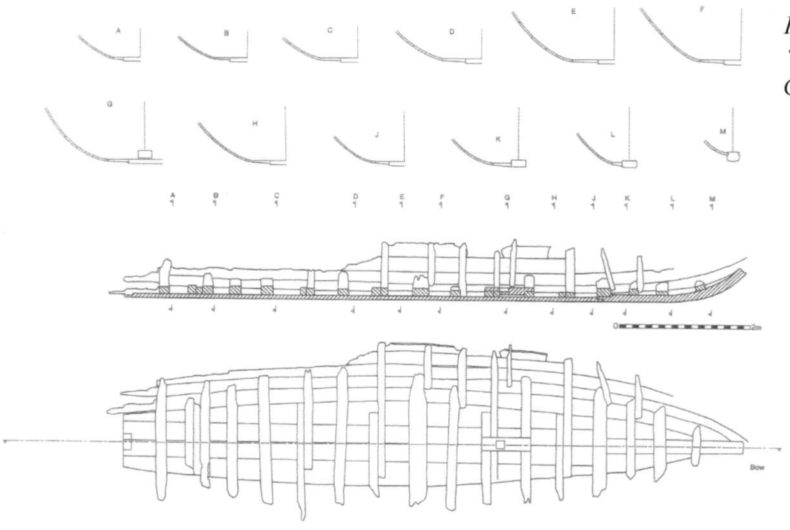

Fig. 2.2B Phase B measured drawing of the 'as-found/torso' model in Fig 2A. (Glamorgan-Gwent Archaeological Trust)

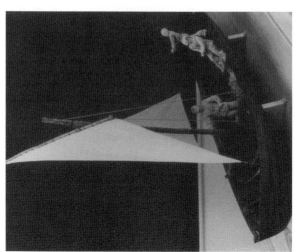

Fig. 2.3B Phase C model of the reconstructed Barland's Farm boat from the drawing in Fig. 2.3A and other evidence. (Glamorgan-Gwent Archaeological Trust)

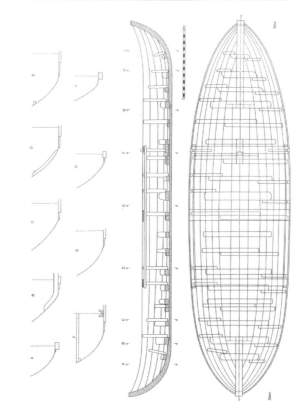

Fig. 2.3A Phase C reconstruction drawing of the Barland's Farm boat developed from the phase B drawing in Fig. 2.2B. (Glamorgan-Gwent Archaeological Trust)

single unit in an articulated state, but the remains were then dismantled for recording, from which an 'as-found/torso' model could also be built. When a vessel is recovered articulated but not subsequently dismantled, on the other hand, as, for example, the Mary Rose (Marsden 2003), an 'as-found/torso' model may still be built using information from every type of recording undertaken.

'Incomplete' Experiments

The Barland's boat project is an example of an 'incomplete experiment' – incomplete in the sense that the final Phase D, the building of a full-scale model, has not yet been attempted – and may never be. The project ended at Phase C with a small-scale reconstruction model or drawing from which performance has been estimated using naval architectural methods (McGrail 1993: 8). Other incomplete projects include: the three Bronze Age sewn plank boats Ferriby 1 (Wright 1990: 85–116; Clark, 2004) Brigg 2 (McGrail 2001: 187–8; Roberts 1992); the Iron Age Hasholme logboat (McGrail 2001: 176–8); and the medieval Graveney boat (McKee 1978). There are many others. Two questions should be asked of such projects:

1) Have these reconstructions been sufficiently criticised and are they now accepted internationally?
2) Would it be both justifiable and cost effective to build an experimental, full-scale model in order to learn more about the original boat; that is, progress from Phase C to D? Would the potential gains in knowledge at least balance the costs?

In both the Ferriby 1 and the Brigg 2 projects, two alternative, and significantly different, reconstructions have been published:

Ferriby 1.
a) A reconstruction drawing of Ferriby 1 based on a Greenwich minimum reconstruction model (McGrail 2001: fig. 5.17) specified by excavator Ted Wright, with performance estimates by naval architect Dr. Ewan Cortlett.
b) Another reconstruction drawing subsequently compiled by Ted Wright which, as John Coates has shown, would have a significantly improved performance (Wright 1990: 113–116, fig. 5.17).

Brigg 'raft'.
a) A Greenwich reconstruction scale model specified by the present author, with performance estimates by John Coates (McGrail 1994; 2001: fig. 5.20).
b) A recent reconstruction model built by Owain Roberts which would have superior performance (Roberts 1992).

The competing reconstructions in both cases were based on different ideas of what was excavated. In other words, different conclusions were reached at the end of Phase A (the assessment of evidence) and therefore different models were built in Phases B and C. How can such differences be resolved? The only sure way is for an independent group of specialists to undertake an audit of the Phase A evidence upon which the reconstructions were based: that is, the excavated timbers, the site archive and the research archive. After critical evaluation of this evidence, the investigators should then attempt to build a Phase B 'as-found/torso' model which would then be compared with the competing models or drawings.

Rules for Experiments?

In his lecture at ISBSA 1, Professor John Coles (1977) lamented that, despite the fact that the experimental approach to archaeology had been in use for over a century, no-one had yet devised a set of rules and procedures. The result of this, he maintained, had been a chaotic mixture of subjective and objective observations, and wide differences of opinions about the reliability and validity of experimental results. Coles made the further point that conclusions drawn from experiments had rarely been subjected to critical scrutiny by impartial observers. Does this criticism sound familiar?

Twenty years later, in a belated response to Professor Coles' lament, John Coates and nine colleagues (1995) published a paper 'Experimental Boat and Ship Archaeology: principles and methods'. This suggested that scholarly standards could best be achieved in future archaeological experiments if participants complied by a set of 'rules and procedures'. The coalition forces that produced this paper did not always agree amongst themselves, indeed two of the original twelve authors opted out before publication: the result is a compromise. Nevertheless, this paper still constitutes a 'road map', a structure within which would-be archaeological experimenters can plan and execute a project. Regrettably, no instances are known of this paper being so used.

There have been written responses to the Coates' paper, notably by Ole Crumlin-Pedersen (1995, 1996). The latter's responses do not adversely criticise Coates' paper: they are complementary to it. They deal, in the main, with practical matters such as the choice of builder and building site, timber, tools and techniques, themes which Coates et al (1995) generally speaking, had not discussed. In these and in other recent papers by Crumlin-Pedersen, a glimpse is given of the experimental 'rules and procedures' used at Roskilde, none of which appear to transgress, as it were, the 'principles and methods' set out in Coates et al (1995). Indeed, Crumlin-Pedersen and Coates have very much in common in their approach to experimental research.

The Future

What then of the future of Experimental Boat Archaeology? Two projects, Hjortspring and Skuldelev, are in their final stages. Those responsible for publication of these experiments are in a very strong position to set standards and to indicate the way ahead for experimental research during the coming decades. Time is needed to assess fully the recently published Hjortspring volume (Crumlin-Pedersen and Trakadas 2003). It is very clear, even after a rapid reading of selected parts, that much thought has gone into the planning of this experiment, but it is also noticeable that the two key papers on reconstruction principles and methods, Coles (1977) and Coates *et al* (1995), are not quoted.

Several very informative papers have already been published about the Skuldelev experiments (for example, Crumlin-Pedersen 1986A, B and C; Andersen *et al* 1997), and a comprehensive and most informative volume (Crumlin-Pedersen and Olsen 2002) sets out the history of the project from excavation to conservation and display. We can now look forward to two further volumes describing the post-excavation research, including the design, building and trials of reconstructions of all five ships – a tremendous achievement. In this context, the term 'design' is intended to mean "the process used at Roskilde to ensure that each reconstruction was built to the size, shape and structure of the corresponding original Skuldelev vessel" i.e. phases A, B and C of the four-phase reconstruction process.

In his recent account of the building of the Roskilde reconstruction of Skuldelev 3, Henrik Juel (2000) noted that Roskilde had had to tackle a fundamental paradox of experimental boat archaeology: Roskilde 'rules and procedures' require that an 'exact copy' of the original vessel be built using Viking Age materials, tools and methods. However, as those Viking Age methods were 'free-arm' and 'by-eye', how can the experimenter control hull shape so that reconstruction is an 'exact copy' of the original?

Crumlin-Pedersen (1996: 115) has described how this paradox was resolved: an 'as-found/torso' small-scale model of each Skuldelev wreck was transformed into a reconstruction model by 'adding the missing sections'; this was done in such a way that the main dimensions of the original hull could be estimated with an uncertainty of less than 2%. Control measurements taken off the reconstruction model then ensured that the full-scale reconstruction could be built to the 'exact shape' of the original hull, without recourse to moulds.

Maritime archaeologists everywhere eagerly look forward to the forthcoming Skuldelev volumes in which we shall be able to study the details of these and other research techniques evolved at Roskilde over the past 25 years. It would be a bonus for the discipline if the Roskilde team were also able to publish a re-assessment of the Coates *et al* (1995) paper on 'principles and methods', in the light of their unique experience of the Hjortspring, Skuldelev and other experiments.

This then is where the future of Experimental Boat Archaeology principally lies – at Roskilde, in the Viking Ship Museum, in its research and in its publications.

There is therefore every reason to believe that both the practice and the theory of this important archaeological technique are in good hands.

References

Andersen, E., Crumlin-Pedersen, O., Vadstrup, S. and Vinner, M., 1997, *Roar Ege – Skuldelev 3 skibet som arkaeologisk eksperiment*. Vikingeskibshallen. Roskilde.

Basch, L., 1987, *Le musée imaginaire de la marine antique*. Institut Hellinque pour la Préservation de la Tradition Nautique. Athens

Baykowski, U., 1994, Kieler Hanse-Cog. In C. Westerdahl (ed) *Crossroads in Ancient Shipbuilding: proceedings of the sixth International Symposium on Boat and Ship Archaeology, Roskilde, 1991*, 261–264. Oxbow Monograph 40. Oxford

Bednarik. R.G. 1997, Earliest evidence of ocean navigation. *International Journal of Nautical Archaeology* 26: 183–191.

Bednarik. R.G. 1998, Experiment in Pleistocene seafaring. *International Journal of Nautical Archaeology* 27: 139–149.

Bednarik. R.G. 2003, Seafaring in the Pleistocene. *Cambridge Archaeological Journal* 13: 41–66

Bischoff, V., 2003, Reconstruction of the Ladby ship. In C. Beltrame (ed), *Boats, Ships and Shipyards: proceedings of the Ninth International Symposium on Boat and Ship Archaeology, Venice 2000*, 71–80. Oxbow Books. Oxford.

Brandt, H. and Hochkisch, K., 1995, Sailing properties of the Hansa cog in comparison with other cargo sailing ships. *Technology Research Schiffstechnik* 42.1: 1–20.

Brown, D.K., 1998, *Experimental boat architecture seen as reverse engineering*. Unpublished Paper presented to the Trireme conference at Corpus Christi College, Oxford in September 1998.

Bruce-Mitford, R., 1975, *Sutton Hoo Ship-Burial*. British Museum Press. London.

Clark, P. (ed), 2004, *The Dover Bronze Age Boat*. English Heritage. Swindon.

Coates, J., McGrail, S, Brown, D., Gifford, E., Grainge, G., Greenhill, B., Marsden, P. M., Rankov, B., Tipping, C. and Wright, E., 1995, Experimental boat and ship archaeology. *International Journal Nautical Archaeology* 24: 293–301.

Coles, J. M., 1966, Experimental Archaeology. *Proceedings of the Society of Antiquaries of Scotland* 99: 1–20.

Coles, J. M., 1977, Experimental archaeology: theory and principles. In S. McGrail (ed) *Sources and techniques in Boat Archaeology*: 233–243. B.A.R. 29. Oxford.

Coles. J. M. 1979, *Experimental Archaeology*. Academic Press. London.

Crumlin-Pedersen, O., 1966, Two Danish side rudders. *Mariner's Mirror* 52: 251–261.

Crumlin-Pedersen, O., 1970, Viking ships of Roskilde. In J.S. Morrison, et al. (eds), *Aspects of the history of wooden shipbuilding*, 7–23. Maritime Monograph 1. Greenwich

Crumlin-Pedersen, O., 1986a, 'Roar' project. In O. Crumlin-Pedersen and M. Vinner (eds), *Sailing into the Past. Proceedings of the International Seminar on Replicas of Ancient and Medieval Vessels, Roskilde, 1984*, 94–103. Vikingeskibshallen. Roskilde.

Crumlin-Pedersen, O., 1986b, Aspects of wood technology in medieval shipbuilding. In O. Crumlin-Pedersen and M. Vinner (eds), *Sailing into the Past. Proceedings of the*

International Seminar on Replicas of Ancient and Medieval Vessels, Roskilde, 1984, 138–147. Vikingeskibshallen. Roskilde.

Crumlin-Pedersen, O., 1986c. Aspects of Viking-Age Ship-building in the Light of the Construction and Trials of the Skuldelev Ship-Replicas Saga Siglar and Roar Ege. *Journal of Danish Archaeology* 5: 209–228

Crumlin-Pedersen, O., 1995, Experimental archaeology and ships. *International Journal of Nautical Archaeology* 24: 303–6

Crumlin-Pedersen, O., 1996, Problems of reconstruction and the estimation of performance. In R. Gardiner (ed), *The Earliest Ships: the evolution of boats into ships*, 110–119. Conway's History of Ships. Conway Maritime Press, London.

Crumlin-Pedersen, O. and Olsen, O. (eds), 2002, *The Skuldelev Ships 1. Topography, Archaeology, History, Conservation and Display*. Ships and Boats of the North 4.1. Vikinge-skibshallen. Roskilde.

Crumlin-Pedersen, O. and Trakadas, A. (eds), 2003, *Hjort-spring. A Pre-Roman Iron-Age Warship in Context*. Ships and Boats of the North 5. Vikingeskibshallen. Roskilde.

Fenwick, V. (ed), 1978, *Graveney Boat*. B.A.R. 53. Oxford.

Giesecke, H.E., 1983, Akroteri ship fresco. *International Journal of Nautical Archaeology* 12: 123–143

Gilmer, T. C., 1978, Thera ships: a re-analysis. *Mariner's Mirror* 64: 125–133.

Gilmer, T. C., 1985, Thera ships as sailing vessel. *Mariner's Mirror* 71: 401–413.

Heyerdahl, T., 1978, *Early Man and the Ocean*. Allen and Unwin. London.

Hoheisel, W. D., 1994, Full-scale replica of the Hanse Cog of 1480. In C. Westerdahl (ed), *Crossroads in Ancient Ship-building: proceedings of the sixth International Symposium on Boat and Ship Archaeology, Roskilde, 1991*, 257–260. Oxbow Monograph 40. Oxford

Irwin, G. 1992, *Prehistoric Exploration and Colonisation of the Pacific*. Cambridge University Press. Cambridge.

Johnston, P. F., 1997, Thera. In J. P.Delgado (ed), *Encyclopaedia of Underwater and Maritime Archaeology*, 419–420. British Museum Press. London.

Johnstone, P., 1972, Bronze Age sea trial. *Antiquity* 46: 269–274.

Johnstone, P., 1973, Kalnes Bronze Age boat. *Antiquity* 47: 60–61.

Juel, H. 2000, *Spaner: omkring et vikingeskib*. Holst and Son. Copenhagen.

Katzev, M. L. 1989, Kyrenia 2. In H. Tzalas (ed), *Tropis I, 1st International Symposium on Ship Construction in Antiquity*, 163–175. Hellenic Institute for the Preservation of Nautical Tradition. Athens.

Katzev, M. L., 1990, Analysis of the experimental voyages of Kyrenia 2. In H. Tzalas (ed), *Tropis II, 2nd International Symposium on Ship Construction in Antiquity*, 245–255. Hellenic Institute for the Preservation of Nautical Tradition. Athens.

McGrail, S. (ed), 1977, *Sources and techniques in Boat Archaeology*. B.A.R. 29. Oxford.

McGrail, S., 1986, Experimental boat archaeology. In O. Crumlin-Pedersen and M. Vinner (eds), *Sailing into the Past. Proceedings of the International Seminar on Replicas of Ancient and Medieval Vessels, Roskilde, 1984*, 8–17. Vikingeskibshallen. Roskilde.

McGrail, S., 1992, Replicas, reconstructions and floating hypotheses. *International Journal of Nautical Archaeology* 21: 353–5.

McGrail, S., 1993, Experimental archaeology and the Trireme. In T., Shaw, (ed) *Trireme Project*, 4–10. Oxbow Monograph 31. Oxford.

McGrail, S., 1994, Brigg 'raft': a flat-bottomed boat. *International Journal of Nautical Archaeology* 23: 283–8.

McGrail, S., 2001, *Boats of the World*. Oxford Oxford University Press. Oxford.

McGrail, S. and McKee, E., 1974, *Building and Trials of the Replica of an Ancient Boat: Gokstad faering*. National Maritime Museum Monograph 11. Greenwich. (2 volumes).

McKee, E., 1978, 'Reconstruction' and 'Replicas'. In V. Fenwick (ed), *Graveney Boat*, 265–302; 307–9. B.A.R. 53. Oxford

Marsden, P., 2003, *Sealed by Time: the loss and recovery of the Mary Rose*. Archaeology of the Mary Rose Vol.1. Mary Rose Trust. Portsmouth.

Morgan, L., 1988, *Miniature Wall Paintings of Thera*. Cambridge University Press. Cambridge.

Morrison, J. S., and Coates, J. F., 1986, *Athenian Trireme*. Cambridge University Press. Cambridge.

Morrison, J. S., Coates, J. F. and Rankov, N. B., 2000, *Athenian Trireme*. Cambridge University Press. Cambridge.

Nayling, N., 1998, *Magor Pill Medieval Wreck*. CBA Research Report 115. Council for British Archaeology. York.

Nayling, N., and McGrail, S., 2004, *Barland's Farm Romano-Celtic Boat*. CBA Research Report 138. Council for British Archaeology. York

Roberts, O., 1992, Brigg 'raft' re-assessed as a round bilge Bronze Age boat. *International Journal of Nautical Archaeology* 21: 245–258

Rosenberg, G., 1937, *Hjortspringfundet*. I Kommission hos Gyldendalske Boghandel, Nordisk Forlag.Copenhagen.

Severin, T., 1978, *Brendan Voyage*. Hutchinson. London.

Severin, T., 1982, *Sindbad Voyage*. Hutchinson. London.

Severin, T., 1985, *Jason Voyage*. Hutchinson. London.

Severin, T., 1987, *Ulysses Voyage*. Hutchinson. London.

Severin, T., 1994, *China Voyage*. Little, Brown and Co. London.

Sorensen, A. C., 2001, *Ladby: a Danish ship-grave from the Viking age*. Ships and Boats of the North Vol.3. Viking Ship Museum in cooperation with the National Museum of Denmark. Roskilde.

Steffy, J. R., 1994, *Wooden Shipbuilding and the Interpretation of Wrecks*. Texas A and M University Press. College Station.

Throckmorton, P. (ed), 1987, *History from the Sea: shipwrecks and archaeology; from Homer's Odyssey to the Titanic*. Mitchell Beazley. London.

Toby, A. S. 1986, World's first warships. *International Journal of Nautical Archaeology* 15: 339–346

Wachsmann, S., 1998, *Seagoing Ships and Seamanship in the Bronze Age Levant*. Texas A and M University Press. College Station.

Wright, E. V., 1990, *Ferriby Boats: Seacraft of the Bronze Age*. Routledge. London.

3 Experimental archaeology at the Viking Ship Museum in Roskilde

Søren Nielsen

Reconstructing a Viking Age longship of which only 25% is preserved (Fig. 3.1) is a big challenge, and it is no coincidence that Skuldelev 2 is the last of the five Skuldelev ships to be reconstructed at the Viking Ship Museum in Roskilde. The experience gained by building the other ships plays a huge part, but what further sources do we use when reconstructing? We reconstruct the ships and the trades related to their construction, compiling results on the way in order to provide archaeologists, historians, etc., with the possibility to create a more varied image of the past and to place the archaeological finds in a larger cultural-historical context.

Our background is not anchored in a distinct boat-building tradition, although we have traditionally skilled boatbuilders among us. Our background lies in the trade of boatbuilding itself in a broad sense, but with the Nordic clinker-built boat as our starting point. We consider the maintenance and sailing of our own collection of boats from Norway (Fig. 3.2), the Faeroe Islands, Sweden, Finland and Denmark an important background for our work. Furthermore, we make use of the knowledge and experience of traditional boatbuilders, sailors of square-

rigged boats and other persons within this line of work and interest.

As an example, we wanted to include a traditional Norwegian boat in our collection, and so we contacted boatbuilder Harald Dalland, from Tysnes in Western Norway. He builds the traditional *oselver*, which is characterized by particularly wide planks of pine, as in Skuldelev 1 and 6. We asked him to help us choose appropriate wood from "his" forests to be used for the

Fig. 3.2. Rana, a north Norwegian storåttring, built in 1892 (Werner Karrasch).

Fig. 3.1. The Viking Age longship Skuldelev 2, built in 1042 (Werner Karrasch).

first boat in pine that we were going to reconstruct, Skuldelev 6. His help was necessary, as we did not have expertise in picking out this sort of wood. Harald Dalland showed us a traditional, specialized, detailed and varied trade full of experience and knowledge of boatbuilding, materials and the utility of boats. He said "look at the shape of the hull and tell me for what purpose the boat was originally built." The ability to evaluate a boat is an important part of understanding and building it, in the first place.

We did not learn Harald's trade, nor were we fully taught how to choose the right pine trees for planks – it would take many years and many boats to achieve his skills. However, we did learn the level of detail in his trade. And this can be compared to the trade of a Viking Age boat-builder, as the boats then (Fig 3.3) were just as advanced. Now it is up to us to retrieve all the finer points of a trade where we know the result – the boat – but not all the steps leading up to it.

Apart from living bearers of tradition, we also use a diversity of sources in the process of reconstruction. The most important of them all is, of course, the find material,

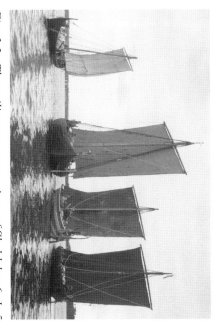

Fig. 3.3. The sailing reconstructions of Skuldelev 6, 1, 5 and 3 (Werner Karrasch).

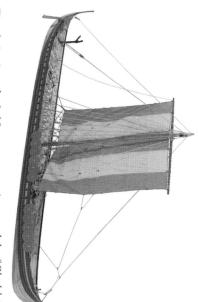

Fig. 3.4. A scale 1:10 reconstruction model of Skuldelev 2 (Werner Karrasch).

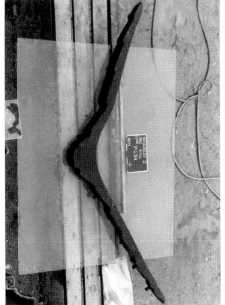

Fig. 3.5. A floor timber from Skuldelev 2 (The Viking Ship Museum).

along with other comparable archaeological finds, preferably from the same period and same geographical area. Then we have the iconographical sources (picture-stones, graffiti on timber etc.), historical sources and scientific sources as pollen-analysis, wood anatomy and so on.

In 1993 the display of the remains of Skuldelev 2 in the museum was at long last finished. A new reconstruction model in cardboard was created, from which a drawing of the inner edge-lines of the strakes was made. A few years later, funds from the Tuborg Foundation made it possible to reconstruct the ship with a view to building a wooden model in scale 1:10 (Fig 3.4). Erik Andersen threw himself at reconstructing the missing parts, the sail and the rig for the ship.

In 2000 the Tuborg Foundation again made a large donation to the Viking Ship Museum, this time to fund a full-scale reconstruction of Skuldelev 2. For this project, nine boatbuilders (Ture M. Møller, Thomas Finderup, Tom Nicolajsen, Hanus Jensen, Birger Andersen, Rasmus B. Jensen, Pernille Voss, Jacob Schroll, Lene Christensen, and Petter Mellberg) and other specialists with a combined experience from traditional Scandinavian boatbuilding, restorations and reconstructions of Viking Age and Medieval boats and ships, were employed by the museum.

The wooden model and the inner edge-line drawing are the starting points for building the ship in full scale. The hull shape, which was reconstructed on the basis of the cardboard model, is seldom altered when building the full scale ship. It has happened that we have had to go back and alter the inner edge-line drawing, as inch-thick radially split oak planks do not behave in the same way as downscaled cardboard when twisted and bent on to a stem. However, the basic reconstruction of the hull takes place in the cardboard model, where you can look at all the recovered parts of the ship simultaneously.

After considering the influence of a thousand-year stay in the ground, and what the object originally looked like (Fig 3.5), all the recovered parts of the ship are copied according to the 1-to-1 documentation of the original parts, including the finish and the peculiarities of each piece. It is an important process to be able to find and practise the ship's level of craftsmanship and later to be able to transfer this experience to the parts which were not found.

As a starting point, the parts that were not found are reconstructed on the wooden model, but these solutions are then discussed in a drawing and reconstruction committee, and according to its decisions a working drawing is made. This drawing is passed on to the boatbuilder along with photographs of corresponding original material, and he or she examines the original ship or comparable ship-parts in the Archaeological Workshop. Roskilde 6, a 36-meter-long warship from the Viking Age, was recently documented here. The following then have to be determined:

- Wood species
- Position of the pith in the finished piece
- Direction of the wood fibres
- Pattern of the medullary rays
- Quality of the material in general
- Tool marks

It can be difficult to observe details on the conserved ship, Skuldelev 2, whereas the unconserved timbers of Roskilde 6 hold an inexhaustible amount of information. The close cooperation between the boatbuilders and the Archaeological Workshop contributes to a better reconstruction, as well as a better documentation.

According to these observations, the trees are chosen in the forest (Fig 3.6) and the production method and the range of tools are decided upon. If the boatbuilder can match both the tool marks and the position of the object in the tree, as it can be seen on the original ship, we are reasonably certain that we have chosen the same technique as they used a thousand years ago.

In other words, the final drawings are not produced before the ship is finished. They are the result of the ongoing reconstruction and not the result of decisions made only on the drawing table. The ship we build is the documentation and a publication of our work; it is the concrete result of the experimental-archaeological work.

But there are also topics that extend beyond the concrete ship reconstruction process. I have chosen two examples on these parallel topics.

The planks on Skuldelev 2 are made of radially split oak. Dendrochronologists have determined that the trees were felled in the year 1042 near Dublin, Ireland. The cross sections of the original planks show that the trees had grown very slowly. Modern oak grows much faster, with wider annual rings, and it is known that the wider the rings, the stronger and more durable the wood is. Slowly grown oak is more porous, easier to split and work, and is more bendable and flexible. Faster grown oak is preferred when it comes to the large carvel-built ships of modern times. Was slowly grown oak of decisive importance to the strength of the longship's flexible hull, or was the light construction the most important factor with relation to the strength, meaning that the type of oak was irrelevant? To answer this question we need the help of wood-technologists and engineers.

The planks clearly reflect a high quality – clean planks free of knots. But as we can see from the medullary ray pattern, they were not all straight-grown (Fig 3.7). In order to split an oak log a meter in diameter into 16 to 24 boards with a final width of 33 cm, you need a tree without branches and overgrown knots, without rot or other defects in the centre of the tree, and which did not twist when growing (Fig 3.8a). From this tree we got 24 planks.

If you climb down one step on the quality ladder, to where the tree is smaller (Fig 3.8b), the trunk slightly twisted, perhaps with a sudden bend, or has irregular bark (a sign of small internal defects), we only obtain 10 planks as a rule (Fig 3.9). And even this quality can be hard to find in modern monocultural forests! However, the ray pattern in the boards of this quality is clearly different, and they look more like the planks in the original ship. From an economic point of a view, it is our experience that it pays off to buy logs of the finest quality, costing twice as much as the quality just below. The

Fig. 3.7. Detail of a radially split, Viking Age oak plank (Ivan Conrad Hansen).

Fig. 3.6. Compass timber of oak for the production of floor timbers (Werner Karrasch).

Fig. 3.8 a/b. First and second choice oak trees for plank production (Werner Karrasch).

cheaper logs have been by far the most expensive per board-meter as the level of utilization is lower and it takes longer to work. Working on the finest quality is faster because the splitting is cleaner and more straight, which makes the rough hewing that follows easier and faster.

However, this does not mean that we can deduce that people in the Viking Age only chose (or for that matter even had access to) timber which matched today's best quality. If trees as well as manpower were cheap, it did not matter if you got fewer planks from a tree and therefore had to use a larger number of trees for the ship. The trees were split and the boards were hewn out roughly in the forest, and probably the distance from the forest to the place where the ship was built also played a role in which trees were chosen.

This question is related to the following larger questions about the use of the forest resource:

• How was the mixed-culture of the Viking Age forest able to produce these big, almost clean, straight, long oak trees?

Fig. 3.9. Second choice split logs of oak for plank production (Werner Karrasch).

Fig. 3.10. Traditional tar burning at Kuhmo, Finland (Werner Karrasch).

Fig. 3.11. Full scale reconstruction of Skuldelev 2 in progress (Werner Karrasch).

• How widely spaced were the usable oak trees in the Viking Age forest?

• How large an area of the then existing forest-type was necessary to build just one longship?

- How many longships were built during this period?

Perhaps the answers can provide us with an idea on why the construction of the ships changed through time, that it is not just a question of changed routes and trade goods, but that the lack of good timber can have played a crucial role. These are questions that can only be solved through interdisciplinary cooperation.

The second example is about the requirement for human resources and about clarifying which further disciplines should participate in fulfilling the project of building a longship. We would like to know how much time had to be committed to such an enterprise and we would like to throw some light on the complete organisation involved.

We have been watching boatbuilders, blacksmiths, ropemakers, sailmakers and weavers over many years. Recently we had the opportunity to participate in the production of tar in Kuhmo in Finland (Fig 3.10), and not surprisingly we realised that tar burning is also a trade based on the experience of generations and handed down knowledge. From a big stack of 60 cubic metres they extracted approximately 2000 litres of tar by burning roots and resinous pine in the same way as they have probably done for the last thousand years.

To get an impression of which specialists were needed, we have tried to add it all up. Building a longship demands at least:

- Iron workers   ?
- Traders   ?
- Farmers   ?
- Forest workers   10 men for 3 months
- Transporters   ?
- Boatbuilders   10 men for 7 months
- Stem-smith (master boatbuilder)   1 man for 7 months
- Shield-makers   1 man for 5 months
- Riveters   2 men for 3 months
- Tar-burners   4 men for 2 months
- Blacksmiths   2 men for 5 months
- Weavers   ?
- Sailmakers   ?
- Ropemakers   ?
- Etc.

These figures are still very much based on estimation, but they are becoming more likely as we approach the end of building the ship because every process is timed exactly. Our current estimate is that 10 boatbuilders, 10 forest workers, 5 unskilled workers, etc., would be able to build a longship in approximately half a year.

Everybody at this symposium agrees on the importance of experimental archaeology. But if projects of reconstruction shall be more than communicating the past to the public (Fig 3.11), it requires a close and thorough cooperation between relevant specialists, such as wood analysts, museum conservators, archaeologists, engineers, ethnologists, sailors, foresters, skilled workmen, historians etc. It requires furthermore that all involved take an active part in the process and influence its course with their own professional skill. We are each professionals at the different things we do and this has to be taken advantage of. Cooperation is inspiring and necessary in order to maintain and develop experimental archaeology as an important method of research.

4 History written in tool marks

Thomas Finderup

The boatyard at the Viking Ship Museum has worked in experimental archaeology for over 17 years, since the construction of the copy of Skuldelev find 3 in 1984. Today (2003) we are eight boatbuilders with a combined 50 years of experience in the construction of replicas. We have built copies of the following finds: Skuldelev 1–6, the Gislinge boat, the Gokstad *færing*, the Gokstad *sexæring*, Kalmar 3, Ralswiek 1, the Egernsund pram and the Gedesby ship (the first eight from the Viking Period and the last four from the Middle Ages), although not all of these were built at the Viking Ship Museum. Through these we have developed a broad and deep experience in the construction of Nordic craft spanning several centuries.

Questions

An explanation for why we build replicas can be found in normal human curiosity. Almost anyone, whether amateur or professional, who stands over a ship find begins to ask many questions. Questions such as:

- Sensory questions – how did the ship look when it was new? How did it smell in the builder's yard?
- Human questions – was the work hard? Were they skilled craftsmen?
- Resource questions – How much wood and what kind was used? How long did it take to build?
- Technical questions – which tools did they use? How long was the ship?

Some of these questions can be answered exactly through analysis of the find material, while others will never be answered. We could choose to concentrate only on the former and leave the rest, but our curiosity forbids it. Here is where experimental archaeology comes into the picture.

One can compare it to a police detective's analysis of a crime scene. In some cases, there are witnesses who can be interrogated, while in others there is only physical evidence of what happened. In the best case, one can collect an overwhelming combination of testimony to prove what happened. To reach a result, the detective follows many trails through sources and disciplines. He tests his theories through experiments, through the recreation of how the crime might have occurred, and the result is a combination of answers and new questions. Our working methods in experimental archaeology have many similarities to this technique. Often we find no direct evidence, but must explore the possibilities of how something might have happened. In the course of the work, we are constantly aware of how we find answers to our questions and how we can form new questions.

In the following, I will try to show how we have worked with the technical question of Viking tools and craftsmanship in the reconstruction of Skuldelev 2, a longship 30m in length, originally built in Ireland in the 11th century.

Tools

Some of the questions we have investigated with all of our replicas include:

- What tools were used?
- What techniques were used?
- How long did construction take?
- How efficiently was the raw material used?

Answers to the first two technical questions are the prerequisite for answering the latter resource questions. Here we start by trying to discover what tools were used on the original ship. Our source material, in order of priority, is:

1. Tool marks
2. Tool finds
3. Iconography
4. Historical documents
5. Ethnographic parallels
6. The boatbuilder's own experience

Now I will try to provide a short description of how we use these sources.

Thomas Finderup

Tool marks

Our choice of tools is supported by all of these sources, but original tool marks are always the most important, as they are the only "primary evidence." In some cases, we have no evidence of any kind that can give us a clue as to how the Vikings solved a particular problem, and we have to experiment our way to a solution. As with any other source material, we must cite it properly. We can in this case refer to the find number for original timbers and tool finds.

During the construction of replicas we use all of the information that can be extracted from the original timbers. Where we lack this sort of data, we use information from parallel finds. During the construction of the replica of Skuldelev 2, which is very poorly preserved, we have also used information from Roskilde 6, a longship of 37m, dated to AD 1030. Roskilde 6 has been in the process of documentation at the museum immediately next to the boatyard.

Ivan Conrad Hansen of the Viking Ship Museum's Find Receiving Facility (formerly part of the National Museum), has focused on squeezing the maximum amount of information out of the material, initially recorded in 1:1 drawings on plastic sheet and analog photography (Fig. 4.1) and more recently using a FaroArm coordinate

measuring machine (CMM) and digital photography. Following documentation, he has worked on interpreting the tool marks in collaboration with the museum's boatbuilders.

In this way, we have been able to determine such things as the lengths of axe edges, the types of planes and scrapers and how they were used, how skilled the users were, how they appreciated the qualities of the wood, and what hewing techniques they used, etc.

Tool finds

After interpreting the tool marks, we try to match them with tool finds from the Viking Period. In order to create an adequate comparative database, we decided to catalogue a "collection" of Viking tool finds. All of the Danish museums and a number of museums abroad were contacted and asked to report what finds they held. We received answers from 45 museums in Denmark, Sweden, Norway, England, Ireland and Germany. Several of the most interesting collections were visited and tools photographed, drawn, weighed and described. In this way we were able to develop a database of over 300 tools (Fig. 4.2).

From these we chose which tools we would use to build the replica. The criteria used in the selection were:

1. They should match the marks found in the original timbers or agree with other primary source material.
2. They should be as contemporaneous to the ship as possible.
3. They should come from sites in Ireland.
4. The type should be richly represented in the find material.

Iconographic sources

There are no known contemporaneous Danish images of boatbuilding from the Viking Period. Axes are shown on individual picture stones from the broader Viking world, but they are typically weapons. There are a number of illustrations from elsewhere in Europe, but they have to

Fig. 4.2. Documentation of tool finds (photo Werner Karrasch, Viking Ship Museum).

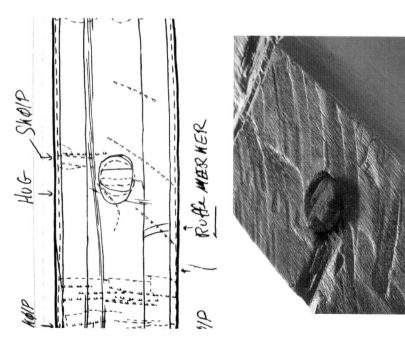

Fig. 4.1. Documentation of tool marks: a. (top) full-size tracing on clear plastic (drawing Ivan C. Hansen): b. (bottom) macro photography in raking light (photo Ivan C. Hansen).

be used with great care. The Bayeux tapestry is the best known of these. Such source material should always be corroborated by other evidence. The Bayeux tapestry shows a broadaxe in use for the hewing of plank (Rud 1994: 61), but there are only three axes of this type in the Danish archaeological material, three from Hedeby/Haithabu (Germany), none from Norway and a single example from Sweden. The two best preserved are from the Danish finds and are both heirlooms, highly decorated with inlaid copper and silver (Nielsen 1991), as is the Swedish example. They were probably never used, even if they are clearly decorated examples of working axes rather than weapons, as can be seen from the edge bevel on only one side. There are no marks made by such broadaxes found on Danish Viking ships.

Written sources

We have made little use of this material up to the present. As none is contemporaneous with the ship, they must be used with great care and only where they can be corroborated by several of the other sources.

Ethnological parallels

Sometimes, it can be nearly impossible to figure out a reasonable explanation of how the Vikings carried out a particular task from the primary evidence. The study of how similar problems were solved in both our own and other regions over time can provide some inspiration.

Boatbuilders' experience

The craftsmen who participate in the experiment can use some of their own experience from previous projects with care. It is important that he or she enters the experiment with curiosity and free from preconceptions, and does not rule out possibilities with thoughts such as "my grandfather would never have done it this way." Still, there are things which may be common to both Viking and modern craftsmen, as they both wanted/want to carry out the work

Fig. 4.3. Cutting off rivet ends with chisel and hammer (photo Werner Karrasch).

Fig. 4.4. Difference in nail ends cut off with a chisel (left) and nippers (right) (photos author).

in the easiest and most practical way, and the craftsman is entitled to use his or her experience when choosing a tool or technique.

The experiment

Once all of the sources have been considered, we determine how the work will be carried out. In some cases, the source material is unequivocal about how the job was done, while in others we are completely in the dark. A report is written describing which tools, equipment and techniques will be employed and how. All choices are justified with citations from the source material. Once this is done, accurate copies of the chosen tools are ordered and the project can begin. What follows here are some examples of how we work with this method.

Nippers

One of the questions we have long wanted to ask the Vikings is how they cut off the ends of rivets before peening them over the roves. There are no preserved nippers from the Viking Period, only fragments of one from Viborg Søndersø (Jantzen 1998: 211) which are without context, yet during the construction of a ship such as Skuldelev 2, over 5000 rivets have to be cut off. We have no sources that tell us how this should be done. With the inspiration of oral tradition from Norway and the Faroe Islands of how they did it in the "old days," we began to experiment. After several attempts, we arrived at a method that seems to work reasonably well. With a copy of a chisel from Hedeby (Westphalen 2002: Table 7/16), a large hammer from Dublin (unpublished) and a small hammer from Dublin (unpublished) we could cut off the ends of the nails. The large hammer is held against one side of the nail, and a nick is made in the opposite side with the chisel and the small hammer (Fig. 4.3). The nail end can then be bent back and forth until it breaks off. At the new end of the nail are tool marks that show how the cut was made, marks that are very different from the marks at the end of a nail that has simply been nipped off (Fig. 4.4).

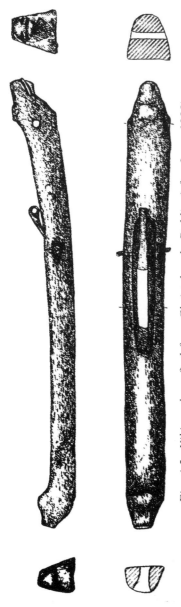

Fig. 4.5. Viking plane find from Christchurch, Dublin (after Lang 1988).

Fig. 4.6. Plane tool marks a. (left) in original plank from Roskilde 6 (photo Ivan C. Hansen); b. (right) in replica plank from Skuldelev 2 reconstruction (photo author).

We now have the possibility to compare our cut ends to cut ends we may find from the Viking Period. We have thus answered how we might nip off nail ends without a pair of nippers, and created a new question: is our method one that was actually used? We have also sharpened our examination of the archaeological find material.

This method provided the introduction to a lively debate among participants at ISBSA 10, and on the practical day they had the chance to test our methods and their own theories. In this way, experimental archaeology showed its potential as a catalyst for a good professional debate.

Drill

We have many different types of evidence that show how holes were bored in the frames: cross-sections of the holes themselves, chips from boring, iconography, and many finds of drills. All of this evidence agrees that spoon bits were the type used in boatbuilding, so we use copies of a spoon bit from Hedeby (Westphalen 2002: table 22/13). Unfortunately, there are no handles preserved from the Viking Period, and so we have used a copy of a handle found in the Gedesby ship of c. 1280 (Bill 1992: 59). The chips made by this drill are photographed and compared to those we know from the Viking Period. Only through the examination of the chips have we been able to say with certainty that a spoon bit was used.

For making the 7000 smaller (8mm) holes in the ship, we decided at the start of the project to make a copy of an auger from Hedeby (Westphalen 2002: table 22/5), but the tool proved to be very difficult in practice. Inspired by modern Indian boatbuilding, we decided to try a bow drill, which is still used there. There are no known Viking finds of a completely preserved bow drill, but many fragments are interpreted as the remains of bow drills. These include a bow from the Viking settlement at L'Anse aux Meadows in Newfoundland (Wallace 1992: 35), which was found with ship parts dated to c. 1000 and is interpreted as the bow to a drill. For the bit, we have used a copy of a small spoon bit from Hedeby (Westphalen 2002: table 22/7). This drill has shown itself to be very

efficient and we now bore nail holes with it. Still, we cannot say that the Vikings used the bow drill, but we have raised a research question. How did Viking boat-builders manage to drill 7000 holes? At the same time, we have developed a great deal of knowledge about how a bow drill works and the chips it produces, which can help us to interpret finds better and possibly identify traces of bow drill use in the original material.

Plane

There are no tool marks preserved on the surfaces of Skuldelev 2's planks, due to the condition of the material. We thus turned to the remains of Roskilde 6, such as plank 1482, where there are many marks to be seen. Together with the experts cleaning and documenting the find, we studied the marks on the plank and agreed that they seem to have been made by a block plane. The basis of this identification was that the marks were flat at the bottom (axes and adzes leave bowl-shaped marks).

There is a single find of a tool of this type from the Viking Period (Fig. 4.5), from under a Viking house in Dublin, dated to the 11th century (Lang 1988: 33). Based on this, we made a slightly scaled-up copy, so that the width of the iron would correspond to the width of the tool marks in the planks of Roskilde 6. After tests, the marks were compared with the originals, which they resembled closely (Fig. 4.6). The plane functioned, but left a lot of torn grain, due to the large throat (the gap in the sole in front of the iron). We could easily improve on this, on the grounds that the excavated plane was a badly made example, but how far down this road should we go? We must return to the source material and search for other examples of planes.

The tool database

We have provided above a few examples of how, in the daily work in the boatyard, we try to discover how the Vikings built their ships. One of the results will be a database of the tools we use at the museum. This is planned as a resource for experimental archaeologists, maritime archaeologists and artists, a key to understanding the history that is written in tool marks. The database will contain the following information about the copies we use (Fig. 4.7 and 4.8):

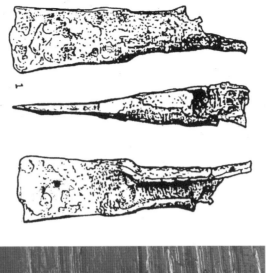

Fig. 4.7. Documentation of original tool, in this case a chisel, in drawing (after Jantzen 2002) and photos of original tool marks (photo Ivan C. Hansen).

Fig. 4.8. Documentation of replica tool: the tool, how it is used, the marks it leaves, and the chips it produces (photos Werner Karrasch).

- Catalogue data about the original tool find
- Drawings of the original find
- Photos of the original find
- Photos of tool marks in the original timbers
- Photos of the copy
- Drawings of the copy
- Photos of the copy in use
- Photos of the marks made by the copy
- Photos of the chips/shavings produced by the copy

We think that this database will be a good tool, one that will help everyone who works with Viking ship finds and tool finds. We also hope that it will create greater interest in the field, so that in the future we can work more closely with historians, archaeologists, blacksmiths, artists, etc. We would like to be able to collect and integrate a wide range of information about how ships were built and how tools developed over time.

Conclusion

It is our experience that a good result requires much more than just the right tools. It requires many years of experience with an axe to appreciate the possibilities of what one can do with it. The same is true of marks that one produces with the tool. It is meaningless to compare the marks made by a modern amateur with those made by a professional boatbuilder in the Viking Period. If we were to sum up our requirements for good experimental archaeology, they might follow these lines:

- Before starting the experiment, all of the source material must be collected and considered.
- To the greatest degree possible, accurate copies of tools and equipment should be used.
- The decisions made in the experiment should be properly documented and published, a process that must start before the experiment itself begins. Things can change in the course of the work, but there should always be a written record of the basis of decisions taken in the building process.
- All the relevant groups of knowledgeable professionals should be consulted.

- The source material should be used as the basis for a critical assessment of how things have been done.
- An external group of experts should follow the project closely, evaluate it and publish their findings.
- The craftsmen who participate should have both high professional competence and a strong interest in the project.
- The results must be published.

If one makes sure that all of these aspects are in order, we believe that experimental archaeology can be a useful tool for the interpretation of the archaeological material. At the same time, in our boatyard we have created a living history that builds on the same source material as all other history. Here we can give the "reader" our most qualified hypothesis about how ships were built, while they have the opportunity to criticise or debate while the "book" is still being written. Experimental archaeology is both research and presentation. It is a delicate balance, but for us research always has the first priority.

References

Bill, Jan 1992, *Beretning for udgravningen af Gedesbyskibet 1990.* Nationalmuseet, Oldtid og Middelalder, Skibshistorisk laboratorium, rapport nr. 5/1992. Unpublished, circulated report. Roskilde.

Jantzen, Connie 1998, Genstande af metal. In Hjermind, J., Iversen, M. and Krongaard Kristensen, H. (eds) *Viborg Sonderso 1000–1300. Byarkaeologiske undersogelser 1981 og 1984–85,* pp.185–213. Højbjerg.

Lang, James T., 1988, *Viking Age decorated wood. A study of its ornament and style.* Medieval Dublin excavations 1962–81, Ser. B, Vol. 1. Dublin.

Rud, Mogens 1994, *The Bayeux Tapestry and the Battle of Hastings 1066.* 2nd English edition, Copenhagen 1994 (transl. from the 3rd Danish edition 1992).

Nielsen, Bjarne Henning 1991, Langbladsoksen. *Skalk* 1991.2: 9–13.

Wallace, Birgitta Linderoth 1992, L'Anse aux Meadows, the western outpost. In Clausen, Birthe L. (ed.) *Viking Voyages to North America,* pp. 30–42. Roskilde.

Westphalen, Petra 2002, *Die Eisenfunde von Haithabu. Die Ausgrabungen von Haithabu* 10. Neumünster.

5 Reconstruction of rope for the copy of Skuldelev 2: Rope in the Viking Period

Ole Magnus

Background

My background for this work with the reconstruction of Viking rope is that of a craftsman. I am a ropemaker and my approach to the material began as that of a craftsman, which means analysis with my hands, the feeling of the material, its form and the shaping of it, together with thoughts on the people who once worked with rope in the Viking Period. Later, I learned how to use a microscope from Kirsten Jespersen, who was a conservator at the Viking Ship Museum and the Danish National Museum. This means analysis with sight that which is not normally visible to the naked eye, and the understanding of the biological construction of the material. These are two inherently different approaches, but they make good partners.

Fig. 5.1. The author at work on a ropewalk (Verner Hyldekrog Sorensen).

Work at the Viking Ship Museum

When the replica of Skuldelev find 3 was built at the Viking Ship Museum in Roskilde in 1984, with great confidence I made the rope for the new ship from hemp at an existing ropewalk, on an electric ropemaking machine. I knew that electrical power was not appropriate for the Viking Age, but I proudly used otherwise traditional methods to produce rope (Fig. 5.1).

When I made the rope for the reconstruction of Skuldelev find 2, starting in 2004, I planned to sit on my stool with the same degree of confidence and spin bast, the fibrous layer just under the bark of the linden tree, into yarns, and later lay them into three-stranded rope with my bare hands, often still sitting down. Despite the great size and length of rope needed, I did not plan to use any machinery, only more human hands (Fig. 5.2).

In one sense, this is a professional step backwards. In any case, my old master ropemaker Johannes Thorsen said that I had now become too primitive, when I told him some years ago that I realised that rope in the Viking Period was made purely by hand, without any tools. He

Fig. 5.2. The author at work making rope by hand (Werner Karrasch).

was angry with me and felt slighted, that I had undermined his proud thoughts about the ropemaker and his long ropewalk as a craft a millennium old.

The greatest part of a traditional ropemaker's work was walking backwards down the ropewalk with hemp fibre would round his belly, spinning one of the many yarns that would become rope. One could say that it was a backwards job to come to an understanding of the fact that the only equipment needed for preparing linden bast and turning it into rope are the hands.

Experience with historic work

When I think back on more than 20 years of collaboration with the Viking Ship Museum in making Viking rope, I can see in it a greater and greater involvement and comprehension that to do it properly required a thorough alteration in my way of working.

From:

The ropewalk's manually or electrically driven spinning wheel, on which hemp fibre was spun into yarns, which were turned into cords and then laid into rope with the help of mechanically turned hooks and the ropemaker's walking with the top.

To:

Spinning with the hands, twisting and arranging raw material such as bast, roots, hair, rawhide strips, or other fibres into cords, which were then laid into rope with the hands.

In the same way, the raw material changed as well.

From:

Hemp fibre, which has been the dominant material for rope in the West for many hundreds of years

To:

Bast from the bark of the linden tree (*Tilia* sp.), which seems to have been the most commonly used material for rope in the Viking Period

Source material – insight and choice

The most direct source of information about Viking rope is, of course, archaeological finds (Fig. 5.3). Over the last 15 years, in collaboration with the Viking Ship Museum and the Danish National Museum, I have catalogued the greater part of the Danish archaeological rope finds. In the course of cataloguing, a large number of finds have been measured, described and analysed, and the information collected in a database, which now contains over 800 Danish finds, dating from the Stone Age up to modern times. There are 66 Danish finds of bast rope dating to the Viking Period; all of those examined in detail (34 finds) have been identified as linden bast (Fig. 5.4). Preservation is not equally good for all materials. The fact is that plant fibres such as hemp, straw or nettle break down much more quickly than bast, and that animal fibres, such as hair and rawhide, last as well in the ground

as bast. Therefore, the archaeological material can only be part of the truth about Viking rope.

If one looks at the finds from the periods before and after the Vikings, the picture does not change. The dominant material for rope is consistently bast. There are only a few short pieces made from horse hair. In the written sources, the materials mentioned in connection with rope are hair, skin and bast. Today there is not a thorough comprehension of what the exact meaning of these words was in relation to the physical material, and certainly no understanding of the functional meaning of words in relation to the names of the different lines used in rigging a ship.

It is easier and cheaper to develop a comparative collection of ethnological parallels. The range of material used for rope is very wide. This material differentiates itself from the archaeological material in that it does not represent the actual amount of use, but it can be seen as a series of examples and possibilities. This collection is kept in the museum's stores.

Written sources well into the Middle Ages for the most part mention only bast in connection with rope. Ethnological parallels as well as preserved artefacts from later periods show a broader range of raw material for rope. From this material it can be seen that the development of the Danish economy in the 18th and 19th centuries concentrated the greater part of rope production in professional ropewalks, in contrast to Norway and Sweden, where the greater distances meant that home production of rope preserved older technologies and especially the use of material other than hemp.

Of the material seen in the ethnological parallels, practical requirements limit the possible raw materials to rawhide, withy, bast, and plant fibre, if the rope is going to be used in the standing rigging. A wider range of materials can be used for the running rigging (Fig. 5.5).

Rope finds in situ

The surviving rope finds that can be related to the standing

Fig. 5.3. Original finds of bast rope from medieval ship find Rodskilde 1 (author).

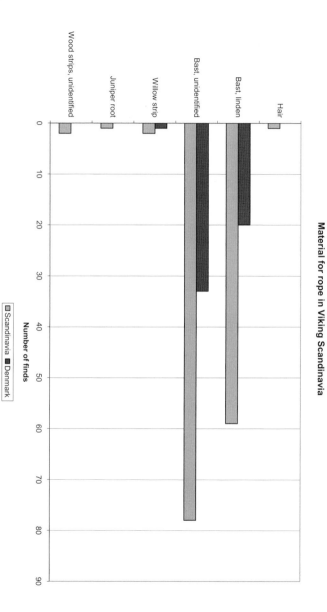

Material for rope in Viking Scandinavia

☐ Scandinavia   ■ Denmark

Number of finds

Fig. 5.4. Materials used for rope as shown by Scandinavian finds of the Viking Period.

Material for rope rope	Ethnological material	Written source 1100-1900	Written source before 1100	Archaeological material
hemp fibre	■	■		
flax fibre	■	■		
nettle fibre	■	■		
wood	■	■		
tree root	■	■		
tree bast	■	■	■	■
skin	■	■	■	
hair	■	■	■	■
strips of wool	■	■	■	■
strips of fabric	■	■		
synthetic fibre	■	■		
hops	■	■		
rush	■	■		
fish skin	■	■		
crowberry	■	■		
straw	■	■		■
paper	■	■		
grass	■	■		

Fig. 5.5. Evidence for usage of different materials for rope.

rig are not extensive. There are many fragments of rope from ship finds, but only a few that have been found attached to the ship, so that one can be sure that the fragment was part of the standing rig.

The first find that can show the rope's function with certainty comes from the Gedesby ship (dendrochron-ologically dated to 1280). Here, a fragment of one of the shrouds was still fastened to the ship's side, along with its strop and shroud pin (Fig. 5.6). All of the rope in this find is of bast. This shows that ships still sailed with bast

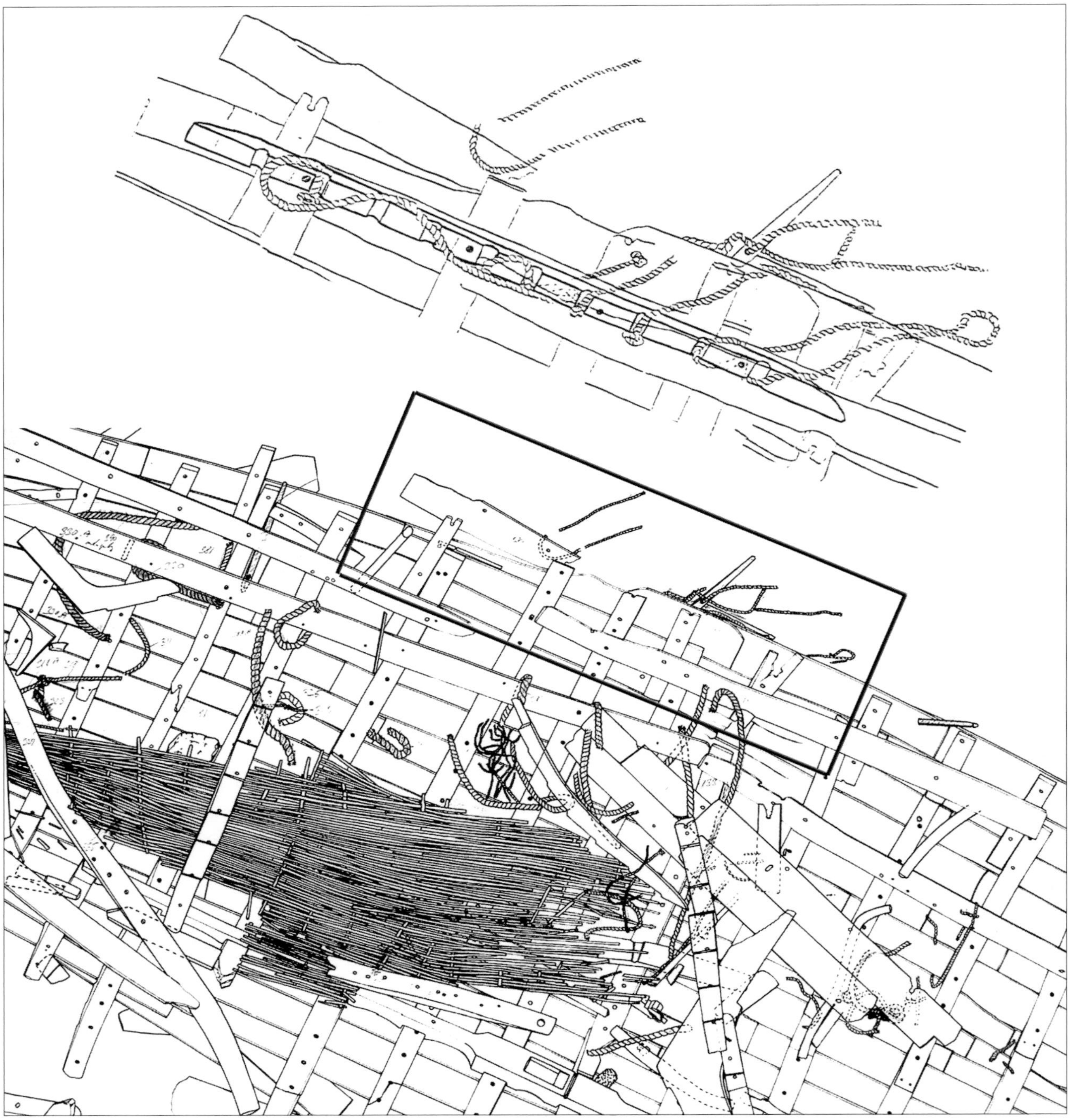

Ole Magnus

Fig. 5.6. Portion of site plan of Gedesby wreck (s. 1280) with outlined section enlarged to show rope detail on the outside of the plank (Morten Gøthche).

rigging in the Middle Ages, but it is not possible to say that Skuldelev 2 had a bast rig, just because bast was used on a sailing ship from Falster several centuries later.

Rope and its use

A different way to approach the study of the archaeological material is to compare it with modern use of rope. If one looks at the dimensions of the finds and compares these with the dimensions of rope used at the end of the 19th century in agriculture, fishing and sailing, it is apparent that it is first in the Viking period that we encounter ropes finds greater than 18 mm in diameter (Fig. 5.7). When I see a 72-mm bast rope found on the shore of Copenhagen harbour and dated to after 1250, I cannot imagine it was used to tie up a cow. It must have been used on a ship. Large dimensions in 19th-century rope are related to seafaring. It must also have been thus with

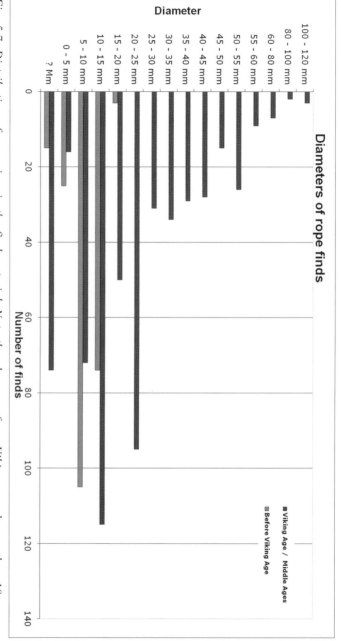

Fig. 5.7. Distribution of rope sizes in the find material. Note the absence of pre-Viking rope larger than 18 mm.

Fig. 5.8. Bast ropes of different sizes prior to tensile testing (author).

large-diameter archaeological finds, as there was hardly any other use for such heavy rope.

Rope structure

Another aspect of the certainty of using linden bast for the rigging of Skuldelev 2 is the finding of bast rope with an entirely new structure, a structure than means considerably more work in the production process. This new type of rope appears in ship finds after the 13th century and in large quantity and in ropes over 18 mm in diameter. Linden bast is still the raw material, but the question is if one wanted to invest so much energy in the development of a new method of work, if there was an easily accessible better material. Tensile tests of the two types of rope in

dimensions up to 32 mm show no difference in strength, but tests were not conducted on larger rope (Fig. 5.8).

Access to material

One must also consider how accessible potential raw materials for use in Viking ships were in Denmark. Linden bast can be harvested from the forest and costs no more than the labour involved in collecting it, cutting off the limbs and removing their bark in order to expose the bast layer underneath. Linden is among the best woods for renewing the resource, as new branches grow to harvesting size in 10–12 years. At this point, the branches are about as thick as a human arm and produce a useful amount of bast. In contrast, hemp fibre had to be purchased from abroad or cultivated. This required surplus agricultural production and affected the use of arable land (Fig. 5.9).

Something else occurs to me concerning the use of the raw material. If my Viking wife saw me in 1040 with a bundle of fine hemp fibre and thought that I might use it to make rope, I doubt she would allow me, and she would have good reason. I would at that point have thousands of years of tradition behind me for making bast rope, but none with hemp. The fibre from the hemp plant's stem is much finer, as fine as hair and nettle fibre, and its use for spinning into thread for textiles is much more effective than turning it into simple rope (Figs 5.10 and 5.11).

A test

It is one thing to think about and be certain that it is

Ole Magnus

Fig. 5.9. Harvesting the raw material: bast from the forest (left) and hemp from the field (right) (author).

Fig. 5.11. Macrophoto of bast after retting, showing how the layers of fibre separate and the structure of the layer at a microscopic level (author).

to produce rope from materials such as bast, roots and hair using modern, rational techniques and tools, the result has been unsuccessful. Only when I began to use my hands and gain an understanding of the properties of the different materials and the ways that they "want" to be formed, was I able to produce a satisfactory copy of an archaeological find (Fig. 5.12).

In all of the trials with the new material, there has been support to be found in the archaeological material and the ethnological parallels. The ethnographic descriptions need to be treated with caution, as time has in may cases altered the work with simple materials to a quicker and cruder form. Because the requirements for rope for rigging a ship are different from those for agricultural use (where bast rope survived the longest), there have been changes in how the material is worked.

Fig. 5.10. Two different materials for rope: hemp (left) and linden bast (right) (author).

possible to equip a ship like Skuldelev 2 with standing and running rigging of bast, it is another thing entirely to produce the rope! As a professional ropemaker, it has been a backwards realisation that each time I have tried

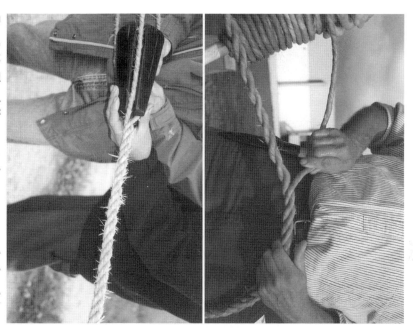

Fig. 5.12. The difference in laying up rope by hand (top; Hans Erik Lund) or on a ropewalk with a top and winding gear (bottom; Jon Hune).

Technique

There are clear indications in the archaeological material that rope was laid by hand. The first find that showed this was a 34-meter length of 8-mm, three-stranded rope from the excavation of Illerup bog. This rope was laid up from a single, long strand, folded back on itself twice and twisted together. This cannot be done on a ropewalk, where each of the three strands is fastened to its own hook and twisted while it is laid up. After this I registered many other details in finds that showed that they had been laid up from a single spun strand into two- or three-stranded rope. An end finished off with a turn of the single strand is seen in many finds, as are blocks laid into the rope during manufacture and laid eyes, produced while the rope is being made (Fig. 5.13). Tensile tests have shown that a laid eye is stronger than an eyesplice.

A complicated working process can be seen in the find of a net from the excavations at the Nydam bog. After laying up a thin, two-stranded rope, the remaining length of the single strand was twisted further while being laid up as the third strand, at the same time that is was used to connect the rope into a gridwork, a net. There are several other examples of nets made in this way, where the strands are twisted at the same time as the net is being formed.

To make rope

In this way it was possible to reach the point where there was sufficient documentation for a linden bast rig for a ship of the Viking Period, a reconstruction of Skuldelev 2. With the help of microscopic analysis of the archaeological material and a craftsman's appreciation of the material, we can understand some of the truth about Viking rope. The production of a full bast rig for a Skuldelev 2 reconstruction would be the largest such project to date, and would provide practical knowledge about the manufacture and handling of ropes of such great length and thickness. It would provide information about the quantity of raw material needed for a large ship and variations in the material's qualities based on different harvesting and processing methods. In short, it would provide insight into the practical reality of making a significant quantity of rope from bast. This is not trials with short lengths and a mass of theory about how it might have been done in the Viking Age.

For me personally, it would mean sitting on my backside for many months, sitting on a stool with a reel for the finished rope on one side and a pile of split bast

Fig. 5.13. Finished bast rope use for the forestay and bowline block pendant on one of the replicas at the Viking Ship Museum (author).

fibre in front of me. A tent for protection from wind and sun, or a booth as it was called. It is a picture that agrees quite well with a description in the town records of Malmö in 1412. There it states that only those who have it as a profession may work with bast, while in another place in the same work permission is given for 24 *rebvindere* (literally, "rope twisters") inside the city walls. It does not talk about *rebslagere* (literally "rope layers," the modern term for a rope maker) and their ropewalks, but rope twisters, and presumably their booths, just as the St. Clemens area of Copenhagen was once called *Rebvinderboderne*, the rope twisters' booths (Fig. 5.14).

The area immediately to the east of the Viking Ship Museum is known as Vindeboder, perhaps because the ropemakers of Roskilde once worked there long ago. In any case, I will find a place near to the water for my workshop, the *vindebod*. It is best to keep the bast wet during the process of separating the bast layers, spinning the strands and laying up the rope (Fig. 5.15). I am proud of my craft, and would be glad to be called a *rebvinder*, or as some have said, *reblæger*.

Fig. 5.14. A 16th-century illustration of a rebvinder on his characteristic stool, with raw material hanging close to hand and the finished rope taken up on a reel.

Fig. 5.15. Making rope in the medieval manner (Hans Erik Lund).

6 Trial voyages as a method of experimental archaeology: The aspect of speed

Anton Englert

Sailing trials have become an important component of the experimental analysis of ship-finds. This paper stresses the potential of a dual approach: the combined results of standardised sailing and rowing trials *and* systematically documented trial voyages provide essential empirical data for a better understanding of the use of vessels in the past. In this paper, the aspect of 'travel speed' is used to exemplify the potential of the trial voyage as a method, by looking at recent voyages of reconstructed Viking and medieval vessels in the Baltic Sea area.

Standardised sailing and rowing trials

Standardised sailing and rowing trials and the use of advanced measuring devices portray the sailing and rowing properties of a specific vessel in terms of specifically chosen parameters. This method makes it possible to compare one vessel's properties to those of other tested vessels, based on absolute data.

Despite the constantly changing nature of wind and sea, standardised trials can be carried out under circumstances which come close to the chosen conditions of a laboratory. A suitable, trial theatre under minimal influence of currents may be chosen, where the vessel under trial can be exposed to open, undisturbed onshore winds and wave motion on some days, and to land winds with a relatively calm sea on other days. Experience has shown that it is better to sail numerous trials over short distances rather than a few trials over long distances (pers. comm. Max Vinner). In that way, many different manoeuvres with varying combinations of course, propulsion and trim can be carried out and documented within the same state of wind and sea. This trial scenario applies to rowed vessels as well as to sailing craft. A large number of instruments can be employed to collect absolute data (Table 6.1).

A typical example for the results of standardised sailing trials can be seen in a polar diagram published by Max Vinner in the monograph *Roar Ege*, on the testing of a reconstruction of the Danish Viking ship-find Skuldelev 3 (Andersen *et al.* 1997: 262) (Fig. 6.1). Standardised trials make it possible to compare directly four different vessels through ten centuries: Two reconstructed ship-finds of the 11th century (*Saga Siglar*, representing Skuldelev 1, and *Roar Ege*, representing Skuldelev 3), one original, traditional working boat with single square rig of the late 19th century (*Rana*) and one modern racing yacht (X-99 with and without spinnaker). The diagram shows the velocity made good (VMG) of these vessels at various angles to the wind. It demonstrates that the single-square-rigged boats, with their shallow draft, share a modest windward performance. At the same time, the modern Bermuda-rigged racer cannot outrun a 900-year-older design on the dead run without setting the spinnaker. Clearly, this kind of sailing experiment is a valuable tool for exploring the history of naval architecture with its ship types. However, in order to relate a vessel type to its former use and its former function within society, a second, complementary method should be considered: the trial voyage.

Instruments	Resulting data
GPS	Ground track
	Speed over ground
	Velocity made good (VMG)
	Standard time for the trial
Wind indicators	Wind direction & speed, apparent and true
Log	Speed through the water
Compass	Heading
Stop watch	Duration of manoeuvres
Inclinometer	Heeling angle
Scales	Weight of hull, rigging, equipment, ballast, cargo and crew

Table 6.1. Typical instruments used in a standardised trial and the resulting absolute data.

Trial voyages

Trial voyages are real voyages at sea or on inland waters, carried out in the original nautical environment, under conditions known for the time of the original use, and with a minimum of modern aids. Providing the opportunity for a variety of valuable as well as unpredictable observations, trial voyages provide an authentic insight into the length of time and the precautions required to carry out a certain voyage with a certain type of vessel within the experienced weather pattern. The performance of vessel and crew delivers first-hand data and physical experiences, which can be compared with historical sources and used to aid the interpretation of archaeological evidence for nautical activities like goods exchange, naval warfare and fishing. Whereas standardised sailing and rowing trials help us to understand the history of naval architecture, the trial voyage is an experimental tool for the study of nautical history in general.

Trial voyages of reconstructed ancient vessels have a long and popular ancestry, which can be illustrated with the following well-known examples (Table 6.2).

These voyages have in common that they were carried out by amateurs who wanted to prove a certain hypothesis in the most practical way: by re-enacting the voyage in question with all the hardship and joy involved. The popularity which these voyages enjoyed in public, suggests that the idea of such a voyage may be associated by the actors as well as by the audience with a certain archetype of adventure, such as is known from the *Odyssey* or from the *Argonautica*, with its perilous search for the Golden Fleece. Brushing aside all emotional excitement and admiration for heroic deeds, one may now argue whether these floating hypotheses have contributed to experimental archaeology. In fact, only a few projects were built on firm archaeological evidence, as in the case of *Viking* and *Saga Siglar*. It is therefore necessary to identify and define conditions of authenticity for trial voyages (Table 6.3).

It may be difficult, if not impossible, to comply with all these demands at the same time and during the entire voyage. An essential point is the setting up of a certain geographical goal and the avoidance of any arrival appointments. A trial voyage is very much the opposite of a pleasure cruise, where boat and crew follow the wind and coast at leisure, in order to be back in their homeport on a given day. In the absence of engines and timetables, time is no longer a limiting factor, but a wheel of fortune, which can turn adverse winds and currents into propelling forces.

The most problematic demand is that of authentic navigational methods. Many ship losses in the past were caused by imperfect methods of positioning. Today, charts and GPS have almost neutralised this problem. For centuries, it has been considered good seamanship to employ all available means of navigation to ensure the safety of vessel and crew. Disregarding this basic rule for the sake of an experiment leads to a legal and ethical dilemma. Navigational buoys, beacons and lights are difficult to ignore for responsible navigators. Modern shipping, traffic separation schemes and military practice areas cannot be ignored without running into immediate danger. This dilemma can partly be solved by gaining sufficient local knowledge in advance, either personally

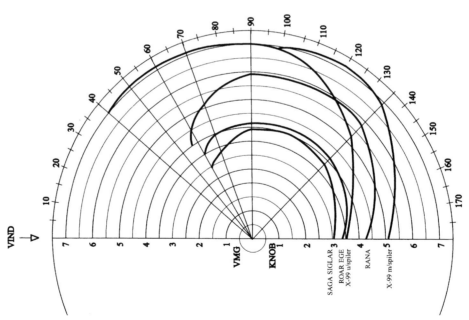

Fig. 6.1. Speed under sail through ten centuries (Andersen et al. 1997: 262).

Year	Vessel and design	Voyage	References
1893	Viking (Gokstad)	Norway – USA	Andersen 1895
1947	Kon Tiki (freely reconstructed raft)	Peru – Polynesia	Heyerdahl 1948
1976/1977	Brendan (freely reconstructed hide boat)	Ireland – Canada	Severin 1978
1984–1986	Saga Siglar (Skuldelev 1)	Around the world	Thorseth 1988; Vinner 1995

Table 6.2. Famous voyages in search of the conditions of ancient seafaring.

Vessel & maritime environment	Use an authentically built reconstruction of a well-documented ship-find. Sail through waters related to the use of the original vessel. Use natural harbours instead of constructed harbours.
Navigation	Employ only navigational methods or instruments known at the time under study (however, if you do not have sufficient local knowledge, charts and other topographic literature may be necessary for safety). Do not use engines! Do not accept external assistance except in emergency! Do not follow a timetable. Do not make appointments for your arrival!
Mental aids	Maintain personal hygiene and sanitation without modern comforts. Eat and drink authentic food and beverages. Use authentic garments.
Safety	At all times, care for sufficient equipment and competence to ensure the safety of the crew!

Table 6.3. A catalogue of ideal conditions for a trial voyage.

Fig. 6.2. Weather – Ship – Crew. A typical scene from the Danish-German-Polish trial voyage with Bialy Kon (Ralswiek 2) in August 1998 (photo David Gregory).

or by hiring a 'pilot'. But when in doubt, safe return must weigh more than scholarly ambition, and a sealed box of modern aids must always be within reach.

Moreover, it is more important to concentrate on some of the proposed conditions and to maintain them, than to try to keep them all at once, only to lose sight of them one by one. The conditions concerning personal hygiene, authentic food and clothing are not mandatory, but can provide mental and physical aid for the understanding of past voyages.

One of the physical observations to be gained is the main order of factors and resources of a voyage without engines: weather, ship and crew (Fig. 6.2). The weather is dominating and unalterable; the ship is an artefact with limitations; since it has to resemble a certain archaeological find, only the handling of the boat can be improved, but hardly the boat itself. The only variable in this trinity is the crew; although easily exhausted, man is the most adaptable resource. Can these three main factors of a trial voyage compare to the conditions of the past? The weather may follow a similar pattern; the ship can come quite close to the quality of the original vessel; but you yourself

can hardly replicate the routine-hardened sailors of the past. However, your own performance may set a minimum level for what was possible at the time in question.

There are no certain standards for the recording of trial voyages. It may prove useful to develop recording methods based on traditional navigation with its mix of absolute data and observations. Minimum recording equipment comprises firstly a logbook with times, positions, observations on weather, ship and crew, secondly a chronometer for logbook entries, and thirdly a track-recording GPS can supplement the manual record. In that case, the GPS-time gives a useful frame of reference for the logbook, too.

Trial voyages and the Viking Ship Museum

Under the optimal research conditions of the Centre for Maritime Archaeology in Roskilde (1993–2003), George Indruszewski and Anton Englert were able to acquire experience with the trial voyage as a method. The newly-built reconstruction of the Slavic boat-find Ralswiek 2, *Bialy Kon*, owned by the Archaeological Museum of Mecklenburg-Vorpommern, was sailed and rowed through inshore waters from Ralswiek in Germany to the ancient trading centre of Wolin in Poland in August 1998 (Englert *et al.* 1998; Englert *et al.* 1999).

However, this was not the first replica voyage in which researchers from Roskilde took part. When the Norwegian adventurer Ragnar Thorseth set out for his round-the-world voyage with the Skuldelev 1 reconstruction *Saga Siglar*, Erik Andersen and Max Vinner from the Viking Ship Museum took part in and recorded the first two legs from Bergen to Iceland and from Iceland to Greenland (Andersen and Andersen 1989: 285–327; Vinner 1995).

In general, sailing experiments have been part of the work of the Viking Ship Museum ever since the acquisition of the *storåtring Rana* from northern Norway (Nordland) in 1971 (Andersen *et al.* 1980). The art of sailing the single square rig with *Rana* having been learned, methods of measuring and comparing performance became very important. Standardised tests were developed. (Vinner 1980; Vinner 1986). In 1984, the first of five sailing reconstructions of the Skuldelev finds, *Roar Ege*, was launched and ready for use (Andersen et al. 1997). Since then, amateur boat guilds (*bådelaug*) have grown up around many vessels of the Viking Ship Museum, spending many hours sailing and rowing on the fjord as well as in inshore waters. Usually, the boat guilds sail summer holiday cruises with about half a dozen of the museum's ships. Since these voyages take place without built-in engines and with hardly any external assistance, they can result in valuable experimental data.

It is not by accident that the best-known voyage projects originate from private initiative. The Viking Ship Museum cannot carry out trial voyages without voluntary help and external resources. In order to make use of the many sea miles sailed by the boat guilds, all summer cruises have been recorded since 2002. This recording project will continue, in order to build up a database of voyage data. The most useful data so far are from *Ottar's* cruise to Norway in 2003. *Ottar* is a sailing reconstruction of the cargo ship Skuldelev 1.

In August 2004, the last and largest of the Skuldelev reconstructions, a replica of the longship Skuldelev 2, left the building stocks. In order to exploit its experimental and educational potential, the Viking Ship Museum is planning a circumnavigation of Britain in 2007, starting from Roskilde, with Dublin, the assumed home port of the original ship, as the turning point of the voyage. This voyage will be a trial voyage on most of its legs.

Voyage recording at the Viking Ship Museum

In documenting voyages with boats of the Viking Ship Museum, the following simple elements are used. Each vessel carries a user-made logbook, which is kept by the watch on duty. For better comparison, all these logbooks follow the same design with parameters such as number of persons on board, time, wind direction and force, sail area in use, sail position, course steered, position, observations on weather, ship and crew, etc (Fig. 6.3). Sea state is described by estimate and by recording the number of persons affected by seasickness. In addition, the degree of seasickness is of importance (still active, passive or severely suffering). While the established parameter of sea state is an absolute and neutral assessment of sea motion, seasickness is an indicator of the specific motion of the boat, which varies with the angle to the wind and sea. Positions are given either in relation to the coast and navigational marks or as GPS-readings. Since *distance through the water* is of minor relevance for a trial voyage compared to the *distance over ground* given by GPS and terrestrial positions, log and log readings are not used. A handheld GPS-receiver, continuously supplied by a 12V car battery, records the vessel's track over ground. Occasionally, the museum's photographer records parts of the cruise in still and video formats. Finally, interviews and individual reports are helpful to record the experiences of the voyage, and to explain the motives behind important decisions and manoeuvres. During an annual analysis, all relevant data are collected to build up a database.

The aspect of speed

The analysis of standardised trials and trial voyages leads to several definitions of speed. Standardised sailing and rowing trials result in at least three different forms of speed:

Speed through the water
= distance logged/time
(on the log)

Date: __17/06/2003__　Day of Voyage: _8_　From __Anholt Harbour__　To _____

Page: _6_

Skipper: __Halfdan Rohde__　　Crew: __See page 5__

Persons on board: _11_

Analysis (keep blank)	Time 00.00	Wind dir/force	Sail Area FU L1 L2 L3 rowing/row	Sail Position CH CR BE BR RU no. of rowers	(Course) steered 000°	Position, Weather change, Watch change, Important events and observations 00°00,0'N; 00°00,0'Ø or in relation to the coast and nautical marks
	0645	SE 0-1	F	BR PO	-----	Set sail in the inner harbour and cast off stern lines
	0741	SE 3	F	BE SB	020°	56° 43.9' N; 011° 29.3' E, course corrected to 350
	1310	SE 3	F	BR SB	335°	Kobbergrund E bouy (SE of Læsø) passed on starboard side

Fig. 6.3. A simple logbook for trial voyages.

Speed over ground
= distance over ground/time
  (along the ground track)
Velocity made good (VMG)
= distance made good/time
  (between start and end points)

A log measures the speed difference between the boat and the surrounding medium, water. This parameter, *speed through the water* is of interest for measuring the efficiency of the hull form and surface. *Speed over ground* presents the speed of a boat in relation to the Earth. Since the ground track of a boat in most cases is not a direct line, speed over ground is usually higher than the resulting *velocity made good* (VMG) between any chosen start and end point on the ground track. With standardised trials under sails, the concept of VMG is important in order to measure the effective speed to windward, which is always considerably lower than the corresponding speed over ground.

The concept of VMG is also important for the assessment of voyages. Here it is relevant how much time was spent between two geographical positions, say harbours:

Travel speed (VMG) at sea
= distance made good between harbours/time at sea (incl. breaks at anchor)
Travel speed (VMG) total
= distance made good between harbours/duration of voyage
Days of travel
= duration of voyage
24-hour distance
= distance made good between two positions at sea/24 hours

Regarding voyages, distance made good is the shortest

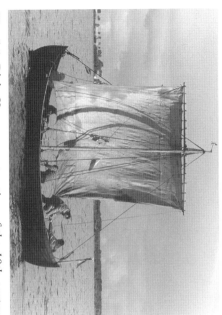

Fig. 6.4. Bialy Kon, reconstruction of the 10th century Slavic boat-find-Ralswiek 2 by the Archaeological Museum of Mecklenburg-Vorpommern (photo David Gregory).

navigable distance along the chosen route. This means that the distance made good of a voyage can be much shorter than the ground track of the vessel which sailed the voyage. This distinction is necessary in order to compare the speed of several voyages along the same route. *Travel speed at sea* results from the shortest navigable distance between two harbours over the time spent at sea, including breaks at anchor. This parameter is mainly an expression of the sailing qualities of the vessel and crew under the observed conditions, whereas *travel speed total* includes unavoidable delays to the duration of a voyage. Here, it is a matter of conscience to decide what delays should be accounted for. One may well exclude the time spent waiting for the arrival of a new crew, but one should include the time spent waiting for fair wind. Finally, there is the traditional and still useful way of expressing the speed of a voyage by counting days or 24-hour distances. Table 6.4 shows examples for the different types of speed as recorded on the 1998 trial voyage through inshore waters with *Bialy Kon* (L: 9.0 m; B: 2.5 m) (Figures 6.4 and 6.5).

Speed analysis of Ottar's cruise to Norway

The 2003 summer cruise of *Ottar*, the Viking Ship Museum's reconstruction of Skuldelev 1 (L: 16,5 m; B: 4,5 m) provides valuable data from a voyage across the open waters of the Kattegat and Skaggerak (Fig. 6.6). *Ottar* travelled under sail only, from Hundested on the north coast of Zealand (*Sjælland*) to Lyngor on the south coast of Norway, and returned from the southern Norwegian harbour of Stavern to Gilleleje at the north tip of Zealand. A first step in the speed analysis of this voyage is to plot the GPS-ground track into a chart and to establish the distances over ground as well as the distances made good (Fig. 6.7). On the second leg from Anholt to Lyngor, *Ottar* sailed only four nautical miles more than the shortest possible distance of 143 nautical miles. However, on the first leg from Hundested, *Ottar* had to return half way to Anholt because of strong headwinds and problems with the rudder withy. This resulted in a ground track of 87 nautical miles for a distance made good of 46 nautical miles. In order to establish the travel speed of this voyage, the distances over ground has to be divided by the time spent at sea (23 hrs), resulting in a poor travel speed at sea of 1.4 knots for the first leg. Table 6.5 presents a data sheet for the outbound and homebound voyage.

Of all four legs, only the second leg of the outbound voyage took place under good conditions. With a moderate breeze from astern, speed over ground averaged 4.5 knots. During the outbound voyage, *Ottar* was delayed by a northwesterly gale at the island of Anholt for almost four days. During the homebound voyage, *Ottar* interrupted the voyage for almost 32 hours at the island of Læsø for pleasure and without being forced to do so. Therefore, the hours spent on Læsø are not included in the travel speed assessment.

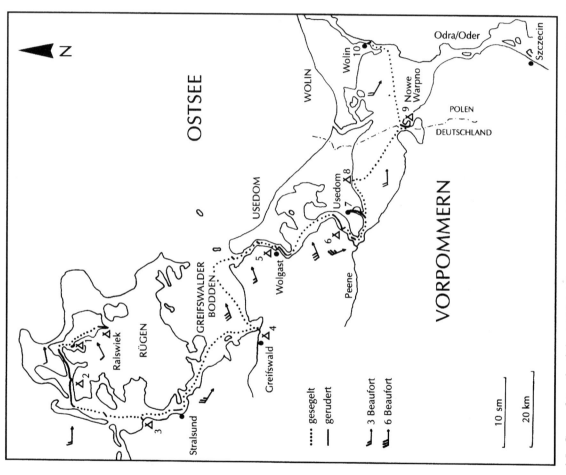

Fig. 6.5. Ground track of the 1998 trial voyage with Bialy Kon (Englert et al. 1999: Abb. 2).

22 August 1998 — **Greifswald-Wolgast**

At 1358	8.9 knots maximum *speed through the water*
1220–1415	5.3 knots *average speed over ground*
Entire day (7½ hrs)	2.9 knots *travel speed at sea*

log reading under sail
10.2 nm, 1 h 55 min under sail
21.4 nm, 4 h 05 min under sail
1 h 10 min rowing
2 h 15 min resting at
anchor

Entire voyage Ralswiek-Wolin through inshore waters, August 1998

Distance made good (connecting all night camps)	135.6 nm
Time at sea (sailing, rowing, breaks at anchor)	57 h 20 min
Travel speed at sea	2.4 knots
Days of travel	10 days
(Travel speed total)	(0.6 knots)

Table 6.4. Speed examples from the 1998 trial voyage with Bialy Kon (Ralswiek 2, 10th-century Slavic boat).

Fig. 6.6. Bound for Norway: Ottar, the Viking Ship Museum's reconstruction of the 11th-century Norwegian cargo ship Skuldelev 1 (photo Werner Karrasch).

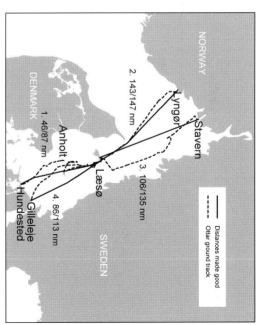

Fig. 6.7. Ottar's cruise to Norway in 2002. Ground track and distances made good (drawing Søren Laursen).

Date	Route	Wind (dir./force Bft)	Time at sea /ashore	Dist. ov. gr. (nm)	Speed ov. gr. (kts)	DMG (nm)	VMG (kts)	No. of Crew, remarks
12-13 June	Hundested-Anholt	W 4-6, occ 7	23h	87.2	3.8	46.2	1.4	(12) 7 seasick & still active, rudder probl.
14-16 June	Anholt	NW gale	94h / 45'	------	----	------	----	waiting for favourable wind
17-18 June	Anholt-Lyngør (N)	SE 3-4	32h / 45'	146.8	4.5	143.0	4.4	(incl.) (11) 1 seasick & still active, fine conditions
Outbound voyage	total		150h 30'	234.0	(4.2)	189.2	1.3	A seven days voyage to Norway
13-15 July	Stavern (N) – Læsø	Var 0-3	54h 30'	134.7	2.5	106.0	1.9	(11) little wind, drifting at times
16 July	Læsø	Var calm	(31h 35')	------	----	------	----	landed on Læsø for pleasure (excl.)
17-19 July	Læsø - Gilleleje	NE v SW	38h / 25'	113.4	3.0	85.6	3.4	(11) veering, unstable wind
Homebound voyage	total	0-5	92h / 55'	248.1	(2.7)	191.6	2.1	A 'four days' voyage to Denmark

Table 6.5. Ottar's first visit to Norway: Speed analysis. DMG: distance made good. VMG: travel speed.

Boat speed and travel speed

Ottar's cruise to Norway demonstrates the great value of experimental voyage data. The voyage record provides long-term observations of the boat's speed potential as well as real data about the time required for a certain voyage under the observed weather conditions. The difference between boat speed and travel speed becomes clear in the answers to these two questions:

How fast did Ottar sail? Under good conditions, 4.5 knots over ground or ca 108 nautical miles in 24 hours.

How long did it take the crew to travel the distance of ca 190 nautical miles? Between four and seven days, averaging 1.3–2.1 knots or ca 31–50 nautical miles in 24 hours.

Interpretation of historical sources

A major advantage of voyages with reconstructed ships is that they can contribute directly to the interpretation of written sources. The sea route from Denmark to Norway has been a key to the close relations between the two countries for over a thousand years. The oldest known travelogue by a Scandinavian, Ohthere's account in the late 9th-century Old English *Orosius*, tells how Ohthere sailed from *Sciringesheal* (Kaupang) in Norway to *Hæpum* (Hedeby) at the foot of Jutland in five days (*Orosius* I.1; Lund et al. 1984: 22). Since both ports have been identified geographically, the distance made good can be established as ca 400 nautical miles. Therefore, the average 24-hour distance cannot have been less than 80 nautical miles. It can also be deduced from Ohthere's account that he had passed North Zealand after three days. Assuming that Ohthere used sail as his main means of propulsion, *Ottar's* summer cruise of 2003 can help to answer two questions which have been debated among scholars (i.e. by Crumlin-Pedersen 1984: 33 and Korhammer 1985: 158–161):

Did Ohthere have favourable wind? Yes, most likely, he enjoyed favourable wind.

Did he sail day and night? Most likely, in order to make 400 nautical miles in five days, partly through narrow-winding waters, he had to take advantage of the wind whenever it blew from the right quarters.

Can experimental voyages really count as research?

The scientific value of trial voyages and the recording of boat guilds' summer cruises may be doubtful for a number of readers. However, with the use of an authentic reconstruction, with a certain amount of sailing experience and without the use of engines, the basic requirements for a pre-industrial voyage are met. The careful establishment and maintenance of trial conditions in combination with the recording and publishing of the results turn the voyage in question into a scientific experiment, ready to create debate and receive criticism.

Acknowledgements

Many thanks to the members of the boat guilds (*bådelaug*) who, year after year, commit part of their spare time to the collecting of research data for the Viking Ship Museum. Many thanks also to Fred Hocker, Max Vinner, Erik Andersen and Janet Bately for proof-reading and discussing the manuscript.

References

Andersen, Bent and Erik Andersen 1989. *Råsejlet – Dragens Vinge*. Roskilde.

Andersen, Erik, Andersen, Bent, Gøthche, Morten and Vinner, Max, 1980. *Nordlandsbåden – analyseret og provesejlet af Vikingeskibshallens Bådelaug*. København.

Andersen, Erik, Crumlin-Pedersen, Ole, Vadstrup, Søren, and Vinner, Max, 1997. *Roar Ege. Skuldelev 3 skibet som arkæologisk eksperiment*. Roskilde.

Andersen, Magnus 1895. *Vikingefærden. En illustreret Beskrivelse af "Vikings" Reise i 1893*. Kristiania.

Crumlin-Pedersen, Ole 1984. Ships, navigation and routes in the reports of Ohthere and Wulfstan. In: Lund, Niels (ed.) *Two Voyagers at the Court of King Alfred. The ventures of Ohthere and Wulfstan together with the Description of Northern Europe from the Old English Orosius*. York, 30–42.

Englert, Anton, Indruszewski, G., Jensen, H. and Gülland, T., 1999, *Bialy Kons Jungfernreise von Ralswiek nach Wollin – Ein marinarchäologisches Experiment mit dem Nachbau des slawischen Bootsfundes Ralswiek 2. Bodendenkmalpflege in Mecklenburg-Vorpommern, Jahrbuch 1998* 46, 171–200.

Englert, Anton, Indruszewski, G., Jensen, H., Gülland, T. and Gregory, D., 1998. Sailing in Slavonic waters. The trial voyage Ralswiek – Wolin with the Ralswiek 2-replica Bialy Kon. *Maritime Archaeology Newsletter from Roskilde, Denmark* 11, 14–27.

Heyerdahl, Thor 1948, *The Kon-Tiki Expedition*. Oslo.

Korhammer, Michael 1985. Viking Seafaring and the Meaning of Ohthere's *ambyrne wind*. In: Bammesberger, Alfred (ed.) *Problems of Old English Lexicography. Studies in Memory of Angus Cameron*. Eichstätter Beiträge 15. Regensburg, 151–173.

Lund, Niels, Crumlin-Pedersen, O., Sawyer, P. and Fell, C.E. 1984. *Two Voyagers at the Court of King Alfred. The ventures of Ohthere and Wulfstan together with the Description of Northern Europe from the Old English Orosius*. York.

Severin, Tim 1978, *The Brendan Voyage*. London.

Thorseth, Ragnar 1988, *Saga Siglar – Århundrets seilas jorda rundt*. Ålesund.

Vinner, Max 1980. Forsøgssejladser. In: Andersen, Erik et al., *Nordlandsbåden – analyseret og provesejlet af Vikingeskibshallens Bådelaug*. Working Papers 12. København, 237–285.

Vinner, Max 1986. Recording the Trial Run. In: Crumlin-Pedersen, Ole and Max Vinner (eds.) *Sailing into the Past. The International Ship Replica seminar. Roskilde 1984*. Roskilde, 220–225.

Vinner, Max 1995. A Viking-ship off Cape Farewell 1984. In: Olsen, Olaf et al. (eds.) *Shipshape. Essays for Ole Crumlin-Pedersen on the occasion of his 60th anniversary February 24th 1995*. Roskilde, 289–304.

7 An example of experimental archaeology and the construction of a full-scale research model of the Cavalière ship's hull

Sabrina Marlier

Introduction

The program of experimental archaeology presented here was founded in 2001 in the Centre Camille Jullian (CCJ – Aix-en-Provence – France) as part of my PhD research under the supervision of Patrice Pomey. The objective of this program is to contribute to the study of different sewn techniques used in shipbuilding in the Mediterranean Sea in antiquity. It is based primarily on the construction, at full-scale, of hull sections of various boats that display different methods of sewn construction techniques.

The sewn construction technique in ancient Mediterranean shipbuilding

Recognition that some ancient Mediterranean shipbuilders assembled boats using sewn construction techniques only recently came to our attention at the beginning of the 1980s with the discovery and study of the Bon-Porté Greek Archaic shipwreck (Pomey 1981). Subsequently, a number of sewn shipwrecks were found in the Mediterranean basin (note 1). These shipwrecks provide evidence for the use of vegetable fibre stitches whether entirely or partly in the assembly of components of the hull. Moreover, the increasing number of these discoveries indicates that several types of stitching methods existed depending on the "geography" and the "chronology" considered (Pomey 1985). Studies of these various sewing systems are only just in their infancy, one drawback being the poor state of preservation of the vegetable fibres.

Why construct a full-scale research model?

Inspired by the work of Richard Steffy, who led the way in the construction of research models of Mediterranean shipwrecks in the 1970s (Steffy 1994), the staff from the Centre Camille Jullian decided, in 1995, to realise a research model, at full-scale, of the lower hull section of the Greek sewn boat Jules-Verne 9 (Pomey 1999: 150, fig.6; 2003: 60). The objective was to reproduce and study its sewn construction and assembly techniques.

In order to pursue this line of research, it seemed appropriate to set up a program that adopted similar research models that addressed different boats that displayed different sewn construction techniques. This approach should allow a record, at full-scale, of the construction techniques adopted and for the reproduction of the sewn construction techniques used in the boats concerned. The construction of various models from different sewn boats having a different construction technique should also allow comparison of the various systems, especially concerning the level of technology and the principle function of each construction technique. The research models will allow analysis of the phases and techniques used to realise the various sewn construction techniques and to observe the subtleties of these different systems. Thus, this program was developed to extend previous studies.

The choice of the sewn boats

Three criteria for selection were used to select the sewn boats destined to be the subject of a detailed study that lead to the construction of a study model:

1. the boat must be representative of a group of sewn boats that presents a similar sewn construction technique;
2. the shipwrecks must be in a good state of preservation;
3. the data and the recorded documentation of the shipwrecks must be accessible.

According to these criteria, several sewn boats were chosen to be modelled at full-scale.

The first model that adopted the same approach used to model the Jules-Verne 9 boat, was the Roman boat of Cavalière (Fig. 7.1).

The Cavalière shipwreck and Roman sewn framed ships

The Cavalière shipwreck, dating from around 100 BC,

Sabrina Marlier

was found in 1972 on the French Mediterranean coast (Fig. 7.2) (Charlin et al 1978). This boat is a good example of a specific family of ships found in the northwest Mediterranean Sea that date from the 3rd century BC to the 1st century AD (Fig. 7.2). They are characterised by frames that are fastened to the shell with stitches that are secured with treenails; the shell is fastened by the mortise-and-tenon technique (Fig. 7.3) (Pomey 2002; Wicha in this volume). The stitches are made from vegetable fibres lashed in a loop and fed through channels that were drilled through the frames and corresponding strakes. Between the channels, small grooves are notched in the back of the frames and in the outer part of the planks, in order to collect the stitches and connect the channels. This system prevents the stitches protruding outside the assembled pieces. Finally, treenails are used to secure the stitches in their channels and ensure a watertightness which is

Fig. 7.1. The full-scale research model of the Cavalière ship's bottom (builders: S. Marlier, R. Roman (Centre Camille Jullian, CNRS); photo: Ph. Foliot (Centre Camille Jullian, CNRS).

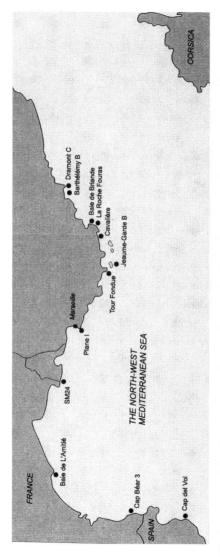

Fig. 7.2. Location of the Roman sewn frame shipwrecks from the NW Mediterranean Sea (drawing: S. Marlier).

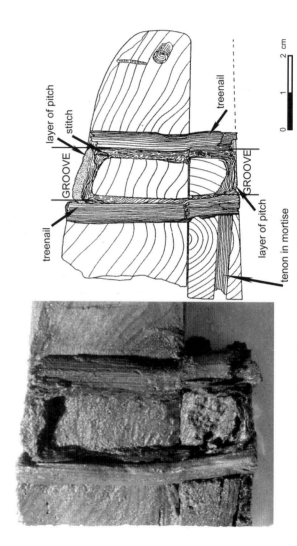

Fig. 7.3. Attachment of the frame to the shell by stitching from the Dramont C shipwreck (photo: G. Réveillac (Centre Camille Jullian, CNRS). Drawing done from the Cavalière shipwreck (drawing: M. Rival (Centre Camille Jullian, CNRS).

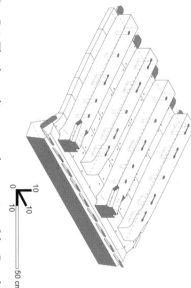

Fig. 7.4. The three-dimensional projection of the Cavalière ship's bottom (drawing: S. Marlier).

subsequently strengthened by a thick layer of pitch that seals the grooves.

At the time of the excavation of the Cavalière shipwreck in the 1970s, this assembly system was not observed (Charlin et al 1978). It was only when the site was reopened in 1995, for the "*Dendrochronologie et dendromorphologie des épaves antiques de Méditerranée*" program (Guibal and Pomey 1998; 1999), that this system was observed and recorded (Pomey 1996: 56–57).

Thus, in light of the high quality research undertaken on this shipwreck, the fact that an important part of the hull has been conserved, and that we have a relatively complete documentation of its study (note 2), it was decided to choose the Cavalière shipwreck as a an initial study of the sewn construction technique.

The construction of the Cavalière research model
The three-dimensional projection (Fig. 7.4)

The research model focused on the central part of the bottom of the hull including a part of the keel, six strakes, two frames and two half-frames. A three-dimensional projection was derived from the transverse sections (from M19 for the frames and from M26 for the half-frames) taken during the excavation of the shipwreck (Charlin et al 1978: fig. 34), and was used as a reference plan for the construction of the model.

The wood (Table 7.1)

Concerning the wood used for the construction of the research model, we tried to employ the same or very similar woods to those used by the shipwrights for the construction of the Cavalière vessel. However, it was not always possible to acquire the required materials, particularly for the pegs and the treenails.

The tools

Likewise, we employed traditional carpentry tools for the model construction, including a small handsaw, a rabbet

plane, a wood chisel, a mortising chisel, a hammer and a gouge. But, since the principal objective was the restitution of the sewn construction technique, we also used electric tools used in modern carpentry in order to ease the work, such as a band saw for straightening out the pieces, an electric planer, a planing machine, an electric mortiser, and a power drill.

Constitution of the shell

When the keel, the garboard and the strakes were cut according to the original measurements (Charlin et al 1978: 60, 67 and fig. 34, M19, M26 transverse sections), these pieces were assembled with mortises and tenons secured by wooden pegs according to the drawings provided by the archaeological remains (Charlin et al 1978: 67). One of the mortises was cut by hand with a mortising chisel and a hammer in order to experiment with the method of manual cutting of the mortises. The other mortises were fashioned with an electric mortiser. The shell of the hull fastened by this technique presents a perfect cohesion and we observed that this assembly was particularly solid, especially between the keel and the garboard. Thus, this part forms practically one perfectly homogeneous piece.

The frames

The frames and the half-frames were also cut according to the archaeological data (Charlin et al 1978: 72, fig. 34, M19 transverse section) with the help of a cardboard template.

Localisation of the assemblies and arrangements (Fig. 7.4)

Before proceeding to attach the frames to the shell, the position of the channels, the passage of the stitches, and the position of the single treenails, had to be marked on the frames and half-frames. Starting from the second

	Original wood	Research-model wood
Keel	Bosnia Pine (*Pinus leucodermis*)	Scotch Pine (*Pinus sylvestris*)
Shell	Bosnia Pine (*Pinus leucodermis*)	Scotch Pine (*Pinus sylvestris*)
Frame	Bosnia Pine (*Pinus leucodermis*)	Scotch Pine (*Pinus sylvestris*)
Tenons	Holm Oak (*Quercus ilex*)	Holm Oak (*Quercus ilex*)
Pegs	Holm Oak (*Quercus ilex*)	Beech (*Fagus sylvatica*)
Treenails	Fir (*Abies alba*)	Beech (*Fagus sylvatica*)

Table 7.1. Original wood used for the Cavalière ship's construction and wood used for the construction of the research model.

Sabrina Marlier

Fig. 7.5. The "test wood" with the five tests (photo: Ph. Foliot (Centre Camille Jullian, CNRS)).

strake, the archaeological observations (from Pomey's notebook) included the following alternating pattern on the frames: two single treenails, a stitch passage, two single treenails, etc. Moreover, on the garboard, a nail, driven from the outside of the shell, strengthened the attachment of the frame to the shell (Charlin *et al* 1978: fig. 34, M19 transverse section). In contrast, the pattern for the half-frames was different: also starting from the second strake, an alternation of two stitch passages, one single treenail, two stitch passages, etc. So, a 'global pattern' arranged in a quincunx was observed; and the alternate method of assembly is noted on each strake. When the 'global pattern' was determined, the implantation of the single treenails and of the channels was traced on the frames.

The holes for the single treenails (diameter 18 mm) and the channels (diameter 18 mm) were then drilled with a brace, while the grooves between the channels (average distance between the channels was 48 mm, with an average breadth of 14 mm and an average depth of 12 mm), were cut with a gouge.

Once these arrangements were complete, the corresponding channels and grooves were fashioned on the outer part of the shell, in order that the passage for the ligatures corresponds exactly with those of the frames: both channels bored into the height of the frame and of the corresponding strakes, as well as the grooves cut on the back of the frame and of the external part of the strakes, thus form a rectangle (on this part of the hull, the grooves have an average depth of only 5 mm) (note 3).

Experimentation with the sewn attachment of the frames to the shell

Archaeological remains of all the known sewn frame shipwrecks reveal that the original stitches were likely vegetable fibres. But it is difficult to determine how many strands formed each stitch: was it a stitch made up of two strands twisted together, or was it a braid made up of three strands? From the drawings and the majority of the photographs, it would appear to be a braid (note 4).

The stitches were passed through the channels in the frames and the corresponding strakes (Fig. 7.3). They made several turns and were probably blocked, without a knot, by the treenails in their passages. The treenails also had a flat in order to leave a passage for the braid. From the drawings of Rival, this flat appears to have an average thickness of 4–5 mm. Moreover, the archaeological remains of the Cap Béar C shipwreck (this aspect is not on the Cavalière remains) seem to indicate that the treenails were driven in opposing directions i.e. for each stitch, one treenail is inserted from the back of the frame into the channel and the other treenail is inserted from the external part of the strake into the other channel (cf. the unpublished excavation rapport).

But what was the diameter of the strands used to make the braids and how many times were the braids passed through the channels before being blocked by the tree-

nails? And were the blocking treenails driven from opposite directions? The archaeological remains do not give an answer. Thus, several tests were undertaken in order to experiment with different hypotheses concerning this assembly system.

These experiments were done on a piece that we called the "test-wood" that is composed of two pieces cut according to the heights of the frames and the strakes (Fig. 7.5). On this piece, as for the model, we drilled pairs of channels linked by grooves cut on the back of the frames and on the outer part of the shell. Tests were undertaken using hemp. The reason for the use of a hemp fibre is two-fold: firstly, none of the results of the analysis done on the fibres used to secure the frames to the hulls, are yet known (Wicha this volume). Secondly, although we think it is unlikely that hemp was used for this type of stitching, and that sparta or halfa would more likely have been employed (note 5), for procurement reasons, we had to use hemp. Either way, the use of these fibres does not negate the validity of the experimentation.

For each test, the strands, making up a twist or a braid, had a variant diameter. And for each test, the number of turns that was possible to make through the channels and the grooves before the insertion of the treenails, was also recorded. For all the tests, the end of the stitch was always threaded in the same manner.

For all the tests the following procedure was adhered to (drawings Fig. 7.6): at the beginning, one end of the stitch had to be left free on the frame's back. The other end was driven into the right hand channel and picked up on the outer shell groove. Then the stitch was driven into the left hand channel and picked up and laid in the groove on the back of the frame, before being turned again in to the right hand channel. Hence, once the first turn is done and the tightness is realised on the stitch located on the outer face, the same process will be repeated several times; on each turn the stitch would be tightened. Thus, the stitch is passed in a loop and care is taken to ensure that it should not protrude above the grooves. Once the maximum possible number of turns was achieved, the extremity

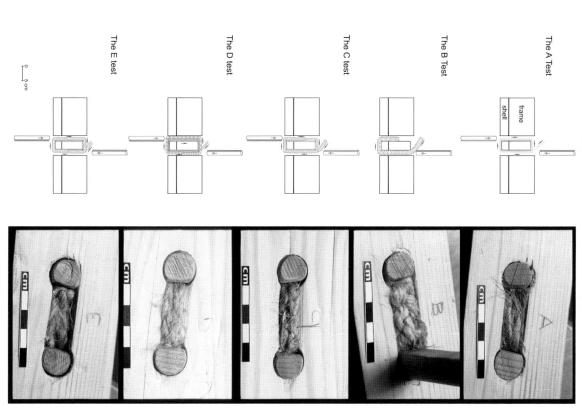

Fig. 7.6. Results of the trial-tests (drawings: S. Marlier; photo: Ph. Foliot (Centre Camille Jullian, CNRS).

The A Test

The B Test

The C test

The D test

The E test

frame
shell

0   5 cm

of the stitch was blocked by a treenail wedged into the passage. Then, a second flattened treenail is used to block the other channel in the opposite direction.

For our experimentation, five tests were done (Fig. 7.6):

- Test A, that comprised a twist composed of two 3 mm diameter strands but not a braid, was rejected because it had no braid;
- Test B comprised a braid composed of 5 mm diameter strands, was too big and thus rejected;
- Test C comprised a braid composed of 3 mm diameter strands, was rejected because the length of the braid was too short (cf. 50 cm);
- Test D, comprised a braid composed of 2.5 mm diameter strands, was rejected because the strands were too fine;

Finally, Test E was successful. For this test, the diameter of the strands in the braid, were of 3 mm each, as in Test C. However, with this length (min. 60 cm), the number of turns through the channels and the grooves, was more than two. Thus, this braid having been threaded still allowed sufficient passage for the insertion of the treenails, without protruding above the grooves.

The attachment of the frame to the shell

When the experimentation was complete, the model's frames were attached to the shell with the use of single treenails driven from the outer part of the shell inwards. The insertion, in the first instance, of these single treenails, allowed the frames and the half-frames to be positioned in place against the shell prior to them being secured in place by the stitches. The sewing was then undertaken according to Test E (above). This process requires the involvement of two people, one on each side of the hull. This practise is illustrated through ethnographic parallels documented in India (Varadarajan 1998: 71, fig. 84). It facilitates the passage and the tightness of the braid through the channels. It is important to achieve this tightness, especially in the case of the sewn frame ships, as it allows a strong join between the elements. When the sewing is complete, each person drives a blockage treenail into the passage of the stitch from both sides. Once this is complete, the frames are further secured to the shell by a nail driven from outside the shell into the garboard (Fig. 7.4).

Observations and results

The realisation of this research model allows the reconstruction of a method by which the frame is lashed to the shell. It also permits an understanding that the alternation between the stitches, blocked by treenails, and the single treenails, is probably explained by the advantages presented by these two assembly types. The lashing technique blocked by treenails indeed allows a strong attachment in order to fasten the frames and to maintain their attachment to the shell: as long as the stitch is firmly secured i.e. not used or distended, this system ensures that the frame is firmly secured to the shell.

The single treenails deter sliding of the frame on the shell and help avoid the risks of the stitches' snapping. The drawings and the photographs of the Cavalière shipwreck clearly show a sliding of the frames on the shell for those vessels constructed with stitches and blockage treenails (Fig. 7.3). The single treenails prevented the frames from sliding completely and the stitches from breaking under the tension.

Finally, a research model was realised, measuring about $1m^2$ in area, has 10 single treenails, 6 m of braid (equivalent to 28.5 m of hemp) and has 20 blockage treenails, that were used to attach the frames (the two frames and the two half-frames) to the shell. From these figures, we calculate that for the construction of the Cavalière ship which measured 13 m in length (Charlin et al 1978: 79), the shipbuilders must have used about 750 single treenails, 450 m of braid and 1500 blockage treenails, in order to fasten all the frames to the shell (note 6).

Conclusion and perspectives

After the construction of the Jules-Verne 9 and Cavalière research models, a third research model will soon commence. This model will aim to explore the construction of the Roman Comacchio ship, found in the Po Delta region. The hull of this ship was stitched and the frames were also attached to the shell by stitches (Berti 1990: 29–31). These construction techniques present further variations on the sewn construction technique than those yet tested in the previous models. As for the fourth vessel, we aim to model the Nin shipwreck (Brusić and Domjan 1985), which will allow us to improve the comparison between the various sewn construction techniques that existed in ancient Mediterranean shipbuilding.

Acknowledgements

I am most grateful to Patrice Pomey, my director, and to Robert Roman who provided technical help in building the Cavalière model, without him I could not have realised my research program. I dedicate this paper to him.

I would also like to thank Michel Rival for his kind collaboration concerning all the graphic restitutions.

I would like also to thank Mohamed Abd el Maguid and Lucy Blue for very kindly editing my paper.

Notes

1   Cf. in the Mediterranean basin, the Giglio shipwreck (Italia) (Bound 1991), the Gela shipwrecks (1 and 2) (Sicily-Italia) (Panvini 2001), the Ma'agan Mikhael shipwreck (Israel) (Linder and Kahanov 2003), the Mazarron shipwrecks (Spain) (Negueruela et al 1995), the Jules-Verne 7 and 9 and the César 1 shipwrecks (Marseille-France) (Pomey 1999, 2001). In Adriatic Sea, the Nin shipwrecks (Croatia) (Brusiº and Domjan 1985), the Comacchio boat (Italia) (Berti 1990), the Cervia and the Pomposa shipwrecks as well as the many remains of sewn boats found in the Po delta region (Bonino 1985; Beltrame 2000). Lately, new sewn shipwrecks have been discovered: the Grand Ribaud D shipwreck (France) (Pomey and Rival 2002), the Cala Sant Vicenç shipwreck (Baleares, Spain) (Nieto et al 2002), and the Pabuç Burnu shipwreck (Turkey) (Greene 2003). These wrecks are in the process of being excavated.

2   During the 1970s excavation, whilst J.-M. Gassend did not observe the sewn construction technique employed to attach the frames to the shell, he nevertheless realised a comprehensive study of the hull published in Charlin et al 1978. Moreover, despite the fact that the information concerning the sewing observed on the Cavalière shipwreck during the "dendrochronology" campaign has not yet been extensively published, M. Pomey kindly entrusted me with his excavation notebook that has provided all the necessary details.

3   All these measurements were directly taken from M. Rival's drawings done during the "dendrochronology" campaign in 1995.

4   Cf. the photographs presented by D. Colls in the 1986 unpublished excavation report from the Cap Béar C shipwreck (report stored and in free consultation in the Département des Recherches Archéologiques Subaquatiques et Sous-Marines (DRASSM), Marseille-France). Cf. also the photos taken during the 1998 "dendrochronology" campaign on the Dramont C shipwreck (cf. note 2).

5   Hemp fibre (Cannabis sativa – Cannabinaceae) is frequently used in the Middle Ages, while halfa (Stipa tenacissima L. – Graminae-Poacea) or sparta (Lygeum Spartum) grass was more frequently used in antiquity – the ancient authors (cf. Pliny, N.H., 19.29, Livy, 22.20.6) talk about Spartum/Sparti. Even so, it is difficult to know

if the ancients did recognise the difference between sparta and halfa as they are very similar grasses (Janville 1902: 146, 67). *Spartum* is moreover adapted to this type of assembly as it is extremely resistance and has anti-rot qualities. Pliny indeed stated that *Spartum* "is of un-rivalled utility, especially for use in water and in the sea, though on dry land they prefer ropes made of hemp; but esparto is actually nourished by being plunged in water..." (*N.H.*, 19.29). Moreover, the stitch fragments that were analysed from the Cheops bark (Lipke 1985: 21), from the ships timbers discovered in Lisht (Haldane 1992: 104), and from the Comacchio boat (Berti, 1990: 29), were all of *Spartum*.

6   The calculations were made from the transverse sections and the lines reconstructed from the Cavalière shipwreck by R. Roman in his unpublished Masters thesis (1988: 38); *Etude architecturale comparative de six navires de commerce antique*. The results given by these calculations remain of course approximations.

References

Beltrame, C., 2000, *Sutiles Naves* of Roman Age. New evidence and technological comparisons with the pre-Roman sewn boats. In J. Litwin (ed) *Down the river to the sea: Proceedings of the Eighth International Symposium on Boat and Ship Archaeology, Gdansk 1997*, 91–96. Polish Maritime Museum. Gdansk.

Berti, F., 1990, *Fortuna Maris: La Nave Romana di Comacchi.*, Nuova Alfa. Bologne.

Bonino, M., 1985, Sewn boats in Italy: *sutiles naves* and barche cucite. In S. McGrail and E. Kentley (eds), *Sewn Plank Boats: archaeological and ethnographic papers based on those presented to a conference at Greenwich in November 1984*, 87–104. BAR Int. Series 276. Oxford.

Bound, M., 1991, The Giglio wreck. *Enalia* supplement 1:31–34.

Brusić, Z. and Domjan, M., 1985, Liburnian boats – Their construction and form. In S. McGrail and E. Kentley (eds), *Sewn Plank Boats: archaeological and ethnographic papers based on those presented to a conference at Greenwich in November 1984*, 67–85. BAR Int. Series 276. Oxford.

Charlin, G., Gassend, J.-M. and Lequement R., 1978, L'épave antique de Cavalière (Le Lavandou, Var). *Archaeonautica* 2: 9–93.

Greene, E., 2003, The 2002 Excavation Season at Pabuç Burnu, Turkey, *The Institute of Nautical Archaeology Quarterly* 30.1: 3–11.

Guibal, F. and Pomey, P., 1998, L'utilisation du matériau-bois dans la construction navale antique: analyse anatomique et dendrochronologique. In E. Rieth (ed) *Méditerranée antique. Pêche, navigation, commerce, Actes du Congrès National des sociétés historiques et scientifiques, Nice 1996*, 159–175. Editions du CTHS. Paris.

Guibal, F. and Pomey, P., 1999, Essences et qualité des billes employées dans la construction navale antique: étude anatomique et dendrochronologique, *Forêt et Marine*, 15–32. Paris.

Haldane, C., 1992, The Lisht Timbers: A Report on Their Significance. In D. Arnold (ed), *The Pyramid Complex of Senwosret I. The South Cemeteries of Lisht*, Vol. III. Metropolitan Museum of Art. New York.

Janville, P., 1902, *Atlas de poche des Plantes utiles des Pays Chauds les plus importantes pour le commerce*. Bibliothèque de poche du Naturalise XII. P. Klincksieck. Paris.

Linder, E. and Kahanov, Y., 2003, *The Ma'agan Mikhael Ship, Volume 1.* Israel Exploration Society and University of Haifa. Jerusalem.

Lipke, P., 1985, Retrospective on the royal ship of Cheops. In S. McGrail & E. Kentley (eds), *Sewn Plank Boats: archaeological and ethnographic papers based on those presented to a conference at Greenwich in November 1984*, 19–34. BAR Int. Series 276. Oxford.

Nieto, X., Terongi, F. & Santos, M., 2002, El pecio de Cala Sant Vincenç, *Revista de Arqueologia* 258: 18–25.

Negueruela, I., Pinedo J., Gomez M., Mivano A., Arellano I. & Barba J.S., 1995, Seventh-century BC Phoenician vessel discovered at Playa de la Isla, Mazarron, Spain. *International Journal of Nautical Archaeology* 24.3: 189–197.

Panvini, R., 2001, *La nave arcaica di Gela (e primi dati sul secondo relito greco).* S. Sciascia. Palermo.

Pomey, P., 1981, L'épave de Bon-Porté et les bateaux cousus de Méditerranée. *Mariners Mirror* 67.3: 225–243.

Pomey, P., 1985, Mediterranean sewn boats in Antiquity. In S. McGrail & E. Kentley (eds), *Sewn Plank Boats: archaeological and ethnographic papers based on those presented to a conference at Greenwich in November 1984*, 35–48. BAR Int. Series 276. Oxford.

Pomey, P., 1996, Dendrochronologie et dendromorphologie des épaves antiques de Méditerranée, *Bilan Scientifique du Département des Recherches archéologiques sous-marine...* 1995, 56–57. Ministère de la Culture. Paris.

Pomey, P., 1999, Les épaves grecques du VIe s. av. J.C. de la place Jules-Verne à Marseille. In P. Pomey & E. Rieth (eds), *Construction navale maritime et fluviale. approches archéologiques, historique et ethnologique: actes du septième Colloque international d'archéologie navale. Proceedings of the seventh international symposium on boat and ship archaeology; Ile Tatihou, Saint-Vaast-la-Hougue, 1994*, 147–154. Archaeonautica 14. CNRS éditions. Paris.

Pomey, P., 2001, Les épaves grecques archaïques du VIe s. av. J.-C. de Marseille: épaves *Jules-Verne* 7 et 9 et *César 1*. In H. Tzalas (ed), *Tropis VI. Sixth International Symposium on Ship Construction in Antiquity. Lamia 1996*, 425–437. Hellenic Institute for the Preservation of Nautical Tradition. Athens.

Pomey, P., 2002, Une nouvelle tradition technique d'assemblage antique: l'assemblage de la membrure par ligatures et chevilles. In H. Tzalas (ed) *Tropis VII. Seventh International Symposium on Ship Construction in Antiquity. Pylos 1999*, 597–604. Hellenic Institute for the Preservation of Nautical Tradition. Athens.

Pomey, P., 2003, Reconstruction of the 6th century BC Greek ships. In C. Beltrame (ed), *Boats, Ships and Shipyards. Proceedings of the Ninth International Symposium on Boat and Ship Archaeology, Venice 2000*, 57–65. Oxbow. Oxford.

Pomey, P. & Rival, M., 2002, Epave Grand Ribaud F. In L. Long, P. Pomey & J.-C. Sourisseau (eds), *Les Etrusques en mer. Epaves d'Antibes à Marseille*, 117–119. Musées de Marseille. Marseille.

Steffy, J.R., 1994, *Wooden ship building and the interpretation of shipwreck*. Texas A & M University Press. College Station. Texas.

Varadarajan. L., 1998, *Sewn Boats of Lakshadweep*. Dona Paula. National Institute of Oceanography.

8 Reconstruction of the large Borobudur outrigger sailing craft

Erik Peterson[1]

At the famous Buddhist Borobudur Temple, built between 760–830 AD and located in Central Java, Indonesia, as many as fifteen hundred scenes are depicted on bas-reliefs (Miksic 1990). Among these are images of five large double-outrigger sailing craft (Fig. 8.1). Borobudur was constructed during a period when Indonesia, via the Srivijaya Empire with its centre in southern Sumatra, was a dominating sea-power in South East Asia, controlling sea-traffic to and from the region, towards China and towards India and Arabia (Wolthers 1967; Manguin 1983, 1993a; Ray 1994) (Fig. 8.2).

Fig. 8.1. The five Borobudur panels with ships.

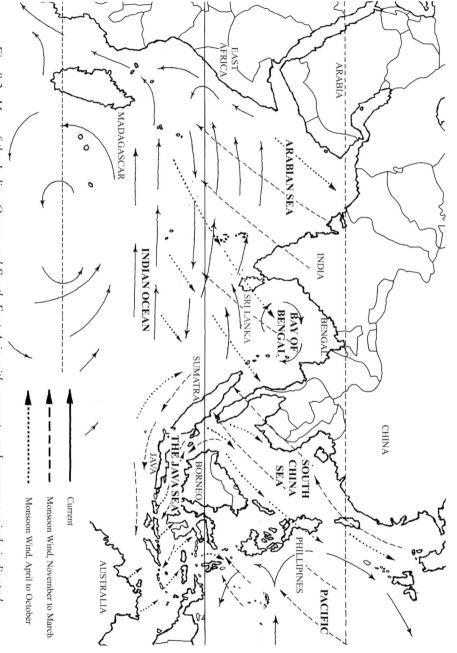

Fig. 8.2. Map of the Indian Ocean and South East Asia with currents and monsoon winds indicated.

Monsoon Wind, April to October

Monsoon Wind, November to March

Current

Fig. 8.3. The largest of the Borobudur craft. Panel no 1 b 86.

plenty of outrigger canoes of Indonesian type may still be found. Further there is linguistic and other evidence that Madagascar was populated by Indonesians from Borneo at some stage during the first millennium AD (Southhall 1975; Verin 1975; Mack 1986; Dahl 1991; Moseley and Asher 1994).

The Borobudur reliefs are the best available source of information on the Indonesian ships of the first millennium. At this stage there is little evidence to gain from excavated wrecks, and no other descriptions or pictures of ancient Indonesian ships have been found.

As a type, the Borobudur ships are unique. They are different from the Chinese junks and also from the Indian-Arab ships which often frequented South East Asia during the Srivijaya period (Hourani 1951; Needham 1971; Flecker 2000; McGrail 2001). When the Europeans came to South East Asia they did not find any vessels of a type similar to the Borobudur ships; evidently, by this stage they had all disappeared.

The Borobudur ships

The Borobudur ship reliefs have been known since 1850, and were described from the early 20th century (Erp 1923; Heide 1928; Swamy 1997), but no serious attempts to

But even before the Srivijaya Empire existed, the Indonesians had sailed in the Indian Ocean. After initial contacts between the Indonesian kingdoms and Bengal, sea trade expanded and the large cultural-religious move from India to South East Asia began (Manguin 1996). Simultaneously, the Indonesians sailed directly westward to southern India, Sri Lanka, and even East Africa, where

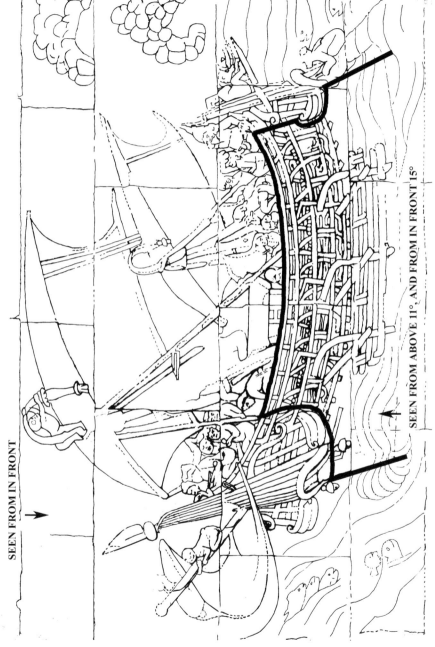

SEEN FROM IN FRONT

SEEN FROM ABOVE 11°, AND FROM IN FRONT 15°

Fig. 8.4. The principles of representation of the large Borobudur craft on the relief

reconstruct the ships seem to have been previously carried out. Based on this knowledge, an attempt to reconstruct the largest vessel, and in the opinion of the author, best documented of the five ships (Fig. 8.3), started in 2001.

This ship evidently had a basic hull which extended upwards with an elevated grid-construction, here called the rowing gallery. At bow and stern, the rowing gallery is hidden by large forward leaning stem and sternpost. On the side of the ship that is visible, a large outrigger structure is seen, and a similar structure was probably also present on the other side of the original ship.

The ship's two masts are forward leaning and square sails hung on yards. A relief of one of the other ships shows that they had bipod masts. Aft is a rudder which according to Burningham (2000) can be identified as a quarter rudder, similar in construction to many Indonesian rudders still in use today.

Reconstructing the ship

When starting the reconstruction, the method by which the sculptor represented the ship on the relief was first studied (Fig. 8.4). Evidently he had tried to be realistic. As far as could be seen, he had started by making a precise picture of the ship as seen from the side. Then in order to illustrate the grid construction and the outriggers,

he presented the side of the ship under the deck line and between stem and stern, as seen from above and from in front. The stem and stern and everything over the deck were only largely visible as if viewed from the front. The relative size of all ship-parts seemed to be accurately represented, only the size of the people seem to have been exaggerated.

In order to determine the size of the ship, it was anticipated that each of the modules in the rowing gallery was 1 m long. With this assumption, the length of the ship was 16.4 m at the waterline, and 23.4 m overall length.

In order to reconstruct the Borobudur ship from the relief, it is necessary to make many assumptions: there are no clear indications of the width of the vessel; many construction details are hidden; and there is not much to be seen of the basic hull shape. However, a faint curved line in the water under the outriggers could be seen on the relief, and it is assumed that this represents the bottom or keel-line of the hull.

According to these observations and assumptions, the basic hull consisted of three parts:

The bottom element or keel was probably made from one half of a trunk as a dugout (Petersen 2000). Over the keel, timbers cut in triangular shapes and fixed to the keel-piece by means of dowels and tenons, the so-called

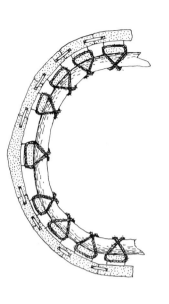

wings, were probably present fore and aft since this type of construction is seen on Philippine wrecks from about 1200 AD.

Over the keel and wings, which jointly determine the sheer of the hull, the basic hull is built up with planks, cut with nearly parallel sides, and fastened together mainly with dowels along the edges (Fig. 8.5). Inboard, the planks

are carved with protruding lugs, provided with holes for lashing the flexible frames. This is the so-called 'lashed-lug' construction, which was believed to have been a common construction technique of South East Asian vessels during the first millennium AD and until about 1400, when frames attached to the planks with the use of iron nails apparently superseded the flexible frames (Clark 1993; Green 1995; McGrail 2001: 304–307).

As the basic hull (Fig. 8.6) and the rowing-gallery must have been strongly fixed together, it was assumed that the frames were extended to the full height of the rowing-gallery. The grid structure (Fig. 8.7), placed upon thwarts which reached out over the sides of the basic hull, was then tied to the extended frames, leaving a gap which gave room for a light-weight wall of bamboo poles. This is a flexible construction by which the rowing ports could easily be opened or closed. The outrigger structure

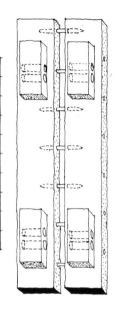

Fig. 8.5. The lashed-lug planking technique used for the Butuan 5 boat. Based on sketches by P.-Y. Manguin and T. Vosmer.

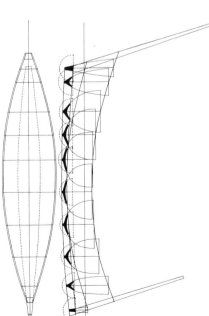

Fig. 8.6. The basic hull, consisting of keel, stem and sternpost, wings and boards. Ten cross-sections are shown with the keel in black.

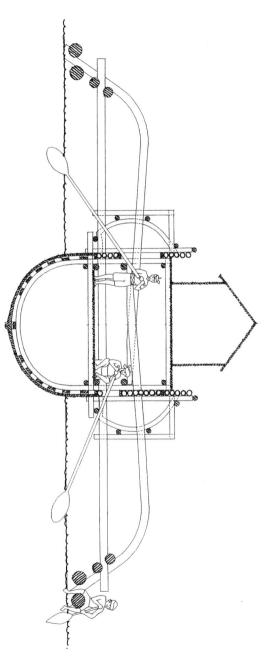

Fig. 8.7. Cross section amidships with possible positions of rowers and paddlers shown.

Fig. 8.10. The model prepared for the initial sailing test.

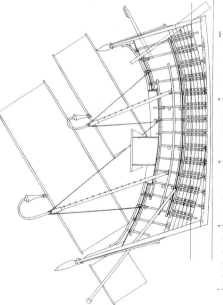

Fig. 8.8. Longitudinal section of the large Borobudur craft as reconstructed.

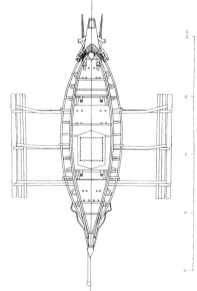

Fig. 8.9. Reconstructed deck plan.

is lashed, both to the basic hull and to the grid structure. On three of the ship illustrations, oars are seen sticking out from the rowing-galleries, showing that these craft, in addition to sails, used oars for propulsion. The rowers were probably facing forward, standing on the lower deck, maybe with members of the crew sitting on the floats and paddling simultaneously.

The panel shows that the stem and sternpost were covered by poles tapering towards the top. These poles were probably lashed both to the posts and to the ends of the grid structures.

The longitudinal section (Fig. 8.8) shows the bowsprit fixed to the side of the stem. At the double quarter rudder construction rudder stocks find their way in between the beams and the grid-construction, ending over the deck with longitudinally oriented tillers. On top of the masts and the stem and sternpost are placed decorations, which have received limited detailed attention.

The suggested position of the bipod masts is also shown with their base-thwarts resting on the upper pair of long heavy beams inside the frames (Figs 8.8, 8.9). The masts can thus be adjusted in forward or aft positions. The stays

of the masts are passing under beams before they are fastened to bitts.

In preparation for the construction of the model, a sketch of the ship was produced at scale 1:50, and later 1:20 scale drawings were prepared as a basis for the model, shown in Fig. 8.10 in its final shape. The hull was narrow, only 2.7 m, based upon the assumption that it had a form like most of the double outrigger canoes known from South East Asian waters (Hornell 1946: 253–269).

The craft's stability, with the support of the outriggers, was believed to have been adequate. This assumption, however, was wrong. When the model was tested in the river, it capsized both in clam and windy conditions, making it necessary to reconsider the construction. It was evident that the ship's stability had to be improved. The hull had to be wider, thereby enlarging the craft's carrying capacity and necessitating the requirement for ballast to be placed in the bottom of the hull when unloaded.

The stability could also be improved by lowering the centre of gravity, and by making the outrigger booms longer and increasing the carrying volume of the floats. The hull should be stable enough by itself under normal conditions, and the floats should be placed a little above the water surface, so that they only contributed to the stability of the ship in critical situations.

As a consequence of these reconsiderations, the model was then fitted with foam cushions making it wider and enabling it to float higher. At the same time, extensions were fitted to the outrigger booms, enlargements added to the floats, and 2.2 kg of ballast was placed in the bottom of the hull.

The model was then tested again in the river (Fig. 8.11), and the stability of the model was much improved. The floats were in a better position, and it was now difficult to get the model to capsize. With a strong current in the river it was difficult to undertake reliable tests of the model's sailing capabilities. Observation revealed that it was fairly capable of keeping on course when the wind was a little aft of the beam.

After this, the reconstruction drawings were revised at a scale of 1:50 (Figs 8.7–8.9), and the width of the hull ended up being 3.6 m and the outrigger system spanned 14.2 m. The displacement of the ship was now calculated to be 38 m³, and with a calculated total weight of 18 tons for the empty ship, the carrying capacity would be about 20 tons, including crew and load or ballast.

The Borobudur reliefs depict Buddhist legends which tell us that the ships were trading ships carrying holy people on long voyages. But probably some were also used for warfare and raids and some for controlling foreign ships sailing to and from Srivijaya. The ship type had no doubt been developed for the calm conditions of the Java Sea, where it could utilise the monsoon wind. Even if it originated in the Java Sea, however, it is quite possible that it had also been sailing in the Indian Ocean, the Bay of Bengal and the South China Sea, using favourable currents and monsoon winds. In these waters it would have encountered very high waves and extremely strong winds and such tough conditions were, no doubt, dangerous for the Borobudur ship-type, since it could easily capsize or wreck.

In conclusion, this study is not the definitive word on the interpretation of the Borobudur ships. It is essential to know the real width of the ships and their outrigger structure. This knowledge is probably best achieved when wrecks of the Borobudur type are found and excavated and a reconstruction design undertaken.

Until then several other questions also deserve further study. Are the assumptions made here concerning the

Fig. 8.11. Final test of the model with foam cushions and extra floats fitted to improve stability.

construction of the basic hull correct? At what time and why did the Borobudur ship-type disappear? Where were the ships of the Borobudur type built, from where did they sail, who were the owners and who formed the crews? What can we learn from existing or from extinct but recorded, double outrigger vessels about the structure, use and correct proportion of the outriggers in relation to the hull of the ship, and how can this knowledge be used for the reconstruction of the Borobudur ship-type?

In southern Borneo there are at present two 'traditionally' constructed boat types, the Sangkilang and the Bolos, which are both constructed over logboats made from cleaved half-trunks (Petersen 2000: 7). Is their construction historically related to the Borobudur ship-type?

In Sri Lanka, James Hornell (1944) saw the *Yathra Dhoni* which he considered to be part of the same family as the Borobudur ships, and in Sumatra there existed during the 20th century, the *Tjangkal*, a ship-type which also has features in common with the Borobudur ships.[2] Are these two types descendants of the Borobudur ships?

I would appreciate if other researchers would continue the work so that the present understanding of the larger Indonesian ships of the first millennium AD could be improved.

Notes

1   (by Ole Crumlin-Pedersen): As a participant of ISBSA 10 in September 2003, Erik Petersen was evidently not in good health. His son Joakim Gundel read his paper in the auditorium but Erik was able himself to answer questions and offer further information on the subject of early Indonesia ships and their reconstruction. However, his condition rapidly deteriorated, and after returning to his home in Banjarsamin, Borneo, he died on 17 February 2004 and was buried there.

Born in Denmark in 1930, Erik Petersen graduated as an architect from the Academy of Fine Arts in Copenhagen. He worked until 1990 as a town planner and university lecturer in Denmark, Kenya, Pakistan, Tanzania and Indonesia. After retirement he lived in Borneo and was engaged in the design of locally-produced furniture.

His main interest, however, was the study of boats and boating, and in this capacity he was a determined and skilful observer and recorder of the boat building traditions and skills of various indigenous groups of craftsmen in southern Borneo. After having contacted the Viking Ship Museum in Roskilde in 1996, he prepared several reports on these studies, including his monograph *Jukung-Boats from the Barito Basin, Borneo*, published in Roskilde in 2000. The present paper on the studies leading to a hypothetical reconstruction and a scale model of one of the major vessels shown in the Borobudur reliefs on Java was Erik Petersen's last scholarly work, and according to his will the model has been offered for display at the Maritime Museum (Museum Bahari) in Jakarta.

2   In the Kronborg Maritime Museum, Denmark, there is an example of a Sumatran *Tjangkal* ship-type that displays

square sails hung on yards in a similar fashion to the Borobudur ships.

References

Burningham, N., 2000, Indonesian quarter-rudder mountings. *International Journal of Nautical Archaeology* 29: 195–217.

Clark, P., 1993, The Butuan Two Boat, known as the Balangay in the National Museum, Manila, Philippines. *International Journal of Nautical Archaeology* 22.2: 143–159.

Dahl, O. C., 1991, *Migration from Kalimantan to Madagascar*. Norwegian University Press. Oslo.

Erp, Th. van, 1923, Voorstellingen van Vaartuigen op de Reliefs van Boroboedoer. *Nederlandsch-Indie, Oud an Niew*, 1923: 227–255.

Evans, M.A., 1927, Notes on the remains of an old boat from Pontian, Pahang. *Journal of the Federated Malay States Museums* 12.

Flecker, M., 2000, A 9th-century Arab or Indian shipwreck in Indonesian waters. *International Journal of Nautical Archaeology* 29: 199–217.

Green, J., 1995, Interim Report on the joint Australian-Philippine Butuan Boat Project. *International Journal of Nautical Archaeology* 24.3: 177–188.

Heide, G. J. van der, 1928, Die sammenstelling van Hindoo vartuigen uitgewerkt naar beldwerken van den Borobudur. *Nederlandsch-Indie, Oud an Niew* 1928: 343–357.

Hornell, J., 1944, The outrigger canoes of Madagascar, East Africa and the Comoro Islands. *The Mariners Mirror* 1944.1/4: 3–17, 170–184.

Hornell, J., 1946, *Water Transport. Origins and early evolution*. Cambridge University Press. Cambridge.

Horridge, G. A., 1978, *The design of planked boats of Moluccas*. Maritime Monographs 38. National Maritime Museum. Greenwich.

Horridge, G. A., 1979, *The Konjo Boatbuilders and the Bugis Prahus of South Sulawesi*. Maritime Monographs 40. National Maritime Museum. Greenwich.

Horridge, G. A., 1982, *The lashed-lug Boat of the Eastern Archipelagos, the Alcina MS and the Lomblen whaling boats*. Maritime Monographs 54. National Maritime Museum. Greenwich.

Hourani, G. F., 1951, *Arab Seafaring: in the Indian Ocean in ancient and early Medieval times*. Princeton University Press. Princeton.

Hudson, A.B., 1963, *Deadceremonies of the Padju Epat. Ma'anyan Dayaks*. Sarawak Museum Spec. Monographs 1.

Hudson, A.B., 1967, *The Barito Isolects of Borneo*. Cornell University Press. Ithaca, New York.

Hudson, A.B., 1972, *Padju Epat. The Ma'anyan of Indonesian Borneo*. Michigan State University. Holt, Rinehart and Winston Inc. New York.

Mack, J., 1986, *Madagascar. Island of the Ancestors*. British Museum Publications Ltd. London.

Manguin, P-Y., 1983, Relationship and cross influences between SE-Asian and Chinese Shipbuilding Traditions. Unpublished paper. Ninth Conference of International Association of Historians of Asia, Manilla, Philippines 1983.

Manguin, P-Y., 1985, Sewn-Plank Craft of SE Asia, a preliminary survey. In S. McGrail, *Sewn plank boats. Archaeological and ethnographic papers based on those presented to a conference at Greenwich in November, 1984*, 319–343. B.A.R. International Series 275. Oxford.

Manguin, P-Y., 1989, The trading ships of Insular Southeast Asia: New evidence from Indonesian archaeological sites. In *Proceedings, Pertemuan Ilmiah Arkeologi V, Yogyakarta 1989*, vol. I, 200–220. Ikatan Ahli Arkeologi Indonesia. Jakarta.

Manguin, P-Y., 1993a, Pre-modern SE-Asian Shipping in the Indian Ocean, the Maldive Connection. Unpublished paper presented at the Conference of International Commission of Maritime History, Fremantle 1993.

Manguin, P-Y., 1993b, Palembang and Srivijaya: An early Malay harbour-city rediscovered. *Journal Malaysian Branch of the Royal Asiatic Society* 661: 23–46.

Manguin, P-Y., 1996, SE-Asian Shipping in the Indian Ocean during the first millennium AD. In H.P. Ray and J.-F. Salles (eds) *Tradition and Archaeology: Early maritime contacts in the Indian Ocean. Proceedings of the International Seminar Techno-Archaeological perspectives of seafaring in the Indian Ocean 4th century BC – 15th century AD*. New Delhi, February 28 – March 4, 1994. 181–198. New Delhi.

McGrail, S., 2001, *Boats of the World, from the Stone Age to Medieval Times*. Oxford University Press. Oxford.

McGrath, W. H., 1988, Some Notes on the Navigation of 1985 Trans-Indian Ocean Canoe Voyage. *Journal of Navigation* 41: 2

Miksic, J., 1990, *Borobudur, Golden tales of Buddhas*. Periplous. Singapore.

Miller, J. I., 1969, *The spice trade of the Roman Empire*. Clarendon Press. Oxford.

Moseley, C. and Asher, R. E., 1994, *Atlas of the World's Languages*. Routledge. London and New York.

Needham, J., 1971, *Science and Civilisation in China IV, 3: Nautical Technology*. Cambridge University Press. Cambridge.

Petersen, E., 2000, *Jukung-Boats from the Barito Basin, Borneo*. Viking Ship Museum. Roskilde.

Ray, H. P., 1994, *The Winds of Change, Buddhism and the Maritime Links of Early South Asia*. Oxford University Press. Delhi.

Shaw, T., 1993, *The Trireme Project; Operational Experience 1987–90, Lessons Learnt*. Oxbow Monograph 31. Oxford.

Southhall, A., 1975, The Problem of Malagasy Origin. In H. N. Chittick and R. I. Rotberg (eds), *East Africa and the Orient: cultural syntheses in pre-colonial times*. Africana. London.

Swamy, L.N., 1997, *Boats and Ships in Indian Art*. Harman Publishing House. New Delhi.

Verin, P., 1975, Austronesian contributions to the culture of Madagascar. In H. N. Chittick and R. I. Rotberg (eds), *East Africa and the Orient: cultural syntheses in pre-colonial times*. Africana. London.

Wolthers, O.W., 1967, *Early Indonesian Commerce. A study of the origins of Srivijaya*. Cornell University Press. Ithaca, New York.

9 The construction and trials of a half-scale model of the Early Bronze Age ship, Ferriby 1, to assess the capability of the full-size ship

Edwin Gifford, Joyce Gifford and John Coates

This paper is dedicated to Ted Wright, who discovered the remains of at least three ships in the Humber Estuary in 1937 and who endured a long struggle to excavate, record and interpret them. He frequently attended ISBSA conferences where he attempted to arouse interest in this work. It was to Tatihou in 1997 that he brought his model of Ferriby 1 and first saw the Giffords' half-scale model of the Sutton Hoo ship (Fig. 9.1). The recent re-dating of the most complete vessel, Ferriby 1, to 1780 BC, making it one of the earliest known sewn planked vessels in NW Europe (Wright *et al* 2001), encouraged Ted to bequeath his research to the three of us, shortly before his death in May 2001, with the agreement that we should build and test a half-scale model along the lines of the reconstruction published in his book (Wright 1990).

After excavation of Ferriby 1 in 1946, the recovered parts were reassembled at the National Maritime Museum at Greenwich (Fig. 9.2). These amounted to the two keel planks, butt-jointed amidships (each 8 m x 520 mm x 150 mm), the two full-length outer bottom planks (each

10.5 m x 600 mm x 80 mm), and one end of a lower side strake. The latter was to give the vital clues to the angle and shape of the upper strakes. All were sewn together with yew withies, still well preserved.

When laid upon a flat floor, the soft, water-logged timbers, already cut into short lengths to assist the excavation, naturally took the shape of the surface on which they had been placed so that it was at first believed that the ship had a straight, horizontal keel. Later re-examination of the reconstructed lengthwise section of the pre-1946 Ferriby 1 excavations (Fig. 9.3), and the results of Wright's 1937 probes into the mud, led him to an alternative interpretation, that the vessel clearly showed

Fig. 9.1. Ted Wright at Tatihou.

Fig. 9.2. Ferriby 1 at Greenwich (Wright 1990: fig. 2.17; National Maritime Museum: Greenwich).

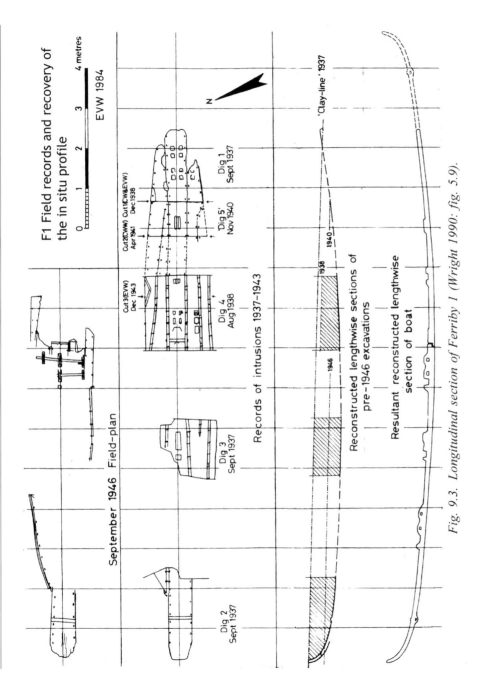

F1 Field records and recovery of the in situ profile

EVW 1984

0   1   2   3   4 metres

September 1946 Field-plan

Cut 3(EVW)
Dec 1943

Dig 4
Aug 1938

Dig 3
Sept 1937

Dig 2
Sept 1937

Cut 2(CWW) Cut 1(CW&EVW)
Apr 1941   Dec 1938

Dig 5
Nov 1940

Dig 1
Sept 1937

Records of intrusions 1937–1943

'Clay-line' 1937

1938
1940

1946

Reconstructed lengthwise sections of
pre-1946 excavations

1946

Resultant reconstructed lengthwise
section of boat

Fig. 9.3. Longitudinal section of Ferriby 1 (Wright 1990: fig. 5.9).

a rockered keel (Wright and Coates 1990: 89–92). There are several advantages to be gained from the inclusion of a rockered keel; seaworthiness, ease of movement onto skids or when being "walked" broadside up soft beaches.

The published hypothetical reconstruction drawing by John Coates (Fig. 9.4), is based on Wright's pre-1946 excavation reconstruction, and forms the basis of the reconstruction described below. Note that the flare of the side strakes enabled straight planks to fit the elliptically curved bottom. This enabled the economical cutting of long, wide planks 'dory' fashion.

The midships butt-joint in the keel plank puzzled us as it was not fastened in any way and thus, because of the long overhang and fine lines of the ends, the ship, with its buoyancy concentrated amidships, would almost always be hogging with the ends tending to droop, putting the keel plank into compression. The hull would thus be acting as an inverted arch, with the top strakes in tension and always being forced inwards. This in fact simplified the building process as there was no need to lock the thwarts through the upper strakes. Another advantage of the hogging mode is that the force on the stitches would only be in one direction, thereby reducing wear.

It would thus appear that Early Bronze Age builders had a profound understanding of the forces acting on the ship's structure. The vessel also represented a major step

forward in terms of technological innovation as the shape is primarily derived from the planks rather than being hewn from a whole log. Therefore, the size of available trees was no longer such a limiting factor in determining the size of a ship.

The building of the model was a challenge, involving the hewing, bending and carving of green oak to achieve a close fit of joints and then sewing the planks together. A part model was built in softwood which could be more readily carved and adjusted to achieve the complex shapes than working with oak (Fig. 9.5). The finished parts were used as templates in the hewing of the final shapes.

A major challenge was bending the middle part of the keel and bottom planks to fashion the rocker (the forward part of the plank having been carved from a solid log). This was done by steaming the planks inside a PVC sleeve, the green oak requiring a temperature of only 70°C for a period of three hours, with 200 kg of weight, in order to permit bending (Fig. 9.6). Such a temperature could have been obtained in the Early Bronze Age by heating water with hot flints in a long clay-lined "cooking-trough". It was determined that the full-sized planks would probably have needed a weight of 1500 kg for about six hours. Carved cleats were left proud of the bottom planks and holes were cut into them in order to take the transverse timbers. This appears to have been the method employed

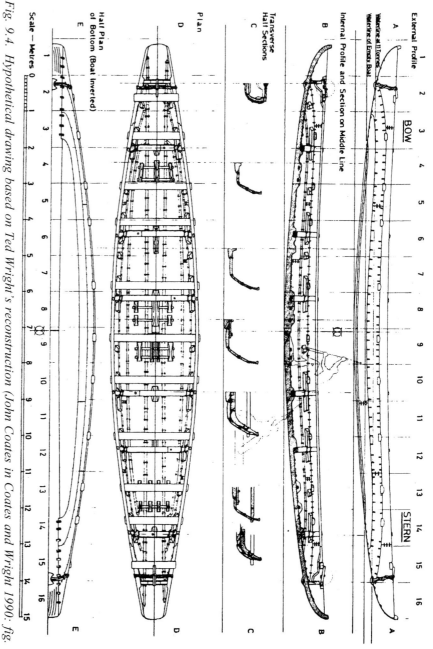

Fig. 9.4. Hypothetical drawing based on Ted Wright's reconstruction (John Coates in Coates and Wright 1990: fig. 5.17).

Fig. 9.5. Part model in soft wood.

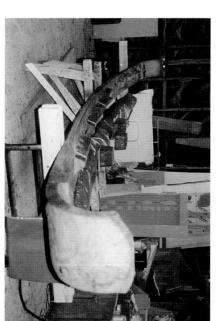

Fig. 9.6. Bending the keel.

to align the bottom planks during assembly and stitching. This worked well, as did the carved "bird-mouth" joints between the planks (Fig. 9.7).

In the absence of half-scale yew withies and the skill to create them, Marlow pre-stretched, polyester 8-plait rope was used as a substitute as this is close to yew in strength and elasticity, as demonstrated by tests at Southampton University Department of Engineering. Mastic jointing was used for caulking instead of moss, a

Edwin Gifford, Joyce Gifford and John Coates

Fig. 9.10. Craft almost complete.

Fig. 9.7. Carved cleats and cross timbers.

Fig. 9.8. Tightening and wedging stitches.

Fig. 9.9. Lower side planks.

developed so that the stitches could be tightened and wedged by one man. Its suitability for yew withies has yet to be tested (Fig. 9.8).

Figure 9.9 shows the lower side planks being placed in position; it also shows the transition between stem and side planking, the rebated joint for the next plank above not yet completed. Figure 9.10 illustrates a more general view of the almost complete craft, showing the connection between thwart and gunwale. All the oak planking was soaked in water prior to use and subsequently dressed with a mixture of linseed oil and white spirit. The boat has always been stored under cover and to date there has been no significant cracking.

Figure 9.11 shows the craft ready for launching and demonstrates the buoyancy amidships and the fine lines of the overhanging ends. The girth-lashing at the bow passes through a "winged cleat" on the underside of the keel. When tightened with a tourniquet it keeps the gunwale tight against the stem. It was useful during construction and gave strength to the hull.

On completion the bare hull weighed 570 kg as compared with the previously calculated 480 kg that had been based on moderately dry oak.

method previously tested in France, at the Park Archéologie de Samara, la Chausee-Tirancourt, Somme. The space between the stitches was doubled so that the shear strength of the model was to scale. A tool different from that found and experimented with by Ted Wright, was

Fig. 9.11. Ready for launching.

Trials

The first trial was made by one man, with two oars, to test the ability of the vessel to run straight and also to turn. This it did well, but required strong correction after a sharp turn, as would be expected from a rockered hull. With an impromptu crew of paddlers, steering was more difficult, although the addition of a longer steering paddle helped (Fig. 9.12). Carrying capacity was checked with nine people on board, equivalent to 72 on the full size ship.

Following the authors experience of curraghs in Aran and the Giffords' *naevog* from Dingle that were propelled by oars, it was decided to experiment with testing the vessel under oars. This proved to be more efficient than paddling, particularly in the open sea. A double sculler rig, with two oars each side, produced a speed of 4.4 knots (the equivalent of 6 knots on the full size vessel).

Despite its somewhat later date, we believe that the c. 950 BC Canewdon "paddle", found in Essex, could be an oar (Wright 1990: 151–155). On the Malabar coast of India, fishermen row dugout *vallams* with oars of similar length (c. 2 m) to that discovered at Canewdon. Subsequent trials with a pair of these oars found them well balanced, and under oar the model rode a moderate swell very comfortably. For a more severe test we rowed through the short steep wash of fast ferries, approximately 1 m high and 10 m long, taking little water aboard (Fig. 9.13).

The presence of the two "saddle features" on the keel plank, one amidships (Fig. 9.14, which also shows the butt joint) and one forward (Fig. 9.15), have been interpreted as possible supports for a mast. The vessel was subsequently tested under sail and a mast supporting a 5 sqm sail was stepped on the midship saddle. In a 10-knot breeze the model reached a GPS measured speed of 4 knots when running and broad reaching (Fig. 9.16). This agrees with Coates' prediction of a 6–7 knots speed for the vessel in a fresh breeze. Leeway when reaching was 15°, and the steering was well balanced, but when the speed of the model under tow exceeded 5 knots (7 knots full size) it became more difficult to steer. As this speed

Fig. 9.12. The builders paddling.

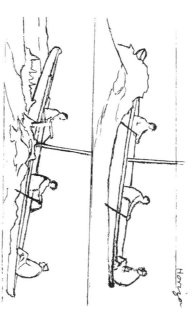

Fig. 9.13. Passing through a 1 m high wash – Sketch made from video tape by John Coates.

Fig. 9.14. Midship "mast step" and butt joint.

could be exceeded when running before a strong wind down the face of a wave, perhaps causing a broach, the forward mast position may have been used to help steer in such conditions.

Edwin Gifford, Joyce Gifford and John Coates

Fig. 9.16. Under sail in a gentle breeze.

Fig. 9.15. Forward "mast step".

Conclusions

The building and trials of the model have demonstrated that this shape and method of boat construction could produce vessels of much larger size and improved shape in the Early Bronze Age, that would have been faster than the logboats they succeeded, and more suitable than skin boats for landing on rough beaches. Such vessel types would have enabled longer offshore voyages, the ability to land safely on unfamiliar coasts, and when the weather was suitable, they may have been able to cross the North Sea in three to four days.

Several aspects of the vessel construction impressed the authors; in particular, an understanding of the structural forces, and the skill of the shipwrights in shaping and fitting the planks, particularly the "bird-mouth" joints; all remarkably advanced for c. 1800 BC and potentially requiring a large, well organised community to construct. The oldest bottom timbers at Ferriby, those of Ferriby 3, c. 1905 BC, do not have saddles, perhaps indicating that if their interpretation as mast supports is correct, the sail might have been introduced to the North Sea some time between 1900 and 1800 BC. This then raises questions about the material used for the sail.

Could suitable woven fabrics have been available for sails or would they have used skins? Could the delicate shaping of the timbers, particularly the joints between planks, have been done with stone tools in the Neolithic? The discovery of Ferriby 1 and construction of the Ferriby 1 model serves to highlight possible approaches to construction and reconstruction and in so doing raises many more questions that remain to be answered.

Acknowledgements

We wish to thank Richard Darrrah for selecting and cleaving a fine oak tree and successfully producing such difficult shapes; Damian Goodburn for finding and shaping the oak crooks for the frames; and Jeff Bird and his team of shipwrights for their ingenuity and hard work in building the ship. They were all present at the launch (Fig. 9.12).

References

Wright E.W., 1990, *The Ferriby Boats: Seacraft of the Bronze Age*. Routledge. London.
Wright, E.W. and Coates, J., 1990, Reconstruction and performance. In E. Wright *The Ferriby Boats: Seacraft of the Bronze Age*, 85–116. Routledge. London.
Wright, E.V., Hedges, R.E.M., Bayliss, A. and Van de Noort, R., 2001, New AMS radiocarbon dates for the North Ferriby boats – a contribution to dating prehistoric seafaring in northwestern Europe. *Antiquity* 75: 726–734.

10 The value of experimental archaeology for reconstructing ancient seafaring

Timm Weski

Experimental archaeology has long been part of nautical archaeology (Goodburn 1993; Coates *et al.* 1995; Crumlin-Pedersen 1995; Weski 1997). In fact, if we regard the reconstruction of a trireme in France in 1861 as a proper experiment (Lehmann 1982), it is at least as old as boat and ship archaeology as an academic discipline. Some of the projects are well known and are mentioned in several publications, while others have received very little attention (e.g. Fee 1958). Though some additional knowledge is gained from experimental archaeology, its value from the scientific point of view is seldom debated. Sometimes it is questionable whether certain topics are of historical or archaeological interest at all, for example the problem of dehydration of rowers in a trireme (Coates *et al.* 1990: 18; Coates *et al.* 1993: 108; Coates 1995: 130). In antiquity these men were used to hard physical work in a hot climate from their youth, therefore dehydration is only of significance for modern sports medicine. Another question is: Can we really conduct tests under realistic conditions? It would be very interesting to see how the hoofs of the horses and their droppings affect the wood and which repairs would be necessary after a couple of years of using a ship for the transport of livestock, or how many of the horses and cows died if transported in an open Viking Age replica from Norway to Iceland. It is hard to imagine that anybody would try such an experiment today. Colin Mudie, the naval architect of several replicas (Mudie 1984), pointed out quite rightly that nowadays the necessary raw materials are often no longer available, therefore other construction methods must be chosen. Further to this, modern safety regulations make more ballast, stronger rigs, etc. compulsory. For example, *Matthew*, the reconstruction of Cabot's ship, had to be equipped with an auxiliary engine for safety reasons (Mudie 1996: chap. 11.0; Mudie 1994: 3).

This paper will deal only with the results concerning actual seafaring and will omit any questions dealing with boatbuilding techniques, but the question does arise whether it is always necessary to build a whole vessel. In several cases, a scale model or the construction of only a part of the hull would have served the same purpose. The value of replicas as part of a museum's exhibitions will also not be discussed.

What did the *Kon Tiki* expedition teach us (Heyerdahl 1948)? Rafts are on one hand seaworthy, but on the other hand they are slow, difficult to steer and there is the constant danger that they might fall apart. Perhaps it should be mentioned that the historical background for most of the raft voyages is rather weak, and one has even been labelled "delightfully wrong" (McKusick 1979: 123). In spite of negative outcomes, rafts have been used for further expeditions not only by Thor Heyerdahl, but by other people as well. For example, the *Hsu Fu* dissolved itself successfully after a couple of months when Timothy Severin tried to cross the Pacific some years ago (Severin 1995).

What is the historic outcome of *Hokule'a's* trip from Hawaii to Tahiti and back in 1976 (Finney 1979: 101)? Most likely it is the ability of modern men to learn the ancient Polynesian art of navigation without instruments. The ability of catamarans to cross open water is well known from other sources. Therefore the safe arrival of a boat constructed with modern materials is nothing surprising.

One of the unsolved questions of seafaring in classical times in the Mediterranean was the arrangement of rowers in a trireme. The solution to how it was possible to place the rowers in such a manner that they were able to handle their oars was practically tested by a full-scale mock-up (Morrison *et al.* 2000: fig. 7; 8). So what else did we learn from the trials of *Olympias* (Coates *et al.* 1990)?

Kyrenia II was built along the lines of the Kyrenia wreck in authentic technique (Katzev *et al.* 1989; Steffy 1989). In 1987 she was sailed from Piraeus, Greece, to Paphos, Cyprus, and back (Katzev 1990). Under certain conditions she was towed by another vessel. In spite of this it was a successful cruise during which winds with gale force were encountered, but did we learn more from it, if we compare the results with those of *Galateia*? She was constructed from modern materials as a half-scale model (Braemer 1991: 80). Unfortunately this was done at a time before the final lines were published. Therefore the shapes of the bows of the two vessels differ. The sailing ability of *Galateia* was tested in 1984 on Außenalster in Hamburg and in 1985 on the Kieler Förde in the Baltic Sea (Braemer 1991: 87). For recording wind force, speed, leeway etc. modern professional equipment was used (Braemer 1991: 85). The data were later converted to the larger size of the original wreck (Braemer 1991: 234). Another example is *See Wylfing*, which follows the lines of the boat in the Sutton Hoo burial, even if the depth of the false keel differs. Again, modern materials for the hull, rigging and sails were used (Gifford 1995; Gifford 1996, Gifford 1998).

Icelandic sources tell us that of the 25 boats of the first settlers which sailed from Iceland to Greenland only 14 arrived, the others were either forced back by bad weather or were lost at sea (Genzmer 1944: 248). If this was the normal rate of casualties for oceanic passages, seafaring must have been very dangerous in the Viking Age. So what do we learn from the cruise of *Saga Siglar* in 1984 to Greenland, in which her auxiliary engine was used during calm spells (Vinner 1995: 302)? This machinery and the additional stern rudder were also used when her side rudder broke in a storm off Cape Farewell (Vinner 1995: 300). That open boats can cope with strong winds? Countless shipwrecked sailors have survived in open boats as long as they could bail fast enough, could prevent capsizes, had enough food and drink and did not die of exposure (e.g. Brown 1974: 119; Veer 1970: 82; Robin 1981; 63; Merrien 1963: 30; Kennedy 1978: 113; Luckner 1921; 211; Horder 1988: 84; 107). Already in 1893 the *Viking*, a replica of the Gokstad wreck, had crossed the Atlantic successfully (Christensen 1986). So what does the *Saga Siglar* expedition tell us apart from the fact that sailing a late Viking Age replica in high latitudes is adventurous and fun? The same applies to the passage of *Snorri* from Greenland to Newfoundland in 1997 (Carter 1999). Both boats were constructed along the lines of the wreck Skuldev 1.

Viking age navigation without instruments was successfully tried on a cruise around the North Sea a couple of years ago by using a traditional Norwegian West Coast vessel built in Åfjord in 1863 and a replica of a boat constructed originally in 1872 in the same area (Engvig 2001a; Engvig 2001b). This experiment shows that one can test certain topics without a reconstruction of an archaeological find built as closely as possible to the original.

What do we gain from the crossing of the Atlantic of *Mathew* in 1997, apart from the positive identification of the people of Bristol with this ship? We know that Cabot succeeded in 1497, but he certainly did not have the comfort of electrical power, GPS or hot and cold showers (Matthew 2002).

We know that the Pilgrim Fathers in 1620 sailed with 135 people on board of *Mayflower* across the Atlantic.

What did we learn from the passage of *Mayflower II*, apart from the fact that modern sailors used to steel hulls and rigging were totally unprepared for the constant trimming of hemp standing rigging on a wooden ship (Villiers 1962: 145)? After all she carried modern equipment like wheel steering and radio communication and a crew of only 33, who wore historic costumes on public occasions (Villiers 1962: 144; 146; 150). In addition, a southerly route to North America was chosen instead of the direct route steered by the Pilgrims. The fact that *Mayflower II* could weather a storm by lying a-hull, because her high stern castle kept the bow close to the wind is not really surprising looking at her lines (Villiers 1962: 151). But was this result really worth building a vessel of 105 feet length over all? Most likely we would learn more about 17th-century seamanship by studying paintings. For example, that Dutch East Indiamen were brought to anchor under backed foresail and partly brailed up mizzen (Giltaij et al 1997: 119). Under storm conditions reefed lower courses and a partly brailed mizzen were carried (Giltaij et al. 1997: 143), and the top masts were struck as one can see on other paintings.

Another example is *Duyfken*, which recently sailed from Australia to Europe. Again we know that the original vessel had made the passage the other way round. If we want to show how leach buntlines work, we do not have to build a whole ship. Using the same technique as the crews of Humber keels for setting and lowering a flying topsail, recorded in the 19th century, shows only the cleverness and practical mind of these sailors, but nothing about seamanship in the Age of Discovery (Burningham 2001: 77).

Let us have a closer look at the Bremen wreck of 1380, which has been reconstructed in full size three times. Before the Kiel replica was constructed, a 1:25 model was tested in a wind tunnel (Sauer 2003: 22) and a 1:15 model was tank tested (Brandt *et al.* 1994: 32; Sauer 2003: 23). The lines of the original wreck are slightly distorted, if one compares the port with the starboard side. Therefore this had to be eliminated, though it is not said which side was chosen (Brandt et al 1994: 8). During the building process, moulds were used as well as stainless steel for the nails and the sintels. Another historic inconsistency are steam bent planks (Hoheisel *et al.* 1994: 257). For the trials the vessel had no mechanical power, although two water jet engines have since been installed (Yacht 1995). She was tested on the Baltic Sea off Kiel, Roskilde and Warnemünde in 1992. The aims of these tests were mainly those used by modern naval architects for comparing various ships with each other, which are necessarily not those of interest for nautical archaeologists or historians.[1] This is not really surprising, as the whole project was led by naval architects.

The difficulty with the wind tunnel test was that the modern computer programs developed for yachts had to be adapted for a late medieval vessel. In addition, the sail area used for this test differs from that of the replica.

Therefore the results had to be recalculated. This showed that the results of wind tunnel testing did not agree with the full-size, real world test (Brandt et al 1994: 49). The question arises, is there anything we can learn from the wind tunnel test? Or could we perhaps use in future these corrected data for analysing other Late Medieval vessels without having to build replicas?

For the real tests, which were done in varying wind speeds up to force 7, the vessel had been loaded with 28 tons of stones as ballast(Brandt et al.1994: 32), because the empty ship had insufficient stability. The heeling stability was tested with the yard set, but without the sail. This is a completely artificial situation, because in real life there would always have been a sail set from the yard while at sea. On the other hand, the stability of the empty ship was most likely greater, because in harbour or at anchor the yard was lowered to the deck. The stability of the ship in ballast is sufficient (Brandt et al 1994: 33). The author claims that the vessel must have always had this amount of ballast for safety reasons, even when carrying cargo (Brandt et al. 1994: 54). It is rather doubtful whether this statement is really true, because we know from later periods that merchant ships often did not carry any ballast when fully loaded. In fact, organising the discharge of the cargo or ballast and taking in ballast or cargo without endangering the ship has long been one of the most important tasks in harbour for the officer in charge (e.g. Wells 1994). From historic sources we know that ships often sailed with as little ballast as possible to keep the costs down (e.g. Burmeister 1978: 51; Wahlde 1989: 114). Therefore it would have been very interesting to know what the minimum amount of ballast was to keep the vessel upright, in harbour as well as at sea.

Another practical test concerned roll and pitch periods. Again this was done with the ship in ballast and with the yard set, but without sail (Brandt et al. 1994: 34). It must remain open which historic questions can be connected to this test, because most likely Late Medieval sailors cared little about the movements of their ships, but looked upon it as part of daily life at sea.

Trials showed that the vessel could not tack against the wind in calm weather, but did not gain any ground to windward in a force seven wind (Brandt et al. 1994: 48). This is not really surprising, looking at the hull lines and considering the high wind resistance of the hull, particularly with a reefed mainsail (Brandt et al. 1994: 47). From this the author concluded that ships similar to the Bremen wreck of 1380 were unable to enter harbours and anchored in open roadsteads to be discharged or loaded (Brandt et al.: 1994: 69). This is certainly wrong, because we know from historic documents that ships sailed up rivers, even non-tidal ones, to reach their port of call, e.g. up the Trave to Lübeck, the Elbe to Hamburg, the Weser to Bremen or the Swin to Brugge. To reach ports like Bergen or Stockholm the sailors had to pass the narrow, winding waterways through the skerries. Therefore they had to know how to handle clumsy ships in narrow waters.

The results of the trials were compared with those of other sailing vessels. As no data from other replicas apart from *Galaeia* were ready at hand, data collected from traditional square-riggers at the beginning of the 20th century were used (Brandt et al. 1994: 69). It is very doubtful, if one can learn anything of historic relevance from this kind of comparison.

For imitating a full cargo additional to the ballast, 35 concrete blocks weighing 1.05 ton each were put into the hold (Brandt 1994: 34). Of course one can test the sailing qualities with this kind of cargo, but it is somewhat unrealistic, as the density of the concrete is higher than that of a full load of grain. From an historical point of view, it would have been very interesting to see how the vessel behaved when loaded with a mixed cargo. Further one wants to know what the maximum loading capacity was, because it is known that before the introduction of the international load line (Plimsoll Mark), it was not unusual for ships in storms to jettison parts of their cargo in order to lighten them (Heinsius 1986: 233; 242). In a single-masted, square-rigged sailing ship, the longitudinal trim is very important for steering ability (Andersen 1986: 212 Fig. 3; Godal 1986: 201). From toll lists we know that vessels often carried mixed cargoes owned by different merchants (Lechner 1935: 506). How was such a cargo stowed? On one hand, the necessary stability and longitudinal trim must be gained, on the other hand it must still be possible to identify the goods of a single merchant. What kind of wear marks occurred during loading and discharging which may explain certain repairs? In toll lists it is laid down that horses were sometimes transported. Were they lifted on board utilising the ship's rigging or were other methods possible? How did the vessel behave in strong winds? Is it safe to run before the wind or will she have the tendency to broach? Can she run before the wind without a sail? How much green water will be shipped when close hauled in the open sea, for instance in the Gulf of Biscay? How can one heave to with a single-masted, square-rigged ship? Does the method developed by Norwegian fishermen to stay more or less stationary in order to wait for the change of the tide or the lifting of the fog also work for this kind of ship (Godel 1986: 205; Fig. 10)? Is it safe to lie a-hull in a storm with heavy seaway, because the bow will be kept close to the wind due to the great windage of the stern castle?

To get answers to these questions it will be necessary to sail the vessel on a trial voyage, for example from Lübeck to Gdansk with a mixed cargo only partly loaded. From there one should sail to the Baie de Bourgneuf (at the Gulf of Biscay) with grain in bulk and return to the Baltic Sea at Schonen with salt in bulk, then load herring in barrels for Lübeck. Then one should proceed in ballast to Hamburg to load beer in casks for Bergen. In Norway a full cargo of stockfish is collected for Brugge. From there it goes back to Lübeck with a full, mixed cargo. To accomplish such a program could take several years. During this period one has to feed and pay the crew, even if they can be enlarged by volunteers. In addition, a standby ship for emergencies has to be organised, etc. All this is financially beyond the scope of any academic institution. Therefore we must admit that a realistic test of a vessel of this size is impossible, but why are we then building a full size replica as authentically as possible?

Another drawback is that most of the experiments have been conducted in "laboratory" situations e.g. sea trials were mostly done in sheltered waters and not in the open sea in unfavourable conditions. Most tests have been conducted only in a limited number and not over a longer period. In the latest publication about the Bremen wreck of 1380 some doubts about the usefulness of the trials of the replica of Kiel have been put forward (Sauer 2003, 26; 31).

Perhaps it is a little too exaggerated, if I claim that experimental boat and ship archaeology in authentically reconstructed vessels is mainly adventure and fun, but adds very little or even nothing for the understanding of earlier seafaring. What we can learn, can often better be done by analysing ethnographic, written and iconographic sources and by using scale models and mock-ups with modern materials (e.g. Schnall 1975; Godal 1986; Weski 1991; Andersen 1995; Gifford 1995; 1996; 1998).

Acknowledgements

I am thankful to Trixi Gülland and Kai Zausch who introduced me into the art of sailing the single-masted, square-rigged Slavonic replicas *Biały Kon* and *Dziki Kon* in 2001. Further I would like to thank the students of the Humboldt University Berlin, who took part not only in this course, but also presented papers in my seminar "Ausgewählte Beispiele der experimentellen Schiffs-archäologie" in the winter semester 2001/02, for their critical remarks and questions.

Notes

1   Wie groß ist die Querstabilität und das Segeltragvermögen? Reichen die Steuerkräfte der projektierten Ruderfläche aus?
Wie ist das Manöverierverhalten, geht das Schiff beim Wind durch den Wind?
Welche Schiffgeschwindigkeiten werden bei welchen Windgeschwindigkeiten und Kursen zum Wind erreicht? Können Hansekoggen Wasser gegen den Wind gut machen? Welche Luvgeschwindigkeiten werden erreicht? Wie groß ist bei einem derartigen Schiff mit flachem Boden, ohne Kiel und Seitenschwerter, die Abdrift? Die Sicht des Steuermanns unter dem Kastell ist durch das hohe Schanzkleid und den Steven völlig verdeckt. Wie kann die Kogge auf Kurs gehalten werden? Wie ist das Seegangsverhalten der Hansekogge? Ist Trimm empfehlenswert?

Welche Roll- und Stampfperioden hat das Schiff, welche Amplituden werden erreicht?
Wie unterscheiden sich die Segeleigenschaften der Hansekogge in Ballast ($T_m = 1,65$m) von denjenigen mit Ladung ($T_m = 2,07$m) (Brandt 1994: 30).

References

Andersen, E., 1995. Square sails of wool. In: O. Olsen, J. S. Madsen and F.Rieck (Eds.), *Shipshape. Essays for Ole Crumlin-Pedersen*, 249–270. Roskilde.

Braemer, H., 1991, *Studien und Experimente zur Schiffsarchäologie im mediterranen Raum*. Institut für Schiffbau der Universität Hamburg Bericht 519. Hamburg.

Brandt, H., Hoheisel, W.-D- and Hochkirch, K., 1994, *Experimentelle Ermittlung der Segelleistung von einem originalgetreuen Nachbau der Hansekogge von 1380*. Technische Universität Berlin/Institut für Schiffbau und Meerestechnik-Bericht 94/5. Berlin.

Brown, A. C. (Ed.) 1974, *Longboat to Hawaii. An Account of the Voyage of the Clipper Ship HORNET of New York Bound for San Francisco in 1866*. Cambridge.

Burmeister, H., 1978, *Mit der Pamir um Kap Horn*. Oldenburg, Hamburg.

Burningham, N., 2001, Learning to sail the Duyfken replica. *International Journal of Nautical Archaeology* 30: 74–85.

Carter, W. H., 1999, Discovering Vinland. The Voyage of SNORRI. *Wooden Boat* 148: 62–70.

Christensen, A. E., 1986, "Viking", a Gokstad Ship Replica from 1893. In: O. Crumlin-Pedersen and M. Vinner (Eds.), *Sailing into the Past. Proceedings of the International Seminar on Replicas of Ancient and Medieval Vessels, Roskilde, 1984*, 68–77. Roskilde.

Coates, J. F., Platis, S. K. and Shaw, J. T., 1990, *The Trireme Trials 1988. Report on the Anglo-Hellenic Sea Trials of the Olympias*. Oxford.

Coates, J. and Morrison, J., 1993, Summary of lessons learned. In: T. Shaw (Ed.), *The Trireme project. Operational Experience 1987–90. Lessons Learnt*. Oxbow Monograph 31, 108–109. Oxford.

Coates, J., 1995, The Naval Architecture and Oar Systems of Ancient Galley. In: R.Gardiner and J.Morrison (Eds.), *The age of the Galley. Mediterranean Oared Vessels since pre-classical Times*, 127–141. London.

Coates, J., McGrail, S., Brown, D., E.Gifford, E., Grainge, G., Greenhil, B., Marsden, P., Rankov, B., Tipping, C. and Wright, E., 1995, Experimental Boat and Ship Archaeology: Principles and Methods. *International Journal of Nautical Archaeology* 24: 293–301.

Crumlin-Pedersen, O., 1995, Experimental archaeology and ships – bridging the arts and the sciences. *International Journal of Nautical Archaeology* 24: 303–306.

Engvig, O. T., 2001a, The Viking Way. Part 1. *Viking Age Heritage Magazine* 1: 3–7.

Engvig, O. T., 2001b, The Viking Way. Part 2. *Viking Age Heritage Magazine* 2: 24–28.

Fee, R. G. C. 1958, Design and Construction of the Jamestown Ships. *The Society of Naval Architects and Marine Engineers* 17: 1–12.

Finney, B. R., 1979, *Hokule'a. The Way to Tahiti*. New York.

Genzmer, F., 1944, *Germanische Seefahrt und Seegeltung*. München.

Gifford, E. and J., 1995, The sailing performance of Anglo-Saxon Ships as derived from the Building and Trails of Half-Scale Working Models with Special Reference to the Sutton Hoo Ship. *International Journal of Nautical Archaeology* 24: 121–131.

Gifford, E. and J., 1996, The sailing performance of Anglo-Saxon Ships as derived from the Building and Trails of Half-Scale Models of the Sutton Hoo and Graveney Ship Finds. *The Mariner's Mirror* 82: 131–153.

Gifford, E and J., 1998, The Sailing Characteristics of Saxon Ships. In: P. Pomey and E. Rieth (Eds.), Construction navale maritime et fluviale: Approches archéologique, historique et ethnologique. Proceedings of the Seventh International Symposium on Boat and Ship Archaeology Ile Tatihou 1994, *Archaeonautica* 14: 177–184.

Giltaij, J and Kelch, J., 1997, *Herren der Meere – Meister der Kunst. Das holländische Seebild im 17. Jahrhundert*. Berlin.

Godal, J., 1986, Recording Living Traditions of Square-Sail Rigged Norwegian Boats. In: O. Crumlin-Pedersen and M. Vinner (Eds.), *Sailing into the Past. Proceedings of the International Seminar on Replicas of Ancient and Medieval Vessels*, Roskilde, 1984, 24–37. Roskilde.

Goodburn, D. M., 1993, Some further thoughts on reconstructions, replicas and simulations of ancient boats and ships. *International Journal of Nautical Archaeology* 22: 199–203.

Heyerdahl T., *The Kon-Tiki Expedition*. Oslo.

Heyerdahl, T., 1984, Testing Wash-Through Watercraft in Three Oceans. In: O. Crumlin-Pedersen and M. Vinner (Eds.), *Sailing into the Past. Proceedings of the International Seminar on Replicas of Ancient and Medieval Vessels*, Roskilde, 1984, 24–37. Roskilde.

Hoheisel, W. D., and Baykowski, U., 1994, A Full-scale Replica of the Hanse Cog of 1380. In: C. Westerdahl (Ed.), *Crossroads in Ancient Shipbuilding. Proceedings of the Sixth International Symposium on Boat and Ship Archaeology Roskilde 1991*. Oxbow Monograph 40, 257–264. Oxford.

Horder, M., 1988. *On their Own. Shipwrecks and Survivals*. London.

Irwin. G., Bickler, S. and Quirke, P., 1990, Voyaging by canoe and computer: experiments in the settlement of the Pacific Ocean. *Antiquity* 64: 34–50.

Katzev, M. L., 1990, An Analysis of the Experimental Voyages of Kyrenis II. In: H.E.Tzalas (Ed.), *Tropis II. 2nd International Symposium on Ship Construction in Antiquity; Delphi 1987. Proceedings*, 245–255. Athens.

Katzev, M. L. and Katzev, S. W., 1989, Kyrenia II: Building a Replica of an Ancient Greek Merchantman. In: H.E.Tzalas (Ed.), *Tropis I. 1st International Symposium on Ship Construction in Antiquity, Piraeus 1985, Proceedings*. 163–175. Athens.

Kennedy, G., 1978, *Bligh*. London.

Lechner, G., 1935, *Die hansischen Pfundzollisten des Jahres 1368. Quellen und Darstellungen zur hansischen Geschichte* N.F. 10. Lübeck.

Lehmann L. Th., 1982, A trireme's tragedy. *International Journal of Nautical Archaeology* 11: 145–151.

Luckner, F., 1921, *Seeteufel. Abenteuer aus meinem Leben*. Leipzig.

McKusick, M., 1979, The North American periphery of Antique Vermont. *Antiquity* 53: 121–123.

Matthew, 2002, http://www.matthew.co.uk/ship_statistics/ statistics.html.

Merrien, J., 1963, *Sie segelten allein*. Bielefeld. Berlin.

Morrison, J. S., Coats J. F. and Rankov, N.B., 2000, *The Athenian Trireme: The History and Reconstruction of an Ancient Greek Warship²*.Cambridge.

Mudie, C., 1984, Designing Replica Boats. The Boats of St. Brendan, Sindbad and Jason. In: O. Crumlin-Pedersen and M. Vinner (Eds.), *Sailing into the Past. Proceedings of the International Seminar on Replicas of Ancient and Medieval Vessels*, Roskilde, 1984, 38–59. Roskilde.

Mudie, C., 1994, *Designing the Matthew*. http://www.matthew. co.uk/ship_statistics/designing_matthew.html.

Mudie, C., 1996, *Matthew and Naval Architecture*. International Conference on Historic Ships Bristol 24 May 1996. http:// www.matthew.co.uk/ship_statistics/design2.html.

Robin, B., 1981. *Survival at Sea. A practical manual of survival and advice to the shipwrecked, assembled from an analysis of thirty-one survival stories*. London, Melbourne, Sydney, Auckland, Johannesburg.

Sauer, A., 2003, Segeln mit einem Rahsegel. In: G. Hoffmann and U. Schnall (Eds.), *Die Kogge. Sternstunden der deutschen Schiffsarchäologie. Schriften des Deutschen Schiffahrts-museum 60 = Die Kogge von Bremen 2*, 18–33. Bremerhaven, Hamburg.

Schnall, U., 1975, *Navigation der Wikinger. Nautische Probleme der Wikingerzeit im Spiegel der schriftlichen Quellen. Schriften des Deutschen Schiffährtsmuseums 6*. Oldenburg, Hamburg.

Severin, T., 1995, *The China Voyage. A Pacific Quest by Bamboo Raft*. London.

Steffy, J. R., 1989, The Role of Three-Dimensional Research in the Kyrenia Ship Reconstruction. In: H.E.Tzalas (Ed.), *Tropis I. 1st International Symposium on Ship Construction in Antiquity, Piraeus 1985, Proceedings*, 249–262. Athens.

Villiers, A., 1962, Sailing Mayflower II across the Atlantic. In: A.Villiers (Ed.), *Men, Ships and the Sea*, 142–153. Washington.

Vinner, M., 1995, A Viking-ship off Cape Farewell 1984. In: O. Olsen, J. S. Madsen and F.Rieck (Eds.), *Shipshape. Essays for Ole Crumlin-Pedersen*, 189–204. Roskilde.

Wahlde, F. V., 1989, *Ausgebüxt*. Bremerhaven, Hamburg.

Wells, T. W., 1994, Ballast and Cargo Handling on Board the Bark Passat. *The Log of Mystic Seaport*, Spring: 110–115.

Weski, T., 1991, Technische Beobachtungen zur Schalenbauweise anhand von rezenten Beispielen in Indonesien und die archäologische Nachweismöglichkeit von Schiffbau. *Archäologisches Korrespondenzblatt* 21: 145–149.

Weski, T., 1997, Ausgewählte Beispiele der experimentellen Boots und Schiffsarchäologie. *DEGUWA Rundbrief* 12.7: 38–49.

Yacht, 1995, 320 PS für die Kieler Hansekogge. *Yacht* 8, 12. April 1995: 10.

11 The Pacific migrations by canoe-form craft

James Wharram and Hanneke Boon

The Pacific Migrations

It is now generally agreed that the Pacific Ocean islands began to be populated from a time well before the end of the last Ice Age by people, using small ocean-going craft, originating in the area now called Indonesia and the Philippines. It is speculated that the craft they used were based on either a raft or canoe-form, or a combination of the two. The *homo sapiens* settlement of Australia and New Guinea shows that people must have been using water craft in this area as early as 60–40,000 years ago. The larger Melanesian islands were settled around 30,000 years ago (Emory 1974; Finney 1979; Irwin 1992).

The final long distance migratory voyages into the Central Pacific, which covers half the world's surface, began from Samoa/Tonga about 3,000 years ago by the migratory group we now call the Polynesians (Irwin 1992). They continued to populate every remaining island in the Pacific, covering vast distances. These migrations are believed to have been accomplished with craft based on

the canoe-form, which the Polynesians developed into superb ocean-voyaging craft.

The Pacific double-ended canoe is thought to have developed out of two ancient watercraft, the canoe and the raft; these combined produce a craft that has the minimum drag of a canoe hull and maximum stability of a raft (Fig. 11.1).

As the prevailing winds and currents in the Pacific come from the east, these migratory voyages were made against the prevailing winds and currents. More logical than one would at first think, as it means one can always sail home easily when no land is found, but it does require craft capable of sailing to windward.

The Migration dilemma

By the 1950s, based on a combination of 'bad press' relating to the sailing abilities of Polynesian vessels that was proffered by early 19th-century missionaries, and the innate European cultural attitude that such lightly built 'native' craft could not be seaworthy, it was a widely held western belief that the Pacific canoe-form craft 'could not sail to windward', 'would break up in strong winds or gale seas', or that 'life on board would be so hard that many crew would die from cold' (Sharp 1956; Finney 1979).

This created a dilemma. The Pacific Ocean islands were settled by migrating sailors, who from studying genetics and linguistics appeared to have originated from South East Asia, but their observed canoe-form craft were condemned by westerners as unsuitable to sail to windward or of surviving gales (Sharp 1956; Finney 1979) (Fig. 11.2).

Theory A: Thor Heyerdahl – sailing with winds and currents

In 1947, Thor Heyerdahl (1950, 1952) entered the debate. He presented a theory based on his study of the South American Indians, of downwind, down current, settlement of the Central Pacific by sailing rafts from South America

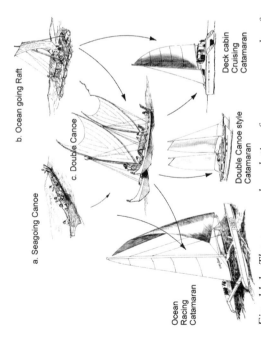

Fig. 11.1. The proposed evolution from canoe and raft into double canoe and ultimately the modern catamaran. (Drawn by Hanneke Boon).

single
outrigger
proa

double outrigger

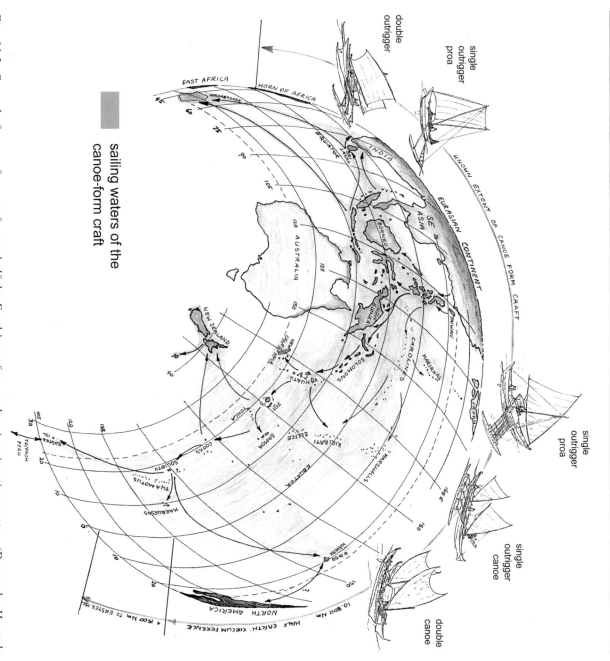

sailing waters of the
canoe-form craft

single
outrigger
canoe

double
canoe

Fig. 11.2. Spread of canoe-form craft over half the Earth's surface and main migration routes. (Drawn by Hanneke Boon).

(rafts that were observed by the first Spanish explorers in the early 16th century) (Heyerdahl 1952: Chapter VIII; Francesco Pizarro 1524–26).

Heyerdahl was one of the first proponents of 'Experimental Sea Archaeology' and set the scene for many later replica ship voyages. Unfortunately, he never sailed his *Kon-Tiki* raft against the wind, which is essential in proving that a vessel is capable of Pacific migratory voyages.

Theory B: Eric de Bisschop – sailing against the wind

Unknown to Heyerdahl, probably because the academics

of Hawaii refused to acknowledge or record it due to technical disagreements, a 20th-century double canoe voyage was made by the Frenchman Eric de Bisschop (1940). In the 1930s, de Bisschop had been studying ocean currents and wind systems with reference to ancient Pacific sea migrations whilst sailing into the Western Pacific from Formosa (now Taiwan) on a 40-ft Shanghai Junk. His junk was wrecked in Hawaii. Bravely, he announced: "I will build an ancient Pacific double canoe and carry on with my research work", which he did. In early 1937, he left Hawaii on his self-built 38-ft double canoe *Kaimiloa*. He sailed from Hawaii to Futuna and the Australian Barrier Reef, and from Surabaya to Cape Town, during which he endured severe gales. From Cape Town, he then sailed non-stop to Cannes in the Mediterranean – a total voyage of 18,000 Nm in fourteen and a half months. By 1938, Eric de Bisschop was the first to prove, by what we now call 'Experimental Archaeology', the windward/storm sailing ability of the Pacific double canoe craft.

Unfortunately, Eric de Bisschop, as an 'experimental' archaeologist, disagreed with the 'academic' archaeologists in Hawaii on canoe design principles and his voyages were not regarded as 'of value' and therefore not used in 1947 to examine the theories of Thor Heyerdahl.

In 1956–57 de Bisschop, who was still intrigued by the Polynesian migration theories, made a raft voyage from Tahiti to South America, against wind and currents. This voyage effectively completed the Heyerdahl experiment and examined whether or not rafts from South America could have made the return voyage. This voyage was not totally successful as the raft was too heavy and slow, the voyage took a very long time, during which the raft deteriorated. The raft was eventually badly damaged in a storm off the islands off the South American coast (Danielson 1959).

By the early 1950s, Eric de Bisschop had a few disciples of his theory of the ancient double canoe as voyaging craft (de Bisschop 1940), who were also prepared to take replicas out into the ocean and test sail them in gales and sail them to windward. I was one such disciple, the other was Rudy Choy in Hawaii.

More experimental voyages

The 1950s were a time of new ideas and new fields of adventure. As a youth in the late 1940s, I dreamed of sailing the oceans in 'ethnic' boats. In Britain's excellent libraries and museums I studied drawings, descriptions and models of Chinese junks, Viking ships, Arab dhows and Indo-Pacific canoe-form craft, the latter of which are documented in *Canoes of Oceania* (Haddon and Hornell 1936–38 [1975]).

The easiest and cheapest 'ethnic' boat to build – with respect to materials and labour time – was a Pacific double canoe. The South Kensington Science Museum houses a model of a Tahitian reef canoe (Photograph Neg. Nr. 396/53) based upon which I built a 7 m double canoe and called it *Tangaroa* (the Father God of Pacific religious myth).

Fifty years later, this double canoe design looks incredibly crude, but by 1955, with a crew of two, I had sailed her across the Bay of Biscay to northern Spain where we encountered our first sea gale. Contrary to perceived opinion, we found that the 7 m double canoe rode the Biscay gale seas in surprising comfort, which enabled us to publish a positive article on her sailing abilities in *Yachting Monthly* (Wharram 1956). By the end of 1956, we had sailed this double canoe across the Atlantic Ocean from the Canaries to Trinidad. Arriving in the West Indies, we had proven, as Eric de Bisschop had, that the double canoe was an incredibly safe craft,

could sail to windward and even had a surprisingly 'sea kindly' motion, even one as small and crude as the 7 m *Tangaroa*. Such are the inherent sailing abilities of the Indo-Pacific Ocean canoe-form craft.

Modern catamaran development

As we were exploring the ocean-going capabilities of the double canoe in the 1950s, other western naval architects were exploring the speed potential of the double canoe for day yacht racing. In 1955, the Prout brothers in England developed a 16-ft day-sailing catamaran called *Shearwater*. Subsequently the Duke of Edinburgh sailed in one, and thus, catamarans 'arrived' on the yachting scene.

Even so, in the second half of the 1950s, there were still serious doubts about the seaworthiness and sailing abilities of the double canoe, misnamed 'catamaran', particularly when operating offshore in the cold waters of the North Atlantic.[1] This scepticism was promoted by Sharp in his book *Ancient Voyagers in the Pacific* (Sharp 1956, 1957) and was still being quoted in academic circles into the 1970s.

First successful double canoe/catamaran voyage across the North Atlantic

In 1957 in Trinidad, we decided to challenge Sharp's assumptions. With our transatlantic sea knowledge, we began building a new 40-ft double canoe design (called *Rongo*) and on 11th August 1959 sailed her up the West Indian Archipelago to New York, then proceeded to cross the 3,000 Nm stretch of the cold North Atlantic encountering gales and head winds, arriving in Britain at the end of September.

This voyage in the Atlantic, together with another by Rudy Choy in the Pacific (developing the Hawaiian canoe concept for ocean racing), and the speeds achieved by the day-sailing catamarans, were all written about in the world's yacht magazines. As a result came a surprising development – the 'ancient' canoe-form concept, now generally termed 'catamaran', was enthusiastically taken up by the single-hulled world of modern yachting.

Experimental archaeology continued by 'ordinary' sailing people

By 1965, 'multihulls', a generic term for 'catamarans' and 'trimarans' (a western word for an adaptation of the Indonesian double outrigger canoe), were a vital new element of the western yachting scene. Choy and Wharram were early providers of catamaran designs for modern adventurous yachtsmen. By 1976, we had sold 3,000 sets of boat plans of 'Polynesian Catamarans' for self-building. Many world-wide ocean voyages were made by the Wharram Catamarans ranging in length from 27 to 50 ft, and crewed by 'Mr and Mrs Adventurous Urban Human'.

That these voyages were successful is again tribute to the innate seagoing qualities and windward abilities of the previously academically derided double canoe craft.[2] These many voyages undertaken with the minimum number of accidents raise the possibility that early Pacific exploration could have happened by a 'slow Clan group seepage' over many generations on small craft for the 'pleasure and adventure values of sailing and exploration', and not necessarily by highly organised fleet voyaging as the result of war or overpopulation.

Research in the 1990s

Building and sailing a new experimental craft

As professional catamaran designers, we have had to develop and use general analytical yacht design formulae to find out the 'real' (as against the advertised), sailing abilities of competitive designs. These analytic formulae combined with our accumulated sailing experience on canoe-form craft, can also be applied to understanding the performance of recorded historic canoe-form ships or canoe-form craft still sailing today.

In the late 1980's we were asked to design a replica 19-m Pacific Voyaging Canoe for a member of the Andean Explorers Foundation and Ocean Sailing Club. While designing this craft we decided to build a modified version for ourselves, with a wider overall beam to give more stability for a larger western sail rig. We built the 19-m *Spirit of Gaia*, launched her and began sailing her across the Bay of Biscay in 1992.

The *Spirit of Gaia* sailed in the various different winds off the Canaries at speeds of 14–16 knots. She has surfed down waves at 18 knots. She sailed from New Zealand to Fiji encountering a three-day storm, with winds of up to 50 knots, sailing under a storm jib 70 degrees off the wind and still made 60 Nm a day and kept on course. She sailed 600 Nm non-stop to windward in the Red Sea, heavily reefed into the force 7–8 northerly winds for which the Red Sea is famous (Morgan and Davies 2002), 60 Nm 'made good' to windward per 24 hours. She sailed in the Canaries, island to island, for one month with 20 people on board, giving us practical experience on possible crew numbers of ancient migratory groups (Fig. 11.3).

Sailing data acquired

During all the voyages, Spirit of Gaia was monitored with electronic speed and wind instruments, backed up with GPS satellite navigation. After the first 6,000 Nm of sailing we were able to publish accurate polar sailing diagrams. These give a comprehensive picture of double canoe sailing abilities, showing much better windward ability than had ever been suggested in previous academic Polynesian ship studies (Wharram 1994).

The 19 m *Spirit of Gaia* has deck space for 20 people, load carrying ability to carry food and water (by basic

western standards) for this crew for 22 days, which at a conservative 100 Nm/day average means a voyage of 2,200 Nm (30–35 days if rain water and fresh-caught fish are added, extending the voyage to 3,000–3,500 Nm). A crew of 20 would be able to hoist and handle two 40 m² Polynesian style sails without blocks and pulleys (which the Polynesians had not developed), and be sufficient to run watches for the hand held steering paddles they would have used. All this data confirms that Polynesian double canoes the size of *Spirit of Gaia* could have made the migratory voyages.

Waka Moana Symposium

In 1996 the Auckland Maritime Museum, with UNESCO funding, organised the 'Waka Moana Symposium' on Pacific ships, and invited participants of the 1995 Tahitian Voyaging Society 'Great Gathering of Canoes', in which we had participated the year before, to speak. One of my lectures was on the establishment of the Roskilde Viking Ship Museum and its endeavors to develop experimental archaeology. This symposium subsequently encouraged more attention on the sailing of replica canoes and the gathering of data in the Pacific region.

Pacific Canoe hull shapes

Tikopian hull shape

The Auckland National Museum houses a 9 m Tikopian

Fig. 11.3. Double canoe Spirit of Gaia. (*Photo by Hanneke Boon*).

Sacred Outrigger Canoe, that had been presented to the Museum in 1916 when the island was converted to Christianity.[3] Admiral Paris (Haddon and Hornell 1975: Vol II: 52) recorded identical canoes nearly 100 years earlier showing this canoe shape is a possible descendant of Pacific craft that were operating prior to the arrival of the Europeans.

This small craft immediately struck us as being a seaworthy craft and we were confident that we could sail it offshore. Thus, we photographed and recorded the hull lines and when we returned home, to our excitement, we found that the underwater profiles and cross sections were so very close to the profiles and cross sections of our 19 m *Spirit of Gaia*, that the collected sailing data of *Gaia* could be used to predict the sailing performance of the 100-year-old Tikopian canoe and other recorded Pacific V-shaped hull forms.

Tikopian hull shape developed

Recently, we were asked to design an 'ethnic' double canoe for an American, who 20 years ago was sailing the Pacific in one of our 8 m designs. We have designed for him an 11.5 m double canoe using Tikopian hull lines. This 'Tama Moana' double canoe will be able to make voyages of the same duration as the Spirit of Gaia, but carrying 8 people instead of 20. A predicted 100–150 Nm sailed per day gives this craft a sailing range of 2,200 Nm (with minimum speed/maximum food consumption), or 5,000 Nm (maximum speed/minimum food) – data that suggests that ancient Pacific migrations could have been made with small groups on small ships. Thus, future voyages using a traditional Pacific 'crab claw' sail will provide invaluable experimental archaeological sailing data that hopefully will confirm our calculated predictions.

Double canoes or outriggers?

The question arises, did the proto-Polynesians always use double canoe craft for their ocean voyages? If you take the Tikopian 11.5 m hull, described above, and assemble it as an outrigger canoe, as is the practice in Tikopia, you halve the labour and material required in the hull building. This size outrigger craft can still carry four to five people the same distances as the same size double canoe (Feinberg, 1974). For scouting voyages to discover new islands, this would seem the most cost-effective craft, with minimum loss if the vessel never returned. Later settlement voyages to already discovered islands could then be made in double canoes (assembled from two outrigger main hulls) with the extra load carrying capacity and deck space for settlement stores and animals. In the present day Pacific it is the outrigger canoe that has survived, whereas the use of the double canoe has disappeared. This suggests that the cost/labour efficiency of the outrigger canoe is still a major factor in choice of vessel.

Melanesian Canoes

In 1996, we sailed north from New Zealand into the Melanesian Pacific, Fiji and Vanuatu. The Melanesian Pacific Islands are to the ancient sailors the stepping stone route, that Melanesian man, on canoe craft or rafts, began colonising at least 30,000 years ago from Sundaland (present day Indonesia) east into the Central Pacific (Emory 1974; Irwin 1992).

In Fiji and Vanuatu we met many outrigger canoe sailors. In Vanuatu the small dugout outrigger canoe is still universally used as a commuter craft, with daily trips to gardens on nearby islands, every family in a village would own one. Large canoe sailing only died out within living memory, and as such our large double canoe fascinated the older men. We invited them on board and took some out sailing. We could talk to them as equal canoe builders/sailors, on windward sailing, leeway angles, storm handling. We particularly noticed how they understood design elements like hull shape and bow angles. We in return learned how to sail on outrigger canoe with a steering paddle, something we have continued to study and have built a number of small outrigger canoes for this specific purpose.

A visit to Tikopia

From the North of Vanuatu it is 200 Nm to the Polynesian outlier island, Tikopia. We made a pilgrimage there to meet the chief whose great-grandfather presented the sacred outrigger to the Auckland Museum in 1916. Though the Tikopians still have paddling canoes, they are no longer sailed, but on the nearby island of Anuta the building and sailing of these same type of canoes was until recently, still practised, as studied and recorded by Richard Feinberg (1988) in his book *Polynesian Seafaring and Navigation*.

Conclusion

From all our studies described in this paper of Pacific Ocean canoe-form craft (and further studies of canoe-form craft in the Indian Ocean not described here), through study of their design through mathematical yacht design formulae and means of experimental voyages; and we can confidently conclude that the canoe-form craft used by the Polynesians for their migratory voyages were seaworthy and capable vessels able to sail to windward and travel long distances. It is thus a pity that there is such a dearth of actual archaeological ship finds upon which more accurate replica ships could be based.

We hope by building future craft, outrigger canoes, proas and more double canoes, on which we intend to carry out further studies of the Indo-Pacific hull shapes, rig types and the use of steering paddles, to gain further insights into the sailing qualities of the Indo-Pacific canoe-form craft, which covered a sailing area of half the Earth's surface.

Notes

1 'catamaran' is a misappropriated western term for a double-hulled vessel, that originally described an Indian log raft, the *kattumaram* or tied/lashed-log raft, as literally translated in Tamil (Rajamanickam 2004).

2 The writings of Sharp (1956) deride the abilities of the double canoe craft and Finney (1979) makes several long references to this attitude in the 1950s.

3 Tikopia is a small remote Polynesian outlier island at the eastern end of the Solomons.

References

Bader, H.-D. and McCurdy, P., 1999, *Proceedings of the Waka Moana Symposium 1996*. New Zealand National Maritime Museum. Auckland.

Best, E., 1976, *The Maori Canoe*. Dominion Museum Bulletin No. 7. A.R. Shearer, Government Printer. Wellington, New Zealand.

Bisschop, E. de, 1940, *The Voyage of the Kaimiloa*. G. Bell and Sons Ltd. London.

Bisschop, E. de, 1959, *Tahiti-Nui. By Raft from Tahiti to Chile*. Collins. London.

Buck, P.H., 1959, *Vikings of the Pacific*. The University of Chicago Press. Chicago.

Dodd, E., 1972, *Polynesian Seafaring*. Dodd, Mead and Company. New York.

Danielson, B, 1959, *Von Floss zu Floss, Eric de Bisschops letzte Fahrt*, Verlag Ullstein. Berlin.

Emory, K. P., 1974, Coming of the Polynesians. *National Geographic* December: 732–45.

Feinberg, R., 1988, *Polynesian Seafaring and Navigation*. The Kent State University Press. Kent, Ohio.

Finney, B.R., 1979, *Hokule'a, The Way to Tahiti*. Dodd, Mead and Company. New York.

Gatty, H., 1943, *The Raft Book*. George Grady Press. New York.

Gladwin, T., 1970, *East Is a Big Bird*. Harvard University Press. Cambridge, Massachusetts.

Haddon, A.C. and Hornell, J., [1936–38], 1975, *Canoes of Oceania*. Bishop Museum Press. Honolulu, Hawaii.

Heyerdahl, T., 1950, *The Kon-Tiki Expedition*. George Allen and Unwin Ltd. London.

Heyerdahl, T., 1952, *American Indians in the Pacific*. Bokförlaget Forum AB. Stockholm.

Holmes, T., 1981, *The Hawaiian Canoe*. Editions Limited. Kauai, Hawaii.

Irwin, G., 1992, *The Prehistoric Exploration and Colonisation of the Pacific*. Cambridge University Press. Cambridge.

Kane, H.K., 1976, *Voyage. The Discovery of Hawaii*. Island Heritage Limited. Honolulu.

Kane, H.K., 1991, *Voyagers*. WhaleSong, Incorporated. Washington.

Lewis, D., 1972, *We, the Navigators*. The University Press of Hawaii. Honolulu, Hawaii.

Malinowski, B., 1922, *Argonauts of the Western Pacific*. E. P. Dutton and Co., Inc. New York.

Morgan, E and Davies, S., 2002, *Red Sea Pilot*, Imray, Laurie, Norie and Wilson. UK.

Neyret, J., 1976, *Pirogues Océaniennes, Tome I and II*. Association des Amis des Musées de la Marine. Paris.

Rajamanickam, G.V., 2004, *Traditional Indian Ship Building*. New Academic Publisher. Delhi, India.

Sharp, A., 1957, *Ancient Voyagers in the Pacific*. Pelican. Penguin Books.

Wharram, J., 1956, Twin Hulls Across the Bay. *Yachting Monthly* March: 142.

Wharram, J., 1969, Two Girls Two Catamarans. Abelard Schuman. London.

Wharram, J., 1977, *History and Problems of Design of Modern Multihulls*. HISWA Symposium. Netherlands.

Wharram, J., 1994, Nomads of the Wind. *Practical Boat Owner* October: 41.

Wharram, J., 2000, Lessons from the Stone Age Sailors. *Water Craft* October: 11, November: 37.

12 New light on the false clinkers in ancient Mediterranean shipbuilding

Patrice Pomey

In the volume *Shipshape*, published in 1995 on the occasion of Ole Crumlin-Pedersen's 60th birthday, Honor Frost gave a paper entitled "Where did the Carthaginians see clinkers?" (Frost 1995).[1] In this paper, she tries to explain the strange anomaly observed on the Marsala Punic ship where four stakes resemble clinker strakes (Fig. 12.1).

The Punic ship excavated by Frost during the years 1971–1974, near Marsala in Sicily, is considered as a warship according to the ram found on the so called "sister ship". She dates to around the mid-3rd century BC and probably sank during the First Punic War (Frost *et al* 1976).

The construction technique of the ship is quite typical of ancient Mediterranean shipbuilding and is characterised by a smooth hull in which the strakes are assembled edge-to-edge by mortise-and-tenon joinery locked by little wooden pegs. In such a construction, it is very odd, indeed, to find at the waterline level, near the turn of the bilge, four planking strakes looking like clinkers. In fact, the planks are carved like clinkers but they do not overlap each other and that is the reason why Frost speaks of "false clinkers". The four stakes in question are n° 12, 13, 14, 15 from the keel. The first three are complete and n° 15 is very fragmentary. But, according to Frost, there was probably "a belt of waterline clinkers" up to the first wale. The thickness of each strake extends from 4 cm, in the upper thinner part, to 6 cm in the lower thicker part. Like all the rest of the hull planking, the false clinkers are united edge-to-edge by mortise-and-tenon joinery.

To explain this peculiar architectural anomaly, Frost, considering the Marsala Punic ship as a fast, oared long ship, suggests, on the advice of the naval architect Austin Farrar, to interpret the false clinkers like spray deflectors in order to reduce the physical "Coander effect" and to avoid the water creeping up over the sides, spilling into the boat itself. But the Punic ship is dated from the middle of the 3rd century BC, which is a very early date for clinker construction and that is the reason why Frost asks the question "Where did the Carthaginians see clinkers?".

Recent new discoveries on the French Mediterranean coast yield new lights on the interpretation of the false clinkers (Fig. 12.2): in 1995, a hull fragment with false clinkers was found by the French Département des Recherches Archéologiques Sous-Marines on the beach at Les-Saintes-Maries-de-la-Mer, in Camargue, on the delta of the Rhône River. It was studied and published by Frost in 1997 (Frost 1997) (Fig. 12.3). The fragment (1.25 x 1.10 m) consists of nine strakes, and part of a tenth, joined edge-to-edge by mortise-and-tenon, and two surviving frames. But the presence of three other frames is attested by the marks of their seatings and by the remains of the treenails that attached the frames to the planking. Among the planks, the uppermost four are carved on the outside to look like clinkers (their thickness extends from 4.4 cm to 5.4 cm), then there are two series of one flat plank and one slightly sculpted plank (from 4.5 to 4 cm) and the rest

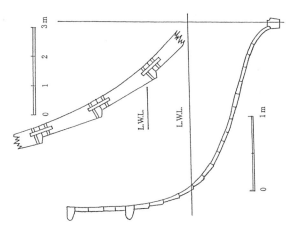

Fig. 12.1. Schematic sketch showing the Punic Ship's mortise-and-tenon joined planking with "false clinkers" at the level of its water line. (From Frost 1995).

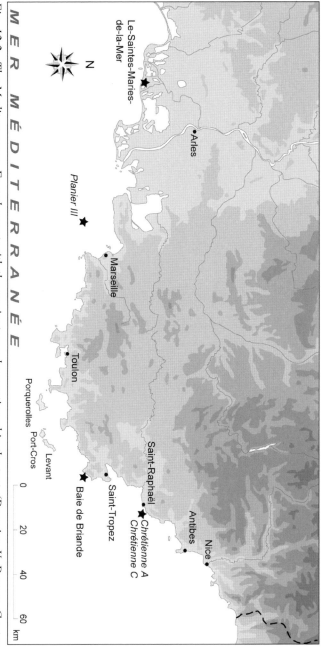

Fig. 12.2. The Mediterranean French coast with the ancient wrecks mentioned in the text. (Drawing V. Dumas, Centre Camille Jullian, CNRS Aix-en-Provence).

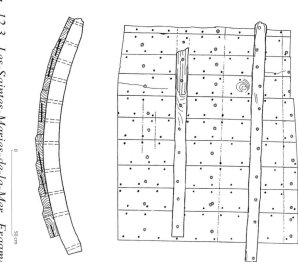

Fig. 12.3. Les-Saintes-Maries-de-la-Mer. Fragment of hull from wreckage found on the beach. (From Frost 1997).

wreck of the Baie de Briande, near Saint-Tropez (Var), which is dated to the first half of the 2nd century BC. The wreck, known since 1965 (Tchernia 1969), was largely plundered and the hull was partly excavated for the first time in 1995 by the author as part of the dendrochronological program on ancient Mediterranean wrecks (Guibal 1998; Guibal and Pomey 2003). The hull studied was 5.50 m in length and 3.50 m wide at the central part of the boat around the area of the mast step timber (Pomey 2002). Its structure corresponds to a typical Mediterranean hull with the planking joined edge-to-edge by mortise-and-tenon and the framing made up of floor timbers alternating with half frames. On the cross section, around the turn of the bilge, we can see, at least, three false clinkers planks (n° 17, 18, 19) (3.3 cm to 5 cm) comparable to the Punic ship (Fig. 12.4). Visible also between the keel and the turn of the bilge, are some others strakes (n° 12, 14, 15) which are thicker (4.8 cm) than the normal planking (3 cm). Obviously, these strakes situated under the waterline, reinforce the hull, particularly near the turn of the bilge at the level of the junction between the floor timbers and their futtocks. The floor-timbers and futtocks are not connected at this point in fact there is a large gap between them.

Due to the cargo of amphorae, it is quite clear that the Baie de Briande wreck is a merchant ship, or merchant galley. Consequently we are presented with a slow ship and not a fast moving vessel. Therefore, it is quite unlikely that the false clinkers are spray deflectors and it is more probable they were made to reinforce the hull as is the case with other thicker strakes that are found below the waterline.

The same system of strakes, thicker than normal

remain smooth. According to the curve of the remaining frames, the hull fragment probably came from the turn of the bilge. There is no doubt this fragment belongs to an ancient Mediterranean ship due to the system of fastening by mortise-and-tenon joinery, but there is no evidence to determine the date or the archaeological context and we do not know if the fragment comes either from a long warship or from a round cargo ship.

Further evidence is provided by the Greco-Roman

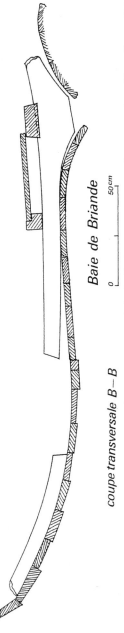

Baie de Briande

coupe transversale B – B

0   50cm

Fig. 12.4. Baie de Briande wreck. Central cross section of the hull. (Drawing M. Rival, Centre Camille Jullian, CNRS Aix-en-Provence).

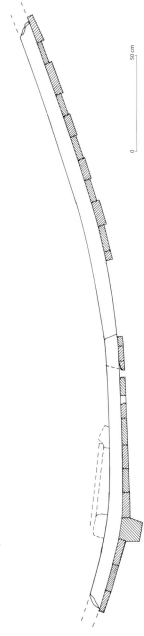

0   50 cm

Fig. 12.5. Chrétienne C wreck. Central cross section of the hull. (Drawing M. Rival, Centre Camille Jullian, CNRS Aix-en-Provence).

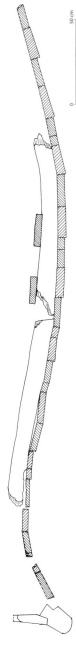

0   50 cm

Fig. 12.6. Chrétienne A wreck. Central cross section of the hull. (Drawing M. Rival, Centre Camille Jullian, CNRS Aix-en-Provence).

planking and located below the waterline in order to strengthen the hull between the keel and the turn of the bilge, can be observed on two others wrecks off the Mediterranean French coast. These wrecks were recently reconsidered in 1996, again as part of the dendrochronological program on ancient wrecks.

The first one is the Chrétienne C wreck, near Saint-Raphaël (Var), excavated in 1971–1973 by Joncheray (1975). It is a Greco-Roman wreck from the first half of the 2nd century BC with a huge cargo of about 500 Greco-Italic amphorae. The hull belongs to the Mediterranean type with planking joined edge-to-edge by mortise-and-tenon. However, on the cross section of the central part of the hull, along the curve of the hull, a series of at least five thick strakes (n° 11, 13, 15, 17, 19) (4–4.5 cm), have been identified, regularly alternated with thinner strakes (3 cm) (Fig. 12.5).

The second is the wreck of Chrétienne A, also near Saint-Raphaël and situated adjacent to the wreck of *Chrétienne C*. The wreck has been known since 1948 and the hull was partly studied by Dumas during the years 1961–1962 (Dumas 1964), before being reconsidered during the 1996 dendrochronological campaign (Pomey 2002). The wreck belongs to a merchant ship, according

to its large cargo of amphorae, and dates to the beginning of the 1st century BC. On the midship cross section, we can observe the same system of reinforcement of the hull by some strakes (n°12, 14, 16, 18, 20) also thicker (5.5 cm) than the current planking (3.5 cm) (Fig. 12.6), although the pattern looks less regular than on the Chrétienne C wreck.

Lastly, on the Planier III wreck, a Roman cargo ship with amphorae from the middle of the 1st century BC that sank at the entrance of the Bay of Marseille and was excavated in 1968–1971 by Tchernia and the author (Tchernia 1968–1970; Liou 1973), we have an outstanding example of reinforcement of the hull around the waterline at the level of the first main wale. Indeed we can observe a system of wale with a pre-wale, which recalls the system of false clinkers observed on the Punic ship but of a different shape, simpler, with an increasing thickness from the current planking (6 cm) to the pre-wale (10 cm) and to the wale (19.5 cm), and with a transition by bevelled edge (Fig. 12.7).

In conclusion, false clinkers have been observed not only on the Marsala Punic ship, but also on at least two other ancient ships. This evidence proves that such false clinkers were neither an anomaly nor an exception.

Furthermore, the Baie de Briande wreck shows that such false clinkers can also be found on cargo vessels and that their interpretation as spray deflectors is quite unlikely. As emphasised on the Baie de Briande wreck, these false clinkers are also associated with thicker strakes than the normal planking in order to reinforce the hull according to a tradition that is now well attested on other wrecks such as Chrétienne A and Chrétienne C. Lastly, on the Planier III wreck, we have a device which recalls a different way but probably for the same purpose, the Punic ship system of false clinkers. Therefore, it seems very likely that these false clinkers are made to reinforce the hull around the water line, according to a tradition that seems to have been in use particularly during the Hellenistic era or the Roman Republican period. But the question is why are these strakes shaped like false clinkers? In this regard the interpretation of Honor Frost makes some sense as she suggests that the false clinkers of Les-Saintes-Maries-de-la-Mer vessel were reproduced for reasons of snobbery to give the ship a "touch of class". However, the interpretation that they were spray deflectors has nothing to do with this snobbery and therefore, the false clinkers shape is merely a coincidence.

Notes

1   This question was first discussed by Honor Frost at the occasion of the seventh ISBSA held on the Île Tatihou, France, in 1994 (Frost 1999).

References

Dumas, F., 1964, *Épaves antiques: introduction à l'archéologie sous-marine Méditerranéenne*. Maisonneuve et Larose. Paris.

Frost, H., et al., 1976, The Punic Ship: Final excavation Report. *Notizie degli Scavi di Antichità*. Supplement vol. XXX, Accademia Nazionale dei Lincei. Roma.

Frost, H., 1995, Where did the Carthaginians see clinkers? in O. Olsen, J. Skamby Madsen and F. Rieck (eds), *Shipshape. Essays for Ole Crumlin-Pedersen. On the occasion of his 60th anniversary, February 24th 1995*, 283–288. The Viking Ship Museum, Roskilde.

Frost, H., 1997, False clinkers on a hull fragment from "Saintes-Maries-de-la-Mer wreck N°5". Structural comparison with the Marsala Punic Ship. In M. Baudat (ed) *Crau, Alpilles, Camargue. Histoire et Archéologie. Actes du Colloque d'Arles. Novembre 1995*, 117–122. Groupe Archéologique Arlésien. Arles.

Frost, H., 1999, Simulated clinkers in the 3rd century BC Mediterranean. In P. Pomey and E. Rieth (eds), *Construction navale maritime et fluviale. approches archéologiques, historique et ethnologique: actes du septième Colloque international d'archéologie navale. Proceedings of the seventh international symposium on boat and ship archaeology, Île Tatihou, Saint-Vaast-la-Hougue, 1994*, 161–164.

Guibal, F., 1998, Dendrochronologie des épaves de navires antiques de Méditerranée. In P. Pomey and E. Rieth (eds), *Construction navale maritime et fluviale. approches archéologiques, historique et ethnologique: actes du septième Colloque international d'archéologie navale. Proceedings of the seventh international symposium on boat and ship archaeology, Île Tatihou, Saint-Vaast-la-Hougue, 1994*, 303–308. Archaeonautica 14. CNRS éditions. Paris.

Guibal, F. and Pomey, P., 2003, Timber Supply and Ancient naval Architecture. In C. Beltrame (ed), *Boats, ships and shipyards: Proceedings of the Ninth International Symposium on Boat and Ship Archaeology, Venice 2000*, 35–41. Oxbow Book. Oxford.

Joncheray, J.-P., 1975, *L'épave C de la Chrétienne*. Cahiers d'archéologie Subaquatique Supplément 1. France.

Liou, B., 1973, Informations archéologiques. Recherches sous-marines. *Gallia* XXXI: 586–589.

Pomey, P., 2002, Remarque sur la faiblesse des quilles des navires antiques à retour de gabord. In L. Rivet, M. Sciallano (eds), *Vivre, Produire, Échanger: reflets Méditerranéens. Mélanges offerts à Bernard Liou*, 11–19. M. Mergoil. Montagnac.

Tchernia A., 1968–1970, Premiers résultats des fouilles de 1968 sur l'épave 3 de Planier. *Études Classiques* 3: 51–82.

Tchernia, A., 1969, Informations archéologiques. Recherches sous-marines. *Gallia* XXXVII: 465–499.

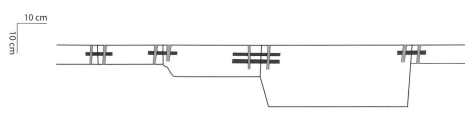

10 cm

10 cm

Fig. 12.7. Planier III wreck. The system of reinforcement of the hull, with a pre-wale and a wale, at the level of the water line. (Drawing M. Rival, Centre Camille Jullian, CNRS Aix-en-Provence).

13 A preliminary report on the hull characteristics of the Gallo-Roman EP1-Taillebourg wreck (Charente-Maritime, France): archaeological evidence of regional practices of ancient flat-bottomed construction?

Eric Rieth

Introduction

The EP 1-Taillebourg wreck was discovered in the River Charente in 2001 during an underwater survey organized by the archaeological service of the region Poitou-Charentes, under the direction of J.-F. Mariotti. The wreck is situated at a depth of about 7.50 m, a little more than 1 km upstream of the village of Taillebourg (Charente-Maritime). Dominating the village on the right bank of the River Charente are the vestiges of the medieval castle of Taillebourg (Fig. 13.1). Taillebourg, despite the fact that it is situated some 57 km from the mouth of the river, is in a very tidal section of the Charente.

The first campaign of excavation was conducted from 9th of September to 4th October 2002, with the aim of making an archaeological assessment of the constructional characteristics of the wreck. The underwater excavation

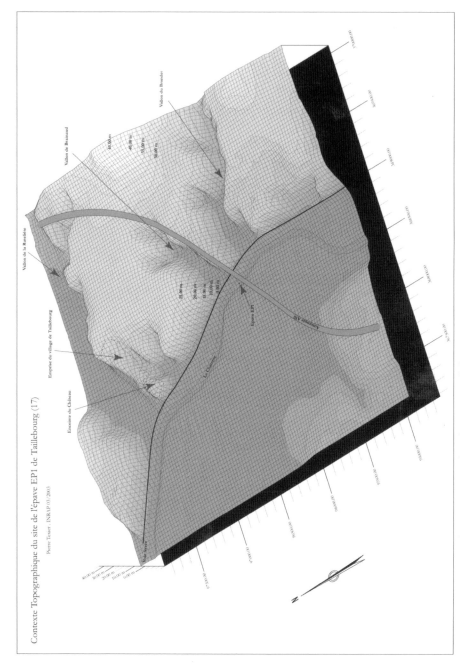

Contexte Topographique du site de l'épave EP1 de Taillebourg (17)

Pierre Texier, INRAP 03/2003

Fig. 13.1. Topographical context of the wreck (Topography by Pierre Texier, INRAP).

lies within a broader project that commenced in 1971, that aims to investigate the ancient and medieval river craft of the Charente. The main aim of the research is to undertake a study of the different morphological, structural and functional characteristics of the regional boats and ships. The vessels will be addressed within their physical (riverine and maritime) environment on one hand, and their socio-economical environment on the other.

The excavation of the EP 1-Taillebourg wreck is a collaborative scientific venture between the National Center for Scientific Research (CNRS) and the Department of Underwater Archaeological Research (DRASSM). The regional unit of Annecy (Haute-Savoie) of DRASSM, which specialises in inland underwater archaeology, provided technical support without which it would not have been possible to excavate the wreck. The archaeological team was composed of students of nautical archaeology and of some sports divers interested in archaeology.

The EP 1-Taillebourg wreck: its constructional characteristics

The EP 1-Taillebourg wreck has the peculiarity, along with the Merovingian wreck of Port Berteau II situated 10 km upstream (Rieth, Carrière-Desbois and Serna 2001), to be preserved in an inverted position on the bottom of the Charente River. It is located in the central section of a minor river bed, orientated northwest/southeast. Many factors have contributed to a change in the appearance of the river since the first centuries AD when the boat would have sailed on the Charente. These factors include an increase in the water height as a result of the building of a dam downstream and the widening of the minor river bed, amongst others. Thus, the ongoing geomorphological and geoarchaeological studies of the

wreck environment should make it possible to locate the position of the wreck within the context of the ancient limits of the river bed. The discovery of an alignment of piles, of which several cross a part of the remains of the wreck, could indicate that the boat was abandoned or deliberately sunk in order to be used as a reinforcement bank or to protect a structure located on the edge or within the bed of the Charente. It is important to note that the EP 1-Taillebourg wreck is not isolated but that in fact the 2002 survey by the archaeological service of the Poitou-Charentes region revealed an interesting and complex landscape of archaeological remains (Mariotti et al 2002), that include groups of piles, wrecks of logboats and plank-built boats, with many artefacts (in particular ceramics and weapons) that date mainly to the Early Medieval Age.

The EP 1-Taillebourg wreck appears to have been preserved in its present state to a length of over 8.70 m and a breadth of 1.50 m (Fig. 13.2). The bottom of the hull is completely destroyed, only the two sides (planks and frames) and a crossbeam, as well a number of other significant timbers, remain. The complex nature of the find is highlighted by the fact that a logboat was also discovered within the context of the wreck site lying over the wreck. Excavation was further hindered by bad visibility, and the fact that extensive records of each architectural feature had to be taken, limited the first campaign of excavation to just one half of the wreck.

The EP 1-Taillebourg wreck is a flat-bottomed river barge. The only frame well preserved (MBG 18) indicates that the hull had a sharp bilge, clearly seen on the starboard side (Fig. 13.3), with an interior angle between the flat bottom and the side of about 140 degrees. In relation to this form of cross section, the planks are rectilinear, with a generally consistent breadth. These characteristics of planking are in accordance with 'simple

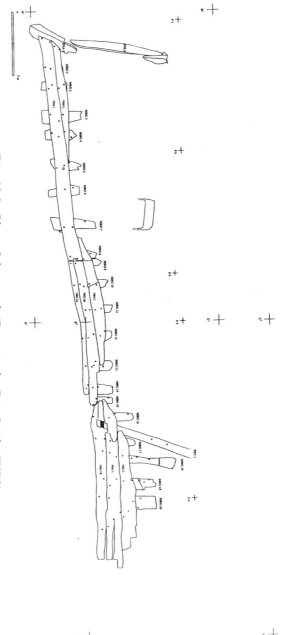

Fig. 13.2. Plan of the wreck (Drawing by Eric Rieth, CNRS).

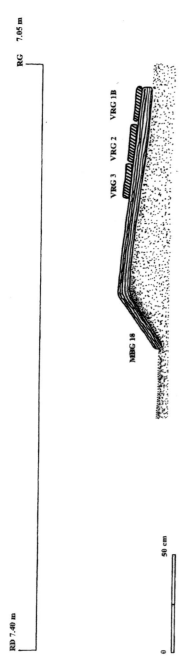

Fig. 13.3. Record in situ of the frame MBG 18. According to the inverted position of the wreck, the strakes VRG 3, VRG 2 and VRG 1B correspond to the planking of the side (Drawing by Eric Rieth, CNRS).

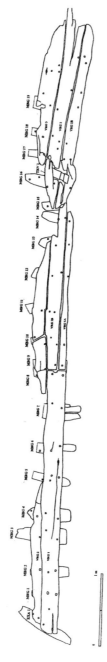

Fig. 13.4. Unfolded, developed plan of the planking (Drawing by Eric Rieth, CNRS).

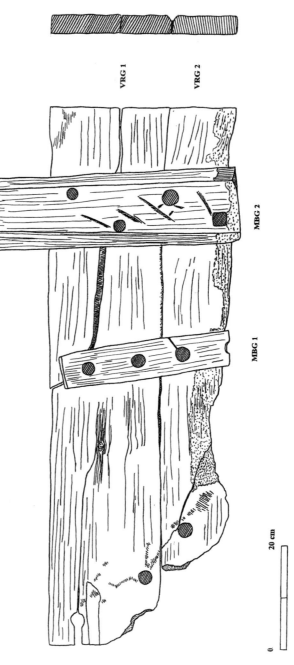

Fig. 13.5. A sample of the hull (inner part of planking and frames) recorded on the ground (Drawing by Eric Rieth, CNRS).

and undeveloped' hull shapes (Fig. 13.4). The down-stream extremity of the hull, partially preserved, seems to be closed with an inclined board. It is not possible, at the current stage of excavation, to associate this board with the bow or stern section of the hull.

From a structural point of view, the most significant characteristics are of four types:

- the sides are built with non-edge fastened, flush-laid planking
- the planks, with an average thickness of 3.5 cm, have their edges bevelled. In the triangular seam between the two bevelled edges, caulking (vegetable fibres) has been driven in from the outside of the planks (Fig. 13.5)

- the fastenings between the planks and the pre-erected frames were treenails of 2.5 cm diameter driven in from the outside of the planking
- the hull is reinforced in its upper part with a cross-beam, the extremity of which fits into a rectangular notch in the strake and extends beyond the planking.

A number of samples were taken in order to determine the wood species and examine how the timbers were fashioned. A sample of the hull some 1.05 m in length (planks VRG 1 and VRG 2, frames MBG 1 and MBG 2), indicates that the oak carvel planks, which do no have any traces of sawing, were firstly cleaved and then fashioned, probably with an axe. As for the frames, they were shaped by reduction with an axe or/and an adze.

From a functional point of view, the EP 1-Taillebourg wreck equates to a river barge although it is not yet possible to determine its dimensions, the nature of the cargo or its capacity.

Dendrochronological analyses of sixteen samples taken from the frames should provide a more accurate date for the vessel which is currently based on radiocarbon analysis and lies between AD 145 and 420 (calibrated radiocarbon date).[1] It would appear, that the EP 1-Taillebourg wreck is the first archaeological record of a Gallo-Roman river boat discovered in the Charente River.

The EP 1-Taillebourg wreck in its regional context.

Identified as a flat bottomed barge, concerned with inland navigation, the EP 1-Taillebourg vessel is believed to have been built along the banks of the River Charente, or one of its tributaries. It is thus within a regional techno-economic framework that the historical interpretation of the wreck should be considered. With this in mind, it is interesting to note that the EP 1-Taillebourg wreck has several primary characteristics in common with the Merovingian Port Berteau II wreck that dates from the beginning of the 7th century. The Port Berteau II wreck has been interpreted as a regional sailing coaster, carvel built "frame-first", whose zone of maritime and inland navigation was believed to have been limited to the coast and rivers of Aunis and Saintonge (Rieth 2003).

The primary characteristics attested to both wrecks are as follows:

- non-edge-fastened, flush-laid planking
- bevelled seams between planks
- planks and frames fastened with wooden treenails driven from the outside of the planking inwards
- a crossbeam, the extremity of which fits into a rectangular notch in the strake and extends beyond the planking;
- seams caulked with vegetable fibres driven in from the outside of the planking
- planks cleaved.

These six characteristics are identified in both vessels, both of which operated within the same "fluvio-maritime" zone of transport. As a result, it could be hypothesised that a regional boat building practice of "frame-first" constructed, flat bottomed vessels operated within this particular "fluvio-maritime" zone of transport.[2] On account of its localisation within the "Atlantic Gulf" region, this hypothesised regional boat building practice could be called the "fluvio-maritime Atlantic shipbuilding practice".

The EP 1-Taillebourg wreck in the Gallo-Roman framework

In the geographical frontier of Gaul, the construction of the EP 1-Taillebourg wreck can be ascribed similar archaeologically determined regional boat building characteristics as two other wrecks of Gallo-Roman flat bottomed, river barges: that of the square Tolozan, in Lyon, on the River Rhône (Becker and Rieth 1995), and of the ancient bridge of Chalon-sur-Saône, Saône-et-Loire (Lonchambon 2000). However, it must be noted that such comparisons are made in the knowledge that the chronological context and construction detail of the vessels differs. Both the Lyon and Chalon-sur-Saône wrecks date to the 1st century AD, and thus pre-date the EP 1-Taillebourg wreck. Likewise, the construction of both wrecks differ from EP 1-Taillebourg wreck, the Lyon and Chalon-sur-Saône vessels being joint-monoxylons with transition strake.[3] Moreover, the planks of their flat bottom have a very particular method of fastening which was probably used to temporarily fasten the planks before the frames were introduced. This method is characterised by the use of small iron nails driven obliquely into the edges of the planks, and of mortises and unpegged tenons localised along the edges of the seams.

Thus, two characteristics clearly distinguish the Gallo-Roman wrecks of Lyon and Chalon-sur-Saône from that of the EP 1-Taillebourg wreck: the exclusive use of large iron nails for attaching the planks to the frames, and the caulking or, more exactly, the luting of the seams by means of pitched cloth laid on the edge of a plank before placing the next plank. In contrast, in the EP 1-Taillebourg wreck, fastening is exclusively by means of wooden treenails, and caulking is stricto sensu, by means of vegetable oakum driven into the triangular seams from the outside of the planking.

These peculiarities of fastening and caulking could be considered as "archaeological fingerprints", amongst others, of different regional shipbuilding practices. However, the Gallo-Roman wrecks of Lyon and Chalon-sur-Saône would seem to be wrecks that belong to a different regional shipbuilding practice to that of the classic "Romano-Celtic" practice (Arnold 1992; McGrail 1995; 2001, 2003).[4] Indeed, they could be indicative of a regional shipbuilding practice[5] that was peculiar to the nautical region of the "Rhône-Saône".[6] This particular nautical region would be located at the crossroads of different construction practices: the inland "Romano-Celtic" practices and those of the maritime Mediterranean.

The presumed regional shipbuilding practice of the Gallo-Roman flat-bottomed construction within the "Romano-Celtic" tradition) which, in the current research environment must be considered before any hypothesis can be proposed, can also be assessed in relation to construction characteristics of different traditional European zones of transport such as those proposed by Westerdahl (Westerdahl 1995). The three zones of transport which are of concern to this study are: zone 6 ("southern Jutland and the Rhine and the Schelde estuaries, including the rivers system up to Switzerland"), zone 12 ("inner parts and rivers of the Iberian Peninsula and South France"), and zone 17a ("the inner sea of western Spain with the Balearic Islands united since Roman times with the Saône-Rhône river systems of France") (Westerdahl 1995: 224–225). It is striking to note that these three zones of transport could be superimposed on the geographic territories of our proposed different regional shipbuilding practices.

Let us add a second cartographic argument. In his definition of the nautical geography of Europe, François Beaudouin (Beaudouin 1995) determined, in relation to the watershed which acts like a natural/geographical and also cultural/historical frontier, two vast hydrographic territories: that of the "nautical Europe of the North and of the South". Interestingly Westerdahl's zones of transport 6 and 12, fall within the hydrographic territory of the "nautical Europe of the North" as determined by François Beaudouin; and the zone of transport 17a falls within Beaudouin's hydrographic territory of the "nautical Europe of the South". No doubt, it is too early to pursue this argument to any conclusion but it is important to begin the debate.

Conclusion

In concluding this preliminary report on the hull characteristics of the Gallo-Roman EP 1-Taillebourg wreck, it is important to remember that the vessel is not yet fully excavated, and that current hypothesis must be compared with the results of future campaigns of excavation. In relation to the new data provided by the EP 1-Taillebourg wreck and, also when compared with the Lyon and Chalon-sur-Saône wrecks, the archaeological reading of "Romano-Celtic" flat-bottomed constructed vessels can now be considered from a more diverse perspective than had previously been possible. And whilst we cannot yet be definitive in our interpretation, the excavation of the Gallo-Roman EP 1-Taillebourg wreck has certainly permitted a broadening of the debate.

Acknowledgments

Etienne Champelovier, chief diver and technical director of the excavation (DRASSM -Annecy), for his collaboration over the last 20 years.

Notes

1 Catherine Lavier, Laboratory of Chrono-Ecology, CNRS, Besançon.

2 According to the archaeological evidence, the two wrecks discovered in the River Charente, the concept of a "construction tradition" seems too broad. The concept of "regional shipbuilding practices" seems more suitable. In this respect McGrail (McGrail 2001: 127) emphasises that: "… The Romano-Celtic tradition, like other boat and ship-building traditions, is an archaeological construct, an abstraction from reality. Not being mass produced, each boat or ship is unique in one way or another and, in ultimate detail, each vessel could form a class of its own. Only by simplifying complexities of form and structure, by ignoring variations in detail, and by taking a generalised view, it is possible to identify a group of vessels as 'Romano-Celtic' ". An excellent recall to caution in the interpretation of archaeological data!

3 In the wreck EP 1 the planks near the chine are not preserved.

4 In our publication (Becker and Rieth 1995: 85), we wrote, as an hypothesis: "… ne pourrait-on pas supposer que la présence de l'assemblage secondaire par mortaises et clous observés dans l'épave de la place Tolozan d'une part, et celle du calfatage à base de tissu et de brai d'autre part, pourraient-être les signes d'une éventuelle influence de techniques méditerranéennes sur des pratiques de construction navale fluviale de tradition purement régionale et continentale?"

5 These regional shipbuilding practices could also be interpreted as a "sub-group within the Romano-Celtic tradition" (McGrail 1995).

6 In the conclusion of her study, Catherine Lonchambon (Lonchambon 2000: 178) suggests a similar hypothesis. She notes: "… ces données suggèrent l'existence d'un groupe d'embarcations propre à la vallée du Rhône – comprenant les bateaux de Chalon, de Lyon et éventuellement d'Arles … Mais la signification historique de ce groupe reste encore à définir: s'agit-il d'un sous-groupe des embarcations de tradition "romano-celtique" (le groupe 1 étant alors scindé en deux sous-groupes, celui des embarcations calfatées à la mousse et celui des embarcations lutées avec du tissu poissé), ou bien est-ce un groupe à part, à la jonction entre la tradition méditerranéenne et la tradition romano-celtique? Dans ce cas, la date précoce des bateaux chalonnais et lyonnais serait-elle tout à fait aléatoire ou est-elle un signe du rôle précurseur de ces embarcations?".

References

Arnold, B., 1992. *Batellerie gallo-romaine sur le lac de Neuchâtel*. Archéologie Neuchâteloise, 12–13. Saint-Blaise.

Beaudouin, F., 1994. L'économie motrice nautique pré-mécanique. Les chemins qui marchent. *Neptunia* 193: 1–13.

Becker, C. and Rieth, E., 1995. L'épave gallo-romaine de la place Tolozan à Lyon: un chaland à coque monoxyleassemblée. In *L'arbre et la forêt, le bois dans l'Antiquité*, Publications de la bibliothèque Salomon Reinach, Université Lumière-Lyon 2, 77–91. Lyon.

Lonchambon, C., 2000, Un bateau monoxyle-assemblé à Chalon-sur-Saône (1er siècle ap. J.-C.) In L. Bonnamour (ed), *Archéologie des fleuves et des rivières*, 174–178. Errance. Paris.

McGrail, S., 1995, Romano-Celtic boats and ships: characteristic features. *International Journal of Nautical Archaeology* 24: 139–145.

McGrail, S., 2001, The Barland's Farm boat within the Romano-Celtic tradition. *Archäologisches Korrespondenzblatt* 31.1: 117–132.

McGrail S., 2003, Celtic Boats and Ships. *Maritime Life and Tradition* 20: 24–33.

Mariotti, J.-F., Pichon, M., Dumont, A., Degez, D., Henriet, J.L. and Hulot, O., 2002, *Prospection thématique sub-aquatique fleuve Charente Taillebourg-Port d'Envaux 2002*. Service régional de l'archéologie Poitou-Charentes, Direction régionale des affaires culturelles, Poitiers.

Rieth, E., Carrierre-Desbois, C. and Serna, S., 2001, *L'épave de Port Berteau II. Charente-Maritime. Un caboteur fluvio-Maritime du haut Moyen Age et son contexte nautique*. Maison des sciences de l'Homme. (DAF 86) Paris.

Rieth, E., 2003, Essay to Restore the Operating Process of a Shipyard in the Early Medieval Period: the Example of the *Port Berteau II Wreck*, Charente-Maritime, France. In C. Beltrame (ed), *Boats, Ships and Shipyards. Proceedings of the Ninth International Symposium on Boat and Ship Archaeology, Venice, 2000*, 113–118. Oxbow Books. Oxford.

Westerdahl, C., 1995, Traditional zones of transport geography in relation to ship types. In O. Olsen, J. Skamby Madsen and F. Rieck (eds), *Shipshape. Essays for Ole Crumlin-Pedersen*, 213–230. Viking Ship Museum. Roskilde.

14 The Dor 2001/1 wreck. Dor/Tantura Lagoon, Israel: Preliminary report

Yaacov Kahanov and Hadas Mor

General Description

Tantura Lagoon is located on the Mediterranean coast of Israel, 30 km south of Haifa. For many years this natural lagoon, which is south of the promontory of the ancient city of Dor, has been a fruitful area for archaeological survey, and during recent years for underwater excavations and research (Kingsley and Raveh 1996; Wachsmann and Kahanov 1997; Wachsmann *et al* 1997). A water-jet probing survey was carried out in the lagoon in November 2001 by students of the Department of Maritime Civilizations of the University of Haifa. During the work, fragments of wood of at least two species surfaced, indicating the possibility of a wreck. The wood was dated by ^{14}C analysis to between the 3rd and 6th centuries AD, which equates to the Late Roman–Byzantine period in this region. Based on these results, it was decided to excavate the site of the suspected wreck (Mor 2002–2003: 15–17).

A few days into the first season of excavation in 2002 the remains of a ship were exposed. The ship is oriented roughly northwest/southeast, about 70 m offshore, 2–3 m southeast of the lagoon's navigation channel, at a water depth of 1 m, and buried under 1.5 m of sand. The total length of the find is about 11.5 m, and the maximum width is 4.5 m. The hull remains include: keel, false keel, keelson, frames, planking, ceiling planking, chine strake and stringer.

Hull Remains

(Fig. 14.1) The major part of the hull is still covered by the stone cargo. However, several components were exposed, though some have still not been thoroughly examined due to various obstacles. Further discoveries are expected in future excavations.

The **keel**, of *Cupressus sempervirens*,[1] which was

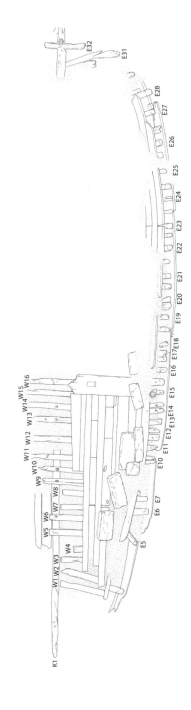

DOR 2001/1
NAS + CMS + AQUADORA
Drawn by Kitty + Jamie Brandon

Fig. 14.1 Plan view of hull remains after first season (C. Brandon).

exposed at the southeastern end and for a length of 2.04 m, is 11 cm sided × 16 cm moulded (Fig. 14.2).

The **false keel**, of *Quercus coccifera*, is 5 cm thick, and it is not yet clear how it is joined to the keel itself.

A **keelson**, of *Quercus coccifera*, measuring 15 cm sided × 18 cm moulded, was exposed at the northwestern end of the hull. It was laid above the frames and pointed towards the endpost, which is 8 cm sided × 12 cm moulded (Fig. 14.3).

Frames (Fig. 14.4). Thirty-two frames, the majority flat floor-timbers that would all have originally extended across the full floor, were found, with average dimensions 10 cm sided × 8 cm moulded, and room and space of 24 cm. Some are larger: 13 cm sided × 10 cm moulded, and some smaller: 8 cm sided × 7 cm moulded. They alternate: large frame, small frame, etc, at least in the central section of the hull. Limber holes were visible above the planking near the keel, their dimensions being 2.5 × 2.5 cm on average. All frames are joined directly to the keel by 5 mm square-section iron nails.

The frames were made of several tree species: *Fagus orientalis*, *Ulmus campestris*, *Quercus cerris*, *Quercus coccifera*, *Ziziphus spina christi* and *Tamarix*. Except for the latter two, all the wood species of the hull originated in western Turkey. Since *Tamarix* and *Ziziphus spina christi* are local trees, and frames of this species were only found in the northern end of the hull, it would appear that these frames were later repairs using local wood. This may give a clue to the ship's service life.

Planking (Fig. 14.5). The planking, of *Cupressus sempervirens*, is connected to the frames from the outside by square iron nails, with 5 mm cross-section. Plank dimensions are 2–3 cm thick by 8–15 cm wide.

After careful examination, where accessible, no evidence of any mortise-and-tenon, or any other plank edge joints, was found between planks. It seems that they were simply placed one next to the other and connected to the frames with the use of iron nails. A butt-joint was identified at frame station W22 – Strake 7. Traces of caulking material, as yet unidentified, were found in the seams.

Ceiling planking (Fig. 14.6). Eleven ceiling planks survived in the eastern part of the wreck, all made of *Pinus brutia*. Ceiling planks 1 to 8 are mostly covered by matting and stones, and are 2–2.5 cm thick and 6–9 cm wide, narrowing towards the end, using drop strakes. Ceiling planks 9 to 11 change attitude from horizontal

Fig. 14.3 Keelson at the north-west end of the wreck (I. Grinberg)

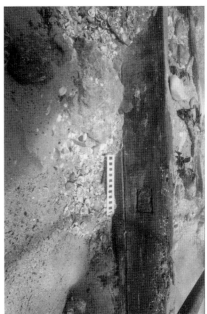

Fig. 14.2 Keel and false keel (N. Sheizaf)

Fig. 14.5 Planking (I. Grinberg)

Fig. 14.4 Frames (note the limber holes) (I. Grinberg)

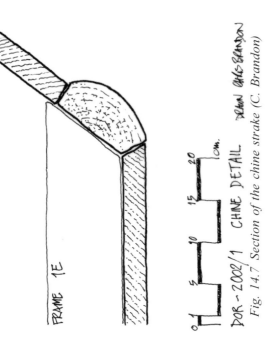

DOR - 2002/1 CHINE DETAIL ... Chris Brandon

FRAME 1E

0 1 5 10 15 20 cm.

Fig. 14.7 Section of the chine strake (C. Brandon)

Fig. 14.6 Ceiling planking (N. Sheizaf)

over the bottom, to vertical, parallel to the ship's sides. They are generally 2 cm thick and 6–19 cm wide, narrowing towards the end. One was a maximum of 4 cm thick and 32 cm wide. This relatively large strake served as a significant internal longitudinal reinforcement member. The ceiling planks were nailed from the inside of the hull to the frames by square-section metal nails, apparently iron, with a cross-section side between 4 and 8 mm, two nails for each ceiling plank–frame junction.

A **chine-strake** of *Cupressus sempervirens*, with a radius of 6 cm and width of 10 cm, was observed at the southeastern end of the vessel (Fig. 14.7).

The **mast step** position has yet to be located. A timber, lying at 90° to the hull's longitudinal axis, 122 cm long, 35 cm wide and 6 cm thick, with a rectangular groove measuring 8 cm x 16 cm, was initially considered to be part of the mast step assemblage. However, it was probably a base for a supporting stanchion for a transverse beam, or might have served as a support for one of the mast partners.

The flat **floor timbers** dictated the shape of the hull's bottom, which was evidently suited to carrying building stones.

The north-western end of the ship was found almost

complete. The other end, which did not survive, can be reconstructed by extrapolation. The total length of the ship can be estimated to have originally been 17 m in length, with a beam of about 5–6 m.

The presence of strong skeleton components: keel, false keel and a heavy keelson, as well as significant long-itudinal reinforcing timbers; chine strake and stringer, together with the specific method of joining the frames to the keel and the attachment of the planks, suggest that the ship was built based on frames, apparently a skeleton construction. The sequence of building was probably that of a general skeleton construction; that is, firstly frames were attached to the keel by rectangular metal nails, then the keelson was fitted on top, then the planks were nailed to the frames from the outside, and then the ceiling planking was nailed from the inside. Finally, the seams were caulked, and the exposed timbers were coated with protective layers of resin.

The finds

The wreck was found loaded with about 100 building stones (Fig. 14.8). They were stacked in two layers of three to seven rows, one next to the other. They are probably *kurkar* (coarse calcareous sandstone), and though their precise origin has yet to be determined, they are probably local, as this type of rock is common in the region. The stones are all about the same size, with average dimensions of 57 x 28 x 18 cm. They were laid on top of the ceiling planking, with a woven mat beneath to provide protection for the wood.

The site is rich in Byzantine ceramics, which are found above the wreck, above and between the stones, and within the ship's hull. Most of these were severely damaged (Fig. 14.9). However, due to the nature of Tantura Lagoon, where the heavy seas of strong winter storms can easily move pottery and stones, it is not certain that the ceramic remains belong to this ship. Finds from inside the hull that may be discovered in future excavations could perhaps, after careful examination, be considered as *in situ* artifacts, and would thus help determine a more precise date for the wreck. Currently all the ceramics, including the Byzantine assemblage, whatever their relation to the ship, are suspect.

Ropes of several sizes were found, and also matting protecting the ceiling planking from the stones. These have not yet been analysed.

Dating

A great deal of pottery from the 4th to 7th centuries AD was found in association with the wreck. At this stage, however, as explained above, a sceptical and conservative approach to accepting these as *in situ* ceramic evidence for dating, is being adopted. It is therefore preferred to date the wreck by ^{14}C analysis. About ten ^{14}C samples have been analysed, which included samples of wood from the hull and short-living organic materials such as rope and matting. The results range from the 3rd to the beginning of the 7th century AD.[2] It is thus logical to date the ship provisionally to the 5th century AD.

Analysis

In the ninth ISBSA in Venice, Royal presented analysis of construction components of contemporary shipwrecks.[3] The analysis of some of his results, including Dor 2001/1, revealed similarities with other wrecks from Dor/Tantura. The coefficient of the average keel cross-sectional area divided by the estimated vessel length of Dor 2001/1, is very similar to that of Tantura A. The coefficients of average frame cross-sectional area to the estimated vessel length of both vessels, are also almost identical. The preliminary frame measurements of Dor 2001/1 also fall close to those of Tantura A. However, when comparing the planking dimensions, Tantura A and Dor 2001/1 do not show similar frame spacing. These analyses and numerical comparisons are preliminary, as

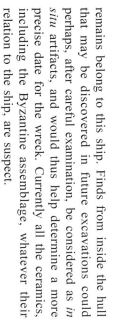

Fig. 14.8 Stone cargo (N. Sheizaf)

Fig. 14.9 Byzantine pottery in the site (N. Sheizaf)

they are based on incomplete information from Dor 2001/1, and are compared with the sparse information from Tantura A. However, they may serve as an analytical tool for future study, particularly when extending the study to Dor 2001/1 to compare it with other Mediterranean shipwrecks, including those from the central and western Mediterranean.

Transition in Construction[4]

The Dor 2001/1 wreck adds to earlier evidence from Tantura Lagoon, which suggests that the transition in ships hull construction from strake-based to frame-based was completed some centuries earlier in the eastern Mediterranean than had previously been accepted (Steffy 1994).

Tantura A, dated to the 6th century AD, was the first wreck that raised this possibility (Kahanov 2001; Kahanov *et al* 2004). The adoption of frame-based hull construction was at the time, attributed to the fact that Tantura A was a small coaster that naturally adopted changes earlier than larger seagoing ships.

Tantura B, dated to the 9th-century AD, was excavated immediately after Tantura A, and also supported the earlier introduction of frame-based hulls in the region (Kahanov 2000). Whether she was a galley, or a merchantman designed for shallow-water sailing, is still subject to debate. Whatever the case, her hull was frame-based, without mortise-and-tenon joints, and with caulking material between the seams.

Dor D, dated to the 6th century AD,[5] was also of frame-based construction, but with many unpegged mortise-and-tenon joints (Kahanov and Royal 2001; Kahanov 2003).

Fortunately, the proposed 5th-century AD Dor 2001/1 was subsequently discovered. The plank seams were carefully scrutinized and checked wherever accessible, but no mortise-and-tenon, or any other construction components functioning as edge joints, were found. The planking was clearly nailed to the frames, and several longitudinal members, such as the keel, false-keel and keelson, combined with the frames and longitudinal reinforcing components, present a skeleton-based construction. This supports the argument that ships were constructed frame-based without mortise-and-tenon joints in the eastern Mediterranean possibly as early as the 5th century AD, and that this construction is not limited to lightly-built hulls, but now includes a heavier vessel.

Thus, the typology of ship construction and the transition in construction from strake-based to skeleton-based in the eastern Mediterranean has to be redated to about five centuries earlier than previously accepted, to around 5th century AD.

To summarise: the information from Dor 2001/1, a cargo carrier, dated to about the 5th century AD, when considered in relation to the data from Tantura A and Tantura B, appears to shed new light on the typology of ship construction, especially with regard to the date of the transition from strake-based to skeleton-based construction in the eastern Mediterranean.

Notes

1   The tree-species analysis was carried out by Prof. Nili Liphschitz of the Botanical Laboratories of the Institute of Archaeology, Tel Aviv University, Israel.
2   ^{14}C analyses were made by E. Boaretto of the Weizmann Institute of Science, Israel, and by G. Bonani of the Institute of Particle Physics, Zurich, Switzerland.
3   The presentation by J. G. Royal in Venice, which was not published in the Proceedings, was based on his PhD dissertation, submitted to Texas A&M University in May 2002: *The Development and Utilization of Ship Technology in the Roman World in Late Antiquity: Third to Seventh Century AD*.
4   For 'Transition in Construction' see Steffy 1994: 83–85.
5   Based on two ^{14}C tests.

References

Kahanov, Y., 2000, Tantura B Shipwreck. A Preliminary Report on its Hull Construction. In J. Litwin (ed), *Down the River into the Sea. Eighth International Symposium on Boat and Ship Archaeology, Gdańsk 1997*, 151–154. Polish Maritime Museum. Gdańsk.

Kahanov, Y., 2001, A Byzantine Shipwreck ("Tantura A") in Tantura Lagoon, Israel: Its Hull Construction. In H. Tzalas (ed), *Tropis VI, Proceedings of the 6th International Symposium on Ship Construction in Antiquity, Lamia 1996*, 265–271. Hellenic Institute for the Preservation of Nautical Tradition. Athens.

Kahanov, Y., 2003, Dor D Wreck, Tantura Lagoon, Israel. In C. Beltrame (ed), *Boats, Ships and Shipyards, Proceedings of the Ninth International Symposium on Boat and Ship Archaeology, Venice 2000*, 49–56. Oxbow. Oxford.

Kahanov, Y. and Royal, G. J., 2001, Analysis of Hull Remains of the Dor D Vessel, Tantura Lagoon, Israel. *International Journal of Nautical Archaeology*, 30.2: 257–265.

Kahanov, Y., Royal, J. and Hall, J., 2004, The Tantura Wrecks and Ancient Mediterranean Shipbuilding. In F. M. Hocker and C. A. Ward (eds), *The Philosophy of Shipbuilding*, 113–127. Texas A&M University Press. College Station.

Kingsley, S. and Raveh, K., 1996, *The Ancient Harbour and Anchorage at Dor, Israel: Results of the Underwater Surveys 1976–1991*. BAR International Series 626. Oxford.

Mor, H. 2002–2003, The Dor (Tantura) 2001/1 Shipwreck. A Preliminary Report, *RIMS (Recanati Institute for Maritime Studies) News* 29: 15–17.

Royal, G. J., 2002, *The Development and Utilization of Ship Technology in the Roman World in Late Antiquity: Third to Seventh Century AD*. Unpublished PhD dissertation, Texas A&M University, Ann Arbor.

Steffy, J. R., 1994, *Wooden Ship Building and the Interpretation of Shipwrecks*. Texas A&M University Press. College Station.

Wachsmann, S. and Kahanov, Y., 1997, Shipwreck Fall: The 1995 INA/CMS Joint Expedition to Tantura Lagoon, Israel. INA *(Institute of Nautical Archaeology) Quarterly*, 24.1: 3–18.

Wachsmann, S., Kahanov, Y. and Hall, J., 1997, The Tantura B Shipwreck: The 1996 INA/CMS Joint Expedition to Tantura Lagoon. INA *(Institute of Nautical Archaeology) Quarterly*, 24.4: 3–15.

15 A hypothesis on the development of Mediterranean ship construction from Antiquity to the Late Middle Ages

Carlo Beltrame and Mauro Bondioli

The problem of the evolution in Mediterranean ship construction from Antiquity to the Middle Ages has been the topic of various theoretical studies. These have tended to focus attention on the principles and procedures of execution, and are based on the distinction between "shell-first" and "skeleton-first" processes of construction related to a longitudinal or a transverse conception (Pomey 1994 and ref.).

Although such theoretical speculation is conceptually useful, the growing corpus of wrecks belonging to the Late Antique and Medieval periods is increasingly challenging the limits of an approach focused only on the definitions of constructive principles and methods of realization. This is demonstrated by the fact that, in response to the question regarding how we arrive at given skeleton-based construction, we can actually answer only with an ambiguous and generic definition such as "mixed construction". This term is currently used to explain a transitory phase, characterized by a large number of archaeological exceptions, in which some constructive solutions have been employed which simultaneously share aspects of both concepts (Rieth 1996: 21–29; Pomey 1998: 68).

Although this approach can be theoretically correct, it helps us to understand the long process which led to the building of complete pre-erected frames, to the drawing of moulds and to the application of methods of geometrical reduction based on these moulds. The mixed construction definition does not permit us to define the method of building of a hull, in order to be able to place the technical solutions, noted within it, in a relative chronological sequence. Apart from their geographical, typological and cultural differences, is it possible to suppose that, for example, the medieval wrecks of Serçe Limani (Steffy 1982), Cala Culip (Nieto and Raurich 1998) and San Marco in Boccalama are part of an evolutive *continuum*? Or should they be considered examples which are unrelated to one another?

In our opinion, if we want to answer these questions, we have to look in a different direction from one connected

to theoretical principles. Through new readings of archaeological data and by the study of written sources, it becomes possible to identify traces of the transformation process of the constructive method, and to put these in an evolutionary sequence.

Undoubtedly, it is a fantasy to extend this research to the entire Mediterranean. What we can try to do is to hypothesize a general course of development, which is independent of any context and which can be modified as new data emerge. The following hypothesis is simply a theoretical reference proposal for the analysis of archaeological data, in order to attempt to place a wreck in a more precise moment within an evolutionary sequence.

To formulate a theory of constructive development it is useful to have a theoretical model of gradual technological advancement. Although such a model cannot perfectly reflect historical reality, it does allow us to simulate a logical sequence, whereby the passage from one phase of development to another requires the introduction of new conditions which, consequently, produce the loss of another part belonging to the previous phase (Fig. 15.1). In fact, a novel construction is always based on previous experiences. Thus these last ones will remain more or less significant until their final disappearance during the passing of the evolutionary phases.

Because the theory must relate to the objective difficulties of realising a ship, we have turned our attention to the practical problems of any shipbuilder. For example, after he has defined the shape and built the ship, he will have to face the problem of recording and transmitting the most important construction data in order both to derive replicas of his constructions and to introduce changes.

Regarding the replication process or 'cloning', it is necessary to make a distinction: we must distinguish between building a ship's shape *ex novo*, and cloning one ship from another one. The majority of shipwrights were, in fact, mere executors, who produced hulls of the same shape following handed-down experiences. Masters who built new ships or who added changes to the shape were rare.

Carlo Beltrame and Mauro Bondioli

It is possible that in Antiquity, the problem of 'cloning' was tackled in an instinctive way, by the use of mobile floor timbers or of moulds (Fig. 15.2). Pegs found on the military boats of Oberstimm of the 2nd century AD (Bockius 2002: 17–19) were not used for the frames, but constitute potential traces of the use of a mould which could be temporarily fixed and then removed and, possibly, re-used on another ship.

It is likely that the shipwrights soon noticed that the role of this element could have been developed further, more efficiently, by one or more floor timbers fixed to the keel. After the phase of using a simple mould to replicate more ships from an initial shape, it is in fact possible that they began to lay floor timbers, curved according to a default shape, before laying planking for the hull bottom (Fig. 15.3).

The pre-erection of a few floor timbers nailed to the keel would have determined the shape of the hull bottom, and probably, at the same time, would have assured a structural solidity that permitted a reduction in the number of fastenings between the strakes, and consequently in shipyard labour (Basch 1972: 50).

Indeed, from the Imperial period onwards, there was a slow and progressive reduction of junctions between planking. Tenons in fact became more and more widely spaced and even smaller. This phenomenon had already begun in the 2nd century AD, and by the 5th century, some ships even featured tenons which completely lacked pegs to fix them in the mortises (one is the Ravenna wreck: Medas 2003: 46).

On these last hulls, tenons no longer fastened the planking: they simply functioned to facilitate laying the planks in the building of the shell, in particular at the extremities.

The master, building this kind of ship, probably had two problems: one of structure, compensating for the almost total lack of plank fastenings, and one of procedure, assembly of the components.

On the one hand, Pomey (1998: 66–67) explains the bolts on the floor timbers as simple strengthenings useful to avoid the loss of the keel if the ship would have crashed against a reef. On the other hand, Steffy (2000: 265) believes that the widely spaced tenons reflect the relative lack of slave workers at the end of the Empire.[1] Con-

Development process diagram

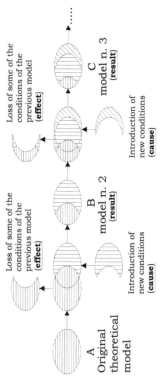

A
Original
theoretical
model

Introduction of new conditions (**cause**)

Loss of some of the conditions of the previous model (**effect**)

B
model n. 2
(**result**)

Introduction of new conditions (**cause**)

Loss of some of the conditions of the previous model (**effect**)

C
model n. 3
(**result**)

Loss of some of the conditions of the previous model (**effect**)

Fig. 15.1. Theoretical model of gradual technological advancement (authors).

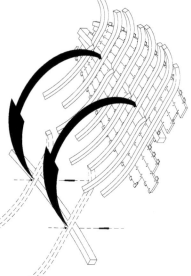

Fig. 15.3. Use of floor timbers bolted to the keel (authors).

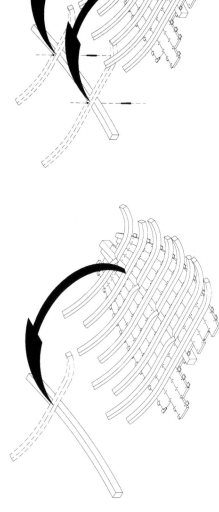

Fig. 15.2. Use of a mobile floor timber or mould (authors).

Fig. 15.4. Schematic diagram of the port side planking of the Serçe Limani wreck (after Steffy 1982).

 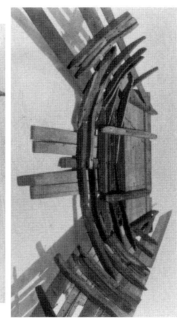

Fig. 15.5. Wooden model of the hull from Pantano Longarini (Siracusa) (after Bass 1972).

sequently, this last phenomenon would have caused the appearance, in the same period, of metal junctions between floor timbers and keel.

However, changing perspective and looking at the widening of the junctions of the planking as an effect, rather than as a cause, of other technical innovations, the panorama radically changes. Main innovations could have been simply the junctions between keel and floor timbers, which became quite common in the 2nd century AD and then more and more frequent and numerous as the mortises became increasingly widely spaced (Basch 1972: 50). This becomes increasingly widespread up to the 7th century: in this century in fact, both the Pantano Longarini (Throckmorton and Throckmorton 1973) and Saint Gervais 2 (Jézégou 1985) hulls have all the floor timbers nailed to the keel, and rare unpegged tenons.

Even if the erection of a sufficient number of floor timbers could guarantee a good support for the nailing of the planking without the help of junctions between strakes,

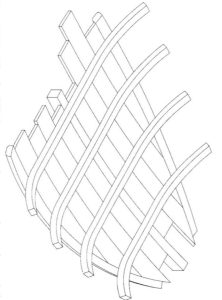 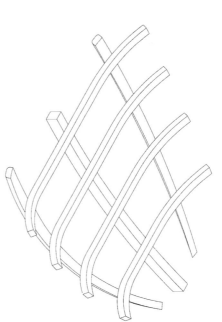

Fig. 15.6. The wale nailed to the knee of the floor timbers defines the ship's shape (authors).

Fig. 15.7. Planks fill the space between the wale and the keel (authors).

it was still necessary to find a technique to define the shape of all the floor timbers, especially at the extremities. Looking at the models and documentation of the Pantano Longarini and Serçe Limani wrecks (of the 7th and 11th centuries respectively), we can hypothesise about the subsequent phase of evolution.

Note that the Serçe Limani hull has a thicker strake than the others, connecting the posts at the level of the knee. In addition, notice how the disposition of the planking between this strake and the keel is radically

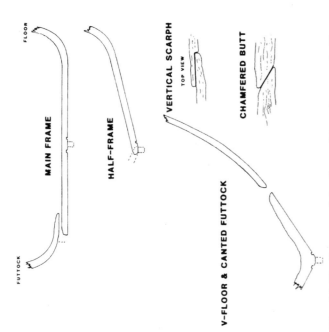

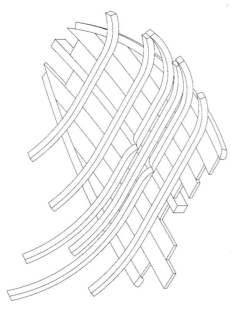

Fig. 15.8. Half-frames can be nailed to the bottom of the hull (authors).

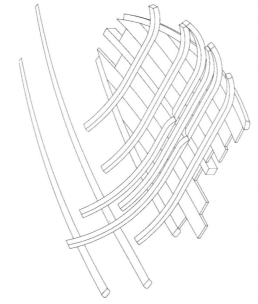

Fig. 15.9. Other wales can be used to align the half-frames and thus to define the uppermost shape of the hull (authors).

Fig. 15.10. Frames of the Serçe Liman1 wreck. Note the lack of strong junctions between floor timbers and futtocks (after Steffy 1982).

different from that above the plank (Fig. 15.4). These characteristics, which are also present on the Pantano Longarini hull (Fig. 15.5), permit us to think that, after the erection of some floor timbers on the keel, an external wale was nailed on each side at the level of the keel.

The laying of the wale, in addition to having a role in the structural strengthening – that is, of fixing the floor timbers – defines the ship's shape based on frames (Fig. 15.6). Keel, posts and wale in fact defined the bottom and thus the most important part of the ship. Now, it was necessary only to fill the space between wale and keel (Fig. 15.7).

Next, on the completed bottom, half-frames were perhaps nailed down to fix the side planking (Fig. 15.8). Thus, as the Pantano Longarini wreck would show, it is likely that this last operation occurred in repeating the laying of a second and perhaps of a third external wale,

used to align the half-frames and so to define the highest shape of the hull (Fig. 15.9).

If we note the Arab ships wrecked in the 10th and 11th centuries – Agay, Bateguier (Darmoul 1985; Jézégou and Joncheray 1997), Marsala (Ferroni and Meucci 1995–1996) and Serçe Limani – we can see that they present new and common characteristics. They are flat-bottomed hulls with almost straight sides and thus with knees with a very marked angle. The transverse skeleton is slowly becoming more regular, but it is still far from the 'logical order' visible on the Cala Culip wreck of the end of the 13th century.

Although all or almost all the floor timbers have taken on an active role, it is not possible to say this for the rest of the skeleton still composed of half-frames and futtocks, used simply to connect and strengthen the uppermost part of the planking.

Available documentation about the Agay wrecks indicates that floor timbers and futtocks still have no junctions. Only after the shipbuilder had formed the bottom did he have the bearing surface for the nailing of the L-shape half-frames. Once the planking was nailed to these, it was probably possible to lay futtocks extending the flat floor timbers.

The builder of the Serçe Limani ship probably followed the same sequence: in fact, analyzing Steffy's publication, we have noted that what he calls junctions between L-shaped floor timbers and futtocks are not connections which permitted the shipwright to lay a complete frame on the keel (Fig. 15.10). In fact, on some floor timbers the nails are sometimes insufficient or completely absent and, instead of having hook scarps, there are just simple scarps.

With the growing complexity of the constructive system, a simplification of the mechanisms which regulate the building process is required. It is probable that, already at this point, the shipwrights tried to concentrate all the information in one mould to determine the shape of the hull bottom. In this way, it was possible to eliminate the use of too many moulds. The concept of *sesto* is born: this is a mould with reduction markings, used to obtain numerous floor timbers and simply derived from the ship's shape. It is a primitive *sesto*, generated by the observation that most of the development of the hull bottom comes from the mould of the central floor timber.

The next phase in the design evolution was the laying of complete frames, that is of strongly linked floor timbers and futtocks, before the nailing of the planking. The first wreck showing characteristics which reflect this sequence is the Cala Culip vessel. Here, in fact, the extremities of the floor timbers have real hook scarps and large metal nails to connect the futtocks in an integral way (Nieto and Raurich 1998: 152–154).

At this point, the technique of defining the bottom shape by an external wale had probably become obsolete, because the hull was no longer being built in consecutive stages. In fact, the profiles, suggested by complete frames, defined the ship's shape, at least in its central part. At the most, it is probable that a temporary wale, that is a ribband (*maistra*), was used to define the profile of the frames to be put at the extremities and to control the bevel of the frames (Fig. 15.11). The ribband could be an inheritance from the earlier use of the external wale.

The role which the external wale had of strengthening the transversal structure is now carried out by an internal element. In this period, in fact, an important element of the inner planking appears: the *parascossola*, a thick bilge stringer nailed to the junctions between floor timbers

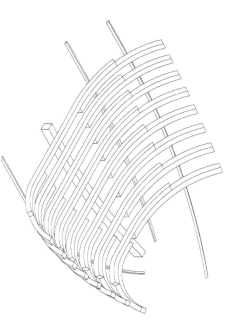

Fig. 15.11. A temporary wale (maistra) could be used to define the profile of the frames to be put at the extremities and to control the bevels of the frames of a hull (authors).

and futtocks. The first archaeological traces of its presence has been seen on the same wreck of Cala Culip (where the stringer itself was no longer present but the fastenings for it were) and on the Venice galley (Fig. 15.12).

This last observation concerns the techniques of reduction of the *sesti* which, because they permit the shipwright to draw the frames before their use and to define the shape of the central part of the hull, represent the most practical and effective method to "clone" hulls. We have already seen that these could have appeared in an empirical and instinctive form, a long time before the introduction of geometrical systems. However, considering what Ousterhout (1999: 72) defines as the "Byzantines" unproductiveness, lasting at least five centuries, in the fields of mathematics and geometry — that is, considering the elementariness of the Byzantines' methods of geometrical drawing and design — we do not feel like ascribing to them the invention of such a solution, which would imply considerable scientific knowledge which appears lacking.

The Cala Culip wreck, which seems to represent the most ancient evidence of the use of *sesti*, lets us conjecture, instead, that this last method has to be ascribed to the western world's Renaissance of the 12th century. This is an age of cultural renewal, encouraged by the translation of Arab and Greek texts, but also constituting a period of transition from the Romanesque architectural style to the Gothic one, in a vision of universal order, regulated by geometrical forms and rules.

In conclusion, we hope that our proposal might offer a simple but useful outline for the interpretation of the numerous medieval wrecks found in the Mediterranean in recent years, and that it might inspire further discussion on the development of ship construction in this area.

Fig. 15.12. The parascossola of the 14th-century galley of San Marco in Boccalama (Venice; authors; by permission of the Ministro per i Beni e le Attività Culturali).

Acknowledgement

We would like to thank Claire Calcagno for her careful corrections of the translation of the original Italian text.

Note

1   Steffy believes that slavery offered cheap manpower and that its disappearance coincided with the change from jointed planking techniques to the less labour-intensive skeleton construction. This idea does not take into account the real *status* of slaves, who were often no cheaper than *humiliores* (Štaerman and Trofimova 1975: 95–97). In late antiquity, in fact, although there were no slaves, a community of *humiliores* would have been ready to work for little pay.

References

Basch, L., 1972, Ancient wrecks and the archaeology of ships. *The International Journal of Nautical Archaeology and Underwater Exploration* 1: 1–58.

Bass, G. (Ed.), 1972, *A History of Seafaring Based on Underwater Archaeology*. London.

Bockius, R., 2002, *Die Roemerzeitlichen schiffsfunde von Oberstimm in Bayern*. Mainz.

Darmoul, A., 1985, Les épaves sarrasines. Contribution à l'étude des techniques de constructions navales musulmanes et méditerranéennes. In M. Galley, L. Ladjimi Sebaï (Eds), *L'Homme méditerranéen et la mer. Actes du Troisième Congrès International d'études des cultures de la Méditerranée Occidentale (Jerba, Avril 1981)*, 152–163. Tunis.

Ferroni, A. M. and Meucci, C., 1995–1996, I due relitti arabonormanni di Marsala. *Bollettino di Archeologia Subacquea* 1–2: 283–350.

Jézégou, M.-P., 1985, Éléments de construction sur couples observés sur une épave du haut Moyen Age découverte à Fos-sur-Mer (Bouches-du-Rhone). In *VIe Congreso Inter-*

nacional de Arqueologia Submarina, Cartagena 1982, 351–356. Madrid.

Jézégou, M.-P. and Joncheray, J.-P., 1997. Les épaves sarrasines d'Agay et de Cannes. *Archeologia* 337: 32–39.

Medas, S., 2003, The Late-Roman « Parco di Teodorico » Wreck, Ravenna, Italy: Preliminary Remarks on the Hull and the Shipbuilding. In C. Beltrame (Ed), *Boats, Ships and Shipyards. Proceedings of the Ninth International Symposium on Boat and Ship Archaeology, Venice 2000*, 42–48. Oxford.

Nieto, X. and Raurich, X. (eds.), 1998, *Excavacions arqueològiques subaquàtiques a Cala Culip 2: Culip VI*. Girona.

Ousterhout, R., 1999, *Master Builders of Byzantium*. Princeton.

Pomey, P., 1994, Shell conception and skeleton process in ancient Mediterranean shipbuilding. In C. Westerdahl (ed.), *Crossroads in Ancient Shipbuilding. Proceedings of the Sixth International Symposium on Boat and Ship Archaeology, Roskilde 1991*, 125–130. Oxford.

Pomey, P., 1998, Conception et réalisation des navires dans l'Antiquité méditerranéenne. In E. Rieth (Ed), *Concevoir et construire les navires. De la trière au picoteux*, 49–72. Ramonville Saint-Agne.

Rieth, E., 1996, *Le maitre-gabarit, la tablette et le trébuchet. Essai sur la conception non-graphique des carènes du Moyen Age au XX siècle*. Paris.

Štaerman, E. M. and Trofimova, M. R., 1975, *La schiavitù nell'Italia imperiale*. Roma.

Steffy, R., 1982, The reconstruction of the 11th-century Serçe Limani vessel. A preliminary report. *The International Journal of Nautical Archaeology and Underwater Exploration* 11.1: 13–34.

Steffy, R., 2000, Influences on shipbuilding technology. In J. Litwin (ed.), *Down the River to the Sea. Eighth International Symposium on Boat and Ship Archaeology, Gdansk 1997*, 263–267. Gdansk.

Throckmorton, P. and Throckmorton, J., 1973. The Roman wreck at Pantano Longarini. *The International Journal of Nautical Archaeology and Underwater Exploration* 2.2: 243–266.

16 Geometric rules in early medieval ships: Evidence from the Bozburun and Serçe Limanı vessels

Matthew Harpster

Introduction

Recent research indicates that the designs of the 9th-century AD Bozburun vessel and the 11th-century Serçe Limanı vessel were developed using similar geometric processes. The elements and applications of these two geometric processes, moreover, bear similarities to Renaissance-era proportional methods. This paper will discuss these geometric methods and their similarities to later methods such as the system of *partisoni* and that outlined in the *Fabrica di Galere*.

The sites at Bozburun and Serçe Limanı were discovered during the first survey of the Turkish coast by researchers from the Institute of Nautical Archaeology (INA) in 1973 (Bass and van Doorninck, Jr. 1978: 119, 121). Excavation of Serçe Limanı (dated to c. 1025 by coin and weight finds) occurred between 1977 and 1979, and in addition to examples of the glass and personal items recovered, the conserved hull remains are now on display in the Bodrum Museum of Underwater Archaeology, in Bodrum, Turkey.

The hull remains and artefacts from Bozburun (dated to AD 874 by dendrochronology and excavated between

1995 and 1998), are in varying states of analysis (Fig. 16.1). Final reports on the galley ware and macrobotanical evidence are now available, while research on the hull and amphoras is nearing completion (Gorham 2000; Danis 2002; Harpster 2002). The artefacts from Bozburun are held at the Bodrum Museum of Underwater Archaeology, while the hull remains are in storage awaiting conservation nearby, at the Turkish headquarters of INA.

The evidence

Elements of the construction of these two vessels are very similar. The midships floor timbers of each are located halfway along the length of their keels, and both vessels are framed with asymmetrical L-shaped floor timbers (Figs 16.2, 16.3). The Bozburun vessel only contains seven such asymmetrical floor timbers, all near amidships, while the Serçe Limanı vessel was constructed with more, extending between the vessel's fore and aft tailframes (Bass *et al* 2004: 155–58). Elements of the geometric methods used to design these craft are very similar as well. One such element is a standard unit of length.

Fig. 16.1. *Excavation of the hull material from Bozburun, Turkey (Don Frey, INA).*

Fig. 16.2. *The asymmetrical shape of the Serçe Limanı floor timbers, as indicated by the dashed lines (after Steffy 1994: 88).*

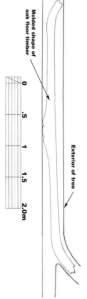

Fig. 16.3. *The asymmetrical shape of the oak floor timbers in the Bozburun vessel (author).*

Matthew Harpster

The standard length in use on the Bozburun vessel is a unit of 345 mm, and multiples and divisions of this length are evident throughout the vessel's design. The midships floor timber, for example, is 3.45 m wide between the bilges, and is located 345 mm forward of the next frame aft. The keel, moreover, is 7.41 m long, or 21.5 of these units.

In the design of the Serçe Limanı vessel, a standard length of 32 cm is evident in various elements of its design. The keel, for example, is 16 cm deep and 12 cm wide, or one-half of a unit by three-eighths of a unit (Bass *et al* 2004: 154). The beam of the vessel is 16 units wide, and the vessel's length is approximately 48 units (Bass *et al* 2004: 167). More significant, however, are the roles that these standard units played in the geometric methods used to design the shapes of each vessel's midships floor timber and the locations of key floor timbers in each vessel's structure.

The tripartite division of the Bozburun and Serçe Limanı midships floor timbers

The width of the midships floor timber from the Bozburun vessel is divided into three distinct sections, as demarcated by a partially-eroded scribe mark on the floor timber's bow face (Fig. 16.4). One section, at the center, is 1.38 m wide, and encompasses the area over the keel, the limber holes, and both garboard hollows. This center section is bracketed by the 1.035-m long arms of the floor timber that extend to either bilge. As these arms are flat, all of the deadrise in the floor timber is encompassed within the garboard hollows, which rise 115 mm. Applying the 345-mm long standard unit to these measurements, it is apparent that the center section of the midships floor timber is 4 units wide, either arm extends 3 units to each bilge, while the floor timber rises one-third of a unit through the garboard hollow (Fig. 16.5).

A similar tripartite division is apparent in the design of the midships floor timber from Serçe Limanı. The floor timber's center section is 32 cm, or one unit, wide, while arms to either side extend approximately 1.28 m, or four units, to either bilge (Bass *et al* 2004: 156) (Fig. 16.6). As there are no garboard hollows, the vessel's deadrise is instead incorporated in the arms to either bilge, which rise 4 cm, or one-eighth of a unit (Bass *et al* 2004: 156).

Arrangement of key floor timbers in the Bozburun vessel

Both vessels were built by fastening key floor timbers in place prior to attaching some of the planking. These collections of key floor timbers, however, not only derived their shapes from the midships floor timbers in each vessel, but their locations along the keel were determined by multiples of the distance between the vessels' bilges as well.

After the midships floor timber was fixed in place halfway along the length of the Bozburun keel, a second floor timber – identical in design to the midships frame but with its long arm on the opposite side – was nailed in place 345 mm, or one unit, abaft amidships. By fixing this second floor timber in place, the builders had defined the cross-sectional shape of the vessel, but they still had to demarcate what extent of the vessel would retain that shape, where the vessel would begin to taper to the endposts, and where the tailframes would be placed. To determine all of these locations along the keel, the builders utilized the width of the vessel between the bilges, which was ten units in the Bozburun vessel (Fig. 16.7). To demarcate the length of the ship that retained the vessel's full cross-section shape, this 10-unit length was reoriented longitudinally along the keel (Fig. 16.8). Next,

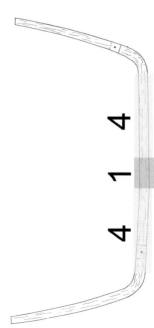

Fig. 16.6. The tripartite division of the midships floor timber in the Serçe Limanı vessel (after Steffy 1994: 89).

Fig. 16.7. The ten-unit width between the bilges of the Bozburun midships floor timber (author).

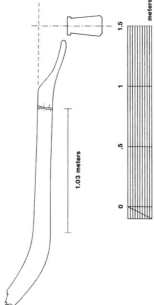

Fig. 16.4. Location of the scribe mark on the bow face of the midships floor timber (author).

Fig. 16.5. The tripartite division of the midships floor timber in the Bozburun vessel (author).

floor timber E, which was identical in design to the midships floor timber, was fixed in place one-half of this length, or five units, forward of amidships.¹ The beam and cross-sectional shape of the floor timbers forward of floor timber E all taper towards the stem. Floor timber 1, 345 mm abaft amidships, represented the after extent of the vessel's original cross-sectional shape; all floor timbers abaft that point diminished in their beam as well.

Defining the locations of the tailframes followed a similar process. Multiplying the same ten-unit length by 1.25, and marking that distance forward of midships defined the location of the forward tailframes. Multiplying the ten-unit length by 1.5, and extending that length aft from floor timber 1 defined the locations of the aft tailframes (Fig. 16.9).

The builders of the Bozburun vessel, with a few simple steps, had effectively defined the locations of – and erected – floor timbers that played key roles in the shape of the hull. Moreover, they had also demarcated the extent of the cargo space in the vessel. All of these characteristics, importantly, this process was completed in an easily understood and repeatable manner.

Arrangement of key floor timbers in the Serçe Limani vessel

The tripartite division of the midships floor timber in the Bozburun vessel defined a 10-unit length between the vessel's bilges. In the Serçe Limani vessel, the same tripartite division defined a nine-unit length, and this length was applied to the vessel's design in a similar manner. After the midships floor timber was fixed to the keel at a point midway along its length, and an identical floor timber was in place 32 cm forward, the builders

next had to demarcate the same areas along the keel's length: the extent of the vessel's original cross-sectional shape, the areas that taper to either post, and the locations of the tailframes.

Determining the extent of the vessel's original cross-sectional shape consisted of extending this nine-unit length forward of amidships; floor timber E, which retained the vessel's original beam, was then fixed in place half of that length forward. Unlike Bozburun, the same process was repeated aft. Floor timber 4, also retaining the original beam of the vessel, was fixed to the keel one-half of this nine-unit length abaft floor timber A – the floor timber 32 cm forward of amidships. All of the floor timbers forward and abaft these two floor timbers taper in beam towards the stem and sternpost.

Establishing the location of the tailframes consisted of a process similar to that practiced on Bozburun, but the multiples were reversed. In this case, the nine-unit length was multiplied by 1.5 and extended forward of amidships to demarcate the location of the forward tailframes; the aft tailframes were 1.25 times this nine-unit length abaft floor timber A.

Discussion

The particulars of these two methods differ slightly. In the Bozburun vessel, the first two floor timbers fixed in place were amidships and that immediately aft, while in the Serçe Limani vessel, it was amidships and the floor timber immediately forward. Additionally, the multiples used to determine the locations of the tailframes in the two vessels are reversed. Whereas in Bozburun the forward tailframes are 1.25 times the beam forward of amidships and the aft tailframes are 1.5 times the beam aft, the multiples used in the Serçe Limani vessel are opposite. Nonetheless, the relative results of these two methods are the same. By using one unit of length and an easily reproducible arithmetic method, the builders of each craft were able to define the cross-sectional shapes of their craft, the vessel's overall form, and their effective cargo space.

Moreover, the development of these geometric methods is evident as well. Multiples of the 345-mm Bozburun unit were used to define both the rise of the midships hollow from the keel, and the width of the floor timber to either bilge. There is no indication, however, that a geometric system was also used to determine the floor timber's curve through the bilge, or any rising or narrowing of particular floor timbers. In the vessel from Serçe Limani, advances in these techniques are evident. The same tripartite division of the midships floor timber is in use, as is a very similar system to determine the location of key floor timbers along the vessel's length. Also apparent is the use of geometric methods and offsets to determine the floor timber's curve through the bilge, and the narrowing and rising of some of the floor timbers. Greater geometric complexity, but a similar process, is

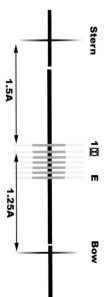

Fig. 16.9. Determining the locations of the fore and after tailframes (author).

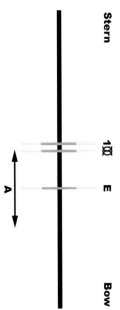

Fig. 16.8. Determining the location of floor timber E forward of amidships (author).

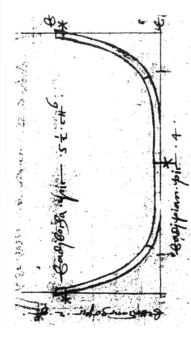

Fig. 16.10. Proposed design of a midships frame in the Trombetta manuscript. Note the similarity between the demarcated divisions of this frame and the midships floor timbers in the Bozburun and Serçe Limanı vessels (after Zorzi di Modon, 1444).

demonstrated in the *Fabrica di Galere* (1410), the *Trombetta* (1444) manuscript, and the 16th-century system of *partisoni*. The *Fabrica di Galere* continues the use of multiples of the width of the midships floor timber between its bilges, or the flat, to determine the dimensions of components of the vessel's structure, while the *Trombetta* manuscript displays a division of the midships frame similar to that in the design of the Bozburun and Serçe Limanı midships floor timbers (Fig. 16.10) (Bellabarba 1988: 16). The *partisoni* system, moreover, develops the shapes of the *cavi di sesto* from the design of the midships frame and proceeds to erect these three frames first (Alertz 2003: 212–214). This is a process and a pattern very similar to that employed in the construction of the Bozburun and Serçe Limanı vessels. These three Renaissance-era methods may be more complex, but the elements key to the Bozburun and Serçe Limanı methods are still present. Each is built around a standard unit of measurement and a tripartite division of the floor timbers is still evident, as is the use of multiples of the flat amidships to determine the dimensions and layout of the ship.

Conclusions

The vessels from Bozburun and Serçe Limanı appear to contain early stages of the design methods later exemplified in Renaissance-era Italy and elsewhere. All of these methods have the same elements, all the elements are used in similar manners and, among them, continuity and progression from the Byzantine to the Renaissance methods is apparent. Their significance in the Byzantine era lies not only in their presence – indicating the age and potential origins of the later processes – but perhaps in their application as well. The use of the geometric method of design in the Bozburun vessel, currently the oldest fully-excavated ship built in a frame-first manner, may be more than coincidence. It is entirely possible that

the transition to the frame-first method, a method which requires the careful shaping of a ship's framing, could not have occurred without the development of such a design method, and vice versa. The transition to more modern methods of assembling a ship, it appears, may be intertwined with the development and application of methods to design the ship as well.

Acknowledgements

The creation of this essay would not have been possible without the help of numerous people. First and foremost, the support and guidance of the members of my committee, who patiently awaited the completion of my dissertation, as well as Professor J.R. Steffy, whose thoroughly original analysis of the 11th-century Serçe Limanı vessel provided the basis for this research. Dr. Felipe Castro was also kind enough to present this paper in my absence in 2003, for which I thank him. Friends such as Athena Trakadas, Kathryn Thomas, Cassady Yoder, and Glenn Grieco stood by while I blathered about my ideas, and always nodded patiently; I hope I can repay them soon.

Note

1 Floor timbers 1, midships, and A through E are identical in moulded shape, although the location of the longer arm above their bilges alternates from the port to starboard side.

References

Alertz, U. 2003, The Venetian Merchant Galley and the system of *Partisoni* – Initial steps towards Modern Ship Design. In C. Beltrame (ed.), *Boats, Ships and Shipyards, Proceedings of the Ninth International Symposium on Boat and Ship Archaeology, Venice 2000*, 212–221. Oxford.

Bass, G. and van Doorninck Jr., F., 1978, An 11th century shipwreck at Serçe Liman, Turkey. *International Journal of Nautical Archaeology* 7.2: 119–132.

Bass, G., Matthews, S., Steffy, J. R. and van Doorninck, Jr., F.H., 2004, *Serçe Limanı, An Eleventh-Century Shipwreck. Vol. 1, The Ship and Its Anchorage, Crew and Passengers.* College Station

Bellabarba, S., 1988, The Square-Rigged Ship of the *Fabrica di Galere* Manuscript. *Mariners' Mirror* 74.2: 113–130.

Danis, D.. 2002. *An Analysis of the Galley Ware from a Ninth-Century Shipwreck at Bozburun, Turkey.* Unpublished MA thesis, Texas A&M University.

Gorham, L. D. 2000, *The Archaeobotany of the Bozburun Byzantine Shipwreck.* Unpublished Ph.D. dissertation, Texas A&M University.

Harpster, M. 2002. A Preliminary Report on the 9th-century AD hull found near Bozburun, Turkey. In H. Tzalas (ed.), *TROPIS VII, 7th International Symposium on Ship Construction in Antiquity, Pylos 1999*, 409–418. Athens.

Steffy, J.R., 1994, *Wooden ship building and the interpretation of shipwrecks.* College Station.

17 Oak growing, hull design and framing style. The Cavalaire-sur-Mer wreck, c. 1479

Brad Loewen and Marion Delhaye

During the investigation of a late 15th-century armed vessel at Cavalaire-sur-Mer (Provence), evidence was found of a controlled timber source for the oak frames and of a geometrically-derived hull design. The relationship between these indicators of a sophisticated naval architecture is interesting since the Cavalaire vessel has a 'mixed' framing style that is characteristic of several wrecks dating to the 16th century, especially those having an Ibero-Atlantic or perhaps Basque provenance. Triangular links among framing style, hull design and tree shape suggest that the Basque coast possessed a cohesive shipbuilding culture divided into at least three trades that were conscious of each others' needs, without necessarily having any direct contact. Carpenters, shipwrights and oak growers observed mutually dependent practices that formed a cultural whole. The approach used to study the Cavalaire vessel reveals the structures of a maritime culture with a specific space-time, namely the Basque coast in the 15th-16th centuries. However, a similar approach could be used to examine the structures of shipbuilding cultures from other places and times.

The Cavalaire-sur-Mer vessel

Investigation of the Cavalaire shipwreck from 1993 to 1996 was directed by Marion Delhaye, with funding from the French, Vars and Cavalaire-sur-Mer governments (Delhaye *et al* 1996, 1997). Field operations included the full dismantling of the hull remains and their study on land. The surviving hull measured about 18 metres in length and included most of the port side, from the keel to the stern castle (Fig. 17.1). Nearly all the timbers were of European oak (*Quercus robur*). Each frame consisted of three timbers – floor timber, first futtock, second futtock. Frame scantlings were highly regular : 17 cm square at the bilge, narrowing to 14 cm at the beam.

In the central frames, the floor timber and the first futtock were linked by a mortise-and-tenon assembly, reinforced by treenails and iron nails. The assembly was composed of a square, double mortice – one in the floor timber and the other in the first futtock, set in the

overlapping segments of these timbers. In the bow and stern frames, the floor timber and the first futtock were not assembled but simply overlapped. Second futtocks also were not assembled to first futtocks but simply overlapped. This 'mixed' framing style of assembled and non-assembled timbers was similar to that seen in several 16th-century Atlantic wreck sites.

Hull planks were carvel below the water line, and lapstrake above the water line. Carvel planks were sawn tangentially and lapstrake planks were split radially. Joggles in the second futtocks received the lapstrake planks. Carvel planks measured 5.5 cm thick, 34 to 39 cm wide and up to 11 metres long. Lapstrake planks were 1.5 cm thick and 19 cm wide; no complete example was preserved.

Two features suggested that the Cavalaire wreck had an Atlantic and probably Basque provenance, despite its discovery on the French Mediterranean coast. First, growth patterns in the oak timbers reflected Atlantic (and not Mediterranean) climatic conditions (F. Guibal, pers. comm., 1996). Dendrochronology of these timbers showed no correspondance with available reference chronologies from north of the Loire Valley and thus a provenance south of the Loire was assumed. Second, both treenails and iron nails fastened the hull planks and, especially, reinforced the double mortice in the assembled frame timbers. Such a nailing pattern is observed on 16th-century Basque shipwrecks and is a diagnostic feature of the Ibero-Atlantic typology elaborated by Thomas Oertling (1989, 2001, 2004).

The wreck was initially dated to the second half of the 15th century by the style of the cannons found on the site. Subsequently, the tree-ring sequence of a single repair plank made of larch (*Larix decidua*), located in the ceiling and appearing new compared to the surrounding oak timbers, could be matched to a reference chronology from Savoie in the French Alps, yielding a felling date of 1479 (F. Guibal, pers. comm., 1996). Ceramic shards found on the wreck are Ligurian and Provençal in origin and confirm a date in the later 15th century.

No shipwreck appears in the primary sources at Cavalaire-sur-Mer during this period. However, Basque

Brad Loewen and Marion Delhaye

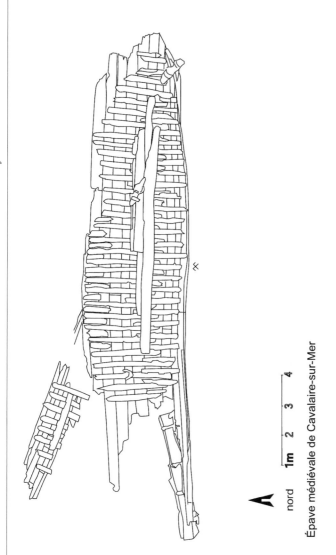

nord

1m 2 3 4

Épave médiévale de Cavalaire-sur-Mer

Fig. 17.1. Site plan of the Cavalaire-sur-Mer (Provence) wreck site (Marion Delhaye).

ships were common on this coast in the later 15th century. They monopolized the wheat trade from North Africa to Genoa (Heers 1955) and, in this period of hostility between Genoa and Venice, armed Basque captains harassed Venetian shipping and took prominent passengers as hostages (Doumerc 1995). Basque shipping into the Mediterranean arose in the 14th-century alum trade from central Italy to north-western Europe and declined with the emergence of Seville as the hub between Atlantic and Mediterranean trade routes at the end of the 15th century (Egaña Goya and Loewen 1995). The Cavalaire vessel thus appears to fit into an historical context when Genoa attracted long-distance Basque captains, outfitting their vessels for trade and arming them as privateers.

Long-distance shipping was synonymous with the Basque ports since the 12th and 13th centuries. Basque ships carried Castillean wool and Aquitanian wine north to the Channel countries, returning with wheat, linseed and forest products that were trans-shipped to southern Iberia. Mediterranean fruit and olive oil paid for the return voyage to the Basque coast. Such a tradition of bulk carriage mixed well with a growing interest in commercial fishing by Basque crews, first in Britanny and Ireland, then in Iceland by about 1412. Shipbuilding was officially encouraged from the 13th century, as is shown by the Basque *fueros*, or provincial customs. In the year 1300,

when the Basque provinces and Castille were united, the *fueros* enshrined an older practice that reserved oak forests within two leagues (11 km) of the sea for shipbuilding. Subsidies for oak planting and shipbuilding were offered to municipalities and private landowners. Again in 1492, these naval customs were renewed by Ferdinand and Isabella and they were strengthened by Philip II when a naval shortage was observed in the 1560s (Egaña Goya and Loewen 1995). History thus reveals a well-developed shipbuilding industry before 1500, but its workings are visible only through the archaeology of Basque ships.

Mixed framing style

The Cavalaire-sur-Mer vessel is characterized by a framing style in which only the floor timber and first futtock of the central frames are assembled. Remaining frame timbers are simply overlapped and held in place by the planking fasteners. This framing style is similar to that of many 16th-century ships and has been the subject of several interpretations. Mark Redknap (1984; 1985), who first described this style based on the Cattewater wreck, called the central frames 'pre-assembled' since their mortices, nails and treenails could only be assembled if the frames were not in place on the keel. He reasoned that the function of the assembled frames was to solidify the hull during construction. Robert Grenier (Grenier 1988; Grenier *et al* 1994), whose work on the 1565 *San Juan* allowed a hull assembly sequence to be inferred from the mixed framing style, suggested that this 16th-century style formed an evolutionary link between medieval 'shell-first' and modern 'skeleton-first' sequences in the Atlantic. The mixed framing style was linked to an 'alternating' construction sequence in which each level of frame timbers was raised, held in place with ribbands, planked and solidified with internal structures before the next level of frame timbers was raised.

Richard Barker suggested that the 'pre-assembled frames' might correspond to the *madeiras da conta*, or group of calculated frames in the central hull that are mentioned in early Portuguese texts on naval architecture (Barker 1988). However, no thorough-going correspondence can be demonstrated in shipwrecks (Loewen 1999). Thomas Oertling (1989, 2001, 2004) has taken a typological approach in suggesting that the mixed framing style, along with other characteristics, forms a regional Ibero-Atlantic style.

Our goal is to document links among the mixed framing style, methods of geometrical hull design and practices of obtaining naval timber in the Cavalaire vessel. Three aspects of the mixed framing style are important for this analysis. First, the upper ends of each level of frame timbers form an uneven but generally fair 'sheer line'. The floor timber wrongheads lie above the turn of the bilge and the heads of the first futtocks above the lowest deck. Timber length is thus linked to sheer lines. Second, the overlapping ends of the timbers lie at positions where two internal timbers clamp them in place. At the bilge, a footwale and the bilge stringer play this role; at the first deck, the beam shelf and the waterway wale clamp the timber ends in place. Timber length is thus also linked to deck height. Third, despite the relative regularity of timber heads, there is no absolute regularity. Timber lengths vary as much as 30 cm and the heads are staggered by at least this amount. Since no frame timbers are butted against each other, timber length is flexible within reasonable bounds. Thus, some variation is allowed in the preparation of timbers.

Renaissance hull design

Reconstruction of the Cavalaire frames has shown that the hull was designed according to geometrical principles found in the earliest texts on naval architecture, dating to the period 1430–1620. The earliest of these texts originate in Venice, while the Atlantic naval centres of Lisbon, Seville and London produced the remaining works in a 50-year period from 1570 to 1620. This corpus of about 15 texts is well known (Loewen 1994; Barker 1991; Rieth 1996; Bellabarba 1996) and our intention here is to draw out key aspects of their study. For example, all begin the process of designing a hull by laying out the basic proportions, then they conceive the master frame within

these proportions and, finally, they modify the master frame so as to mould the remaining frames forward and aft of the master. Closer study reveals that these early texts fall into two 'families', based on the method of modifying the master frame. The English texts describe a method called 'hauling down the futtock', which is a geometrical approach based on the manipulation of tangent circular arcs (Barker 1991). The Venetian, Sevillean and Portuguese texts describe a second method (*legno in sesto, joba, espalhamento*) which produces a non-geometrical arc in the bilge area (Apestegui 1992).

The method of 'hauling down the futtock' has also been documented in the English *Mary Rose* and the Basque-built *San Juan*, both prior to the earliest Atlantic shipbuilding text. These findings suggest that the 'hauling down' method was in fact common to much of the Atlantic at the beginning of the 16th century (Loewen 2001).

The Cavalaire vessel was also designed according to this method (Fig. 17.2). Two aspects of 'hauling down', as observed in the Cavalaire vessel, help to demonstrate links between the framing plan, hull design and timber supply. First, the arc segments used in this method are arranged in a sequence which closely follows that of the frame timbers. The master frame, as well as each assembled frame forward and aft of the master, contains five components connected tangentially, from keel to railing:

- the floor (a straight, horizontal line)
- the bilge arc (a circular arc, generally with a relatively short radius)
- the futtock arc (a circular arc, generally with a relatively long radius)
- the breadth arc (a circular arc, generally with a medium radius)
- the tumblehome (a straight, sloping line)

This regular design meant that all second futtocks in a ship, for example, could have an identical curvature and

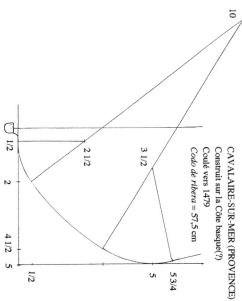

CAVALAIRE-SUR-MER (PROVENCE)
Construit sur la Côte basque(?)
Coulé vers 1479
Codo de ribera = 57,5 cm

Fig. 17.2. The geometrical conception of the master frame, Cavalaire-sur-Mer (Brad Loewen).

Brad Loewen and Marion Delhaye

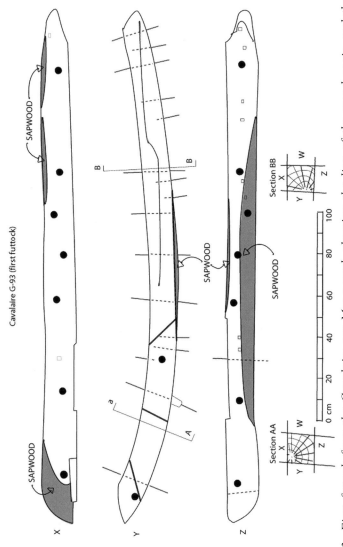

Cavalaire G-93 (first futtock)

Fig. 17.3. First futtock from the Cavalaire-sur-Mer vessel, showing the line of the wood grain and the mortice assembly with the floor timber (Alison McGain and Dominique Lalande).

length, and thus could be mass-prepared in the forest without fear of error. First futtocks as well could be mass-prepared if the radii of the arcs was known.

Second, the bilge arc covers the overlap of the floor timber and the first futtock. This is also the zone affected by the process of 'hauling down the futtock'. To modify the master frame, the futtock arc is lengthened downward, while the bilge arc is reduced by a similar length from one frame to the next, until the bilge arc disappears. This meant that the first futtocks had a variable shape in their lower half. However, due to the ability to slide the futtocks up or down slightly (their ends did not butt against any other timber), it was not necessary to shape them precisely. In fact, several successive frames could contain identical first futtocks, whose overlap with the floor timber and the second futtock could be varied as needed, within reason. Again, this flexibility meant that first futtocks could be moulded ahead of time. The precise geometrical control of the 'hauling down' method could thus be applied efficiently thanks to the mixed framing style.

Timber supply

Data was gathered from the Cavalaire frame timbers to evaluate the correspondance between the tree's original shape and that of the finished timber. Three comparisons were made : the tree's curvature versus that of the timber; the tree's branch-free length versus timber length; the tree's diameter versus the timber's squared dimensions (Loewen 2000).

To compare the curvature of the tree and that of the timber, the centre of the wood grain was traced on the fore or aft face of the frame timber (Fig. 17.3). If the centre of the grain remained within the central part of the timber, correspondance was considered good. While some trees did not have a smooth arc, all showed a high degree of correspondance with the finished shape of the frame timber. In all cases, however, the tree was slightly straighter than the finished timber. This was apparent in the consistent locations of waney edges : on the inboard face at the ends of the timber and on the outboard face in the central portion of the timber's length. In no case, however, did the timber' curvature deviate significantly from that of the parent tree.

The presence of waney edges simplified the comparison of the tree's diameter with the timber's squared dimensions. A diameter of 26 to 29 cm was found for the base of the first and second futtocks. In no case was a tree split in half to produce two futtocks.

Finally, when comparing the branch-free length to that of the finished timber, the first and second futtocks were all found to be free of major branches. This finding would appear to signify that the trees had been pruned so as to produce a better quality of naval timber.

These results suggest that the Cavalaire timbers were obtained in an oak forest where prime naval timber abounded and, likely, careful pruning and selection were practiced. In an effort to determine to what extent this forest was managed, tree age was determined by counting the rings. This was done visually and, in order to limit the margin of error, great care was taken to double check the counts. Finally, the age was rounded off to the nearest five years (Fig. 17.4). Despite the limits of this method, it was clear that the majority of trees used to build the Cavalaire ship had been felled about the age of 65 years (± 5 years). This trend was clearest among the first and second futtocks. Such uniformity of tree ages suggests that the majority of the trees had been used as futtocks had been cultivated and harvested as a single crop.

On the other hand, trees of various ages, including some much older trees, were used for floor timbers. This result appears to reflect a more opportunistic selection process in which forks were collected from all available sources. For example, the forks may have been found in the crowns of 'standard' oaks, normally between 80 and 140 years old at felling, very long in the trunk with a small crown and reserved for planking, beams or internal reinforcements.

When the findings on tree shape and tree age are combined, a picture of a systematic naval forestry trade emerges, especially for the futtocks. In 65 years, no surplus wood was produced and all trees had attained the correct curvature, branch-free length and diameter for use in the Cavalaire vessel. These findings would be compatible with the practice of pollarding, in which old trees are cut at a height of about two metres and four to six new shoots springing from the stump are left to grow into branches. Pollard groves also served as pastures, since high stumps protected new growth from foraging animals. These young branches of a uniform age could be 'trained' to a desired curvature by spreading them apart forcibly with props, while allowing the heads to return naturally to a vertical position (Albion 1926: frontispiece; Marzari 1991: 63; Marzari 1994; Ballu 2000: 76–77). Preparing the trees in this manner was possible in part because of the pre-dictability allowed by the geometrical hull design and the mixed framing style.

Conclusion

The Cavalaire vessel appears to have originated on the Basque coast and is likely a precursor of the 16th-century Basque ships found in the New World. Its mixed framing style is typical of many 16th-century shipwrecks, and can

be linked to the geometrical, 'hauling down' design method that was widespread in 16th-century Atlantic Europe. Study of timber and tree shape, and of tree age at felling, brings naval forestry into focus as a component of the hull design and construction process. Use of a geometrical hull design method and a standard framing style brought a significant degree of predictability to timber shapes, and oak growers appear to have reacted to this predictability by producing timber of a specific diameter and branch-free length and 'training' trees to a specific curvature. In turn, the long growing period for these timbers, about 65 years, kept shipwrights and ship carpenters from innovating new hull shapes or framing styles. Once in place, the triangular relationship among hull design, framing style and timber supply had a tendency to self-perpetuation and only a crisis – a timber shortage, for example – could bring about change.

In another study of Basque shipbuilding in the period 1560–1580 (Grenier et al 1994), archival material was used to show that frame timbers were entirely moulded in the forest by workmen hired by oak planters. Shipowners lent their frame moulds to oak planters, and ship car-

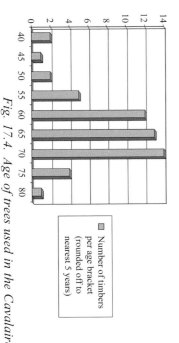

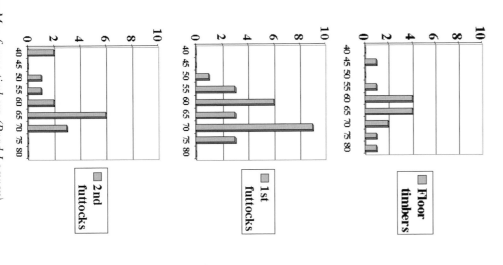

Fig. 17.4. Age of trees used in the Cavalaire-sur-Mer frame timbers (Brad Loewen).

Floor timbers

1st futtocks

2nd futtocks

Number of timbers per age bracket (rounded off to nearest 5 years)

penters merely assembled the pieces that were delivered to them. The community of naval oak planters was therefore an important repository of hull design knowledge. The Cavalaire vessel shows that such a culture of naval forestry was already well developed in the 15th century. Trees destined to be futtocks were 'trained' in the period 1400–1420.

This three-part approach to studying the Cavalaire vessel's frame timbers brings greater clarity to the idea of a regional shipbuilding culture, in which naval forestry, hull design and framing methods are closely related, even though they might be carried out by different people. The Basque coast may represent an especially well-developed paradigm, perhaps because the mountainous terrain and short rivers limited the area that could be devoted to timber production. The mutual dependence among forestry, architecture and carpentry that is suggested by the Cavalaire findings helps us to understand the emergence and perpetuation of regional shipbuilding traditions. The slow regeneration of oak trees meant that naval forestry practices constrained hull design and framing practices to a certain extent. Research is needed to discover whether distinctive traditions of design and framing style arose in regions where oak was abundant and could be obtained in natural or loosely managed forests, as in England, France or the New World colonies, or in regions where the European oak was in limited supply, as in Holland, Portugal or the Mediterranean.

References

Albion, Richard G. 1926, *Forests and Sea Power: The Timber Problem of the Royal Navy, 1652–1862*. Cambridge.

Apestegui Cardenal, Cruz 1992, Análisis técnico de la obra, in F. Fernandez Gonzalez et al (eds.), *Arte de fabricar Reales de Antonio Gastanieta Yturribalzaga, 1680*, pp. 13–32. Barcelona, Lunwerg.

Ballu, Jean-Marie 2000, *Bois de marine. Les bateaux naissent en forêt.* Paris.

Barker, Richard A. 1991, Design in the dockyards, about 1600, in R. Reinders, K. Paul (eds.), *Carvel construction techniques*, pp. 61–69. Oxford.

Barker, Richard A. 1988, 'Many may peruse us.' Ribbands, moulds and models in the dockyards. *Revista da universidade de Coimbra* 34 : 539–559.

Bellabarba, Sergio 1996, The ancient methods of designing hulls. *Mariner's Mirror* 79 :274–292.

Delhaye, Marion, Thirion, G., and Loewen, B., 1996, *L'épave médiévale de Cavalaire-sur-Mer. Bilan des activités de 1992–1995 et programme de fouilles pour 1996.* Unpublished report on file, Marseille, Directorat des recherches en archéologie subaquatique et sous-marine (DRASSM).

Delhaye, Marion, Loewen, B., and Thirion, G.,1997, *L'épave médiévale de Cavalaire-sur-Mer. Bilan des fouilles programmées de 1996.* Unpublished report on file. Marseille, Directorat des recherches en archéologie subaquatique et sous-marine (DRASSM).

Doumerc, Bernard 1995, Pirates basques et galères vénitiennes. La confrontation inévitable (XVe siècle), in *L'aventure maritime, du Golfe de Gascogne à Terre-Neuve. Actes du 118e Congrès annuel des sociétés historiques et scientifiques, Pau, octobre 1993*, pp. 309–318. Paris.

Egaña Goya, Miren and Loewen, Brad, 1995, Dans le sillage des morutiers basques du Moyen Âge. Une perspective sur l'origine et la diffusion du mot bacallao. *L'aventure maritime, du Golfe de Gascogne à Terre-Neuve. Actes du 118e Congrès annuel des sociétés historiques et scientifiques, Pau, octobre 1993*, pp. 235–250. Paris.

Grenier, Robert. 1988, Basque whalers in the New World, in G. Bass (ed.), *Ships and shipwrecks of the Americas*, pp. 69–84. London.

Grenier, Robert, Loewen, B., and Proulx, J.-P., 1994, Basque shipbuilding technology ca. 1560–1580: the Red Bay project. In C. Westerdahl (ed.), *Crossroads in Ancient Shipbuilding. Proceedings of 6th International Symposium on Boat and Ship Archaeology, Roskilde, 1990*, pp. 137–141. Oxford.

Heers, Jacques. 1955, Le commerce des Basques en Méditerranée au XVe siècle. *Bulletin hispanique*, 57: 292–320.

Loewen, Brad 2001, The structures of Atlantic shipbuilding in the 16th century. An archaeological perspective. In F. Alves (ed.), *Proceedings of the International Symposium on Archaeology of Medieval and Modern Ships of Iberian-Atlantic Tradition*, pp. 241–258. Lisbon.

Loewen, Brad 2000, Forestry practices and hull design, ca. 1400–1700. In F. Contente Domingues (ed.)., *Fernando Oliveira e o Seu Tempo. Humanismo e Arte de Navegar no Renascimento Europeu (1450–1650)*, pp. 143–151. Cascais.

Loewen, Brad 1999, The morticed frames of XVIth century Atlantic ships and the madeiras da conta of Renaissance texts. In P. Pomey, É. Rieth (eds.), *Construction navale maritime et fluviale. Approches archéologique, historique et ethnologique. Archaeonautica 14. Actes du 7e Colloque international d'archéologie navale*, pp. 213–221. Paris.

Loewen, Brad 1994, Codo, carvel, mould and ribband: the archaeology of ships, 1450–1620. *Mémoires-vives*, 6–7: 6–21.

Marzari, Mario 1994, Dalla Foresta al Mare. In *Alle soblier della rivoluzione tecnologica, 1793–1993. Josef Resel : un inventore a Trieste*, pp. 91–106. Trieste.

Marzari, Mario 1991, *Uomini e Barche. Cinque secoli di costruzione navali.* Mariano del Friuli.

Oertling, Thomas J. 2004, Characteristics of Fifteenth- and Sixteenth-Century Iberian Ships. In F.M. Hocker and C.A. Ward (eds.), *The Philosophy of Shipbuilding. Conceptual approaches to the study of wooden ships*, pp. 129–136. College Station, Texas.

Oertling, Thomas J. 2001, The concept of the Atlantic vessel. In F. Alves (ed.), *Proceedings of the International Symposium on Archaeology of Medieval and Modern Ships of Iberian-Atlantic Tradition*, pp. 233–240. Lisbon.

Oertling, Thomas J. 1989, The few remaining clues. In J.B. Arnold III (ed.), *Underwater archaeology proceedings from the Society for Historical Archaeology Conference, Baltimore, 1989*, pp. 100–103.

Redknap, Mark 1985, The Cattewater wreck. A contribution to 16th-century maritime archaeology. In C.O. Cederlund (ed.), *Postmedieval Boat and Ship Archaeology*, BAR International Series 256, pp. 39–59. Oxford.

Redknap, Mark. 1984, *The Cattewater wreck. The Investigation of an Armed Vessel of the Early Sixteenth Century.* BAR British Series 131. Greenwich.

Rieth, Éric. 1996, *Le maître-gabarit, la tablette et le trébuchet.* Paris.

18 Ship design in Holland in the eighteenth century

Ab Hoving

Introduction

This paper is not about the slowly growing outdatedness of Dutch ships and shipbuilding methods in the early 18th century compared with other European countries, nor is it about the growing demands that both the Navy and the VOC made on the shipbuilders of those days (Lemmers 1996: 48). I will not explain how the Dutch Republic had five Admiralties, the most important next to Amsterdam being Rotterdam and Middelburg in Zealand (nor the fact that most of the time they were rivals more than allies), nor will I speak about the introduction of English shipwrights into the Amsterdam Admiralty shipyard in 1727 (Bruyn 1998). I will not touch upon the insulting article the Amsterdam Admiral Schrijver wrote in 1756 about the lack of quality of the Dutch shipwrights in general and those of the other Admiralties in particular and I will not sum up the list of books and publications that were written by Dutch shipbuilders to defend themselves against his contemptuous insinuations (Hoving and Lemmers, 2001: 157 and bibliography).

My paper is about a method of ship design that was developed in Rotterdam by the master shipbuilder of the Admiralty shipyard there, Paulus van Zwijndregt, a member of a shipbuilding family which worked in Rotterdam from late in the 17th, up to the middle of the 19th century. Paulus built the first ship in Holland ever to be built from previously made draughts in 1725. She was called *Twikkelo*, and she was a 56-gun man-of-war. I want to demonstrate his techniques to you just to show you the sheer beauty of his geometrical solutions, developed in the same years Johan Sebastian Bach wrote his fugues with the same sort of mathematical logic, inventiveness and taste.

Van Zwijndregt applied his method of design two years before the English shipwrights arrived in Amsterdam, which proves that, contrary to what has been assumed up to now, ship design on paper was not after all introduced in Holland by the British (Lemmers 1996: 45). What a relief.

The English method

I am aware of the fact that you all know much better than I do how the British designed their ships, but I will give a short abstract of the method, adopted from a description that Charles Bentam, one of the imported British shipwrights, wrote in the 1730s about his drawing techniques for his master, the Admiral Schrijver, mentioned above. Bentam writes that he starts with an elevation drawing, in which keel, stem and stern are indicated. Next he places the decks and draws in the gunports. The regular frame stations were then fixed between the gunports. This, Bentam emphasises modestly, is very clever compared to the Dutch practice: they built their hull first and cut in the gunports later, thus destroying beautiful and expensive, long pieces of wood. The shape of his main frame is put together from a couple of segments of different circles. Now in both the plan view and the elevation draught he draws four very important lines: the *rising line of floors* and the *rising line of breadth* in his elevation, and the *narrowing line of floors* and the *narrowing line of breadth* in his plan view. In my perspective drawing in Fig. 18.1, you can see that they actually represent only two lines on each side, that define the lines of the ship. There are geometrical methods to construct those lines, but Bentam, not being a top designer, probably used moulds he brought from England when he ran away to get his Dutch appointment. Next he takes the shape of his main frame and fits the main part of it between the two lines and moving it forwards and backwards, the same frame shape is repeated over and over again, but the centre of the circles move with the narrowing and rising lines inwards and upwards. As the drawing is eventually to be enlarged on the mould loft floor by illiterate persons, the radii that indicate the circle-segments are represented in the draught and can be seen as very characteristic of British technical shipdraughts.

It is most time consuming to work your way through three dimensions to produce a lines plan for a ship to be built and the system hardly guarantees fine lines.

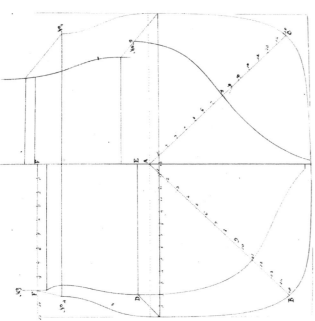

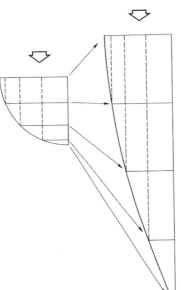

Fig. 18.2. Body plan showing key frame shapes in the 'Continental' method (author).

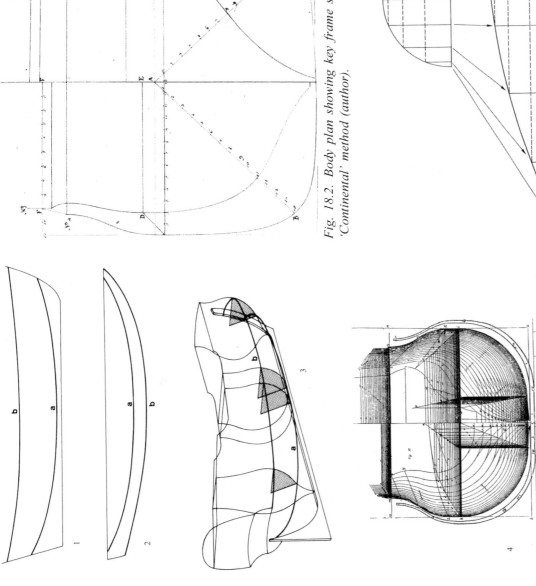

Fig. 18.1. The key components (sections, rising and narrowing lines) in Bentam's design method (author).

Fig. 18.3. Geometrical device for determining the intermediate frames in the 'Continental' method (author).

The 'Continental' method

So far nothing new I suppose. There is however a completely different method, that may be a little bit more abstract, but works a lot more simply and faster. I call it the Continental method, although that is probably because of my lack of knowledge over the entire field. The fact is that both in France and in Holland variations of the method were applied. It works with a body plan only.

The length of the ship between perpendiculars was divided into twelve equal intervals, requiring eleven frames. The starting point is the main frame (Fig. 18.2), which was decided by the shipwright and placed at 5/12 of the length from the bow. Quarter frames were then defined at 1/12 (no 1) and 11/12 (no 11) positions. The variation of the eight moulded frames between those three frames was controlled by the geometric device in Fig. 18.3. Thus for the fore part, he uses a quarter of a circle,

which he divides into four equal pieces, which brings him three intermediate points. Projecting these to the base line finds his division for frames 2, 3 and 4. For the after part he divides the quarter circle into six which produces the required division for five frames (nos 6,7,8,9 and 10). As the parts of the base line are stretched with equal lengths the quarter circle changes into a line we call a sine. A sine is a good line to start from if we want a ribband-line on a ship's hull. These eleven frames were sufficient to run ribbands from stem to stern.

Van Zwijndregt's contribution

How was this applied to the drawing? As you can see in this sequence strip (Fig. 18.4) a piece of paper is placed over the diagonal that runs in the frame drawing between deck-height and the corner of the square and the distance between frame number 1 and 5 is notched on it (let's limit ourselves to the ship's fore-part). From the division a 'triangle' is made, which has equal sides (isosceles). By putting the card parallel to the base line in the triangle, in such a way that both notches coincide with the outside lines, the division can be copied on the card and brought back into the frame drawing. The division is marked on the diagonal in the frame drawing and more diagonals are drawn and treated in the same way. Now the shipwright can draw a line along a flexible batten that connects the marks on the diagonals. Very simple, probably widely known in those days... but not completely satisfying. The method is beautiful for finding the shapes of intermediate

frames, but it allows no adjustment of the frames into a more useful shape. Leaving the method as it is, no variations are allowed in the shape of the ribbands. The trick was to find a method to do that, to find a way to twist and curve the constructed lines in such a way that they resulted in a fine operating ship shape, that could be corrected as wished for the next ship to be built. Fig. 18.5 shows a very early draught by a French shipwright, Mr Coulomb, who made an effort in 1689 to draw a 'fluit' here. Anyone who knows anything about fluits sees that the shape has nothing to do with what was understood to be a fluit in Holland, but the drawing and its dating show that the method was spreading, long before van Zwijndregt made his adaptations in 1725, because the triangles and the parallel lines are in the drawing.

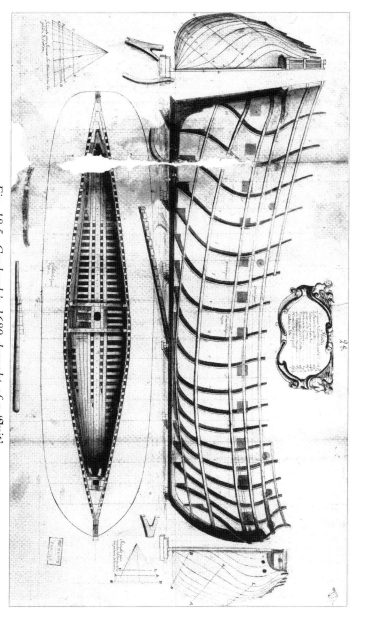

Fig. 18.5. Coulomb's 1689 draught of a 'fluit'.

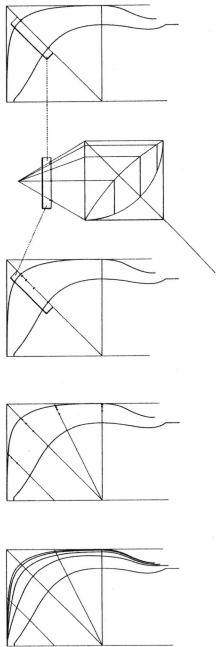

Fig. 18.4. Sequence of use of card device for generating intermediate frame shapes (author).

Ab Hoving

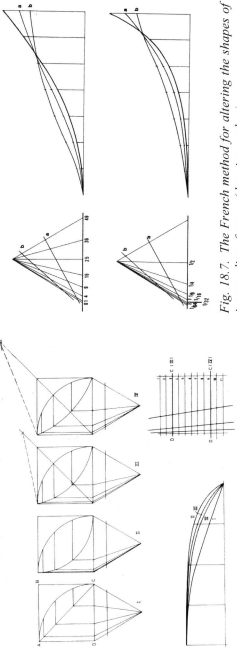

Fig. 18.7. *The French method for altering the shapes of intermediate frames (drawing author).*

Fig. 18.6. *Van Zwijndregt's invention (author).*

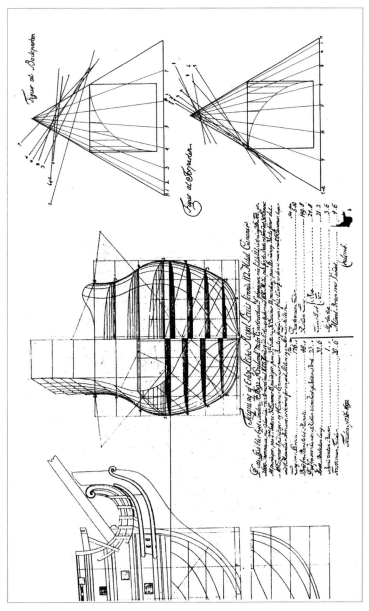

Fig. 18.8. *French draught of the period.*

Fig. 18.6 shows what van Zwijndregt invented: He introduced a second circle segment, drawn from the diagonal of the square. The three points on the initial curve are projected on to the second circle segment and next to the base line. By varying the radius of the second curve, van Zwijndregt had a system to manipulate his lines. The shorter the radius, the fuller the line, the longer the radius, the shallower the curve.

Was it unique? Yes. As a comparison it is interesting to see what solutions the French had to this variation problem, because they used a method basically similar to van Zwijndregt's, and were famous for it.

The French method

In France, the geometrical method was exchanged for a mathematical one (Fig. 18.7). The starting point was no longer a geometrical figure, but a division of the base line, derived by mathematical or arithmetical progressions, such as points decided by squared numbers or repeatedly halving a line, producing ellipses and parabolas as ribband-lines. The triangle was made in the same manner as van Zwijndregt's, but to manipulate the curves, the French did not carry the divisions over parallel to the base line, but at different angles, which also causes the line to curve in different ways (Boudriot 1988). In Fig. 18.8, you can see

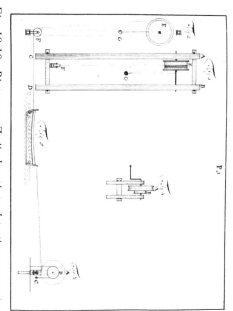

Fig. 18.10. Pieter van Zwijndregt's tank testing apparatus.

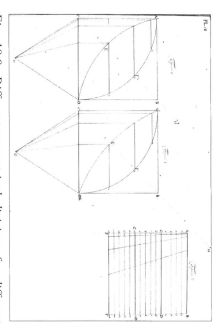

Fig. 18.9. Different geometrical divisions for different sized ships (after van Zwijndregt).

Van Zwijndregts inventiveness

When we return to the Rotterdam method, we see a completely different solution to register the lines and to make them reproducible (Fig. 18.9). By using one division for a very full ship and another one for a very slender ship, all possibilities in between could be found without executing the whole procedure over and over again and by numbering the different divisions it became very simple to register the curves used for any specific ship.

Van Zwijndregt's son Pieter probably was the first to execute valid water resistance tests, which was before 1757, the date given to his manuscript (Fig. 18.10), in order to be able to choose a good set of lines. The method he used in testing resistance of different shapes in water was not applied to ship models, but to planks (Fig. 18.11), sawn in the shape of different waterlines, and he used a swinging pendulum to register the time it took the planks to be towed over a distance of 163 feet. He also tested

that the triangles used were drawn together with the draught, to register the origin of the lines.

reversed curves and the effect of the rudder combined with different waterline shapes. A close look at the contraption he used for his tests gives us a strong conviction that Chapman had seen van Zwijndregt's apparatus when he visited Holland around 1755, as the one he used for his own tests (as illustrated in his book in 1775) looked very similar (Fig. 18.12; Chapman 1775).

The divisions I showed you were called triangle-scales and were scribed into copper plates, to be used over and over again, just as van Zwijndregt had copper plates in which he scribed dimensions for stems, sterns, placing of masts, etc., using different formulae for different types of ships as well as for big and small ships, so that all the sizes in between could be taken from the plates without the necessity of any calculation (Fig. 18.13). Here we see the predecessor of the slide rule.

Fig. 18.14 shows the draught of Twikkelo of 1725, containing all the information needed to build a ship. When he became Master of the Admiralty dockyard in the 1760's, Pieter van Zwijndregt made draughts for all the different rates of men-of-war that the Dutch navy used. He was, in effect, the first to take the first uncertain steps on the long path to standardisation of the Dutch navy.

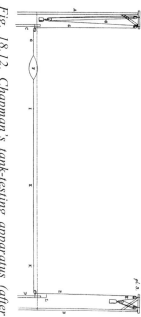

Fig. 18.12. Chapman's tank-testing apparatus (after Chapman).

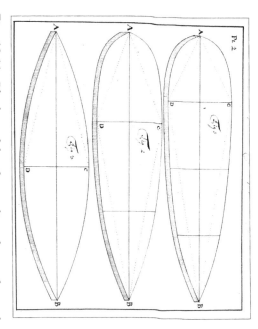

Fig. 18.11. Plank models of waterline shapes for tank testing (after van Zwijndregt).

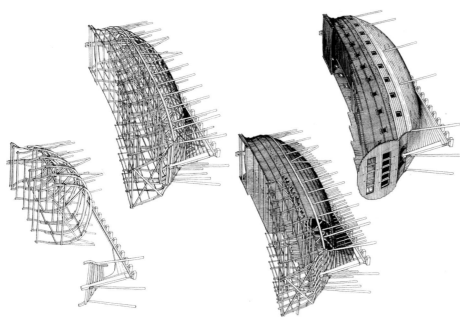

Fig. 18.15. Building method resulting from van Zwijn-dregt's design technique (author).

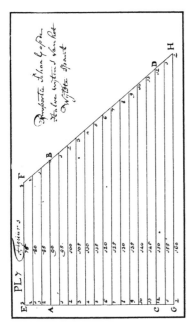

Fig. 18.13. One of van Zwijndregt's triagular scales.

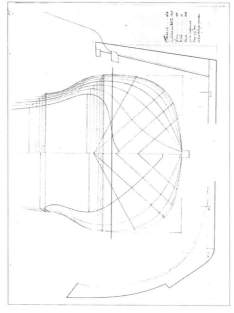

Fig. 18.14. Draught of Twikkelo (1725) by Paulus van Zwijndregt.

Conclusion

Making draughts changed the method of building in the yard: eleven frames were erected, connected by ribbands and the missing frames were filled in using the ribbands as a reference (Fig. 18.15). That is how the advantages of traditional methods were maintained, because neither speed of building, nor the costs, changed, and yet ships could still be improved systematically. Besides these advantages, draughts changed the role of the shipwright: his presence was no longer necessary in the yard and he became a naval engineer more and more, although real calculations about stability, speed and resistance were not made by master-shipbuilders during the eighteenth century in Holland.

Although Van Zwijndregt did not publish his method for the benefit of his colleagues, the conclusion must be that Dutch 18th-century shipbuilders and the level on which they carried out their craft were by no means as backward as we have always thought they were.

Acknowledgement

Thanks to Richard Barker for correcting the text.

References

Unpublished primary sources

Bentam, C., *Memorie over de Scheepsbouw, opgetekend uit de mond van* – (s.d.). Manuscript in the Fagel Archive, Royal Library, The Hague.

van Zwijndregt, P. Pzn. *De Groote Nederlandsche Scheepsbouw op een Proportionaale Reegel Voor Gestelt.* Manuscript in Nederlands Scheepvaartmuseum, Amsterdam. Set of 20 draughts in Maritime Museum Rotterdam.

Published sources

Boudriot, J. March 1988, La conception des vaisseaux royaux sous l' ancien regime. In *Neptunia* 169.

Bruyn J.R., 1998, *Varend Verleden. De Nederlandse oorlogs-vloot in de 17de en 18de eeuw.* Amsterdam.

af Chapman, F.H. 1775.*Tractat om Skeppsbyggeriet.* Stock-holm.

Hoving, A.J. and Lemmers, A.A., 2001, *In Tekening Gebracht.* Amsterdam..

Lemmers, A.A. 1996, *Techniek op schaal. Modellen en het technologiebeleid van de Marine 1725–1885.* Amsterdam.

19 Archaeobotanical characterisation of three, ancient, sewn, Mediterranean shipwrecks

Stéphanie Wicha and Michel Girard

Introduction

An archaeobotanical project has been in place since 1991 entitled *"Dendrochronology and dendromorphology of ancient shipwrecks in the Mediterranean"*. This program, which is run by the CNRS and supported by DRASSM and the French Ministry of Culture (Guibal and Pomey 1998), aims to establish a set of reference samples for the dendrochronological analysis of Mediterranean wood, in order to meet the needs of archaeological dating.

In addition to this program, a previously unknown ancient sewing construction technique was discovered for the first time on the Cap Béar 3 wreck (c 60–70 BC), excavated by Colls between 1982 and 1987. This system

was evidence of a previously unknown tradition of ship construction (Pomey 2002), and has been subsequently identified on twelve other ships found in the western Mediterranean, near Spain, France, and Sicily, dating to between the 3rd century BC and the 1st century AD: Tour Fondue (v. 250–225 BC); Roche Fouras (v. 150–100 BC); Cavalière (v. 100 BC); Dramont C (v. 75–50 BC); Plane 1 (v. 50 BC); Cap Béar 3 (v. 50–25 BC); Cap del Vol (v. 25 BC–25 AD); L'îlot Barthélémy B (v. 25–50 AD); Saintes Maries 24 (v. 50 AD); Baie de l'Amitié (50–100 AD); Port la Nautique (v. 100 BC–70 AD) and Perduto 1 (100 AD) (Fig. 19.1). Two other wrecks, the Jeaume Garde B (v. 125–75 BC) and Marsala (v. 250 BC) also

Fig. 19.1. Baie de l'Amitié shipwreck discovered in western Mediterranean, France (photo: Ch. Durand, Centre Camille Jullian, CNRS, Aix en Provence, France).

Stéphanie Wicha and Michel Girard

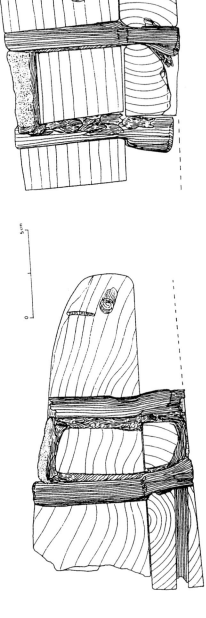

Fig. 19.2. Cavalière shipwreck, sewing assembly that joins the planks to the frame (drawn by M. Rival, Centre Camille Jullian, CNRS, Aix en Provence, France).

display this construction technique but only for repairs or in short sections.

With the exception of the Marsala shipwreck, all these ships were intended for trade; the dimensions of the most wrecks vary between 10 to 13 m, although three of them are larger, from 20 to 30 m (Baie de l'Amitié, Cap del Vol and Saintes Marie 24). Between them, these wrecks offer substantial evidence of a tradition of shipbuilding which dates to at least the end of the 3rd – beginning of 1st century BC, as shown by the wreck of Marsala, and one that appears to have been widespread in the western Mediterranean between the 1st century BC and the 1st century AD. At present, both the chronology and origin of this technique remain unknown. In order to locate the geographical origins of the shipyards where these ships were built, we have carried out wood identification and palynological analysis of pitch samples taken from these ships.

"*Ces navires qui se composent pour l'essentiel d'une quille, d'un bordé assemblé à franc-bord par tenons et mortaises, d'une membrure alternée composée de varangues et de demi-couples, d'une emplanture encastrée sur les varangues, de vaigres et de serres, sont d'un type habituel en méditerranée antique*"

"These ships, which are essentially composed of a keel, planks fastened with mortises and tenons, alternating frames of floor timbers and half-frames, a stepped recess on the floor timbers, ceiling planks and inboard clamps, are typical of traditional ancient Mediterranean shipbuilding" (Pomey 2002).

There is little difference in the structural characteristics of the wrecks, with the exception of Baie de l'Amitié (Wicha 2001: 43–44) and Cap del Vol (Nieto and Foerster 1980), both of which have an original flat keel.

The principal interest in studying these shipwrecks is the use of a particular technique for attaching the frames to strakes.

Two construction techniques have been identified on these ships:

• the first is the traditional ancient Mediterranean

shipbuilding construction technique, with planks secured by mortises and tenons;

• the second was until recently unknown, and features a sewing assembly system which joins the planks to the frames. Stitches were passed through two holes in order to attach the frames to the strakes. Subsequently, long treenails were put into these two holes to secure the stitches, and then a large quantity of pitch was applied in order to protect and waterproof the stitches (Fig. 19.2).

The discovery of original tree species in three ships: Cavalière, Cap Béar 3 and Baie de l'Amitié (Table 19.1)

Of these thirteen wrecks, three are of particular interest due to the identification of the species of wood used in their construction: Cavalière, Cap Béar 3 and Baie de l'Amitié.

The Cavalière wreck (c 100 BC)

The Cavalière wreck (c 100 BC) is located in the Bay of Cavalière (Var, France), at a depth of 43 m. It was approximately 13 m long, and was found with its cargo. The cargo comprised amphorae originating from different parts of the Mediterranean region: Italy, France, Spain and Africa. Forty-four wood samples were taken: from the keel (2), strakes (22) and frames (20), and show a substantial use of a single tree species, the Bosnian pine (*Pinus heldreichii* Christ.). This wood is well known for its mechanical qualities, and is found living in extreme edaphic and climatic conditions (Avolio 1996). This pine species was used for the longitudinal structural members, strakes, and transverse structural elements, such as floor timbers and half-frames. Two additional strakes were made using wood from *Pinus sylvestris* L. (1991: 324).

	Cavalière (1)	Plane 1 (1)	Roche Fouras (1)	La Tour Fondue (1)	Barthélemy B(2)	Dramont C (2)	Cap Béar 3 (2)	Baie de l'Amitié (3)	SM24 (3)	Jeaume Garde (B)	Marsala
Framing	Bosnian pine	Poplar, alder, Aleppo pine	Oak, willow, elm	Aleppo pine	Aleppo pine	oak	Spruce, holm oak, fir, Aleppo pine	Elm, ash, beech, plane, oak, walnut, Aleppo pine, pear	Elm, ash, oak, Bosian pine, poplar, fir	Aleppo pine, elm	Oak, fir, Bosnian pine, elm
Keel	Bosnian pine			Holm oak, Aleppo pine	Aleppo pine	Holm oak					oak
Upper false keel					beech						
Planking	Bosnian pine	Scots pine	fir	Aleppo pine	Aleppo pine	Aleppo pine	Fir, spruce, Aleppo pine, Scots pine				
Ceiling planking		Aleppo pine	fir		fir			oak	oak	Scots pine	oak
Stringers		Aleppo pine				Aleppo pine	Spruce, fir				
Keelson							alder			Scots pine	
Floor Ceilings		Aleppo pine									
Wedging elements		ash									
Stanchion									boxwood		

Table 19.1. Synoptic table: Wood species employed in the selected wrecks and different constructional parts of the selected wrecks (by Wicha). The following categorises the wrecks listed by differentiating shape:

1. Vessels that have a quadrangular shape or are higher than they are broad, with a wine glass shaped lower hull.

2. Vessels that are broader than they are high and have a round or angular form shaped hull.

3. Vessels that are broader than they are high and have a flat bottom.

Stéphanie Wicha and Michel Girard

The Cap Béar 3 wreck (c 50–25 BC)

The Cap Béar 3 wreck (c 50–25 BC) is located near Port Vendres (Pyrennées Orientales) at a depth of 40 m. It was exceptionally well conserved, with its cargo in place. This merchant vessel was approximately 12 m long, and was carrying materials from Spain. Forty-nine samples were collected and analysed from the Cap Béar 3 wreck. Five tree species were identified, with the largest variety of wood found for the frames and strakes – *Picea abies* Karsten (29), *Abies* Mill. (7), *Pinus halepensis* Mill. (10), *Quercus ilex* (1) and *Pinus silvestris* L (1), and *Alnus glutinosa* Gaertn, as well as an unidentified part made using wood from *Carpinus betulus* L. *Quercus ilex* L. was used to make the pegs and tenons, and *Abies alba* was used for the treenails associated with the stitches.

The Cap Béar 3 wreck is primarily composed of resinous species, in particular *Picea abies* Karsten (56%). This species, which can usually live for 300–400 years, can reach 45 to 50 m in height. The wood of this species is easy to work and had previously been discovered in the Planier 3 wreck, where it was used in the formation of a curved timber. This is the only other evidence of the use of *Picea abies* Karst. in the construction of frames, strakes and inboard planks (Rival 1991: 324). In addition to this species, *Pinus halepensis* Mill., *Abies alba* Mill. (only one sample) and *Quercus* sp. (also for only one sample) were identified from samples taken from strakes and inboard planks, and *Abies alba* Mill. and *Pinus* type *sylvestris* were identified. The two latter species are commonly used in the construction of ancient ships as the "Dendrochronology and Dendromorphology of the ancient wrecks of the Mediterranean sea" research program has demonstrated (Guibal and Pomey 1998).

The Baie de l'Amitié wreck (c 70–80 AD)

The Baie de l'Amitié wreck (c 70–80 AD) is located near Agde (Herault) at a depth of 3 m. This merchant vessel was approximately 20 m long and the majority of its cargo (amphora, ingots) came from Spain. Forty-one samples were collected and analysed and ten tree species have been identified. This ship is remarkable, because it is the only known occurrence of a hull which was entirely made from deciduous species, with eight identified: *Ulmus* sp., *Fraxinus* sp., *Fagus* sp., *Platanus orientalis* L, *Pirus* sp., *Juglans* J., *Acer pseudoplatanus* L and *Quercus* sp., the latter representing the main wood species used in the construction, particularly for some of the frames and for all strakes. This is the first time that deciduous oak has been recognised in the construction of the strakes of an ancient ship. In addition, this is the first time that the plane tree (*Platanus orientalis* L.) has been identified in the construction of an ancient ship. Theophrastus described the use of this species for shipbuilding, but it appears that ancient shipbuilders preferred *Ulmus* sp. or *Fraxinus* sp. *Platanus orientalis* L. has similar technical properties to *Fagus* sp., but this is perishable and rather unsuitable for

outdoor use. In total, nine species were identified in the remains of the Baie de l'Amitié ship. In addition to the traditional use of *Quercus ilex* L. for the tenons and pegs, *Abies alba* Mill. was used for the treenails associated with stitches. This choice is probably justified by the need for a non-astringent and flexible wood.

Palynological study

In the same study, resin samples were collected from the Baie de l'Amitié and Cap Béar 3 shipwrecks for palynological analysis. Their analyses showed that most samples coming from these ships contain only a low quantity of pine pollen. Furthermore, the presence of many carbonised elements in the majority of samples may originate from the use of a mixture of pitch and resin; pitch obtained by the distillation of wood is characterised by an abundance of carbonised elements. Once solidified, these pitches will not be contaminated by further pollen deposition, although they may have been melted several times. For a small trading vessel, we can assume that the vessel was coated in pitch at the same time and in the same place as it was constructed.

Baie de l'Amitié ship

One of the eight samples from the Baie de l'Amitié wreck was particularly rich in pollen. The sample is characterised by a high number of mesophile taxa (32%) such as *Quercus* sp., *Carpinus betulus* L. and *Fagus sylvatica* L., as well as typically Mediterranean species (13%), such as *Pinus* t. *pinaster*, *Quercus* t. *ilex/coccifera* and *Platanus orientalis* L., and other taxa which represent crop plants, such as *Olea* and *Vitis*. Herbaceous plants were also represented in the pollen sampled and were dominated by Graminaceaeous pollen, including several cereal crop pollens that indicate open-land with a small amount of cultivation, waste areas that were covered by Graminaceous, *Helianthemum*, *Malva*, *Heliotropium*, *Sanguisorba*, Filicales, zones of high human impact that contain species such as *Polygonum* t. *aviculare*, or plowed areas indicated by Chenopodiaceae, *Artemisia* sp. and Cichoriae, *Plantago* species. The existence of a wetland located nearby is suggested by the presence of *Alnus* sp., *Fraxinus* sp., and Isoetaceae and Cyperaceae which prefer the banks of wide calm waters.

Cap Béar 3 ship

The three samples taken from the Cap Béar 3 wreck are dominated by mesophyte species. Each sample shows the presence of Mediterranean taxa, with highly variable percentages. Amongst the herbaceous taxa there is a relatively high proportion of cereals as well Graminaceous, Chenopodiaceae and Cruciferae. The presence of *Ononis* is notable as it occurs in dry and even rocky places. At the same time, evidence is found of aquatic plants such as *Sparganium* and the *Lemna* and taxa that occur in wet terrestrial and aquatic places, for example Cyperaceae, *Equisetum* and *Lythrum*. In the last sample *Quercus suber* L. pollen was found, which grows on acid substrate, and *Ostrya carpinifolia* Scop. pollen, which has a primarily eastern distribution. The large number of herbaceous taxa, the marked presence of cereals and the messicoles-partners, particularly the group of plants indicative of meadows or waste lands, show that the landscapes in which the pitch was made had a strong anthropogenic influence.

Conclusion

The three boats show a number of similarities but also differences that therefore prevent a definitive interpretation of a common geographical origin, although the possibility that the ships were constructed using the same techniques suggests that they may have come from the same region. However, they were not contemporary as the varying dates of the cargo indicate: Cavalière (c 100 BC), Cap Béar 3 (c 50–25 BC) and the Baie de l'Amitié (c 70–80 BC). The observed differences in the ship construction over time could represent changes in ancient shipbuilding.

Bosnian pine, discovered on the wreck of Cavalière, is common in some mountainous areas of the Mediterranean region. It is present from Calabria to as far as Bulgaria, but the most significant stands are in Bosnia, Serbia, Montenegro, Albania and in Greece (Quézel and Médail 2003: 573). The plane tree (*Platanus orientalis* L.) identified at Baie de l'Amitié, is one of the dominant

riparian species of the valleys of the central-eastern Mediterranean, in southern Italy (Campany, Calabria, Sicily), the Balkan Peninsula, the coasts of Macedonia and those of Asia Minor. Spruce (*Picea abies* Karst) identified at Cap Béar 3, is found in large areas throughout central Europe, the transalpine Alps, the Apennines, the Croatian coast and the coasts of Macedonia. This species, which is located at some distance from the coasts, was undoubtedly brought to the shipbuilding site (Fig. 19.3).

There is a large variation in the composition of tree species found in the Cavalière, Cap Béar 3 and Baie de l'Amitié hulls, nevertheless, they appear to define a possible area of timber supply in either the central or eastern Mediterranean, at least for Cavalière and Baie de l'Amitié. However, this raises the question of the relationship between the shipbuilding and operation areas, as these ships sank in the western Mediterranean Sea, off Cavalière (Var), Port-Vendres (Pyrennées Orientales) and Cap d'Agde (Hérault).

Generally, the xylological and palynological results are coherent. The occurrence of similar taxa in the results from Baie de l'Amitié, notably *Platanus orientalis*, suggests that construction of the hull and the application of resin were contemporary. The palynological results allow us to construct a more general view of the landscape in which this ship was built: a strongly anthropogenic landscape, with a substantial amount of cultivation and in close proximity to wet or humid environments. The discovery of *Picea abies* in the xylological analyses of the Cap Béar 3 ship suggests the transportation of timber to the construction site. This appears to be confirmed by the palynological analysis. When both sets of results are

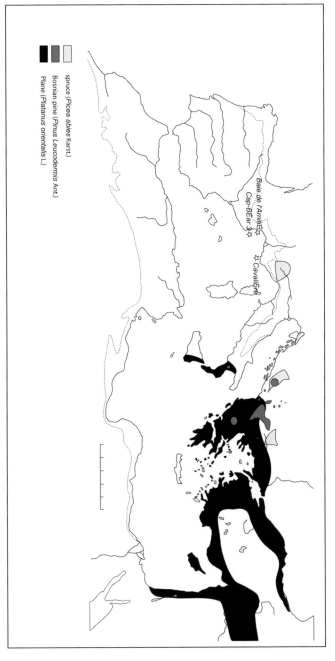

Fig. 19.3. Localisation of the three shipwrecks (in western Mediterranean) and the wood species which are used in their construction (in central-eastern Mediterranean (according to Quézel and Médail 2003).

spruce (*Picea abies* Karst.)
Bosnian pine (*Pinus Leucodermis* Ant.)
Plane (*Platanus orientalis* L.)

combined a number of key points emerge: the association of the species with acid ground, the identification of *Ostrya carpinifolia*, and the presence of *Picea abies*, which combined make it possible to limit the zone of construction to the eastern Mediterranean.

References

Avolio, S., 1996, *Il Pino Loricato (Pinus leucodermis Ant.)*. Emblema del Parco Nazionale del Pollino.

Guibal, F. and Pomey, P., 1998, Dendrochronologie et dendromorphologie. Archeologia Subacquea, come opera l'archeologo storie dalle acque. In *VIII Ciclo di Lezioni sulla Ricerca applicata in Archeologia Certosa di Pontignano (Siena), 9–15 Dicembre 1996*, 425–446. Edizioni All'Insegna del Giglio. Firenze.

Nieto, F. and Foerster, F., 1980, El pecio romano del Cap del Vol (Campanas de 1978 y 1979). In *Cypsela*, III, 163–177. Diputació de Girona, Servei d'Investigacions Arqueològiques, Conservació i Catalogació de Monuments. Girona.

Pomey, P., 2002, Une nouvelle tradition technique d'assemblage antique: l'assemblage de la membrure par ligatures et chevilles. In H. Tzalaz (ed) *Tropis VII, Seventh International Symposium of ship Construction in Antiquity*, 597–604, Pylos. 1999. Hellenic Institute for the Preservation of Nautical Tradition. Athens.

Quezel, P. and Médail, F., 2003, *Ecologie et biogéographie des forêts du bassin méditerranéen*. Elsevier. Paris.

Rival, M. (ed), 1991, *La charpenterie navale romaine. Matériaux, méthodes, moyens*. Éditions du Centre national de la recherche scientifique. Paris.

Théophraste, 1916, *Historia plantarum: with English translation by Sir Arthur Holt*. Heinemann. London.

Wicha, S., Guibal, F. and Médail, F., 2004, Archeobotanical characterisation of three ancient Mediterranean shipwrecks. In Fouche, E. (ed) *Actes du colloque international 2002: Dynamiques environnementales et Histoire en domaines méditerranéens*, 229–234. Elsevier. Paris.

Wicha, S., 2003, Un bateau antique (Barthelemy B) détenant un assemblage original par ligatures végétales chevillées. Une tradition technique dont l'origine reste à préciser. *Cahiers d'archéologie subaquatique 2003*, 135–143. Ministère de la Culture (SDA). Paris.

Wicha, S., 2001, L'épave antique de la *Baie de l'Amitié* (vers 70–80 BC). Cap d'Agde (Hérault). In *Bilan scientifique du Département des recherches archéologiques sous-marines 2001*, 43–44. Ministère de la Culture (SDA). Paris.

20 Coating, sheathing, caulking and luting in ancient shipbuilding

Ronald Bockius

Introduction

As reflected by many shipwrecks found in the Mediterranean and north of the Alps, shipyards took particular care to ensure watertightness and protection. Both caulking and luting of seams, as well as coating of plank shells by watertight materials applied to the outboard face and — in the case of double skins — between planking layers, are features well-known from pre-medieval ship finds. Even lead sheathing was carried by many Graeco-Roman wrecks. Archaeological clues of such technical measures can be distinguished by means of their geographical distribution, by links to peculiar shipbuilding traditions and by the technological character of certain procedures, but also with regard to the substances used by shipwrights or owners to build or to repair vessels. Literary evidence of coatings, whether of fabric, resin, pitch, or wax, points to the significance of such treatments even for seagoing vessels, but very little is said about caulking and luting. This paper provides some observations and ideas on the latter (References and Table 20.1).

Materials and procedures

Coating and sheathing

As reflected by ancient literature and ship finds as well, coating vessels with substances like pitch or resin was a widespread procedure in classical shipbuilding. Additional sheathing with lead patches nailed onto the planking over layers of either soaked fabric or vegetable material is also indicated by a series of shipwrecks which are mainly dated to the period from the 4th c. BC until the 2nd c. AD. Lead sheathing apparently was concentrated on Mediterranean vessels of mortise-and-tenon construction (Fig. 20.1). The earliest evidence from the Gela wreck (Sicily) does not contradict such an observation, because that late archaic ship revealed a mixed system of edge-joined planking.

In current discussions, lead sheathing is interpreted as a measure to make vessels watertight. Nevertheless, the toxic property of lead points to other functions as antifouling agent and protection against marine borers. Watertightness may have been achieved by the coating underneath the lead patches, which therefore should be treated as an isolated feature.

Luting connected with vessels of stitched construction

Remarkably, on ancient ships of sewn planking neither lead sheathing nor coatings seem to play a role worth mentioning. But, as opposed to the mass of Mediterranean ships, on such vessels seams were sealed by products applied to the interior surface of the shell, where the substances had been integrated into the system of stitches (Fig. 20.2). As indicated by a small number of findings, strands of linden bast fibres (Comacchio and Ljubljana wrecks) or of textile fabric (Marseille, La Bourse 7 and 9 wrecks; Gela wreck), or in once case (Comacchio: Fig. 20.3) both, were used as luting material that, in at least three cases, was soaked with pitch or resin. Whether these references from the 6th, 2nd, and 1st c. BC exemplify a procedure typical for the entire group of ancient sewn ships remains an open question. But it is striking that the same substances, i.e. pitch and resin respectively, occur as with coating. Moreover, wood fibres and fabric are frequently preserved in Roman ships from Central and Northwest Europe belonging to different ship building traditions.

Caulking and luting in prehistoric and Roman ships of local tradition outside the Mediterranean

As shown by B. Arnold of Neuchâtel, the peculiar method used to caulk Roman prams and related vessels from western Switzerland and, probably, from Belgium, by strands and cords made from moss, with seam fillings usually covered by laths (Fig. 20.4), can be paralleled with the specific luting indicated by mid- and late Bronze Age ship finds from England (Fig. 20.5). An exception may be made in cases where the process of application

WRECKS	MOSS	GRASS/ REEDS	FIBRES/ OAKUM	FABRIC	INTE- GRATED	COATED	PROCEDURE
Dover (GB)	■						●
North Ferriby 1 (GB)	■						●
North Ferriby 2 (GB)	■						●
North Ferriby 3 (GB)	■						●
Brigg (GB)	■						●
Avenches (CH)	■				↔		▲
Yverdon 1 (CH)	■	■			↔		▲
Bevaix (CH)	■	■			↔		▲
Yverdon 2 (CH)	■	■			↔		▲
Olbia (I)		□			↔		△
Pommeroeul (B)		□			↔		○
Xanten-Wardt (D)		■					○
Zwammerdam 2 (NL)		■			↔		○
Zwammerdam 2a (NL)		■					●
Chalon (Caisson) (F)		■			↔		●
Oberstimm 1 (D)			■		↔		●
Oberstimm 2 (D)			■		↔		●
Mainz 1 (D)			■		↔		●
Mainz 3 (D)			■		↔		●
Mainz 4 (D)			■		↔		●
Mainz 5 (D)			■		↔		●
Blackfriars (GB)			■		↔		●
New Guy's House (GB)			■		↔		●
Guernsey (GBG)			■		↔		●
Barland's Farm (GB)			■				●
Port-Vendres A (F)			□		↔		○
Dramont E (F)			□		↔		○
Zaton A (HR)		□					○
Laibach (SLO)			■			→	●
Comacchio (I)			■	■		→	●
Mainz 6 (D)				■		→	●
Marseille 7 (F)				■		→	●
Marseille 9 (F)				■		→	●
Gela (I)				■		→	●
Lyon (F)				■	↔	→	●
Chalon 1 (F)				■	↔		●
Chalon 2 (F)				■	↔		●
Arles (F)				■	↔		●

Table 20.1. Summary of caulking and luting indicated by ancient ship wrecks (until AD 500). ■ substances; ▲ caulking; ● luting; ↔ and ↓ types of seam application. light symbols: identification uncertain.

seems to be different (Fig. 20.6). In the sphere of Romano-Celtic shipbuilding, moss was also used to seal nail heads on the Blackfriars freighter and as leak stopping in one of the late Roman Mainz ships, indicating a N. European prehistoric heritage.

In contrast to Mediterranean ship finds, these clues to ship luting are relatively numerous from the Roman provinces on our side of the Alps (Figures 20.5 and 20.7). The seams of round-framed vessels of Romano-Celtic construction were filled with wood shavings, "macerated wood", or wood or bark fibres respectively (Barland's Farm; Blackfriars; New Guy's House; Guernsey; Mainz wrecks 1, 2, 3, 4, and 5). Prams from the Rhine area (Xanten-Wardt; Zwammerdam wreck 2), on the other hand, have marsh-plants and "straw" luting. Others from the same region reveal a more complex technique (Fig. 20.8): tapes of soaked fabric were glued on top of the seams outboard, protected by iron ribbons fixed to the shell by nails. The procedure and combination of materials resemble the lead sheathing of seagoing ships in the Mediterranean.

Caulking and luting as features of mortise-and-tenon construction

Amongst ships built with mortise-and-tenon joints, the phenomena of caulking and luting are less exceptional appearances than expected. Yet they are evident for

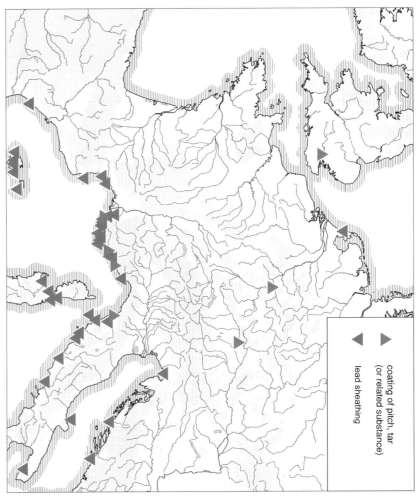

Fig. 20.1. Distribution of ancient shipwrecks with traces of lead sheeting (after Fitzgerald 1996 with additions) and coatings (author).

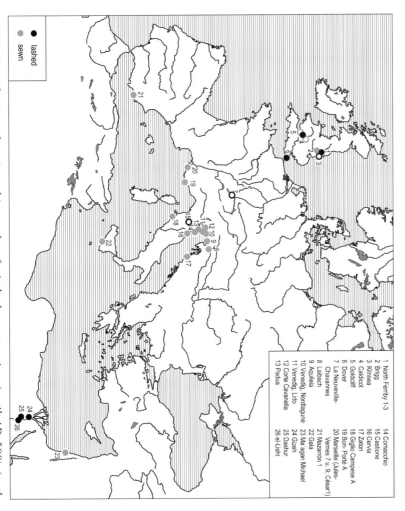

1 North Ferriby 1-3	14 Comacchio
2 Brigg	15 Castione
3 Kilnsea	16 Cervia
4 Caldicot	17 Zaton
5 Goldcliff	18 Giglio Campese A
6 Dover	19 Bon- Porté A
7 La Neuveville-	20 Marseille (Jules-
Chavannes	Vernes 7 u. 9, César)
8 Laibach	21 Mazarron 1
9 Aquileia	22 Gela
10 Venedig, Nordlagune	23 Ma´agan Michael
11 Venedig, Lido	24 Gizeh
12 Corte Cavanella	25 Dashur
13 Padua	26 el-Lisht

● lashed
● sewn

Fig. 20.2. Distribution of ancient shipwrecks of stitched construction (until AD 500) (author).

coating of pitch, tar
(or related substance)

▶ lead sheathing

Ronald Bockius

seagoing vessels in the Mediterranean: Late Roman cargo ships from Dramont (E) and Port-Vendres (A) were luted with "oakum", the former over larger parts of her planking. In both cases the findings are suspected to be of secondary character (repair). This is doubtless true for a

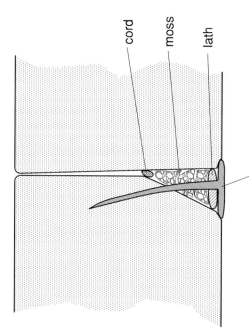

cord

moss

lath

nail

Fig. 20.4. Bevaix, Neuchâtel distr., Switzerland. Roman pram built after AD 182. System of caulking (after Arnold 1992a).

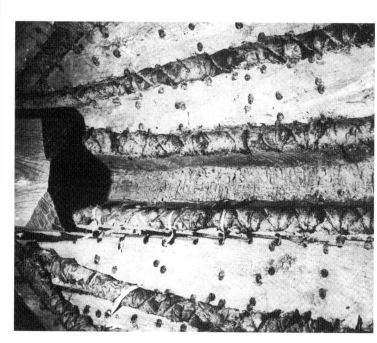

Fig. 20.3. Comacchio, prov. Ferrara. Freighter sunk around the end of the 1st c. BC. Lower parts of the planking sewn with luting material (linden bast covered with fabric) integrated into the stitches (inboard view).

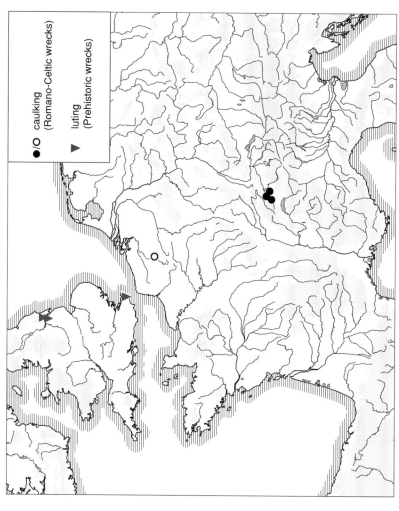

caulking (Romano-Celtic wrecks)

luting (Prehistoric wrecks)

Fig. 20.5. Distribution of ancient shipwrecks (barges/prams) caulked or luted with moss (author).

shipfind of the 2nd to 3rd c. AD from Olbia, Sardinia, because a single seam was caulked on the interior with plant material (*spartium iunceum*) over some frame distances.

More data are available from the Roman provinces: Remains of planking, presumably from a round-framed vessel, found in Zwammerdam (wreck 2a), contained reeds, thus reflecting a relationship to the treatment of Rhenish prams. In contrast, strands of fibre material

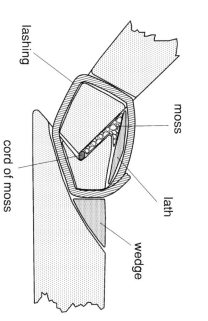

moss

lath

wedge

lashing

cord of moss

Fig. 20.6. North Ferriby, Bronze Age shipwreck F3. System of lashing and luting (after Wright 1990).

discovered in the Oberstimm oared ships was identified as linden bast; the findings clearly indicate luting. Luting – made from a grass species – is also evident in a wooden bridge caisson from the early 3rd c. AD, the planking of which was edge-joined by mortises and tenons to some extent, whereas flat-bottomed vessels found in the rivers Rhône and Saône (Arles; Chalon wrecks 1 and 2 [Fig. 20.9]; Lyon) were luted with fabric, either impregnated or not, which had been applied during the progress of planking. The latter group seems to link the Mediterranean with the northern frontier provinces in several respects: although found at the periphery of the highly civilized Roman world, the influence of mortise-and-tenon construction could be detected in three of these barges. The same might be true for their specific luting material, which can be understood as an integral component of Mediterranean ship construction. Furthermore, from a typological point of view such vessels belong to a category of prams different from Rhenish shipfinds according to their structural features. These are only to be found in the hinterland.

Conclusions

Examinations of ancient shipwrecks confirm the multiform appearance of sealing. As to luting, pre-Roman plank

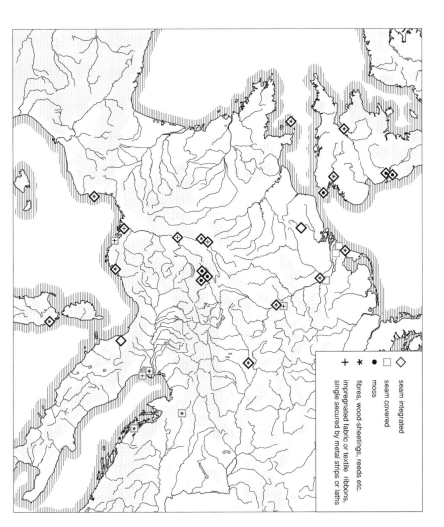

+   seam integrated
*   seam covered
●   moss
□   fibres, wood-sheetings, reeds etc.
◇   impregnated fabric or textile ribbons, single secured by metal strips or laths

Fig. 20.7. Distribution of ancient shipwrecks with traces of caulking and luting (author).

Ronald Bockius

Fig. 20.9. Chalon-sur-Saône, France. Roman pram (1st c. AD). Seams of bottom planking luted with fabric (inboard view).

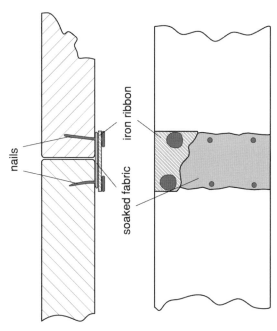

Fig. 20.8. Mainz, Rheinland-Pfalz, Germany. Roman pram built AD 81. System of luting (author).

ships of stitched construction from NW Europe and from the classical world already shared technical procedures of shell construction and treatment of plank seams. Yet materials are different and techniques vary in detail. Even Romano-Celtic shipwrights were acquainted with caulking and luting: the substances used not only indicate a regional background (moss caulking protected by laths) and technological transfer from the Mediterranean (textiles as seam fillers), but probably also the amalgamation of practices outside the old-world routine of boatbuilding, the embodiment of interpretations rather than genuine innovations (soaked fabric protected by seam battens; luting of lime-tree fibres unrelated to stitched construction). On the other hand, the role of inland navigation as a participant in the concert of ancient shipbuilding traditions should not be underestimated. Nevertheless, caulking and luting found in seagoing ships of mortise-and-tenon construction only from a period when that

practice was already in decline, may point to such a direction. Regrettably, too, less is known about the character of inland vessels of the Mediterranean. The same is true, however, for archaic and older shipfinds.

References

Bockius, R., 2002a, Abdichten" und „Kalfatern". Schiffsversiegelung und ihre Bedeutung als Indikator für Technologietransfers zwischen den antiken Schiffbautraditionen. *Jahrbuch des Römisch-Germanischen Zentralmuseums Mainz, 49.2*.

Bockius, R., 2002b, Die römerzeitlichen Schiffsfunde von Oberstimm in Bayern. Monographien des Römisch-Germanischen Zentralmuseums Mainz, vol. 50, Mainz 2002, pp. 17. 34. 50–52.

Bockius, R., in press, Caulking and Luting. Technological Exchange between Ancient Shipbuilding Traditions? In: H. Tzalas (ed.), *Tropis VII. 8th International Symposium on Ship Construction in Antiquity, Hydra 2002. Proceedings*, Athens (in press).

21 Roman techniques for the transport and conservation of fish: the case of the Fiumicino 5 wreck

Giulia Boetto

Among the wrecks found about forty years ago at Fiumicino Airport, the Museum of the Ships displays a small fishing craft, called Fiumicino 5 that is dated to the 2nd century AD (Boetto 2001: 123).[1] This boat displays a fish-well amidships (Fig. 21.1). This paper will outline the main constructional features of the vessel and will then attempt to define:

- the type of ship;
- the type of fishing in which it was involved;
- the functioning of the fish-well.

Fig. 21.1. *Fiumicino 5 wreck during the excavation (Photo Soprintendenza per i Beni Archeologici di Ostia).*

Constructional characteristics of Fiumicino 5

Fiumicino 5 is preserved to an overall length of 5.20 m. The beam measures 1.50 m, while the amidship depth measures 55 cm, on the starboard side (Fig. 21.2).

The original keel is not preserved. The replica keel is flat and rectangular in section. The garboards are chamfered against the upper sides of the keel. Pegged tenons are visible only on the starboard garboard. Modern tenons connect the keel to the stern and stem gripes (timber that attaches the keel to the stem and/or stern post). One scarf is preserved on the stern gripe extremity that served to connect the stern post (not preserved) to the keel. Stern and stem gripes are both made of oak (*Quercus* sp.). Garboards and planking ends are fastened with copper nails (head diameter 2 cm) and wooden treenails (diameter 8 mm to 1 cm) into the rabbets of these gripes.

There are eleven bottom planks on the starboard side of the hull and thirteen on the port side. The planking is made of cypress (*Cupressus sempervirens* L.)[2] and is about 2 cm thick (1.8–2.3 cm). The hull was constructed in the classical shell-first fashion with plank edges joined by pegged mortise-and-tenon joints. The measurements taken between the centres of the tenon pegs vary from 12 cm to 46 cm (average of 27.7 cm). The few mortises that it was possible to examine averaged 6 cm in width and 5-6 mm in thickness. A few diagonal scarfs, some stealers and one repair, have also been recorded.

The pegs that locked the tenons seem to have been driven from outside the hull. The exterior diameters ranged from 8 mm to 1 cm, and the interior diameters from 7 mm to 9 mm.

The preserved 18 frames are made of juniper (*Juniperus communis* L.), stone pine (*Pinus pinea* L.), cypress (*Cupressus sempervirens* L.) and oak (*Quercus* sp.). These are fastened to planks by olive treenails, but also by a few

Guilia Boetto

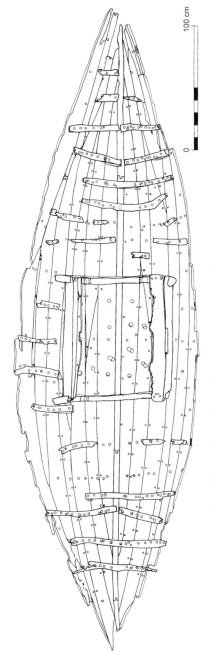

Fig. 21.2. *Plan of the Fiumicino 5 wreck (Drawing by G. Boetto).*

Fig. 21.3. *Cross planking of the fish well (Photo by G. Boetto, courtesy Soprintendenza per i Beni Archeologici di Ostia).*

Fig. 21.4. *The bottom of the fish well with the holes and the plugs (Photo by G. Boetto, courtesy Soprintendenza per i Beni Archeologici di Ostia).*

copper and iron nails. Treenails average from 9 mm to 1 cm in diameter; copper nails have a head diameter of 2 cm.

The cross-sectional dimensions of frames average from 4.5 cm to 6.5 cm in width, from 2.5 cm to 10 cm in height. Space between frames varied between 5 cm and 23 cm (14 cm in average). The alternating floor and half-frame pattern is not respected. The bottom cross girders of the central fish-well can be considered as floor timbers. Another floor timber, not preserved, was placed amidships inside the well. The well was flanked by five futtocks: only four of which are still preserved on the starboard side.

It is likely that the boat was propelled by oars as no trace of a mast step survives. The fish-well is placed at the centre of the boat. It is 89 cm long, 85 cm wide and 55.8 cm high. The total water capacity is about 314 litres. The cross planks separating the wet and dry area have a thickness of 5 cm, while the longitudinal planking is thinner and measures 2–3 cm (Fig. 21.3). The tree species utilised are: elm (*Ulmus minor* Miller), oak (*Quercus* sp.), cypress (*Cupressus sempervirens* L.) and stone pine

(*Pinus pinea* L.). The bottom planks are attached to the hull planking by copper nails driven from outside, while the fish-well planking is connected by mortises and tenons. A few wooden treenails and iron nails have been recorded. Some angular notches were probably used to fix a lid.

The bottom of the hull is bored with 19 holes (Fig. 21.4). The average diameter of the holes ranges from 2.5–3 cm. Some of these holes are stopped by plugs chopped from stone pine (*Pinus pinea* L.) branches. The plugs measure between 10–14 cm in height and have a maximum average diameter of 3–4 cm.

Type of ship

A graphic research model has been realised following the methodology established by the staff of the Centre Camille Jullian and inspired by the work of J.R. Steffy (1994).[3] It is not possible here to examine all the stages of the reconstruction of Fiumicino 5, however the reconstructed main dimensions are: a length of 5.61 m, a breath of 1.50 m and a depth of 75 cm.

The next stage was to try and identify the type and function of the Fiumicino 5 vessel. No representations of fish-well boats have been identified in the contemporary iconography; however, the written sources testify to the use of such ships. We know from Atheneus (5.208a) that the *Syracusia*, a giant vessel built by Hieron II of Syracuse in the 3rd century BC, included a fish-tank filled with live sea fish. This fish-tank, built with wooden boards and coated with lead, was an integral element in the ship's structure and it was filled with sea water (MacIntosh Turfa and Steinmayer 1999; Zevi 2001: 100–105). In the principate of Tiberius (14–37 AD), one of his freed-men, Optatus, Commander of the Fleet of Misenum, imported some wrasses (*Scarus*) from the Carpathian Sea. He distributed and scattered the fish between the mouth of the Tiber and the coast of Campania (Pliny *N.H.* IX, 62–63). The ships are referred to as *naves vivariae* (Macrob. *Sat.* III, 16, 10). Probably similar vessels were used to repopulate the Lake of Latium with marine fish, and to transport special types of oysters from Brindisi to Baia, near Naples (Gianfrotta 1999: 24). Thus, thanks to the *naves vivariae*, particularly desirable fish could arrive at the market in Rome. These included species such as red mullets (*Mullus surmuletus* L.) of Corsica and Taormine or moray eels (*Muraena* sp.) from Sicily (Iuv. *Sat.* V, 92–99). Moreover, it also became possible to directly supply the banquets of the wealthy Roman aristocracy (Suet. *Vitellius* 13).

Fish are a highly perishable foodstuff that decay quickly in ambient temperature. When a fish is dead, bacteria, present in low quantities when it is alive, increase exponentially. Their reproduction velocity could be reduced by cold, salt or drying (Davidson 1997: 162). Another way is to keep the fish alive for as long as possible.

The *naves vivariae* served to keep the fish alive for as long as possible when ice was not available and, as is so frequently demonstrated in naval ethnography and traditional ship construction, this proved to be an extremely reliable system. Moreover, a live fish is a better guarantee of freshness; however, it could be argued that other means of preservation suited different tastes. The predilection for live fish is shown by Seneca (*N.Q.* III, 18), who tells us that the Roman gourmets "cannot taste a fish unless they see it swimming and palpitating in the very dining-room". The famous cook Marcus Apicius thought it especially desirable for red mullets to be killed in a sauce made with the entrails of other similar fish (Pliny *N.H.* IX, 66.). Pliny the Elder (*N.H.* IX, 95) asserts that "the spiny lobster is the only animal whose flesh is of a yielding texture with no hardness, unless it is boiled alive in hot water". In Rome, this crustacean was demanded, and Apicius (409) developed several kinds of preparation.

Thus, returning to the Fiumicino 5 wreck, it would appear that it is the only archaeological example of a *navis vivaria* known from the Roman world.

The Zwammerdam 1 and 5 pirogues found in the

Netherlands, dating from the 2nd to the 3rd century AD, can not really be considered as fish-well boats. In fact, they were re-used as floating fish-tanks after having a multitude of holes drilled through the hull (De Weerd 1988; Arnold 1995: 118–119). Ethnographic parallels exist not only in Italy (in the Adriatic lagoons and on the rivers and coastal lakes of Tuscany and Latium) as floating fish-tanks in the form of boats were built, but also in France. The *marote* of the Venice and Comacchio lagoons were up to 14 m in length (Fig. 21.5). On the other hand, the *burcielli*, a vessel of more limited dimensions, equipped the fishing vessels named *bragagne*. The capacity of these fish-tanks varied from 5 quintals (or 500 kg) to more than 20 quintals (2000 kg) of fish. The *marote* were punted or towed to the fishing areas and were generally used for the storage and transportation of eels. In the second half of the 19th century, convoys of *marote* could reach Naples through the Straits of Messina, or Milan via the Po River (Bullo 1940; Ninni 1940: 253–254; Marzari 1983: 152, fig. 6; 1984: 55–56; Cecchini 1990: 132–136).[4]

The *serve* was a floating fish-tank used on the Thau Lagoon, in southern France. The biggest model could contain 25 quintals (2500 kg) of eels (Gourret 1897: 48–49). When utilised on the Rhône River, the *serve* was equipped with a yard and a sail (Roussiaud 2002: 323–324). On the Saône River, the *bêche*, a big floating fish-tank 10 m long, had a capacity of up to 4 tons of fish (Bonnamour 1986: 10).

If we examine traditional ship construction, the examples of fish-well ships are numerous. In China, from the Song Dynasty (10th century) well-boats were used to transport live fishes, especially different varieties of carp, harvested in ponds and transported to the market centres (FAO 1977: 16–17; Sahrhage and Lundbeck 1991: 221; Huss 1998: 93). In Europe fish-well ships have a large geographical distribution and are used inland, on lakes and rivers, along the coasts and on the open sea (Boetto in press b). Their form and dimensions change in relation to their navigation space and to the type of fish they carry. In Central Europe pirogues have been recorded with a fish-well built into the log and with the bottom bored by holes. They date from the Middle Ages up to the 20th century, and are used in rivers and lakes (Arnold 1995: 138, 180; Ossowski 1999a: 46, 114–115, 1999b: 65).

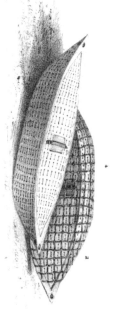

Fig. 21.5. Marota from the Comacchio lagoon (Drawing from Coste 1855).

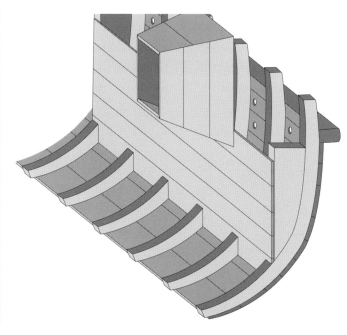

Fig. 21.6. Fish well of the carloforina boat (Drawing by G. Boetto after a sketch of A. Sanna).

In Sardinia, from the 19th century a flourishing lobster fishing activity developed. Small welled boats, 5 m to 7 m long, such as the *gozzo* of Alghero and the *carlofortina*, could contain 10 kg to 40 kg of spiny lobsters. The second strake of the hull bottom was drilled with 6 or 12 holes with a diameter of 4 cm (Fig. 21.6). After the lobster fishing season was over, the well was used to keep moray eels alive. The lobsters, after having been stored for a period in wooden fish-tanks, or in special coastal constructions, were carried on big fish-welled vessels to markets in Spain, France and Italy (Santucci 1928; Marzari 1997: 56–57; Damonte 1994).

Included amongst the biggest vessels that have fish-wells, are:

- the *waterschepen*, known from from the 14th century in the Netherlands, with a carrying capacity of about 10 tons of water and fish (Reinders et al. 1986: 29; Pedersen 1996: 80);
- the welled smacks built in England on the Dutch model, for the purpose of transporting live cod (March 1953: 13–15, 311–313, pl. 1–2);
- the flat-bottomed vessels of the Loire River, named *fûtreau*, and used to fish eels (Chasse-Marée 1988: 21–23);
- the ships used in Brittany (Domenech de Celles 1990; Malbosc and Ménélec 1998) and in the Mediterranean for the purpose of fishing and transport of live spiny lobsters (*Palinurus vulgaris*).

Amongst the smallest fish-well crafts, it is worth mentioning the Thames peter boat and the Medway doble, two clinker-built fishing boats provided with a fish-well amidships. In use as late as the middle of the 19th century, these vessels were intended not only for the purpose of river fishing, but also for shrimping and probably for oystering. The central wet-well allowed the catch to be kept alive and fresh during the voyage home to market. This wet-well was supplied with an ever-changing flow of water as it was open to the river through holes bored in the bottom of the hull at the position of the storage well (March 1953; Pollard 1963).

Finally, welled boats are represented within the collection of replicas of Danish traditional boats in the Viking Ship Museum of Roskilde (Vinner 2002: 60–63). Similar vessels are also known in Norway and Poland.[5]

Fishing activity

Is it therefore possible to define the type of fishing for which a boat like Fiumicino 5 was employed?

To try to answer this question, it is necessary to know where it navigated. Fiumicino 5 was abandoned in a marginal area of the harbour of Claudius, probably not so far from the place where it was constructed and operated. Unfortunately, the navigation space connected to the port of Rome and to the Tiber Delta, has changed a great deal since this period. The configuration of the coast has changed enormously. The principal transformation has been the considerable progradation of the coast in the last 2500 years. This change also includes the diminution of coastal lagoons and their transformation into marshy lakes and then their reclamation at the end of the 19th century (Bellotti 1998). If we consider the historic cartography, as seen on a map of Benedetto Cingolani from the end of the 17th century (1692), we recognise two coastal lakes, the eastern lake near Ostia and the western lake near Portus. During the Roman period, these brackish areas were exploited as salt marshes (Giovannini 1985; 2001) but it is possible that they were also important for fishing as presumed elsewhere in ancient times (Sternberg 1998, 2000). Today, this kind of exploitation of the territory survives on the coastal lakes of Latium, to the south of Rome (Della Valle 1961; Pacini 1967).

As archaeological traces of an ancient fishing activity have not be identified in this region (probably because of the use of perishable materials for the construction of traps, and the fixed fishing structures), the medieval sources have informed our analysis of the activities of fishing groups on the western lake. Here, eel was the most important species exploited (Fea 1831: 28; Tomassetti 1848: 497–498). Moreover, the Trajan Lake, the only body of water to have survived the siltation of the Imperial harbour of Rome, was an important fishing reserve, and gave its name to a particular fish, the *cefalo trajano*, the Trajan grey mullet (Chevallier 1986: 37).

On the basis of its function and dimensions, it is assumed that Fiumicino 5 was locally constructed, and as a consequence of its dimensions and the type of pro-

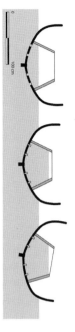

Fig. 21.7. Functioning of the fish well in Fiumicino 5 (Drawing by G. Boetto).

pulsion, its navigation was probably limited to the Tiber Delta, within the lagoons, along the coast, in the river-mouth and, probably, on the stretch of the river up to Rome.[6] Fiumicino 5 was used for both active and passive fishing,[7] assured good conservation of a perishable product, and was effective in the transportation of fish or crustaceans to the markets of Rome or, more probably, to Portus and Ostia. It may also have been used to introduce young fish into the fishing ponds.[8]

Of course, it is hard to establish the species of fish for which the fish-well was used. If we discount the imported ones, the species varied in accordance to the seasons and their availability. The species probably included those fish living in a fluvio-maritime environment, such as mullet (*Mugil* sp.), gilt-head bream (*Sparus aurata* L.), bass (*Dicentrarchus labrax* L.) – the Tiber's one was particularly popular[9] – and, naturally, eels. We can add shrimp (*Crangon crangon* L.) and sole (*Solea solea* L.), which were plentiful in the Ostian waters (Pliny the Younger, *Ep.* II, 17).

Functioning of the fish-well

In conclusion, the question of the function of the Fium-icino 5 fish-well will be addressed (Fig. 21.7). The water filled the container up to the boat's flotation line. If the quantity of water was insufficient for the catch, the fisherman had to put in more water after having stopped the holes. In this case, the wet-well was not kept supplied with an ever-changing flow of water open to the sea through the holes, as demonstrated in the English and Sardinian traditional small well boats. However, the Sardinian fisherman would have regularly had to take out some water from the well, in order to maintain its quality.

Finally, in the case of the Fiumicino 5 boat, the plugs served to improve the capacity of the container. These could also be useful to keep in water when the gradient of salinity differed from outside. This may have been necessary for the survival of the species of the fish transported.[10] In any case, when the boat was hauled, they were removed for its speedy draining.

Notes

1   Fiumicino 5 is known in previous literature as *Barca del Pescatore*: cf Testaguzza 1970: 132–133; 143–144; Scrin-ari 1979: 21–25, fig. 4.)

2   Only two planks (T20/24) are made of stone pine. Planks

T22 and T23 (stone pine), T10 and T11 (cypress) and T9 (spruce) probably do not belong to the wreck.

3   For the reconstruction method cf Pomey, 2003; The study of the Fiumicino 5 wreck is part of a doctorate research on the Fiumicino ships under the direction of Patrice Pomey and the collaboration of Michel Rival and Robert Roman of the CCJ. For Fiumicino 1 cf Boetto 1998; 2003.

4   For Latium: Della Valle 1961: 20, n. 34. For Tuscany: Casaccia 2001: 122; Franceschini 1994: 62–63, fig. 4–6.

5   Personal communications of Arne Emil Christensen and Robert Domzal during the conference.

6   The importance of fluvial fishing activities in Roman times is well attested by the sources and, in less measure, by the archaeology: Le Gall 1953: 83–84; Meiggs 1973: 268; De Grossi Mazzorin 2000.

7   Active fishing uses nets and trawls, passive uses traps or other fixed devices: Sternberg 1998: 90–91.

8   Hypothetically these fishing ponds could be situated within the coastal lakes. Higginbotham (1997: 34) inter-prets Fiumicino 5 as a supply vessel for the *piscinae* annexes to the maritime villas of Latium. In reality, the location of the archaeologically known *piscinae* is too far from the operational area of the boat (Giacopini et al. 1994; Pellandra 1997; Gianfrotta 1997, 1999: 28–29; Rustico 1999).

9   It is the *lupus inter duos pontes*: cf Le Gall 1953: 83–84, 267–268.

10 Hypothesis suggested by Beat Arnold.

Acknowledgements

Vincent Dumas, Anna Gallina Zevi, Alexandra Grille, Chantal Godet, Cinzia Morelli, Gilberto Penzo, Salvatore Pomata, Patrice Pomey, Edoardo Riccardi, Philippe Rigaud, Michel Rival, Robert Roman, Antonio Sanna, Joan Seal, Myriam Sternberg, Kevin Walsh.

References

Arnold, B., 1995, *Pirogues monoxyles d'Europe centrale. Construction, typologie, évolution. Archéologie neuchât-eloise, 20. Musée cantonal d'archéologie. Neuchâtel.

Bellotti, P., 1998, Il delta del Tevere: geologia, morfolgia, evoluzione. In C. Bagnasco (ed.), *Il delta del Tevere. Un viaggio fra passato e futuro*, 19–29, Fratelli Palombi Editori. Roma.

Boetto, G., 1998, *Il porto di Claudio, Museo delle Navi. Soprintendenza archeologica di Ostia. Roma.

Boetto, G., 2000, New technological and historical observations on the *Fiumicino 1* wreck from Portus Claudius (Fiumicino, Rome). In J. Litwin (ed), *Down the river into the sea: Proceedings of the Eight International Symposium of Boat and Ship Archaeology*, 99–102. Gdansk 1997. Gdansk.

Boetto, G., 2001, Les navires de Fiumicino. In J.-P. Descœudres (ed), *Ostia, port et porte de la Rome antique*, 121–130. Catalogue de l'exposition. Musée d'art et d'histoire/Georg Editeur. Genève.

Boetto, G., 2003, The Late Roman *Fiumicino 1* wreck: recon-structing the hull. In C. Beltrame (ed), *Boats, Ships and Shipyards: Proceedings of the Ninth International Sym-

posium of Boat and Ship Archaeology, 66–70. Venice 2000. Oxbow Books. Oxford.

Boetto, G., in press a, L'épave romaine *Fiumicino 4* (fin du II – III siècle ap. J.-C.): navire de pêche ou petit caboteur? In H. Tzalas (ed), *Tropis 8, Proceedings of the 8th International Symposium on Ship Construction in Antiquity*, Hydra, 2002. Athens. Hellenic Institute for the Preservation of Nautical Tradition.

Boetto, G., in press b, Le imbarcazioni vivaio: uno studio etnoarcheologico. In *Atti del III Convegno Italiano di Etnoarcheologia*, Mondaino, 2004. (British Archeological Reports).

Bonnamour, L., 1986, Bateaux de Saône. In *Bateaux de Saône. Mariniers d'Hier et d'Aujourd'hui*, 1–14. Société d'Histoire et d'Archéologie de Chalon-sur-Saône, Pont-de-Veyle.

Bullo, G., 1940, La vallicoltura. In G. Brunelli, G. Magrini, L. Miliani, P. Orsi, *La laguna di Venezia. La pesca nella laguna*, vol III, VI, XI, 49–212. C. Ferrari. Venezia.

Casaccia, M., 2001, Il lago e il suo circondario: cultura materiale, ecologia, tradizioni popolari, dialetto. In P. Tamburini (ed), *Un museo e il suo territorio. Il Museo Territoriale del Lago di Bolsena. 2. Dal periodo romano all'era moderna*, 109–148. Città di Bolsena Editrice. Bolsena.

Cecchini, F. (ed.) 1990, *Sorella anguilla. Pesca e manifattura nelle valli di Comacchio*. Nuova Alfa Editore. Bologna.

Chasse-Marée, 1988, Une voile carrée sur la Loire. *Le Chasse-marée. Histoire et ethnologie maritime*, 35: 19–32.

Chevallier, R., 1986, *Ostie Antique. Ville et Port*. Société d'édition "Les Belles Lettres". Paris.

Coste, J.-J.,1855, *Voyage d'exploration sur le littoral de la France et de l'Italie*. Paris. (Italian ed.) 1989, Industria della laguna di Comacchio. A. Forni Editore. Bologna).

Damonte, L., 1994, Marseille au soir de la voile. *Le Chasse-Marée. Histoire et ethnologie maritime* 78: 14–27.

Davidson, A., 1997, *Poissons de la Méditerranée. Comment les reconnaître et les cuisiner*. Édisud. Aix-en-Provence.

De Grossi Mazzorin, J., 2000, État de nos connaissances concernant le traitement et la consommation du poisson dans l'Antiquité à la lumière de l'archéologie. L'exemple de Rome. *Mélanges d'archéologie et d'histoire de l'École Française de Rome* 112.1: 155–167.

De Weerd, M.D., 1988, *Schepen voor Zwammerdam*, Unpublished dissertation, University of Amsterdam.

Della Valle, C., 1961, *La pesca nei laghi costieri del Lazio*. Pubblicazioni dell'Istituto di geografia dell'Università di Roma, n.s. 2. Roma.

Domenech de Celles, F., 1990, En Mauretanie à bord de la Belle Bretagne. *Le Chasse-Marée. Histoire et ethnologie maritime* 48: 16–31.

Food and Agricultural Organisation of the United Nations, *Aquaculture Bulletin* 8.20, 1977: 16–17.

Fea, C., 1831, *Storia delle saline di Ostia introdotte da Anco Marcio quarto re di Roma dopo la fondazione di quella città*. Stamperia della Rev. Camera Apostolica. Roma.

Franceschini, F., 1994, *Lago, palude, fiume: il lessico delle pesche tradizionali nella Toscana occidentale*. Saggi ALLI. Rux Edizioni. Perugia.

Giacopini, L., Belelli Marchesini, B. and Rustico, L., 1994, *L'itticoltura nell'antichità*. IGER. Roma.

Gianfrotta, P.A., 1997, Le peschiere scomparse di Nettuno (Rm). In *Atti Convegno nazionale di archeologia subacquea*, 21–24. Anzio 1996. Edipuglia. Bari.

Gianfrotta, P.A., 1999, Archeologia subacquea e testimonianze di pesca. *Mélanges d'archéologie et d'histoire de l'École Française de Rome* 111.1: 9–36.

Giovannini, A., 1985, Le sel et la fortune de Rome. *Athenaeum* 73: 373–387.

Giovannini, A., 2001, Les salines d'Ostie. In J.-P. Descœudres (ed), *Ostia, port et porte de la Rome antique*, 36–38. Catalogue de l'exposition, Musée d'art et d'histoire/Georg Editeur. Genève.

Gourret, P., 1897, *Les étangs saumâtres du Midi de la France et leurs pêcheries*. Typographie et lithographie Moullot fils aîne. Marseille.

Higginbotham, J., 1997, *Piscinae. Artificial fishponds in Roman Italy*. Studies in the history of Greece and Rome. The University of North Carolina Press. Chapel Hill and London.

Huss, H.H., 1998, *El pescado fresco: su calidad y cambios de su calidad* FAO Documento Tecnico de Pesca, 348. Roma.

Le Gall, J., 1953, *Le Tibre. Fleuve de Rome dans l'Antiquité*. Presses Universitaires de France. Paris.

MacIntosh Turfa, J., and Steinmayer, A.G. Jr., 1999, The *Syracusia* as a giant cargo vessel. *International Journal of Nautical Archaeology* 28.2: 105–125.

Malbosc, G. and Ménélec, R., 1998, *Les années langouste*. Retia Graphic éd. Spézet.

March, E.J., 1953, *Sailing Trawlers. The story of deep-sea fishing with long line and trawl*. Percival Marshall and Company Limited. London.

Marzari, M., 1997, Typologie des bateaux de Sardaigne. *Le Chasse-Marée. Histoire et ethnologie maritime* 111: 56–57.

Marzari, M., 1983, The Bragagna, a study. *Mariner's Mirror* 69.2: 143–156.

Marzari, M., 1984, *Vecchie barche adriatiche. Bragozzo – Bragagna – Tartana*. Rivista Marittima. Roma.

Meiggs, R., 1973, *Roman Ostia*. Oxford University Press. Oxford.

Ninni, E., 1940, Attrezzi e sistemi di pesca nella Laguna. In G. Brunelli, G. Magrini, L. Miliani and P. Orsi, *La laguna di Venezia. La pesca nella laguna*, vol III, VI, XI, 213–258. C. Ferrari. Venezia.

Ossowski, W.,1999a, *Studia nad Lodziami jednopiennymi z obszaru polski*. Polish Maritime Museum's Proceedings, IX. Marepress. Gdansk.

Ossowski, W., 1999b, *Some results of the study of logboats in Poland*. In J. Litwin (ed), *Down the river to the sea. Eight International Symposium on Boat and Ship Archaeology*, 59–66. Gdansk 1997. Polish Maritime Museum. Gdansk.

Pacini, P., 1967, *Atlante della pesca in Italia*. Sadea/Sansoni. Firenze.

Pedersen, R.K., 1996, *Watership ZN 42: a clenched-lap fishing vessel from Flevoland, the Netherlands*. Excavation report 17. NISA, Lelystad.

Pellandra, I., 1997, Due poco note peschiere romane a Santa Severa e a Santa Marinella. *Archeologia subacquea. Documenti, studi e ricerche II*: 21–33.

Pollard, A.O.Jr., 1963, Medway Doble. *Small Craft* 22: 490–491.

Pomey P., 2003, Reconstructing of Marseilles VIth century BC Greek ships. In C. Beltrame (ed), *Boats, Ships and Shipyards: Proceedings of the Ninth International Symposium of Boat and Ship Archaeology*, 57–65. Venice 2000. Oxbow Books. Oxford.

Reinders, H. R., Van Veen, H., Vlierman, K., and Zwiers, P.B. 1986, *Flevobericht nr. 140. Het wrak van een 16e eeuws vissersschip in flevoland, het onderzoek van een vissersschip gevonden op kavel W 10 in Flevoland.* Opgravingsverslag, 1. NISA, Lelystad.

Roussiaud, J., 2002. *Dictionnaire du Rhône médieval.* Centre alpin et rhodanien d'ethnologie. Grenoble.

Rustico, L., 1999, Peschiere romane. *Mélanges d'archéologie et d'histoire de l'École Française de Rome* 111.1: 51–66.

Sahrhage, D. and Lundbeck, J., 1991, *A History of Fishing.* Springer Verlag, Berlin.

Santucci, R., 1928. *La pesca dell'Aragosta in Sardegna. Notizie scientifico-pratiche e conclusioni preliminari.* Premiate Officine Grafiche C. Ferrari. Venezia.

Scrinari, V.S.M., 1979, *Le navi del porto di Claudio.* Tipografia Centenari. Roma.

Steffy, J.R., 1994, *Wooden Shipbuilding and the Interpretation of Shipwrecks.* Texas A & M University Press. College Station.

Sternberg, M., 1998, Les produits de la pêche et la modification des structures halieutiques en Gaule Narbonnaise du IIIe siècle av. J.-C. au Ier siècle ap. J.-C. Les données de Lattes (Hérault), Marseille (Bouches-du-Rhone) et Olbia-de-Provence (Var). *Mélanges d'archéologie et d'histoire de l'École Française de Rome* 110.1: 81–109.

Sternberg, M., 2000, État des connaissances sur la pêche dans le monde ibérique (VIème s.-IIIème s. av. J.-C.). In C. Mata Parreno and G. Pérez Jordà (eds), Ibers, agricultors, artesans i comerciants: *III Reunió sobre Economia en el Món Ibèric, Saguntum-plau, Extra-3,* 93–97. Universitat de València, Departament de Prehistòria i d'Arqueologia. València.

Testaguzza, O., 1970, *Portus.* Julia Editrice. Roma.

Tomassetti, G., 1848, *La Campagna Romana antica, medievale, moderna.* II. *Via Appia, Ardeatina ed Aurelia.* Arnaldo Forni Editore. Roma.

Vinner, M., 2002, *Viking Ship Museum Boats.* Viking Ship Museum. Roskilde.

Zevi, F., 2001, Le invenzioni di Archimede e le grandi navi. In M. Giacobelli, *Lezioni Fabio Faccenna,* 95–114. Edipuglia. Bari.

22 Land and sea connections: the Kastro rock-cut site (Lemnos Island, Aegean Sea, Greece)

Christina Marangou

Introduction

The island of Lemnos, in the northeast Aegean Sea, located in front of the entrance to the Dardanelles Straits, has been the focus of both mythical and actual travels and population movements since at least the end of the 4th millennium BC. Since the time of Homer, the island has frequently been mentioned by Classical and later authors, partially due to the fact that it was inhabited by non-Greeks, until Athenian occupation around 500BC. The first named possibly Bronze Age inhabitants, were the Sintians "of wild speech" (Odyssey 8.294; Iliad 1. 593–594), reputedly from Thrace (Heubeck et al 1988: 366). According to the myth, the Sintians of Lemos received the pre-Hellenic divinity, who became the god Hephaistos, who became the god of fire and metalworking. Lemnos was his favoured island (Iliad 21.58; Richardson 1993: 58) and became his main cult-centre in Greece (Kirk 1985/1990: 113). Jason and the Argonauts (Minyans) are reported to have stopped here on their way to the Black Sea (Iliad 7. 467–468). Jason's son, Eunos, King of Lemnos, despatched wine-ships to the Acheans during the Trojan war (Iliad 7. 467–468). Finds of Mycenaean figurines and pottery seem to confirm connections to the Acheans, while Lemnian spinners are mentioned on a Linear B tablet (PY Ab 186, Ventris and Chadwick 1973: 410).

The descendants of the Sintians and the Minyans were replaced, according to Herodotus (VI 137), after the second millennium BC, by Pelasgians, or rather Tyrrhenians possibly from the East (Torelli 1975; Sakellariou 1977: 186 ff, 217–221; Giuffrida 1983: 9 ff). Evidence of their non-Hellenic language survives in inscriptions recovered from the Archaic period (de Simone 2000). The 'Homeric hymn' to Dionysos, refers to the Tyrrhenians as dreadful pirates and raiders. The name 'Sintian' is said to derive from the verb 'to harm, damage, or rob' (Giuffrida 1983: 16). This relates either to their early ability to manufacture harmful weapons, or to their piratical activities; the latter confirmed by the Sintians' raid of Thrace. However, despite the fact that piracy was wide spread and frequently synonymous with trade through Archaic times (Giuffrida

1983: 4–8), the Athenians later used this as an excuse to colonize the island as a form of punishment.

It was probably the Tyrrhenians who at the end of the 8th century BC, introduced the mystic cult of 'Kaveiri' or 'Great Gods' to Lemnos – their sanctuary having been located and excavated on the north coast of the island. The 'Kaveiri' (Hemberg 1950), also known to be metallurgists, were the sons or grandsons of Hephaistos and the pre-Hellenic 'Great Goddess' with the same name as the island, Lemnos, a divinity of nature. In the Archaic period the 'Great Goddess' Lemnos was assimilated with the Phrygian Cybele and was related to the Thracian Bendis (Beschi 1990: 29). The goddess of hunting and wild nature, Artemis, also became incorporated with Bendis, and probably succeeded Lemnos, after Athenian colonisers likely adopted the latter's pre-Greek worship.

The site

The modern-day port of the capital of Lemnos, Myrina, is situated on the west coast of the island, facing the Athos-Chalkidiki Peninsula on the Greek mainland (Fig. 22.1).

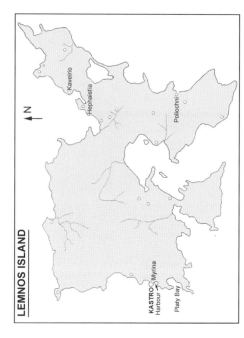

LEMNOS ISLAND

Fig. 22.1. Map of Lemnos Island showing main places mentioned in the text (Compiled by author).

Fig. 22.2. *General view of the Kastro Peninsula from the east (Photo by the author).*

Fig. 22.3. *Carved rocks in Area N/Z from the north. View towards the entrance of the harbour (Photo by author).*

The northern part of the harbour, the rocky Kastro Peninsula projects towards the west (height c. 115 m; Fig. 22.2). The rock formation dates from the Tertiary period, and the coastal deposits of the surrounding low areas, from the Holocene (Geological map of Greece, 1993).

Various structures have been carved out of the Kastro Peninsula, exploiting the natural shapes and locations of the outcrops and boulders: cavities, platforms, "rooms", flights of steps, niches, conduits (Marangou 2002a). The current research commenced in 2002 with the recording of the visible rock-cut features, and is being completed since 2002, by the unearthing of rock-cut structures in selected areas. In 2003, work resumed in two areas on the southern slope of the Kastro Peninsula located in the outer port. Both areas command a view over the entrance to the harbour and are surrounded by cliffs that overlook dangerous shallows and reefs. Preliminary results suggest that these areas had been occupied at least since the Bronze Age until the Hellenistic period (c. second half of the second millennium–3rd century BC). Subsequently a Byzantine, Genovese, Venetian and finally, a Turkish castle was built on the northern side of the headland (Castrorum Circummavigatio 1999: 56–57), partially destroying earlier remains.

Observation posts and industrial/trade activities?

In Area N/Z some carved rocks offer a convenient observation post (39 m above current sea level) over-looking the entrance to the harbour (Fig. 22.3). Behind them, towards the north, an area of probable industrial activities and/or trade as well as cult, was revealed. Rock-cut cavities and conduits, attesting to the containment and management of liquids, might have been used for metallurgical activities, partially indicated by traces of slag. A rock-cut feature with such a function has been identified at the Early Bronze Age (EBA) settlement of Palamari, on the island of Skyros; located on an abrupt slope, it was exposed to prevailing winds, a necessary requirement to obtain the high temperatures necessary for melting the copper (Hadzipouliou 1997: 359). The

location of ancient furnaces close to the sea would have facilitated ships unloading and the requirement of sand for extracting lead from litharge (Papadimitriou and Kordatos 2001: 687), would also have been benefited from a coastal location. However, there is no evidence for the existence of metals on Lemnos, which would have had to have been imported by sea, despite the advance in metal working in prehistory, and this particular spot is high above the current sea level, overlooking a rocky coast. Nevertheless, communication with the coast was facilitated (see below).

Finds from the area include a small probable lead or tin ingot (Fig. 22.4), various pieces of metal artefacts, including jewellery, in lead (or tin?), iron and copper-based metal and clay lamps, loom-weights (one of which has a bull imprinted on the top), an unusual bat(?) figure, as well as some later female figurine fragments, possibly related to a female goddess (see below), as well as a small "hoard" of copper-based coins with complex represent-ations, that were discovered near the foundations of a stone wall.

Tin and/or lead ingots are known to have been rep-

1 cm

Fig. 22.4. *Small lead or tin ingot from Area N/Z (Photo by author).*

that ships lie offshore below the castle, towards the north-eastern part of the bay "moor up on shore and drop anchor into the sea" (Piri Reis 1988: 233, 240, pl. 52/b, 241). However, the bay was treacherous ("malsaine") even more so for smaller boats (Ploigos 1955: 50), with shallows of 4–5 m (Instructions Nautiques 1929: 239). The difficulty of entering the harbour in the dark was mentioned in the beginning of the 19th century, although it was less dangerous in daylight, as both the peninsulas that delineate the bay are volcanic and thus dark-brown in colour and thus not easily discernable, in contrast with the coast of the two bays on either side of the Kastro, sandy and light coloured. After entering, the rocky coast was indistinguishable and abrupt (Marangou 2002a).

One of the epic adjectives attributed to Lemnos 'amichthaloessa' (Richardson 1993: 356; Dumézil 1998: 73), meant either smoke enshrouded, foggy, misty and hard to catch sight of, apparently because of Hephaistos' metallurgical activities[3] or because of fumarolic gases (Forsyth 1984), or because it was difficult to come ashore, being rocky and steep, with inhospitable harbours that were difficult to access. The difficulty of approaching the island is also illustrated by the impossible conditions the Lemnians presented to the Athenians: they would only surrender if the Athenians arrived sailing against the north wind from Athens, conditions only satisfied when the Athenians sailed from the Athenian Chersonese (Herodotus VI. 138).

Anchoring was possible in the harbour in nice weather, the best area being at a depth of 18 m (Instructions Nautiques 1929: 239). Similar instructions are still given in Ploigos (1955: 50): the best anchoring was between the two shallows, although the seabed was sandy and unstable and the ships had to be on the alert to put off immediately as soon as the wind changed to a westerly.[4] The Myrina harbour is "like open sea" when exposed to western winds. Piri Reis warned "vessels cannot lie at anchor against winds blowing from the sea, for the place is exposed", and suggested an alternative natural harbour (Platy Bay), four miles to the southwest which "may be entered by large galleys, ... is sheltered" ...(and)... offers anchorage "suitable for all winds" (1988: 233, 240, 241).

Euneos, the King of Lemnos, purchased a slave at Troy in exchange for a silver krater (Iliad 7.467–468) that had been offered to his grandfather, King Thoas, by Phoenician merchants, possibly in return for the right to moor in the harbour or to trade in Lemnos (Richardson 1993: 252). The necessity for pilotage (McGrail 1996: 315) and the importance of a friendly or at least non-aggressive, attitude to the islanders, is self-evident. It would not have been easy if they were pirates or wreckers themselves. It seems significant that areas inhabited by the Tyrrhenians also included the coast opposite Myrina, including that of Mount Athos Peninsula, as well as Imbros and other areas along the route to the Black Sea. As attested in the later Hellenistic and Roman periods, it was common for notorious piratical populations to occupy barren coastal regions, such as Cilicia, bordering crucial sea-lanes, in

resented on Egyptian reliefs since the 15th century BC (Bass 1967: 62–67, 70), and tin ingots were traded in the eastern Mediterranean from at least the Late Bronze Age (LBA) as the Uluburun (Parker 1992: no 1193; Bass 1997: 157; Pulak 1998: 199–201), Cape Gelidonya (Bass 1967: 30, fig. 17; 52, 82–83; Parker 1992: no 208) and Kefar Samir (also lead ingots; Parker 1992: no 540; Muhly 1998: 319)[1] wrecks indicate.

In the northeast Aegean tin has often been found (Pernicka et al 2003: 163): an almost pure tin artefact comes from EBA Thermi, Lesbos (Lamb 1936: 171, fig. 50, pl. XXV). The source of the tin ore remains conjectural (Hall and Steadman 1991; Rapp 1999, 703; Pernicka 2001: 369–371; Pernicka et al 2003: 164, 170–171). Tin may have been traded through the Caucasus area (Colchis) and the Black Sea (Doumas 2002: 53).[2] Lead is more common in the Aegean and was involved in the production of silver since EBA Troy (Papadimitriou and Kordatos 2001: 681). It was mined at Laurion (Attica), Thasos, Siphnos and other Cycladic islands since at least the Bronze Age (Bass 1967: 73, 131; 1997: 158; Stos Gale et al 1996; Vavelidis et al 2001: 634; Pernicka et al 2003: 166). Lead was known in Anatolia since the Neolithic (Sayre et al 2001) and several archaeometallurgical sites including lead have been identified in NW Turkey (Pernicka et al 2003: 148 ff, Fig. 1). Numerous different metal ores are known in Kassandra, northwest of the Chalkidike Peninsula (opposite Myrina) (Begemann et al 2003: 198).

Overseas contact for the acquisition of raw metal in Lemnos is without question. In the Iliad (7.467–475) the Lemnians are said to have traded with the opposite Anatolian coast, exchanging wine for "copper", "glistening iron", hides, cattle and slaves (21.40–41, 58). Archaic Lemnian exports were found in the northern Aegean islands and mainland Greece, imports to Lemnos originated from the eastern and southern Aegean (Beschi 1998: 75). Direct contacts with the eastern Aegean continue to be attested in the Hellenistic period (Archontidou 2000: 43).

A dangerous harbour and offshore anchorage

Area N/E is located a little more to the east on the Kastro Peninsula, about 10 m below Area N/Z, overlooking a small rocky island that served as a sea-mark until recent times. In fact, ships entering the harbour would have had to avoid two shoals situated almost in the middle of the entrance, at an equal distance from this island and from another protruding rock at the end of the opposite peninsula; in the 1950s, the shoals were destroyed and the port dredged. Prior to the destruction of the shoals in the middle of the bay, they were marked with a red buoy in 1929 and a beacon was sometimes placed there at night (Ploigos 1955: 50; Marangou 2002b). The submerged rocks at the entrance of this bay and several shoals close to its southern coastline, are indicated on the 16th-century map of Lemnos by Piri Reis, who also mentions

order to exact "transit dues" in exchange for guarantees of safe passage (Rauh 2003: 169–201).

Crossroads, access routes and cult

Area N/E is a crossroads of a partly preserved, ascending ramp intersected by a flights of steps that climbed up from the edge of the cliffs. Natural and rock-cut segments of ramps and steps, sometimes zigzagging, extended down towards the sea. The main ramp, which was parallel to the coast, continued towards other parts of the site and had probably at some time been transformed into a stone platform that was placed in full view of the harbour and that covered a large part of the Area N/E. A number of vases were found in connection with the ramp/platform.

Two of the flights of steps that crossed the platform arrive either side of a stepped rock. The largest flight of steps turned and continued up above the intersection, leading to another large, carved rock, with a symmetrical flight of a few steps on its opposite side.

A preliminary study of the pottery from both Area N/Z and Area N/E indicates that the area was utilised from the Bronze Age, through to the Archaic, Classical and Hellenistic periods. Pottery from the base of the ramp – thus from its initial occupation – that is still under study, likely dates from the end of the Late Bronze Age (Troy VII, if not already Troy VI) and the beginning of the Iron Age (roughly Troy VIIb), thus including the period around the Trojan war (see Marangou in press), without excluding the possibility of extending the occupation to the time of the Argonauts. This is followed by Archaic pottery of the Tyrrhenian "pirates", to whom the above mentioned industrial activities should possibly also be attributed. Later phases have a strong Athenian bias, the functions of both areas having probably changed in the Classical and Hellenistic periods to now involve, besides that of possible military observation posts and trade, ritual and cult practices.

In fact, a number of clay, female figurine fragments and a few clay artefacts were found in the area of a small stone structure, a single row of stones based on the stepped rock mentioned above, by the inner side of the ramp. One could interpret this as a small open-air altar, or at least a significant place, located at the intersection of access routes to the sea, that may have been used by visitors in the Classical and Hellenistic periods. Small open-air altars are not a rarity outside temples or sacred enclosures, in particular in harbour areas. However, an alternative interpretation of the area as possibly being an observation post must also be retained, or even a double function was feasible. Additional figurine fragments were found in Area N/Z and Hellenistic figurines in other areas of the Kastro Peninsula (Archontidou 1994: 55, figs. 12–13).

The figurines often represent a woman wearing a *polos* (high hat) and veil and/or seated on a throne (Fig. 22.5). *Polos* iconography is known since the 6th century BC

from Thasos. Oriental and Neo-Hittite influences on the type, characterising divinities, have also been noted (Weill 1985: 147–202). This style of headgear is characteristic of pre-Hellenic Lemnos (Beschi 2001; Archontidou 2000: 27, fig. 40), of the Phrygian Cybele, probably related to the Lydian Kybebe and the Syrian-Anatolian Kubaba (Haas 1994: 406–409), but also of 5th–4th century BC Artemis, Demeter, Hera or Hecate (Weill 1985: 193–196). Up until now all the figurines appear to be female and often with attributes of Cybele or Lemnos, however, they are not all of the same type; yet, figurines of Greek gods/goddesses are known to "visit" sanctuaries of other divinities (Alroth 1989: 108–113), while some could also represent mortals.

Artemis was the most important goddess of the island in Classical times, with at least two precincts in Myrina (Archontidou 2000: 32–34; Beschi 2001: 218). Besides, a priestess of Artemis collected and sealed the "Lemnian earth" from Mount Mosychlos, where Hephaistos supposedly first fell, close to Hephaistia, the second town of the island (Parker 1994: 344–345); and Archaic to Roman vestiges, interpreted as a sanctuary of Artemis, have been excavated on the shore, a few kilometres to the north of Myrina (Archontidou 2000: 32–34; Beschi 2001: 218).

Since the Archaic period, both Lemnos and Cybele are usually represented seated on a throne (Acheilara 2000: 11, fig. 10); while, the Anatolian Cybele is often represented carved on "rock facades" and occasionally related to "step-altars" (Haspels 1971: 73–111) – she may also be connected with entrances and boundaries, "liminal" areas (Rein 1996: 234). The cult of Artemis is related to headlands, coastal areas and offshore anchorages (Romero Rocio 2000: 118; Fenet 2002: 339–340). She is a divinity

1 cm

Fig. 22.5. *Clay figurine head from Area N/E wearing a high polos hat and veil (Photo by author).*

of mariners, as well as of doorways, a guardian of ports and itineraries (Romero Rocio 2000: 77–78), and is then particularly connected with crossroads, doorways, boundaries, transitional and liminal places. Artemis has borrowed some of Hekate's epithets of liminality, such as "of the (cross)roads", and "watching the harbour"; harbours too being liminal points (Johnston 1990: 21–28 and notes 10, 24). Rituals performed in such places usually protect transitions, beginnings or departures.

Crossroads, carved flights of steps and combinations of natural and artificial passageways are omnipresent on the Kastro Peninsula. Such rock-cut installations have similarities with the Late Bronze Age and Phoenician remains particularly in relation to marine structures (Frost 2001: 197). On an area of rocks closer to the sea, flights of steps that symmetrically ascend towards a flattened space or ramp are attested by old photographs before the destruction of the 1950's. Further sinuous and often invisible flights of steps lead eventually towards the abrupt summit of another rock, strategically located (Marangou 2002b). The pattern of these structures is frequently repeated – a rock with steps on both sides and steps or ramps leading down to the water and up to the summit, although many of these structures are not always visible from the sea, such as those of the above mentioned abrupt rock. Thus, besides the hypothesis of maritime rituals, a practical function can also be proposed when interpreting these elevated places, for example for use in transit, observation or the transmission of optical (fire or smoke) signs (Frost 1999: 356–357), also relating to friendly or otherwise, ships and the sea (Marangou 2002b). In fact, ships sailing into the bay were vulnerable, being exposed both to the natural dangers and to the power and good will of the Lemnians, who would be entirely at the latters' mercy, if wrecked or damaged.[5]

Special ships

The nautical connections of the Kastro Peninsula also include a symbolic component: an oared ship, possibly of (Late?) Bronze Age type, about 2.20 m long, has been observed carved on a rock complex, close to the sea on the same side of the peninsula (Marangou 2002c). It is located where boats were repaired up until the beginning of the 20th century, facing the area where ships moored and dropped anchor in Piri Reis time. Similar symbolic or ritual activities are attested by a 3rd-century AD Lemnian ritual involving a famous ship (Dumézil 1998): a *theoris* (sacred ship) was sent every nine years (or every year) to the island of Delos, in order to bring back new fire (Parker 1994: 345; Burkert 1998: 133). Purification ceremonies took place and fires were extinguished, while the *theoris* was away. According to the Lemnian Philostratos (c. 215 AD), supposedly well informed about local ritual practices (Maclean et al 2001: xci), if the ship returned before a

period of nine days, she had to wait for the end of the purifications and invocations of chthonian and ineffable gods, before entering the harbour – the Kaveiri were away during this period – and the fire had to be kept pure out on the sea (Heroicus 53, 5–14; De Lannoy 1977; Burkert 1998: 137, note 8):

"Then [if too early] she [the ship] cannot come into harbour anywhere on the island, and rides at anchor [in the open sea] floating off the headlands till the time becomes right to sail into the harbour…". Then "the fire is distributed to the houses as well as to the crafts using fire" – in which were included the metal workers – "and they say that a new life starts afterwards" (translated by the author).

Conclusions

The sectors of the Kastro headland that have been briefly considered in this paper showed strong maritime connections. If life was naturally connected to the sea through all periods in Lemnos and in particular on the Kastro, for obvious reasons of closeness to the water and insularity, the evidence presented here indicates various aspects of these associations and sometimes change of functions diachronically. In a preliminary interpretation, to be tested in future research, such activities might have included:

- Navigation: control of the approach of ships or boats to the land and the entrance into a not-very-hospitable harbour; possible military or piratical observation posts; [Archaic to Hellenistic; end of the Bronze Age-Iron Age not excluded]

- Transit between sea and land: flights of steps and ramps, between low levels, closer to the sea, and higher levels of the occupied area on the rocks; such an itinerary attains a "thoroughfare" located close to the edge of the rocks and parallel to it, leading towards other sectors of the site; [Archaic and later, possibly also earlier]

- Trade and industrial activities: metal ingot [Archaic] and copper-based coins [Hellenistic?]; possibly metal-working in one area [Archaic];

- Cult: clay figurines, a number of which probably represent female divinities of nature, attested in Lemnos at least since the Archaic period, and the Classical and Hellenistic periods (e.g. goddess Lemnos, Cybele, Artemis), included in which are goddesses related to liminality [mostly Classical and Hellenistic].

Metal-working was particularly related to male divinities on the island since pre-Homeric and Archaic times, while ships and navigation are not only represented in the iconography (e.g. ship rock-carvings), but are also associated with myths (Argonauts, the Achaeans and Philoctetes, King Euneos trading on the opposite coast, piratical raids of Sintians and Tyrrhenians) [pre-Homeric] and rituals (Kaveiroi, sacred ship bringing new light) [at least Classical-Hellenistic; 3d c. AD], some of which at least, had likely origins in real and/or historical events. These liminal spaces between sea and land, whether used for observation, cult, communication, or trade, at the same time or consecutively, attest to transition both in real and symbolic terms. Continuation of research on the Kastro will hopefully aid better understanding of the overall structure of the rock-cut elements which seem to present a much more complex pattern that initially suspected.

Acknowledgements

The author wishes to thank: the 20th Ephorate of Antiquities, its director, Mrs Archontidou, and the Council for the Monuments of the Islands, for granting the study and publication permit; the Institute for Aegean Prehistory for financial support for part of this study; the Myrina Museum staff and several collaborators for their help; H. Frost for precious suggestions; L. Beschi and E. Hatzipouliou for fruitful discussions on pottery and other finds.

Notes

1 on lead and tin ingots off the coast of Israel see Pulak 1998: 191, 220.
2 see objections by Muhly 1998: 321 about Colchis gold.
3 "ashy" is also an epithet of Lemnos (Burkert 1998: 125, note 46)
4 Bronze Age or ancient ships could also be forced to anchor by submerged reefs, if at a safe distance from the shore (Frost 1999: 368: 2002: 982–983).
5 Not only the strategic position of the Medieval castle on a steep prominence surrounded by precipices made it impregnable (Piri Reis 1988: 233 and 240, map 52/b) and it did not fear pirates, but already ancient Myrina resisted the Athenians longer than Hephaistia (Marangou 2002a and 2002b).

References

Acheilara, L., 2000, Η θρησκεία των Λημνίων. In Lemnos Amichthaloessa 2000, 11–12. Ministry of Culture. Athens.

Alroth, B., 1989, Greek Gods and Figurines. Aspects of Anthropomorphic Dedications. Acta Universitatis Upsaliensis. Uppsala.

Archontidou, A., 1994, Η Μύρινα υπό το φως των ανασκαφών. Archaiologia 50: 50–55.

Archontidou, A., 2000, Η Μύρινα υπό το φως των ανασκαφών. Ελληνιστικά εργαστήρια της Ηραιστίας και της Μύρινας. In Lemnos Amichthaloessa, 26–34: 42–43. Ministry of Culture. Athens.

Bass, G. F., 1967, Cape Gelidonya: A Bronze Age Shipwreck. Transactions of the American Philosophical Society 57. Philadelphia.

Bass, G. F., 1997, Prolegomena to a study of maritime traffic in raw materials to the Aegean during the fourteenth and thirteenth centuries BC. In R. Laffineur and Ph. Betancourt (eds), Craftsmen, Craftswomen and Craftsmanship in the Aegean Bronze Age, Aegaeum 16: 153–170. Université de Liège and the University of Texas, Liège.

Begemann, F., Schmitt-Strecker S., and Pernicka, E., 2003, On the Composition and Provenance of Metal Finds from Besiktepe (Troia). In G.A. Wagner et al (eds), Troia and the Troad. Scientific Approaches, 173–201. Springer. Berlin-Heidelberg-New York.

Berenson Maclean, J.K., and Bradshaw Aitken, E., 2001, Flavius Philostratus: Heroikos. Society of Biblical Literature. Atlanta.

Beschi, L., 1990, Bendis, the Great goddess of the Thracians, in Athens. Orpheus 1: 29–36.

Beschi, L., 1998, Arte e cultura di Lemno Arcaica. La Parola del Passato LIII: 48–76.

Beschi, L., 2001, I disiecta membra di un santuario di Myrina (Lemno). Annuario della Scuola Archeologica di Atene e delle Missioni Italiane in Oriente LXXIX, ser. III, 1: 191–251.

Burkert, W., 1998, Un feu nouveau à Lemnos. In Burkert, W., Sauvages origines. Mythes et rites sacrificiels en Grèce ancienne, 113–146. Les Belles Lettres. Paris.

Castrorum Circumnavigatio 1999, Κάστρων Περίπλους. Hellenic Ministry of Culture, Archaeological Receipts Fund. Athens.

Conze, A., 1886 (1860), Reise auf den Inseln des Thrakischen Meeres. Hakkert. Amsterdam.

De Lannoy, L., (Ed.), 1977, Flavii Philostrati Heroicus. Teubner. Leipzig.

De Simone, C., 2000, The Tyrrheni of Lemnos. In M. Torelli (ed), The Etruscans, Exhibition Catalogue, Palazzo Grassi. Bompiani. Venice.

Doumas, C., 2002. From Poliochni to Lipari via Akrotiri. In M. Cavalier and M. Bernabò-Brea (eds), In Memoria di Luigi Bernabò-Brea, 53–65. Accessorato Beni Culturali ed. Ambientali e della Pubblica Istruzione.

Dumézil, G., 1998, Le Crime des Lemniennes. Macula. Paris.

Fenet, A., 2002. Les dieux olympiens et la mer: le cas de la Messénie et de la Laconie. In H. Tzalas (ed), Tropis VII, 7th International Symposium on Ship Construction in Antiquity, 335–344. Hellenic Institute for the Preservation of Nautical Tradition. Athens.

Forsyth, P.Y., 1984, Lemnos reconsidered. Echos du monde classique. Classical views XXVIII, 3.1: 3–14.

Frost, H., 1999, Anchors sacred and profane. Ugarit – Ras Shamra 1986; the stone anchors revised and compared. In Ras Shamra – Ougarit VI: Arts et Industries de la pierre, 355–410. ERC. Paris.

Frost, H., 2001. The Necropolis, Trench and other Ancient Remains: A Survey of the Byblian Seafront. Bulletin d'Archéologie et d'Architecture Libanaises 5: 195–217.

Frost, H., 2002. Syria and Lebanon: the rich potential. In H. Tzalas 2002 (ed), Tropis VII. 7th International Symposium on Ship Construction in Antiquity, vol. II, 981–993. Hellenic Institute for the Preservation of Nautical Tradition. Athens.

Geological map of Greece, 1993, 1:50.000. Institute of Geology and Mineral Exploration. Athens.

Giuffrida I., M., 1983, La pirateria Tirrenica. Momenti e fortuna. Bretschneider. Roma.

Haas, V., 1994, Geschichte der Hethitischen Religion. Brill. Leiden.

Hadzipouliou, Elizabeth, 1997, Εξετδικευμένες δραστηριότητες στο Παλαμάρι της Σκύρου. In C. Doumas and V. La Rosa (eds), Proceedings of the International Symposium "Poliochni and the Early Bronze Age in the North Aegean", 357–361. Scuola Archeologica Italiana di Atene and University of Athens. Athens.

Hall, M., and Steadman, S., 1991, Tin and Anatolia: Another look. *Journal of Mediterranean Archaeology* 4.1: 217–234.

Haspels, C.H. Emilie, 1971, *The Highlands of Phrygia*, Vols I–II. Princeton University Press. Princeton, New Jersey.

Hemberg, B., 1950, *Die Kabiren*. Almqvist and Wiksells. Uppsala.

Heubeck, A., West. S. and Hainsworth, J.B., 1988, *A commentary on Homer's Odyssey*. Volume 1, Introduction and books I–VIII. Clarendon Press. Oxford.

Instructions Nautiques, 1929, *Instructions Nautiques. Mediterranée Orientale*, Iᵉ Volume. Imprimerie Nationale. Paris.

Johnston, S.I., 1990, *Hekate Soteira. A study of Hekate's roles in the Chaldean Oracles and Related Literature*. American Philological Association. Scholars Press. Atlanta, Georgia.

Kirk, G.S., 1985 [1990], *The Iliad: A commentary*, Vols I–II. Cambridge University Press. Cambridge.

Lamb, W., 1936, *Excavations at Thermi in Lesbos*. Cambridge University Press. Cambridge.

De Lannoy, Ludo, 1977 (ed). *Flavii Philostrati Heroicus*. Teubner. Leipzig.

McGrail, S., 1996, Navigational techniques in Homer's Odyssey. In H. Tzalas (ed), *Tropis IV: 4th International Symposium on Ship Construction in Antiquity, Athens 1991*, 311–320. Hellenic Institute for the Preservation of Nautical Tradition. Athens.

Marangou, C., 2002a. Rock-art and Landscape in Myrina, island of Lemnos, Greece. In P. Whitehead, W. Whitehead and L. Loendorf (eds), *1999 International Rock-Art Conference Proceedings*, Vol 2: 147–153. American Rock Art Research Association. Tucson.

Marangou C. 2002b. Rocks and Itineraries: Sea and Land Perspectives on an Aegean island. In W. H. Waldren and J.A. Enseyat (eds), *World Islands in Prehistory. International Insular Investigations. V Deia International Conference of Prehistory*, 7–18. B.A.R Series 1095. Oxford.

Marangou, C.. 2002c, The Myrina ship re-examined. In H. Tzalas (ed), *Tropis VII, 7th International Symposium on Ship Construction in Antiquity*, 513–522. Hellenic Institute for the Preservation of Nautical Tradition. Athens.

Marangou, C., (in press), Diachronic maritime aspects at the Myrina Kastro (Lemnos): Overview of ongoing research. In H. Tzalas (ed), *Tropis VIII, 8th International Symposium on Ship Construction in Antiquity*. Hellenic Institute for the Preservation of Nautical Tradition. Athens.

Muhly, J.D. 1998, Copper, tin, silver and iron: the search for metallic ores as an incentive for foreign expansion. In S. Gitin, A. Mazar and E. Stern (eds), *Mediterranean Peoples in transition. Thirteenth to Early Tenth Centuries BCE. In Honor of Professor Trude Dothan*, 314–329. Israel Exploration Society. Jerusalem.

Papadimitriou, G.D. and Kordatos, I., 2001 Μεταλλουργική μελέτη αρχαίων λιθαργύρων από την περιοχή του Λαυρίου. In Y. Bassiakos, A. Aloupi, and Y. Facorellis (eds), *Archaeometry issues in Greek Prehistory and Antiquity*, 679–697. Hellenic Society of Archaeometry, Society of Messenian Archaeological Studies. Athens.

Parker, A.J. 1992, *Ancient Shipwrecks of the Mediterranean and the Roman Provinces*. B.A.R. Series 580. Oxford.

Parker, R., 1994, Athenian religion abroad. In R. Osborne and S. Hornblower (eds), *Ritual, Finance, Politics. Athenian democratic Accounts presented to David Lewis*, 339–346. Clarendon Press. Oxford.

Pernicka, E., 2001, Metalle machen Epoche. In J. Latacz et al, *Troia. Traum und Wirklichkeit* (exhibition catalogue), 369–372. K. Theiss. Stuttgart.

Pernicka, E., Eibner, C., Öztunali, Ö., and Wagner, G.A., 2003, Early Bronze Age Metallurgy in the North-East Aegean. In G.A.Wagner, et al (eds), *Troia and the Troad. Scientific Approaches*, 143–172. Springer. Berlin-Heidelberg-New York.

Piri Reis, 1988, *Kitab-i Bahriye* (re-edition of the 1526 book), Vol 1. Ministry of Culture and Tourism. Ankara.

Ploigos 1955, Πλοηγός του Ελληνικόν Ακτόν, Δ τόμος. Hydrographic Service of the Royal Navy. Athens.

Pulak, C., 1998, The Uluburun shipwreck: an overview, *International Journal of Nautical Archaeology* 27.3: 188–224.

Rapp, Jr., G., 1999, Copper, tin and arsenic sources in the Aegean Bronze Age. In P.P. Betancourt, R. Laffineur and W-D.. Niemeier (eds), *Aegeaum 20, Meletemata. Studies in Aegean Archaeology presented to Malcolm H. Wiener as he enters his 65th year*, 699–704. Vol. III. Université de Liège, Liège

Rauh, N., 2003, *Merchants, Sailors and Pirates in the Roman World*. Tempus. Gloucestershire.

Rein, M.J., 1996, Phrygian Matar: emergence of an iconographic type. In E. Lane (ed), *Cybele, Attis and related cults. Essays in memory of M.J. Vermaseren*, 223–237. Brill. Leiden.

Richardson, N., 1993, *The Iliad: A commentary*, Vol VI. Cambridge University Press. Cambridge.

Romero Rocio, M., 2000, *Cultos Marítimos y Religiosidad de Navegantes en el Mundo Griego Antiguo*. B.A.R. Int. Series 897. Oxford.

Sakellariou, M. 1977, *Peuples préhelléniques d'origine indo-européenne*. Ekdotikè Athenon. Athens.

Sayre, E.V..Joel, E.C., and Blackman, M.J. 2001. Stable isotope studies of Black Sea Anatolian ore sources and related Bronze Age and Phrygian artefacts from nearby archaeological sites. Appendix: New central Taurus ore data. *Archaeometry* 43.1: 77–115.

Stos-Gale, Z.A., Gale, N.H., and Annetts, N, 1996, Lead isotope data from the isotrace laboratory, Oxford: Archaeometry data base 3, ores from the Aegean, Part 1. *Archaeometry* 38.2: 381–390.

Torelli, M., 1975, Τοppανοί. *La Parola del Passato* CLXV: 417–433.

Tzalas, H., (ed), 1996, *Tropis IV: 4th International Symposium on Ship Construction in Antiquity, Athens 1991*. Hellenic Institute for the Preservation of Nautical Tradition. Athens.

Tzalas, H., (ed) 2002, *Tropis VII, 7th International Symposium on Ship Construction in Antiquity, Vols I–II*. Hellenic Institute for the Preservation of Nautical Tradition. Athens.

Vavelidis, M., Gialoglou, G., Trontsios, G., Melfos, V, and Weisberger, G., 2001, Ενα αρχαίο μεταλλείο όχρας και μολύβδου-αργύρου στην περιοχή Ελιά της Θάσου. In Y. Bassiakos, A. Aloupi, Y. Facorellis (eds), *Archaeometry issues in Greek Prehistory and Antiquity*, 633–644. Hellenic Society of Archaeometry, Society of Messenian Archaeological Studies. Athens.

Ventris, M. and Chadwick, J., 1973, *Documents in Mycenaean Greece*. Cambridge. Cambridge University Press.

Wagner, G.A., E. Pernicka and H.-P. Uerpmann (eds), 2003, *Troia and the Troad. Scientific Approaches*. Springer. Berlin-Heidelberg-New York.

Weill, N., 1985, *La plastique archaïque de Thasos. Figurines et statues de terre cuite de l'Artemision. I. Le haut archaïsme*. Etudes Thasiennes 11. Ecole Française d'Athènes. Athens.

23 Local boat-building traditions in the Bristol region

Anthony J. Parker

Bristol and the Severn Estuary region: situation and environment

The long, funnel-shaped estuary of the River Severn in the west of England provides access for sea-going ships to large areas of central and southern England and south Wales (Fig. 23.1). The force of the tides, with their great range (up to 13 m at the mouth of the Bristol Avon), assists sail- and oar-powered craft long distances into the land – especially to Bridgwater on the River Parrett in Somerset, Gloucester on the Severn, and Bristol itself (Parker 2001a: 23–24). Bristol in particular is situated in a safe, secure position, surrounded by hills but within easy reach of the estuary and the open sea; the port lies in a fertile basin, rich in mineral resources, and with good land communications to Southampton and London. All the estuary ports have made full use of coastal and inland shipping to distribute imports and collect stores and exports, especially by means of the River Severn, which is navigable inland for some 260 km without locks or weirs (Willan 1967; Green 1999). A busy network of different kinds of shipping was an essential part of the infrastructure of the Bristol region, at least until the coming of the railways in c. 1840 (Hussey 2000).

There were also difficulties inherent in the natural conditions of the region. Up till 1810 there were almost no floating quays at Bristol and ships of any size had to take the ground between tides, and the situation was not much better at the other estuary ports (Parker 1999). The vigorous runoff of rainfall from the catchment areas of the rivers could make upstream travel, even with a flood tide, difficult in winter, while in summer the inland Severn could be affected by low water (Waters 1949). Out in the estuary, the strong tidal currents had more effect than the wind on the direction in which a boat moved, with resulting hazards of running aground or striking rocks, especially in fog (Waters 1947). The speed with which the tide came in meant that a grounded boat was in danger of being overset by the flood, while, out in the channel, wind against tide resulted in nasty, steep seas which could easily swamp even fair-sized craft. These difficulties resulted in special

techniques of ship-handling, as recounted in the 20th century by Eglinton (1982; 1990), and possibly also in appropriate, robust types of construction, as proposed by Farr (1977). The Severn Estuary is included with the sea areas of St George's Channel and the outer Bristol Channel

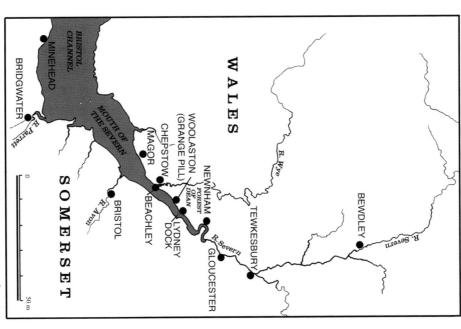

Fig. 23.1. Bristol and the lower Severn region, showing places mentioned in the text (Susan Grice, University of Bristol).

in a single 'transport zone', according to Westerdahl (1995), but its special combination of features suggests that it should be separate; in such a case, one might expect there to be a special grouping of boat- and shipbuilding types as well.

Shipbuilding

Shipbuilding was an important activity at Bristol from the beginnings of the city in the 11th century (Farr 1977). References to 'Welsh boards' show that the main sources of ship-timber were south Wales and the Forest of Dean in Gloucestershire. Although ships were built at Chepstow, Newnham and other Forest locations, it seems that sea-going merchantmen and warships were mostly constructed in Bristol. No direct evidence has been discovered of special characteristics of Bristol ships prior to the 19th century, but there are occasional suggestions in official papers that Bristol-built ships were highly regarded, even in the 16th century. The phrase 'ship-shape and Bristol fashion' is interpreted by Farr (1977) to reflect the supposedly sturdy construction of Bristol ships, but the first definite use of the whole phrase (according to the *Oxford English Dictionary*) dates only from 1839.

There is very little archaeological evidence for the procedures used to build ships at Bristol in the centuries up to c 1800, but finds suggest that lapped planking was normal, even up till c 1600 (cf. Farr, notes relative to construction of Bristol ships, in the *Shipbuilding in the Port of Bristol*, at Bristol Record Office). In the later 17th century, a visiting Navy Surveyor found Bristol shipwrights unable to make or use a draught, although this is scarcely a reliable source for what actually went on in the yards! In the 18th century, the draughts which exist of Bristol-built ships, and drawings of shipyards by Nicholas Pocock (Greenacre 1982: 22 ff), do not suggest anything out of the usual, nor does a view of a ship's frames standing proud at Tippett's Yard, Bristol, in 1826 (Stoddard 2001: 98). However, when working boats are taken into account, both documentary evidence and also vernacular tradition of the region suggest that alternative procedures may have operated. Moreover, there is a hint of something different in *A Poetical Description of Bristol* by William Goldwin, published 1751 (Martin and Pickard 1973):

> Here active scenes of naval labour reign,
> And wooden cradles infant Ships sustain …

Although they are scarcely a technical analysis, the lines could be read as meaning that even large ships were at least sometimes built on a cradle or former at Bristol. If this were so, it would chime with some aspects of vernacular boat-building in the region, as will be shown below.

There are a number of suggestions from antiquarian drawings of the 18th and 19th centuries that a variety of structural techniques were in use in the Bristol region for building smaller craft. In a view of Bristol in 1826 by

Thomas Rowbotham, the most reliable for nautical detail of the artists who worked for the collector George Braikenridge at that time, a boat of about 5 m is shown with what appears to be lapped planking, whereas other ferry or river fishing boats are usually smooth-skinned (Stoddard 2001: 80). Conversely, two fishing boats (one lug-, the other gaff-rigged) are shown on the strand at Minehead c 1800, both with very broad lapped planks (Dunning 1999: 58–59). Contemporary sloops shown at Bristol in Braikenridge's collection are smooth-skinned (Stoddard 2001: 1), but broad planks are characteristic of the inland river flatners of Somerset (Greenhill, 1995: 28–29), giving a hint of the diversity of construction in the region which may formerly have existed. Hence, some techniques which we know to have been used for smaller boats might also have been employed for sea-going ships, and this might explain the term 'Bristol fashion'.

One example of this may possibly be found in a drawing of c. 1800 by William Delamotte, published by Greenacre (2003). It shows the tidal River Avon at Canon's Marsh in Bristol, one area where shipbuilding was carried on for centuries. A shipwright's yard is indicated by the stack of timber at one side, and, as well as some completed ferry-boats and passenger wherries, the beginnings of a boat, perhaps 8 m long, can be seen. There is a range of baulks on the ground, quite high, to allow for assembly from outboard, and the stem and the transom frame have been erected; however, there is no keel visible in the drawing, and it can be supposed that this boat was being built shell-first with edge-positioned planks. The height of the stem and stern in this case suggest, not a barge, but a trading sloop or a pilot 'skiff'. If this interpretation is justified, one can see the convergence of small- and large-scale ship-building traditions in post-medieval Bristol, and thus a reflection of the close interaction between the port and local waterborne transport networks.

Working boats of the Bristol region

Severn trows

The term 'trow' (normally pronounced like 'snow') is found as a term for working boats of Bristol and the River Severn from the 15th century onwards, and trows certainly filled a key role in the interaction of Bristol with its hinterland (Green 1999). During the 19th century, the inland trade on the River Severn declined in the face of railway competition, and the trow business concentrated on the Bristol Channel and the Severn Estuary. To this end, old trows were rebuilt, and new ones built in carvel style, with a hull-form similar to that of other coasting sloops and ketches, and this is the form recorded by McKee (1983: 37, 39, 97). Before c 1840, however, trows were built long, wide and shallow in order to allow them to ascend the Severn, and their characteristic appearance, in striking contrast to that of seagoing ships, is well rendered by 18th- and early 19th-century artists including

Rowlandson, Turner and Pocock (cf Greenacre 1982: Figure 22). Fortunately a trow of this period, still partly visible at Lydney Dock, has been excavated archaeologically, and her construction analysed by a shipwright (Williams 1992). The hull, as in other types of coastal barge, was built up from a keel-less bottom of flush-laid planks. To port and starboard of the central keel-plank were seven flat planks, edge-assembled by skew (cant) nails, the seventh on each side having an upwards-facing bevel on to which was set the first of two edge-positioned planks (also bevelled) which gave a rounded turn to the bilge. The sides were of lapped planks, which were carried round at the bow and towards the transom stern, with lapped strakes substituted for flush planking below at each end. The hull assembly in general was by iron nails, clenched over roves as necessary. The futtocks overlapped the floor timbers but were not joined to them, 'discontinuous framing' as termed by McKee (1983: 60–61); the planking at each end was erected before the frames – 'the fitting is done by spiling and eye only' (Williams 1992: 15). In the main part of the hull, the 'side pieces' (top timbers) were, apparently, stood on top of the floor timbers at their outboard ends but were not fastened to them, implying that they, too, did not serve as active frame elements. The structural procedure, in summary, is 'rafted' in the terminology of McKee (1983: 53–55) or 'bottom-based' as termed by Arnold, Hocker and others (and conveniently explained by Fenwick, 1995).

Illustrations of trows before c 1750 are, unfortunately, not exact enough to determine their general appearance (pace Farr, 1946); indeed, the term 'trow' may not in earlier periods have had a single corresponding boat-shape, as could, for example, be implied by a Bridgwater man's account of sailing to and from Wales in 1673 in 'a barke or trough' (Hussey 2000: 36). However, the structural features of the Lydney Dock trow, described above, may be represented by some earlier remains found at Magor Pill in south Wales. Some elements of a boat, apparently inverted, and possibly only a fragment, were found in a silted-up former creek 75 m north of the medieval wreck previously excavated by Nigel Nayling (1996: 85–88). This second wreck was not excavated: no tree-ring date was possible, but ^{14}C suggests a 15th, 16th or early 17th-century date. Nayling interpreted the visible planks as the keel plank, the first bottom strake (edge-positioned to the keel plank) and the second strake (lapped on the first) of what he termed 'a clinker-built vessel'. An alternative interpretation of the remains is possible: the supposed keel plank is very narrow, and would be better seen as a bilge strake or a rubbing strake; the outboard face of the frame timbers where they are not masked by planking shows no sign of joggle or rebates, suggesting that the missing planks were flush-laid, and that the supposed keel plank was not centrally located. The effect is to suppose that the Magor Pill 2 boat resembled later up-river trows, with flush-laid bottom planking and lapped side planking. This interpretation requires confirmation from excavation, but shows that a regional style of boat-building can be traced back as far as the use of the term 'trow' for boats which linked Bristol and the Estuary with inland regions.

Documents suggest that pre-1840 trows were particularly associated with inland places such as Bewdley or Tewkesbury, and it is likely that most were built on the banks of the Severn, even if they were frequently seen in estuary ports such as Bridgwater and Bristol. Later trows, flush-planked on standing frames, tended to be built lower down the Severn, and in estuary ports; however, there is an interesting reference by McKee (1983: 123) to the persistence of a regional construction procedure. He describes how a Bridgwater shipwright described to him the method used there to build coasting ketches and trows up till 1914: "They would construct and erect the complete midship frame first and then work from ribbands without any lofting". In the same area, at Highbridge, he refers to the use of a 'mould', i.e. a former or jig, to build small boats in the 1930s (McKee 1983: 51). These 'free arm' approaches to working up a hull of edge-positioned planking can be seen as natural successors to the methods which one can infer were used to construct the bottom-based boats of earlier centuries.

Barges and lighters

We know little of the barges and lighters formerly used in Bristol and other regional ports. In the later 19th century, flush-planked barges, similar in shape to estuary trows but rather smaller and with a single square sail, were used on the Bristol Avon (Green 1999; 65; Elkin 1995: 124), but no information about their construction has come to light. At Bridgwater, a class of barge survived into the 1950s and was measured afloat by John Coates and Eric McKee (McKee 1983: 30, 85–86, 130). This was classified by McKee as a 'true bateau', a keel-less, flat-bottom boat. In their final years, these barges were normally propelled only by the tide and by poling, but they are known to have sailed with a single square sail in the 1920s, and Bridgwater barges are recorded historically as sailing to Wales in the 17th century; sailing is, in fact, implied by their 'cod's head – mackerel tail' plan and their 'tombstone' (not sharp-pointed) stern (McKee 1983: 81, 209). Their side planking was lapped, and their bottoms flat, of 3-inch (73 mm) planking, apparently not edge-fastened. In his published account McKee puts a question-mark over the details which were submerged and not checked on the floating barge which he studied, but his original structural drawing (as reproduced by Greenhill 1976: 267) shows the outer bottom planks bevelled downwards and the first side strake attached to the bevel, as in his published diagram of 'Longitudinally rafted bottom and ends' (McKee 1983: 54). The structural drawing shows the 'tombstone' stern timber stood on the after end of the median plank, with a rising knee to support it; the stem, however, is shown rabbetted underneath so as to sit over the nose of the keel-plank, as in the diagram 'Rabbetted stempost and knee combined on bevelled flat bottom (Somerset)' (1983: 63). It seems, then, that the Bridgwater barge preserved into the mid-20th century traditional features of shape and structure which are shared with other vernacular boats of the region (Banks 1999: 25).

Stop-Net boats

On both sides of the Severn Estuary there survive examples (no longer in use) of a distinctive type of fishing-boat: the Stop-Net boat. These strongly-built boats (5.5–6.7 m long) were moored across the current to manipulate a large net, supported on heavy poles, though they could also sail out along the estuary. Twentieth-century stop-net boats were built using modern techniques, with galvanized nails, etc., and sometimes from moulds. The type is referred to anecdotally as long ago as the 17th century (information from S. Cooper, 2000), but how such earlier boats were built is not known. The 'Stop-Net Boat' is the label given by Eric McKee to taxon no. 10 in his classification of working planked boats in Britain, being of keel-less, round-section, square-stern form (McKee 1983: 83, 86, 168–171).

Bristol region boats: a typological group

In his *Working Boats of Britain* (1983) McKee examined the hypothesis that there was a link between a boat's work, her surroundings and her shape. He found that this was often true in what he thought of as solitary situations, as in Somerset, where some traditional boat types shared features of construction and shape, but varied in terms of their work and surroundings: 'this group of boats between them,' he wrote, 'present an almost Darwinian progression of forms … each type has developed up to a point where the local requirements have been met to perfection' (McKee 1983: 212). In order to organize the subject-matter of his study, McKee (1983: 78–105) devised a classification based on distinctive keys of shape alone (Fig. 23.2); it has the advantage that it can be applied to boats which are afloat and in one piece, and does not require either destructive intervention by an archaeologist or explanation by the builder, as is needed to analyse structure. McKee saw that the shape of a boat was related to its structure, but in an undefined way; he recognized that the procedure adopted to build a boat would have to be such as would result in the desired shape, but he did not include a detailed analysis of such procedures in his study (1983: 81). He did, in fact, refer to structural procedures when he had opportunity to record

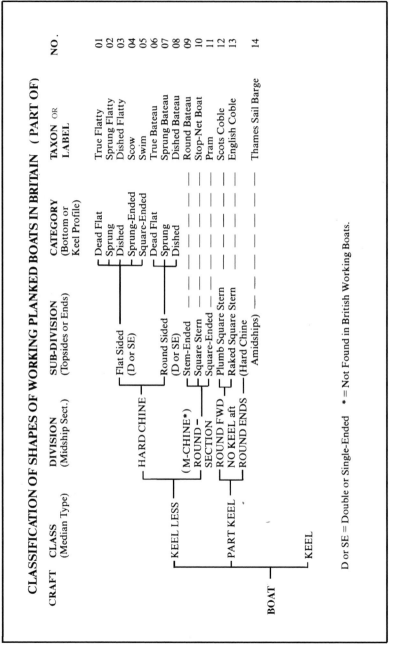

Fig. 23.2. *Morphological taxonomy of keel less and part keel boats of Britain, following Eric McKee (Susan Grice, University of Bristol, after McKee 1983).*

them, and noted that, 'In so far as it can be separated from shape, structure is more regional in nature'.

Meanwhile, however, archaeological and ethnographic studies have emphasized the importance of structural methods in the characterization of boats and boat remains. The traces of the method used may not be visible on a boat which is still in use, and are most readily discerned in the post-excavation study of excavated boat remains (for example, by Maarleveld 1998: 105–133). Structural method may be preserved in local tradition, and may resist changes in the size, function or shape of the boats which are required to be built at a place. A consideration of structural method thus needs to be added to the classification of boats by shape, especially as its distribution may extend beyond the limits of environmental circumstances.

Using only the shape of a boat, McKee (1983: 83) drew up a classification of boat taxa in which, as in other tree-like diagrams, related taxa are grouped together on the plot. It is striking that, of the first ten taxa, seven are represented in the Bristol region. The similarity of the Somerset classes cannot be due to environmental factors, for examination shows that these factors were quite different in each case. What is perhaps more significant is that all the Severn region boats which can be studied in detail show some shared methods of construction. One can posit that it is not the environment which affects a regional grouping of boat shapes, but a shared regional structural tradition. What we do not yet know is how far this tradition goes back in time.

A working boat of round-section form found at Grange Pill, Gloucestershire

In the spring of 2000, Elizabeth Townley, a research student at Bristol University, found the remains of a wooden boat, exposed by run-off erosion from the marsh, at one side of a creek named Grange Pill, at Woolaston, on the western side of the Severn, 24 km north of Bristol. Excavation by volunteers showed that much of the boat had disappeared, and that it appeared to have been abandoned (with a load of local limestone still on board) close to a revetment of the sea-bank (Townley 1998: 84). A one-meter-thick layer of brown alluvium had then formed over the site, and is now being actively eroded back again. The remains of the boat were raised and studied (Parker 2001b) and have now been reburied near the find spot.

The boat was round-section in form, and mostly of oak; the futtocks and floor timbers (7 x 10 cm [3 x 4 ins] or more) were fastened to thick planks by treenails. Iron nails were used in places, but there were no modern materials or other evidence for recent construction or use. Part of a railing and a wale were found, but no deck, rigging, stem, or stern structure. Although the remains were waterlogged, it was possible to lay out much of the wood in a workshop at Bristol University; this enabled the two surviving portions of the boat (which had become repositioned after deposition) to be placed in their correct relationship. The boat must have been originally about 10 m (32 ft) long and over 2.9 m (9 ft 6 in) beam. The planking rises and the strakes taper towards the stern; the stern is missing, but was perhaps square rather than pointed. The bow was clearly very full-cheeked. Neither the keel (or central bottom-plank) nor the stem and sternpost survive; however, it seems likely that all the bottom planks (of elm, at least one being a replacement) were of equal thickness, and that the stem was combined with a knee which was rabbeted to fit on the fore-end of the keel-plank, as in Somerset boats, as noted above (Faine 2001: 62). Only one floor timber (broken) survives; the floor timbers and futtocks alternate but are not joined. The framing timbers appear to be of one phase. Some iron nails are used in fastening the planking, but the main fastenings are treenails, which appear to have been driven from outboard. The planks are not edge-fastened, and the framing elements are discontinuous, so the hull must have been erected by some 'free-arm' method, in McKee's phrase.

The hull, temporarily refitted for study, turned out to have been distinctively rounded in both plan and cross-section. The bow is fuller than the stern, so far as one can tell, and the main frame station (which can be inferred from the spacing of the floor timbers) appears to have lain forward of amidships, indicating a 'cod head – mackerel tail' plan (unlike the parallel-sided stop-net boat, described above). The inboard end of every preserved futtock is set on a wedge, which appears to be original, not a repair; this clearly serves to accentuate and reinforce the rounded cross-section. It may be that the setting of the futtocks had to be adjusted in this way when they were set on the bottom and made ready to receive the side planking, as happened with the Lydney Dock trow (above). This rounded shape places the Grange Pill boat in McKee's taxon no. 10, the 'Stop-Net Boat' type, although its construction differs in many respects from that of 20th-century stop-net fishing boats.

Study of the bottom planking, some of which survived in good condition, showed that the planks are bowed, or sprung, fore-and-aft as well as athwartships. The hull is, therefore, dished, like the Somerset boats classed in McKee's taxon no. 03, 'Dished Flatty', who notes that they were at one time formed with the aid of fire (McKee 1983: 84, 53). However the Grange Pill boat was formed, it is too large to have been built upside-down conveniently, so it must have rested on some kind of cradle which would help create the bottom shape.

Date and function of the Grange Pill boat

The date of the boat is unknown: there were no datable finds from the excavation and no tree-ring date could be obtained by Nigel Nayling from the sawn timbers. The seawall near which the boat lay is not shown on an estate map of 1787 (Gloucestershire Record Office), so it may have been built, and the boat then abandoned, after that date; on the other hand, the pale brown silts which covered the boat formed in the second half of the nineteenth century (Allen 1999; 2003: 62). A search of photographic archives has revealed no obviously similar local boats in the period after c 1850, so a date earlier than this is likely. A ^{14}C date was determined as 30±80 BP (Beta-151769), 'outside of the calibration range'; this at least allows the boat to be dated in the first half of the 19th century, but on its own it does not provide any more detailed dating evidence.

The Register of Coastal Shipping (National Archives; also summarized at the National Maritime Museum) reveals at least one boat in the Woolaston area in the early 19th century which was owned by partnerships of farmers and mariners. Such ownership could explain the carboniferous limestone rubble left lying in the abandoned hull, which was most likely brought 5 km along the coast from Sedbury Cliffs to reinforce a seawall or other farm structure (information from J.E. Jones). A boat of generally similar shape can be seen in an early 19th century view of the ferry-house at Beachley Passage, 8 km south-west of Grange Pill, and it may be possible to recognize her rounded profiles in a small drawing of a river-barge on the Avon above Bristol Bridge in Millerd's late 17th-century view. Where there is evidence for details of shape, the Grange Pill boat can be compared with the Bridgwater barges and other, smaller boats of Somerset, as well as with the stop-net boats of the area where she was found. More important than shape, however, is the structural method used to build the boat: in several ways this is shared with the coast and rivers of the Severn. Despite differences of appearance and of detailed techniques, the approach adopted to build the Grange Pill boat is akin to that used for the Lydney Dock trow. In both cases, the boats were built 'free-arm' in a bottom-based method, and perhaps this was also the essential difference between Bristol ships and those of eastern England in the 17th and 18th centuries. If this were so, one could relate large-scale to small-scale shipbuilding at Bristol, and see both as belonging to a regional school, as their common engagement with the Severn Estuary as a transport zone would imply.

References

Allen, J.R.L., 1999, Two probable wooden jetties at Cone Pill, Lydney Level, Gloucestershire. *Archaeology in the Severn Estuary* 10: 132–134.

Allen, J.R.L., 2003, Intertidal archaeology at Old Passage, Aust, Gloucestershire: a sketch of the surviving evidence. *Archaeology in the Severn Estuary* 13: 53–64.

Banks, L., 1999, *Flat-bottomed boats of the Bristol Channel region*. Unpublished MA dissertation, University of Bristol.

Dunning, R., 1999, Somerset towns, 1340–1642. In T. Mayberry and H. Binding (eds.), *Somerset. The Millennium Book*, 51–60. Tiverton.

Elkin, P., 1995, *Images of Maritime Bristol*. Derby.

Faine, C.M. 2001, *Interpretative Reconstructions of Archaeological Boat Finds*. Unpublished MA dissertation, University of Bristol.

Farr, G.E. 1977, *Shipbuilding in the Port of Bristol*. Greenwich.

Fenwick, V., 1995, Review article: B. Arnold, *Batellerie gallo-romaine sur le lac de Neuchâtel*. *International Journal of Nautical Archaeology* 24: 167–170.

Green, C., 1999, *Severn Traders. The West Country trows and trowmen*. Lydney.

Greenacre, F., 1982, *Marine Artists of Bristol. Nicholas Pocock 1740–1821. Joseph Walter 1783–1856*. Bristol.

Greenacre, F., 2003, Cityscapes. *Bristol Evening Post* 3 June 2003: 36–37.

Greenhill, B., 1976, *Archaeology of the Boat. A new introductory study*. London.

Greenhill, B., 1995, *The Archaeology of Ships and Boats. An introduction*. London.

Hussey, D., 2000, *Coastal and River Trade in Pre-Industrial England: Bristol and its region, 1680–1730*. Exeter.

Maarleveld, T., 1998, Archaeological heritage management in Dutch waters: exploratory studies. *Scheepsarcheologie* 5, Lelystad.

McKee, E., 1983 (reissued 1997), *Working Boats of Britain: their shape and purpose*. London.

Martin, E. and Pickard, B. (eds.), 1973, *600 Years of Bristol Poetry*. Bristol.

Nayling, N., 1996, Further fieldwork and post-excavation: Magor Pill, Gwent Levels intertidal zone. *Archaeology in the Severn Estuary* 7: 85–93.

Parker, A.J., 1999, A maritime cultural landscape: the port of Bristol in the Middle Ages. *International Journal of Nautical Archaeology* 28: 323–342.

Parker, A.J., 2001a, Maritime landscapes. *Landscapes* 2: 22–41.

Parker, A.J., 2001b, Mystery Boat Rescued at Grange Pill, Woolaston. *Nautical Archaeology* 2001.1: 6–7.

Stoddart, S., 2001, *Bristol before the Camera: The City in 1820–30. Watercolours and drawings from the Braikenridge Collection*. Bristol.

Townley, E., 1998, Fieldwork on the Forest shore: Stroat to Woolaston, Gloucestershire. *Archaeology in the Severn Estuary* 9: 82–85.

Waters, B., 1947, *Severn Tide*. London.

Waters, B., 1949, *Severn Stream*. London.

Westerdahl, C., 1995, Traditional zones of transport geography in relation to ship types. In O. Olsen, J.S. Madsen and F. Rieck (eds.), *Shipshape. Essays for Ole Crumlin-Pedersen*, 213–230. Roskilde.

Willan, T.S., 1967, *The English Coasting Trade 1600–1750*. Manchester.

Williams, A., 1992, (ed. C. Clark), *A River Severn Trow at Lydney, Gloucestershire. An archaeological and naval architectural investigation for English Heritage*. Ironbridge Archaeological Series No. 27. Ironbridge: no publication date given.

24 The harbour of Haiðaby

Sven Kalmring

Topographical introduction

Considering the significance of Haiðaby as one of the major commercial centres of the Viking Age, it is important to take a look at its topographical situation first, for it formed the basic requirement for trade. Haiðaby is situated at a most favourable position for trade and communication, at the narrowest point of the Cimbrian peninsula, the Schleswig isthmus. This is even more restricted by natural barrier landscapes of marshes and lowlands in the west and the fjord-like Schlei in the east to a narrow strip only 15 km wide (Fig. 24.1). The site itself is located far inland at the inner end of the Schlei. Two vital marginal inlet at the inner end of the Schlei. Two vital traffic routes ran through the Schleswig isthmus and could be controlled by the fortifications of the Danevirke/ Danewerk and by the settlement of Haiðaby itself. A north-south axis was formed by the Heervej/Ochsenweg, which ran overland from Viborg in the north down to the river Elbe in the south and which can be traced back to the Bronze Age. Even more important to trade was the east-west axis between the Baltic and the North Sea, from the Schlei in the east, over the land bridge and down the rivers Eider and Treene to the Waddensee. The counterpart to the harbour of Haiðaby on the Baltic side was most presumably Hollingstedt, which formed the North Sea harbour for the traffic crossing the isthmus (Jankuhn 1986: 117; Brandt 2002: 83, 102). Beyond this, the topographical situation was geostrategically characterized by its position within the borderland between the Danes, Frisians, Saxons and Slavs (Obodrites), which constituted another important factor for trade and cultural exchange.

The harbour excavation 1979/80

Since Haiðaby as a major commercial centre had to have had a special harbour area to handle trade activities, the question of the construction of the harbour and its facilities arose already in the 1930s (Jankuhn 1936: 98). Interest in the harbour of Haiðaby has persisted and led to the harbour excavation in 1979–1980 (Fig. 24.2) under direction of K.

Schietzel (1984), which required an immense financial and logistic effort and represents the climax of research within the harbour until now. However, apart from a few short preliminary reports, only a small section in connection with the publication of the Haiðaby ships by O. Crumlin-Pedersen (1997: 63f) has hitherto been dedicated to the harbour features revealed in this campaign.

In connection with the excavation of wreck 1, a long, slender personnel carrier of prime workmanship from the end of the 10th century (Fig. 24.3), the substructures of some harbour facilities were encountered. They appeared in outline as regularly spaced rows of posts and continued from the Haddebyer Noor right to the shore and were readily interpreted as the supports of landing-stages or jetties reaching into deeper water. Including expansion of the excavation to the north and south in the second season, around 2000 m² were excavated, representing approximately 1.5 % of the former harbour area within the Noor. In addition, two small, adjacent parts of the shore were uncovered in the extensions of 1980.

The general plan of the excavated area in 1979–80 shows all the registered posts and postholes, and through these the outlines of different harbour facilities appear in the straight lines which are formed by the rows of posts (Fig. 24.4). Six different jetty structures, a shore defence

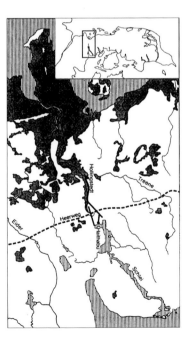

Fig. 24.1. Map showing location of Haiðaby/Hedeby.

Sven Kalmring

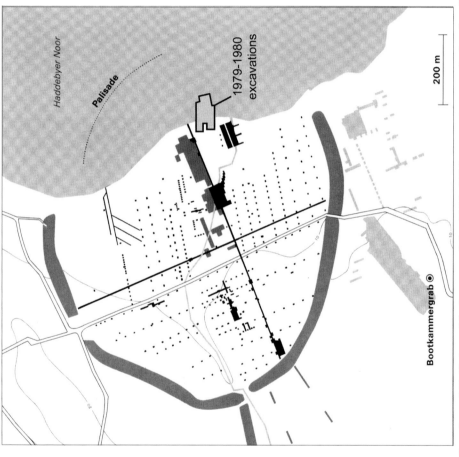

Fig. 24.2. Site plan of Haiðaby, with the area of the 1979–1980 excavations marked with a bold outline.

Haddebyer Noor

Palisade

1979-1980
excavations

200 m

Bootkammergrab ◉

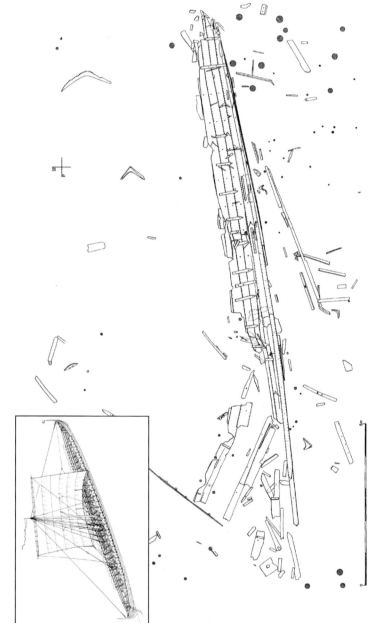

Fig. 24.3. Site plan and reconstruction of Haiðaby wreck 1 (after Crumlin-Pedersen 1997).

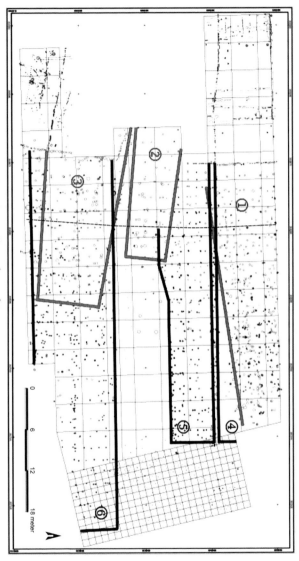

Fig. 24.4. Site plan of jetty structures.

and parts of the former landward development next to the excavated area of the harbour. The harbour facilities themselves must belong to at least two distinct phases with three installations each, because they partly overlap each other and therefore cannot be contemporary.

Stratigraphy and water level

A problem for the analysis of the features was the more or less indistinct stratigraphy within the deeper waters of the Haddebyer Noor. For the most part there were only three main layers, of which the middle layer carried the cultural material. At this stage of work, one very important piece of information can be extracted from at least one of the profiles. During the excavation, one layer was described as "sandy, honeycombed with turf – activity of waves recognizable", which would indicate the shore of the Haddebyer Noor in the Viking Age. This single spot indicates not only the location of the shore, but also provides information about the much-discussed Viking Age water level. It was not, as D. Hoffmann (2001: 132pp.) supposed, 0.8 to 1 m below NN, or even -1.5 m, as W. Kramer assumed (1998/99: 111f), but only 0.5 to 0.6 m below NN (Kalmring 2002: 58pp.). This result has lately been proved by S. Labes (2002: 10) in her work on the water level variation between the Flensburger Förde and the Eckernförder Bucht. With this information, we are able to reconstruct the whole Viking Age shoreline within the excavated area and to distinguish between the dry area or foreshore and the sea.

The knowledge of the Viking Age water level in connection with the recorded profiles makes it possible to determine the depth of the sea at the individual harbour structures. With information on the draught of ships, it is

therefore possible to reconstruct the possibilities of lying alongside the excavated structures. With a terminological framework, one can even arrive at a classification of the harbour facilities of Haiðaby on this basis (Kalmring 2002: 37,106).

The harbour facilities

Although wood preservation in Haiðaby is extremely good because of the deposition of sediments and the rise of the water level, only the substructures of the harbour facilities have survived in the form of regularly placed rows of posts, which can be complemented by the inclusion of postholes. From these it is possible to reconstruct the facilities as open pile works, through which water could flow. Individual structures vary in length from 18 to more than 51 m, and from 6 to 13 m in breadth.

Even though it is not possible to say to which structure every post or post hole belonged, we can catch a glimpse of the interior structure as well as the outlines of the jetties. The structures have been repaired several times and have been built over in some parts by the succeeding structures, but there are regularities in the positions of the posts of the interior bays and the position of the bays in relation to each other are clearly discernable. There even seem to be certain regularities within the interior structures themselves.

From slight discrepancies from the overall alignment within the construction of the substructures, and from rope marks around individual posts at the seaward ends, later extensions can be deduced. They probably became necessary as a result of a combination of silting up of Haddebyer Noor and the development within shipbuilding towards specialized cargo-carriers with more draught (Kalmring 2002: 116).

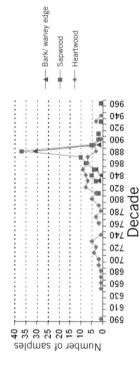

Fig. 24.5. Plot of results from dendrochronological analysis of samples from the 1979–1980 excavations.

Dendrochonology

During the excavation, more than 1500 samples with sufficient annual rings for dating were taken from the oak structural timbers. Dendrochronological analysis of 50% of these samples produced 15% that could be dated, and it was possible to arrive at a dating of the structures (Eckstein and Schietzel 1984). Overall distribution of felling dates showed a strong peak around AD 880–890 and a weaker one around 840 (Fig. 24.5). This indicates that the development of the harbour of Haiðaby took place in two main phases of construction. The earlier suggestion of an extremely early dating for one jetty to around 725–750 (Crumlin-Pedersen 1997: 68), which would be even older than the oldest artefacts from the central settlement area of Haiðaby, could not be sustained (Kalmring 2002: 97p.). On the other hand, the second, younger phase of construction of the harbour corresponds well with the strong peak in the overall chronological distribution of finds around 880–890. The question of the situation of the harbour of late Haiðaby in view of the chronological overall distribution remains open. The main activities did not move to Schleswig, Haiðaby's successor on the Schlei, earlier than c. 1000, and the end of Haiðaby is connected with the attacks of Harald Harderada around 1050 and of the Slavs in 1066.

Prospects

The results of the harbour excavation from 1979–1980 discussed above could only have arisen in this context. Nevertheless, it demonstrates an enormous potential for further research, not only because of the significance of the harbour of Haiðaby during the Viking Age, but also due to the superb wood preservation and the opportunities for dendrochronological analysis. The documentation of the harbour excavation, in the form of drawings of plans and profiles, photo-documentation and dendrochronological data, are currently being worked up and transferred into a Geographical Information System (GIS) within the scope of the *Forschungsprojekt Haithabu*, in order to improve and increase our knowledge on the harbour of Haiðaby, early-medieval harbour facilities and seafaring.

References

Brandt, K., 2002, Wikingerzeitliche und mitelalterliche Besiedlung am Ufer der Treene bei Hollingstedt. Ein Flusshafen im Küstengebiet der Nordsee. In K. Brandt. M. Müller-Wille and Ch. Radtke (eds.). *Haithabu und die frühe Stadtentwicklung im nördlichen Europa.* Schriften des Archäologischen Landesmuseums 8, 83–105. Neumünster.

Crumlin-Pedersen, O., 1997, *Viking-Age Ships and Shipbuilding in Hedeby/Haithabu and Schleswig.* Ships and Boats of the North 1. Schleswig – Roskilde.

Eckstein, D. and Schietzel, K., 1984, Dendrochronologische Gliederung der Baubefunde von Haithabu. In H. Jankuhn, K. Schietzel and H. Reichstein (eds.). *Archäologische und naturwissenschaftliche Untersuchungen an ländlichen und frühstädtischen Siedlungen im deutschen Küstengebiet vom 5. Jahrhundert v.Chr. bis zum 11. Jahrhundert n.Chr. 2. Handelsplätze des frühen und hohen Mittelalters,* 171–184. Weinheim.

Elsner, H. 1994, *Wikinger Museum Haithabu: Schaufenster einer frühen Stadt.* 2nd edition. Neumünster.

Hoffmann, D., 2001, Archäologische Beiträge zu Wasserstandsveränderungen der Ostsee. Eine kritische Betrachtung. *Arch. Nachr. Schleswig-Holstein* 11: 125–137.

Jankuhn, H., 1936, Die Ausgrabungen in Haithabu 1935/36. *Offa* 1: 96–140.

Jankuhn, H., 1984, Die Geschichte der Haithabuforschung und die Entwicklung der Fragestellung. In H. Jankuhn., K. Schietzel and H. Reichstein (eds.), *Archäologische und naturwissenschaftliche Untersuchungen an ländlichen und frühstädtischen Siedlungen im deutschen Küstengebiet vom 5. Jahrhundert v.Chr. bis zum 11. Jahrhundert n.Chr. 2. Handelsplätze des frühen und hohen Mittelalters,* 3–15. Weinheim.

Jankuhn, H. 1986, *Haithabu. Ein Handelsplatz der Wikingerzeit.* 8th edition. Neumünster.

Kalmring, S.. 2002, *Zu den Hafenanlagen von Haiðaby. Dendrochronologische und kulturgeschichtliche Untersuchung zu den Befunden der Ausgrabung 1979/80.* Unpublished MA thesis, Kiel University.

Kramer, W., 1998/99, Neue Untersuchungen im Hafen von Haithabu. *Arch. Nachr. Schleswig-Holstein* 9/10: 90–118.

Labes, S., 2002, Zum Meeresspiegelanstieg an der südwestlichen Ostseeküste aus archäologischer Sicht. *Starigard:* 5–13.

Schietzel, K., 1984, Hafenanlagen von Haithabu. In H. Jankuhn, K. Schietzel and H. Reichstein (eds.), *Archäologische und naturwissenschaftliche Untersuchungen an ländlichen und frühstädtischen Siedlungen im deutschen Küstengebiet vom 5. Jahrhundert v.Chr. bis zum 11. Jahrhundert n.Chr. 2. Handelsplätze des frühen und hohen Mittelalters,* 184–191. Weinheim.

25 Money, port and ships from a Schleswig point of view

Christian Radtke

Money

The Baltic economy was, from its very beginnings, based on imported silver.[1] The period of the inflow of Arabic dirhams between the start of the 9th century and the end of the 10th century lies, however, outside the discussion here as do also the reasons behind the sudden ending of this influx round about the turning of the millennium. As a result of this radical change in the main direction of trade, large numbers of silver coins streamed in several phases and waves from around 970 out of the towns of the German Empire into the Baltic region. The material basis certainly lay in the Rammelsberg silver mines near Goslar, which opened in the year 968. Mirrored in the finds, this influx occurred in several waves, reached its peak sometime before 1050, declined after 1070 and thereafter found sole expression on Gotland and on the opposing Baltic and Russian coastlines, when Gotland began minting its own coins about 1140, and Estonia and Russia likewise later.

According to the latest statistics, we have more than 270,000 coins minted on the continent and found in hoards from the Baltic, concentrated in southern Sweden, on Gotland, in Russia and the west Slavic region, dating approximately to between 1000 and 1150. The numismatists have calculated that this stock (assuming 10,000 strikes per die) represents a minting output of around two thousand million coins. This is equivalent to a silver weight of 2000 metric tons, with about 50–100 million coins (representing 50–100 tons of silver) in circulation at any one time. These are immensely high numbers.

Everyone agrees that the coins have to be seen as indicators of long-distance trading activity. Turning away from the statistical view of matters to look at the largely unknown aspect of trading practice, it may be supposed that these coins were, once upon a time, transported to the north individually, or in larger amounts. Since money cannot move itself, it must have been moved by a correspondingly high number of long-distance traders. The trading system of this period largely functioned according to the principle of 'goods for money'. Of course, the long-distance traders of the western part of the continent, to whom the discussion here is restricted, also had goods on offer for the Baltic markets. In the case of the Schleswig market, mention is made of textiles, weapons and gold jewellery for example, which most obviously came from the continent. The most important operations of such traders, however, were in minted silver, i.e. money, with which the goods of the Baltic region could be acquired. Most important among these were furs for luxury clothing and bee's wax for church candles.

Summing up so far: from the numismatic point of view, the German coins from the late 10th to the early 12th century "nearly all streamed out to the Baltic, as if they had been minted purely for export",[2] to quote Bernd Kluge (1978: 186). The hoard finds have revealed that they were used in their hundreds of thousands for import transactions in the Baltic, thus earning the title "long distance trade denarii".

About one third to one half of these coins stem from the catchment area of the North Sea, i.e. from the large trading centres on the Rhine and surrounding area and from the Frisian coast. Cologne undoubtedly formed the centre of this economic region, with other important places including Dortmund and Soest in Westphalia and Tiel, Utrecht and Deventer more towards the coast. Here were located the mints for the coins found in the Baltic region and thus the starting points for the long-distance trade using the coins.

The journey to the Baltic taken by the traders and their 'accompanying' coins from the Rhineland and the Frisian ports took them inevitably from the west to the east across the North Sea and the Schleswig isthmus into the Baltic region. As already known from the Viking Period, the two transhipment stations in this transit traffic were Hollingstedt on the river Treene in the west and Hedeby/Schleswig at the most inner part of the Schlei fjord in the east. It was thanks to this transit highway that Hedeby enjoyed such great significance in the 9th and 10th century, Schleswig taking over as its successor in the 11th century.

In the 11th and the first half of the 12th century, two economic blocks encountered one another at Schleswig: the continental trading system in which silver coins were legal tender according to their nominal value and the Baltic system in which coins were valued according to their weight of precious metal. The two systems were hermetically isolated from each other, did not penetrate one another but butted against each other at this border. This means that at every business transaction completed in Schleswig, money had to be "demonetised" and converted from its value as coin money into weight money. It changed its character from being struck and minted and authorised by a ruler and became weighed silver or bullion. Schleswig was the 'bureau de change'. From here the 'new' money spread into the economic circulation of the Baltic. On the way it was halved and quartered piece by piece and tested for its silver content whenever it changed ownership. And finally it landed in one of the thousands of hoards, buried in an earthen treasury. The end of this business cycle had come at the latest about 1150 with the minting of new types of coins in the German Empire, whose circulation was reduced to the neighbourhood of the respective minting places. In this very moment from a historical point of view a new place of contact between the continent and the Baltic was built up, that is Lübeck.

The conversion of coin and weight money required scales and weights. These are richly evidenced as archaeological finds in Schleswig. Like coins, this source of evidence is able to illustrate spheres of trade and communication within far-flung business relations. According to this, a circle which embraces all the coastal lands of the Baltic during a phase spanning 970/1000 to 1050/1070, intersects with a circle oriented towards the North Sea. The intersection is located in the central part of Denmark, whose economic and communications centre, tangential to both circles, was formed by Schleswig. In this macro-structure Schleswig clearly becomes important in its function as a broker's place to buy and sell, as a trading centre and meeting place. The number of finds of balances and weights confirms this picture convincingly (Steuer 1997).

Alongside the trading activities one may also have to reckon with a systematic import of silver to Denmark, which was of immense interest to the Danish king because he was continually in need of large amounts of silver for his coin minting. As an example: 500,000 coins with a silver content of 800 pro mille (.800 fine) require 400 kg of silver. It has been calculated that for each one of the numerous types of coins which were struck in Lund and Roskilde in the 1070s, some 300–500,000 pieces were produced. Therefore thousands of kilograms of silver were required, supposedly mostly in the form of coins which were then melted down for reminting – as is known archaeologically from a 12th-century find from Lödöse, Sweden.

If, as can be assumed, a large part of these coins reached the Baltic via Schleswig – and where else otherwise? not via Old Lübeck at the Trave river or Wolin at the mouth of the Oder river – these numismatic findings have consequences for the port topography in Schleswig as well as for ship activities, consequences which to date have not been thoroughly considered by research.

Port

The function of the town of Schleswig as an arterial gateway for continental silver into the Baltic, as implied above, inevitably demands a corresponding structure in the topography, in market trading, in legal customs and in the constitution. Of prime interest here is the port. According to our hypothesis it must have been present since the beginnings of this influx, that is the turn of the millennium. Unfortunately the archaeological picture for the years between around 1000 and 1070 is not very clear and it is not until the end of the 11th century that archaeology confirms the numismatical and historical sources. The port waterfront with its seven known massive jetties is the largest known port of the High Middle Ages in Northern Europe. The waterfront constructions, quays and piers which have been excavated were erected in the years between 1081 and 1095. They were over 10 m wide, reached into the open water for up to 45 m, and were later extended even further. Considering the analysis of the town layout, the port apparently stretched over the whole southern waterfront of the settlement and took up a major part of it.

The principles of construction were simple: bulkhead boxes (caissons) were made of oak beams and filled with an earthen mass, consisting partially of settlement rubble which had been dug out elsewhere and which contains interesting archaeological information such as 11th-century weights and fragments of silk. This material is therefore older than the dated structures on the external palisades. It is possible that the material consisted of the demolished remains of structures from a precursor settlement. The fill rested on a layer of brushwood which was originally 30 cm thick and which had itself been sealed by layers of rich farmyard manure above and below, to keep it airtight and watertight. Three construction phases can be differentiated: 1087, 1095 and after 1095. These later dates are not based on dendrochronology as in this period the stock of thick oak trunks had strongly declined, leading to the use of thin posts that cannot be used for this dating method. This tendency towards dwindling resources may also be observed in house construction (Vogel 1999). Along one road running parallel to the waterfront, building was carried out from 1075. The pottery lying below, however, points to a period well before 1070.

The enlarging and extending of the port structures in quick succession in the direction of the open water between the years 1087 and 1095 signalise the pressing interest of the town lord and long-distance traders to provide ample port capacities to the growing traffic in shipping. The size of a port directly mirrors the shipping tonnage. This tonnage must have rapidly increased, therefore, from around 1080 to 1095 – quite in contrast to the numismatic findings in the countries of destination of this shipping traffic, where the amount of German import money in the Scandinavian hoards clearly declines. This reduced depositing of hoards, however, should not be misinterpreted as a drop in the volume of trade. Most probably, correspondingly large amounts of silver were melted down for Danish mints which were flourishing, as exemplified by Lund and Roskilde. From the historical viewpoint, there was a dramatic upswing about 1100 in trading activities between the Lower Rhineland and Westphalia on the one hand and the Baltic lands on the other.

The plots, houses and roadways comprising the port settlement were aligned at right angles to the landing-bridges. The dense development bordered gable to gable close to the trackways. The houses were like the others in Schleswig, being one-roomed post dwellings on raised wooden floors with vertical plank walls and having a hearth. Since workshops and stables are missing, it appears that this area of settlement was made for the business of trading and storage so that topographically, the impression prevails of a settlement structure laid out mainly for marine trading. Single buildings also stood on the piers themselves and presumably served as warehouses. It is possible – as suggested by the excavator Volker Vogel (1999: 193) – that the individual piers were in private ownership.

The picture of intensive port business is confirmed by the written sources, which not only mention the *portus* frequently, but which also place it earlier in time than the *civitas*, the royal and episcopal town. We are quite well informed, both historically and archaeologically, about life in the port area. Finds of coins and weights and central terms from the town charter such as *gubernator*, the steersman and ship owner, *nautae*, the ship's crew and merchants, *nautum*, chartering, *emptor* and *venditor*, buyers and sellers, and others speak clearly. One of the most important legal arrangements consisted of storing other persons' goods as if they were one's own. Paragraphs from Maritime Law with rules concerning life on board and in foreign ports go back to seafaring laws extending back to old Nordic times and presumably into the Viking Age. As demonstrated archaeologically, the definite end of the port came with the monastery of the Dominicans being built in 1238 on the ground of the major part of the waterfront area.

Ships

As reported in the written sources, for example in Adam of Bremen and the Schleswig Town Charter, ships hailing from and going off in all directions of Baltic trading could be found in the port of Schleswig. The most important trade route was certainly that going to Gotland and further on to Novgorod, the export port for furs and bee's wax, two commodities which brought the greatest profit. Other destinations lay in Norway, in Southern Sweden, on the island of Bornholm and on the southern Baltic coast.

Several examples of the types of ships used for Schleswig's long-distance trading are now known. As in the case of the port facilities, the ships too had to correspond to the volume of trade in terms of construction type and capacity. The merchantman built on the Schlei about 1025 which went down in Haddeby Noor opposite Schleswig port, referred to technically as Wreck III from Hedeby, fully complies with these requirements. Built in the Nordic clinker technique and having 25 m length, maximum beam of 6.2 m and depth of 2.5 m, it is particularly high-sided and robust and can be identified as one of ships of *knorr* type, which were navigable in the high seas. The cargo capacity totalled some 60 tonnes. Seen from the viewpoint of ship archaeology, it stands at the beginning of a line of large trading ships (Crumlin-Pedersen 2002: fig. 5) well known also from the finds from the port of Roskilde.

Belonging to this group is also the Karschau ship, which was recently raised from the middle Schlei (Englert *et.al.* 2002). Built sometime after 1138, it stands somewhat at the end of the series of large trading ships of Scandinavian type of construction. With a total length of 25 m, beam of 6.6 m and capacity of 50 to 60 tons, it is among the largest of cargo ships of its age and can at best be compared with the well documented Lynaes I ship, which was built about 1150. Many of the details show its affiliation with the Nordic boat-building tradition: the iron rivets used to connect the planking, the caulking with animal hair, the decorative profiling of structural timbers and the insertion of *bien* over every floor-timber. The ship sank presumably on the voyage to Schleswig. Small finds from its interior yield interesting information. Animal bones and the remains of deep sea and fresh water fish give insights to the daily diet, while hazelnut shells and pips and stones from sloes, apples and plums attest to a supplementary diet rich in vitamins and minerals. In addition to the ceramic and wooden vessels on board ship, there were also combs for personal hygiene and gaming pieces for leisure activity. Most interesting is the large number of about 300 wooden pins with which – according to my theory – perhaps furs were tied up into bundles. Most likely we are dealing with a fur freighter on its way from Gotland or Novgorod to Schleswig and which foundered shortly before its port of destination, being plundered perhaps and partially broken up.

Another 'big ship,' a third one, is known from the outer Schleswig harbour area lying just at the southern shore of the island with the *castellum ante portum* of Schleswig. Built about 1150 it reaches – as far as is known today – a tonnage of 50 to 60 tons, that is like Hedeby III and the Karschau ship.

From Schleswig itself has been retrieved a large quantity of ship parts which were used secondarily in the building of houses and roads. There are over 50 timber fragments from various areas of construction, giving information about ships which were broken up there, including frames and planks from a "largish cargo vessel of Nordic type" (Crumlin-Pedersen 1997: 266) which was built in 1095, the year when the port underwent large expansion.

A *navis magna* which, according to written sources, was built about the year 1175 in Schleswig was another large ship with such generous proportions that it had difficulties being launched (Radtke 2002b: 47). Characteristic details such as lubricants (*lubricum aliquid*) and sliding cushions (*pulvini suppositi*) are not necessary for the archaeological finds but are useful when it comes to the keel-less ships of cog type. After a centuries-old tradition and practical experience in ship-building, it seems to me implausible that building a normal ship in the Nordic keel and clinker technique would have been asking too much of a wharf. The launching of a new and untested type of ship with flat bottom for whose construction there was of yet not the accumulated experience, could, however, have given rise to problems as with the cog. This could fit into recent considerations by Jan Bill and Fred Hocker (2004) that the archaeologically known early Danish cogs were built in southeastern Jutland. Perhaps the construction plans were provided by the Frisians, who have been clearly attested to in Schleswig in the written sources.

Alongside these large merchant ships engaged in overseas traffic, a vessel used on the inland waterways has recently been discovered (Kühn 2004). This craft is a flat-bottomed vessel built about 1184 and was 14.5 m long and 2.7 m wide. It had open gates in the bow and stern between vertical sides about 0.5 m high. The bottom and side planks were held together by 22 floor timbers. The bottom is built in carvel fashion. The features of such construction are distinct from the Nordic ship-building tradition and approaching the cog type. It is possible that the above mentioned 'big ship' and this barge belong to the same construction milieu (cf. Bill and Hocker 2004). The barge most probably served as a ferry over the River Schlei. Recent studies have shown that the overland routes leading to Schleswig from the south and the west ended on the southern banks of the Schlei, meaning that the town was only accessible via the river. All the heavy traffic, therefore, had to cross the Schlei. This historically-based thesis, however, has yet to be substantiated by archaeology (Radtke 2004a).

Conclusions

In the 11th and 12th centuries, Schleswig was one of the most important international trading centres in the Baltic region (cf. Radtke 2004b). Its significance was based on its function as a 'bureau de change' between the two

prevailing economic systems – the coin money of the continent and the weight money of the Baltic. As continental long-distance merchants did not travel the Baltic themselves until about 1160, it must have been that the hundreds of thousands of Western European coins known to us from the hoards of the Baltic changed ownership at one stage in Schleswig. The town is structurally geared to this function. Apart from the king's area with the royal palace and the church with the episcopal cathedral, the port covers the greatest area. With its seven known piers, it extends some 150 m along the waterfront. In the year 1095 alone, five piers were erected. The maritime face of the town was above all visible in the shipping traffic. As reported by the town charter and as can be recognised by the archaeological finds, ships from the whole of Scandinavia put into port at Schleswig. Numerous structural fragments from 11th- and 12th-century Nordic ships are known from secondary building activity. In the harbour of Hedeby, a cargo ship built in 1025 went down (Hedeby 3), while in the middle course of the River Schlei at Karschau another ship with a building date of about 1140 was wrecked, and a third one of about 1150 is known near the island in front the harbour itself. All of them have capacities of around 60 tons, placing them among the largest known merchant vessels of Nordic type of construction. In the light of the recently discovered flat-bottomed barge of about 15 m length and 2.7 m breadth (which was built about 1180), the question again arises as to whether the port of Schleswig was participating in the new type of ship, the cog, already in the 12th century. A written source referring to the difficult launching of a very large ship about 1175 could be interpreted as in that year Schleswig saw the launching of one of the first cogs of the Baltic. That would be a new indication of tradition and innovation in shipbuilding in Schleswig in the 11th and 12th centuries.

It is hoped that this paper has drawn attention to the fact that under no circumstances should ships be considered in isolation. They are always a reflection of processes undergone by society as a whole. Merchant ships mirror economic relations. In this case these are especially discernible through the money hoards found in the coastal lands of the Baltic. Money, ports and ships are three parts of one system.

Notes

1   This text is mainly based on Radtke 2002 a; please see the more extensive references given there; further references are given here in a few characteristic cases, for new literature and for quotations. This text was translated by Amanda Loughran M.A.. Kassel.

2   [*Sie sind*] *nahezu komplett in den Ostseeraum abgeströmt, ja, geradezu für den Export geprägt worden.*

References

Bill. J. and Hocker, F. 2004, Haithabu 4 seen in the context of contemporary shipbuilding in Southern Scandinavia. In K. Brandt and H. J. Kühn (Eds), *Der Prahm aus dem Hafen von Haithabu ("Wrack Haithabu IV") in seinen regionalen und überregionalen Bezügen*. Schriften des Archäologischen Landesmuseums. Ergänzungsreihe 2. Neumünster.

Crumlin-Pedersen, O. 1997, *Viking-Age Ships and Shipbuilding in Hedeby/Haithabu and Schleswig*. Ships and Boats of the North 2. Schleswig and Roskilde.

Crumlin-Pedersen, O. 2002. Schiffahrt im frühen Mittelalter und die Herausbildung früher Städte im westlichen Ostseeraum. In K. Brandt, M. Müller-Wille and Chr. Radtke (eds.), *Haithabu und die frühe Stadtentwicklung im nördlichen Europa*. Schriften des Archäologischen Landesmuseums 8, 67–81. Neumünster.

Englert, A. et al. 2002, Das Wrack von Karschau. *Beretning fra enogtyvende tværfaglige vikingesymposium* 7–25. Højbjerg.

Kluge, B. 1978: Bemerkungen zur Struktur der Funde europäischer Münzen des 10. und 11. Jahrhunderts im Ostseegebiet. *Zeitschrift für Archäologie* 12, 183–190. Berlin.

Kühn, H. J. 2004: Ein hochmittelalterlicher Fährprahm im Haddebyer Noor. In K. Brandt and H. J. Kühn (eds.), *Der Prahm aus dem Hafen von Haithabu ("Wrack Haithabu IV") in seinen regionalen und überregionalen Bezügen*. Schriften des Archäologischen Landesmuseums. Ergänzungsreihe 2. Neumünster.

Radtke, Christian 2002a. Schleswig im vorlübischen Geld- und Warenverkehr zwischen westlichem Kontinent und Ostseeraum. In K. Brandt, M. Müller-Wille and Chr. Radtke (eds.),

Haithabu und die frühe Stadtentwicklung im nördlichen Europa. Schriften des Archäologischen Landesmuseums 8, 379–429. Neumünster.

Radtke, Christian 2002b. Die Kogge. In H. Mehl (ed.), *Historische Schiffe. Vom Nydamboot zur Gorch Fock*. Volkskundliche Sammlungen vol. 7, 38–50. Heide.

Radtke, Christian 2004a. Der Prahm "Haithabu IV" in seinem historischen Kontext: Schleitransit, Fährstation, Überlandwege und die Kirche von Haddeby. In K. Brandt and H. J. Kühn (Eds), *Der Prahm aus dem Hafen von Haithabu ("Wrack Haithabu IV") in seinen regionalen und überregionalen Bezügen*. Schriften des Archäologischen Landesmuseums. Ergänzungsreihe 2 (in press). Neumünster.

Radtke, Christian 2004b. Schleswig c. 1000 – 1250. Systems theory sketches for profiling urbanisation. In N. Engberg et al. (eds.), *Archaeology of medieval Towns in the Baltic and North Sea Area*. Publications from the National Museum. Studies in Archaeology and History. Copenhagen.

Steuer, H. 1997: *Waagen und Gewichte aus dem mittelalterlichen Schleswig. Funde des 11. bis 13. Jahrhunderts aus Europa als Quellen zur Handels- und Währungsgeschichte*. Zeitschrift für Archäologie des Mittelalters. Beiheft 10. Köln.

Vogel, V. 1999, Der Schleswiger Hafen im hohen und späten Mittelalter. In J. Bill et.al. (eds.), *Maritime Topography and the Medieval Town*. Publications from the National Museum. Studies in Archaeology and History 4, 187–196. Copenhagen.

26 Inland water transport in the Pre-Roman Iron Age in Northern Germany and its role in intra- and intercultural communication

Ulrike Teigelake

Introduction

This article gives a short overview over the results of a doctoral thesis carried out in cooperation between Södertörns Högskola (University College), Stockholm, and the Unversity of Kiel.

Despite the fact that prehistoric Germany's geographical conditions were much more favourable for river transport than for land transport, the question of inland water transport in this area has so far rather little been taken into consideration by historians and archaeologists. The geographical frame of the investigation is defined by the river Rhine in the West, the river Odra in the East, the German-Danish boarder in the North and an east-west line roughly defined by the river Lippe, a tributary of the Rhine and an important axis in prehistoric times, in the South.

Evidence for water transport usually comes from a certain number of source catagories, such as shipwrecks, pictorial evidence, harbours or landing places, ship's cargo and, finally, historical sources. For Iron Age

Northern Germany, however, there is a rather special situation. Pictorial evidence is completely missing. Harbours or landing places have so far hardly been identified, and the same is the case for clearly identified ship's cargo. Written evidence only starts in the second half of the period under study. Finally, the number and distribution of ship finds is not at all representative.

As shown in the map (Fig. 26.1), there are no ship finds dated to the Pre-Roman or Roman Iron Age in the eastern part of Northern Germany. However, the distribution of all log boat finds from Stone Age to Early Modern times (Hirte 1987: 40, Map 1), which is relatively even from east to west, shows that this picture is mainly a result of the state of research. There are a number of ship finds in the East, but the bulk of them are dated either to another period or not at all. Until more logboat finds are dated by carbon 14 or dendrochronological methods, the distribution map of Iron Age ship finds in Northern Germany can thus not be taken to be representative.

Another restricting factor is the number of ship finds,

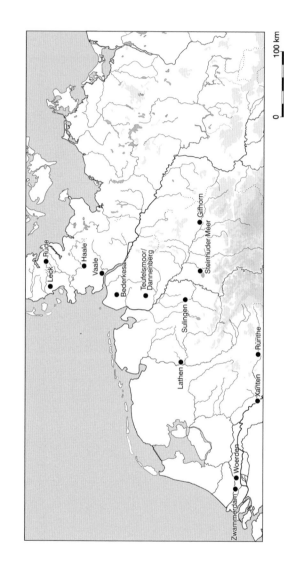

Fig. 26.1. Distribution of Iron Age ship finds in the area under study (Teigelake/Rothe 2003).

which is too small to draw valuable conclusions about the original Iron Age boat traffic, regional boatbuilding traditions or the like. Therefore a combination of different methods has been chosen to treat the question of what role inland water transport played in Iron Age Northern Germany.

The three main starting points of the investigation are boat finds, written sources and secondary sources (see Teigelake 2003a). From written sources we can gain an impression of the use of boats in Germanic society. Secondary sources, which means secondary goods that are believed to have been transported by water, give clues about the location of water routes or combined land-water routes. The technical investigation of the available ship finds gives information about the standard of boatbuilding techniques, sizes and types of boats, type and size of inland routes used for ship traffic, and finally about the degree of specialisation employed in Iron Age boat-building in Northern Germany.

Archaeological and written evidence

Boat finds

The boat finds represent three general types of boats. These are the dugout, the extended dugout and the flat-bottomed barge or "prahm" (Table 26.1). Out of 22 ship finds, there are 12 simple dugouts, two extended and one expanded dugout, and six flat-bottomed barges.

At the present stage, two of the three types show a regional concentration within the area under study. While the flat-bottomed barges appear only to the west of the river Rhine, the extended dugouts are found in a larger region west of the Jutland peninsula, but the number of finds is too small to allow a conclusion regarding regional boatbuilding traditions. Further, both types have been found out of the working area as well. The flat-bottomed barge has been found in a Gallo-Roman context in different western European countries (see Arnold 1992). Extended dugouts have also been found in different contexts in the area of the Baltic (Crumlin-Pederson 1972; Ossowski 1999: 215).

The main purpose of the investigation of the ship finds is to determine the probable function of each boat, in order to put it into the general context of inland water transport. Further, it is suggested that the degree of specialisation of a vessel is related to the degree of organisation of water transport. While a smaller multi-purpose vessel is ideal for use by a private person or a family, a long slender boat for rapid transport of a larger number of people can hardly be used in a private context. An organisation, bringing the required number of crew together, must stand behind it. Viking longships might serve as an example. Without a considerable number of people, strictly organised and led by a king or chieftain, the building, maintaining and sailing of longships was not possible. Even if they were smaller and more simple in shape, the long, slender dugouts made for rapid transport in Northern Germany must be a similar case. The conclusion is that the existence of specialised boats shows the existence of an organisation in water transport. To show this was one of the main aims of the investigation.

To learn about any specialisation, the characteristics of the boats had to be analysed with regard to their function. This was to a large part done by comparison to other archaeological and ethnological investigations of logboats and barges (see, for example, McGrail 1988). The characteristics in question were, for example, the shape of cross section and longitudinal section, the shape of bow and stern, the height of the sides, as well as internal construction like ribs, futtocks, thwarts, cleats, etc., further the overall size and several ratios, such as the length-to-beam ratio. The find situation and the type of waterway in which a vessel was found were also taken into consideration. From the overall picture gained from each find, the finds were set into different functional groupings. Since flat-bottomed barges are a boat type designed as slow, but effective, cargo carriers or working boats, only the dugouts had to be analysed concerning their general function. These are shown in Table 26.2.

After this first functional grouping (see Teigelake 2003b: Table 3.9 for more details) it was possible to divide the main functions into "specialised" and "non-specialised". Specialised are such boats which can only or mainly be used for one purpose, for example, rapid

Dugout	Extended Dugout	"Prahm"
Bederkesa	Leck	Woerden
Githorn	Vaale	Xanten-Lüttingen
Haale		Xanten-Wardt
Lathen		Zwammerdam 2, 4, 6
Rüde 1-3		
Rünthe		
Steinhuder Meer		
Sulingen		
Teufelsmoor		
Zwammerdam 1, 3, 5		

Table 26.1. Types of boats found in Iron Age Northern Germany

Simple and extended dugouts	
Main function	Number of boat finds
Fishing	-
Hunting	1
Mainly personal transport	4
Mainly cargo carrier	3
Specialised ferry function	1 (counted in personal transport)
Multi-purpose vessel	5
No grouping possible	2

Table 26.2. Functional grouping of the boat finds

personal transport of a large group of people – in other contexts called "war canoe" – or for slow but effective cargo transport. Non-specialised are those which can be used for personal transport as well as for cargo transport or for fishing, for example. Of the dugouts and boats examined, six could be described as non-specialised and 13 as specialised. The relatively high number of specialised boat finds can serve as evidence for a considerable degree of organisation existing in Northern German prehistoric boat traffic. This picture is supported by the evidence from written and secondary sources, too.

Written sources

Historical and ethnological reports from ancient authors, such as Caesar, Tacitus, Pliny and others, contain numerous descriptions of boat transport on the sea or inland waters in the area of prehistoric Northern Germany. In the middle of the first century BC, Caesar (*BG* IV,4.1–7) writes about tribes living on both sides of the Rhine, obviously using boats to get from shore to shore, as well as about several river crossings by Germanic warriors or whole tribes, where not only people and cargo, but also horses and possibly other beasts, were transported on the water. This not only shows the need for boats, but also the ability to build them. Later, in the first century AD, Tacitus (*Hist.* V.22.2–3) writes about battles between the Low German tribe of the Batavi together with their allies and the Romans, carried out on the Rhine, in which the Batavi succeed and steal part of the Roman Rhine fleet. Following this, a parade in which the Germans show their whole fleet to the Romans in the mouth of the Rhine is described (*Hist.* V.23.1–2). From this we learn about several different types of ships possessed by the Batavi, some made for up to 40 people and most of them propelled by sails. Battles between Romans and Germans on other rivers are also described (Tacitus, *Ann.*, XI.18). The fact that the Romans bring up considerable numbers of biremes and triremes for this purpose makes it clear that on the German side there must have also been a certain strength in boats, and not only a few dugouts, as is sometimes written. The written sources thus present a picture of well-equipped and organised boat traffic on the sea, as well as on inland waters.

Secondary sources

Finally, to find out about the geographical expansion of inland water traffic within Northern Germany, the distribution of characteristic find categories has been analysed. For this purpose, from the available written and archaeological sources about imports, exports and transports within Northern Germany, those finds, for which there is a high likelihood that they have been transported on water, have been selected. Reasons for water transport would have been great weight or size, or a very fragile constitution (see Teigelake 2003a for a fuller discussion). As result, a group of find categories, mainly made up

from imported vessels of Mediterranean and Celtic origin, has been put together: bronze vessels, terra sigillata and other fine Roman ceramics, glass vessels, silver vessels, iron vessels and rotary querns from the Eifel region.

Based on comparisons to other regions and periods (Pauli 1993; Salač 1998; Sorokin 1997) these find categories should function as an indicator for water transport so their distribution has been mapped and viewed in relation to the river systems of Northern Germany. To exclude any coincidence, the general find distribution has also been mapped and has in most cases been shown to be much different. The results of this mapping of characteristic import finds can be summarised as below (Fig. 26.2).

The distribution of the complete find material shows a definite concentration near waterways, but the different categories vary in their distribution. For the Pre-Roman Iron Age (Fig. 26.2), the imported bronze vessels give a clear picture of transportation by water, even though Northern Germany is both the area of production and consumption (see Kimmig 1983: 43, Figure 34, 35 and 42). In the Roman Iron Age, the number of find categories increases, as does the density of finds. Here we have at least one category that is certain to have been transported on the water from the place of production to the purchaser: Terra Sigillata (Fig. 26.3). The same is probably true for glass vessels (Fig. 26.4), based on the distribution.

While terra sigillata was transported down the Rhine and through the North Sea eastwards, it apparently did not go further than the Elbe estuary, nor did rotary querns, but glass vessels can be found east of the Elbe (Fig. 26.5). They seem to have been subject to another transport organisation. Their distribution within the eastern part of Germany seems to point towards a transport along the Baltic coast and up the small rivers leading southwards.

In this context there is a very interesting region, between the lower Elbe near Lauenburg and the town of Wismar by the Baltic coast. Here we find a concentration of glass finds, lying in a row between the Elbe and the Baltic, as well as several bronze, silver and other valuable vessels. This find situation is interpreted as an indicator for a Roman Period land route between the North Sea and the Baltic, comparable to the later land route at the foot of the Jutland peninsula connecting the waters of the the Eider, the Treene and the Schlei, controlled by the Viking Age town of Hedeby. More research is necessary to verify (or falsify) this thesis, but it is indeed an intriguing situation.

Summary

The question of the organisation of water transport within prehistoric Northern Germany has been treated in three different approaches. Each of them, but particularly combining all three of them, has shown not only that the region saw a significant amount of inland water transport, but also a considerable degree of organisation within it.

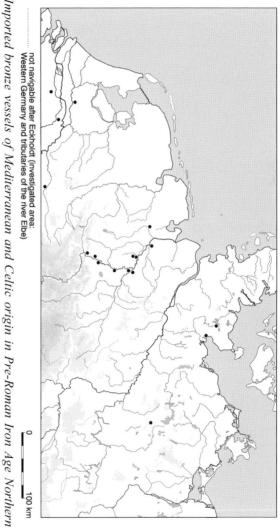

not navigable after Eckholdt (investigated area:
Western Germany and tributaries of the river Elbe)

Fig. 26.2. Imported bronze vessels of Mediterranean and Celtic origin in Pre-Roman Iron Age Northern Germany
(Teigelake/Rothe 2003).

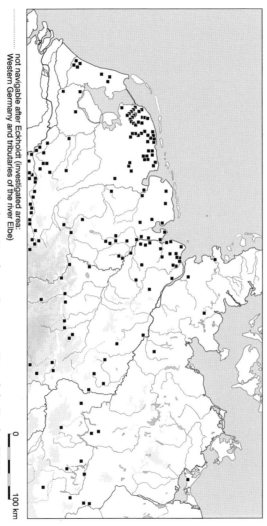

not navigable after Eckholdt (investigated area:
Western Germany and tributaries of the river Elbe)

Fig. 26.3. Terra sigillata finds in Northern Germany (Teigelake/Rothe 2003).

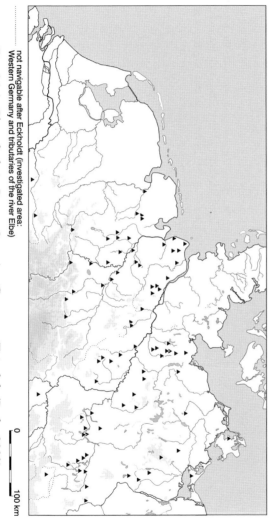

not navigable after Eckholdt (investigated area:
Western Germany and tributaries of the river Elbe)

Fig. 26.4. Glass finds in Roman Iron Age Germany (Teigelake/Rothe 2003).

Ulrike Teigelake

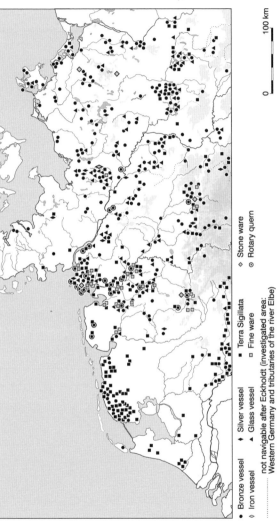

● Bronze vessel   ♦ Silver vessel   ■ Terra Sigillata   ◇ Stone ware
◇ Iron vessel   ▲ Glass vessel   □ Fine ware   ⦿ Rotary quern
- - - not navigable after Eckholdt (investigated area:
     Western Germany and tributaries of the river Elbe)

0   100 km

Fig. 26.5. Characteristic import finds in Roman Iron Age Northern Germany (Teigelake/Rothe 2003).

This is a result at odds with those historians and archaeologists who have written that the organisation within Germanic society (even in the Roman Iron Age) was at too low a level to allow any organised transport system on the water (e.g. Kunow 1983: 55). Many individual aspects of this organisation, such as evidence for regular patterns of landing stations already in the Pre-Roman Iron Age, or the aforementioned land route between the North Sea and the Baltic, are future targets that will help to clarify the picture of Early Germanic water transport.

Acknowledgements

For help and support with developing and finishing the PhD thesis this paper is based on, I owe my thanks to many people. I would like to thank my colleagues at Kiel University and Södertörns Högskola, Stockholm, the Archaeological Museum of Schleswig-Holstein in Schleswig, the Deutsches Schiffahrtsmuseum, Bremerhaven, and the Viking Ship Museum, Roskilde. I am particularly grateful to Carl Olof Cederlund for inviting me into Södertörns Högskola's maritime archaeological research project and for many fruitful discussions and support. The studies have been financed by the Swedish Östersjö Stiftelse and the German Alfried Krupp von Bohlen und Halbach – Stiftung.

References

Ancient Sources

G. Julius Caesar, *De bello Gallico.*
Cornelius Tacitus, *Historiae.*
Cornelius Tacitus, *Annales.*

Modern works

Arnold, B., 1992, *Battellerie gallo-romaine sur le lac de neuchâtel. Vol. 2, Archéologique neuchâteloise* 12. 13. Saint Blasie
Crumlin Pedersen, O., 1972, Skin or wood? A study of the origin of the Scandinavian plank-boat. In O. Hasslöf, H. Henningsen and A. E. Christensen, Jr. (eds.), *Ships and shipyards, sailors and fishermen*, pp. 208–234. Copenhagen.
Hirte, C., 1987, *Zur Archäologie monoxlyer Wasserfahrzeuge im nördlichen Mitteleuropa*, unpublished PhD dissertation, Kiel University.
Kunow, J., 1983, *Der römische Import in der Germania libera bis zu den Markomannenkriegen, Studien zu Bronze-und Glasgefäßen.* Neumünster.
McGrail, S., 1998, *Ancient Boats in N.W. Europe, The Archaeology of Water Transport to AD 1500*, 2nd edition. London/ New York.
Ossowski, W., 1999, *Studia nad Lodziami jednopiennymi z obszaru Polski – Study on Logboats from Poland*. Gdańsk.
Pauli, L., 1993, Hallstatt- und Frühlatènezeit. In H. Bender, L. Pauli and I. Stork (eds.), *Der Münsterberg in Breidach II, Hallstatt- und Latènezeit*, pp. 21–172. München.
Salač, V., 1998, Die Bedeutung der Elbe für die Böhmisch-Sächsischen Kontkte in der Latènezeit. *Germania* 76/2: 573–617.
Sorokin, P., 1997, *Waterways and Shipbuilding in north-west Russia in the Middle Ages.* St. Petersburg.
Teigelake, U., 2003a, Tracing ship traffic without ships – alternative methods of finding evidence for pre- and early historical inland water transport. In C. Beltrame, *Boats, Ships and Shipyards. Proceedings of the Ninth International Symposium on Boat and Ship Archaeology, Venice 2000*, 154–169. Oxford.
Teigelake, U., 2003b, *Eisen- und Kaiserzeitliche Binnenschiffahrt in Norddeutschland und ihre Rolle im regionalen und überregionalen Austausch*. Unpublished PhD dissertation, Kiel University.

27 Staraya Ladoga:
a seaport in medieval Russia

Petr Sorokin

The year 2003 marked 300 years of St. Petersburg's existence, and at the same time it was the 1250th anniversary of the town of Ladoga, now Staraya (Old) Ladoga, a small settlement in Leningrad *oblast'*, 128 km east of St. Petersburg. The founding date of 753 has not been attested by any historical document; instead, the jubilee resulted from the dendrochronological dating of the oldest house yet excavated in Ladoga.

Ladoga, on the Lower Volkhov River, was founded in the middle of the 8th century and occupied by Slavs, Finns and Scandinavians. As attested by Russian chronicles, in 862, a Scandinavian Prince Rurik, the founder of the Russian princely dynasty, was invited to Ladoga by local tribes. For a few years, this settlement became his seat in Northern Russia. Later, the capital was moved southward to Ryurikovo Gorodishche, near Novgorod on the Upper Volkhov (Fig. 27.1). In 1019, Prince Yaroslav the Wise presented Ladoga as a wedding gift to his wife, the Swedish princess Ingigerd. Scandinavian sagas, in which Ladoga is mentioned as Aldeguborg, tell about visits of Norwegian nobility to this town in the late 10th and early 11th centuries. Since the beginning of the 12th century, Ladoga served as a fortress on the northwestern border of the Novgorodian country (Kirpichnikov and Sarabiyanov 2003: 178–181).

The formation of Ladoga was influenced by its geographical position on international trade waterways: Baltic Sea – Volga and Baltic Sea – Dnieper. The common section of these waterways was via the Volkhov River, Lake Ladoga, and the Neva River as far as the Gulf of Finland. It connected northwestern Russia with the Baltic Sea region. This was the most important route in Viking Age and medieval communication. From the middle of the 8th until the 14th century, the settlement of Ladoga, situated at a key point on this route, was the main port in northwestern Russia.

The Volkhov rapids, which extended for about 18 km, began ten kilometers up the Volkhov River from Ladoga. For many centuries the place served as a portage that was controlled and managed by the local population. The boats

were towed or hauled overland, depending on their size and the water level in the season. Travelers of the 17th–18th centuries described how boats surmounted the Volkhov rapids (Olearius 1906: 20–21, Sorokin 1997:14–17) (Fig. 27.2). Many of the boats were wrecked during that difficult part of their passage.

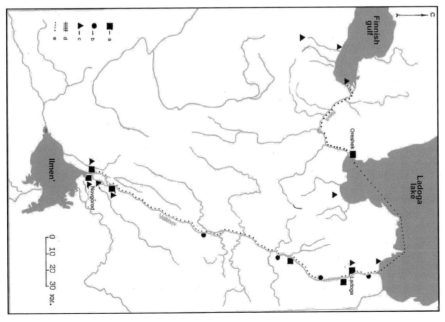

Fig. 27.1. Neva – Ladoga – Volkhov waterway; 8th–13th Centuries: a – hillforts; b – navigation key-points; c – hoards; d – rapids; e – water routes.

Petr Sorokin

For over a century, archaeological excavations in Ladoga have yielded hundreds of ship details and about 30 areas of concentration where they were reused – mostly for construction and paving streets. However, careful investigation of these finds started only about 10 years ago.

Studies of archaeological finds and historical documents of the Viking Age lead us to the conclusion that cargos were transported via this waterway using a combination of different types of vessels. Special ship types were used for every particular section of the route. Three basic types of vessels existed in Ladoga during the period: clinker ships and boats, ferry boats and log-boats. The clinker ships and boats built in the Scandinavian tradition are dated by archaeological finds from the middle of the 8th to the 10th century. Ferry boats are known from the

9th century. Log-boats, which were used in Novgorod on a large scale since the 11th century, were according to archaeological evidence rather uncommon in Ladoga (Sorokin 1997: 80–89).

The first part of the route which ended in Ladoga was covered by travelers on seagoing ships. Farther on, small keel-boats, flat-bottomed ferry boats and log-boats were used. There is evidence for the stationing and wintering of Scandinavian seagoing ships in Ladoga, which are concerned with travels of the Norwegian princes Magnus and Harald from Novgorod to Sweden. In Scandinavian sagas, these ships are mentioned under the general term of a "*scipa*". The rank of the visitors suggests the presence here of large Viking ships belonging to kings or jarls. Runic lapidary inscriptions of the 11th century from central Sweden telling about voyages via the eastern route to the eastern Baltic regions refer to such types of ships as "*knorr*" or "*skeid*" (Mel2nikova 1977: 77, 89–111, 191). In Russian medieval chronicles, among the ship types in use throughout the section of the water route under consideration we find Scandinavian "*shnek*", Russian "*morskaya lodiya*" and Finnish "*loiva*" (Sorokin 2002: 140–145).

The evidence for the presence of Scandinavian clinker-built vessels in Staraya Ladoga includes iron rivets and riveted wooden parts uncovered in archaeological layers or graves with cremations. In addition to these hull remains related to sea-going ships, certain details of their rigging, *e.g.* various toggles, have also been found. One of these was connected with a bast rope about 1.5 m long (Fig. 27.3).

A large section of a deck gives us an idea of the shape of the bow of a fairly large vessel. Probably, rowlocks

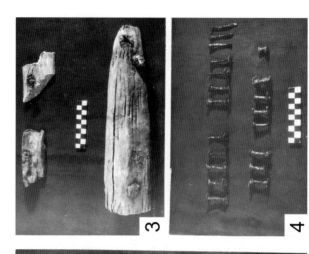

Fig. 27.3. Parts of keel-boats from Staraya Ladoga: 1 – a toggle with a bast rope; 2 – toggles; 3 – wooden parts with rivets; 4 – iron rivets from graves with cremations (necropolis of Placun)

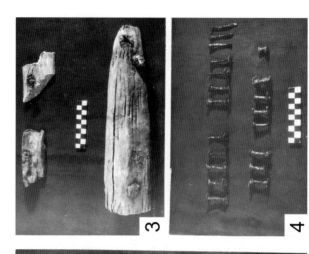

Fig. 27.2. The Volkhov rapids. Engraving from Adam Olearius's book.

with holes (horizontal or vertical) left by nails in their bases also belonged to Scandinavian type of vessels. A post for a tent or a mast 2.4 m high is similar to certain parts of the ship found in Gokstad (Fig. 27.4). On the top of the post, there is a graffito representing an old Scandinavian god. A similar representation is known from a wooden part of a tent from the Oseberg ship (Brøgger et al. 1917:327). As attested by these images, some tradition connected with religious protection for sailors probably existed. Who is the deity represented on the ship dwellings? The images of a male with a pointed beard and long moustaches on the tents from the Oseberg ship and from Staraya Ladoga suggest that it was a Scandinavian god, close in terms of iconography to Thor (Fig. 27.5). His representations on ship tents testify that he must have been regarded as the protector of a ship and its crew. The two identical representations found in similar contexts suggest the existence of a certain ritual tradition among Vikings related to seafaring (Sorokin 1997: 41).

The parts of boats common in Ladoga during the Middle Ages were made mostly from pine or fir. Some of the ship details, however, were made from other kinds of wood, such as oak or ash, although the former was very

rare here and the latter has not as yet been found at all in the course of palaeobotanical researches. According to the Scandinavian tradition, mast parts must have been made from oak or ash.

In the Viking Age layers of Staraya Ladoga, a number

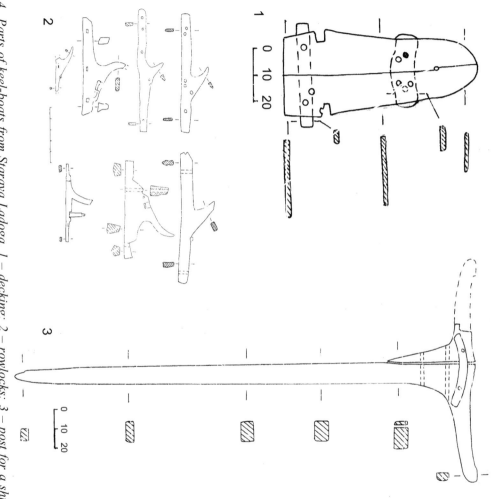

Fig. 27.4. Parts of keel-boats from Staraya Ladoga. 1 – decking; 2 – rowlocks; 3 – post for a ship tent.

Fig. 27.5. Graffito representation of an ancient Scandinavian god on the top of a tent post.

Petr Sorokin

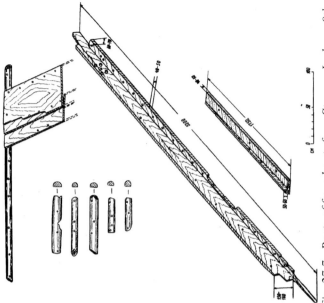

1

2

Fig. 27.6. Graffiti with representations of ships from Staraya Ladoga: 1 – ship with high stems, equipped with a central mast and onboard rudder: graffito of the mid-9th century on birch-bark; 2 – schematic depiction of a vessel with a triangular sail, a bone engraving, mid-8th century.

of ship graffiti have been uncovered (Fig. 27.6). On a birch-bark graffito of the middle 9th century, a large Scandinavian ship with a high stem and rigged with a central mast and side rudder is represented. Another schematic representation of a vessel, now with a triangular sail, engraved on a bone, was dated to the mid-8th century. This latter drawing, found together with a set of tools and numerous ship rivets, is of special interest. This is the most ancient representation of a triangular sail found in Northern Europe. The type of sail cannot be regarded as lateen, but resembles rather the triangular sails represented in Byzantine chronicles as symmetrical to the mast. It could be a similar situation to that which is represented on one image of the Bayeux Tapestry, which shows a sail partly brailed up. The graffito with a vessel bearing a triangular sail is, however, too schematic and uncommon to allow any conclusions to be drawn on the rigging of ships from the region under consideration.

Ferry boats were used for river transportation. This

Fig. 27.7. Parts of ferry boats from Staraya Ladoga. 9th–10th centuries.

kind of boat had a flat bottom and upright sides. Boats of this type are represented by their masts, uncovered in various archaeological complexes where they constitute about 2/3 of all vessel parts found. In addition, this collection includes several side planks, also upright, connected in a carvel manner and also straight and angled frames. It allows us to derive some information on the general parameters of this kind of boat: their length exceeded 14 m, the width was up to 3.2 m, and height of the side was 0.6 to 1.2 m (Ryabinin and Sorokin 1998: 192–194). Ferry boats may have been used also for transportation of cargos downstream on the Volkhov River, similarly to post-medieval barks, for the construction of which they had served as a pattern (Fig. 27.7).

Significant growth in the navigation mentioned above took place during the later period, in relation to Novgorod and the Hanseatic League (12th – 15th centuries). From trade contacts between Novgorod and Gotland, different Hanseatic towns obtained information on the system of navigation via this water route. Merchants from Gotland and towns of northern Germany arrived twice a year, in spring and autumn, to the Novgorodian court (GVNP 1949). According to historical documents, Russian merchants visited Gotland, northern Germany and Denmark, most frequently during the 12th century. The type of ships used for these travels was known as *lodiya* or *morskaya lodiya*. As to the Hanseatic cogs, they probably reached only the delta of the Neva River, very seldom entering Lake Ladoga because it was difficult for heavy sailing ships to pass upstream through the shallows and rapids. Trans shipping of cargos from sea going ships of this type into river boats was carried out somewhere in the lower

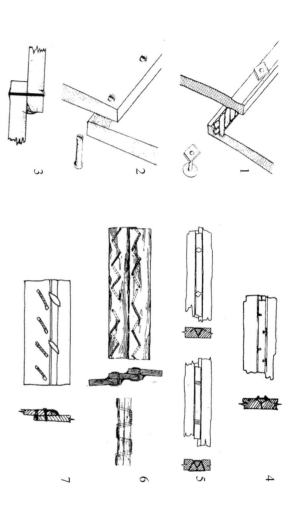

Fig. 27.8. Types of caulking: 1 – Scandinavian; 2 – Slavic; 3 – German tradition of cogs (according to O. Crumlin-Pedersen); 4 – ferry boat from Staraya Ladoga, beginning of the 10th century (according to the author); 5 – ferry boats from Novgorod of the 11th–14th centuries (according to B. Kolchin); 6 – koch from Mangazeya, 17th century (according to Belov et al.); 7 – a vessel from Staraya Ladoga, 16th century (according to the author).

reaches of the Neva River. For this reason, the next section of the waterway via the Neva River, Lake Ladoga and the Volkhov River was a service zone with Russian boatmen and pilots. Some of them, according to historical documents, were natives of the Lake Ladoga region. During that period, the local traditions of 'sewn' ships were transferred to the building of clinker boats.

A part of a ship side consisting of two clinker planks connected by the sewing technique was found in the Ladozhka River. The seam was caulked with moss, a lath and iron clamps. This find is dated by ^{14}C to the middle of the 16th century. The sewing technique is known by finds from Novgorod from the end of the 10th to 15th centuries. It was the oldest local technique of shipbuilding. The technique of caulking by means of iron clamps became widespread in northwestern Russia from the 12th century, when intensive communications with the Hanseatic League started. This technique may be considered therefore as a result of the western influence upon Russian boatbuilding. Most commonly it was used in ferry boats. An older method of caulking, known since the beginning of the 10th century in Staraya Ladoga, employed oak pegs instead of iron clamps (Fig. 27.8).

Numerous remains of river boats found indicate the existence of a developed boatbuilding tradition. Some archaeological finds suggest that not only boats but also larger ships were repaired or possibly even built in Ladoga. The place where these works were carried out has not as yet been discovered, the investigation of the riverside areas of the settlement having been started only in recent years. In the central part of the settlement, two areas with smithies have been excavated, yielding various contexts which included iron rivets. Finds of separate ship parts from the settlement of Ladoga, such as rowlocks, toggles stored for reuse and a special blade with a woollen covering for tarring ship hulls testify that ships were prepared for navigation here. A set of tools used in shipbuilding was found in a layer of the mid-8th century during E.A. Ryabinin's excavation. This set included tongs for forging and fitting, shears for cutting metal, drills, an implement for making nails, various chisels, and a small anvil (Ryabinin 1985: 55–64).

The natural harbour at the mouth of the Ladozha River was traditionally regarded as a place for anchorage in Ladoga (Fig. 27.9). However, research in recent years has shown that in the Viking Age, this stream was very shallow and it must have been difficult even for small ships to enter its mouth. Throughout the Middle Ages, the water level in the Volkhov River system changed considerably as a result of transgressions and regressions of Lake Ladoga. A cultural layer of the 10th–14th centuries found in the Ladozhka riverside zone is 0.8 m below the present-day mid-summer water level in this river. Underwater archaeological research at the mouth of the Ladozhka river has shown that sediments are not thick here, amounting to only about 0.1–0.8 m, while in some spots in the middle of the river, the stone surface is completely free from sediments. Taking into account that the depth changes nowadays here from 2 to 3 m, we are right to suppose that in the 10th–11th centuries the water-level was at least 1–1.5 meters lower. In other words, this river was about 1 m deep and accordingly 15–20 m wide. Ships had no space to maneuver on it. If so, they possibly anchored near the bank of the Volkhov River opposite the settlement.

poles may have been used for mooring. The most probable place for mooring of large boats and ships was the bank near a Viking Age site a few hundred meters up the Volkhov from the mouth of the Ladozhka.

It is possible to trace a distinct tendency to gradual colonization of the zones along the banks of the inland waterways during the Middle Ages. The process was closely connected with the formation and evolution of the system of navigation services. As a result, the frontier bases for Russian ships were transferred from the more inland district of the region, the town of Ladoga, closer to the sea coast: to Oreshek (founded in 1323 on the Neva, where it issues from Lake Ladoga) and the settlements at the delta of the Neva River. Thus important prerequisites for the development of Russian navigation in the Baltic Sea were created. Russian seagoing vessels of the medieval and post-medieval periods generally retained their old features until the early 18th century, when special programs of Peter the Great gave Russia modern shipbuilding technology and fleets.

It is of significance that the anniversaries of St. Petersburg and Staraya Ladoga are celebrated simultaneously. The two cities both were based on a single idea, as Russian seaports on the Baltic Sea – "the Window to Europe". The realizations of that idea, however, were separated by a time-span of almost a millennium – from the mid-8th to the beginning of the 18th century.

References

Belov, M.I., Ovsyannikov, O.V. and Starkov, V.F., 1980, *Mangazeya, Mangazeyskiy morskoy khod.* Leningrad.

Brogger, A.W., Falk, H.J., and Schetelig, H.. 1917, *Oseberg fundet.* Kristiania.

Olearius, Adam, 1906, *Opisanie puteshestviya v Moskoviyu i cherez Moskoviyu v Persiyu i obratno.* Saint-Petersburg.

Kirpichnikov, A.N., and Sarabianov, V.D., 2003, *Staraya Ladoga: Ancient Capital of Rus.* St. Petersburg.

Kolchin, B.A., 1989, *Wooden Artefacts from Medieval Novgorod.* BAR 495. Oxford.

Mel'nikova, E.A.. 1977, *Skandinavskie runicheskie nadpisi.* Moscow.

Ryabinin, E.A.. 1985 Novye otkrytiya v Staroy Ladoge (itogi raskopok na zemlyanom gorodishche v 1973–75 gg.). In *Srednevekovaya Ladoga,* pp. 27–75. Leningrad

Ryabinin, E.A., and Sorokin, P.E.. 1998, Nekotorye sudovye nakhodki iz raskopok v Staroy Ladoge. *Izuchenie pamyatnikov morskoy arkheologii* 3: 187–194.

Sorokin, P.E.. 1997, *Vodnye puti i sudostroenie na Severo-zapade Rusi v srednevekov2ye.* St. Petersburg.

Sorokin, P.E.. 2000, The medieval boatbuilding tradition of Russia. In Jerzy Litwin (ed.) *Down the river to the sea,* pp. xxx. Gdańsk.

Sorokin, P.E.. 2002. The medieval boats in north-west Russia. In *Botnisk kontakt XI. Maritimhistorisk konferens,* pp. 140–145. Härnosand.

GVNP.1949 *Gramoti Velikogo Novgoroda i Pskova.* Moscow, Leningrad.

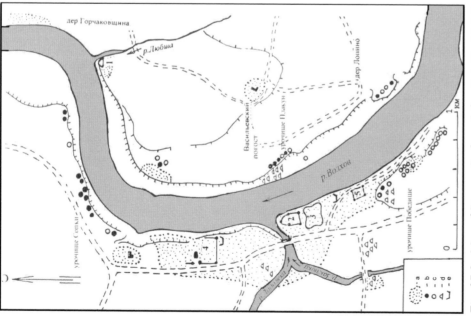

Fig. 27.9. Map of Staraya Ladoga (after E.A. Ryabinin): 1 – archaeological sites (a – medieval settlement layers, б, в, г, д – graves); 2 – the medieval fortress on the Ladojca river mouth; 3 – earthen fortress 16th century (the site of a Viking Age settlement of the 8th–11th centuries); 4–5 – medieval monastery.

Keel ships of the Scandinavian type and medieval Russian *lodiyas* were able to moor directly to the banks or at some anchorage nearby. In the latter case, for unloading cargos from ships to the land, ferry boats may have been used as lighters. No wooden structures have been found close to the banks in the course of underwater archaeological studies conducted in the river, near some settlement sites. Probably this is due to the stony surface of the river bottom and movements of ice during the winter periods. Nevertheless, this question needs further investigation.

Large keel-boats of the Viking Age required no special conditions for mooring – the boats were just dragged out onto the bank. Nevertheless, certain special harbour structures did exist. They included wooden bulkheading of the bank to protect it from destruction and wooden platforms allowing boats to stay at some distance from the bank in the case of shallow waters. Also, some special

28 The APES Archaeological Study: The North Carolina Sounds, an interface between land and sea

Lawrence E. Babits, Frank Cantelas and Keith Meverden

Fig. 28.1. The APES project area.

The Albemarle-Pamlico Estuarine System (APES)(Fig. 28.1) is one of North America's largest, composed of four sounds and many rivers. The APES is separated from the ocean by the Outer Banks, beyond which lies the "Graveyard of the Atlantic," where over 8,000 known wrecks await investigation. The estuary saw the earliest English settlement in North America (1586) and the first powered flight (1903). As a discrete environmental unit, the APES is a complete universe. Defining the cultural resources within the APES is a preliminary step toward understanding the human, land and water interface. Since 1995, on-going research has attempted to examine the APES archaeological resource. Most of our vessels are hopelessly modern by European standards but we are trying to use the direct historical approach to building models about where to look for earlier material.

Four major and several minor rivers empty into the APES. South to north, the major streams are the Neuse, Tar, Roanoke and Chowan. Together, the rivers deliver an average of fifteen billion gallons of water per day (Stick 1958:5–6). Each river system is supported by numerous smaller streams that offer sites for ferries, landings, shipyards and mills. These exploitation sites shift through time and provide clues to predicting archaeological sites. As late as 1900, these waters were the primary transport net in the region.

With so much water, it is not surprising that the area's population was somewhat "amphibious."

The broad waters of the Sound, and its tributaries which leave few points more than a few miles distant from sloop navigation, give old and young, male and female, a semi-amphibious turn. It is rather startling to a mountaineer to see a party composed of two or three women and one man lift anchor and hoist sail in the gloaming, and steer straight into dusk toward a horizon all of water. And wind and wave at times make matters quite lively on the surface of the Sound. The six or eight feet of sand [the Outer Banks]... offers slight obstruction to the east wind, and north and south the sweep is as free. This universal familiarity with sails possessed by what may be called our inland coast people (Bruce 1859:762).

Three major and several minor canal systems enhance regional transportation. Chronologically, the Dismal Swamp Canal connected lower Chesapeake Bay to the APES in 1805. In 1828, expansion of the canal provided Norfolk, Virginia, with 90% of its trade (Turner 1999:23). Water taken from Lake Drummond to maintain canal levels so depleted back pressure that Currituck Inlet closed up the same year and the sound now has fresh water.

The Albemarle and Chesapeake Canal, opened in 1858, connects the Chesapeake with the APES via Currituck Sound. The canal bisects the Currituck peninsula but larger vessels could now avoid Currituck Narrows and get to Norfolk without going offshore (Brown 1981:3–4). Finally, a canal avoiding Croatan Sound's shallow waters connected Pamlico and Albemarle Sounds by linking the Pungo and Alligator Rivers. All three canals are now part of the Atlantic Intracoastal Waterway. Several minor canals provided crucial drainage on interior wetlands as well as short distance transportation routes (Thompson 2002).

Chronological History

Native Americans optimally sited their camps to ensure maximum exploitation of the estuarine environment. The main camps were usually on a ridge between sound and swamp, providing immediate access to at least three major environmental zones. Tools from the outlying sites seem to reflect some specialized activities: woodworking tools in swampland, fish and mammal bones and shell middens on sound or river banks, and a mixture, including hunting implements, on ridge camps. A ridge also provided well drained soils necessary for maize horticulture and provided access to seasonal winds that blow away mosquitoes (Byrd 1997:64–68).

In a maritime area such as the APES, many prehistoric sites first identified from the land as separate entities are actually continuous, very long, coastal sites. They are seen from the water as a band of dark, shell-laden soil along extended parts of the eroding shoreline. The coriolis effect imparted by the earth's rotation determines general patterns of erosion and deposition in coastal environments. The west-facing shore builds up while the east-facing shore erodes. In many cases, so much material has eroded, that visible evidence reflects only the landmost remnants of a once extensive site. Sites that once faced west across the sound are now buried by built up marsh. There is a warning here because most sites have been built upon in the last 40 years.

The numerous waterways dictated a riverine settlement pattern for the region's first European settlers, who utilized the same natural products but changed exploitation strategies, including more intensive and deeper fishing, agriculture, production of naval stores and shipbuilding. The diversified subsistence economy continues today, although over-exploitation of crabs, shrimp and fish have so reduced the take that sea harvesting is rapidly dying.

In colonial times, there were initially three official customs clearing stations in the APES. These were Port Currituck at Indiantown Creek/North River (Jones 1996: 10), Port Roanoke at Edenton (Barber 1931:1), and New Bern. Generally speaking, Currituck vessels went in and out New Currituck Inlet; Roanoke and New Bern vessels used Ocracoke Inlet.

Even given the distance inland, across shallow, rapidly shifting channels in the sounds, colonial vessels in excess of 100 tons called at Edenton, New Bern and Washington, and smaller vessels went as far inland as Halifax. During the nineteenth century, larger vessels, under both steam and sail, were utilized. It may come as a surprise, but steamboats continued in use on the Neuse, Tar and Roanoke until after 1910. In many cases, these shallow draft vessels kept the river open to navigation by continually breaking channels when the river shoaled.

Vessels from the APES went out to the northern colonies, Europe and the West Indies. In the five years between 1771–1776, 232 vessels departed Port Roanoke for New England, 82 more went to New York and Philadelphia, and only 21 departed for the Chesapeake (Barber 1932:12–13). It may be that more Chesapeake-bound voyagers left from Currituck, or because they were small and the region is large, many short-haul vessels did not declare their departures. Only seven cleared for Charleston, and one for St. Augustine. The West Indies drew at least 55 vessels, including about 14 to St Thomas and St Croix. At least 100 vessels went to the British Isles (Barber 1931:15).

These vessels carried local products out, including naval stores (tar, pitch, turpentine, barrel staves and heads), meat, fish, some hides, tobacco, shingles and beeswax. More than 93,000 barrels of tar and another 5800 barrels of pitch went from Roanoke between 1771 and 1776 (Barber 1931:17). Currituck sent out similar amounts.

Exploitation of Albemarle Sound's tributary rivers can be documented for even marginal, tertiary streams. Often, there was a deep "hole" providing good flotation even in periods of low rainfall. In close proximity were live oak and pine, plus swamp-growing cypress and cedar. Of particular importance were the live oaks and cypress described as "excellent for Ship Timber being all crooked and very lasting" (NCSR 6:606–07). The cypress or white cedar was the prime tree used to make periaugers, the most common work boat in the sounds (Pecorelli *et al.* 1996). Exploitation generally involved a shipyard that produced one or two vessels a year until the surrounding area was stripped of useful timber. Smaller trees were incised to produce pine tar.

Statistics show multiple uses of timber resources. The APES produced over half the shingles (58%) and over 60% of the staves from North Carolina between 1768 and 1772 (Jones 1996:24). The APES produced 65% of North Carolina's shingles and 85% of the staves in 1768 alone (Jones 1996:25). Between 1750 and 1790, the APES produced approximately 80% of North Carolina-built vessels (Jones 1996:13). The interrelationship of shingles, staves and ships demonstrates how down time between ship orders, and remnant wood stocks, utilized far more of the harvested timber than otherwise might have been suspected. Even today, the local word for shingle is shake, a term that also refers to damaged trees with cracks deep in the wood making them unsuitable for log boats such as canoes and periaugers. Shake, as in shingle, might well reflect a use for this damaged timber.

While it did not take a large crew or a formal boat yard to make these vessels, some operations were extensive. In 1775, Thomas MacKnight had:

On each side of this river ... I had built very large wharfs and convenient warehouses thereon, and I had erected on the north side of the river, at very great expense, the most commodious, and I will venture to say, the best shipyard in the province, where I had every conveniency for careening as well as for building vessels. From this yard, I have launched a ship (one hundred ft. long) into fourteen ft. water, upon sliding boards not more than thirty ft. in length; the whole run did not exceed twenty-five ft.; and from the top of the keel blocks to the surface of the water was a fall of little more than two ft. (Loyalist Claims Papers 1785, P.R.O., Audit Office 13, Bundle 121).

This operation involved a sideways launch because the North River is quite narrow at the site. There was enough

Type	Cu'tuck	Camden	P'tank	Chowan	Tyrell	Wash'ton	Total
Schooner	64	9	66	40	28	39	246
Sloop	5	0	0	0	3	0	8
Brig	3	0	6	1	0	2	12
Bark	0	0	0	0	0	1	1
Ship	0	0	0	0	0	1	1
Steam	0	0	1	0	0	1	2

Table 28.1 Albemarle Sound Vessels built 1800–1865.

(after Turner 1999:31)

material readily available upstream and downstream to keep a sawmill in operation until the 1940s. MacKnight's labour force was slaves, "they were almost all Tradesmen and House Servants and thee most valuable collection of Negroes in that Country – They were able to build a ship within themselves with no other assistance than a Master Builder" (Loyalist Claims Papers 1785, P.R.O., Audit Office 13, Bundle 121). When MacKnight fled in 1775, his slaves were taken by the state and marched inland, to produce, not ships, but cannon, wagons and gun carriages. Truly, these fifty men and women must have been very skilled.

An 18th-century sloop at the lumber mill site was investigated in 1995. This proved to be 45 feet (13.7 m) in length by 13'10" (4.2 m) in beam. The depth of hold was estimated as 4.5' (1.3 m) (Jones 1996:53). These dimensions yield a vessel rated about 27 tons. This vessel fit very well within the newly defined Southern low country boatbuilding tradition (Pecorelli 2003:106–108). Whether it was built by MacKnight or not, it was certainly used about that time and the yard reopened after 1783.

The North River was still productive in 1862 when Union forces burned the *Scuppernong* about 270 yards (250 m) downstream. The *Scuppernong* was a schooner carrying live oak compass timber when it was set afire. Measuring 77 feet (23.5 m) in length, 17 feet (5.2 m) in beam and nearly 6 feet (1.8 m) depth of hold (Turner 1999:45), the vessel reveals a key change in APES watercraft that occurred in the nineteenth century: the beam does not exceed 17 feet. Anything over 17 feet prevented access to the locks on the Dismal Swamp Canal through which most Albemarle produce reached outside markets (Turner 1999:32). Thus, any wider vessel was intended to operate offshore through Hatteras or Oregon Inlets (after 1846) or Ocracoke Inlet. To allow operation in water deeper than the canal, these narrow vessels were also equipped with a centerboard (Turner 1999:46).

Late 18th-century shipyards were located on the Perquimans River, at Edenton on the Chowan River, on Salmon Creek off the Chowan, at Plymouth on the Roanoke River, and many other tributary streams. Workboats are still constructed in the APES, often without a formal boatyard, conveniently built next to house and water. Boat types shifted over time but gross numbers are misleading. Most figures reflect only registered vessels after the colonial period. Still, the most popular APES vessel in the antebellum period (1800–1860) was the schooner (National Archives n.d.; Turner 1999).

During the Civil War (1861–1865), the APES turned out warships (Fig. 28.2). Three major streams had an ironclad under construction after 1862. Warship construction was not simply building a vessel out of local materials. Iron came from the interior, engines and weaponry from Richmond and Charlotte. The worksites had to be protected. Downstream from each construction site were massive fortifications. Exposed shipyards at Washington and Elizabeth City were captured in 1862, but not before at least one unfinished vessel was taken 15 miles away, up a narrow creek, and burned (Babits 1981).

Numerous single vessel site reports (Fig. 28.3) have been prepared for vessels located in the APES since 1981. These include colonial vessels (Alford 1990; Askins 2000; Goodall 2003; Jones 1999), Antebellum and Civil War vessels (Babits 1981; Bright *et al.* 1981; Jackson 1991; Lawrence 1996; Lawrence 2003; Olson 1996; Spirek 1993) and at least one late 19th-century vessel (Merriman 1995). These are placed in context by regional historical reports about shipping and ports (Cox 1989; Marcinko 2000; McGuinn 2000; Merriman 1996; Morgan 1985; Newell 1987). These formal reports are supported by a great many site inspections conducted by students, contractors and the state's Underwater Archaeology Branch (Brooks, *et al* 1996).

Prior to about 1980, most archaeology in the APES was site specific. Since 1980, several sub-regional surveys (Fig. 28.4) have been completed. The surveys included North River (Wilde-Ramsing 1992), Edenton Harbor (NC UAAU 1980; Watts 1981), Bath Harbor (Lawrence *et al.* 1984; Pietrowski in prep), and the Blackwater, Chowan, Meherrin and Wiccacon rivers (Lawrence 1992). Surveys to develop and test regional models were also completed (Babits and Corbin 2000; 1995; Babits, Kjorness and Morris 1995). These surveys led to testing assumptions about boat disposal, wrecking patterns and associated terrestrial sites within an entire sound (Babits and Meverden, in prep).

Currituck workboat construction occurred on both sides of the sound, and outside the sound on the North River/

Lawrence E. Babits, Frank Cantelas and Keith Meverden

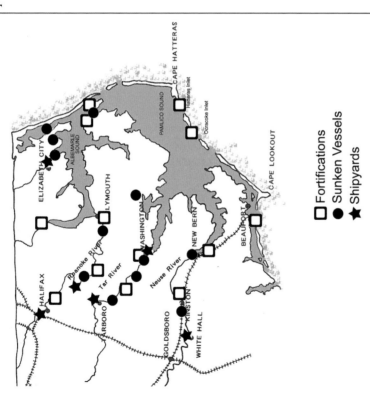

Fig. 28.2. Civil War sites in the project area.

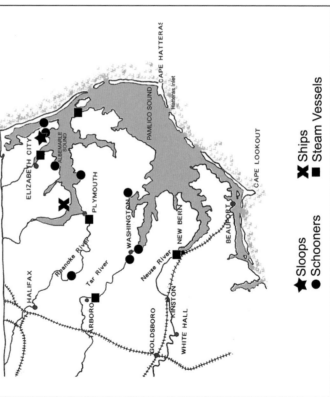

Fig. 28.3. Sunken vessel site reports.

Indiantown Creek swamp complex. Surprisingly, most registered vessels were by different builders. Between 1810 and 1830, only 8 men built more than 1 registered vessel and no one built more than six. However, some families – Walker (8), Jarvis (4) Etheridge (7), and Knight (6) – built several vessels. After the Civil War, many families switched to small workboats for fishing, oystering and

duck hunting. Some did, however, produce larger vessels for use on the Albemarle and Chesapeake Canal and local trading, especially Wilton Walker, who continued operations at the "Launch." Another shipyard operated on the canal bank at Coinjock. This turned out 65-foot-long vessels in the 20th century. Most boat yards were hardly that. Boats were simply built at home, as needed. Those who turned out really good watercraft often built others for sale as their reputations grew (Bates 1985:27–30).

Currituck Sound covers approximately 450 square kilometers. During 2001, East Carolina University conducted a five-week remote sensing survey of Currituck Sound. Fifty-two, 500-meter-square quadrats were searched, a 2.8% sample. The plan was to survey with four different methods for comparative purposes and to ensure that we did not overlook anything. We conducted a visual shoreline survey of all western shoreline, including waterways. On the sound, most eastern shoreline and informant interviews. On the sound, we used a side-scan sonar and a magnetometer.

The remote sensing was designed and conducted using Hypack Max marine survey software. Hypack Max controlled vessel navigation and collected magnetometer data from a Geometrics 886 proton procession magnetometer. Due to the shallow waters, the magnetometer towfish and cable were floated behind the survey vessel with layback set at 80 feet (25 m). Vessel and data positioning were controlled and recorded via a Garmin differential global positioning (DGPS) system connected to Hypack Max.

Side-scan sonar data were collected using a Marine Sonics Sea Scan PC software package and a 600 kHz towfish hung from the side of the research vessel. Range

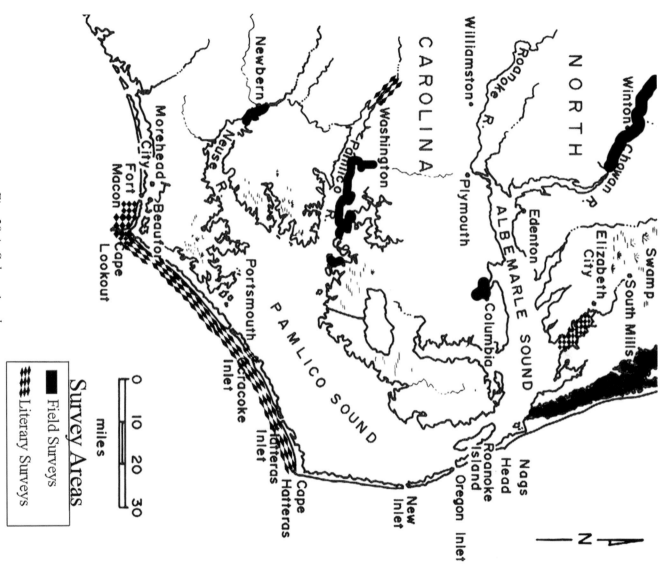

Fig. 28.4. Sub-regional survey areas.

Survey Areas

■ Field Surveys

✠ Literary Surveys

Lawrence E. Babits, Frank Cantelas and Keith Meverden

was set at 33 feet (10 m) to each side, ensuring adequate overlap between magnetometer survey lanes. The survey lane interval was based on recommendations by Murphy and Saltus (1990). A 100-foot (30 m) interval might miss small craft, a 33-foot (10 m) interval was recommended for contour mapping and target mass location.

The 50-foot (15 m) interval provided adequate coverage while allowing search quadrats to be completed within a reasonable time. Some 16.5 linear kilometers were covered searching each quadrat. With a survey speed of 4.5 knots, each quadrat was completed in approximately 2.5 hours. An average of three quadrats was completed each day.

This methodology allowed statistical projections about the likelihood of sites existing in an area we did not survey. The quadrats covered a diverse array of environmental zones. In conjunction with the shoreline survey,

some 849 sonar targets, 320 magnetic anomalies, nearly 60 watercraft, two underwater roadways and 40 eroding terrestrial sites were identified. We stopped counting duck blinds and their little docks because there are so many, regularly placed at 500 yard (476 meter) intervals. We also found at least five ship graveyards.

Among the most promising magnetic and sonar underwater anomalies were those found in Tull's Creek. This creek is the northern channel into Tull's Bay. The southern channel is silted up but was once the main thoroughfare and associated with a long term shipyard identified as "The Launch." This boatyard operated from the late 19th well into the 20th century. Eighteenth-century ceramics eroding from the bank suggest even earlier occupations. Informants stated that a "graveyard" was across the water from the "launch." The graveyard could not be located and it is possible that, until the south channel silted up, the north channel was the grave yard.

In the north channel, Tull's Creek, at least seven sonar targets included at least one duck blind, a flat, a skiff's (Fig. 28.5) keelson and frames, and additional broken-up vessels (Fig. 28.6). Each had a single monopolar magnetic signature of some size and duration.

The outermost fringe of the APES is the Outer Banks. This line of constantly shifting sand islands separates the sounds from the Atlantic. The banks are pierced by a few inlets that open and close depending on back pressure from the APES's water supply and storms that wash over the shoreline. Generally speaking, a combination ranging from three large inlets to eleven small inlets seems required to dispose of water coming from the interior. The inlets "migrate" in a southerly direction as littoral drift deposits sand on the northern side of inlets and currents remove sand from the southern edge. Modern inlets are not at the same location as their earlier namesakes (Table 28.2)(Stick 1958:6).

It was surprising that our initial predictive models did not work from one stream or sound to another. As an example, with shallow water in western Albemarle Sound,

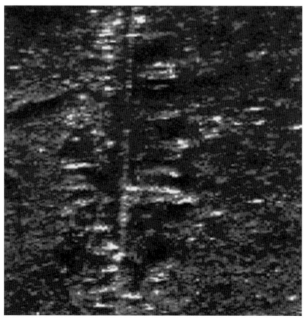

Fig. 28.5. Sonar image showing the remains of a skiff.

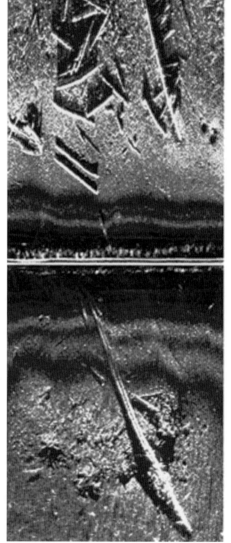

Fig. 28.6. Sonar image showing vessel remains on the right and left channels.

workboats were expected to be primarily flat-bottomed while those in the deeper eastern sound were thought to be round-bottomed. The opposite is true. Ship graveyards in Currituck Sound only exist in conjunction with the Albemarle and Chesapeake Canal system, except for a single complex in southern Currituck. The shallow water and duck hunting in northern Currituck play a major role. The marsh is routinely burned off to provide better forage for wild fowl and clear sight lines. The burning also disposes of abandoned vessels away from the canal. The canal has three graveyards associated with the Currituck peninsula cut, at the southern and northern ends and across the bay from the northern end. These all seem to belong to the 20th century.

During surveys, we learned that "everyone" built skiffs. A sailing skiff lasted about 20 years while motorized versions (post 1910) lasted half as long. For Currituck Sound, there are currently fewer than 100 known skiffs extant today. This covers the 175-year period since Currituck Inlet silted up in 1828. No sail powered skiffs survive. Only one, possibly, prehistoric canoe has been found (Wilde-Ramsing 1993). Of the approximately 100 extant vessels, only about 30 are still used on the water and another 40 are being curated; the others are flower boxes, junk or wrecks. This means that ANY sailing skiff is significant in terms of the universe of approximately 4,000 boats built after 1828. We are not including those before that time. We have no estimation on skiffs prior to 1825 but written accounts suggest they were numerous.

Inlet	Dates
Old Currituck Inlet	1585–1731
New Currituck Inlet	1713–1828
Musketo Inlet	1585–1671
Carthys Inlet	1585–?, 1798–1811
Roanoke Inlet	1585–1811
Oregon Inlet	1585–1770, 1846–present
New Inlet	1708–1922, 1932–1945
Cape Inlet	1585–1657?
Old Hatteras Inlet	1846–present
Hatteras Inlet	1585–1755
Ocracoke Inlet	1585–present
Swash Inlet	?
Drum Inlet	? – present

Table 28.2. Outer Banks Inlets over time.
(after Dunbar 1958)

References

Alford, Michael B., 1990, The Trent River Flatboat: Report to the Kellenberger Historical Foundation. MS on file, North Carolina Maritime Museum, Beaufort, NC.

Askins, Adrian, 2000, *Archaeological and historical site investigation/Thesis of the John's Island Wreck (EDS0001)*. Unpublished MA thesis, Program in Maritime Studies, East Carolina University, Greenville, NC.

Babits, L. E., 1981, The Chicod Creek wreck, Pitt County, North Carolina. *In Underwater Archaeology: The Challenge before Us*, Proceedings of the 12th Annual Conference on Underwater Archaeology, pp. 3–9, San Marino, California.

Babits, L. E., and Corbin, Annalies, 2000, A derelict small boat survey, Pamlico Drainage, North Carolina, USA. In J. Litwin (ed.), *Down the River to the Sea. Proceedings of the Eighth International Symposium on Boat and Ship Archaeology, Gdańsk, 1997*, pp. 193–196, Gdańsk.

Babits, L. E., and Corbin, Annalies, 1995, A survey of the Pungo River, Wade's Point to Woodstock Point, Beaufort County, North Carolina. Report on File, Office of the State Archaeologist, Raleigh, North Carolina.

Babits, L. E., Kjorness, Annalies C., and Morris, Jeff, 1995, A survey of the North Shore Pamlico River: Bath Creek to Wade's Point. Report on File, Office of the State Archaeologist, Raleigh, North Carolina.

Babits, L. E. and Meverden, Keith N., in prep. Preliminary report, regional maritime survey of Currituck Sound. MS on file, Program in Maritime Studies, East Carolina University, Greenville, NC.

Barber, Ira W., Jr., 1931, The ocean-borne commerce of Port Roanoke 1771–1776. Unpublished MA thesis, Department of History, University of North Carolina, Chapel Hill, North Carolina.

Bates, Jo Anna Heath (ed.), 1985, *The Heritage of Currituck County North Carolina 1985*. Winston-Salem, NC.

Bright, Leslie S., Rowland, William H and Barden, James C., 1981, *CSS Neuse: A Question of Iron and Time*. Raleigh, NC.

Brooks, Barbara Lynn, Merriman, Ann M. and Wilde-Ramsing, Mark, 1996, *Bibliography of North Carolina Underwater Archaeology*. Kure Beach, NC.

Brown, Alexander C., 1981, *Juniper Waterway: A History of the Albemarle and Chesapeake Canal*. Charlottesville, VA.

Bruce, Edward C., 1859, Loungings in the Footprints of the Pioneers. *Harper's* 17: 741–763.

Byrd, John E., 1997, *Tuscarora subsistence practices in the late Woodland Period: The zooarchaeology of the Jordan's Landing site*. North Carolina Archaeological Council Publication 27. Raleigh, NC.

Cox, James M., 1989, The Pamlico-Tar River and Its Role in the Development of Eastern North Carolina. Unpublished MA thesis, Program in Maritime Studies, East Carolina University, Greenville, NC.

Goodall, Katherine, 2003, The Burroughs wreck: A key to eighteenth-century ship construction techniques and the life and death of the port of Edenton. Unpublished MA thesis, Program in Maritime Studies, East Carolina University, Greenville, NC.

Jones, Sheridan R., 1966, Historical and archaeological investigation of the MacKnight Shipyard wreck (0001NCR). Unpublished MA thesis, Department of History, East Carolina University, Greenville, North Carolina.

Lawrence, Matthew S., 2003, "A fair specimen of a Southern River steamer," The Oregon and Tar/Pamlico River steam navigation. Unpublished MA thesis, Program in Maritime Studies, East Carolina University, Greenville, NC.

Lawrence, Richard W., 1996, Eastern North Carolina Civil War Shipwreck District multiple property nomination. MS on file, NC Underwater Archaeology Branch, Kure Beach, NC.

Lawrence, Richard W., 1992, A report on reconnaissance surveys in the Blackwater, Chowan, Meherrin, and Wiccacon Rivers. MS on file, NC Underwater Archaeology Branch, Kure Beach, NC.

Lawrence, Richard W., *et al.*, 1984, Bath Harbor Survey: Report on the activities of the 1979 Field School in maritime history and underwater archaeology. MS on file, NC Underwater Archaeology Branch, Kure Beach, NC.

Loyalist Papers, 1785, Copies from British Public Records Office, Audit Office 12 and 13, Bundles 36 and 121, North Carolina State Archives, Raleigh, NC.

Marcinko, Thomas, 2000, The maritime history of Hatteras Inlet, North Carolina, 1846–1862. Unpublished MA thesis, Program in Maritime Studies, East Carolina University, Greenville, NC.,

McGuinn, Phillip, 2000, Shell Castle, a North Carolina entrepot, 1789–1820: An historical and archaeological investigation. Unpublished MA thesis, Program in Maritime Studies, East Carolina University, Greenville, NC.

Merriman, Ann M., 1996, North Carolina schooners, 1815–1901, and the S. R. Fowle and Son Company of Washington, North Crolina. Unpublished MA thesis, Program in Maritime Studies, East Carolina University, Greenville, NC.

Merriman, Ann M., 1995, The Cypress Landing vessel: A North Carolina sailing scow, Chocowinity Bay, Beaufort County, North Carolina. MS on file at the Program in Maritime Studies, East Carolina University, Greenville, NC.

Morgan, W. Stuart, III, 1985, The Commerce of a southern port: New Bern, North Carolina.Unpublished MA thesis, Program in Maritime Studies, East Carolina University, Greenville, NC.

National Archives, n.d. Vessel Documents, Record Group 41, National Archives, Washington, DC.

Newell, Samuel, 1987, A maritime history of Ocracoke Inlet 1584–1783. Unpublished MA thesis, Program in Maritime Studies, East Carolina University, Greenville, NC.

North Carolina Underwater Archaeology Unit, 1980, Field Notes on a magnetometer survey and site assessment of Edenton Harbor and surrounding areas. MS on file, NC Underwater Archaeology Branch, Kure Beach, NC.

Olson, Christopher J., 1996, An historical and archaeological investigation of the CSS *Curlew*. Unpublished MA thesis, Department of History, East Carolina University, Greenville, NC.

Pietrowscki, Andrew, in preparation, Unpublished MA thesis, Department of History, East Carolina University, Greenville, NC.

Pecorelli, Harry III, 2003, Archaeological investigation of the B and B wreck (38BK1672): An eighteenth-century plantation-built vessel, Charleston, South Carolina. Unpublished MA thesis, Department of History, East Carolina University, Greenville, NC.

Harry Pecorelli, III, Alford, Michael and Babits, L. E., 1996, A working definition of "periauger." In *Proceedings of the 29th Annual Conference on Historical and Underwater Archaeology*. Society for Historical Archaeology, pp. 22–28, Tucson.

Spirek, James D., 1993, The *USS Southfield*: An historical and archaeological investigation of a converted gunboat. Unpublished MA thesis, Program in Maritime Studies, East Carolina University, Greenville, NC.

Stick, David, 1958, *The Outer Banks of North Carolina*. Chapel Hill, NC.

Turner, Cecil A., 1995, Historical and archaeological investigation of the schooner *Scuppernong*. Unpublished MA thesis, Department of History, East Carolina University, Greenville, NC.

Watts, Gordon P. Jr., 1981, The Edenton Harbor wrecks. *Archaeology* 34 (3): 14–21.

Wilde-Ramsing, Mark U., 1993, Indiantown Log. MS on file, NC Underwater Archaeology Branch, Kure Beach, NC.

Wilde-Ramsing, Mark U., 1992, Underwater archaeological examination of North River, Currituck and Camden Counties. MS on file, NC Underwater Archaeology Branch, Kure Beach, NC.

29 The ends of the earth: maritime technology transfer in remote maritime communities

Valerie Fenwick

Introduction

As a maritime archaeologist, my adult life has been spent in an Eurocentric academic environment. In 1999 I had an opportunity to take part in the first Cambridge University Expedition to Micronesia, to the remote Eastern Caroline Islands. This paper will essentially compare this region with an ostensibly different study area, the southern Orinoco Delta of Venezuela, where I had previously undertaken two lengthy journeys in Pemon and Amacuro logboats. Societies in both regions still rely upon logboats as a primary means of communication and livelihood and many of the challenges, choices, and responses to the outside world were, or are, paralleled in both regions.

The Amacuro peoples of Venezuela

The southern Orinoco Delta is a world centred on water. The deltaic environment is a vast accumulating area of quaternary sediments, divided by a labyrinth of *caños*, cloaked by macropluvial vegetation. It is inhabited by the Amacuro or Warao who are archetypical 'boat-people'. This is how they style themselves: *Wa – arao* 'canoe – people'. They live on palafittes constructed on stumps of felled palm-trees. Land is the boundary of the mental template; the area is one of the wettest places on earth. Logboats are therefore crucial to survival, they are needed for the journey to school, to go fishing, to fetch firewood, or to visit a neighbour.

The Warao are estimated to have occupied the Delta for 7,000–10,000 years and to have established a nautical tradition of migration, travel and trade (Wilbert 1996). Warao settlements were formerly hidden on islands in naturally created clearings within the mangrove forests. There, fish and the moriche palm provided for most of their needs. Their language is unlike other Amerindian languages. Their kinship system is of the Hawaiian type (Wilbert and Leyrisse 1980), the *Wa'a* syllable being shared with numerous Pacific cultures, including the Hawaiian. Language is their ethnic bond (Wilbert and Leyrisse 1980: 4).

Misión de Guayo is located at the mouth of the Delta, and is the Warao trading-post. Tucupita is situated at the apex of the Delta. Both settlements lie at either end of the main shipping artery that provides access to modern cities upstream. Through the centuries the Warao have monitored passing ships, picked up ideas, and altered their own technology accordingly. A trip along the waterways to the trading-post at Misión de Guayo was sail-assisted by giant, hand-held, teniche fronds, triangular cloth sails, or square sails of moriche leafstalks (Wilbert and Leyrisse 1980: 93, 96, pl.5). By 1980 however, small outboard motors were already being fitted to unmodified Warao logboats, while motor-coasters were introduced by the missions. Subsequently, the Government subsidized large outboard motors. The coasters now lie unused and there is a rush to transform double-ended logboats into speed-boats. The conversion kit includes a plane, square and saw, and is undertaken in a clearing on a sandbank (Fig. 29.1 and Fig. 29.2).

Until the 1940s, the Warao took their goods to trade to Trinidad and Balleras to exchange for iron tools. For this open-sea voyage they paddled their larger, round-bottomed, expanded logboats. The logboats were also extended by a strake on each side, that are attached by transverse boards at bow and stern. Vertical poles along the sides retained the cargo (Suarez 1968: 36ff). An accomplished canoe maker has high status. They also exported logboats; in the 1840s they were recorded as supplying the whole colony of Demerera (Schomburgk in Raleigh 1848: 44). Unfortunately, however, loggers now target the large cedars (*Cedrela odorata*) required for building the logboats, as they are easily accessible from the water.

The Micronesians

The Eastern Carolines are at the terminus of a 2,000-km-long island-chain, along a mean axis 8° north of the Equator, with the tiny 'low' Mwoakilloa and Pingelap atolls lying between the 'high islands' of Pohnpei and

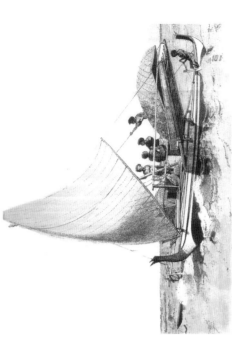

Fig. 29.3. Caroline Archipelago: a flying proa at sea. French circumnavigators were impressed by Micronesiam seafaring skills (after Paris, 1841).

both the logs and the fibres to bind the component parts together; their leaves were used for sails, and sea-shells were the sole tools with which to craft them.¹ These 'flying proas' were extremely fast, cruising with the outrigger float clear of the water when the sea-state permitted (Fig. 29.3). They kept the wind on the outrigger side, by moving the sail 180° round the mast, 'shunting', so the stern became the bow and then the stern again. To increase capacity a platform jutted out on the lee side. The outrigger was a complex arrangement of poles lashed together with coconut twine (coir) or sennit (braid). Fast *proa* hulls were asymmetrical in cross-section (Lewis 1994: 61).

In 1824, landing with the first Europeans on Kusaie, a botanist provided precise descriptions of the islands, the islanders and their technology prior to European contact (Lesson 1835: III, 131ff). Admiral Paris admired the East Caroline canoes, "le type de la perfection de ces petits bateaux, ce sont les mieux construits du grand Océan" (Paris 1841: 96). For Lesson "Ils construisent leurs pirogues avec un talent d'exécution ignoré de tous les autres insulaires de la mer du Sud" (Lesson 1828: 123). Modern research indicates that the Micronesian canoe rig was a technological transfer to Polynesian Fiji and Tonga in the 1770s (Clunie 2001).

High Islands of the Eastern Carolines

The so-called 'high islands' of Pohnpei and Kusaie are essentially formed of the peaks of old volcanoes, now partially submerged. Rain forest and mangroves restrict access on the land. Both islands have Megalithic settlements. They have been dated by ceramics to some 1,500 years ago (Morgan 1988). On Pohnpei, Nan Madol, natural lava 'columns', as much as 7.5 m in length, were stacked horizontally to form walls and even roofs (Morgan 1988). The ocean crashes on long walls built as coastal defences. Huge blocks had to be brought to the sites by

Fig. 29.1. Orinoco Delta: logboat-yard. Planks jammed in trees come from an up-river sawmill. Foreground: a medium logboat is being extended. Its transom will be set well forward of the chopped-off stern. Framing will support a ceiling and thwarts (Photo: Author).

Fig. 29.2. Orinoco Delta: Misión de Araguaimujo – twin-engined logboat now only 15 m long. It has 48 hp Yamaha engines mounted on a 10cm-thick transom and needs to carry two drums of fuel. Fully loaded, a 230 km journey can now be completed in a day (Photo: Author).

Kusaie. More than 2,000 years ago, Austronesian people voyaged to these islands (Morgan 1988). They are believed to have reached the islands in logboats that would later 'flying astonish circumnavigators, who called them 'flying proas'. Trees provided the raw material for these boats,

water (Spengler 1990; Allen 1997). But as to the mechanisms of this colonisation there is no evidence.

The island of Pohnpei was first discovered by de Quiros in 1595, but Spain did not attempt annexation until 1885. The Carolines then passed successively through German, Japanese and American hands before achieving independence as the Federated States of Micronesia in 1979.

On Pohnpei an Irish castaway in the 1820s, James O'Connell, saw canoe-houses 30 m in length. Relic canoes hung from the roof. By this time ocean voyaging had already been abandoned and sailing canoes were now elaborate state barges with cabins for the chiefs (O'Connell 1972). A century later Hornell and Haddon were compiling their masterpiece, *Canoes of Oceania* (1937, 1997). The Eastern Carolines were however not forthcoming in providing relevant information. Hornell relied upon what had previously been published by the German Sudsee Expedition (Hambruch 1912; Eilers 1934), an indistinct photo taken in 1900, and a diagram of a canoe with curved diagonal braces (Hornell 1936: figs 292–4). Today such canoes can be found hidden in the mangroves; their fine finish, long floats and spindly supports echoing a grander past. They materialize for races in the lagoon.[2] Canoes no longer go to sea, yet they still retain a cultural importance, as do the canoe-houses occupied by the Nahnken (Talking Chief) of each tribe. Once every man was buried with his paddle, and each possessed a ritual paddle. For the 1999 presidential inauguration of the Federated States of Micronesia the High Chiefs made a rare public appearance and the sacred paddle dance was performed.

Nan Madol was the most important site on the island of Pohnpei. Recently, the island's field archaeologist arranged for a large boat model, built in the Kiti chiefdom, to be placed at Kolonia. It is a model of a *warasapw*, or state canoe, the last full-size version of which had been built on the island in 1910. It is no less than 5.51 m long and has a red hull and white outrigger. The diagonal braces are straight, not curved. This ceremonial model was built, not with drawings or plans, or by the original builders, but with knowledge passed down within the Kiti tribe, precise knowledge that included the identity of innumerable strange spars – their labels seen in place on the model (Fig. 29.4). Coir bound the component parts of the vessel in intricate patterns. The model accords with the description in 1861–63 of a state canoe by Sherzer (Hornell 1936: 399). Until recently, women, through whom land was inherited, bore tattoos that matched the decoration of the boat.[3] Thus, women and the state canoe had an immediate and directly perceived symbolic significance and were therefore of direct cultural significance.

But how was this detailed knowledge transferred over the generations? Pierre Lemonnier in his volume *Technological Choices* (2002) recently observed:

"any technique, in any society...be it a mere gesture or a simple artefact, is always the physical rendering of mental schemes learned through tradition and concerned with how things work, are to be made, and to be used"

..."non-technical phenomena, like magic, superstition, ritual can be materially efficient in preserving techniques not otherwise used" (Lemonnier 2002: 3,27).

In the past the *warasapw* or state canoe with the house in which it lived, was the tribal focus. Feasts surrounded the construction of a canoe, as did taboos and rituals, from the felling of the giant tree to its first sailing and first fishing feasts. This vocabulary is embedded in the language even though the activity is no longer practised (Rehg and Sohl 1979).

Low Islands of the Eastern Carolines

When Duperrey discovered the atoll of Mwoakilloa in 1824, he saw *proas* (Duperrey 1827: V, 296–302; Paris 1841: pl 3.6–10). However, later authors considered that they had disappeared and had even less to say about the canoes of its neighbouring atoll, Pingelap. Unfortunately, the German Sudsee Expedition took place after the Low Islands had been devastated by a series of typhoons so no further information was available.

A visit to Pohnpei's outlying atolls on the government ship permitted observation of the remaining canoes. Outrigger canoes sit in the shallows and on the beach, but the canoe-houses, *najs*, illustrated in 1934, have long since disappeared (Eilers 1934: pl. 3). Some curved booms are

Fig. 29.4. Pohnpei: detail of complex outrigger attachment arrangement of a 5.5 m ceremonial model *warasapw* or state canoe (Photo: Author).

Fig. 29.5. Mwoakilloa: outrigger of an old 4.4 m canoe. Note the horizontal tensioning cable which increases the curvature of the yoke above it. 30 cm ruler rests on the float (Photo: author).

Fig. 29.6. Mwoakilloa: smaller canoe with a sail of blue plasticized sheet (Photo: Author).

no longer of hibiscus but of PVC pipe supplied for rainwater catchment. Many outrigger platforms are of marine-ply flotsam and monofilament line. Six canoes are under construction (for a New Year paddling race).

The village of Mwoakilloa is sheltered out of sight. The roofs of the *najs* still line the waterfront of coral lumps that were photographed about 1900 (Eilers 1934: pl.3). The Mwoakilloans are famed for their woodwork. Under the Japanese they were forced to build wooden whalers for use on other islands. Still known as 'Mwoa-killoa-boats' (Ashby 1993: 285), these competently-made whalers and delicate canoes (Fig. 29.5 and Fig. 29.6) contrast with the rough 'Ralik' canoe sketched by Eilers (1934: fig. 256), that were referred to by Hornell, as the Mwoakilloa type (Haddon and Hornell 1936: fig. 294).[4] Mwoakilloa did have *proas* when sighted by Duperrey in 1824, and Hornell based his descriptive text on Duperrey's little sketches which Paris redrew for publication in 1841.

People spend much of the day under the *najs*, or near the waterfront processing copra and plaiting mats. The fine grade is what can be used to make sails, but such sails have drawbacks and men prefer cotton or blue plasticized tarpaulin. Women still make coconut twine, by twisting it on their thighs. For a three-strand cord three of them squat under a *naj* to which the strands are tied and pass the hanks round anticlockwise.

Wrecked canoes and boats marked the path of the most recent typhoon. Upon the rafters are treasured remains of old *proas*, one destroyed in 1950. Others are remnants of small sailing canoes. One has a sheer-strake that is stitched to the logboat through tiny square mortices, not through drilled holes. Under the *najs*, too, are the whale-boats now replaced by fibreglass dories that are afloat outside.

On one evening during my visit to the island, the generator was run and people gathered to comment excitedly on a video. In some eight hours of footage, the

construction, three years before, of a Mwoakilloan 'proa' had been commissioned and carefully recorded by an Overseas Program Volunteer, who had then sailed it to Pohnpei.[5] Three skilled old men had built it; there was no dedicated boatyard; the less experienced joined in, pausing whenever the 'expert' re-folded a palm-leaf to measure stations and a sooty line was snapped on the log. Mainly European hand-tools were used in the construction.

Environment

While it may be fashionable to play down the role of the environment in technological development, the 'environment' has dealt these particular cultures a bad hand. The climates are hot and humid and natural resources limited.

The old approach was to view small communities as failures because they did not develop mechanisms to raise their economic level. Another approach is to view them as successful, because they have fully utilized available meagre resources and have learned mechanisms for survival in a stark environment. Surplus population in 'fringe' environments could be forced to emigrate: Pohnpei has discrete communities from the two atolls. Males were sometimes forcibly removed to work elsewhere. The Warao, too, have suffered in this way. In addition, the women in both study-areas were noted as being subject to the depredations and diseases of foreign mariners. The biggest environmental factor for both High and Low Islands, impacting on population, natural resources and canoe design, is the typhoon, the shortage of suitable timber radically affecting canoe construction (Lesson 1835 III: 124). It also precipitated population movement. Today Mwoakilloans evacuate to Pohnpei. In the past survivors sailed to safety to the Marshall Islands. There they remained until the vegetation had recovered sufficiently for them to return home. This factor was not taken into account in previous assessments of Mwoakilloan canoes which were dismissed as being of 'Marshallese design'. Despite obvious and explicable similarities, the islanders are very clear about the differences in their craft.[6]

Technological choices

All the communities were quick to prioritise their needs. The introduction of iron edge-tools and long nails (to use as chisels) reduced the strain on food resources that resulted from labour being tied up in canoe construction.[7] In both study areas dangerous sea voyages were initiated to acquire such cultural 'loans' (Heinen 1985: 30; Reisenberg 1968: 1ff)

In the Carolines 'the agents of change' were most welcome, but their ships had difficulty in getting in and out of harbour, and even their rowing boats, which the canoes could out-perform, did not invite imitation. More recently, Mwoakilloans preferred to paddle the whaleboats they were required to build.

In the atolls, the use of heat to curve hibiscus branches for outrigger booms may have a long history. However, another technological choice was not to use heat technology to expand narrow *proa* hulls. By contrast, in the Orinoco Delta, heat was used to expand already large logs (Suarez 1968: 3, fig.12). This is likely to have been an incidental discovery. Logboats of unmodified semi-circular cross-section may be seen today sailing upstream. In both cultures restraint and selectivity has been exercised over innovation.

Conclusion

As Kirch *et al* (1997: 2) observed, there was a long-held implicit assumption that the pre-European inhabitants of the Pacific Islands were simply actors on a changeless stage. It was assumed also that their water transport had altered little before European arrival and declined after contact. The diffusion-focussed approach of Haddon and Hornell, followed by Father Neyret in 1959, set in stone, as it were, the 'classic' forms of Oceanic canoes and inhibited further research. For the tiny populations of the Carolines, the model of colonization in large voyaging canoes should perhaps now be reconsidered. To a greater extent than generally realised, people in both study areas made open-sea voyages. Nevertheless their comparative isolation permits quantification of external influences and the selection or rejection of 'choices'. As Forde observed (1939: 207), the wide stretches of sea that separate Pacific islands have proved far less serious barriers than the equatorial forests of South America.

These small populations and their comparatively late contact with the outside world make them attractive subjects for research. However, sea-level rise and fragile economies mean that they are unlikely to survive much longer.

Notes

1   Basalt axes are rare in the archaeological record of the High Islands (Ayres 1990: 189ff).

2   On my first visit to Madoleniuw harbour the only visible wooden boat out fishing was a decrepit canoe of 'Truuckese' form. As Truk is an island in the Caroline Archipelago some 150 km distant, this illustrates the pitfalls of misidentification that 'observers' have always faced.

3   I am grateful to Isohtik Reti Lawrence for sharing this knowledge with me.

4   To compound matters Hornell's cross-section is actually of Eilers' Pingelap model (1934: fig. 279).

5   On the Marshall Islands, Dennis Allessio has stimulated canoe-building using non-traditional materials to conserve trees (Alessio 1989).

6   Marshallese help and influence extended to intermarriage and contribution to repopulation after a disastrous typhoon in the early 19th century (Asby 1975: 284).

7   Asby (1975: 212) records that before the introduction of iron tools a builder with ten assistants could take four months to shape a *proa*.

Acknowledgements

I am grateful for the help and advice of the following: Andrew Scourse; Reti Lawrence; Sophia Fenwick-Paul; The Micronesia Seminar: Kolonia, Murphy Lihpai; Mario Sanoja Obediente; Erik Steffen; Nick Burningham, Rouley and Albera; Rev Ichiro John; Oltrick Alex; Francia Medina; Veronica Valarino de Abreu; The Venezuelan Embassy, London.

References

Allen, M.S., 1997. Coastal morphogenesis, climatic trends and Cook Islands. In P.V. Kirch and T.L. Hunt (eds), *Historical Ecology in the Pacific Islands: prehistoric environmental and landscape change*, 124–146. Yale University Press. Newhaven.

Alessio, D., 1989, *The Jalwoj (Jaluit) Malmel*. Waan Aelon Kein Project Report 1. Majuro, The Republic of the Marshall Islands.

Ashby, G., 1993, *A Guide to Pohnpei. An Island Argosy*. Rainy Day Press, Pohnpei, Federated States of Micronesia.

Ashby, G. (ed.), 1975, *Some Things of Value*. Public Education Dept, Trust Territory of the Pacific Islands. Saipan.

Ayres, W. S., 1990. Pohnpei's position in eastern Micronesian prehistory. *Micronesia Supplement* 2: 187–212.

Clunie, F., 2001, *Tongiaki to Kalia, pedigree of the last great Western Polynesian voyaging canoe*. Unpublished report.

Diamond, J., 1998, *Guns, Germs and Steel*. Vintage. London.

Duperrey, L.I., 1827, *Voyage autour du monde de la Corvette, La Coquille*. Atlas. Paris.

Eilers, A., 1934, Inseln um Ponape. Kapingamarangi, Nukuor, Ngatik, Mokil, Pingelap. In Prof. G. Von Thilenius (ed), *Ergebnisse der Südsee-Expedition 1908–1910*. L. Friederichsen. Hamburg.

Forde, C.D., 1939, *Habitat, Economy and Society. A Geographical Introduction to Ethnology*. Methuen. London.

Haddon, A.C. and Hornell, J., 1997 [1936], *Canoes of Oceania*. Bishop Museum Press. Honolulu.

Hambruch, P., 1912, *Die Schiffahrt in den Karolinen und Marshall Inseln*. Meereskunde. Berlin.

Heinen, H.D. (ed.), 1985, *Oko Warao, We are the Canoe People*. Acta Ethnologica et Linguistica 59. Stiglmayr. Wien-Föhrenau.

Hezel, F.X., 2001, *The New Shape of Old Island Cultures*. University of Hawaii Press. Honolulu.

Kirch, P.V. and Hunt, T.L., (eds), 1997, Introduction. In *Historical Ecology in the Pacific Islands: prehistoric Environmental and Landscape Change*. Yale University Press. Newhaven.

Lemonnier, P. (ed), 2002, *Technological Choices. Transformation in Material Cultures since the Neolithic*. Routledge. New York.

Lesson, P., 1828, Memoire surs les Peuples de la Mer du Sud, Nommés Carolines ou Mongols-Pelagiens. *Journal des Découvertes et Navigations Modernes ou Archives Geographiques du XIX siècle*. Paris.

Lesson, P., 1835, *Voyage autour du Monde sur la Corvette la Coquille*. 4 vols. Bruxelles. Gregoir, Woutes et Cie.

Lewis, D., 1994, *We the Navigators: the Ancient Art of landfinding in the Pacific*. University of Hawaii Press. Honolulu.

Morgan, W.N., 1988, *Prehistoric Architecture in Micronesia*. University of Texas Press. Austin.

Morton, N.E., Little, G.F., Lew, R. and Hussels, I.E., 1972, Pingelap and Mokil atolls – historical genetics. *American Journal of Human Genetics* 24.3: 277–289

Neyret, J., [1959] 1974, *Pirogues Océaniennes*. 2 vols. Assoc. des Amies des Musées de la Marine. Paris.

O'Connell, J.F. (ed S. Reisenberg), 1972, *A Residence of Eleven Years in New Holland and the Caroline Islands*. Australian National University Press. Canberra.

Paris, F.E., 1841, *Essai sur la construction navale des peuples extra-européens*. Paris

Raleigh, W. (Schomburgk, R.H., ed), 1848, *The Discovery of the Large, Rich and Beautiful Empire of Guiana...performed in the Year 1595*. London Hakluyt Society.

Rainbird, P., and Wilson, M., 1999, *Pohnpeian Petroglyphs*. Unpublished report to the FSM National Historic Preservation Office. Pohnpei, Federated States of Micronesia.

Rehg, K.L.and Sohl, D.G., 1979, *Ponapean-English Dictionary*. University of Hawaii Press. Honolulu.

Reisenberg, S.H., 1968, *The Native Polity of Ponape*. Smithsonian Institution Press. Washington.

Sacks, O., 1996, *The Island of the Colour-Blind*. Macmillan. London.

Spengler, S., 1990, *Geology and Hydrogeology of Pohnpei*, FSM Unpubublished PhD thesis, University of Hawaii.

Suarez, M.M., 1968, *Los Waraos*. Dept de Anthropologia Instiut Venez. de Inv. Cientificas. Caracas

Wilbert, J., 1996, *Mindful of Famine: Religious Climatology of the Warao Indians*. Harvard University Press. Cambridge, Massachusetts.

Wilbert, J., and Layrisse, M. (eds), 1980, *Demographic and Biological Studies of the Warao Indians*, 91–116. UCLA Latin American Center Publications. Los Angeles.

30 The ships that connected people and the people that commuted by ships: The western Baltic case-study

George Indruszewski, Marcus Nilsson and Tomasz Ważny

Introduction

Late 19th-century historiography left not only an enduring legacy in respect to the translation and compilation of early and high medieval written documents, but also it laid down the basic framework of historical thinking for the next century. The interethnic relations in the Western Baltic occupied a special place within this framework, where much credit and emphasis was put on the *ad literam* interpretation of older Saga literature and native chronicles written in Latin that pictured the Wends (Western Slavs) as a *de facto* ethnic polarity associated with warfare on land and at sea. A central place among the later category is taken by the *Historia regnum Danorum* written by Saxo Grammaticus in the late 12th century, a work which had a decisive impact on how historians and archaeologists envisioned the relationship between the Danes and the Wends from the dawn of the Viking Age until the beginning of the High Middle Ages. In formulating their historical interpretation, these scholars were unable to discard the ideological content of Saxo's work in spite of C. Weibull's' critical analysis at the beginning of the 20th century (Weibull 1915: 2–285). They were in fact prisoners of conscience of Saxo's dichotomous world of we – the good and they – the bad. While this interpretation started to loose its grip in recent decades partly due to new results in linguistic, archaeological, historical, and palaeobotanical research, there is still confusion and uncertainty around the exact nature and the mechanism of cultural and ethnic exchange in the Western Baltic as a whole and between the Danes and the Wends in particular.

The ship material from *Vindeboden* in Roskilde

Salvage excavations carried out north of St. James Street by the Roskilde Museum in 1996 unearthed a 7-meter-long, Y-shaped oak keel, two oak plank fragments 1–2 cm thick and a long piece of wood with holes spaced ca. 30–40 cm apart, probably a stringer. Both the keel and the planks showed iron rivets used as fasteners spaced about 15–18 cm apart, and it was found that wool was used as luting material for the plank seams (Bill *et al* 2000: 248).

This ship material was used to consolidate the wattle walls of a canal that drained the fresh water coming from the spring uphill into Roskilde Fjord. The technological characteristics of the ship material show indisputably traits assigned to the Scandinavian style in shipbuilding, and thus there should be no wonder that they were found next to the capital of medieval Denmark.

Dating

The poles affixing the wattle, dated to 1265–1280 (calibrated ^{14}C), were driven directly into a cultural layer dated to the 11th –12th century (Ulriksen 2000: 172, n. 34; Malmros 2000a: 205). These two dates give the approximate time period when these reused ship parts could have been in use, discarded and then reused as canal reinforcements.[1] The dating of the timbers thus ranges from 1000–1300 according to ^{14}C analysis of wood remains and geo-stratigraphical correlations (Malmros 2000: 204–205).

Artefacts

A large number of artefacts were recovered, the most interesting being the skeletal remains of mammals and fish, a large amount of so-called Baltic Ware/Late Slavic ceramics,[2] metal finds including knife sheath mountings of Wendish type with the sharpened type as unrepresentative for Sjælland, an earring of Wendish type, antler objects, such as combs, needles, and 'primitive' short punchers typical for the Southern Baltic but rare in Scandinavia (signs of major textile manufacture in the St. James quarter), rope, miniature boats showing double-ended ships, remains of fishing nets and float manufacturing, with evidence of shoemaking and smithing among the lesser manufacturing enterprises at Vindeboden.

Site context

What is most interesting however, is the site context. The drainage canal was dug through a shore dike that protected the 11th-century lowland from storm flooding. The place behind the dike was a market area in the 11th and 12th centuries where items such as combs, ceramics, textiles, and leather objects were manufactured and traded. It was this beach market that connected the urban centre of Roskilde with long distance sea trade, the place being known in the 13th century as Vindeboder, the Wendish Booths.

The corroboration of excavation results at St. James Church (Olsen 1953–1961), in the City Park (Engberg, 1980), and those from St. James Street (Ulriksen 2000; Malmros 2000a) indicates that Vindeboder was actually located on the moraine height around St. James Church, with some activity areas located in the lowland on both sides of the spring that drained through the shore dike. The area north of the dike was used as a midden and dumping ground, with the stream carrying away refuse and other by-products from the activity area. St. James Church is one of the three oldest churches in Roskilde, the other two being St. Clemens on St. George's Hill and the precursor of the present Roskilde Cathedral. The market and manufacturing quarters of Vindeboden centred around St James Church, apparently the Merchants' Church, were thus situated between the bishop's seat on the high plateau in the town's centre in the south, the 12th-century fortress of St. Clemens, the sea-farers' church, to the west just across the Magle Spring (Maglekilde).

Toponymy

Vindeboden, as a place-name, appears in historical sources between 1291 and 1491 and is, as in other numerous cases from Denmark and North Germany, not a name given by its inhabitants, but by those coming in contact with them. The name was used long after the activities in Vindeboden ceased, as an appellative relic of the function and the ethnic connotation of that place. There are two other localities on Sjælland that have similar names: Vindbyholt in Præstø County and Windebothe in Copenhagen County. It is important to note M. Andersen's observation that all three place names are to be found on the coast, strongly indicating overseas connections (Andersen 1988: 50).

The town was founded by political will and with ecclesiastic blessings much on the template of the Viking Age trading centres; a comparison with Ralswiek on Rügen shows a striking similarity of geographic settings. Artefacts recovered from the sunken ships excavated in the Peberrenden channel near Skuldelev offer a good example of how manufactured goods could have travelled to and from Roskilde. The bone needles found in Skuldelev 1 and the ceramic fragments of the Baltic /Late Slavic Ware (Bobzin or Warder), found in the hull of the low-status warship Skuldelev 5 (Crumlin-Pedersen 2002: 62–63), have plenty of analogies in the Vindeboden quarter.

However, the new urban setting did not remain unchallenged and from the mid-11th century onward defensive works started to appear: the town was surrounded by its first fortification ring and the artificial sea-barrier at Skuldelev was brought in place. These measures apparently failed to deter future attacks on the town itself: in 1131 Niels's royal fleet got through the Skuldelev barrier, and defeated the armed Roskildians at Værebro, and three years later in 1134 the town's fortification ring did not stop the Wends from devastating the town. However painful, these events did not stop the emerging town from becoming what Adam of Bremen later described as "civitas [..] maxima Roscald, sedes regia Danorum."

The ship material from the medieval cemetery in Lund

The excavations from 1974–75 in the St. Clemens quarter in Lund (note again the name of the patron saint of the seafarers) brought to light a residential area together with a cemetery dated from around 1000 to the 13th century (Lundström 1976: 135–143). The first phase of the oldest cemetery in Lund was dated to the first half of the 11th century with several graves displaying coffins made of reused ship-planks.[3] These finds drew the attention of several scholars, among them S. Lundström, W. Filipowiak, and C. Westerdahl (Westerdahl 1985: 7–42).

These ship-planks were documented anew in 2000 when some interesting details were observed (Ahlström et al 2000: 14–15) (Fig. 30.1a and b):

- close to its forward end and along the seam, the plank from grave no. 322 displays a repair lath laid into a hole, onto a layer of moss from inside the hull and nailed in place with 3 mm clenched spikes. The repair work and the hole indicate that an accident happened at some point during the active life of that vessel. The treenails opposite the repair were driven at an angle into the planking, indicating a position about the turn of the bilge in the hull.

- both plank fragments from the same grave displayed hazelnut shell fragments (Corylus avellana) glued to their tarred inner faces, and on one fragment there was also sand mixed with coarse animal hair.

- with one possible exception (fragment no. VMI 101), all planks have shown luting with moss and caulking with animal hair (for grave no. 322 moss of sp. Drepanocladus sendtneri and aduncus) (Filipowiak 1994: 93) The caulking indicates the longevity of the ships in service.

- three different species (pine, oak, and juniper) of wood were used in the planking treenails excavated in three different graves. The oak treenail had a wedge of unidentified deciduous tree species (Malmros 2000b). The choice of wood for treenails fits not only

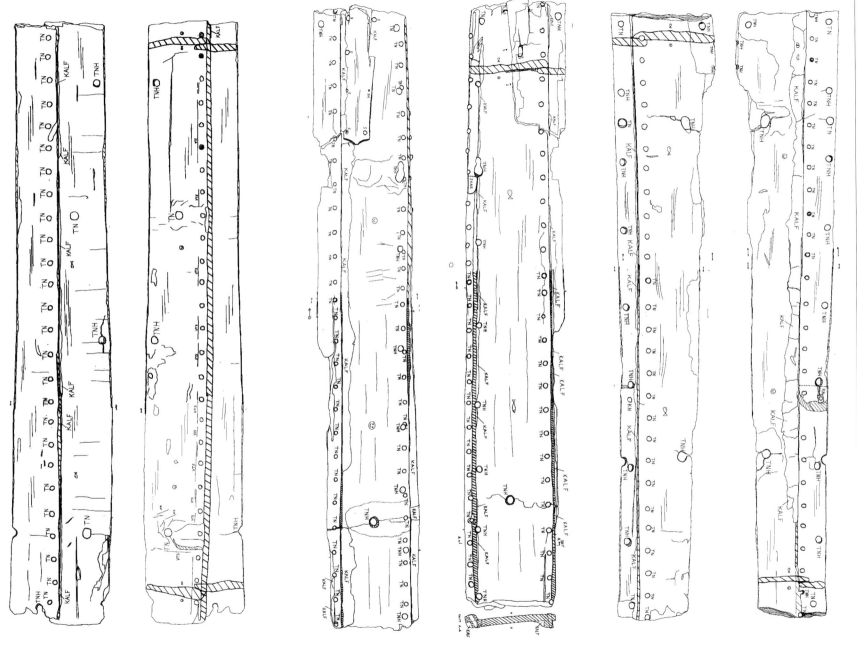

Fig. 30.1a. Treenailed oak ship planks reused in the Lund medieval cemetery in grave no. 322 (no scale) (G. Indruszewski and J. Ahlström).

George Indruszewski, Marcus Nilsson and Tomasz Ważny

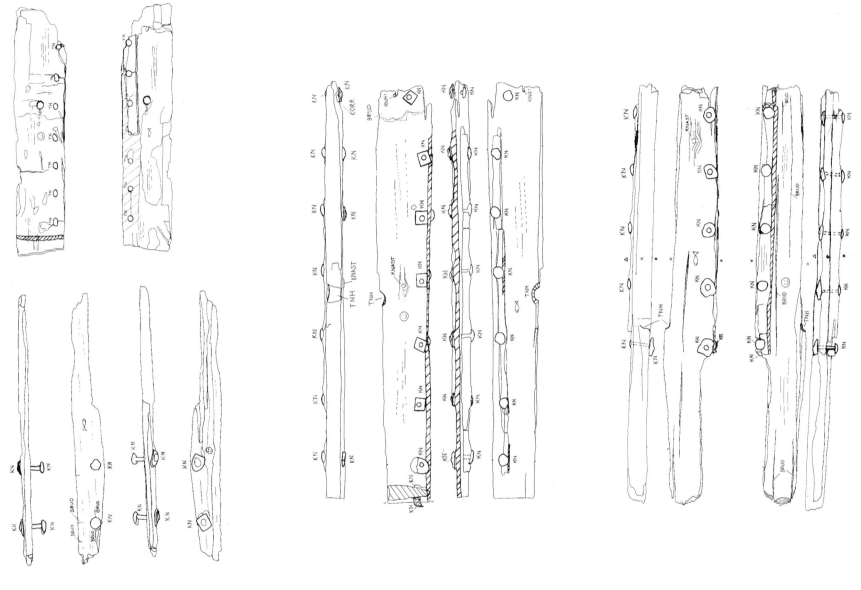

Fig. 30.1b. Riveted pine ship planks reused in the Lund medieval cemetery in grave no. 105 (no scale) (J. Ahlström and M. Nilsson).

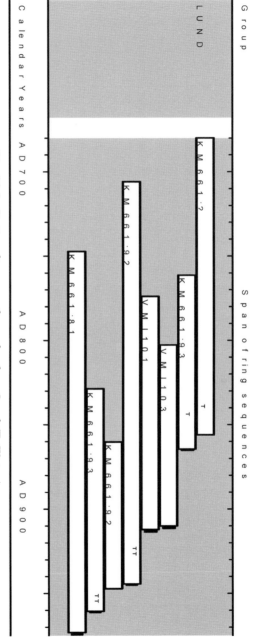

Fig. 30.2. Dating diagram of samples from Lund (T. Ważny).

in the larger Southern Baltic group, but also in the more specific group from the Oder mouth area. Juniper, on the other hand, was more often used in the Oslo Fjord but examples come also from the Southern Baltic. Oak treenails for plank-to-plank fastening remains until now the exception rather than the rule for the area around the Baltic Sea, but later examples from modern times come from continental Europe.

As can be seen, with the notable exception of pine planks fastened with iron rivets, all the other finds exhibit technological traits typical for the Southern Baltic group of ship finds.[4]

Dating

The graves were dated by analogy before 1030, according to the dendrochronological analysis carried out by T. Bartholin on the entire cemetery (Lundström 1976: 135), which gives a general *terminus ante quem* for the lifetime of the ships. *Termini post quem* for the same material are provided by the dendrochronological analysis carried out in 2003 on samples cut from the ship planks reused in the burial coffins (Fig. 30.2). As can be seen, plank dates range with only one exception throughout the 10th century, with clusters in the last quarter of the 9th century, first half of the 10th century, mid-10th century, and third quarter of the 10th century. By taking the earliest dating, one can assess the active life span of these ships at about 30–40 years. According to the analysis, three of these planks come from two tree trunks. Most interesting is that with one exception (which matches the Schleswig-Holstein master curve), all analysed oak planks matched the master curve from Wolin (Table 30.1).

Their reuse in two separate graves and their provenance indicate that here we have at least two different ships.

This result coupled with the presence of sand and that of repairs show altogether that the coffin materials from the first Christian cemetery in Lund came from old ships originally built in the Oder mouth area and around Schleswig, and used in the Baltic area throughout most of the 10th century. The presence of hazelnuts in the tar can be related to the symbolic meaning for the afterlife they had among the Slavs (Niewęgłowski 1993: 47–55) and perhaps in this case they were meant to bring longevity to the ship itself. If the dendrochronological analysis of the cemetery is correct, then they certainly did.

Site considerations and artefact assemblages

Undoubtedly, the site from Lund offers interesting parallels to Roskilde. Both started by the year 1000 not far from Viking Age power centres such as Upåkra and Lejre, both were granted bishopric seats, both were founded by royal will, and both point to the presence of enclaves of non-Scandinavians dedicated to their economic development. In Lund, like almost everywhere in medieval Eastern Denmark, an enormous amount of ceramic material especially of the so-called Baltic Ware (Ger. *Ostsee-keramik*) was uncovered at various locations throughout the medieval precinct of the town (St. Clemens, Apotekaren, St. Maarten). Some of the ceramic material is, according to M. Roslund, identical with that from Usedom at the mouth of the Oder, and it could have been transported in one of the ships whose planks were reused in the Lund cemetery.

Other sites in Scania

The situation from the St. Clemens quarter is not unique. In 1980, other archaeological investigations were carried

No.	Sample	Year rings	Sapwood	Bark	Time series	Dating AD	Tree species	Provenance
1	KM 71839	60	–	–	undated	–	*Quercus* sp.	–
2	KM 71839	74	–	–	undated	–	*Quercus* sp.	–
3	KM 71839	54	–	–	undated	–	*Quercus* sp.	–
4	KM 66166:81	228 (+1)	–	–	747 – 974 AD	992^{+x}_{-7}	*Quercus* sp.	Schleswig (D)
5	KM 66166:929	240 (+1)	–	–	706 – 945 AD	963^{+x}_{-7}	*Quercus* sp.	Wolin (PL)
6	KM 66166:929	89	–	–	860 – 948 AD	965^{+x}_{-7}	*Quercus* sp.	Wolin (PL)
7	KM 66166:?	178	–	–	679 – 857 AD	874^{+x}_{-7}	*Quercus* sp.	Wolin (PL)
8	KM 66166:?	31	4	–	undated	–	*Quercus* sp.	–
9	KM 66166:930	106 (+1)	–	–	760 – 865 AD	883^{+x}_{-7}	*Quercus* sp.	Wolin (PL)
10	KM 66166:930	133 (+1)	–	–	829 – 961 AD	979^{+x}_{-7}	*Quercus* sp.	Wolin (PL)
11	VMI 103	109 (+1)	?	–	803 – 911 AD	929^{+x}_{-7}	*Quercus* sp.	Wolin (PL)
12	VMI 100B	66	–	–	undated	–	*Quercus* sp.	–
13	VMI 100B	121	–	–	undated	–	*Quercus* sp.	–
14	VMI 101A	140	–	–	774 – 913 AD	930^{+x}_{-7}	*Quercus* sp.	Wolin (PL)
15	GRAV 105:2	144 (+3)	–	–	undated	–	*Pinus* sp.	–
16	GRAV 105:1	63	–	–	undated	–	*Pinus* sp.	–

Table 30.1. Provenance and dating of ship timbers from Lund (T. Waźny).

out in Lund, at Apotekaren, and similar ship-related material was found and excavated. The same year traces of reused ship-related material were found in the 11th-century cemetery from Löddeköpinge, but no wood remains were preserved (Cinthio 1980: 54).

The excavations from 2000 in Järrestad have brought to light a Viking Age chieftain's residential area similar to that excavated by L. Jørgensen at Tissø on Sjælland. Several pithouses from around the longhouse yielded quantitites of Menkendorf ceramics in combination with Baltic Ware of an earlier type than Roslund's type a (Söderberg 2000: 48). In addition to ceramic artefacts, the shaft of one of the three excavated wells was built from reused ship planks fastened together with treenails. These artefacts exhibit technological traits characteristic of Southern Baltic ship finds: plank thickness around 2.5 cm, plank width around 25–26 cm, treenails with diameters of around 1 cm spaced about 8.5 cm apart. A 2.5 cm large hole in the middle of the plank recalls the floor-to-plank fastening.

The loose ship material from Varnæs Vig

An unexpected loose find was made in 1983 in the small cove at Varnæs, Aabenraa County. Two tangentially-cut planks of oak, with intact treenails in place, were found on the bottom of the fjord and are presumably part of the same hull. The treenail interval (11–12 cm) and dimensions (1 cm in diameter) fit in the distribution for the Southern Baltic group. All treenails except one are of pine. The exception is of spruce (*Picea abies*) or larch (*Larix var. polonica*), which was growing in early medieval times mostly in the eastern Baltic regions, including the Vistula Lagoon (Malmros 2000b). The combination of technological features and tree species points to the eastern Baltic as a possible provenance for the material and the ship.

Site

The site at Varnæs is interesting in itself. The 13th-century King Valdemar's *Jordebog* describes Varnæs as one of the trading places connected with sea trade, and near the site one can still find a rampart probably related to a possible sea connection of the closed end of the Skov Lake through Vigsmose. Further investigations are needed to identify the character of the site, of the finds, and also of the place-name (since Varnæs has cognates in German – Warnitz, and Slavic – Warnic).

The shipyard from Fribrødre Å

Finally, the well-known site from Fribrødre Å, on the island of Falster, should be mentioned here. More than 1700 ship parts were excavated at this site during the 1982–83 archaeological campaign (Skamby Madsen 1984 and 1991). The following features have been observed at this rich site: wood used for wedges is very diverse and the treenail wedges are coarse, denoting speedy manufacture; treenail wood is not pine but preponderantly willow with best parallels from western Mecklenburg; the relatively high number of mallets is characteristic for a Slavic shipyard; numerous artefacts from this site have their best parallels in the Szczecin material; the repair lath is similar to that from Lund and Wolin site no. 10; plank fragments are of oak with some of beech, similar to those from the Hedeby 2 ship remains; luting was of wool mixed with moss, for which the best parallels are to be found in Ralswiek on Rügen, and in Puck Bay; several hull timbers have good parallels in the Ralswiek and Eckernförder ship material; the scantlings of planks, treenails, etc. fit within the ranges characteristic for the Southern Baltic group of shipfinds.

What can be discerned from this succinct presentation is that Fribrødre Å ship artefacts can be classified according to the principle 'last taken is first dropped' in the following sequence (ranking according to recovered quantities):

1. broken wooden implements used in conjunction with ship repair and construction
2. refuse in form of wooden chips and shavings (mostly oak)
3. internal structure (34 frame fragments of oak, 2 elm, 2 ash, 1 beech)
4. planking (10 fragments)
5. stem and keel assemblage (1 stem fragment, 2 wing fragments)

As can be seen, the numbers of recovered artefacts decrease as the building importance of hull timbers increases. That means that the people that worked in the last quarter of the 11th century in the Fribrødre shipyard left behind the least desirable ship timbers in their quest to build new craft.

Dating

The dendrochronological analysis indicated 1050–1055 AD as the felling date for some of the ship planks left at the shipyard. It is interesting to note that the two averaged curves (M 273 and M 274) yielded similarly low t-values when cross-matched with the master curves from southern Jutland (range 4.84–5.07), Schleswig-Holstein (3.23–3.25), and Lund (2.60–2.67) (Bonde 1984:277). On this basis, and on the lack of comparison with North-German and Polish master-curves, no provenance was indicated for the analysed ship timbers.

Since these were used planks, Skamby Madsen added another 30–40 years to the initial date to accommodate the active life of the vessels. On the other hand, calibrated ^{14}C dating gave a range between 1040–1150, which indicates that the creek shore was reinforced at a later date, sometime in the later 11th century or first half of the 12th century (Skamby-Madsen 1991: 194).

The situation seems similar to that at the Lund cemetery, in that the felling date can be taken as *terminus post quem* for the ships that after being in service several decades underwent major repairs and structural changes at Fribrødre. That happened about the turn of the century and this gives an approximate *terminus ante quem* for the ships.

Artefact assemblages

Besides ship material, the site yielded Late Slavic/Baltic Ware pottery, a musical pipe fragment, which has a good parallel in a similar fragment found in Lund (Skamby-Madsen 1991: 194), Wendish knives and sheath mountings of Knorr type II, and a Wendish-type earring. While M. Müller has questioned whether this musical instrument might have belonged to Vikings (Scandinavians) or to Slavs (Müller 1988), one should note a 10th-century mention in which the Arab traveller Ibrahim ibn Jakub draws attention to the musical instruments used by the Slavs.[5]

Site structure

According to Skamby Madsen's investigations, the shipyard site extended from the Northern Snekke Hill (Norre Snekkebjerg) to the Southern Snekke Hill (Sonder Snekkebjerg) along the left shore of the creek (Skamby Madsen 1984: 265–266). Recent investigations, made on the occasion of hydro-regulation works at the creek, have shown that the cultural layer extends beyond the meander in an eastern direction towards today's Volme Holm bridge. Two high phosphate concentrations have been found in the area, one at the mouth of the creek, and the other south of Volme Holm. Since these areas have not yet been investigated archaeologically, it is difficult to assess the longevity of the site on the basis of scarce stratigraphical information. Nevertheless, the presence of man-made improvements to reinforce the creek shoreline, and spread of the cultural layer, the thickness especially the toponymy that surrounds the site suggest an activity area of a more permanent character than previously thought.

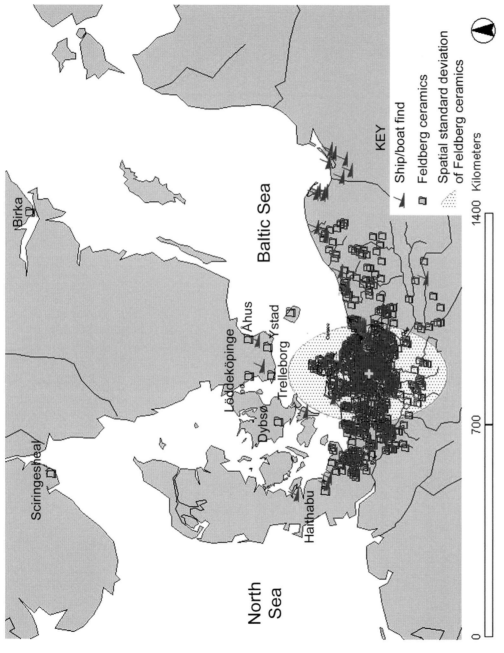

Fig. 30.3. Spatial distributions of ship finds of a Slavic shipbuilding style and Feldberg ceramics (G. Indruszewski).

Toponymy

The surrounding toponymy (Snekke, Fribrodre, Theck-leaggre, Volme Holm) has either a relatively good Slavic background or was used in conjunction with the Slavs.

Conclusion

This short presentation of ship parts and ship-related material in relation to their respective site contexts encourages a perspective at odds with that formulated on the historical background offered by the work of Saxo Grammaticus. While Saxo describes the Wends in general, the Rugians and those from the Oder mouth area in particular, in terms of contempt and enmity, the contextual evidence of both ceramic and ship artefacts point exactly to the opposite. Technological traits, site context, and artefact assemblages presented earlier show clearly that with the exception of the Roskilde case, the ship material fits within the Slavic style in shipbuilding. This style can be traced both in its place of origin and around the Western Baltic region. At the general level of inquiry, it seems

clear that the Western Baltic occupies a pivotal geographic role in meetings between different styles in shipbuilding. It was not a 'melting pot' but an 'assorted pot' of different technological styles that in spite of interaction maintained their own stylistic signatures. During this cultural 'inter-course' the ship became not only the vehicle of connecting people over the Baltic waters, but also a semiotic object for its builders, owners, and users.

Prior to the year 1000, Scandinavia and the Western Baltic knew mostly its own, home-made, coarse Viking Age ceramics and imports of Slavic ware of the Feldberg and Menkendorf type. The fact that Late Baltic Ware appears suddenly and massively in the Danish and Swedish regions, displacing the local Viking Age ceramics, points not only to a technological transfer of know-how in space but to a movement of producers to these regions. More-over, the fact that a larger proportion of these ceramics typologically come from Rügen and the Oder mouth – areas which suffered most from the 12th-century Wendish Wars of Valdemar's reign and historically were seen as the main nests of piracy (see also the Saga of the Joms

Vikings) – puzzled Roslund so much that he described the wave of newcomers as *traelle*, slaves brought in by victorious Danes. This compromise fits neither the archaeological context previously discussed nor the contemporary historical situation, and this can be seen clearly when ship finds with Slavic stylistic character and Feldberg ceramics distributions are overlaid (Fig. 30.3).

We do not know, for example, what Magnus the Good did in Wolin in 1044, other than burning the town. The historical sources are silent in this respect and we are only left to speculate whether he, like Godefrid in the 9th century, carried out a *translatio* of merchants and crafts-men to Scandinavia.

By the end of the 10th century, the Latin world built by the Roman Catholic Church and the Carolingian feudal structures expanded ideologically and culturally for the first time in Scandinavia through the erection of bishoprics in Sliaswich (Schleswig), Ripa (Ribe), and Aarhus (948–965). Preoccupied with imperial ambitions in the North Sea region, the kings of Denmark, from Sven Forkbeard (985–1014) to Sven Estridssen (1047–1074), were interested in the consolidation of the new feudal system at home. Both parties were thus avidly looking at one major resource that was so scarce in those times, namely people. Only with people could the 'new world order' have functioned. For the new Church structure and for the newly established feudal system, the ethnic background of these persons mattered little. What mattered was the ideological, economical, and political advantages they could bring as faithful subjects of the Church and the Crown.

Acknowledgements

Analysis of tree and moss remains for several of the mentioned sites was carried out by C. Malmros, National Museum of Denmark in Copenhagen. The authors wish to thank all institutions and private persons from Sweden, Denmark, and Poland involved in this research initiative.

Notes

1 Ulriksen (2000: 156) makes the point that late medieval items such as double combs and enameled pottery were found in the uppermost layers around the wattle constructions, and that these layers were strongly eroded. Thus, it is possible that the dating suggested by the ^{14}C analysis while the cultural items dated into the High Middle Ages could have been vertically displaced by erosion. The drainage ditch itself was built sometime in the 11th century. The ^{14}C dating was used by J. Bill as a basis for asserting a date between 1200 and 1250 for the recovered ship material (Bill *et. al.* 2000: 157).

2 There were about 8000 ceramic fragments found, 20% of which are rims. The Garz type is specific to the St. James site, since the quantity recovered here is a lot more than the entire ceramic collection recovered inside the medieval town of Roskilde. The Woldegk type, considered by T. Kempke a transition type to late Slavic ceramics (10th-11th century) (Kempke 2001: 240), gives a chronological insight into the dating of the site. Other ceramic imports include the English-style type manufactured in Lund, and the Pingsdorf-type ceramics, but these are sporadic at the site.

3 The coffin fragments KM 66166-930 from grave nr. 322 belonged to two overlapped ship planks of oak fastened with small treenails, about 1.2 cm in diameter driven 6–7 cm apart. Holes of about 2.5 cm in diameter bored in the middle of the planking at 93-cm intevals indicated the position of the floor-to-planking fasteners and the room interval in the ship. Another fragment from the same grave, KM 66166-929, represents part of a sequence of 3 ship planks of oak fastened together with treenails about 1 cm in diameter, and spaced about 6–8 cm apart. Treenail holes used for floor-to-plank fastening were about 96 cm apart.

4 Treenails about 1 cm in diameter, 6–8 cm treenail interval in plank lands no wider than 5 cm, plank scarfs of about 7 cm in length, plank thicknesses between 1.5 and 2.5 cm, luting material of moss. For details see Indruszewski 1997: 106–107.

5 Ibrahim Ibh Iakub in Kowalski (1946:52–53):"The Slavs have various wind and chord musical instruments. Their wind instrument measures more than two ells, and the chord instrument has 8 strings, its lower case is flat and not rounded."

References

Ahlström, J., Indruszewski, G., and Nilsson, M., 2000, Nya undersökningar av skeppsplankor från Lund, *Marinarkeologisk Tidskrift* 1: 14–15.

Andersen, M., 1988, Venderne i Roskilde, *Hikuin* 50: 49–60.

Bartolin, T. S., 1976, Dendrokronologiske og vedanatomiske undersøgelse af fundene. *Uppgrävt förflutet för PK-banken i Lund. Archaeologia Lundensia* 7: 145–169. Lund.

Bill, J., Gøthche, M., and Myrhøj, H.M., 2000, Roskildeskibene. In T. Christensen and M. Andersen (eds.), *Civitas Roscald – fra byens begyndelse*, pp. 211–260. Roskilde.

Bonde, N., 1984, Dendrokronologiske undersøgelser på skibsstømmer fra Fribrødre Å på Falster, *Hikuin* 10: 275–278.

Cinthio, H. 1980, *The Löddeköpinge Excavation III. The Early Medieval Cemetery*. Meddelanden från Lund LUHM New Series 3. Lund.

Crumlin-Pedersen, O., and Olsen, O. (eds.), 2002, *The Skuldelev Ships 1. Topography, Archaeology, History, Conservation and Display*. Ships and Boats of the North 4.1. Roskilde.

Engberg, Niels 1980: Sct. Mikkels kirken i Roskilde. Romu (Roskilde Museums Årbog) 1: 40–58.

Filipowiak, W., 1994, Shipbuilding at the Mouth of the River Odra (Oder). In C. Westerdahl (ed.), *Crossroads in Ancient Shipbuilding, Proceedings of the Sixth International Symposium on Boat and Ship Archaeology, Roskilde 1991*, Oxbow Monograph 40, pp. 83–96. Oxford.

Indruszewski, G. 1997, Metrological aspects reflected in early medieval shipbuilding from the Southern Baltic Sea. In D. C. Lakey (ed.), *SHA Underwater Archaeology*, 104–112. Uniontown.

Kempke, T., 2001, Slawische Keramik. In H. Lüdtke and K. Schitzel (eds.), *Handbuch zur mittelalterlichen Keramik in Nordeuropa*, pp. 209–255. Neumünster.

Kowalski, T., 1946, *Monumenta Poloniae Historica I*. Academia Litterarum Polonica Editionum Collegii Historici 84. Krakow.

Lundström, S., 1976, Båtdetaljer. *Uppgrävt förfluttet för PK-banken i Lund. Archeologia Lundensia* 7: 135–143. Lund.

Malmros, C., 2000a, Geologisk undersøgelse af et vandløb fra vikingetid og middelalder ved Sankt Ibs Vej i Roskilde. In T. Christensen and M. Andersen (eds.), *Civitas Roscald – fra byens begyndelse*, pp. 199–210. Roskilde.

Malmros, C., 2000b, *Bestemmelse af trænagler og kalfatring fra Varnæs Vig – Danmark, Lund – Sverige og Kamień Pomorski – Polen*. NNU Rapport nr. 10. Copenhagen.

Müller, M, 1988, Reed-pipe of the Vikings or the Slavs? An early find from the Baltic region. In E. Hickmann and D. W. Hughes (eds.), *The Archaeology of early music cultures*, pp. 31–38. Bonn.

Niewęglowski, A., 1993, Leszczyna i orzechy laskowe jako materialne korelaty religii w Polsce przedchrześcijańskiej. In M. Kwapiński and H. Paner (eds.), *Wierzenia przedchrześcijańskie na ziemiach polskich*, pp. 47–55. Gdańsk.

Olsen, Olaf, 1962, Sankt Ibs kirke i Vindebode – et bidrag til Roskildes ældste historie. Fra København Amt 1962: 61–87.

Skamby Madsen, J., 1984, Et skibsværft fra sen vikingetid/ tidlig middelalder ved Fribrødre Å på Falster, *Hikuin*10: 261–274.

Skamby Madsen, J., 1991, Fribrødre: A shipyard site from the late 11th century. In O. Crumlin-Pedersen (ed.), *Aspects of Maritime Scandinavia AD 200–1200*, pp. 183–207. Roskilde.

Söderberg, B., 2000, Järrestad i centrum, Väg 11, sträckan Östra Tommarp-Simrishamn. Järrestads sn, Skåne, *IV Syd Rapport* 16: 5–109. Lund.

Ulriksen, J., 2000, Vindeboder – Roskildes tidlige havnekvarter. In T. Christensen and M. Andersen (eds.), *Civitas Roscald – fra byens begyndelse*, pp. 145–198. Roskilde.

Weibull, C., 1915, *Saxo: kritiska undersökningar i Danmarks historia från Sven Estridsens död till Knut VI*. Särtryck ur Historisk tidskrift för Skåneland. Lund.

Westerdahl, C., 1985, Holznägel und Geschichte. Eine Schiffs-archäologische Hypothese. *Deutsche Schiffahrtsarchiv* 8: 7–42.

31 Early cogs, Jutland boatbuilders, and the connection between East and West before AD 1250

Fred Hocker and Aoife Daly

By the end of the 13th century, German merchants had established their economic dominance over two of the major trade routes in northern Europe, the east-west commerce between the Baltic and North Seas and the north-south traffic between the North Sea and interior Russia via the Rhine. Their merchants were found in ports from of the bulk commodities of the Baltic allowed them to dictate commercial terms to town councils and princes alike. Their straight-stemmed, high-sided cogs, the symbol of their power, were featured on the seals of many of the towns from which they came and are irremovably associated with the German towns in the public and academic consciousness.

But the Hanse did not create the routes they came to dominate for nearly two centuries, nor did they create the ship type that carried most of their bulk cargoes. The Rhine had been a major artery since the Romans arrived in Germania. The east-west route over the neck of the Jutland peninsula was not much younger, and had led to the development of Haithabu, one of the great emporia of the early Middle Ages. Long before German colonists had established the towns that would come to be the centres of Hanse power, Saxon, Frisian and Scandinavian traders were busy moving goods between the Baltic and North Seas in heavily built, half-clinker, half-carvel sailing vessels.

Early cogs

Although we can argue about the applicability of the medieval term "cog" to modern archaeological finds (Weski 1999; Crumlin-Pedersen 2000), there is little real doubt that the numerous finds of such vessels must represent, in some fashion, this most commonly mentioned type of large, bulk carrier from the period 1200–1400. Numerous attempts have been made to define what a cog is or was, almost all based on observed physical characteristics of construction (for example Heinsius 1956, Reinders 1985, Dokkedal 1996, Grille 2002). Every

author has his or her own set of diagnostic characteristics, so the number of ship finds that qualify as cogs depends on whom one asks, but most scholars seem to agree on a body of just over 20 ships, plus a few borderline cases. These ships are distributed over the former Hanseatic territory and into the Low Countries, with substantial finds (by our reckoning) in Belgium (1), the Netherlands (10), Germany (2), Denmark (5), Sweden (4 or 5) and Estonia (1). They range in date from the mid-12th century to the first third of the 15th century.

One peculiarity of the distribution of these finds is that the five earliest finds (Kollerup, Kolding, Skagen, Kuggmaren and Bossholmen) are all found in Scandinavia. These early vessels also show clear differences in structural detail from the later vessels, which seem to achieve a great degree of commonality in shape and construction after about 1300, but carry some features reminiscent of Nordic shipbuilding, such as cleft planks and stringers on the inner surface of the planking (Fig. 31.1). All five of these ships seem to have been built in the same region, in southern Scandinavia. Even more intriguing, the origin of the three earliest, perhaps even the four earliest, can be localised to a very small area, in southern Jutland, Denmark (Fig. 31.2).

The Kollerup cog was excavated in 1978 (Crumlin-Pedersen 1981a; Kohrtz Andersen 1983) and the dendrochronological analysis of 17 samples was completed in 2000 (Daly 2000; Daly et al. 2000). Sapwood was preserved on three samples and the felling of timbers for the ship took place around 1150.

The Kolding cog (Fig. 31.3) was partially excavated in 1943 (Hansen 1944) and completed (including recovery and detailed documentation of the hull remains) in 2001 by the National Museum of Denmark (Dokkedal 2001; Hocker 2000; Hocker and Dokkedal 2001). An initial dendrochronological dating of five samples was carried out in 2000 (Eriksen 2000) and an additional 11 samples completed the analysis in 2002 (Daly 2002; in press). Bark edge, preserved on three of the frames, allows a precise felling date: winter 1188–89.

Fig. 31.1. Schematic section through the Kollerup cog, showing some of the features of this and the Kolding find: five flush-laid bottom planks in a rounded bottom, a stringer on the inner face of the planking at the carvel/clinker transition, and futtocks that are notched over the stringer (after P.K. Andersen 1983).

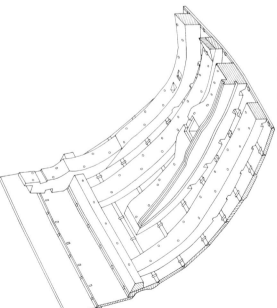

Fig. 31.2. Find locations of the four earliest recognised cogs, as well as the location of the Ellingå vessel (Aoife Daly)

The cog from Skagen was partially excavated in 1994 (Lønstrup and Nielsen 1997) and dendrochronological analysis was carried out on five samples by Eriksen (1994). Felling of timber for this vessel took place around 1193.

The in-water documentation of the cog Kuggmaren I from the Stockholm archipelago, Sweden is reported in Adams and Rönnby (2002). Dendrochronological analysis of three samples were carried out by Eggertsson at the University of Lund and an additional two samples were completed in 2003 (Daly 2003). These two samples had

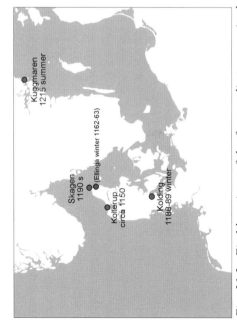

Fig. 31.3. Measured perspective view of the remains of the Kolding cog, as excavated in 2001 (Fred Hocker).

bark edge preserved, providing a felling date of spring or summer 1215.

Dating is only one part of the puzzle, and only half of what dendro analysis can reveal. The annual ring patterns that are distinctive for a particular span of years are also unique to the region where the tree grew.

Dendro analysis

Master chronologies have been built for different regions in Europe over the last 30 years. These chronologies derive from numerous tree-ring analyses of oak timber from living trees, historic buildings and archaeological sites. These chronologies span a considerable period of time and geographically can be taken to represent, climatically, a large region and consist of large amounts of tree-ring data. It has, up to now, been these large chronologies that have been used for dating new oak finds, and these chronologies have also been the basis for the determination of the provenance of archaeological oak timbers, and in the context of this paper of course, ships' timbers.

It should be noted that the determination of provenance of oak from shipwrecks allows us to suggest where the trees grew, but this does not automatically equate with where the ship was built. In earlier periods it is likely that ships were built close to the source of timber, due simply to the cost of transporting timber, but increasing transport of timber as a commodity from the later Middle Ages onward (Fritzbøger 1994) means that a ship can have been built of timber transported a considerable distance from the forest in which it was felled. There is little evidence of long-distance commerce in structural timber in northern Europe before the 14th century, so we feel relatively confident ships built in the 12th century were constructed near the forests where the timber was cut.

Many Danish shipwrecks have been analysed by Daly and colleagues at the National Museum of Denmark, especially over the last 10 years, both with a view to dating and determining the provenance of the timber, using these large regional chronologies (for example Bonde and Crumlin-Pedersen 1990; Bonde and Jensen 1995; Bartholin 2001; Daly, in press). On the other hand, no in-depth analysis of the technique has been carried out. Many questions arise from the numerous shipwrecks from the Viking Age to the Middle Ages to the Renaissance, which have been examined. Why does the determination of provenance work brilliantly for some wrecks and not so well for others? How refined can provenance determination become? How closely can we identify the region in which the trees grew?

The technique

It is possible to date timber from a ship with relatively few samples, by comparing the unique sequence of varying annual ring widths with master curves developed for specific regions and date ranges. However, for identifying the provenance of the timber, a considerable number of samples are needed. The growth pattern of a single tree is a reflection of the many factors, which will have influenced the tree throughout its life. Factors can have local or wider, regional origins. The tree-ring curve is a product of the combinations of local conditions and wider climatic conditions. By analysing and averaging at least 10, even 15 samples from a ship, the variations of the individual trees is ironed out to render a single curve, which represents the trees' collective reaction to the climate where they grew. That pattern is most similar to that of other trees from within the region, which cover the same time span.

In a routine dendrochronological analysis, a fairly standard statistic of correlation, "Student's *t*-test" is widely used. To find a date for a tree-ring curve, this statistic (adapted for dendrochronology by Baillie and Pilcher 1973, and incorporated in a computer program, designed for working with tree-ring data, by Tyers 1997) calculates the correlation, represented as a value for the variable *t*, for every position along a chronology to find positions of high correlation. A date is found when the curve achieves a good correlation with several chronologies, and is confirmed visually. A *t*-value greater than 3.5 is interesting to the dendrochronologist when looking for a date. A *t*-value greater than 10.00 would be expected from the measuring of two samples from the same tree.

This statistic can also be used to suggest the origin of the timber. Once the date is found, the tree-ring curve, in this context from a ship, is checked against master chronologies for Northern Europe as a measure of how

similar the ship's tree-ring curve is to the regional chronologies. The higher the *t*-value, the greater the similarity.

Results

Fig. 31.4a shows the comparison of the curve from the Kollerup cog, at its dated position, with the large regional master chronologies from Northern Europe. The dot indicates the find location of the wreck. It can be seen that the highest *t*-value is with a Jutland chronology.

The attempt here is to examine the possibility of refining this provenance determination by comparing the ship with smaller local chronologies. With dendrochronological analyses, for every site examined, a curve is built. At a later date this data can be assembled into the large regional chronologies. Fig. 31.4b shows the correlation values for individual *site* chronologies from Denmark from the period. Some are from Daly's own analyses and others are from analyses carried out at the National Museum of Denmark (see Table 31.1).

The distribution of the *t*-values speaks for itself. The highest is for a site chronology from Haderslev in southeast Jutland. There are as yet no suitable site chronologies for the island of Fyn from the period but it is on this basis

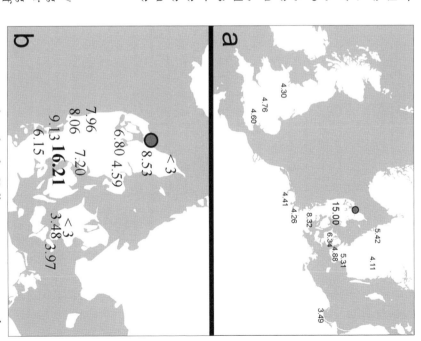

Fig. 31.4. t-values for the Kollerup cog *a. compared to larger regional chronologies; b. compared to local site chronologies (Aoife Daly).*

Country	Name	Source
Denmark	Jutland Funen	National Museum of Denmark
	Zealand	Daly, unpublished
Germany	Schleswig-Holstein	University of Hamburg
	Hamburg	University of Hamburg
	Lübeck	University of Hamburg
	Lower Saxony	University of Göttingen
	Weserbergland	University of Göttingen
	Weser	University of Göttingen
	Northern Lower Saxony	University of Göttingen
	Lüneburger Heide	University of Göttingen
	West Germany	University of Göttingen
	Southern Germany	University of Göttingen
United Kingdom	London	University of Sheffield
	Northern England/Wales	University of Sheffield
	Southern England	University of Sheffield
Ireland	Dublin	Baillie 1977
The Netherlands	Holland	Jansma 1995
Poland	Gdansk Pomerania	Academy of Fine Arts, Warsaw
Sweden	Southwest Skåne	University of Lund
	Lund, Skåne and Blekinge	University of Lund
	West Sweden	Bräthen 1982
	Middle Sweden	University of Lund
Danish site chronologies	Mollestrømmen Haderslev	Eriksen 1996
	Hadsten Watermill	Nationalmuseet
	Vendsyssel	Daly 1998
	Vordingborg	Eriksen 1995
	Løgumgärde	Daly 1999
	Roager Church	Eriksen 2001
	Birkely Bridge	Daly 2003b
	Ribe	Daly, unpublished
	Stegeborg	Bartholin 1978; Daly 2001c
	Viborg Sonderso	Daly 2003a
	Skjern Bridge	Daly 2001b
	Ålborg	Daly 2000b; 2001a

Table 31.1. List of master chronologies and site chronologies used in the maps showing the distribution of t-values.

possible to suggest that the timber for the ship comes from the region around Lillebælt.

A similar analysis for the Kolding cog is shown in Fig. 31.5. Here can be seen again the distribution of *t*-values in Northern Europe, again with the highest similarity appearing with the Jutland chronology. Comparison with Danish site chronologies shows a similar pattern to the Kollerup ship, where the Haderslev site chronology produces the highest correlation.

The third cog, from Skagen in Northern Jutland, does not produce the same extremely high correlation results but it can be said that it is showing a similar pattern (Fig. 31.6). Again the highest regional value is for the Jutland chronology, and southern Jutland once again is strongest

among the local site chronologies. The less striking result compared to Kolding and Kollerup suggests that the trees in the Skagen cog did not grow so close to the source of one of the well-defined local chronologies, but the analysis still points in the direction of a Southern Jutland or Fyn provenance.

In the case of the Kuggmaren cog, the *t*-values (Fig. 31.7) are generally lower than the other examples discussed here, but Jutland is still strongest. It is more difficult to say anything conclusive about the comparison to the local chronologies, as many of the values fall around 6.5–7.0. It is tempting to suggest that the timber for this ship grew in Southwest Jutland but the fact that these correlations are relatively low, and the fact that only five

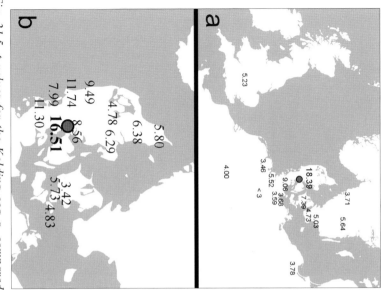

Fig. 31.5. t-values for the Kolding cog a. compared to larger regional chronologies; b. compared to local site chronologies (Aoife Daly).

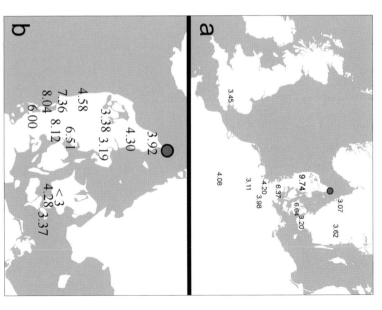

Fig. 31.6. t-values for the Skagen cog a. compared to larger regional chronologies; b. compared to local site chronologies (Aoife Daly).

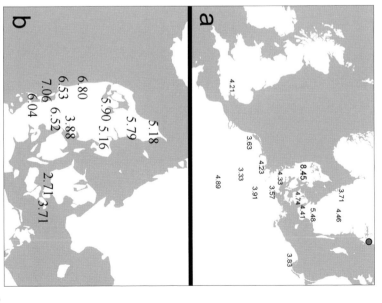

Fig. 31.7. t-values for the Kuggmaren cog a. compared to larger regional chronologies; b. compared to local site chronologies (Aoife Daly).

samples are analysed for this ship, means that the determination of the provenance of this ship is still provisional.

It can be seen for this data that northern German site chronologies are not compared here. Considering the lower *t*-value which appears with the master chronology for Schleswig-Holstein it is unlikely that the provenance of the ship is further south but this cannot be ruled out. Current research is aimed at expanding this analysis to allow comparison of the tree-ring curve from this and other ships with site chronologies from all northern Europe.

It is necessary to be sure that the distribution of *t*-values for the four early cogs is not a product of the site chronologies themselves. There is a danger this is quite simply due to the Haderslev chronology being a particularly well-replicated chronology and therefore more likely to produce higher correlation with a lot of Jutland material. To show that this is not the case, the results of analysis of timber from the Ellingå ship are shown in Fig. 31.8. The shipwreck is a cargo vessel of Nordic type, the timber for which was felled in winter 1162–63 (Bill 1994; Bonde *et al.* 1991). When compared with the master chronologies it gives the highest values with Denmark and Sweden.

When compared with the Danish sites chronologies though, a very different distribution than that of the cogs

		Kollerup	Kolding	Skagen	Kuggmaren	Ellingå
		0013M001	60871M02	0008M001	Z0012M02	0006M001
		Ca. 1150	Winter 1188-89	1190's	Summer 1215	Winter 1162-63
Kollerup	0013M001	*	12,89	5,32	6,07	5,49
Kolding	60871M02	12,89	*	7,85	6,27	4,55
Skagen	0008M001	5,32	7,85	*	-	-
Kuggmaren	Z0012M02	6,07	6,27	-	*	4,74
Ellingå	0006M001	5,49	4,55	-	4,74	*

Table 31.2. Correlation between the oak tree-ring curves from the four early cogs.

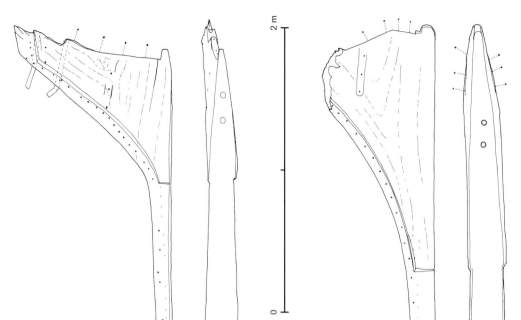

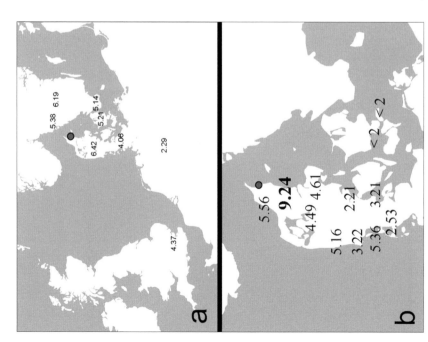

Fig. 31.8. t-values for the Ellingå vessel a. compared to larger regional chronologies; b. compared to local site chronologies (Aoife Daly).

emerges. The highest *t*-value is for a site chronology from the town of Aalborg in Northern Jutland. The local Swedish chronologies have not been checked, so the provenance of this ship is not as yet conclusive.

Table 31.2 shows the correlation of the four cogs to each other. The high value between Kollerup and Kolding can be seen, as can the slightly lower values for Skagen and Kuggmaren. Although there are circa 40 years between the building of the Kollerup and Kolding cogs,

Fig. 31.9. The stern hooks of the Kollerup (top) and Kolding (bottom) vessels, showing similarities in the formation of the rabbet, the sternpost angle and scarf, and the two treenails/plugs in the bottom surface. Note also the indications of rudder gudgeons on both, the earliest known sea-going vessels so equipped (Fred Hocker).

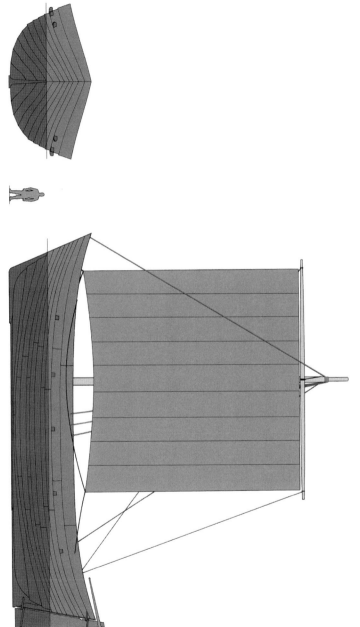

Fig. 31.10. A schematic minimum reconstruction of the Kolding cog, with a displacement probably in excess of 90 tons and a cargo capacity of 70 tons or more (Fred Hocker).

their timber grew in very similar localities. Skagen correlates less clearly, but still with a high enough *t*-value to suggest it was built of timber from the same region if not the same locality. The correlation for the Kuggmaren wreck is even less marked, but the analysis is based on a small number of samples.

Interpretation

If it seems remarkable that ships found from the North Sea coast of Denmark to the Stockholm archipelago might have been built in the same small area, at least the two earliest vessels, Kollerup and Kolding must come from southern Jutland. Their similarity in many fine, even non-functional details of construction despite an age difference of approximately 40 years suggests continuity of this shipbuilding center over several generations (Fig. 31.9). Could the builder of the Kolding cog be the son or grandson of the man who built the Kollerup vessel? Far-fetched, perhaps, but not unthinkable.

As these vessels are also among the largest ship finds from medieval Denmark, they point toward a well-developed shipbuilding center catering for skippers engaged in long-distance commerce rather than vernacular production for local use anf they suggest the existence of a bulk trade well before the Hanse had taken over the commerce in Baltic grain, fish and timber. It should not be surprising that we find such large vessels being built in just this area. As Christian Radtke points out elsewhere in this volume, the port of Schleswig, only

80 km to the south of Haderslev, was a major center of commerce in the 12th century, based on its position at the transshipment point across the neck of the Jutland peninsula. The find of a large, flat-bottomed pram built with similar, "cog-like" techniques and almost exactly contemporary with the Kolding wreck suggests that ships coming to Schleswig in this period may have become so large that lighters were necessary for loading and unloading (Bill and Hocker 2004). The Kolding vessel, which probably displaced over 90 tons and with a draught of perhaps 2 meters or more (Fig. 31.10), may have been part of the traffic contributing to Schleswig's prosperity and putting pressure on its waterfront infrastructure.

The mixture of "nordic" and "cog" features in ships built in this area should also not be a surprise. This region has been a culturally mixed, contested border zone between German and Scandinavian polities for nearly a thousand years, with the current location of the border only resolved in the 1920s. What more likely place to see the early development of large, bulk carriers, engaged not only in Baltic commerce, but even testing the waters of the Skagerak?.

Acknowledgements

Thanks are due to Jan Bill for allowing access to his manuscript prior to publication (Bill, forthcoming). Thanks to Olafur Eggertsson and Hans Linderholm for allowing access to their measurements from the Kuggmaren I cog, and to dendrochronologists who have made chronologies available for dendrochronological and dendroprovenance research, from The Academy of Fine Arts Warsaw, Göttingen University, Hamburg University, Lund University, The National Museum of Denmark, Queen's University Belfast and Sheffield University. The archaeological research for this project was carried out under a grant from the Danish National Research Foundation.

References

Adams, J. and Rönnby, J. 2002, Kuggmaren 1: the first cog find in the Stockholm archipelago, Sweden. *IJNA* 31, pp. 172–181.

Baillie, M.G.L. and Pilcher, J.R., 1973, A simple crossdating program for tree-ring research. *Tree-Ring Bulletin* 33. pp. 7–14.

Bartholin, T. S. 2001, Dendrochronological Dating of medieval Norwegian Ships from Bergen. In: Øye, I. (Ed.) *Ships and Commodities*. The Bryggen Papers. Supplementary Series 7. Bergen, pp. 51–53.

Bill, J., 1994, Iron Nails in Iron Age and Medieval Shipbuilding. In: Westerdahl, Christer (ed.) *Crossroads in Ancient Shipbuilding. Proceedings of the Sixth International Symposium on Boat and Ship Archaeology, Roskilde 1991.* Oxford, pp. 55–64.

Bill, J. forthcoming. *From Nordic to North European – Changes in Danish Coastal Seafaring and Shipbuilding 900–1600.* Ships and Boats of the North. Roskilde.

Bill, J. And Hocker, F., 2004, Haithabu 4 seen in the context of contemporary shipbuilding in Southern Scandinavia. In K. Brandt and H.J. Kühn (eds.), *Der Prahm aus dem Hfen von Haithabu ("Wrack Haithabu IV") in seinen regionalen und überregionalen Bezigen.* Schriften des Archäologischen Landesmuseums, Ergänzungsreihe 2. Neumünster.

Bonde, N., Christensen, K., Eriksen, O.H. and Havemann, K., 1991. Dendrokronologiske dateringsundersøgelser på Nationalmuseet 1990. *Arkæologiske udgravninger i Danmark 1990*, Copenhagen, pp. 226–242.

Bonde, N. and Crumlin-Pedersen, O., 1990, The dating of Wreck 2, the Longship, from Skuldelev, Denmark. A preliminary announcement. *NewsWARP* 7 (April 1990), pp. 3–6.

Bonde, N. and Jensen, J.S., 1995, Dating the coin beneath the mast. In O Olsen, J Skamby Madsen and F. Rieck eds. *Shipshape, essays for Ole Crumlin-Pedersen.* Roskilde. pp. 103–122.

Crumlin-Pedersen, O., 1979, Danish Cog-finds. In: McGrail, Séan (ed.) *The Archaeology of Medieval Ships and Harbours in Northern Europe.* Oxford, pp. 17–34.

Crumlin-Pedersen, O., 1981, Skibe på havbunden. Vragfund i danske farvande fra perioden 600–1400. *Handels- og Søfartsmuseet på Kronborg. Årbog*, pp. 28–65.

Crumlin-Pedersen, O., 2000, To be or not to be a cog. *IJNA* (2000) 29.2. pp. 230–246.

Daly, A., 2000, Dendrokronologisk undersøgelse af skibsvrag, "Kollerup Kogge", Nordjyllands amt. *Nationalmuseets*

Naturvidenskabelige Undersøgelser, rapport 2, 2000. Copenhagen.

Daly, A., 2002, Dendrochronological analysis of timber from a shipwreck from Kolding Fjord, Sønderjyllands amt. *Nationalmuseets Naturvidenskabelige Undersøgelser, report* no. 12, 2002. Copenhagen.

Daly, A., 2003, Kuggmaren cog, Sweden. *Dendro.dk rapport* 9, 2003. Copenhagen.

Daly, A, in press. Results of the dendrochronological analysis of 14 medieval cargo ships from Danish waters. In; Englert, A. forthcoming: *Large Cargo Ships in Danish Waters 1000–1250*. Ships and boats of the north vol ?. Roskilde.

Daly, A., Eriksen, O.H. and Englert, A., 2000, New dendro dates for Danish medieval ships from Eltang and Kollerup. *Maritime Archaeology Newsletter from Roskilde, Denmark* 14, p. 61.

Dokkedal, L., 1996, *Koggen i Nordeuropa fra 1150–1450 e. Kr. – Definition af skibstypen og diskussion af en mulig årsag til dens anvendelse i nordeuropæisk skibsfart.* Thesis. University of Copenhagen, Institute of Archaeology and Ethnology.

Dokkedal, L., 2001, Hvad fjordbunden gemte – om koggen fra Kolding. In: Dedenroth-Schou, Birgitte (ed.) *Koldingbogen 2001.* Kolding, pp. 5–13.

Eriksen, O.H., 1994, Dendrokronologisk undersøgelse af tømmer fra vrag ved det hvide fyr i Skagen. *Nationalmuseets Naturvidenskabelige Undersøgelser, rapport* 17, 1994, Copenhagen.

Eriksen, O.H., 2000, Dendrokronologisk undersøgelse af skibsvrag "Koldingkoggen", Vejle amt. *Nationalmuseets Naturvidenskabelige Undersøgelser rapport* 33, 2000. Copenhagen.

Fritzboger, B. 1994, *Kulturskoven, Dansk Skovbrug fra Oldtid til Nutid.* Kobenhavn.

Grille, Alexandre, 2002, *Les cogues en Europe Septentrionale XIIe–Xve siècles: Approche typologique et définition archéologique.* Unpublished M.A. thesis, Université Marc Block-Strasbourg II.

Hansen, K.E., 1944, Kolding Skibet. Foreløbig Meddelelse om Fund af Middelalderskib. *Handels- og Søfartsmuseet på Kronborg. Årbog* 1944, pp. 119–129.

Heinsius, P., 1956, *Das Schiff der hansischen Frühzeit.* Weimar.

Hocker, F.M., 2000, Relocating the Kolding cog. *Maritime Archaeology Newsletter from Roskilde, Denmark* 14, pp. 50–55.

Hocker, F.M. and Dokkedal, L., 2001, News from the Kolding cog. *Maritime Archaeology Newsletter from Roskilde, Denmark* 16, pp. 16–17.

Kohrtz Andersen, P., 1983, *Kollerupkoggen.* 1 edn. Thisted.

Lønstrup, J. and Nielsen, I., 1997, Mellem tvende have. *Skalk* 1997 (4), pp. 20–30.

Reinders, H.R., 1985, *Cog finds from the IJsselmeerpolders.* Flevobericht 248. Lelystad.

Tyers, I. G., 1997. *Dendro for Windows Program Guide.* Archaeological Research and Consultancy at the University of Sheffield Report 340.

Weski, T., 199, The Ijsselmeer type: Some thoughts on Hanseatic cogs. *IJNA* 28: 360–379.

32 Couronian ship building, navigation and contacts with Scandinavia

Inese Karlina

Late Iron Age

In the Late Iron Age, very important changes took place in Latvia both in the economy and in the social sphere. From the 9th century onwards, events concerning the areas of the present-day Latvia and its inhabitants are mentioned ever more frequently in the writings of northern European Catholic clergymen, in Scandinavian sagas and in the Ancient Russian chronicles. Trade between different peoples became considerably more active, a development linked to the formation of feudal states in both the West and the East, and to the desire of the aristocracy for fine clothes, ornaments, and weapons and craft products from abroad. In Latvia the river Daugava became the main route for east-west trade. This river route remained under the control of local traders until the late 12th century.

Sources on Vessels

Written sources

The later Chronicle of Henricus de Lettis and the Rhyming Chronicle provide information on navigation at the end of the Late Iron Age. The various names of sea vessels, such as *cogge, navis, navigium, pyratica, liburna, cymba,* indicate the different sizes of vessels and diverse ways in which they were used. (Šterns 1988: 73)

Liburna: In the chronicles, *liburna* does not occur so frequently and is not described in great enough detail that it would be possible, with full confidence, to reconstruct it. The chronicler simply writes: "…and the inhabitants of Saaremaa came with big naval forces into the mouth of the River Daugava, taking marauders' ships and boats with them… and some of them went by their boats up to the very town." (*Et venerunt Osilienses cum exercitu magno navili in Dunemunde, ducentes secum pyraticas et liburnas…et quidam ex eis in liburnis suis ascenderunt ad civitatem…*) (*Indriķa hronika* 1993: 196 [XIX, 2]). We can remark that the vessels of the *liburna* type are smaller than vessels of the *pyratica* type, although

specifically meant for sea transport. In another opinion, *liburna* belongs to the big cargo vessel type, carvel-built, with rounded ends, high sides, one firmly fixed mast, and a deck with openings for cargo loading. (Zalsters 1987: 4) But the hypothesis that the *liburna* may be ranked among big cargo ships seems improbable, because the chronicler, when further mentioning *liburna*, writes that "some of them brought wooden crates and old boats, and, having filled them with stones, sank them, thus obstructing our entry into the port." (*Ei quidam ex eis structuras lignorum et liburnas veteres adducentes miserunt in profundum et lapidibus impleverunt et aditum portus nobis obstruxerunt*) (*Indriķa hronika* 1993: 202 [XIX, 5]). Consequently, one may conclude that these vessels could not have been too big.

Cogge: The term *cogge* is used only for the Teutonic crusaders' ships and therefore I will not deal with it in greater detail.

Pyratica: In the chronicles, descriptions of the *pyratica* type of vessel are encountered fairly frequently, consequently, the chances to reconstruct it are much better, and fewer hypotheses as to its appearance are advanced. The chronicler describes them as follows: "… the Couronian, having relieved the bow parts of their marauders' ships, raised them high above the opponents coming from the other direction, and at the same time arranged their ships in pairs, with empty space in between. So, the first two boats or smaller ships of the crusaders traveled into this empty space between the marauders' ships, but, being aboard the smaller ships, they could not reach their adversaries, which were towering high above them" (*Et venerunt Osilienses cum exercitu magno navili in Dunemunde, ducentes secum pyraticas et liburnas…et quidam ex eis in liburnis suis ascenderunt ad civitatem…*) (*Indriķa hronika* 1993: 196 [XIX, 2]). From this, one may conclude that the *pyratica* type was higher than the *cymba* type, and more easily maneuverable than the crusader's *cogge* type, since the necessity to make use of smaller ships would not have crept up to them. In the battle, 30 rowers drove each *pyratica*. The sides of the cargo ship were high, the hull was wide, and the correlation between its width and length was 1:3. As these ships traveled not only in seas and rivers, but also in lakes, they should have been easily transferable from one basin to another (Šterns 1988: 80). Likewise, the mast of the cargo ship could be lifted up and lowered down. The few rowers stood at the beginning and at the end of the hull, on small platforms, as the vessels of this type had neither deck, nor benches. But in one opinion, *pyratica* were a local boat type (both the cargo and the naval type), slender, with low sides, no deck, and a mast which could be easily stepped and struck. It does not necessarily mean that the ships of the Couronians were built in exactly the same manner as those of the inhabitants of Saaremaa and the Estonians, yet it is very likely that they all were built according to the pattern of Swedish Viking ships (Zalsters 1987: 4).

Cymba: In the chronicles, the *cymba* is characterized as a boat or a small ship. Boats or raft-like vessels, both in the local and the crusaders' chronicles, are denoted by the term *cymba* (*Theuthonici vero in cymbis sius, id est minoribus navibus...*) (*Indriķa hronika* 1993: 202 [XIX, 5]). So, it is not logical to place cymba in the rank of boats, which includes boats and rafts, as the chronicle itself states explicitly that they were smaller-size ships. Raft-like vessels include boats with low sides and flat bottoms, as well as rafts for setting ablaze the ships of the adversaries, and rafts made of tree-trunks for transporting people and cargo. (Zalsters 1987: 4)

As regards boats and ships used in river transportation, the chroniclers used the terms *navis, navigium, pyratica,* and *navicula,* but never *cogge, cymba* or *liburna. Navigium* was a smaller ship, more suitable to river transportation, but *navicula* was an ordinary boat, which was never used for traveling in the sea (Mugurēvičs: 66).

Material evidence

There are a number of finds of old ships along the coastline of Kurzeme – in Bernati, Kapsede, the bog of Tirlauki, in Dumele and Briezi, as well as in Riga and Turaida.

The remnants of several old ships were found in Liepaja, in the bed of the former Livu River, and in the vicinity of Liepaja. In the late 1950s, the sea at Bernati washed away a large part of a 5 m high dune, and beneath it a ship, or rather, the carvel-built middle part of a ship, was revealed. As it was thought that the type of the ship is characterized by its bow and stern, this fragment was not considered worth further investigation and so it was left; on the next day it disappeared into the sea. The existence of this ship is attested by the memories of J. Sudmalis, a museum employee, and several photographs, dating back to 1958, which are lost in the museum (Zalsters 1984: 3). Another vessel, possibly dating back to the Late Iron Age, was found in Alsunga. In the 1969 issue of the "Calendar of Nature and History," P. Stepins wrote that in his adolescent years he met with Janis Akots, an inhabitant of Alsunga. In about 1890, the above Akots

was digging a ditch in Tirlauki peat bog. In the peat layer, they found a big boat – a ship. The end of the ship was destroyed while digging the ditch, but the undamaged part of the hull remained in the peat. The ship was built of oak boards, clamped together by copper rivets. But nothing else is known about this ship.

In 1872, after spring floods, in Turaida, remnants of a raft-type boat were revealed. K. Zivers was the first to report on that. It was the so-called "Turaida ship", more than 13.5 m long. It was thought that ship sank in the early 13th century, when the inhabitants of Saaremaa fought with the crusaders at Turaida, but were defeated. In 1873, the remnants of the ship were taken to Cesis, and what happened to them afterwards is not known. The raft-type boat, as to its outer appearance, resembled a big flat-bottomed boat with chamfered stern and a pointed, triangle-shape bow. There was a notch in the central sternpost for a steering oar. The separate elements were joined and fastened together by joinery, wooden pegs, metal nails and small cramps. The components characteristic of this type of ship, L-frames, were also found in the vicinity of Liepāja (Zalsters 1984: 22).

The "Riga Ship" – a typical transport vessel used by the Couronians

The Riga ship was found on the building site of the planned Post Office Savings Bank, but, as World War II broke out shortly afterwards, the building was never erected, and nowadays a small public garden stands in its stead. The excavations of 1939 may provide a little insight on the scorched remnants of a wrecked ship, formerly built of oak, uncovered there. The preserved length of the ship was 16.95 m, the width 4.30 m, and the depth 2.85 m. The ship was found heeled onto the starboard side. It had 20 ribs or frames, to which 12 cloven, clinker strakes were fastened. These were about 30–40 cm wide and 3 cm thick. The inner side of the frames was covered with ceiling in five or six strakes. The ceiling was meant to prevent the goods from coming into contact with the outer planking of the ship. The stern rudder was not found, so one may advance the hypothesis that the ship was steered by means of a quarter rudder or a big oar (Šterns 1988: 35) The tholes for oars and benches for oarsmen were not found, as the upper part of the hull was missing. It is possible that the oarsmen sat on their seachests instead of benches. The forepart of the ship was slender, so the ship was meant for sea voyages. Its anchor was made of oak, to which two heavy stone weights were attached. The archaeologists presumed that this ship was meant for transporting goods over the sea and sank in the 12th century, as no bricks were found under or around the ship. Bricks appeared in Ridzene only in the 13th century, with the building of German Riga (Caune 1992: 73).

Consequently, one may conclude that there is not a sufficient amount of reliable archaeological evidence, to enable us to reconstruct, without doubt, the vessels of the

Late Iron Age. Reconstruction is possible only on the basis of information provided by the Chronicle of Henricus de Lettis, archaeological findings (ships and boats themselves), as well as parallels from the wider Baltic Sea region. Summarizing it all, one may obtain a hypothetical reconstruction of ships, one may conclude that *liburna* and *pyratica* were used in overseas traffic (Heinsius 1956: 73)

Place-names in Scandinavia, linked with overseas traffic of the Couronians

The evidence for contacts and the role of ships in overseas contacts is meager, for example a few individual finds of artifacts, a couple of burial sites in Scandinavia, and several references to nationalities in European chronicles, so place-names are also among the sources revealing traffic and contacts. They give an idea of routes and navigation, on the region of traffic in general, although it is but a hypothesis that needs to be strengthened by archaeological evidence.

The origin of the words *Kursa* and *Couronian* is not clear, because they are not themselves Couronian. So, we can read that in more ancient times, the language of the Couronians bore a very close resemblance to Old Prussian, seemingly even closer than to Lithuanian. It is also said that the *skalvji* were very close to the Couronians and eventually merged with them, or that in the Roman Iron Age the Couronians began to distance themselves from the Old Prussians, although they had not finally distanced themselves from the Lithuanian tribes. In addition to the names of the inhabitants of Kursa encountered in foreign languages, for example Swedish *kurer*, German *die Kuren* etc., place-names with the stem "kur-" are preserved in Sweden, Denmark and Germany. In many cases they are linked with the name Kursa or Kurland. Place-names such as Kūrehorva, Kūreholm, Kurland, Kuredige, Kuregroft, Kuredam, Kurelænge etc, testify to a link with the Couronians (Kursis 1968: 80)

Place-names with the stem *Kur-* in Sweden: *Kuramåla*. *Måla* is an element of place-names, which is widespread only in a very limited area in Småland, Blekinge, Eastern Jutland and Skåne. *Måla* means a parcel of land, usually linked with the name of some person or nation. The name *kuri* might mean *kurlandere*, or may be translated with the meaning guard or reconnoiter. Consequently, one may presume that Kuramala means the land of the Couronians or guards, Kuraholm the island of the Couronians or guards, Kurabacke the hill of the Couronians or guards. Kurön is an island in Lake Mälaren, with an area of 185 ha and a height of 43 m, west of Birka. The name Kurön might be translated as the island of guards, which is included in Birka fortifications, but it does not correspond to the location of the island, because, when approaching Birka from the Baltic Sea, one should cross the Island of Sacred Peace (Helgön). Therefore its significance in the defense of Birka was small. It is possible to remark that, although the word Kurön has not been analyzed, several researchers have assumed that if Kuramāla in Småland is associated with the cultural or ethnic identity, *kurer*, then the same approach could be used in regard to the word Kurön, and it might be translated as the island of the Couronians. There are also other place-names with the stem Kur- to be met in Sweden. (Kursis 1997:98)

Place-names with the stem *Kur-* in Denmark: Place-names, which might be linked with the Couronians, are met only in Bornholm. Kuregaard, which is the long-forgotten name of a country estate, comes from the family-name Kure. In 1914, Kuregaard was renamed Kureander-gaard, replacing the stem *Kure-* with *Kurediged-*, the hill of the Couronians. The hill is associated with an ancient saga about a battle with the Courlanders. We can remark that in the 10th century, P.F. Suum wrote in the History of Denmark: "At the end of the century the Couronian raiders came to Bornholm, with terrible murders and fires..." In historical literature, one can read fairly frequently that the phrase "God, save us from the Couronians", or the like, was said as part of conducting prayers in Danish churches, but rarely with any indication of the source. It has not been possible to find the phrase in reliable sources, which are available today, and so the tale is probably apocryphal. (Kursis 1997:99)

Place-names with the stem *Kur-* in Germany: In 808, the Danish King Gottfred decided to build the border wall called Danevirke. There are several walls stretching along the Danish border fortification system. A part of the wall named Kovirke, which stretched from the Bay of Schlei in the east along the River Rejde to the west, formerly bore the name Kuurburg. And not far from the former Kuurburg stands the German country estate Kurburg. (Kursis 1997:100)

Thus, analyzing the place-names with the stem *Kur-* in the Baltic Region, one can approximately define the possible trade and military routes of the Couronians, and determine the distances, which could be overcome when traveling by Couronian ships, as well as ascertain the shipbuilding schools that had an influence upon the local shipbuilding.

References

Primary sources

Indrika hronika, 1993: no latiņu valodas tulkojis Ā. Feldhūns; Ē. Mugurēviča priekšvārds un komentāri. R.:Zinātne.

Secondary sources

Caune, A., 1992: *Pati Rīga ūdenī*. Zinātne.
Heinsius, P., 1956: *Das Schiff der Hansichen Freuzeit*. Weimar.
Kursis, A., 1968: *Latvijas vietvārdi Zviedrijas rūnakmeņos*. Archīvs.
Kursis, A., 1997: *Ziemeļnieku sāgas par Seno Latviju un latviešiem*. Stockholm.

Mugurēvičs, Ē., 1967: *Svarīgākie ceļi lībiešu un latgaļu teritorijā*, *AE* . Rīga.

Sams M., 1938: *Latviešu senā jūrniecība*. Rīga.

Šterns, I., 1988: *Par kuršu laivām un kuģiem*, UNIVERSITAS, Rīga.

Zalsters A. 1984: Senie kuģi, Padomju Jaunatne, 22. septembris.

Zalsters A. 1984: Tukums un kuģniecības vēsture, Komunisma rīts, 21. aprīlis.

Zalsters A, 1987: Hronika un kuģi, Cīņa, 16. maijs.

Zalsters A, 1989: Senās laivas un kuģi mūsu upēs, Dabas un vēstures kalendārs. Rīga.

Zalsters A, 1995: E Senās Kurzemes kuģniecība in Kurzeme un kurzemnieki, *Latvijas enciklopēdija*.

Zalsters A, 1996: E. XII gadsimta vietējo ūdens satiksmes līdzekļu rekonstrukcija Latvijā, in *XVIII Baltijas zinātņu vēstures konferences tēzes*. Rīga.

33 From Carl Reinhold Berch to Nils Månsson Mandelgren: On the concept of maritime history, (Sw. *sjöhistoria*), and its meanings in Sweden since the latter 18th century

Carl Olof Cederlund

If one starts to trace the interest in maritime history in Sweden through time, one finds a complex situation consisting of different ideas developed by different groups in society. It is in fact a group of historical interests, which already in the latter part of 18th century are defined with one special term. The Swedish concept *sjöhistoria*, meaning maritime history or the history of naval matters, is defined and used in scholarly works from this time. The author of this paper has given a summary of the development up to that period in a paper in *Festschrift* Professor Detlev Ellmers (Cederlund 2003).

Maritime traditions and historical interest exist early, evidently already in prehistory. There are, for example, abundant cases since prehistory of the role of the ship as a symbol in ritual (that is tradition-carrying) documents of many kinds. The projection of ideas of maritime history becomes more tangible when individuals or groups emphasize the importance of the same for special, often group interests. One reason for this is that one thereby wants to motivate oneself or the group one belongs to, and the aims they carry. Out of such interests emanate traditions of maritime history with different origins in society. By studying such interests it is possible to interpret what they represent. It is then also possible to see which roles these motives have in the larger context of the history of ideas.

Currents of ideas connected to maritime history in Swedish society

The following section of this paper is a short overview on the basis of existing sources of different kinds of maritime historical traditions, generally and scholarly.

General maritime traditions and concepts

General interest in sea life and ships as expressed in pictorial art, fiction, poetry, song or music depicting maritime life has existed since long ago. One special form of maritime symbolism has been the frequent and manifold projections of ship symbols and ship symbolist conceptions generally, as artistic symbolism, in print etc. This implies a ship symbolism with manifold meanings, which have existed since prehistoric times in many different forms. As some early examples the following may be mentioned:

- Ship pictures on Bronze Age rock carvings
- Ship pictures on Gotlandic, Iron Age picture stones
- Medieval ship depictions in churches
- Votive ship models, affluent pictorial and sculptural ship symbolism around the big naval ships as well as different types of ship models from the post-medieval period.

Scholarly maritime traditions

The following conceptions of maritime history may be seen as some of the more evident expressions of different kinds of history writing and traditions, and also of ideological aspects of maritime history in Sweden – as the same can be ascertained in different kinds of historical literature.

History writing in general since the early post-medieval period has included different issues of maritime history and ship history. The latter subjects are found within several historical writing traditions, such as:

- The historical works during the 16th and 17th centuries presenting historical/ideological, national value systems. The authors of the same often project ideological aspects onto Swedish history. Examples of such scholars are Olaus Magnus and Johannes Magnus in the 16th century and Olof Rudbeck the Elder in the latter part of the 17th century (Magnus, J. 1554, Magnus, O. 1555, Rudbeck 1937).
- One part of the former was the antiquarian tradition, developed from the end of the 16th century, which focused on surveying and depicting monuments from older periods, such as grave mounds, old churches, ruins, rune stones. Several scholars were active in this field, also with an interest in ship symbolism in

prehistoric and Iron Age art and similar appearances in later times as well as in presentation and treatment of folk tale and saga traditions. Both took up and illustrated motives relating to maritime traditions and history making.

- Naval history and seafaring history were parts in general history works in the 16th and 17th centuries. During the 18th century, this maritime history also generated independent publications in the growing production of historical works (Cederlund 2003: 77). It later successively developed into separate history traditions of naval history, seafaring history, ship history, shipbuilding history or navigation history – a development, which has been continued until the present day (see below).

Maritime history was given in different shapes

Naval history has been presented in special works since the first half of the 18th century. It may be characterized as ideologically inclined naval war history. Its aim was to build up and strengthen fighting and defence morale through the tales of the heroic deeds of naval officers in earlier times, and was often connected to the history of famous naval ships. A central figure in naval history was already in the first works the naval hero as a symbolic figure. He was represented by historical persons, naval officers, often noblemen, who had been the brave defenders of the nation in naval battles in which also famous naval ships were part and also important symbolic expressions. This panegyric tradition was continued into the 20th century. Since the latter part of the 18th century, several special history books on the Swedish navy – sometimes in a popular form – were published for its officers and cadets, but also for a general audience. In the early 20th century naval history literature was written with the intent to emphasise the importance of the navy politically – an expression of the nationalistic / conservative political interests of the time (Cederlund 1994:76).

Seafaring history has been published in Sweden since the 18th century, since the 19th century under the influence of international works on the subjects. It is sometimes combined with commercial history written by representatives of ship owners, politicians with interest in seafaring matters, sea captains after their active years or academic scholars (Cederlund 2003: 77)

Ship history focusing on the technical aspects of ships or ship types, their construction, quality and functional capability can be seen as a forerunner to shipbuilding history, developing from the early 19th century. The former was early contained in general historical works, as for example the work by Olof Rudbeck the Elder and Atland (see for example Cederlund 2003: 72). In the 18th century it appeared in works on naval history in which the qualities of naval ships were described (Cederlund 1994: 76, Cederlund 2003: 76).

Shipbuilding history developed as a special branch

during the 19th century, and expanded and specialized still more during the 20th century. The authors are in principle all marine engineers or civil shipbuilding engineers (Cederlund 1994: 60f).

Marine archaeology started as salvage operations on old wrecks in the 19th century, when the heavy diving apparatus was introduced in Europe. The motives behind the interest in remains and finds from the underwater world usually emanated from interests in naval history. One salvaged guns and artillery equipment or rigging details from wrecks of old naval ships. During the 20th century marine archaeological activities were expanded to cover also other types of find material and developed further. Salvage, underwater investigations and excavations were successively becoming more common and more advanced. One important reason for this was the development of SCUBA diving and other underwater technologies (Cederlund 1998a).

Maritime ethnology emanated in the 20th century from folklife research and Nordic ethnology. Within this field, traditional maritime life and culture were studied from the beginning. Scholars in this field have emphasised the special values one assumes are inherent in maritime culture (see for example Hasslöf 1972: 9, 73). In maritime ethnology one may see the fisherman, another "maritime hero", gaining his livelihood bravely at sea in a harsh struggle against the elements as an example of a symbolic figure. In a way this image of a strong and independent individual striving for his livelihood at sea is born from liberal evaluations (see also Cederlund 1998 b). In this respect he is a counterpart to the naval hero, who in his brave deeds in naval battle serves his king and nation, in other words is envisaged as a hero symbol in a nationalistic context.

The Atlas project of Nils Månsson Mandelgren and its volume for naval matters

As a contrast to this overview let us apply a micro perspective to the development of maritime history by looking in more detail at one period in its development, and on one of those who by his work represents the same. In an earlier paper, I have given a presentation of the conception of maritime history in the 1760s as then presented by the Swedish historian Carl Reinhold Berch (Cederlund 2003). Now we will move forward in time a century by describing how the same subject was presented by a scholar of that time. The scholar is Nils Månsson Mandelgren. His view on maritime history is expressed in the 1860s and 1870s for an atlas volume about maritime and naval matters (Sw. *sjöväsendet*). The volume was part of a grandly planned "Atlas of the History of the Cultivation of Sweden" (Sw. *Atlas till Sveriges Odlingshistoria*), which he started but never finished. After a promising introduction and the printing of a first volume he had to put the project down due to lack of financial support. The manuscript for the volume on maritime matters was all the same made ready for publication, including abundant illustrations. It is preserved in Mandelgren's archives at Folkminnesarkivet at Lund University.

Nils Månsson Mandelgren (1813–1899) was one of the self-educated recorders of Swedish traditional culture in a time when the interest in national history expanded. His work has carried a manifold treasure of information through to our time, especially due to his capability to reproduce evidence of contemporary culture in drawings and watercolours. This desire to document was coupled with an immense curiosity, diligence and perseverance. In his documentation of Swedish material culture he is probably the most prominent among his contemporary recorders of traditional life and matters due to these characteristics (Stavenow 1972; Jacobsson 1975 and 1983).

Mandelgren moved around and registered what he found interesting in many places. We find him on excursions in the landscape, in medieval churches, at international exhibitions of art and industry in the capitals of Europe, in museums and libraries studying and copying scientific literature and also popular magazines. His way to present information is popular and abundantly illustrated.

Just a small part of Mandelgren's energy was spent on maritime material culture. What he left for posterity on this subject gives a comprehensive picture all the same of how it was conceived and appreciated around 1870. This

is one or two generations before maritime museums for the public were permanently established in Sweden. His illustrations are not so different from how one presented the subject of naval matters and maritime history in museum arrangements also a hundred years later, at the time when the author of this paper entered this part of the museum world. One can also see that the selection of subjects in Mandelgren's presentations are more or less identical to those given in the maritime museums of the 1960s – and later too for that matter.

When we look back 140 years into time, into Mandelgren's drafts of his volume on naval matters and also at the illustrations for the final version, we find an astonishing number of illustrations. He wrote ample captions with often-detailed references. It is in this context not possible to make a full presentation or analysis of this material. It is the intention of the author of this paper to do so in a more extensive work on the background and development of maritime history and marine archaeology (Cederlund in progress).

Still, to give an idea of his view on the subject of maritime history, and what he found interesting and worth illustrating, a short overview of the subjects which he included in the concept in question will be given here, together with a few of his illustrations of the same.

He drew plans of ship-shaped stone settings, and also of whole grave fields with this kind of stone settings,

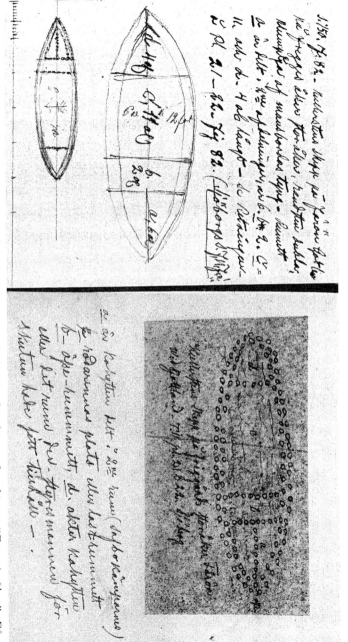

Fig. 33.1. Sketches by Nils Månsson Mandelgren of a stone setting in the shape of a ship at "Freggis åker", Fårö Island, Gotland. He depicts the stone setting like a ship partitioned in different rooms and refers then to the Swedish antiquarian and scholar Nils Henrik Sjöborg (1767–1838), one of the first archaeologists in Sweden and founder of the Historical Museum at Lund University: a) to the right is the cabin divided in two departments; b) is the room where one scoops water out of the bilge; c) is the place for the rowers or the hold; d) is the stern cabin or where the helmsman had his premises.

Carl Olof Cederlund

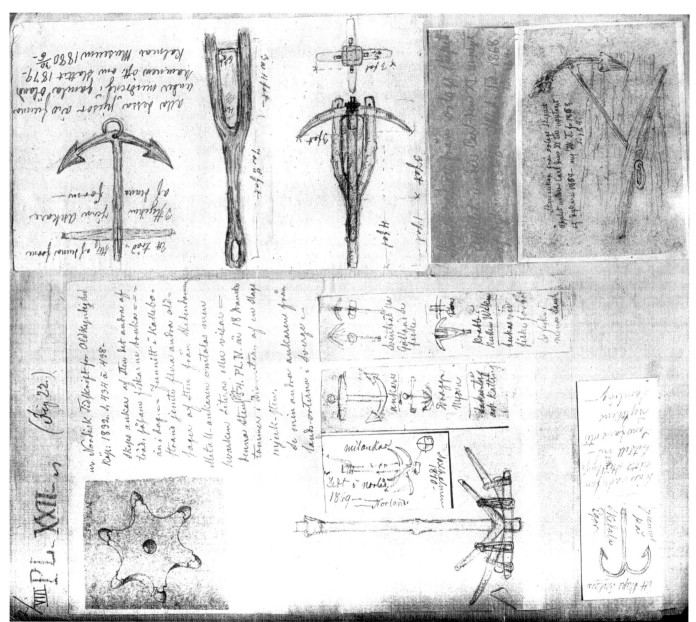

Fig. 33.2. Sketches of different types of primitive anchors made by Mandelgren – some of the originals in museum collections, some from publications.

which he interpreted as ship allegories (Fig. 33.1). Finds from the sea bottom, such as primitive anchors and ship equipment, were drawn from museum collections and from illustrations in books (Fig. 33.2). He transcribed early Swedish antiquarians' studies of rock carvings and the ships in them. He draw primitive craft and water transport systems on location, as well as rural craft and ferries (Fig. 33.3). He draw reconstruction plans on the

basis of archival material of King Gustav Vasa's *Great Carvel* (Sw. *Store Kraveln*), one of the early, big ships in the Swedish navy of the 16th century. He copied out of different works, especially Dutch sources from the 16th century, about early navigation technique and old navigation instruments. He also illustrated different kinds of sea marks and buoys and described naval tactics – from early times to the 19th century – in panorama drawings.

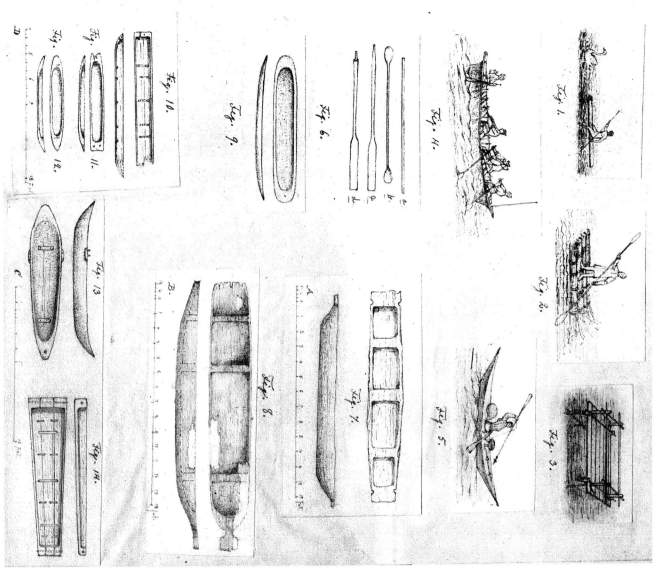

Fig. 33.3. *The first plate of several in the material Mandelgren collected and edited for his atlas volume of the history of naval matters, describing the development of different types of rowing vessels. These depictions of different kinds of vessels are made in a chronological order and with an evolutionary perspective on the subject, something which becomes very evident when one studies the following plates in the same series, and also others by him, describing other aspects of ship history.*

He produced transcripts of contemporary Swedish and foreign works on naval and seafaring history, made notes on maritime and naval matters in libraries and museum collections in Sweden and abroad, and presented oral information, written down by contemporary scholars, on different maritime matters, such as the thoughts of different shipwrights about contemporary shipbuilding. He presented notes on common denominations of maritime

matters and conditions, and he showed pictorial reproductions of naval flag and signal systems during the 18th and 19th centuries.

In his material one also finds lists of a large number of works on early naval matters in Swedish and foreign libraries, for example in the Biblioteque National in Paris. There are transcripts of articles about the Norwegian and Danish burial and sacrifice ships, which at this time had been excavated at Tune and Gokstad in Norway and Nydam in Denmark, as well as other ship finds in Europe. He had included an illustrated atlas from a German encyclopaedia printed 1849, with pictures of ships from Antiquity and the Orient. There are ship construction plans and pictures from the post medieval period, reprints of articles in contemporary, popular journals and other works on ship and seafaring history, as well as texts about the history and the deeds of the Vikings.

The finished plates for his unpublished volume on maritime or naval matters, which survive in his archive, illustrate maritime history in different perspectives. There is a series of drawings showing the development of water craft since its first origin, starting with the log which one floats upon, followed by the dugout, several different types of ships as depicted in the Scandinavian Bronze Age rock carvings, Roman ships, the hide boats used by the Eskimos, sewn boats as depicted by early explorers in Finland and Lapland, drawings of different kinds of "primitive" craft, depictions of the ships on the Bayeaux-tapestry, and the ships on the Iron Age Gotlandic picture stones. He includes drawings and sketches with measurements of log boats, which had been found in lakes or in the ground, along with similar primitive craft, then in use by explorers. He provides drawings of the ship depictions in Olaus Magnus's *Carta Marina* (Magnus 1539), construction plans which had been drawn of church boats in the North of Sweden, similar plans of the Nydam ship as it was recorded and drawn in Engelhardt's then recently published works on the same, as well as plans of the Tune ship. There is a detailed reconstruction drawing of Olav Trygvason's big ship *Ormen Länge*, supposedly by Mandelgren´s imagination and pencil, and his own plan of the 18th-century Swedish Royal Barge *Vasaorden*. Other illustrations include ship depictions in medieval church decorations and on grave stones, depictions of ships from Dutch and English paintings from the 16th and 17th centuries, drawings copied from illustrations in Åke Clason Rålamb's work on ship building *Adelig Öfning eller Skeppsbyggerij* ("The Nobleman's Exercise or Shipbuilding) of 1691, drawings copied from illustrations in Swedish and Danish works on naval history of the 19th century, drawings made of contemporary Norwegian and Swedish rural craft under sail, several construction plans of Swedish rural craft, of the same kind as those made by maritime ethnologists in the 20th century, construction plans of a Swedish gun boat from 1837, drawings of different types of rigging, drawings of ship construction plans from the 17th century. There are also several series of depictions of Swedish lighthouses from the most primitive to the most modern at the time, as well as of light ships of the time. In the material one also finds handwritten manuscripts, which describe maritime matters in the historical perspective — composed in an emphasised evolutionary perspective.

It is surprising to see the extent and the differentiation of the subject of maritime history as collected and depicted by Mandelgren in his atlas material. This is about two

generations before the establishment of permanent maritime museums in Sweden, but already at this time the same pictures and concepts that would be presented in them is already there. It is also possible to follow the ideas contained in the presentation by Mandelgren back to the ideas presented a century earlier by Carl Reinhold Berch (Cederlund 2003). Evidently what we see is the trail of a history tradition, traceable from the middle of the 18th century into the 20th century. This is a part in the Swedish history of ideas, which so far has been investigated very little.

Acknowledgements

The illustrations to this paper have been copied from the Archives of Nils Månsson Mandelgren at the Folklivsarkivet, Lund University.

References

Cederlund, C. O., 1994, The Regal Ships and Divine Kingdom, *Current Swedish Archaeology* 2: 47–85. Also in *L'invention du vaisseau de ligne 1450–1700*, M. Acerra (ed.), Kronos Marine, Editions S. P. M. 1997.

Cederlund, C. O., 1998 a, Från kanonbärgning till akademisk disciplin. Svensk marinarkeologi i ett utvecklingsperspektiv. In *Marinarkeologi och kulturmiljövård. Rapport från seminariet i Kalmar 18–19 mars 1998*, pp. 8–17. Kalmar.

Cederlund, C. O., 1998 b, Inlandets transportbåtar — en samhällshistoriskt betydelsefull men undervärderad grupp av traditionella bruksbåtar. Samverkansprojekt mellan europeiska och nordamerikanska forskare. In *Människor och båtar i Norden. Rapport från seminarium vid Sjöhistoriska museet 29–31 maj 1998*, pp. 73–77. Stockholm.

Cederlund, C. O., 2003. From Olaus Magnus to Carl Reinhold Berch. On the background of Swedish marine archaeology and ship archaeology in the history of ideas. *Deutsches Schiffahrtsarchiv* 25: 65–85.

Cederlund, C. O., in progress, *Marine archaeology in society and research. A study of the Swedish development seen against the background of the ideas of maritime history and naval matters*. Research project at Södertörns högskola (University College, Stockholm).

Hasslöf, O., 1972, Maritime ethnology and its associated disciplines. In *Ships and Shipyards, Sailors and Fishermen. Introduction to Maritime Ethnology*. Copenhagen.

Jacobsson, B., 1975, Nils Månsson Mandelgren som fältarbetare. *RIG. årg.* 58, häfte 3: 73–84.

Jacobsson, B., 1983, *Nils Månsson Mandelgren — en resande konstnär i 1800-talets Sverige*. Höganäs.

Magnus, O., 1539, *Eine kurze Auslegung der neueren Mappen von den alten Goettenreich und andern Nordlendern*. Venedig.

Magnus, O., 1555, *Historia de gentibus septentrionalibus*. Rome.

Magnus, J. 1554, *Historia de omnibus gothorum sveonumque regibus*. Rome.

Rudbeck, Olof, 1937, *Atland eller Manhem*. Uppsala (Facsimile).

Stavenow, Å., 1972, *Nils Månsson Mandelgren*. Nordiska Museets Handlingar 79. Lund.

34 Ships and subsidies

David A. Hinton

Although I was not at the conference from which other papers in this festschrift stem, I am pleased to have the opportunity to pay a tribute to Seán McGrail, whose support for the development of maritime archaeology at the University of Southampton has made him a valued colleague. It will not surprise him that what follows is based on documentary sources rather than on archaeology, let alone on direct contact with anything as dangerous as a boat. It offers little on the technology of shipping, but instead explores a source of information about how medieval people valued their water transport.

'Value' is here meant literally; sources for estimating wealth in medieval England include the Lay Subsidies, taxes intermittently collected from the beginning of the 13th century and, until 1334, based on the estimated cash value of someone's movable property which, in theory at least, included any boats that they owned. There were many exemptions, both of people and of the goods that were to be included in the valuations, and the width of the gap between what people actually possessed and what the assessors recorded is debatable (e.g. Hadwin 1983; Jenks 1998; Nightingale 2004). The first stage in the collection process was to compile inventories of the items which were taxable and their value. These lists can be taken as giving an approximation of the goods' sale value, more often fixed as low as was credible in order to favour the tax-payer, rather than optimistically high to benefit the Crown. Any ship or other vessel would therefore be valued at its estimated second-hand sale price, unlike produce in store or cargoes in transit that would usually be rated at some semblance of wholesale cost. One problem in the assessment of this type of data is the probability of the range of goods assessed being increasingly but tacitly restricted, so that records from the 13th century are more useful than those from the 14th century; another is that the criteria applied to towns were not the same as those applied to rural vills.

Lists of individuals' names with the total that each person owed survive for a number of counties, especially for the 1327 and 1332 assessments, but very few of the preliminary inventories were thought worth retaining in an archive. One of the earliest is for Ipswich, for 1283 (Powell 1904–6, from which are taken all the data in the next two paragraphs). The prologue sets out what was to be assessed, which included ships (*navibus*) and boats (*batellis*) with their equipment (*cum attillamentis eorum*). The richest citizen was Hugo Golding, with movable goods worth £163, including 20 marks (a mark was a unit of 13 shillings 4 pence) in cash, a large sum which shows that he was a merchant and dealer. He was not recorded as owning a ship, however, unlike Roger le Maystre, who owned an unspecified number of ships worth 40 marks, and whose goods, which included wine, totalled £92 18s 4d. Someone taxed for wine was presumably dealing in it, but not all those recorded as holding stocks of wine were necessarily assessed for, or in fact owned, ships: Hugo Reymer, for instance, had £3 8s 0d worth of wine, but no recorded vessel to transport it in.

Whatever criterion the assessors used to distinguish a ship from a boat, it was not simply their relative values; Alanus Yrp had a *navem* worth 5 marks, for instance – but Alexander Lovegood had the value of 6 marks placed on his *batello*. Nor was the distinction made according to the owners' wealth: Lovegood had an overall valuation of £20, whereas Yrp was only worth £17 6s 8d (26 marks). Of the two, Lovegood is the more likely to have been a trader, as he had £11 in cash, yet his was the *batellum*. Hugo Davey had both a *navis* and a *batellum*, each only valued at 5 marks; however, he was not a poor shipwright whose vessels were scrapped for salvage, as he was worth £39 4s 8d overall. Robert Davi, worth £22 14s 0d, owner of ships and equipment valued at only £2, was also too well-to-do for a craftsman – his ships' low valuation probably means that he was a part-owner, like Baldre Horold who was specified as owning the third part of a *navis* for 5 marks, making the vessel worth £10. The assessors did not use the word *navis* of the least valuable vessels, which were the two *naviculae* ('little ships') of Osbertus le Tollere and Roger Fine, both worth 10s, and the *batelli* of Hugo Strangman and Will Horold, also worth 10s each, of Ricardus Love at 8s and of Roger Alleyn at a mere half mark. In all, 33 tax-payers out of a total of some 225 had shipping interests, thirteen having ships and twenty boats, including those who had both.

For most of Ipswich's tax-payers, ships and boats amounted to quite small proportions of their overall property value. In other words, a ship was not a really big investment, though Richard Tollere's undisclosed number of ships, worth 52 marks in total, accounted for two-thirds of his assessment, the same ratio as that of Odo le Evesque, whose ship was worth 10 marks of his £10 total. He was presumably a relative of Johannes le Eveske, whose vessel accounted for 5 marks of his £9 total. Both the Eveskes and the two Horolds could have been families of ship-master-owners, rather than primarily carriers of their own goods, as most probably was Thomas Bo[a]tman, whose *navis* was worth 8 marks of his £10 total. They were successful enough to be taxed, but were not amongst the early 14th-century Devon and Dorset (Kowaleski 1993: 19; Hinton 2002: 14).

Some of those lower down the tax-valuation scales may have been primarily fishermen, like Richard Love, who had an assessable quantity of fish, 15s worth, and was quite possibly catching them from his 8s *batellum*. A hint that such things ran in families comes from the three Baudreseyes, Radulphus, Ranulphus and Herveus, all of whom had *batelli*. The valuations of the boats of such people should be compared to similar valuations of horses, animal, and carts, one of which was worth only half a mark, whilst others were valued together with horses, probably for similarly small sums; eight marks (£5 6s 4d) from 3s to 10s but £1 for one presumably exceptional was the largest amount that anyone had invested in overland transport.

In 1334, when for the first time there is a reasonably complete list of what each vill paid throughout England, Ipswich ranked nineteenth by taxable wealth, though it should probably have been higher; even so, it would have been a little lower than another East Anglian port, Lynn, which was eleventh (Dyer 2000: 755). For Lynn, there is a local assessors' roll for the next Lay Subsidy after Ipswich's of 1283, collected in 1291 (Jurkowski et al 1998: 21). All that survives relates to a single ward, and includes the inventories of about 45 tax-payers.

Only four of Lynn's recorded tax-payers were assessed for ships: Thomas de Newerk had a £4 half-share in a *navis*, making the vessel worth £8 in total, with £2 worth of timber on board; Ralph de Bretham had the much less valuable *Rose* at £3, on board which he had chattels and merchandise worth £5 6s 8d. Thomas de Newerk had a total movable property valuation of only £6 12s 1½d, much less than de Bretham at £58 5s 1½d, but even he was not as rich as Henry le Iremonger, who was reckoned at £95 15s 6d and who had a fourth part in a *navis* called *Blithe* that was reckoned at 60s (i.e. the vessel was worth £12 in total), whereas he had £10 worth of merchandise on board (Owen 1984: 245). Henry le Iremonger's half-share in the *Gozer* was reckoned at £6 13s 4d, so she was thought to be worth £1 10s 0d more than the *Blithe*, but again the cargo was more valuable, at £25. Henry le Iremonger did not deal only in iron, though he does seem to have specialised in metals; otherwise, his 5½ 'lasts' of herring (a 'last' should have contained between 10,000 and 13,200 fish, the second figure being the one used at Yarmouth), worth £16 10s 0d, indicates another commodity in which he dealt. This begins to put the value of his ships into perspective. Overall, Iremonger's saleable property was taxed at £95 15s 6d, making him one of the richest men in his ward.

Iremonger's wealth fell far short of that of Philip de Beke, who was worth £246 8s 1½d and who was also recorded as having more specific shipping interests (Owen 1984: 247). One ship was called 'Cog', valued with its equipment at £40. His quarter-share in another cog cost him £10 – so the two ships were valued at the same amount, which shows how round some of the figures are likely to be, even though at that time the valuations of the listed items may still have been less standardised and more reflective of their actual worth than those of the 1297 and later figures (Hadwin 1983: 203–4; Cromarty and Cromarty 1993: 36). Philip de Beke had one other vessel, called 'Hulc', worth only £13 6s 8d. These terms could be specific enough to imply a recognised difference between cogs and hulks, but throw no further light on the vexed question of their distinction (cf. McGrail 2001: 221–2, 232–42), unless the lower value of 'Hulc' implies that it was smaller, rather than older, which would fit the evidence that it was only after the 14th-century that the hulk began to overtake the cog in size. The total value of de Beke's recorded shipping interests was £63 6s 8d, more than the £43 of the cargo on board the vessels, but still only representing a quarter of his overall worth.

Ralph de Brertham, the owner of the £3 *Rose*, also had two boats, *batelli*, worth 13s 4d for the two. This implies the same distinction between *navis* and *batellum* as identified for Ipswich. The Lynn Lay Subsidy has no other information on people's boats, however, and the port's assessors, unlike Ipswich's, may have been reluctant to tax them if they were seen as vital to someone's trade, as a small craft is to a fisherman or boatman. Similarly, Lynn has no entries for carts, only a single record of a stock of iron and charcoal for their repair. There is just one hint in Lynn's other records of local water transport; its overseas customs lists include a 15th-century account of a vessel in a creek, its forfeited cargo interesting for its mixture of wool and rabbit-skins, hardware, jet and glass beads, harp strings, lewd calendars and such-like, said to have been '*in magno batello vocato kele*' (Owen 1984: 382–3), yet able to get up Norfolk's minor waterways. Perhaps like the River Severn's Magor Pill boat, it was a locally made tramping vessel designed for specific conditions; retention of the name 'keel' for such a craft may indicate the long-term survival of the Nordic tradition (McGrail 2001: 232).

The records for Lynn are unlike others, as it is the only place for which any of the Lay Subsidy assessments give the names of individual ships. *Rose* was a typical name, as flowers were often chosen; *Blithe* could perhaps also follow a norm, if it was meant in the religious sense of 'Mercy' or 'Goodwill', rather than the more common adjectival usage of 'merry'. It is not the only known ship of that name: not only did *la Blythe* of Yarmouth put into the Exeter out-port at Topsham three times in the early 14th century, but so did vessels with variants of the name from eight other ports (Kowaleski 1993:237). Much more difficult to understand is *Gozer*, which means 'dealer in geese'; unlikely to be a forerunner of the modern 'Flying Goose', the word is not at all typical and is probably a misrendering of something like *Godyer* (ibid.: 16, 237), a popular wish for a happy and prosperous year frequently found in French as *en bon an* (see Jones 2000 for a discussion of ships' names).

Records from only two other sea-ports survive, but are uninformative. A fragmentary list from Grimsby of 1297 includes three people assessed for owning herrings, but only William de Groscale for a boat as well, which at £1 5s 0d is a valuation similar to those of the fishing-boats postulated at Ipswich. Also as was often the case with the Ipswich records, the vessel was only a small proportion of William's total wealth of £3 3s 0d, of which a last of herrings accounted for £1 10s 0d, more than the boat in which presumably they had been caught (Rigby 1979). Three rolls for a minor port in Dorset, Bridport, survive for 1316, 1319 and 1322; they have not been published, but the preliminaries state what was to be assessed. This included cords and hemp, reflecting the town's reputation for its rope and net production, but not ships or boats, or even fish. The assessors seem to have followed their instructions to the letter, and perhaps in consequence the richest person was worth less than £5 (Mills 1971: 104; a preliminary scan of the rolls, undertaken by kind permission of the Dorset Record Office, did not yield any further information). Whether Dartford, Kent, should be classified as a sea-port is arguable; certainly its 1301 Lay Subsidy roll does not suggest any maritime activity. Although it is on the Thames, none of its 218 tax-payers was demonstrably linked to the river, though 'merchandise' implies trade (Coates 1874).

Colchester, Essex, is too far up the River Colne to count as a sea-port in the Middle Ages, but rather was a river-port using Hythe as its maritime outlet (Britnell 1986: 11). In 1297, neither ships nor boats were taxed, although three people's occupation was given as *nautae*. The same term was used several times in 1301, once in reference to an Adam le Schepherde, thus demonstrating how, although surnames were becoming fixed, they cannot be taken necessarily to reflect someone's trade; in fact, his property included nets and fish, clearly demonstrating that he was a fisherman rather than a merchant sailor.

For 1301, there are thirteen entries for boats, including one that was a half-share, and one that was split three ways – Alexander le Delve's boat was *debile*, 'decrepit', so was perhaps split in a different way. These vessels were assessed for very low amounts, £1 being the highest, le Delve's only for 2s, though otherwise the lowest were for 5s and 6s. In both lists, people were taxed for herrings and fish, others for nets, so fishing must have been a source of income for many. No-one had to pay for a *navis*, so any Colchester merchants who owned even part-shares in a *navis* were by now having their ships exempt (Parliamentary Rolls I: 228–38, 243–65; Rickwood 1906; Hadwin 1977).

The only other Lay Subsidy lists that seem at all systematic in their recording of maritime vessels are for a few vills in north Wales; assessments for Bryncelin, Cilan and Neryn have survived for 1291 (Jones Pierce 1929–31: 68, 70–1, 143–7). Many people were assessed for their fishing nets, with five also taxed for a boat, four of which were here called *scafa*, three valued at £1 and one at 10s, and one *batellum*, worth 13s 4d. The former might possibly mean something physically distinct from the latter, but the valuations do not suggest it, and *scafa* is derived from the quite common Latin *scapha*, not from a Celtic native word.

Inland, Huntingdonshire has a roll of assessments of goods for 1290 (Raftis and Hogan 1976). It derives from a single hundred on the edge of the fenlands, and included Ramsey, not a borough or place with a formally chartered market, probably because of the abbey's control there, but nevertheless a town likely to have had a flourishing market and different from the rural places around it (Raftis and Hogan 1976: 14–55). Ramsey was the only vill in the hundred in which residents' valuations included boats, almost certainly all for use on inland waterways, for their owners were also taxed on marshland products such as eels, turves and reeds, although Richard de Marham was assessed for general 'merchandise'. The boats' values were comparable to carts'; three at 1s 6d, two at 2s, and so on, up to 10s, with a few assessed together with nets for up to 13s 4d, and one in such poor condition that it was not considered worth anything. The 10s boat was owned by someone whose other goods were two cows, and whose total assessment was only 18s. The two richest men in Ramsey both had boats valued at only 1s 6d. John Crane's possessions also included 2,500 eels (100 'binds'); although he paid 10 marks for his fish 'in a pond', his overall assessment of £12 16s 2d put him well below some of the rich merchants of Ipswich and Lynn. The phrase 'fish in the pond' might be taken to imply a high-status freshwater pond with pike or bream, but much poorer people than John Crane were assessed for the same thing, so some sort of marshland system may have operated. Altogether, some fifteen of the 119 tax-payers in Ramsey were recorded as having boats, but the actual number must have been a great deal higher judging from the numbers with stocks of eels and other fenland products.

Many people in the hundred's rural vills had similar stocks and products and must therefore have had boats, but none were recorded in their assessments.

It seems likely that only the Lynn merchants were systematically assessed for their bigger ships, perhaps only because of a particularly zealous ward collector. However, Ipswich was also subject to assessment – where the highest amount is le Maystre's 40 marks for more than one ship – as was Shrewsbury, an inland town but one with many wealthy merchants whose wool-trade interests would have made investment in shipping an attractive option. The Shrewsbury assessors were instructed to include the value of goods 'in house, field or on board ship', yet in several different years no *navis* was mentioned (Cromarty and Cromarty 1993: 44–5). No boats were assessed for use on the River Severn, though their use is implied by the surname of John le Boatman – who was also known as John le Carter (ibid.: 59).

Other records surviving for inland places have few or no mentions of boats. A hundred north of Bury St Edmunds assessed in 1283 had a small river forming one short length of its boundary, but no waterway running through it and no marshland; unsurprisingly therefore no boats were taxed (Powell 1910: 87). Assessments from 1297 onwards became more formulaic and less likely to list anything other than grain and livestock (Hadwin 1983: 203–4). Minety in northwest Wiltshire was a community known for its kilns and ceramic products from the 12th to the 15th centuries and from which pots have been found as far east as Oxford and beyond. Located a short distance south of the River Thames, some goods from Minety are likely to have been transported down river by boat (Fuller 1894–5: 197). Floor-tiles made at Penn, Buckinghamshire, were certainly being transported down river; loads sent to Windsor Castle were usually costed *cum cariagio*, with at least one entry being specifically *et batillagio*. Probably therefore most of the tiles from Penn found in London were delivered in the same way, though the transport of 100,000 tiles in 200 carts to Salden, a distance of 30 miles from Penn, shows that land was no barrier to their movement if the purchaser could bear the cost. The 1332 Subsidy shows that some men were doing quite well; two 'tylers' were worth £1 4s and £1 11s 8d, and a 'payyer' £1 19s 8d, valuations that all included stocks of tiles and lime, horses and other farmstock, but neither carts nor boats are mentioned (Hohler 1941–6: 22–3).

Reading must have had people who made a living plying on and fishing in the Thames and its tributaries, but although its assessors' rolls for 1297 frequently list carts, they make no mention of boats, though Thomas Bodde had 4s 9d worth of fish, and the 10s valuation placed on Nicholas the Fisherman's chattels may also have included fish (Dodwell 1962: 108–9). Similarly, Bedford in 1297 had many carts but no-one there was taxed for a boat despite its being on the River Ouse – even William the Fisherman. In the countryside, however,

Richard the Fisherman had a boat valued at 1s, much less than the value of his nets at 3s 4d; he was worth only 9s overall (Gaydon 1958: 6). He lived at Great Barford, which is on the Ouse, but surely he was not the only person exploiting the river?

It is frustrating that the documentary record starts so promisingly at Ipswich, where a community's use and valuation of its different types of merchant and fishing boats begins to emerge. The valuations at Colchester are wayward, though at least show how important small boats were to the many people fishing from them, as the north Welsh rolls also display. But even for Ipswich there is no hint of inland water transport, yet many must have been employed; costs of using barges when feasible appear to have been at least half and sometimes as much as a quarter of those for carts (Masschaele 1993). The networks that carried goods from place to place, be it high-value wool or low-value pottery, are not illuminated by the Subsidy records.

For larger vessels, the record also starts well but deteriorates. The highest value that can be computed for an individual ship in Ipswich is £10. Lynn does not have records of smaller boats, possibly because the only roll that survives is for a single, and wealthy, ward, but the individual vessels were more highly assessed, at up to £40 for cogs, though more ordinary ships were around £13. Assuming that these valuations reflect a fair assessment of the second-hand value of the boats, they are not so much at variance with the other limited information that is available; the great galley built by Londoners for the king in 1294–6 may have cost £326, but a better comparison is probably with the one built at Lyme for only £75 (Friel 1986: 42). Her owners claimed £166 in compensation for the loss of the *Nicholas* in 1318, plus £1337 13s 4d for the cargo and the crew's possessions; the wheat on board was valued at £1 per quarter, which seems very high compared to its taxed value of 4s when safely stored in a Minety barn. Although 1318 was a good harvest year, the overvaluation is probably not enormous, especially since the wheat was already ground (Hutchinson 1994: 96–7; Fuller 1894–5; Farmer 1957: 215). Nor is a value of £1095 for 178 tuns and 9 pipes of wine so unbelievable – what is more questionable is the amount of wine stored on board in the first place. Wreck valuations of *batelli* used by fishermen in late 14th- and early 15th-century Suffolk ranged from 20d to £4; price fluctuations and vessel sizes may account for some of the reckonings being so much higher than in the earlier East Coast subsidy lists (Bailey 1990: 104–5).

It is useful to have evidence to confirm the Exeter implication that shipmaster-owners were well enough off to pay taxes, but were not actually rich, and that a ship's value was usually much less than that of the cargo it carried. Ultimately, the pedestrian values of the *Rose*, the *Blythe*, the *Gozer* and the unnamed cogs, hulks and *naves* of Lynn and Ipswich indicate that the costs of acquiring ships did not involve such huge capital outlays that they were an active bar to investment and to the trade of medieval Europe.

References

Bailey, M., 1990, Coastal fishing off south-east Suffolk in the century after the Black Death. *Proceedings of the Suffolk Institute of Archaeology and History* 37: 102–14.

Britnell, R. H., 1986, *Growth and Decline in Colchester, 1300–1525*, Cambridge University Press. Cambridge.

Coates, R. P., 1874, Valuation of the town of Dartford, 29 Ed. 1. *Archaeologia Cantiana* 9: 285–98.

Cromarty, D. and R., 1993, *The Wealth of Shrewsbury in the Early Middle Ages*, Shropshire Archaeology and History Society. Shrewsbury.

Dodwell, B., 1962, Reading records (3): Taxation Roll 1297. *Berkshire Archaeological Journal* 60: 101–12.

Dyer, A., 2000, Ranking lists of English medieval towns. In D. M. Palliser (ed), *The Cambridge Urban History of Britain Volume I, 600–1540*, 747–70. Cambridge University Press. Cambridge.

Farmer, D. H., 1957, Grain price movements in thirteenth-century England. *Economic History Review* 10: 207–20.

Friel, I., 1986, The building of the Lyme Galley, 1294–6. *Proceedings of the Dorset Natural History and Archaeological Society* 108: 41–4.

Fuller, E. A., 1894–5, The tallage of 6 Edward II (Dec. 16, 1312) and the Bristol rebellion. *Transactions of the Bristol and Gloucestershire Archaeological Society* 19: 171–278.

Gaydon, A. T., 1958, *The Taxation of 1297*, Publications of the Bedfordshire History Record Society 39.

Hadwin, J. F., 1977, Evidence on the possession of "treasure" from the Lay Subsidy Rolls. In N. J. Mayhew (ed), *Edwardian Monetary Affairs (1279–1344)*, 147–66. British Archaeological Reports British Series 36. Oxford.

Hadwin, J. F., 1983, The medieval Lay Subsidies and economic history. *Economic History Review* 36: 200–17.

Hinton, D. A. (ed), 2002, *Purbeck Papers*. University of Southampton Department of Archaeology Monograph 4. Oxford.

Hohler, C., 1941–6, Medieval pavingtiles in Buckinghamshire, *Records of Buckinghamshire* 14: 1–49.

Hutchinson, G., 1994, *Medieval Ships and Shipping*, Leicester University Press. London.

Jenks, S., 1998, The Lay Subsidies and the state of the English economy (1275–1334), *Vierteljahrschrift für Sozial-und Wirtschaftsgeschichte* 85: 1–39.

Jones, M., 2000, The names given to ships in fourteenth- and fifteenth-century England. *Nomina* 23: 23–36.

Jones Pierce, T., 1929–31, A Lleyn Lay Subsidy Account. *Bulletin of the Board of Celtic Studies* 5: 54–71.

Jurkowski, M., Smith, C. L., and Crook, D., 1998, *Lay Taxes in England and Wales*, PRO Publications. Kew.

Kowaleski, M., 1993, *Local Customs Accounts of the Port of Exeter 1266–1321*, Devon and Cornwall Record Society n.s.36.

Masschaele, J., 1993, Transport costs in medieval England. *Economic History Review* 46: 266–79.

McGrail, S., 2001, *Boats of the World, from the Stone Age to Medieval Times*, Oxford University Press. Oxford.

Mills, A. D., 1971, *The Dorset Lay Subsidy Roll of 1332*, Dorset Record Society Volume 4.

Nightingale, P., 2004, The Lay Subsidies and the distribution of wealth in medieval England. *Economic History Review* 57: 1–32.

Owen, D. M., 1984, *The Making of King's Lynn*, British Academy, Records of Social and Economic History n.s. 9. Oxford.

Parliamentary Rolls I. *Rotuli Parliamentorum I...1258–1503*, House of Lords, 1767–1832. London.

Powell, E., 1904–6, The taxation of Ipswich for the Welsh war in 1282. *Proceedings of the Suffolk Institute for Archaeology and History* 12: 137–57.

Powell, E. (ed), 1910, *A Suffolk Hundred in the Year 1283*, Cambridge University Press. Cambridge.

Raftis, J. A. and Hogan, M. P., 1976, *Early Huntingdonshire Lay Subsidy Rolls*, Pontifical Institute of Medieval Studies 8. Toronto.

Rickwood, G., 1906, Taxations of Colchester, A. D. 1296 and 1301. *Transactions of the Essex Archaeological Society* n.s. 9: 126–55.

Rigby, S. H., 1979, The Grimsby Lay Subsidy Roll of 1297. *Lincolnshire History and Archaeology* 14: 39–40.

35 Sea-lanes of communication: Language as a tool for nautical archaeology

Katrin Thier

Over the centuries, seafaring technology has been transmitted along the shores of Europe's waterways by people exchanging goods as well as ideas. Much of this exchange happened through the medium of speech, and the adoption of technical terms into other languages can be traced through time and space just like the progressive spread of material culture. Therefore in areas where archaeology and pictorial sources can provide only an incomplete picture, especially on the more perishable parts of a ship, the study of the history of language can help to fill in at least some of the gaps. In the following, I shall attempt to give a short introduction to the methods and potentials of historical linguistics as a research aid for archaeologists.

Methodology: the Archaeology of language

Periodization

Historical linguistics shares some of its methods with archaeology, and is therefore well suited to assist research in this discipline. Unlike history, which often relies on fixed absolute dates and recorded events and at least attempts to be precise in its chronology, both archaeology and historical linguistics must often make do with imprecise information. Both disciplines use a kind of periodization which uses descriptive labels and subdivisions based to a large extent on the characteristics of a corpus of material culture or text respectively. These periods can be clearly distinguished from each other when they appear in their most typical form, but the boundaries are fuzzy and there is much overlap. So within post-Roman British archaeology, the Anglo-Saxon period is distinguished from the later medieval period, and can in turn be subdivided into early (or sub-Roman), middle and late (Viking) periods. The Middle Ages, in turn, are divided in a similar way. While historians have traditionally put the events of 1066 as the end of Anglo-Saxon England, at least politically, archaeologists do not observe so sharp a break. Similarly, the language of the Anglo-Saxon period is known as Old English, that of the

Middle Ages as Middle English, both again subdivided into three phases.[1] However, despite the arrival of a new aristocratic elite speaking Norman French in 1066, late Old English is recorded as late as the early 12th century and then merges into early Middle English.

Typology and Relative Chronology

Language change can be traced by the study of some key areas: phonology (the study of the development of sound), orthography (the study of the development of spelling), semantics (the study of meaning), morphology (the study of grammatical units, endings etc.), and syntax (the study of sentence structure). Of these, historical phonology is easiest to illustrate and in many cases the most important aspect, since it involves single words and does not rely on long texts (which do not tend to survive from early periods). Historical sound developments can be traced by comparing similar words in several languages and several different periods, collating as many examples as possible. In this way, a kind of typology can be established, and from this a coherent relative chronology. So for example, comparison has shown that a word which had the diphthong (vowel-pair) *eu[2] in Germanic, the surmised ancestor language of English, the Scandinavian languages and a number of others, will have $\bar{e}o$ in Old English and $j\acute{o}$ in Old Icelandic (cf. Noreen 1923 §59, Campbell §115).[3] We also know that Old English $\bar{e}o$ became $\bar{e}$ in Middle English (spelt many different ways), and is now usually spelt *ee* but pronounced /iː/.[4] This illustrates a further problem: since only the spelling survives, it is not always possible to be certain how words were pronounced in the past. Many North European languages, however, adopted the Latin alphabet, and we can assume they adopted it more or less with the Latin pronunciation for the letters, which is well studied. When the language changes, a variety of alternative spellings can develop and correlations between letters and sounds become less clear.

An example for the development just mentioned is the modern English word *keel*, designating a type of boat (different in origin from the name of the centreline structural timber). This was *keula in Germanic, which is known, because the word was borrowed into Finnish at an early stage (as keula) and not subject to further sound changes within Finnish.[5] As expected, Germanic *keula appears as cēol in Old English (8th century onwards). In the 6th century, it must have been pronounced almost as /kiul/, because that is how Gildas, a Welsh author writing in Latin, seems to have heard it: he spells it cyul-, and it is subsequently borrowed into British Latin as ciula. In Middle English, the word comes out as kele, kel, keel, etc., and merges in form with a new loan from Scandinavian: kjölr, the word for the structural timber. Both the timber and the ship type are regularly rendered as keel in Modern English. The ship type appears in Old Icelandic as kjóll, exactly as expected as a descendant of Germanic *keula, and clearly different from kjölr.[6]

Absolute Chronology

Such typologies can be anchored in time and help to form absolute chronologies. The most common kinds of evidence for this are datable texts and inscriptions from archaeological contexts. For instance, the first evidence for the word keel comes from Gildas' British Latin text of the mid-6th century, mentioned above. It describes the arrival of the Anglo-Saxons as follows: "[the Saxons arrived] in three ships such as were called in their language cyulae, in ours longae naves".[7] Incidentally, this makes cyul- one of the earliest attested words in English.

An example for a word first attested on an inscription from an archaeological context is a fragment of an accounts tablet from 13th-century (BC) Knossos, which is inscribed with the symbol for 'man' and the syllables e-re-ta (Chadwick 1986–90 As 5941). This is the Greek word eretas (classical Greek eretes) 'rower' written in a script which cannot represent the final s. This shows both that the common Greek word for 'rower' was already in use, and that it had almost the same form as it did in the classical period many centuries later.

If any word is borrowed from one language into another in a certain form and then begins to change according to the rules of the new language (or stops changing, while the word in the donor language changes), this can be dated relatively in the contexts of known changes. If any of these sound changes are given an absolute date, this can also be used to date the borrowing. So in the example above, Finnish preserves the form keula, which must predate the Scandinavian vowel development (after 600 AD, Noreen 1923, §59).

Back-Projection

Having drawn up detailed typologies and nested them in datable contexts, linguists can do one further thing: they can reconstruct unattested forms and project back both to trace the development of a single term and to establish relationships between languages. To illustrate, here are a number of words with vaguely similar forms and senses, put into a family tree to illustrate their relationships, as shown in Table 35.1 (untranslated nouns designate ships, verbs mean 'to float').

These relationships were established by extensive comparison between large numbers of words in many languages, which produced the kind of rules of sound change used above. The subdivision of languages into groups (Germanic, Celtic etc.), going back to a hypothetical Indo-European proto-language is also a part of this work. Similar work has been done on languages outside the Indo-European group, such as Finnish. The knowledge of these relationships can now be used as a tool to reconstruct the form of words which are not attested at a certain period in time. It is even possible to project back beyond any evidence, but this is too speculative to be of concrete use in interdisciplinary research.

It is also possible to tell that both Old English flóege and Finnish laiva are loans from a Scandinavian word represented by Old Icelandic fley. The spelling -oeg- in Old English is very unusual, but if pronounced would sound somewhat like /øi/, which is the same sound later represented by Old Icelandic ey.[8] The Scandinavian language spoken in Viking Age England was probably very closely related to Old Icelandic. The developments in Finnish are regular (Kylstra 1996: 159), but show that the word must have been borrowed in the form *flauja, confirming a form which can also be reconstructed from Indo-European evidence alone.

Geographical Distribution

In periods where good dating evidence is available, the spread of words can also be traced through space. By comparing dates of first attestation and the changes of form, the regional origin of a word can be established as well as the path it takes as it moves between languages. This can be well illustrated with the example of the word mizzen and its relatives, which make their way from the Mediterranean through Europe as the use of two- and multi-masted rigs spreads.[9] In English and most other

reconstr. root	derived stems	noun	verb	noun (again)

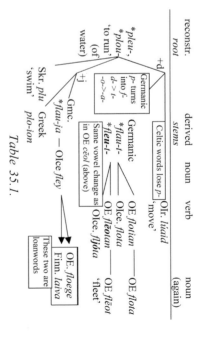

Table 35.1.

West European languages, this word designates the mast and sail closest to the stern in a two- or three-masted rig; in rigs with more than three masts it comes to denote one of the masts towards the stern. In some languages, most notably French, it changes its meaning to denote a sail at the bow; this development will be excluded from discussion here for the benefit of clarity and conciseness.

The term originates in Italy where it is first attested in the form *mezana* around 1348. Italian *mezana* or *mezzana* first and foremost means 'middle', 'mean' or 'medium'. The technology was probably first mentioned about a quarter century previously in a reference to an *arbor de miso*, literally 'middle/medium mast', in a Catalan source of 1325. *Mezzana* and its relatives are repeatedly used to translate *epidromos*, the Greek (and hence Latin) word for the aft-most mast and sail in a three-masted vessel. In Isidore of Seville's influential work, this is already explained as *uelum secundae amplitudinis* (*Etymologiae* XIX iii 3), and an Old English glossary based on Isidore translates this as *se medemesta segl* 'the medium-largest sail' (Antwerp gloss 232.3). This is the same way of thinking that later produces Italian *mezana: Impero che la nave porta tre vele, una grande che si chiama artimone, una **mezzana** la quale si chiama **mezzana**, et un altra la minore che si chiama terzuolo* (Francesco da Buti 1385—95: 546; my highlights).

Related words for the mizzen are attested in other languages of the Western Mediterranean, such as Catalan *mitjana* (1467) and Occitan *mejano* (1525), which like the Italian, mean 'medium etc.'. The Occitan is only attested relatively late, but it has been borrowed into French as *migenne*, which occurs in Normandy as early as 1382 (in galley building accounts from Rouen; Bréard 1893: 93 and *passim*). Here, the Occitan form is reflected and the word no longer literally means 'medium' but exclusively refers to a particular sail. The Spanish *mezana* (1444, later also *mesana*) mirrors the form of the Italian, showing a different path of distribution from Italy west across the Mediterranean. In Portuguese, the main form *mezana*, first attested in the 15th century, also recalls the Italian. In both languages, the direct descendant from the Latin, meaning 'middle, medium', is *mediano*. The term then reaches Dutch in the course of the 15th century, where it is first attested as *besane* in 1480 (now *bezaan*).[10] The reason for this change in initial consonant is not known, but /m/ and /b/ are closely related sounds, Dutch speakers may have assimilated the beginning of the word to sound like the Dutch prefix *be-*. Forms like *mesane* still appear in Dutch as late as 1599. The new form with initial *b* can now be traced from Dutch to other languages like German (*Besan*, from the 16th century, Kluge 1911: 88—90), French (*besane* 'mizzen', 1599, rare), and (through German) Polish *bezan*. In Scandinavia, the word appears in the mid-16th century with an initial *m-*, such as Danish *mejsan* (1550), Swedish *mesan* (1541), as expected. However, in the North, an alternative with a different vowel developed. It is impossible now to tell

where it originated, but it can be seen in variants like Danish *mussan* (1594), Swedish *mösan* (1543) and Scots *mosan* (1505); it also appears in the mid-16th century German form *moysahn* (for forms and dates cf. OED, s.v. MIZZEN) This spread of the word through Europe from South to North from the 14th to 16th century ties in well with pictorial evidence. There are early images from Italy. From Catalonia, where the word appears in 1467, there is an image of some two-masters from the early 15th century; in 1450, a depiction of a three-masted ship comes from land-locked Bourges, from the house of a merchant with interests on all coasts of France. A view of Antwerp of c.1468 confirms the presence of the three-masted rig in the Low Countries at about the same time the word appears. The earliest images in Scandinavia, however, include a Danish seal of 1425, which could be based on a Mediterranean example, and a Norwegian calendar stick of 1457 (on the images see Friel 1995: 162—66). These antedate the earliest linguistic evidence in their areas considerably and serve to illustrate the pitfalls of sticking to any one type of evidence alone.

So far, any mention of England has been deliberately avoided, because it does not fit into the pattern. In fact, English has the earliest use of the word *mizzen* outside Italian: it is first attested in 1416 in the form *mesan*. By itself, this would be interesting, but not necessary suspicious. After all, in all of the above examples, it is almost impossible to tell how long the word was in use before it was first written down in a surviving document. Equally, the depiction of a two-masted ship in Kings Lynn in c.1415 is remarkable for being the earliest outside the Mediterranean, but still does not deviate massively from the timeframe set by the images mentioned above. However, what makes it more significant is that the two date from within a year or so of each other. The 1416 source mentioning the word does actually refer to the first two-master to be built in England to our knowledge, the balinger *Anne*. In the same year, the keel of *Grace Dieu* was laid, also to be fitted with a mainsail and mizzen. The first three-master (*Petit Jesus*) is recorded for 1435 (Friel 1995: 162). All this suggests that the mizzen was indeed known in England unusually early. It would be tempting to suggest that this is due to Norman influence; after all, there was a fleet of Mediterranean ships based in Normandy, and the word for mizzen is recorded in that context as early as 1382 (see above). However, the Norman French word in question is *migenne*, in a form deriving from Occitan; the English word, on the contrary, consistently reflects the Italian form. It must therefore have come to England some other way. A likely solution to the problem is put forward by Friel (1995: 159), who suggests both word and technology were introduced when the English Crown seized a Genoese carrack in 1410, which had been captured by pirates off Milford Haven in the previous year. All first instances of the *mizzen* – word, document and image – appear within a decade of this event, and it provides a direct link between Italy (Genoa) and England, allowing for the Italian word to be borrowed with the technology.' The isolated Mediterranean fleet of Rouen and their Occitan-based term need not have played any part. By the time the French two-master *Roose* was forfeited to England in 1419, both word and thing had already been introduced.

Case Study: What language can do for you

The dilemma of Germanic sails

Evidence for the use of sail in the Germanic world is very thin and starts at a relatively late date, with the earliest secure finds of sailing ships coming from 9th century Scandinavia (Oseberg, Ladby), with pictorial sources and historical texts only a few centuries earlier. The traditional view, on the basis of this evidence and of structural features of Scandinavian ships, has been that sail only developed late in Northern Europe (see McGrail 2001, 211–12 for a summary). It has, however, been argued that the history of sail in the North goes back beyond that, although only very circumstantial evidence is available, as Haywood (1999: esp. 100–110) has discussed in detail.

Much earlier evidence, by contrast, survives from the Celtic world: there are the Broighter boat from 1st century BC Ireland, the ships of the Veneti, which Caesar encountered at roughly the same time in Brittany, and coin images from the mint of Cunobelinus from 1st-century-AD Britain. After these areas become Roman, several types of large ship appear in Roman use which differ from Mediterranean ships in several ways, including the way their planks are joined and their masts are stepped. These are known as Romano-Celtic craft. Seagoing examples are known from London, South Wales, Guernsey and Bruges, river barges e.g. from Zwammerdam and Xanten on the Rhine (McGrail 1995).

Classical sources confirm that Roman military expeditions used both sail and oar to make their way far beyond the bounds of the Roman Empire. Naval fleets had ventured at least as far as the mouth of the Elbe, perhaps further.[11] By the 1st century AD, Roman imports in the Germanic world, including the southern North Sea coast, also indicate intensive trade (Eggers 1951), and a 5th-century carving of a Roman trading vessel from the river Weser bears witness to the involvement of Roman merchant craft (Pieper 1989: 188).

These three cultural (and linguistic) spheres, Germanic, Celtic and Roman, intersect for several centuries in the early part of the first millennium. The history of the word *sail* suggests, how the technology may have developed in this multicultural environment.

The linguistic history of sail

The word *sail* is restricted to the Germanic and some Celtic languages and is very different from the words used in other languages (such as Latin *velum*). It appears in Old English, and Old Icelandic as *segl*, in Old Saxon as *segel*, in Old High German as *segal*, and also in Old Welsh as *huil* (Welsh *hwyl*) and in Old Irish as *séol* (originally *sél*).[12] None of these words is attested before the 8th century AD, although some Old Irish poetry and an early Old English glossary suggest its presence in the 7th century in the respective languages. The Old Irish poem is first recorded in a later manuscript, but the poet lived in the 7th century, and the strict style guarantees that a change would have been virtually impossible. The Old English glossary dates from the early 8th century, but a very similar one survives slightly later, which makes it likely that both go back to an earlier source. Since the two are not identical, this source probably was not a single text they were both copied from, but rather a kind of grandfather text, so that more than one hop was involved to produce the surviving glossaries. This would put the source into the late 7th century at the latest (Pheifer 1974: lxxxix).

Several suggestions have been put forward to explain the presence of these Celtic and Germanic words and their relationship to each other: a common origin in Indo-European or at a later stage, a borrowing from an unattested Latin term or a borrowing from Germanic into Celtic (without further explanation of the origin of the Germanic term). All of these can be tested with the methods outlined above, and this has been done comprehensively elsewhere (Thier 2003). For the present purpose, only two examples shall be discussed in detail. The first is Pokorny's derivation of the term from an Indo-European element (root) *sek-lo- 'something cut to shape', from an underlying *sek- 'to cut' (1959, 895). If this were to be developed into a Welsh word, s- would change into h- (as in *Hafren*, the Welsh name for the Severn), -k- into -g- (as in *dagr* 'tear', which can be compared to Greek *dakru*), and the ending (-o-) would get lost. All these changes are known to have happened before the mid 1st millennium AD, and since the word in this scenario is assumed to have "always" been in the language, further dating of these changes is not an issue. The outcome would thus be *hegl. Since the actual form is *huil*, this is not acceptable.

Szemerényi (1978: 36f) suggests a loan from a Latin *sagellum or *segellum, a variant of *sagulum* 'cloak'. The first problem with this is that there is no evidence for this word in Latin or any Romance language (all of which are descended from Latin). The second is the initial letter: by the beginning of the Roman period, initial s- in British had changed sufficiently to remain distinct from initial s- in Latin loanwords where it would not change to h- as the old British s- did (Schrijver 1995: 381–82). Szemerényi's *segellum, if borrowed in Roman Britain, would therefore have yielded Welsh *swyl, not *hwyl*. So this solution, too, is unacceptable.

Peter Schrijver (1995: 357) has put forward the only solution which works for all attested forms: a derivation from *siglo-, which belongs to early Celtic and Germanic, but cannot be explained any further. The development of *siglo- into the various languages which have the word sail is almost exactly parallel to the development of the Latin loan signum 'sign', which appears as Irish sén, Welsh swyn 'charm' (with s- preserved, because it is a loan), Old English segn 'blessing'. The consequence of the above argument is that the word sail goes back to a base shared by Celtic and Germanic, and that this was present in all these languages by the early 1st millennium AD.

What's in a name?

Celtic and Germanic cultures intersect in the Rhine delta. Classical authors name the Rhine as a border, but modern scholars, both archaeologists and linguists, have shown that things were much less clear-cut, and that especially near the estuary, the cultures and languages overlap. This area has shown so many special linguistic features that in the 1960, Hans Kuhn posited a separate language group in that area which stood half way between Germanic and Celtic and was in fact a remnant of the predecessor of both (Kuhn et al 1962). It is important to remember, however, that in many ways the sound systems as well as the word structures of Celtic and Germanic were very similar, even if similar-looking words could mean quite different things (Schmidt 1986, 243–44). So unless a name can be unambiguously understood and analysed in contrast with other related languages, it is often very difficult to tell the difference. For instance, the tribal name of the Eburones south of the Rhine estuary can be understood as a derivative of the Celtic word for yew (cf. Scottish Gaelic iubhar) or the Germanic word for boar (cf. Old English eofor, German Eber). In this case, a reference to the yew in this context has been suggested to tip the balance in favour of a Celtic name, and the unambiguously Celtic name of their leader Ambiorix supports this suggestion (on the etymologies of the names cf. Birkhan 1970: 205–7, Neumann 1986: 111, also Caesar: Bellum Gallicum VI 31). Additionally, most of the informants to the Roman authors were probably Celtic-speakers and may have Celticized Germanic names where they seemed transparent.

Among these indicators of cultural mixing are a number of tribal names and place-names on both sides of the river. The Frisiavones, for instance, have a Germanic-looking name: the initial f- is one indicator to this effect. They are recorded to the south of the estuary, which in Caesar's account is Belgic territory, but is later given the colonial name of Germania Inferior. Besides, Caesar has a concept of Germani cisrhenani 'Germani' on this side of the Rhine', i.e. the side he was on, the west bank. On the other hand, a tribe known as the Usipii on the east "Germanic" bank of the river, and a bit further upstream, seems to bear an identifiably Celtic name, probably meaning "well-horsed"; they were noted for their horsemanship (Wells 1995:608). The elements of this name have their closest parallels in

Greek eu "good" and hippos "horse" (cf. also the name of the Celtic goddess Epona), the form of the word cannot be Germanic or Latin (cf. Old English eoh, Latin equus "horse" with no p in evidence).

In addition to this, more mixing occurs with the rise of Roman power in the now so-called Germania Inferior, as Germanic tribes are re-settled in areas previously characterized by Celtic names under Augustus, and the new administration adds its own Latin overlay, both in linguistic and cultural terms.

The British Connection

A continuing link between the multicultural Rhine delta and Britain can be traced through the centuries. In the Roman period the Rhine was a highway of trade to Britain, as can be seen from archaeological finds such as Southern Gaulish amphorae, which in the most significant case are distributed along the Rhône and Rhine from their place of origin all the way to Britain (Cunliffe 2001: 419). Germanic troops also served in the Roman army, and among the auxiliary units stationed in Britain there were Germanic Batavi as well as Usipii (who on one occasion stole a sailing ship, albeit unsuccessfully; Tacitus, Agricola 20). Finally, Carausius of the North Sea coastal Menapii (whose name has not been interpreted; cf. Birkhan 1970: 195) became dictator of Britain in the 3rd century.

In the early 5th century, Roman power collapsed in Britain, and in the wake of this, material culture normally associated with Continental Europe and Southern Scandinavia – both traditionally Germanic areas – begins to spread. Among this material culture are the remains of three clinker-built ships with Scandinavian parallels, all found in a small area in Suffolk (two from Sutton Hoo and one from Snape). These are quite different from the Romano-Celtic craft of Roman Britain, and it is quite possible that it was this kind of ship that is referred to by Gildas by its Germanic name (cyul-, see above). By the time of the earliest surviving written evidence (8th century), a Germanic language is in use in a considerable part of the country. Traditionally, arguments were made for a full-scale resettlement of the country. More recently, alternative suggestions have been made to explain the presence of foreign material culture and ultimately the English language by contacts across the North Sea (e.g. Higham 1992). In either case the Scandinavian-style ships from Suffolk are seen as indicative of the type of vessels which dominated this emigration or exchange.

A different picture, however, is suggested by the spread of Germanic place-names on the Continent, in Scandinavia and in Britain, as shown in a comparative study by Udolph (1994). With the help of distribution maps he shows a strong affinity of the Continental European naming practises with those later used in Britain, while Scandinavia is very different. Many elements common to the southern North Sea coast and Britain do not appear north of the Elbe estuary at all or only rarely. In addition, some of these elements are frequent in the south of Britain and largely missing from East Anglia (Udolph 1994: 826f). Place-names are useful for this kind of research, because they are very conservative. Once they are established, they are likely to remain, and if they are replaced (as happened in Anglo-Saxon England), this fact is probably significant: the new names can provide clues about the people who used them.

Schrijver (1999: 33) also shows that the languages of the North Sea Coast, namely Old Frisian, Old Coastal Dutch and Old English, share a number of features which set them apart from other West Germanic languages such as Old High German. He puts this down to the influence of closely related Celtic languages formerly spoken in these areas. Of the Old English dialects, that of Kent is particularly close to its Continental neighbours. Wood (1990) uses historical evidence to show a strong affinity of the English south coast with the Frankish world. His observations tie in with Schrijver's and, taken together, these two approaches and the above arguments suggest a long-standing continuity of contact in these areas.

In Anglo-Saxon East Anglia, by contrast, Hines (1984) and Böhme (1986) observe a cultural link with Scandinavia, mainly supported with distinctive archaeological evidence. It is therefore not surprising to find a number of Scandinavian-style ships in this area. There is, however, no reason for Scandinavian ships to have been in use, let alone dominant, in areas south of East Anglia. On the other hand, most of the above-mentioned Roman ships and barges of Romano-Celtic type come from Britain, the English Channel and the Rhine, areas that have above been identified as areas of contact between Celtic and Germanic, British and Continental (but not Scandinavian). Thus, the indications of both cultural and linguistic continuity around the Rhine delta and the English Channel might suggest that the ships of choice in the Romano-British period, and here were those used in the Romano-British period, and that the word for sail was carried with them to England on this route.

Final thoughts

In the above, I have attempted to give an outline of the basic methods of historical linguistics and to suggest how these may be applied in conjunction with archaeological and historical methods to provide a fuller picture of the past. I do not claim that it is anywhere close to comprehensive, on the contrary, it barely scratches the surface. I do hope, however, that it will be a small step towards integrating a further discipline into the already multi-faceted study of our maritime past.

Notes

1   N.B. These are slightly offset from the archaeological and historical periods, and early Old English only starts around 700, not long before the beginning of the Viking Period.

2   An asterisk means that the form is not attested, see below on back-projection and reconstruction.

3   The bar (macron) on the e in ēo means it is a long vowel, it would have been spelt eo. Linguists add the macron to make their lives easier. The accent on the ó in jó means the same thing, but in this case, the Icelanders did actually spell it that way.

4   Slashes indicate pronunciations. Symbols used within pronunciation slashes are taken from the International Phonetic Alphabet (IPA), which has symbols for every sound used in the languages of the world.

5   Finnish *keula* now designates the stem of a boat, and it is possible that this sense development was influenced by the Scandinavian word for the structural timber, which we know from Old Icelandic as *kjǫlr*; for a different interpretation see Kylstra 1996: 87.

6   The final -ll in *kjǫll* is not irregular, but contains a grammatical ending; Germanic **keula-s* (including the ending) becomes Old Icelandic *kjǫl-r*, and thence *kjǫll*. This ending does not survive in Old English.

7   Old Icelandic manuscripts (and therefore Old Icelandic spelling) only survive from the post-Viking period.

8   I am grateful to all the staff at the Oxford English Dictionary (OED) who were involved in revising the entry MIZZEN, n., now published on http://dictionary.oed.com/cgi/entry/00312747

9   The Netherlands, at this time, were still Spanish, but also becoming a sea-power in their own right.

10   This depends on the interpretation of the account by Velleius Paterculus: *Classis, quae Oceani circumnavigaverat sinus,ab inaudito atque incognito ante mari flumine Albi subvecta.* "The fleet, which had circumnavigated the bay of the Oceanus [i.e. of the Atlantic], [was] borne up the river Elbe from a previously unheard-of and unknown sea" *History* II cvi 3.

11   The o in *seol* represents a later development within Irish.

12   [*erumpens...barbarae,*] *tribus, ut lingua eius exprimitur, cyulis, nostra longis navibus. De Excidio Britanniae* ('the Ruin of Britain') 23.3

References

Birkhan, H., 1970. *Germanen und Kelten*. Wien.

Böhme, H.W., 1986. Das Ende der Römerherrschaft in Britannien und die angelsächsische Besiedlung Englands im 5. Jahrhundert. *Jahrbuch des Römisch-Germanischen Zentralmuseums* 33: 469–574.

Bréard, C., (ed.) 1893. *Le Compte du clos des Galées de Rouen au XIVe siècle, 1382–1384*. Rouen.

Campbell, A., 1959. *Old English Grammar*. Oxford

Caesar: Guthardt, A., 1973. *Caesar: Bellum Gallicum*. Münster. Chadwick J. et al. 1986–90. *A Corpus of Mycenaean Inscriptions from Knossos*, 4 vols. Cambridge.

Cunliffe, B., 2001. *Facing the Ocean*. Oxford.

Eggers, H.J., 1951. *Der römischer Import im freien Germanien*, 2 vol. Hamburg

Francesco da Buti: Giannini, C., (ed.) 1858, *Commento di Francesco da Buti sopra la Divina Comedia di Dante Allighieri*. Vol. I. Pisa

Friel, L., 1995. *The Good Ship*. London

Higham, N., 1992, *Rome, Britain and the Anglo-Saxons.* London.

Hines, J., 1984, *The Scandinavian Character of Anglian England in the pre-Viking period.* BAR 125. Oxford

Isidore of Seville: Arevalus, (ed.) 1878, *Sancti Isidori Hispalensis Episcopi Opera Omnia.* Vol 3. Patrologia Latina 82. Paris.

Kindschi, L., 1955, *The Latin-Old English Glossaries in Plantin-Moretus MS 32 and British Museum Additional 32.246.* Dissertation, University of Michigan, Ann Arbor.

Kluge, F., 1911, *Seemannssprache.* Halle/Saale.

Kuhn, H. et al., 1962, *Völker zwischen Germanen und Kelten.* Neumünster.

Kylstra, A.D. et al., 1996, *Lexikon der älteren germanischen Lehnwörter in den ostseefinnischen Sprachen.* Amsterdam.

McGrail, S., 1995, Romano-Celtic Boats and Ships: characteristic features. *International Journal for Nautical Archaeology* 24, 139–45

McGrail, S., 2001, *Boats of the World.* Oxford.

Neumann, G., 1986, Germani Cisrhenani – die Aussage der Namen. In H. Beck (ed.), *Germanenprobleme in heutiger Sicht.* Ergänzungsbände zum Reallexikon der germanischen Altertumskunde 1, 107–29. Berlin.

Noreen, A., 1923, *Altisländische und Altnorwegische Grammatik.* Halle/Saale.

OED3: Simpson, J., and Weiner, E., (eds) 2000- *Oxford English Dictionary on-line,* new edition. URL: http://www.oed.com

Pieper, P., 1989, *Die Weser-Runenknochen.* Oldenburg.

Pheifer, J.D., (ed.) 1974, *Old English Glosses in the Épinal-Erfurt Glossary.* Oxford.

Pokorny, J., 1959, *Indogermanisches Etymologisches Wörterbuch.* Tübingen.

Schmidt, K.H., 1986, Keltisch-Germanische Isoglossen und Ihre sprachgeschichtlichen Implikationen. In H. Beck (ed.), *Germanenprobleme in heutiger Sicht.* Ergänzungsbände zum Reallexikon der germanischen Altertumskunde 1, 231–47. Berlin.

Schrijver, P., 1995, *Studies in British Celtic Historical Phonology.* Amsterdam and Atlanta.

Schrijver, P., 1999, The Celtic Contribution to the Development of the North Sea Germanic Vowel System. *North Western European Language Evolution (NOWELE)* 35, 3–47.

Szemerényi, O., 1978, Latein in Europa. In K. Büchner (ed.), *Latein und Europa,* 26–46. Stuttgart .

Tacitus: Kretschmer, M., (ed.) 1986, *Tacitus: Germania.* Münster.

Tacitus: Klinz, A., (ed.) 1959, *Tacitus: De vita et moribus Iulii Agricolae.* Münster.

Thier, K.,2003, Sails in the North – new perspectives on an old problem. *International Journal for Nautical Archaeology* 32, 182–90

Udolph, J., 1994, *Namenkundliche Studien zum Germanenproblem.* Ergänzungsbände zum Reallexikon der germanischen Altertumskunde 9. Berlin.

Velleius Paterculus: Shipley, F.W., (ed. and tr.) 1924, *Velleius Paterculus and Res Geastae Divi Augusti.* Loeb Classical Library L152. London.

Wells, C., 1995, Celts and Germans in the Rhineland. In M. Green (ed.), *The Celtic World,* 603–20. London.

Wood, I., 1990, The Channel from the 4th to the 7th centuries AD. In S. McGrail (ed.), *Maritime Celts, Frisians and Saxons,* Papers presented to a conference at Oxford 1988. CBA Research Report 71, 93–97. London.

36 Medieval shipping in the estuary of the Vistula river. Written sources in the interpretation of archaeological finds

Robert Domzal

For most of the Western European countries, the second half of the 12th century and the beginning of the 13th century was the turning point in the history of shipping. Along the southern coast of the Baltic Sea, settlers from Saxony, Flanders and the Rhine basin appeared. They counted on taking over the Slavic and Prussian trading routes, which had been used earlier by the Vikings. A leading role in the colonization of the lower Vistula river was played by knights and merchants from Germany, especially the citizens of Lübeck. Coastal sailing across the Vistula and Kuronian lagoons was an important complement of the Hanseatic route from Lübeck through Visby on Gotland to Inflants (Samsonowicz 1991: 11). The movement of people and goods from Western Europe to the eastern 'peripheries of civilized Europe' could only be done thanks to the new ship types. In the 12th to 14th centuries they were cogs, in the 15th and 16th centuries hulks. Around 1230, the knights of the Teutonic Order first appeared near Torun. They were invited there by Prince Konrad Mazowiecki in order to convert the pagan Prussians to Christianity. After taking over the regions of Chelmno and Torun, the Teutonic Knights started to move down the Vistula towards its estuary.

The rather small number of archaeological finds from this region dating to the 13th through 15th centuries makes us take into consideration the written sources which were gathered in accounts kept by the Teutonic Order. The importance of such sources for the history of medieval shipping and shipbuilding was largely dismissed in the 19th and 20th centuries (Vogel 1915: 466). Both smaller and bigger towns that were ruled by the Teutonic Knights had detailed inventories of the types and number of ships and accounts connected with shipbuilding, including the prices of the materials and equipment and the maintenance of vessels. The most important information is preserved for the larger towns of Elblag (Elbing), Malbork, Torun, and Swiecie, as well as for smaller administrative districts like Tczew and the towns, such as Królewiec, along the shore of the Vistula lagoon like (Figs 36.1 and 36.2).

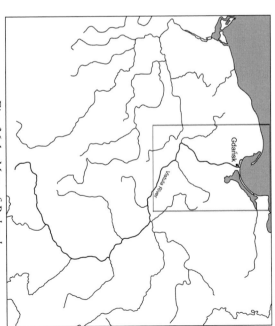

Fig. 36.1. Map of Poland.

Inland shipping

Within the area which is of interest to us we have several rivers: the lower Vistula, Nogat, Elblag, and Dzierzgon. At the turn of the 13th and 14th centuries, the first hydro-technical works on the Vistula and Nogat began in order to protect the land against flooding (Dlugokecki 1993: 39). In 1348 there were works in Elblag, to protect the navigable channel from silting up (Toeppen 1894: 30).

The attractiveness of the area was due to the convenient waterway system which allowed for the carrying of goods down the rivers to the towns on the shore of the Vistula Lagoon and further on towards the open sea. From western Europe, such goods as cloth, herring, wine and weapons were brought here. From the Vistula estuary fur, wax, leather and honey were sent to the West, and in the later Middle Ages bulk cargoes were mainly grain and wood. The exchange of these goods became the basis of subsistence of the indigenous population and newcomers. From the 13th century, Elblag became the main harbour

Warniswald and Mezellenczwald near Malbork (AHM 1911: 221–222). Other forests near Kwidzyn (Marienwerder), Dzierzgon and Ostorda were also famous for their wood (Gierszewski 1961: 20). Medieval shipbuilders from this region had enough good material. They did not have to import it from Poland. This is supported by the dendrochronological dating of the shipwreck from Kobyla Kepa, found on the shore of the Vistula Lagoon and dated to c. 1291 (Ossowski and Krapiec 2001: 94–96). The wood which was exported from Poland was in most cases sent to Western Europe.

Medieval boatbuilding technique in this area is an interesting issue. When German settlers appeared on the lower Vistula, there was already a well-developed boatbuilding tradition in the region. We can add Truso, Gdańsk, and Zantyr in the fork between the Nogat and Vistula to the harbor and shipbuilding centers. In the 13th century, during the wars on the Vistula, the Prince of Pomerania could gather 20 ships in Zantyr and 10 in Swiecie (Dusburg III: 50).

In the Early Medieval times Slavic ships were described as plank-built vessels, having wooden pegs in the plank overlaps and moss as caulking material. From the 13th century, wooden pegs were used much less often. They were used for fastening the inner skeleton of the ship to the planks. For the assembling of the plank shell, iron rivets started to be used, as seen in the ship found in 1920 in Elbing (Ehlich, Steegmann 1923: 152) (Fig. 36.3).

In most cases mentioned in the account books of the Teutonic Knights, boats and ships were caulked with moss and tarred. Occasionally oakum was used (NKR I 1987: 62,156). Most of the ships were clinker built, and the use of clinker nails is specifically mentioned (MKB, 217). The only exceptions so far known can be found in the shipwrecks of Kobyla Kepa and Green Gate in Gdańsk. The later of these is dated around 1332, and they are the oldest finds of inland ships built in carvel technique (Ossowski and Koscinski, in press). So this technique appeared on river vessels in the Vistula estuary more than 100 years earlier than on big, sea-going ships. Vessels of this type are mentioned in the written sources in Gdańsk in the second half of the 15th century (Hirsch and Vossberg 1855: 12, 40).

The accounts from the Old Town of Elblag for the year 1404 mention the construction elements which were needed for the building of the most typical of medieval river vessels, called *skuta* (German *die schute*). It was a plank-built vessel, with flat bottom and inner reinforcements (frames). Stem and stern posts were mentioned. Large and small iron nails were used for the fastening of planks. This vessel had a rudder and 24 long oars. The oarsmen could sit on special benches. There was also a single square sail. As additional equipment two boat hooks were mentioned.

DIE SCHUTE
Parts of the ship in original:

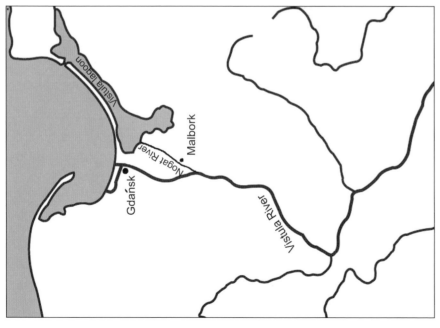

Fig. 36.2. Vistula estuary in enlargement.

and the most important centre for Hanseatic trade for the Teutonic Knights.

Thanks to archival documents we can say that from the 13th until the 15th century, most goods were carried on big river vessels, which were navigated by skippers who belonged to the newcomers from Germany (NKR 1987: 19, 95). Even so, in many towns like Elblag, Gdańsk and Dzierzgon, there were groups of sailors of Polish origin, *die Polan*. They were local fishermen who had their own boats. Teutonic administration paid them also for the water transport of goods, repair and maintenance of vessels, and hauling and launching (Semrau 1936: 38). They inhabited the areas outside the walls of the towns, the *Vorburg*, which were close to the rivers. Small shipyards and river ports were also situated there. Sometimes the name *Vorburg* was used interchangeably with *Lastadia* (Semrau 1936: 38). The first legal rights and duties of the Vistula sailors in the country ruled by the Teutonic Knights were published in the year 1375 (ASP 1874: 35).

Shipbuilding

In the Middle Ages, local wood was used for shipbuilding in the Vistula estuary. We can find the forests where it was cut in the written sources: Ellerwald near Elblag,

Rubencken – benches for oarsmen
wagenscote – planks for boatbuilding
knarholter – roots (natural-grained timber)
wrangen – frame timbers
klusholt – piece of timber with a hawse-hole
kny – knee
dicke delen to dem ruder – thick planks for rudder
1 raholt – yard
24 lange rymen – 24 long oars
mast – mast
beyde steven – stem and stern post
additional equipment – blocks, lines, sail, boat hooks.
(NKR I 1987: 70)

In the 13th century, iron clamps (*sintels*) for the fastening of the wooden laths protecting caulking material were identified as a new element of hull construction along the southern shore of the Baltic Sea (Ellmers 1972: 306). In the Vistula estuary such clamps were very often used for the building of ferries, river vessels, and for the repair of most planked vessels (AHM 1911: 65). They were produced by the local blacksmiths. For the repair of a common ship with a length of 20 meters, about 600 clamps were used. For the building of an inland vessel 600 to 700 clamps were used (AHM 1911: 253). The use of clamps together with the remains of shipwrecks have been observed west of the mouth of the Vistula in Gdansk and Kolobrzeg and of the Vistula in Kobyla Kepa, Elblag, Wladyslawowo near Elblag, and far to the east in Nowogrod. Similar boatbuilding technique was used in the Middle Ages on the lakes in Estonia (Mäss 2000: 55). This technique appeared together with the new settlers of German and Frisian origin. The shape of clamps provides a dating tool for wrecks, and their number is an indication of the size of the ship (Vlierman 1996: 55–58). Cases of repair of river vessels noticed in written sources show that for this work the whole caulking was changed and new clamps for holding it were ordered. The number of clamps for repair and building of a new ship was often the same. Examples of orders of iron elements for ships by the Teutonic administration show that the length of

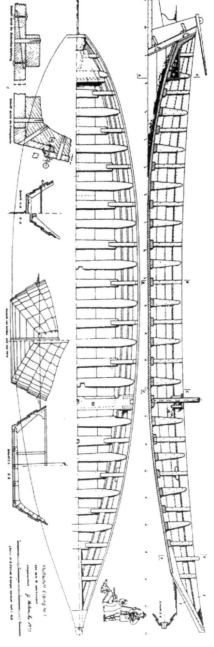

Fig. 36.3. *Medieval River Vessel from Elblag (after G.Salemke 1973).*

Fig. 36.4. *Traditional river boat in which iron clamps were used, from the upper Vistula in the 20th century (J.Litwin).*

most inland vessels was 20 to 25 meters. A surprising parallel in the technique of caulking is found on the upper Vistula (Litwin 1995: 163). It may be there are enclaves far from the sea, where this tradition survived longer than on the coast where it was first used (Fig. 36.4).

The written sources show that the iron for shipbuilding was imported from Sweden and Hungary. The latter was transported down the Vistula and thanks to German

Robert Domzal

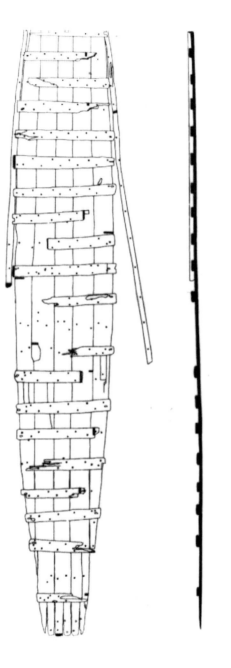

Fig. 36.5. Plan of shipwreck from Kobyla Kepa, built around 1292 (after W.Ossowski 2001).

0 1 2

tradesmen sent to Western Europe. Part of the iron stayed in local shipyards, for example in Gdańsk. In the accounts of a blacksmith shop in Malbork we find a record that 2 lasts (4 tons) of Hungarian iron were sent to the Lastadia in Gdańsk in 1415 (Sarnowsky 1993: 93).

Thanks to the relics of the shipwrecks from Elbląg, Gdańsk, Kobyla Kepa and written sources, we can describe the appearance of a typical river vessel in the 13th to 15th centuries. These were mostly flat-bottomed vessels suitable for inland navigation. They had low sides and straight stems. They carried a single square sail and were steered either with a sternpost rudder or a large steering sweep, with the latter more common on river vessels. They were built primarily in clinker technique, but occasionally carvel. Typical vessels had several strakes of planking caulked with moss fastened with iron clamps. At the plank overlaps, iron nails and rivets were the most common, but wooden pegs were still sometimes used.

Most of the known medieval inland vessels could be described as ferries and *bordings*. The shipwreck from Kobyla Kepa can also be classified as a *bording* (Fig. 36.5). River ships, like the *Weichsellschiffe*, had a different hull shape, similar to vessels from the 17th and 18th centuries which are well known from iconography (Waligorska 1960: 232–235). The *Weichselkanen* mentioned in the Teutonic accounts from Malbork in 1417 had a capacity of 18 to 24 lasts (approximately equal to 36–48 deadweight tons). The *Schute* which sunk in 1499 and belonged to Canrad Dankaw carried 14 lasts (28 tons) (Sattler 1887: 61,65).

The first ships which were built in the Vistula estuary by German citizens in 1236 (probably near Kwidzyn, Marienwerder) were *Pilgrim* and *Friedeland*. They were used for war purposes and for carrying building materials for new towns like Elbląg and Balga (Dusburg III 1861: 60). Both ships had square sails and round wooden fighting platforms, called *mars* (Grunau 1876: 496). The

painting from the church in Krolewiec shows the sails, *mars* and the crew of the Teutonic ships.

Who built the ships? Were they specialist shipbuilders or ordinary carpenters, who also built houses, bridges and other wooden structures? It seems that soon after Elbląg and Krolewiec were founded, a group of shipbuilders also appeared. They were supervisors and master shipwrights. Otto Shipshover was mentioned in Elbląg in 1295. In written sources from this region we have other evidence which mentions craftsmen known as Bootmaker and Shiptymmermanne (NKR I 1987: 156, NKR II 1989: 93). In documents from Elbląg in the 15th century, we find much information about shipbuilders who supervised the building of inland vessels. They were called Niclaus Vogeler and Hennike Botmaker. It seems that there were not enough of these specialists. In case of extensive construction, boat builders had to be sent from town to town. In smaller towns the function of a shipwright was fulfilled by local carpenters (MTB 1896: 276).

Types of vessels

Written sources demonstrate that in the Middle Ages in the Vistula estuary both local and foreign names connected with the types of ships appeared. The western names could come from the lower Rhine, Weser and Laba. Examples of local ship names can be found in the inventory of fishery administration for the Labiau in 1513 (GÄB 1921: 298). We find there one ship called *wittinchen*, which can be associated with *Wicina*, known from the Niemen River (in modern Lithuania). In the Polish language this type of river vessel has been known since the 16th century (Luczynski 1986:198). Some scientists think that a *szkuta* (*schute*) from the Vistula can look much the same as a *wicina* on the Niemen (Brückner 1927: 613). The linguists see the roots of this word in *wicia*, meaning a branch of wicker which was used for fastening of river rafts. Dr. Jerzy Litwin does not exclude the possibility of connecting the elements of plank boats with the use of wicker (Litwin, 1997:279). Such boatbuilding technique could explain the name of those types of vessels.

In the 1415 inventory of the fishery administration in Swiecie, a town on the lower Vistula, 3 *dubas* were mentioned (GÄB 1921: 617, 619). One year later only two such ships were to be found. In 1438, by the ferry at Gniew, near Swiecie, one *czolen* (Slavic canoe) was mentioned, probably a logboat (GÄB 1921: 751). Another ship type found in this region was *nassuta*. Probably this word comes from Polish *nasuc* (to pour), which was used in association with grain which was poured in these river vessels (Kranhals 1942:88).

Thesaurus Lingue Prussicae (Nesselmann 1873: 110) describes *Nassute* as a small, light transport vessel. The name comes from the Lithuanian word *neszu* (Latvian *nesti'*, nest). It shows that the described ship was used for grain transport. If we accept this interpretation, we would have to say that this ship's name came to the lower Vistula from the region of Lithuania and Latvia. This name was adopted in Prussia for small, flat-bottomed river vessels. In this name we can also find the reflection of the building technique – the ship with a snub nose (stem). The prefix *Nase* (*nos*) was used in German and Polish for the description of a raised stem. Röding and Stenzel give an example of the use of this word in association with the position of a ship towards the wind: "*das Schiff hat den Wind auf der Nase*. In Old Polish we find also "boats with raised nose" (Luczynski 1986:185).

Another ship type name is connected with propulsion: *carabas*. In medieval Latin *carabus* meant sail (Diefenbach 1857: 99). In Poland in the 16th century, Jan Maczynski knew *carabus* as a "sailcloth" (Maczynski 1564: 38). This name is also to be found in the Russian language for describing a type of passenger boat used on the Dzwina River. It could also be associated with the Russian *korabi* (Falk 1912: 94). Types of vessels mentioned in written sources could mean other types of ships in different geographical regions. The length of this paper only allows an outline proposal for a general classification of ships and boats which appear in the medieval written sources in the area controlled by the Teutonic Order. Classification of vessels in the 13th – 15th centuries:

1. Names connected with water, for example a river's name: *Weichselkahn, Weichselshiff, Deimeschiff, Haffkan*
2. Names connected with the shipbuilding technique: *Wittinchen, Kyleboth, Kraveel*
3. Names connected with the method of propulsion: *Schelch, Schelschen, Schilling, Carabas*
4. Names connected with the function of a ship: *Nessute,Leichterschiff, Fischerschiff, Keitelshiff, Hoyschiff, Kalkschiff, Speseschiff, Carvanschiff*
5. Names connected with the kind of cargo: *Koleschiff,*
6. Names connected with shape and dimension: *Kleinschiff, Grosschiff, Alteschiff*
7. Names connected with the type of timber used for building: *Dubas, Esping*

Types of inland water vessels evolved more slowly than sea-going types. Thus medieval river ships were probably not very different from the vessels known from the 16th and 17th centuries. German boat builders from the Vistula estuary from the very beginning had contacts with Polish river vessels, for example from Krakow. In 1245, during the battles between the Prince of Pomerania and the Teutonic Order, the latter received provisions sent from Krakow in three vessels (Jasinski 1999: 122).

Until now there are very few iconographic sources which show inland vessels in the described region. One of them, quite controversial, is the painting from the church in Kwidzyn. It shows a ship which is different from ships known from the archaeological excavations. Its hull resembles a cog more than a river boat. It has high, clinker sides, a single square sail and the long steering sweep over the stern as is typical for river vessels. Aside from the more riverine steering oar, the picture shows the ship with the constructional features of a cog.

To sum up, we can say that shipbuilding technique in the Vistula estuary in the later Middle Ages was the result of the encounter of Slavic and Prussian vessels with new types of ships brought by settlers from Western Europe. New archaeological discoveries and analysis of written sources will let us develop this theory.

Abbreviations for primary sources

AHM: *Das Ausgabebuch des Marienburger Hauskomturs für das Jahre 1410–1420* (W. Ziesemer, ed.) Königsberg 1911

ASP: *Acten der Ständetage Preussens unter der Herrschaft des Deutschen Ordens* (M. Toeppen, ed.) Bd.I–V, Leipzig 1874–1886.

GÄB: *Das Grosse Ämterbuch des Deutschen Ordens* (W. Ziesemrer, ed.) Danzig 1921

MKB: *Das Marienburger Konventsbuch der Jahre 1399–1412*, hg. von W. Ziesemer, Danzig, 1913..

MTB: *Das Marienburger Tresslerbuch der Jahre 1399–1409*, hg. von E. Joachim, Königsberg 1896

NKR: *Nowa księga rachunkowa starego miasta Elbląga 1404–1414*, M. Pelech cz. I–II, Toruń 1987–1989

Other published primary sources

von Sattler, C. (ed.), 1887, *Handelsrechnungen des Deutsches Ordens*. Leipzig.

von Dusburg, Petri, 1861, *Chronicon Terrae Prussiae*. Leipzig.

Grunau, Simon, 1876–1896, *Preussische Chronik*. Bd. I–III, Leipzig.

Secondary sources

Brückner, A., 1927, *SB ownik etymologiczny języka polskiego*. Kraków

Diefenbach, L., 1857, *Glossarium Latino-Germanicum*.

Długokęcki, W., 1993: Zmiana koryta Wisły i Nogatu pod Białą Górą od XIII do pierwszej połowy XVI wieku. Przyczynek do historii żeglugi wiślanej. *Rocznik Gdański"* 53: z. 2.

Ehrlich, B., and Stegmann E., 1923, Der Fund eines alten Flussschiffes bei Elbling. *Elbinger Jahrbuch*, H.3.

Ellmers, D., 1972, *Frühmittelalterliche Handelsschiffahrt in Mittel- und Nordeuropa*. Münster.

Falk, H., 1912, *Altnordisches Seewesen*. Wörter und Sachen 4. Heidelberg.

Gierszewski, S., 1961, *Elbląski przemysł okrętowy w latach 1570–1815*. Gdańsk.

Hirsch, T., and Vossberg, F.A., 1855, *Caspar Weinreich's Danziger Chronik*. Berlin.

Jasiski, T., 1999, *Toruń XIII–XIV wieku-lokacja miast toruńskich i początki ich rozwoju (1231- około 1350)*. Historia Torunia I. Toruń.

Kranhals, D., 1942, *Danzig und der Weichselhandel in seiner Blütezeit vom 16. zum 17 Jahrhundert*. Leipzig.

Litwin, J., 1995, *Polskie szkutnictwo ludowe XX wieku*. Gdańsk.

Litwin, J., 1997, Niemen, wiciny i spław do Królewca. *Rzeki* 6. Gdańsk.

Łuczyński, E., 1986, *Staropolskie słownictwo związane z żeglugą w XV i XVI wieku*. Gdańsk.

Maczinsky, J., 1564, *Lexicon Latino-Polonicum* […]. Królewiec.

Mäss, V., 2000, Features of Medieval Frisian Boatbuilding In Estonia Inland Waters. In J. Litwin (ed.), *Down The River*
into the Sea. *Proceedings of the Eight Interenational Symposium on Boat and Ship Archaeology*. Gdańsk.

Nesselmann, G.H.F., 1873, *Thesaurus Linguae Prussicae*. Berlin.

Ossowski, W. and Krąpiec, M., 2001, Niektóre zagadnienia szkutnictwa późnośredniowiecznego na przykładzie wraka z Kobylej Kępy. *Przegląd Archeologiczny* 49: 85–101.

Ossowski W., and Kościński B., in press, *Wrak średniowiecznego statku spod Zielonej Bramy w Gdańsku*.

Samsonowicz, H., 1991, Elbląg w związku miast hanzeatyckich. *Rocznik Elbląski* 12.

Sarnowsky, J., 1993, *Die Wirtschaftsführung des Deutsches Ordens in Pruessen (1382–1454)*.

Semrau, A., 1936, Die Siedlungen im Kammeramt Fischau (Komturei Christburg) im Mittelalter. Elbing.

Toeppen, M., 1894, *Beitrage zur Geschichte des Weichseldeltas*. Danzig.

Vlierman, K., 1996, *Van Zintelen, van Zintelroeden ande Moszen…" Een breeuwmethode als hulpmiddel bij het dateren van scheepswrakken uit de Hanzetijd*. Scheepsarcheologie I, Flavobericht 386. Lelystad.

Vogel, W., 1915, *Geschichte der deutschen Seeschiffahrt*. Berlin.

Waligórska, K., 1960, Konstrukcje statków pływających po Sanie i Wiśle w XVIII w. Kwartalnik *Historii Kultury Materialnej* 8, nr. 2.

37 Linking boats and rock carvings – Hjortspring and the North

John Coles

The publication of the monograph on the Hjortspring boat (Crumlin-Pedersen and Trakadas 2003) provides an opportunity to offer this short contribution to Seán McGrail. His specialised knowledge of ancient boats has for many years guided and inspired archaeologists who have tried to interpret the fragmentary record of such craft from their own excavations and discoveries. My particular interest in such matters has been restricted to commentaries on the various experiments designed to aid a better understanding of the capabilities of the boats (for example Coles 1979: chapter 2), and in the First International Symposium on Boat and Ship Archaeology held in Greenwich in 1976, I was able to contribute a short paper on the role of experiments in such studies (Coles 1977).

In more recent years, my involvement with ancient boats has turned from an interest in their experimentation to observation, not of actual boat remains but of their representation on the rocks of southern Scandinavia, and in a contribution for Ted Wright, a summary of some of the possibilities for interpretation was produced (Coles 1993). The recent publication of the Hjortspring boat (Crumlin-Pedersen and Trakadas 2003) neatly coincides with a current project on a particular rock carving site in Bohuslän, Sweden, where the representations appear to show boats of the Hjortspring style alongside a range of contemporary objects.

The site itself, at Halvorseröd, just south of Tanumshede, was recorded as long ago as 1886 when its general character was identified and illustrated (Baltzer 1886: pl.40). The carvings were upon a very smooth and shallow-sloping granite face which formed part of a long surface of exposed rock, much of which was being quarried away; some blocks still lie immediately beside the site, and it seems that the work was curtailed upon the recognition that carvings existed. It is not known if other carved surfaces were destroyed prior to the cessation of activities, but a few carvings now lie upon one detached block. The carvings extend over an area of about 12 sqm, and were subsequently recorded in the 1950–1970s, and published in a catalogue of parish sites (Bengtsson and Olsson 2000: Tanum 208). The plan published in this catalogue was

subsequently reproduced in the Hjortspring volume in a chapter on the iconography of boats, although in both volumes the scale is incorrect (Kaul 2003: Fig.5.33).

As part of a project to expand and extend the record of rock carving sites in the area, a new examination of the site was undertaken by the author in 2003 and the results appear here insofar as they relate to the Hjortspring boat and its archaeology. These results differ in a number of details from the 1886 recording and also from the more recent plans. Although the surface of the rock itself is fine and unblemished, at least where the carvings exist, and some of the carvings are very clear (Fig. 37.1), others are very shallow and difficult to record in detail; Baltzer in 1886 noted the problems of decipherment. The variations in the published plans are due in part to the scale of reductions in the 1886 and 2000 volumes, but some details do seem to have been missed here and there; further work is planned on the site in the expectation that a fine-tuning operation will expose a few more pieces of information about the boats shown upon the rock, particularly any embellishments of the hulls (see below).

Fig. 37.1. The rock surface at Halvorseröd, Tanum 208, with stacked boat images of Hjortspring type, and severe damage to the right of the carvings. Photo John Coles.

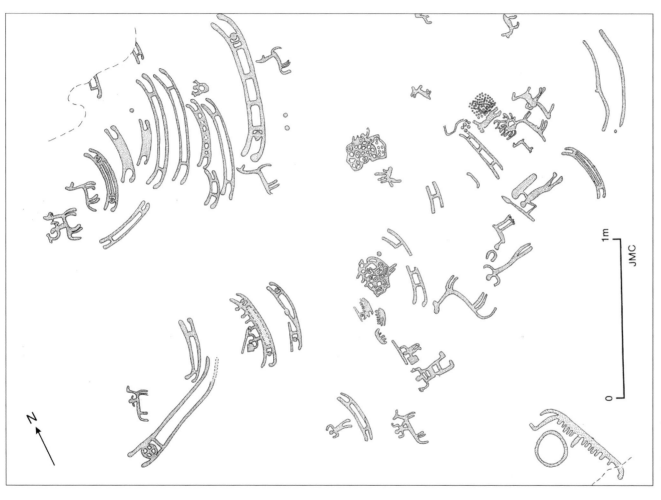

Fig. 37.2. Plan of the rock carving site of Halvorseröd, Tanum 208, based on recordings of 2003. Note the stacked boats at top, the pair of irregular designs near the centre of the panel, and the sloping line of humans and other animals forming a boundary at base. Plan by John Coles 2003.

In essence, the panel of carvings consists of a series of boat images, stacked or otherwise grouped, as well as a smaller number of horse-riders, various miscellaneous images and three very unusual designs or patterns (Fig. 37.2). The representations of these three designs on the published plans are not accurate and the plan reproduced here provides a better impression of their shape, although it is difficult to interpret them at this stage of the investigation. Further comment appears below.

The images on the rock are dated by their resemblance to the Hjortspring boat, and by the position of rock carving sites with similar boat images in the general area of northern Bohuslän; these tend to lie at levels that relate to sea level in the late first millennium BC. The date of the rock carving site lies probably in the decades around 350 BC, the date of the Hjortspring boat. The site itself is on a ridge overlooking a small stream, now channelled, that creeps eventually through bog land to the coast. To the east, some 900 m away, is the great carving site of the Litsleby (Tanum 75) with a number of boat images of the same style, and other smaller sites of similar age (e.g. Tanum 76) are clustered in the same area (Högberg 1995; Coles 2004a).

The images of the boats at Halvorseröd are remarkably consistent, with only a very few seemingly earlier in date, based on the established typology set out in Kaul's contribution to the Hjortspring book (Kaul 2003). Hjortspring boat images on the site number at least eighteen; they have the characteristic slender outline with curving parallel keel and gunwale lines, and five have shield images set fore and aft. Some indication of hull embellishment occurs on several boats, and most are open-hulled in outline. As an aside, it is intriguing to think that in the 1880s, these images of slender boats were being recognised and recorded on rock carving sites of western Sweden, at more or less the same time as the actual Hjortspring boat was being discovered on the island of Als, just off the east coast of Jutland. The connection was not recognised until many decades later.

The Hjortspring boat find also included a huge array of weaponry, including spears, swords, shields, various containers, and the bones of horses, dogs and other animals, although much was lost during the period of discovery of the boat. The rock carving contains images of horse-riders, spear-holders, shield-bearers and various animals, as well as the boats, and it thus duplicates much of the Hjortspring find, but in this case in a more contextual relationship that may link the images with the activities surrounding the boat deposit itself. At its top, nine of the boats are stacked in an orderly manner, and are surrounded by four horses, one with a rider. This could represent a place of actual deposition of boats as much as it could the actual use of boats on water. Most of the other animals, including humans, are placed below the boats and horses, perhaps thereby signifying a land-based element in opposition to the water-based complex set on the upper rock (Coles 2004b).

An earlier style of boat lies misaligned low down on the rock, and two enigmatic designs are central; these perhaps represent emblems on textile or other material, if indeed they ever existed as movable artefacts outside the minds of their makers. It is also a possibility that the two designs could represent jumbled or stacked arrays of objects such as were deposited with the Hjortspring boat; the lowest design, of multiple cupmarks in the rock, could represent the stones, laid out in readiness, that were apparently thrown against the boat as it was laid to rest in the boggy pool at Hjortspring.

This is not the place to embark upon a discourse on the Hjortspring find or its boat capabilities, the latter of which have been demonstrated in part by the experiments outlined in the 2003 report (Crumlin-Pedersen and Trakadas 2003). Nonetheless, it is worth noting the boat's speed and durability, and its postulated role in a presumed

assault and territorial expansion northwards into the island of Als in the 4th century BC. Even further northwards, in northern Bohuslän, the boat style was already well-known, enough at least to persuade the artists of the time to carve the images of such boats into the granites that lay exposed near the contemporary sea, and to record a range and variety of other images to accompany the dominant boat design.

This all speaks of a strong belief in and acceptance of such boats in the seafaring activities of the closing centuries of the first millennium BC. It is likely that, even with the splendid publication of the Hjortspring boat, we may well come to hear more about such impressive craft and their influence on the societies of the time. It is also likely that Seán McGrail will have contributions to make on any future debate about such material.

As an addition to the site description, I might add that work in 2004–5 has revealed more carvings of boats and animals on several blocks of granite detached from the site in the 18th and 19th centuries; these are shown on a new plan in Coles 2005, but do not add much that is new for the discussion above.

References

Baltzer, L., 1886, *Glyphes des Rochers du Bohuslän (Suède)*. Gothenburg.

Bengtsson, L. and Olsson, C. (eds), 2000, *Arkeologisk Rapport 5*. Vitlycke Museum.

The World Heritage Site's Central Area and Grebbestad. Vitlycke Museum. Tanumshede.

Coles, J., 1977, Experimental Archaeology – theory and principles. In S. McGrail (ed), *Sources and Techniques in Boat Archaeology*, 233–243. B.A.R. Supp. Series 29.

Coles, J., 1979, *Experimental Archaeology*. Academic Press. London.

Coles, J., 1993, Boats on the rocks. In J. Coles, V. Fenwick and G. Hutchinson (eds), *A Spirit of Enquiry: Essays for Ted Wright*, 23–31. W.A.R.P., Nautical Archaeology Society and National Maritime Museum. UK.

Coles, J., 2004a, Bridge to the Outer World. Rock carvings at Bro Utmark, Bohuslän, Sweden. *Proceedings of the Prehistoric Society* 70: 173–207.

Coles, J., 2004b, Hjortspring and the North. Review and commentary. *Journal of Wetland Archaeology* 4: 75–82.

Coles, J., 2005, *Shadows of a Northern Past, Rock Carvings in Bohuslän and Østfold*. Oxbow. Oxford.

Crumlin-Pedersen, O. and Trakadas, A. (eds), 2003, *Hjortspring. A Pre-Roman Iron-Age Warship in Context. Ships and Boats of the North*. Volume 5. Viking Ship Museum. Roskilde.

Högberg, T., 1995, *Arkeologisk Rapport 1 från Vitlyckemuseet. Litsleby, Tegneby and Bro*. Vitlycke Museum. Tanumshede.

Kaul, F., 2003, The Hjortspring boat and ship iconography of the Bronze Age and Early Pre-Roman Iron Age. In O. Crumlin-Pedersen and A. Trakadas (eds) *Hjortspring. A Pre-Roman Iron-Age Warship in Context. Ships and Boats of the North*, 187–207. Volume 5. Viking Ship Museum. Roskilde.

38 Aeneas' Sail: the iconography of seafaring in the central Mediterranean region during the Italian Final Bronze Age

Claire Calcagno

Introduction

The study of our maritime past often relies on methods and resources from other research disciplines, especially where the archaeological record leaves enigmatic gaps. Maritime exchanges may be inferred from particular artefact distribution patterns, even though traces of the ships themselves have not been found. Indirect evidence such as boat representations permits us to hypothesise about early seafaring capabilities and maritime cultures in a particular region. A case in point is the central Mediterranean region during the Italian Final Bronze Age (c. 12th – 9th centuries BC), where evidence of 'exotic' objects and foreign technologies testify to significant contacts with both eastern and western Mediterranean societies. Shifting patterns in artefact distribution over time reveal complex and evolving vectors of exchange (Lo Schiavo *et al* 1995; Vagnetti 1991). Such vectors include 11th-century BC Cypro-Phoenician contacts in Sardinia evident through imports as well as technology transfer in the local bronze industry, and technical affinities between 10th/9th century BC Sardinian and Iberian bronzes (Giardino 1995). In fact, although no contemporary wreck sites have yet been identified, the region boasts the largest corpus of prehistoric boat models in the Mediterranean at that time, including over one hundred Sardinian models and at least a score of Villanovan boat models (Depalmas 1996, Calcagno 2000, Lo Schiavo 2000). This paper summarises known evidence for indigenous watercraft in the region as recorded in surviving boat and ship representations, while highlighting particular methodological considerations in iconographic analysis.

The challenges and potentials of iconographic analysis

Throughout antiquity, watercraft have been represented in a variety of media and forms, including two-dimensional vase paintings, wall frescoes, engravings on rocks, seals and gems, and three-dimensional boat and ship models. The analysis of such material can be problematic, particularly because of the subjectivity inherent both in the creation of the representation and its subsequent reading or interpretation. Thus, we can find contrasting attitudes amongst researchers: while Casson has stated that "we are [...] perfectly entitled to take what we see in the ship-pictures at face-value, if necessary" (Casson 1986: 72), Basch suggests a contextual analysis: "Chaque cas exige un examen particulier, tenant compte de toutes les données techniques et culturelles du milieu dans lequel se situe le document" (Basch 1987: 38). For Basch, each type of representation requires its own particular interpretation which will be influenced by various factors ranging from the actual function of the image to its dimensions and medium. There is no golden rule to iconographic analysis; it often entails examining enigmatic images whose reliability may vary enormously. As McGrail puts it, "representations can be [...] invaluable, but they cannot be accepted without rigorous analysis and interpretation" (2001: 2).

Iconographic images can supplement shipwreck evidence in that they may offer information on constructional aspects and gear above the waterline which rarely survive in the archaeological record. Three-dimensional models may offer unique insights into the vessel's cross-section, with implications regarding the vessel's estimated performance. Admittedly, representations will rarely provide data about the construction method of the hull itself, unless details of the outer hull can be demonstrably interpreted as describing aspects of internal construction technique, such as vertical lines suggesting lashings, or marks suggesting nails or other fixtures (McGrail 2001: 2). Compounding the problem of interpretation, it is not always obvious what damage the artefacts have sustained over time which would distort reconstruction hypotheses. Particular chemical properties of painting pigments may lead to differential fading and subsequent loss of some diagnostic features. In all cases, correct interpretation depends on considered hypotheses about artistic conventions and conditions (Janni 1996: 31–37).

The most common hazards encountered in attempting hypothetical reconstructions of watercraft based on iconographic evidence come down to overly ambitious interpretations, where the imagination has been "allowed too much scope" (McGrail 2001: 2). On occasion, three-dimensional reconstructions of painted or engraved ship representations, replete with lines drawings, have been presented with no clear explanation as to how the vessel's transverse sections were extrapolated. Errors of interpretation have also appeared where researchers have been cavalier in their hypothetical restoration of fragmentary pieces, publishing drawings of ship representations as if the surviving artefacts were complete, without indicating damaged or missing portions. Finally, reconstruction drawings have incorporated anachronistic features (e.g., prehistoric vessels with transom sterns, which do not appear until the early medieval period). All these examples have been encountered in studies of proto-historic boat representations from the central Mediterranean region.

The archaeological evidence

There has been a heightened interest over the past two decades in archaeological research encompassing the central Mediterranean region at the turn of the second millennium BC. This has been due primarily to new or re-interpreted excavations as well as re-evaluations of past scholarship, and the advent of innovative provenance methodologies which provide new insights into the mechanisms of cross-cultural contacts. Copper oxhide ingots known from indigenous contexts in Sardinia, which had a significant copper industry of its own, have been determined to be foreign imports, while Aegean-type pottery in southern Italy has been identified as locally produced imitations (Vagnetti 1991). Such examples prompt questions on the mechanisms of local acculturation processes as well as the nature of long-distance exchange.

Nonetheless, the specifically maritime dimensions of this protohistoric period remain rather neglected. In fact, navigation in the region is attested since at least the early Neolithic period, with obsidian from the islands of Pantelleria, Lipari and Sardinia distributed throughout the central Mediterranean (Tykot 1996). A contemporary oak logboat recovered at the submerged Neolithic village site of La Marmotta (Lago di Bracciano, near Rome) confirms the existence of local water transport by this time; if the excavators' interpretations are correct, it might have featured side extensions which would have facilitated its use in coastal sea waters (Fugazzola Delpino et al 1993). Numerous logboats have been recovered from inland sites in northern Italy dating from the mid-third millennium BC onwards (Medas 1993); these include several which may have originally belonged to paired logboats, which theoretically could have managed coastal sea waters with their increased stability. The Capo

Graziano pottery found scattered offshore at Pignataro di Fuori (Lipari) in the southeastern Tyrrhenian area, would seem to indicate a mid-16th century BC shipwreck of a local vessel, although no hull remains or fittings were found (Parker 1992: 312). A hiatus of almost one thousand years separates this site from the seventh-century BC Giglio Campese A shipwreck, located off the northeast Tyrrhenian island of Giglio (Parker 1992: 192). Here, lashed hull construction puts this vessel within an increasingly well documented Archaic boat-building tradition in the region, while the mixed cargo of Etruscan, Greek and Phoenician materials attests to multi-cultural trading patterns.

The iconographic evidence

As the archaeological evidence of watercraft is inconclusive, we must turn to iconographic sources to garner information about indigenous watercraft in the central Mediterranean. The first coherent survey of iconographic sources for pre-Roman maritime imagery in the central Mediterranean region – albeit with a specific political agenda – appeared in Stella's book *L'Italia antica sul mare*, published in 1930. Since then finds of boat representations have been reported sporadically, occasionally gathered in survey volumes (Göttlicher 1978; Basch 1987). The following review of iconographic evidence intends to highlight the most representative examples, but also underscores the challenges in assessing their interpretative potential.

Several clay boat models found in association with the Neolithic Bracciano logboat mentioned above might constitute the earliest boat models in the central Mediterranean region – and indeed, the earliest known in southern Europe (cf. Marangou 1991). No examples of ship depictions have yet been found in the region dating to the Chalcolithic or Early Bronze Age. The hiatus lasts until the Late Bronze Age in Malta. Ship graffiti identified on the pilasters flanking a Hal Tarxien temple entrance have been dated generally to the mid-second millennium BC (Woolner 1957). Numerous depictions of ships, summarily executed and overlapping each other, would appear to represent a remarkable diversity of ship types as well as diversity in illustrators' skills. Their superimposition suggests a votive function: the action of engraving the ship being more important, symbolically, than the image of the ship itself. These forty or so images constitute the earliest known ship depictions from this southern region of the Mediterranean Sea.

Two vessels might be interpreted as sailing ships, one with furled sail and another with a vertical mast and square

in the central Mediterranean during the Italian Final Bronze Age. Based on the author's assessment, at least 170 examples of boat and ship representations have been found from this region, from the 14th to 8th centuries BC (Fig. 38.1; Calcagno 1998). These include graffiti, tomb and vase paintings, and the largest corpus of boat models (c. 140) from the prehistoric Mediterranean.

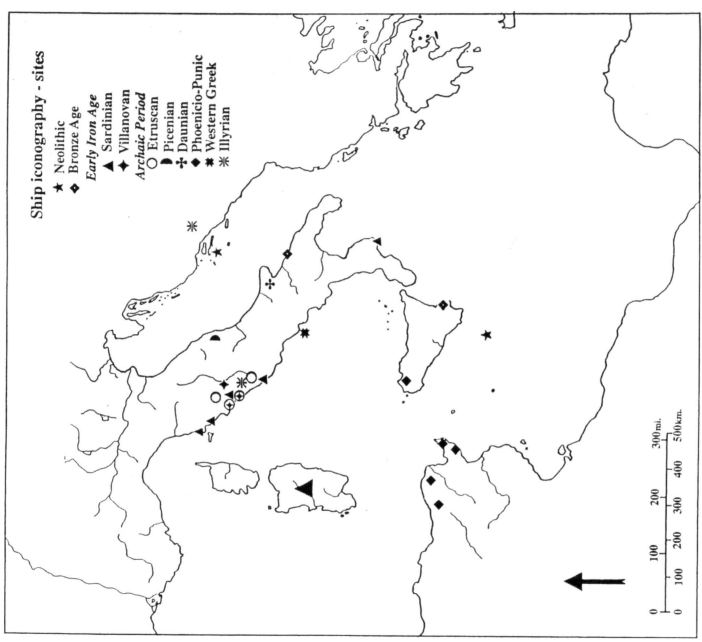

Fig. 38.1. Distribution of nautical iconography in the central Mediterranean region, ca. 14th – 7th centuries BC. Map by C. Calcagno, 1998.

sail (Woolner's n. 5 and 23). Other nautical details might be identified as sheets, steering oars, prow and stern ornaments, oars, deck lines and even possibly banks of oars. However, the hypothesis that many of these graffiti were made using shark teeth, which would produce double lines, illustrates the hazards of reading too much information into such sketchy depictions. Woolner's ident-

ification of several 'spoon-shaped' hulls as Egyptian ships reflects earlier beliefs in far-reaching Egyptian explorations during the Bronze Age. Other figures resembling primitive sausage-like boats with vertical stem and stern have been likened anachronistically to Mesopotamian vessel depictions (Woolner 1957). While Casson distinguishes between what he considers galleys propelled by

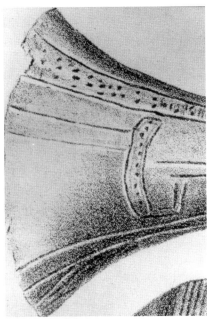

Fig. 38.2. Boat engraved on pedestal of a Thapsos vase, 13th century BC. Museo Archeologico di Siracusa, Sicily. Estimated length of boat image: c. 15 cm. After Basch 1987: 396, fig. 821 (from Monumenti Antichi 1985, Pl. 4a, fig. 7).

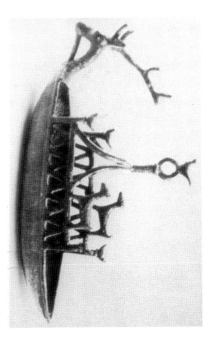

Fig. 38.3. Sardinian bronze boat model from Bultéi (Sassari). Museo di Cagliari, Sardinia. Length: 21 cm. After Basch 1987: 404, fig. 854 (from Göttlicher 1978, n. 424).

numerous oars, rounded hulls and merchantmen, he considers the majority as "too sketchy to yield significant information" (Casson 1986: 32). The real significance of these depictions lies in their apparent sudden appearance on an island where a complex megalithic culture had thrived for several millennia without leaving any ship-like depictions or models, despite its long-term dependence on transmarine contacts with the Sicilian mainland. These images were engraved only after the Hal Tarxien culture collapsed, and 'foreigners' arrived. Theories regarding the identities of these newcomers range from Mycenaeans to Sea Peoples, but the lack of diagnostically relevant cultural material at the site leaves this issue currently unresolved (Woolner 1957).

A very schematic vase graffito from Thapsos in south-eastern Sicily, dating to the 14th or 13th century, illustrates a simple watercraft (Fig. 38.2; Basch 1987: 396, fig. 821). The depiction is engraved on the flared stand supporting a broad cup, and consists of a long, gently upward-curving rectangle studded with ten or eleven round marks, perhaps representing oar-holes. The right-hand end has a vertical projection which turns back at a right angle towards midship; while interpretations regarding bow and stern vary, Basch favors the higher end as the stern (ibid). However, two additional vertical strokes, descending from the left end of the vessel to the lower edge of the stand, might be steering oars – thus identifying that end as the stern. While a structural interpretation of such a modest depiction is unwise, the image merits attention as it constitutes the earliest known representation of a boat from Sicily. The next earliest boat depictions in Sicily only appear in the Archaic period with the arrival of western Greek settlers.

We turn to Sardinia for the most remarkable representations of boats in the region. Over 100 bronze (and one iron) Sardinian boat models have been found on Sardinia, as well as a dozen on the Italian mainland and one in Greece (Fig. 38.3). This assemblage constitutes the largest corpus of ship models in the central Mediterranean – perhaps surprising, coming from an island with a traditional reputation for inward-looking isolationism (Calcagno 1998, 2000). Lilliu (1966) initially catalogued 62 models in his seminal study of the over 500 pieces of Sardinian bronze statuary, which incorporates local as well as Cypriot *cire-perdu* production methods. While this count has continued to be amended over the years, fewer than fifty models and model fragments can be assigned known findspots (cf. Göttlicher 1978: 70–76; Depalmas 1996; Lo Schiavo 2000). Of the provenanced examples, ten were recovered from continental Villanovan/Etruscan contexts, and one was recently found at the Archaic sanctuary of Hera Lacinia near Crotone, Calabria – the first found in a Western Greek context (Spadea 1994). Another found at the 6th-century BC sanctuary of Poseidon near the Corinth isthmus, may well have been commissioned by a Sardinian visitor (Basch 1987: fig. 496.3). Numerous other models from private collections illustrated in occasional exhibition catalogues bring the number of known Sardinian models to at least 104 (personal estimate: Calcagno 2000). Nevertheless, uncertainties regarding the authenticity of unprovenienced models in private collections should be borne in mind in assessing the corpus as a whole (Lo Schiavo 2000: 118–9).

Virtually all surviving models are made of bronze, with two exceptions that incorporate iron fittings (Lo Schiavo 1981; Göttlicher 1978 n. 421). The ubiquitous animal motif frequently depicts a fairly stylised bull's head, or less frequently a horned deer. A variety of creatures sometimes populate the gunwales, while birds often perch on top of the ring from which the object was likely hung. Most models are stereotypically similar, so much so that several have been catalogued twice as distinct examples (e.g., Göttlicher 1978: n.s 419, 432). Gras

(1980: 527) distinguishes two hull types: a longer, 'semi-lunate' convex type, and a more angular type with concave stem and stern. Some would distinguish narrow, naval vessels from broader merchantmen, while others regard the flat-bottomed examples as riverine craft (Lo Schiavo 1981), apparently overlooking the practical requirement of a flat bottom allowing the model to stand without support.

The majority of boat models are sporadic finds, with little information about their specific contexts. Several were reported retrieved from tombs, hanging along the walls of the nuragic temple vestibule, as well as from sanctuaries, prompting their identification as *ex-votos*. Many boat models are equipped with some sort of hanging device, such as a single or double arch joining the two boat sides topped by a ring, implying they were intended to be used not simply as boat representations, but perhaps as lamps or incense-burners, although none reveals traces of such use. Ritual functions have been suggested: they might symbolise the boat of the dead, carrying the soul of the deceased from this world to the next (Lilliu 1966: 16; Johnstone 1988: 142).

The models' date of manufacture was originally estimated to range between the 8th and 5th centuries BC, based solely on stylistic criteria. However, as Sardinian bronzes reflect metallurgical abilities acquired through Cypriot contacts with the island already during the 11th and 10th centuries BC, the models' production date could conceivably shift to a considerably earlier date (Calcagno 1998: 56). It is feasible that the models arrived on the Italian mainland during the 8th century BC if not earlier, based on reassessments of local deposit chronologies (Gras 1985: 533–5; Serra Ridway 1986). The issue remains contested, mainly because models found in Sardinian sites come from unstratified contexts, while those from the Italian mainland may well have arrived (or been deposited) decades if not centuries after their production as heirlooms. The models' geographical distribution, concentrated in the northwest and central part of Sardinia and at Italian mainland sites not far from the sea, attests to active trans-Tyrrhenian exchanges. Southern Sardinia has yielded only a single boat model, despite the archaeological evidence of significant maritime exchanges of the southern Sardinian inhabitants with eastern Mediterranean venturers since the Late Bronze Age.

At least three Sardinian vessels feature columns placed in the centre of the hull, which have been interpreted as masts (e.g. Fig. 38.3). However, none of these boat models have preserved any traces of the rig, such as a mast-step or tabernacle, rigging and gunwale rigging attachments, a crow's nest, yards or sail. Furthermore, none displays a projecting keel, an important structural feature of a true seagoing sailing vessel. The zig-zag structures along the gunwales of several vessels could conceivably be interpreted as protective spray-deflectors, indicating sea-going capabilities (Basch 1987: 404–5). The author hesitates to see any of these few examples as representing true masted

sailing vessels. Nevertheless it is quite feasible that temporary sailing systems to harness the wind were devised on simple craft such as these; these systems would not require permanent fittings on the hulls themselves, and could do with less than ideal sailing hull shape, as amply documented in the ethnographic record (McGrail 1987: 218). The vessels are all hollow, with only one example featuring anything remotely resembling a partial deck or deck cover. Bonino (1995) is keen to interpret these as sewn vessels: he describes one protome as bound to the stem by cordage, and identifies longitudinal hull protrusions as representing external sewing (rather than simply rope fenders). Others see the preponderance of boat models as generally reflecting a high level of shipwrightry (Lo Schiavo 1981). Realistically, the models do not yield sufficient information to determine constructional methodologies. What is more telling is that these boat models constitute over 20% of all known Sardinian bronzes – at the very least suggesting a symbolically high significance of maritime activities for this culture.

Only a few internal rivers have ever been navigable in Sardinia; the Cabras Lagoon near Olbia was once more extensive, and has yielded a continuing tradition of reed rafts that goes back several centuries. It is likely that these island people, rather than exploiting their meager rivers, used the surrounding sea as a highway between Sardinian territories, as well as a means to reach the Italian mainland. The evident maritime exchanges with receptive trading partners across the Tyrrhenian since at least the 10th/9th centuries BC, could have been accomplished with some form of rowed or paddled vessel perhaps fitted with simple sails, presumably crossing at the northern point of the Tyrrhenian via the islands of the Tuscan archipelago and Corsica. This could involve a maximum sea crossing of just over 30 nm. between Elba and the Corsican coast, though a more favourable current pattern might have been exploited across a wider distance roughly at the height of the Argentario Peninsula. At any rate, the maritime distribution of obsidian from southwest Sardinia and Sicilian Channel islands throughout the Neolithic Tyrrhenian amply illustrates seafaring capabilities even in technologically 'primitive' times (Tykot 1996).

Generally contemporary with the Sardinian boat models and often compared with them, the twenty or so boat models found in Iron Age Villanovan contexts in Latium, Tuscany and Emilia-Romagna range between ca. 1000 to ca. 700 BC (Fig. 38.4). Most were found in burials, echoing the Sardinian practice, although once again few come from well-stratified findspots. Göttlicher (1978) provides the nearest to complete catalogue of boat models attributed to Iron Age mainland Italy; to these can be added three *vasi 'a barchetta'* from Bisenzio dated to the second half of 9th century BC (Fugazzola Delpino 1984: 140–1, figs. 54A, B and C), and a couple of poorly provenienced examples in private collections (Chamay 1993: 112 (n.s 23 and 24). All are made of terracotta or impasto with the

Fig. 38.4. Villanovan clay boat model from Tarquinia. Museo Nazionale, Tarquinia. Length: 17.7 cm. After Basch 1987: 401, fig. 843 (from Montelius 1904, Pl. 280 n. 7).

exception of one bronze vessel, and most feature some graffito decoration. While some container-vessels interpreted as boats, have only minimal boat attributes in terms of elongated, double-ended shape, the external fish designs and wave patterns do suggest a maritime context. Others incorporating small dishes at one or both ends might reflect a ritual use, for oil or incense, as lamps or burners (although diagnostic signs of burning or of contents were not recorded). The 'hulls' do not point to any specific boat types—hide, plank or dugout—although it could be posited that they more resemble river or lake craft than seagoing vessels. None displays any indication of a mast or mast-step, perhaps to avoid interfering with their presumed function as containers. Extensions beneath several models could conceivably be protruding keels, but might be better interpreted as supports. Similarly, details such as a pierced forefoot or piercings along the gunwales likely relate to the objects being tied for suspension or pulling, rather than nautical features.

Duck-like figureheads with upturned beaks are a common feature of most Villanovan boat models, recalling images of Urnfield and Hallstatt bird motifs (Götticher 1978, Basch 1987: 401–3) and generating discussions on the nature of trans-alpine influences in peninsular Italy at the time. One example is exceptionally adorned with a birdhead on either end, and two sport horned birdheads. These Villanovan examples have also drawn parallels with the 12th-century BC Skyros stirrup jar painting, which also features a bird-headed vessel (Basch 1987: 403). While birdheads and bird features appear as boat decorations across the length of Europe, there is little need to understand the phenomenon as a consequence of long-distance diffusion. Indeed birds are significant to the maritime environment for navigational as well as symbolic reasons; such imagery surely reflects more nuanced cultural affinities.

Evidence of cultural continuity from the Villanovan to Etruscan phases of later Iron Age Italy, includes the custom of placing boat models in graves, which continues into the full Etruscan period. The corpus of boat and ship representations grows considerably as the Etruscans establish themselves as a maritime power controlling the Tyrrhenian Sea in the face of Phoenician and Western Greek venturers (Paglieri 1960; Cristofani 1983; Hagy 1986). Etruscan vessels are easily differentiated from their Aegean counterparts, consistently featuring distinctive well-rounded hull profiles, downward-jutting cutwaters and crows' nests. Most significantly, the advent of the sail in the central Mediterranean seems convincingly documented only from late 8th century BC Etruria (oenochoe vase paintings: Basch 1987: 409, fig. 870), as the author remains unconvinced that hanging devices on earlier Sardinian boat models are intended to represent masts.

Fig. 38.5. Clay boat model(?) from Punta Le Terrare (Egnazia). Museo Nazionale Archeologico di Egnazia, Apulia. Est. length: ca. 18 cm. Photograph by C. Calcagno.

To complete our rapid central Mediterranean survey, we turn briefly to the Adriatic. Evidence of long-distance maritime exchanges in the southern and northern Adriatic region are well documented during the centuries spanning the turn of the second millennium BC, based on non-indigenous artefact distributions and Aegean-type pottery technologies adopted by locals in the Ionian and Apulian areas and in the Lower Po Valley (Vagnetti 1991). One boat representation might have survived from the area: a vessel recovered at Punta Le Terrare in Apulia, near the natural harbour of Brindisi which has yielded significant evidence of Aegean exchanges into the 11th-century BC (Fig. 38.5). The clay vessel is rounded at both ends and divided internally into two longitudinal compartments, an unusual feature which could indicate a double logboat. If it is indeed a boat model, this 13th-century BC vessel would constitute the only known Bronze Age boat representation from the southern Adriatic region. Nautical depictions next appear only six centuries later, farther up the Adriatic coast in the Picenian and Daunian regions (beyond the remit of this paper; Nava 1988; Bonino 1995).

Discussion

In searching for patterns and trends in the iconographic evidence for central Mediterranean watercraft of the Bronze Age – Iron Age transition period, we must acknowledge that large areas are devoid of any boat depictions over considerable time periods. The northern Adriatic coast lacks ship depictions; a single Sardinian boat model constitutes the only known example from southwest Italy, while the heavily frequented coastal area in around Naples has only yielded a handful of models from a later period. Sicily and Malta, at the crossroads of trans-Mediterranean maritime ventures, have a few sketchy Late Bronze Age examples between the two of them. Only the area of central Tyrrhenian Italy features a significant number of boat models and paintings; meanwhile Sardinia, long touted as an inward-looking island, boasts the largest corpus of boat imagery from anywhere in the Mediterranean. And while groups from the Levant traveled through the central Mediterranean to western territories for centuries, the earliest ship representations from their bases in North Africa and western Sicily only date to the mid-first millennium BC (Longstary 1990). While the distribution may well be distorted by the serendipitous patterns of local excavation, it is also partly determined by the distinctive functions (votive, funerary or other) that boat and ship imagery played within each culture in the region, which actually may have little to do with the utilitarian functions of their referents.

A potential bias in iconographic sources affecting the corpus of surviving images is that ship depictions are less likely to be representative of the range of vessels being used at the time (McGrail 2001: 2–3). Smaller, local-style vessels might not be commemorated in images, or at least not as frequently or with as much interest in detail, as large, more impressive, and novel ships. During the Final Bronze Age in the central Mediterranean region, however, it appears that simple indigenous craft were primarily represented even though 'foreign' vessels would surely have been witnessed over centuries of maritime exchanges. The intended audience for these depictions, at any rate, understood and utilised the images as symbolic paradigms. A ship representation ('re-presentation') is by definition an abstraction: essential features are distilled into a combination of what is known and what is seen, in order to render the image recognizable. The real value contained in such nautical images reflects on the cognitive world of their creators – the symbolic and metaphoric content perhaps greater than the technological information we attempt to glean (Le Bon 1995). Extrapolating nautical information from such a resource pushes the limits on hypothesis-building for scholars attempting theoretical reconstructions of early vessels, even for those well versed in methods of iconographic analysis and familiar with the relevant archaeological record. Without attempting to derive lines drawings from such evidence, as some scholars imaginatively do, we can nonetheless acknowledge the presence of distinctive maritime cultures in the central Mediterranean region, interacting within a shared koiné of maritime connections, whose nautically-related symbolic belief systems merit further examination.

Acknowledgements

I am grateful to have the opportunity to contribute to this volume dedicated to Prof. Seán McGrail, who supervised my doctoral research and whose holistic approach to maritime studies has enhanced my own perspectives in fundamental ways. I thank Dr. H. Tzalas and Prof. L. Basch for their kind permission to reproduce images from *Le musée imaginaire de la marine antique*, as well as the Museo Nazionale Archeologico di Egnazia for permission to photograph its holdings. My paper's title pays indirect tribute to Mary Helm's 1988 book *Ulysses' Sail: an ethnographic odyssey of power, knowledge, and geographical distance*, Princeton.

References

Basch, L., 1987, *Le musée imaginaire de la marine antique*. Hellenic Institute for the Preservation of Nautical Tradition. Athens.

Bonino, M., 1995, Sardinia, Villanovan and Etruscan crafts between the X and VIII c. BC. In H. Tzalas (ed), *TROPIS III: Third International Symposium on Ship Construction in Antiquity*, 83–98. Hellenic Institute for the Preservation of Nautical Tradition. Athens.

Calcagno, C., 1998, *Aspects of seafaring and trade in the Central Mediterranean Region, ca. 1200–800 B.C.* Unpublished D.Phil. dissertation, University of Oxford.

Calcagno, C., 2000, Island in the Stream: Sardinia's evolving role along maritime trade routes during the Italian Final Bronze Age. In *Schutz des Kulturerbes unter Wasser. Veränderunger europäischer Lebenskultur durch Fluß- und Seehandel. Beiträge zum Internationalen Kongreß für Unterwasserarchäologie (IKUWA '99). 18–21.2.1999 in Sassnitz auf Rügen*, 113–120. Lübstorf.

Casson, L., 1986, *Ships and Seamanship in the Ancient World.* Princeton.

Chamay, J. (ed.), 1993, *Art of the Italic Peoples from 3000 to 300 BC.* Geneva and Naples.

Cristofani, M.,1983, *Gli etruschi del mare.* Milano.

Depalmas, A., 1996, Les nacelles en bronze de la Sardaigne. Problèmes de reconstruction des archétypes. *Préhistoire antropologie méditerranéennes* 5: 39–55.

Fugazzola Delpino, M. A., 1984, *La cultura villanoviana. Guida ai materiali della prima età del Ferro nel museo di Villa Giulia.* Rome.

Fugazzola Delpino, M. A., G. D'Eugenio and A. Pessina, 1993, 'La Marmotta' (Anguillara Sabazia, RM): scavi 1989. Un abitato perilacustre di età neolitica. *Bullettino di Paletnologia Italiana* 84 (N. Ser. III): 181–342.

Giardino, C., 1995, *Il Mediterraneo Occidentale fra XIV e VIII secolo a.C. Cerchie minerarie e metallurgiche (The West Mediterranean between the 14th and 8th Centuries B.C. Mining and Metallurgical spheres).* Oxford.

Göttlicher, A., 1978, *Materialen für ein Corpus der Schiffsmodelle im Alterum.* Mainz am Rhein.

Gras, M., 1985, *Trafics tyrrhéniens archaïques.* Paris and Rome.

Hagy, J., 1986, 800 Years of Etruscan Ships. *International Journal of Nautical Archaeology* 15.3: 221–250.

Janni, P., 1996, *Il mare degli antichi*. Bari.

Johnstone, P., 1988, *The Sea-Craft of Prehistory*. New York and London.

Laviosa, C., 1983, Navigazione micenea dal mito alle testimonianze archeologiche. In *Magna grecia e mondo miceneo: Atti. XXII Convegno di Studi sulla Magna Grecia, Taranto, 7–11 ottobre 1982*, 321–335. Taranto.

Le Bon. E., 1995, Ancient ship graffiti: symbol and content. In O. Crumlin-Pedersen and B. Munch Thye (eds), *The Ship as Symbol in Prehistoric and Medieval Scandinavia. Papers given at the International Research Seminar at the Danish National Museum, Copenhagen 5–7 May 1994*, 172–179. Copenhagen.

Lilliu, G., 1966, *Sculture della Sardegna nuragica*. Verona.

Lo Schiavo, F., 1981, Osservazioni sul problema dei rapporti fra Sardegna ed Etruria in età nuragica. In *L'Etruria mineraria. Atti del XII convegno di studi etruschi ed italici, Firenze-Populonia-Piombino, 16–20.6.1979*, 299–314. Florence.

Lo Schiavo, F., E. Macnamara and L. Vagnetti, 1985, Late Cypriot imports to Italy and their influence on local bronzework. *Papers of the British School at Rome* 53: 1–71.

Lo Schiavo, F., 1995, Cyprus and Sardinia in the Mediterranean: Trade Routes Toward the West. In V. Karageorghis and D. Michaelides (eds), *Cyprus and the Sea. Proceedings of the International Conference (Nicosia, 25–6 Sept. 1993)*, 45–59. Nicosia.

Lo Schiavo, F., 2000, I Sardi sul mare: le navicelle nuragiche. In P. Bernardini et al (ed), *ΜΑΧΗ: La battaglia del Mare Sardonio. Studi e ricerche*, 117–132. Cagliari and Oristano.

Longerstay, M., 1990, Représentations de navires archaïques en Tunisie du Nord. Contributions à la chronologie des haouanet. *Karthago* 22: 33–44.

Marangou, C., 1991, Maquettes d'imbarcation: les débuts. In R. Laffineur (ed), *Thalassa. L'Egée préhistorique et la mer*, vol. 3: 21–42. Liège.

McGrail, S., 1987, *Ancient Boats in Northwestern Europe. The archaeology of water transport to AD 1500*. London and New York.

McGrail, S., 2001, *Boats of the World. From the Stone Age to Medieval Times*. Oxford.

Medas, S., 1993, Imbarcazioni e navigazione preistorica nel Mediterraneo. *Bollettino di archeologia subacquea*, 1.0 (Dec. 1993): 103–147.

Montelius, O., 1904, *La civilisation primitive d'Italie depuis l'introduction des métaux*. Stockholm.

Nava, M. L., 1988, *Le stele della Daunia. Sculture antropomorfe della Puglia protostorica dalle scoperte di Silvio Ferri agli studi più recenti*. Milano.

Paglieri, S., 1960, Origine e diffusione delle navi etrusco-italiche. *Studi Etruschi* 28 (serie II): 209–231.

Pallottino, M. 1991, *A History of Earliest Italy*. London.

Parker, A. J., 1992, *Ancient Shipwrecks of the Mediterranean and the Roman Provinces*. Oxford.

Peroni, R. (ed), 1979, *Il bronzo finale in Italia. Atti XXI Riunione Scientifica dell'Istituto Italiano per la Preistoria e Protostoria*, Vol. XXI. Florence.

Peroni, R., 1994, *Introduzione alla protostoria italiana*. Roma and Bari.

Pomey, P., 1985, Mediterranean Sewn Boats in Antiquity, In S. McGrail and E. Kentley (eds), *Sewn Plank Boats*, 35–48. BAR I.S. 276. Oxford.

Serra Ridgway, F. R. 1986, Nuragic bronzes in the British Museum. In M. Balmuth (ed), *Studies in Sardinian Archaeology II. Sardinia in the Mediterranean*, 85–101. Ann Arbor: University of Michigan Press.

Sherratt, S., and Sherratt, A., 1993, The growth of the Mediterranean economy in the first millennium BC, *World Archaeology* 24: 361–378.

Spadea, R., 1994, Il tesoro di Hera, *Bollettino d'Arte* 88: 137.

Stella, L.A., 1930, *L'Italia antica sul mare*. Milano.

Tykot, R. H., 1996, Obsidian Procurement and Distribution in the Central and Western Mediterranean. *Journal of Mediterranean Archaeology* 9: 39–82.

Vagnetti, L. and F. Lo Schiavo, 1989, Late Bronze Age long distance trade in the Mediterranean: the role of the Cypriots. In E. Peltenburg (ed), *Early Society in Cyprus*, 217–243. Edinburgh.

Vagnetti, L., 1991, L'encadrement chronologique et les formes de la présence égéenne en Italie. In J. de la Genière (ed), *Epéios et Philoctète en Italie. Données archéologiques et traditions légendaires. Actes du Colloque Internationale du Centre de Recherches Archéologiques de l'Université de Lille III (Lille, 23–24 Nov. 1987)*, 9–20. Naples.

Wachsmann, S., 1981, The ships of the Sea Peoples. *International Journal of Nautical Archaeology* 10: 187–220.

Woolner, D., 1957, Graffiti of ships at Tarxien, Malta. *Antiquity* 31: 60–67.

39 Western European design boat building in Buton (Sulawesi, Indonesia): a "sequence of operations" approach (SOA)

Daniel Vermonden

When western European explorers first encountered the Pacific islands, they were surprised to discover that the islands were already inhabited. It was subsequently established that the islanders were speaking languages from a single linguistic family called Austronesian. This single linguistic family occupies a huge maritime area, spreading from Madagascar to the Easter Islands, largely occupying the zone between the Tropics (Blust 1995).

In this maritime environment, canoes and boats are an important element of a society's material culture and after some time scholars developed an interest in canoes and boats of the region. Diffusionist studies (Haddon and Hornell 1936–8: 57–85; Doran 1981: 89–94; Neyret 1974; Nooteboom 1932) compiled exhaustive catalogues of boat types and features, covering part or the entire Austronesian area, in order to draw repartition maps and determine migratory patterns and paths. Besides the problem of interpreting present distributions of traits for reconstructing past events, these studies relied upon a conception of the boat as a set of material features (e.g. the number of outriggers, rig type). Typological studies (e.g. Gibson-Hill 1950; Horridge 1985, 1986a) adopt a similar concept of boats (but without the goal of historical reconstruction).

Other ethnographic studies avoided this restrictive concept of boats by tackling the subject in different ways. One approach took into consideration the whole process of boat building rather than just addressing the component features (e.g. Petersen 2000: 81–116; Horridge 1979a: 16–25; Barnes 1985; Feinberg 1988: 32–86; Gladwin 1970: 65–124; Leblic 2000; Nicolaisen and Damgård-Sørensen 1991: 33–81). However, such descriptions align with the classic approach to the study of technology in the sense that they only take into account a limited dimension of the process at work, focusing exclusively on the interaction between tools and the material. Therefore, boat building appears only as a material transformation of a matter into a technical object. Non-directly observable elements (e.g. the actor's choices and representations) are left unexplored, facilitating a view of boat building as simply a 'machine' executing a pre-installed program. In addition, some observable elements are left aside, considered as non-technical (e.g. the social configuration of the work or actions that do not aim to transform the material). Therefore, this approach assumes that technology can and must be studied in isolation, "purified" from certain elements. This results in constructing two dichotomised entities, a dehumanised technology and a dematerialised society, that distracts from understanding the processes at work (Latour 1997; Dobres 2000). Rather, the social dimension should be considered as an intrinsic part of technology, in order to take into account technological choices and local considerations with regard to what determines the nature of the artefacts.

A second approach addresses the "non-technical" aspects of boat building left aside in the first approach (e.g. Horridge 1986b; Tilley 2002; Pelly 1997; Southon 1995: 93–128; Barlow and Lipset 1997; Marshall Carucci 1995; Munn 1977). Such studies make it clear that a boat is certainly not limited to its functional aspect as an instrument of transport. They promote an 'emic' understanding of boats, in exploring the complex networks of symbols, metaphors and exchanges relating to them. "Production becomes a performance through which persons and objects create and define each other" (Tilley 2002: 27) and "through creating, exchanging and ordering a world of artefacts people create an ordering of the world of social relations" (Tilley 2002: 28). Such an approach also makes it clear that societies should not be conceived as homogeneous units, as different meanings, even contradictory ones, can coexist within a society. However, these studies recognise the role of material culture in social construction at the expense of the work of material transformation. A further limitation lies in an emphasis on local specificities, giving the impression that local societies operate as isolated units.

In the wake of Malinowski's seminal work on the Trobriand canoe (1989 [1922]: 164–205), there are studies that combine the two approaches outlined above, some of them maintaining a dichotomy between techniques and rituals (Barnes 1996: 201–249; Horridge 1987; Sather 2000; Feinberg 1995), while others, like Malinowski, adopt a more integrated approach (e.g. Liebner 1996: 4–17; Horridge 1979b: 4–23; Arnaud 2000; Ivanoff 2000). However, these descriptions leave the impression that local societies are bounded and relatively homogeneous entities with no capacity for variations in practices and interpretations. This idea that society operates as a static 'block' is problematic since technical activities are also clearly an arena of social differentiation, competition and integration.

An alternative approach is proposed here. It aims to combine the two previous ones outlined above, while, at the same time to overcome some of the limitations concerning the conception of society and be more sensitive to the actors' perspective on their work, with the aim of offering a more original perspective on change. A boat is the result of a succession of operations that can be divided into different stages (e.g. wood acquisition, keel shaping and assemblage). These stages make up the structure of my analytic framework. The 'sequence of operations' approach (SOA) or 'chaîne opératoire',[1] consists in describing all the operations of the process, taking into account the following characteristics:

1   The operations may be socially distributed and require the acquisition of specific knowledge and skills.
2   Operations may present different alternatives.
3   All the operations implemented are not observable, for example the evaluation of a shape or the motivation behind a measurement. Access to these internal operations is possible through conversations and interviews with the actors.
4   The operations, external (observable) or internal, are not only motivated by what we would consider 'technical' purpose. The motivations of the operations may refer to associations established locally between heterogeneous elements.
5   Operations and the related associations occurring in the context of boat building activity may also occur in the context of other activities.
6   Operations and the related associations may come from different origins and historical strata.

Therefore, for each stage, the SOA describes the different operations that are implemented and their social distribution, and explores the possible variants for a single or different boat type, the process of knowledge and skills acquisition, the motivations behind operations, and the possible associations established between heterogeneous elements, the occurrences of similar operations and associations locally in other activities and, beyond, in other culturally related societies.

This approach allows us to overcome some limits of the previous ones and to bring the study of technical activities to new territories. First, it prevents the a priori distinction between techniques and society but rather invites an exploration of the dialectic relation between technical activities and the continuous constitution of society. Indeed, within the present framework, boat building is no longer simply a transformation of a material into a commodity within a society. Technical activities do not exist outside society but, at the same time, participate in configuring society and are configured by society. On one hand, technical activities involve social relations and cultural representations that participate to shape the process at work and the final product. On the other hand, technical activities like boatbuilding are arenas where knowledge (including cultural represent-ations), skills, social roles and social positions are acquired, enacted, reaffirmed and contested (Dobres 2000: 96–163). Therefore, describing the boatbuilding process according to the framework presented above, consists not only in analysing a specific activity (boatbuilding) but simultaneously, consists in an analysis of the process of the continuous constitution of society.

Second, the SOA prevents us from considering local societies (consciously or not) as bounded wholes by trying to identify the origin of the different elements occurring in the activity or, at least, to point to similarities. In this respect, the local activity and, thence, the local society, appear as blends of elements coming from different origins and belonging to different historical strata.

Third, the SOA offers an alternative framework to the dichotomy between techniques and society for addressing the question of change. One's approach to technical activities is not without consequence to one's conception of the change process. Adopting an approach that dis-tinguishes between techniques and society seriously constrains the understanding of the process at work: change is inherent to each entity separately and/or the result of the interaction between the two entities. Within this framework, efficiency improvement is the major criteria for interpreting technological change, complying with the classic view of a natural, linear evolutionary path to technical improvement (see Pfaffenberger 1992 for a critique of this view). This is problematic. Lemonnier (1993), for example, showed how innovation adoption or rejection are social choices depending on cultural values and social relations rather than on the technology itself. The SOA is able to consider these choices as it takes into account the actors' motivations behind operations. More-over, the present approach acknowledges an understanding of change in another way: through the exploration of the complex relations between boat building and other local activities. Indeed, the upholding of specific operations in the sequence despite the availability of an alternative, may be related to its occurrence in other local contexts. Finally, this exploration of the relations existing between boat building and other local activities (e.g. skills, idioms, operations) provides an original perspective on change as a complex recombination of heterogeneous elements.

Boat building in Buton: a "sequence of operations" (SOA) approach

Two types of planked boat are built and used on Buton island (Southeast Sulawesi, Indonesia): the lambo[2] and

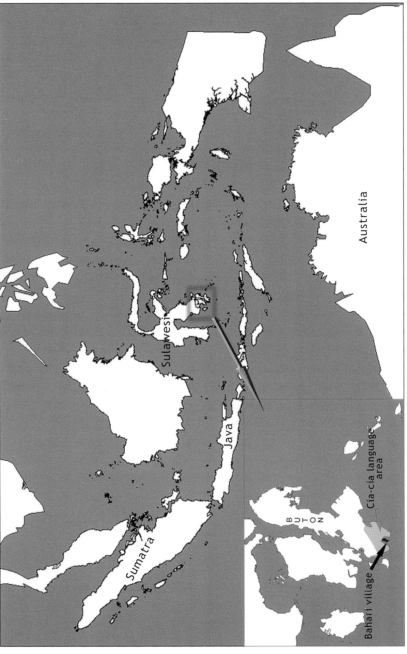

Fig. 39.1. Map of Indonesia and location of Buton Island (produced by the author).

motoro[3] (Fig. 39.1). *Lambo* (Fig. 39.2) is one of the names for a type of sailing boat that has been operating throughout East Indonesia from at least the 1930s.[4] Its distinctive features are a straight keel, a counter stern and fore-and-aft sails. The length usually varies from 8 to 14 m. It is used for trading and fishing expeditions, although less and less so nowadays, as traders prefer to use national ferries, while engine-powered boats (*motoro*) are preferred for shark fishing expeditions (Fig. 39.3).

The data presented here were gathered during an

Fig. 39.3. A Butonese motoro *(Photo by Daniel Vermonden).*

Fig. 39.2. A Butonese lambo *(Photo by Daniel Vermonden).*

ethnographic fieldwork study mostly conducted in Bahari, a coastal village of around 2000 inhabitants situated at the southern edge of Buton Island. Local production consists of agriculture on poor lime soils, sea trading, as well as coastal and offshore fishing. Before the thirties, boat building activity in Bahari was limited to outrigger canoes. Locals say that the first boatbuilder learnt *lambo* building from relatives in a neighbouring village, where people are mostly of noble origin (being Buton). The exact scenario of the emergence of *lambo* boat building in Buton in general and in Bahari in particular, is unknown. What is known is that locals in Buton, at least in the region of the main city of Baubau (the former centre of the Sultanate), were already building planked boats before they 'adopted' the *lambo* type. We also know that, by the end of the 19th century, Australian pearling luggers, very similar in shape to *lambo*, were coming to Buton to pick up Butonese divers and then heading to the Banda Islands (Ligtvoet 1878).

Nowadays, local boatbuilders build *motoro*. *Motoro* appeared around ten years ago as an 'evolution' of *lambo*. The hull shape is narrower and a cabin covers the hull and the counter stern. However, besides the difference in shape and the absence of sails, the building process is very similar to *lambo*.

Acquiring a boat

Until recently the only way for Bahari villagers to acquire a boat was to build one. Now it is possible to buy a boat (new or second hand) as shark fishing provides cash and shark fin buyers (*bos*) supply credit facilities to fishermen. The choice is not limited to determining the best quality-price ratio. For example, in Bahari, two *motoro* boats were ordered from the boat builder La Ndole,[5] while cheaper boats could have been purchased or ordered elsewhere. It must be appreciated that a boat's safety and good fortune is partly dependant upon the manner in which it is built and on who builds it. La Ndole became the most famous carpenter in the village after transforming an old *lambo* into Bahari's most lucrative *motoro*.

Buying a boat also necessitates special precautions. The buyer assesses the shape because "boats and canoes are similar to women: if you don't like the shape, you are already tired before beginning working". The buyer also checks the dimensions that must fit with his own body or wife's body. These remarks illustrate that boats in Buton are not ordinary commodities.

Wood acquisition

Wood is the basic material of both the *lambo* and *motoro* boats. There are two ways to acquire wood: to buy ready shaped timbers or to fell the trees and cut them up yourself. If the boat is to be built in Bahari, wood is usually purchased from the teak plantation nearby. The other choice is to move to a place where wood is abundant, accessible and cheaper, whether in Buton or further afield. Sometimes migration to the wood source can result in the establishment of a new village.

A variety of different types of wood are suitable for boatbuilding but teak (*Tectona grandis*) is preferred for the hull planks, if available and affordable. Carpenters have an extensive knowledge of wood; over 100 vernacular names for wood species were recorded. This knowledge is built up progressively from childhood when accompanying parents in the gardens and in the forest. Apprenticeship relies both on personal attentive observation of tree characteristics (e.g. colour, stem and leaf shape, bark texture and fruit), practical experience of woodwork, and questions to adults, especially for learning the names. Active woodwork can begin at adolescence, helping one's father make fences, a garden hut, houses or boats. If motivated apprenticeship continues. Motivation is of utmost importance: nobody is forced to specialise in boatbuilding if he does not like it.

Yet technical knowledge and skills are not enough. To the people of Bahari, wood is not just an ordinary material, it is a living matter that interacts with humans. Wood holds the potential of becoming 'human-like' through a process modelled on human procreation. Its manipulation deserves special precautions as woodwork also presents a potential danger that can provoke illness or death. First, one must choose an auspicious moment to fell a tree. If the carpenter lacks this knowledge, he will consult an experienced woodworker. It is also wise to pay attention to dreams, the so-called "secret teacher".

Once in the forest, the carpenter selects the appropriate trees, taking into account several elements, notably proximity to the river for ease of transportation, available space and absence of obstacles for trunks once felled. Trunks from garden clearing are also a potential source of boatbuilding wood. Axe handle measurements are important in determining the best trees in the forest: "if one brings a bad tool [meaning dimensions not fitting with one's body], one will not see the appropriate trees".

Before felling the tree, the carpenter asks the (invisible) inhabitants of the tree to leave "because you have enjoyed this tree for long. It is now my turn to enjoy it". On another occasion the carpenter announced to the tree: "I'm not felling you without reason; hopefully you will become human". This is similar to what Munn (1977) noted about canoe building in another Austronesian society, that of the Trobriand Islands in the Solomon Seas: humans give life to immobile trees by transforming them into fast canoes through human action.

In storing wood, the original orientation must be respected: peak up. Orientation will also be respected when the vessel is assembled, again on pain of illness or death. Given all these dangers involved with handling wood, it is not surprising that many village notables in Bahari are former carpenters. One's ability to manipulate wood ensures that you hold the necessary basic knowledge to ensure good fortune.

Daniel Vermonden

Keel shaping and assemblage

Although keels were made of three pieces (plus bow and stern) until recently, a one-piece keel is now preferred (Horridge 1979a: 16). Craftsmen shape the timbers using a large machete (*golo*) and an adze (*bhingku*). These boat tools are widely used in other woodworking activities, like house making. Each craftsman owns his own tools that are adapted to his preferences: model, weight, size. Another similarity between canoe and house building concerns the attention craftsmen pay to measurements. A widespread measurement for the keel length is an odd multiple of the owner's wife's foot. Correct measurements ensure the boat's future safety and good fortune. Ideally, measurements are best taken from measurements on the woman's body, conceived as recipient of the local family's good fortune. This idea relates to the local concept of human reproduction considering that all the elements of the future baby are already contained in the man's semen; the woman's role consists of nurturing this semen in her belly so the semen can become a child. The recommendation to take boat measurements from a woman's body is an extension of this conception of the role of women in human procreation, associating women with development.

This conception of women as ensuring the household's good fortune has concrete consequences on the relation between husband and wife. One example is a boat owner needs to maintain a harmonious relation with his wife in order to ensure the success of his boats. Marital disputes or divorce could lead to a decrease in the boat's success.

The assemblage of the keel piece(s) is a moment of special importance, the first step of creating a human-like boat. The keel pieces are fastened with mortise-and-tenon joints. This task is undertaken by a specialist (*pande*) whose expertise also extends to house building. On the chosen auspicious day and in the presence of the carpenter and the boat owner and his wife, the *pande* sits in front of his mouth, a white cloth enveloping some valuable materials. He murmurs a spell and puts this small piece of white cloth inside the mortise. He then casts a spell on another white cloth and puts it between the two pieces of wood that the carpenter then assembles. Through his ritual, the *pande* transforms the assemblage of the keel pieces into an act of sexual intercourse. A similar idiom organises house building in Buton. This similarity between house and boat building is also present in South Sulawesi (Macknight and Mukhlis 1979).

Design conception

The differences outlined above are also associated with other technical choices that similarly serve to express the builder's identity. La Muru, an experienced boatbuilder, identified three schools or traditions (*kapande*) of boat building distinguished by different criteria such as the set of measurements, the planking model and the orientation of the plank. Knowledge of these criteria is acquired from a master builder upon request. Besides offering him some sort of payment, establishing a relationship with a master builder requires that one gains his confidence and shows him respect for the rest of his life. In this respect, boat building is not only a constituent of social construction; it is also a quest for knowledge and a source of the structure of social relations. Other features of social expression are manifest in the vertical inclination of the prow, the horizontal inclination of the bowsprit, the longitudinal position of the beam, and the position of the mast. Thus, through boat building, social identity is expressed on different scales: island, village and lineage of apprenticeship.

Planking

Boats are built without plans. However, a detailed planking scheme serves as a mental guide for the building process (Fig. 39.4). The first strake must contain an odd number of roughly equal length planks (*dhopi*), for example five or seven. The size of these planks becomes the standard plank length used for the other strakes, except for the planks at the ends of each strake.

For the top three strakes, longer planks are used; their length is a multiple of the standard one. The first 'reference' plank is placed at the centre of the keel. The shape of its ends differs from those of 'non-central' planks. A second plank is placed on top of this first reference plank but is offset over half the length of the first reference plank, to form the basis of the second strake. By the third strake, the reference plank is back at the centre and so the pattern continues as the boat is planked up. As each strake is laid, the central plank is always the first to be fitted. The height of the reference planks is around 15 cm (*acudha*).[6] The number of strakes employed must also be odd, usually nine, finishing with the gunwale (*wiwi kapala*).

For each plank the carpenter chooses the most suitable

Fig. 39.4. Planking scheme (of a motoro) showing reference planks and parapalea join type (produced by La Ode Nilo).

Several variations of ritual exist, depending on the *pande* who performs it. These variations concern the materials that are enveloped within the white cloth, the orientation of the wood pieces used in the construction of the keel, the orientation of the tenons (pointing to the bow or to the stern), and the order of assemblage. These variations determine, affirm and uphold elements of social identity as well as claims of authority.

piece of wood from the ones available. Plank fitting is achieved through successive corrections: the plank is carved, put in place then refined and so on, until it fits perfectly. While boatbuilders use fire to shape the planks when necessary, shaping is mainly performed by hewing, using an adze and two machetes (the small *padhe* and the larger *golo*). The saw is present but is only occasionally used. Why does saw use remain rare? Lemonnier (1994) pointed out the importance of representations of actions on objects, here percussion for cutting. Moreover, machete use is not limited to boat building. It is a very versatile tool used by men and women in a large range of activities in everyday life. Children learn to handle it at a young age. Finally, skill in using the adze and the *golo*, in contrast to the use of the saw, is socially recognized as a testament of one's mastery in woodwork.

Planks are assembled edge to edge and secured by dowels, as additional planks are secured to dugout canoes. The carpenter makes holes in both plank edges; he places the dowel in the hole on the upper edge of the bottom plank, shapes the dowels' edges with the machete and then hammers in the upper plank. Dowel preparation can be undertaken by the apprentice, most often a younger brother or the son of the boatbuilder who is present throughout the boat building process and thus learns through observation. The ends of the planks are cut in order to form a *parapalea* (overlapping) scarf joint. This enables each plank to be joined to the frame. However, in other places in Buton or elsewhere in Indonesia, planks are butted directly with flat edges. This may indicate a different path in the formation of their boat building tradition.

From a local perspective, the method of joining planks by dowels in the shell-first method is more secure than the 'western' method of nailing thin planks to the frames. Indeed, with this later method, as one boatbuilder explained, "the plank is forced in position, therefore it wants to come back to its initial position. This danger is ever present". A second local argument in favour of the Butonese joining method is that the planks are joined in order to form the frames but also between them, at the bottom and at the top. Therefore carpenters lack confidence in the 'western' system where a frame-first method of construction is adopted. The fact that the Butonese carpenters is convinced that his method of construction is superior, whether or not this is justified, is central to the fact that they do not adopt frame-first method. It also demonstrates that change does not impose its pace to passive recipients; actors and their representations must be taken into account.

Moreover, the carpenter does not complete the planking before he begins to insert the frames (*buku*); the process is simultaneous. When three or four strakes of planks are laid, the frames are added, as "baby simultaneous develops skin and ribs", say the locals. Floor timbers alternate with futtock timbers and are secured to the hull by dowels (Horridge 1979a: 19).

In the boatyard, a carpenter can work alone during the whole process of boat building. However, if he can afford it, he may hire carpenters and agree with them a sum for each plank adjusted. This type of payment may lead hired carpenters "to cut large planks in two in order to get paid twice", as a local carpenter remarked. It demonstrates that social organisation of work has direct and concrete consequences on the (material) characteristics of the final product.

Drilling the keel (lamba puse)

Finally, the last operation of the boatbuilding sequence in Buton is the navel drilling (*lamba puse*). A complete boat from a technical point of view is not considered a final product according to the locals. In Buton, a boat is not an inanimate object but is viewed as a child by its owner as 'everything takes its origin in the human body". Therefore, boats need a navel, a centre for rejecting danger and attracting luck. Houses and gardens have similar centres that serve as privileged places of interaction between humans and invisible creatures, including ancestors.

In order to drill a hole in the keel, the *pande* sits cross-legged on the keel, inside the boat, his head and body covered with a piece of white cloth. He faces the boat owner and is surrounded by relatives attending the ritual (Fig. 39.5). The *pande* murmurs a spell, requesting primarily that the boat does not perish at sea, as the seafarers main fear is to die far from their relatives and house. If the boat is to be damaged, it should happen in the village and nowhere else. He then bores a hole through the keel while holding his breath. In this way he transfers potency to the boat.[7] Outside, the boat owner's wife collects the sawdust. She keeps this sawdust in her house, as women keep semen in their womb in order to produce a child.[8]

If *lamba puse*'s main goal is to transform the boat into a living being and hence ensure the safety of the crew, it also contributes to social construction. Indeed, while highly respected, *pande* do not escape criticism. Chal-

Fig. 39.5. Pande *performing the* lamba puse *ritual (Photo by Daniel Vermonden).*

lenges tend to be focused around three key issues: firstly, the 'true' knowledge of the *pande*, as variations exist both in ritual implementation and interpretations (see also Southon 1995: 129–137). A second aspect of social contest relates to the secrecy of the spells. When I tried to know more about the *pande*'s spells I was informed that they were too dangerous for me: "being taught the spell involves a capacity to control its power". The spell holds power in its own right. Navel potency depends on the spell itself and on *pande*'s personality. Despite an ideology of free access to knowledge, I observed that the transmission of *pande*'s knowledge is limited to brothers and sons-in-law. Knowledge is power, and secrecy, combined with a strict control of knowledge transmission, permit the maintenance of this power. The final grounds for criticism focus on the *pande*'s potency, which is assessed by the success and safety of the boat expeditions. Each accident is a potential rebuff for the *pande*, if no other explanation is to be found.

From a historical perspective, *lamba puse* also contributes towards the understanding of the boat building path of diffusion. Indeed, the vernacular word for navel is *tuwuni*, not *puse*, which is the term in Wolio language, the official language of the former Sultanate of Buton. According to linguists, the Wolio language does not belong to the Muna-Buton group, "Instead, together with Laiyolo (the eastern Buton) it links up with Kamaru (at the tip of Selayar Island) and Wotu (at the southern part of the Gulf of Bone in South Sulawesi)" (van den Berg 2002). And, interestingly, similar ritual practices are present in South Sulawesi boatbuilding traditions (Pelly 1997). This tends to indicate that some elements of the boatbuilding tradition implemented in South Buton come from there.

Conclusion

The aim of this paper was to propose an original approach to boats and boat building and to apply this approach to the Butonese *lambo* and *motoro* case study. The SOA considers boats as the result of a sequence of socially distributed operations (1) conducted by knowledgeable, skilled, and socially situated actors and (2) whose motivation may be related to complex associations between heterogeneous elements. For instance, boat building in Buton includes associations between measurements and good fortune; woman, human procreation and good fortune; navel, potency, houses and boats. It is necessary to explore these associations in order to understand the actors' operations and choices (e.g. building or buying a boat; attention paid to wood orientation; simultaneity of framing and planking). As a result, the SOA provides us with an emic understanding of boats and the related boat building process, that is, in Buton, boats as hybrids resulting from a double transformation: of a material into a physical object and, simultaneously, of a material into a kind of human being with its own life principle.

The SOA also explores the dialectic relation between the boat building activity and its social context. On one side, it provides us with a capacity to relate the boat's characteristics with the social context of its building. In Buton, measurements and planking models used depend on the builders' identity and social trajectory, while the length of the planks may vary according to the social organisation of the building (as carpenters are paid "per plank"). On the other hand, boat building activities contribute to the constitution of society, by staging a specific cultural world and by its role as a social arena. The associations lying behind the motivation of the operations (e.g. between woman, procreation and good fortune) are not simple applications of clearly defined cultural representations that exist independently of their staging in the context of activities. Rather, a dialectic relation exists between the enactment of these associations in the context of the technical activity and the production and reproduction of the associated representations.

Moreover, boatbuilding is an arena where actors materialise their identities through the choice of different boat characteristics (e.g. the planking model, measurements), where social relations are established (between master builders and novices, between *pande* and boat builders), where social roles are enacted (*pande*), and social positions confirmed or contested through skill demonstration including the observable quality of wood material transformation, but also the safety and success of the boats built.

In addition, the SOA offers a perspective on the phylogeny of local society through the exploration of the various origins and historical strata of the activities operations and related associations. In this regard, Butonese boatbuilding activity is a blend of a western model, the *lambo*, occurring in East Indonesia in the early 20th century, an association between the navel, potency, houses and boats shared with, and probably inherited from, South Sulawesi Bugis-Makassar societies, and Austronesian idioms about wood and its transformation. Subsequent research could explore more exhaustively these networks and their historical path of diffusion.

Finally, the SOA offers an analysis of change that takes into account three elements: the actor's representation and social values relating to the operations and occurrences of similar operations in other local activities. In the present case study, we have noticed that saw use remains marginal and that this may be explained by the actors' representations of percussion, the use of machete in everyday life and the social conception of skill recognition associated with the adze and the big machete (*golo*). Similarly, the persistence of shell-first building is related to the actor's conviction that it provides the best 'solidity', as well as to the association between boat building and procreation.

Furthermore, the SOA provides a perspective of change that differs from approaches considering technology in isolation. Indeed, if one considers the boat model alone, the adoption of the *lambo* boat type in Buton and the subsequent move from *lambo* to *motoro* might be considered as major changes. If one considers the technical attributes of the boat building process, the range of change is sharply reduced. It appears that the adoption of the *lambo* is limited to borrowing a shape, and the difference between *lambo* and *motoro* is limited to marginal details of the technical process. Now, within the present framework, *lambo* and *motoro* boatbuilding activities appear as complex recombinations of heterogeneous elements from different activities: operations from canoe making, skills from canoes and house building, and idioms from house building.

Acknowledgements

Fieldwork in Buton was conducted between 1999 and 2002. It was sponsored by LIPI and financed by two grants from the "Communauté Française de Belgique" (Action-Nord and Bourse de Voyage) and by a grant from the "Fondation Belge de la Vocation". I would also like to thank O. Gosselain for useful comments on previous versions of this paper.

Notes

1 Originally "chaîne opératoire" (in French). The concept was proposed by Leroi-Gourhan (1964) from an original idea of Mauss.

2 Terms in italic are vernacular terms (*cia-cia* language).

3 Given space limits, I focus on the description of a limited number of stages of the sequence of operations and do not pretend to be exhaustive, neither in describing gestures nor in exploring connected networks.

4 Several studies dealt with Butonese *lambo*. Horridge (1979a) devoted a monograph to its construction process, but from a restricted technical perspective. Southon conducted an analysis of "both the social organization of the perahu economy and the ritual related to boats" (1995: 3). Liebner (1990) conducted a linguistic survey about the vocabulary of boat building and seamanship in the region.

5 Personal names have been modified. Masculine names in Buton are preceded with a 'La' particle.

6 *Cudha* corresponds to a little finger to thumb spread. Depending on boatbuilder's tradition all reference planks are the same height or differ slightly.

7 Consider what Munn says about Gawan canoes (Melanesia): "[…] a senior man can animate the canoe through verbal spells and associated operations, knowledge of which is thought to be stored inside the body" (Munn 1977: 50).

8 In Murik, when the canoe is back from its first voyage, women collect the foamy spray from the bow in a bark container which is then brought home. "As long as they hold onto this "spittle", said the women, the canoe would "always come home to its mother" (Barlow and Lipset 1997: 19). While not an exact copy of the Butonese practice, the similarity is fascinating.

References

Arnaud, V., 2000, Calfatage d'or et éternité (Botel Tobago, Taïwan). *Technique et culture* 35–36: 255–286.

Barlow, K. and Lipset, D., 1997, Dialogics of material culture: male and female in Murik outrigger canoes. *American Ethnologist* 24.1: 4–36.

Barnes, R. H., 1985, Whaling Vessels of Indonesia. In S. McGrail and E. Kenley (eds), *Sewn Plank Boats: Archaeological and Ethnographic Papers based on those presented to a Conference at Greenwich in November 1984*, 345–366. National Maritime Museum Greenwhich (Archeological Series n°10). Oxford.

Barnes, R. H., 1996, *Sea Hunters of Indonesia. Fishers and Weavers of Lamahera*. Clarendon Press, Oxford.

Blust, R., 1995, The prehistory of the Austronesian-speaking peoples: A view from language. *Journal of World Prehistory* 9: 453–510.

Dobres, M-A., 2000, *Technology and Social Agency: Outlining a Practice Framework for Archaeology*. Blackwell, Oxford.

Doran, E., 1981, *Wangka, Austronesian Canoe Origins*. Texas A&M University Press. College Station, Texas.

Feinberg, R., 1988, *Polynesian Seafaring and Navigation. Ocean travel in Anutan Culture and Society*. Kent State University Press, Kent, Ohio.

Feinberg, R., 1995, Continuity and change in Nukumanu maritime technology and practice. In R. Feinberg (ed), *Seafaring in the Contemporary Pacific Islands*, 159–195. Northern Illinois University Press. DeKalb.

Gibson-Hill, C. A., 1950, The Indonesian trading boats reaching Singapore. *Journal of the Malaysian Branch of the Royal Anthropological Society* 23: 108–138.

Gladwin, T., 1970, *East is a Big Bird: Navigating and Logic on Pulawat Atoll*. Cambridge University Press. Cambridge.

Haddon, A. C. and J. Hornell, 1936–8, *Canoes of Oceania*. Bernice P. Bishop Museum (Special publication 29). Honolulu.

Horridge, A., 1979a, *The Lambo or Prahu Boat: a Western Ship in an Eastern Setting*. Maritime Monographs and Reports N°39 National Maritime Museum, London (Greenwich).

Horridge, A., 1979b, *The Konjo Batbuilders and the Bugis Prahus of South Sulawesi*. Maritime Monographs and Reports N°40 National Maritime Museum, London (Greenwich).

Horridge, A., 1985, *The Prahu. Traditional Sailing Boat of Indonesia*. Oxford University Press, Oxford.

Horridge, A., 1986a, *Sailing Craft of Indonesia*. Oxford University Press. Singapore.

Horridge, A., 1986b, A summary of Indonesian canoe and prahu ceremonies. *Indonesian Circle* 39: 3–17.

Horridge, A., 1987, *Outrigger Canoes of Bali and Madura, Indonesia*. Bishop Museum Special Publication 77, Bishop Museum Press. Honolulu.

Ivanoff, J., 2000, *La technologie symbolique chez les Moken. L'histoire d'un mo. Technique et culture* 35–36: 199–232.

Latour, B., 1997, *Nous n'avons jamais été Modernes. Essai d'Anthropologie Symétrique*. La Découverte. Paris.

Leblic, L., 2000, *Une pirogue pontée à l'île des Pins* (Nouvelle-Guinée). *Technique et culture* 35–36: 301–328.

Lemonnier, P. (ed), 1993, *Technological Choices*. Routledge. London.

Lemonnier, P., 1994, Choix techniques et représentations de l'enfermement chez les Anga de Nouvelle-Guinée. In B. Latour and P. Lemonnier (eds), *De la Préhistoire aux*

Missiles Balistiques: l'Intelligence Sociale des Techniques, 253–272. Editions La Découverte. Paris.

Leroi-Gourhan, A., 1964, *Le Geste et la Parole: Technique et Langage*. Albin Michel. Paris.

Liebner, H., 1990, Istilah-Istilah Kemaritiman dalam Bahasa-Bahasa Buton. In *Bahasa-Bahasa Daerah Sulawesi dalam Konteks Bahasa National*, 99–117. Prosiding Konferensi dan Seminar Nasional Ke-5 Masyarakat Linguistik Indonesia Proyek Kerjasama Unhas-Sil.

Liebner, H., 1996, *Beberapa catatan tentang pembuatan perahu dan pelayaran di daerah Mandar, Sulawesi Selatan*. Unpublished MA thesis.

Ligtvoet, A., 1878, Beschrijving en Geschiednis van Boeton. *Bijdragen tot de Taal Land en Volkenkunde van Nederlandsh-Indie* 26: 1–112.

Macknight, C. C. and Mukhlis, 1979, A Bugis Manuscript about Praus. *Archipel* 18: 271–282.

Malinowski, B., 1989 [1922], *Les Argonautes du Pacifique occidental*. Gallimard. Paris.

Marshall Carucci, L., 1995, Symbolic imagery of Enewetak sailing canoes. In R. Feinberg (ed), *Seafaring in the Contemporary Pacific Islands*, 16–33. Nothern Illinois University Press. DeKalb.

Munn, N., 1977, The Spatiotemporal transformations of Gawa canoes. *Journal de la Société des Océanistes* 33: 39–53.

Neyret, J., 1974, *Pirogues océaniennes*. Association des Amis des Musées de la Marine. Paris.

Nicolaisen, I. and Damgård-Sørensen, T., 1991, *Building a Longboat*. Vikingeskibshallen, Roskilde.

Nooteboom, C., 1932, *De Boomstamkano in Indonesie*. E. J. Brill, Leiden.

Pelly, U., 1997, Pengaruh Islam dalam Pembuatan Perahu Bugis Pinisi. In E.K.M. Masinambow (ed), *Koentjaraningrat dan antropologi di Indonesia*, 237–250. Yayasan Obor Indonesia. Jakarta.

Petersen, E., 2000, *Jukung-Boats from the Barito Basin, Borneo*. The Viking Ship Museum, Roskilde.

Pfaffenberger, B., 1992, Social anthropology of technology. *Annual Review of Anthropology* 21: 491–516.

Sather, C., 2000, Bajau Laut boat-building in Semporna. *Technique et culture* 35–36: 177–198.

Southon, M., 1995, *The Navel of the Prahu*. Department of Anthropology Research school of Pacific and Asian studies (Australian National University). Canberra.

Tilley, C., 2002, Metaphor, Materiality and Interpretation. In V. Buchli (ed), *The material culture reader*, 23–55. Berg. Oxford – New-York.

van den Berg, R., 2002, *The place of Tukang-Besi and the Muna-Buton Languages*. Unpublished paper presented at the Ninth International Conference on Austronesian Linguistics, Canberra.

40 *Balagarhi Dingi:*
An anthropological approach to traditional technology

Swarup Bhattacharyya

Balagarh is a small place in southern Bengal lying along the course of the River Ganga (Ganges) (Fig. 40.1). On such a vital stream floats the *Balagarhi dingi*, a unique variety of watercraft, which has its origins in Balagarh and also retains the name of the place as its prefix. Etymologically the term *dingi* is attributed to the small country boat of India, which owes its origin to the Austric term *dingi* (Ray 1993; note 1). Subsequently, westerners borrowed the term (*dinghy*) and used it to denote all small boats. However, in India there is a tradition of nomenclature based on territory, and hence the naming the boats of Balagarh as *Balagarhi dingi*. The patterns of nomenclatures very clearly express the sense of pride and ethnicity that is so intimately associated with the inhabitants of Balagarh, in the Gangetic Plain. However, in a practical sense all *Balagarhi dingi* are not typologically identical. Typological variations in terms of size and shape can be found in the *dingis* of Balagarh although the technological know-how remains specific to the actual trademark of the *Balagarhi* carpenters. This sort of territorial cognition is typical in a pan-Indian context.

West Bengal or Bengal, as it is more popularly known, is encircled by land to the north, east and west, whereas the southern part is covered by a great stretch of the Bay of Bengal. Almost all the rivers that flow down from the great Himalayas in the north towards the sea form the fertile Gangetic Delta, the largest in the world. This river bed acts as a life source to its inhabitants, who depend on watercraft as their traditional economy. Rivers here are the basic, and often only, means of transport, particularly in the rainy season when the monsoons of Bengal prevail over almost a quarter of the year and bring severe floods to low-lying areas.

Balagarh is the most renowned boatbuilding centre in West Bengal and is the only commercial centre where traditional wooden boats are fashioned in the courtyards of boat-makers' houses, on riverbanks and in bamboo groves, or in the garden of the client (Fig. 40.2). With other co-workers, the head carpenter is a special guest in the house of the patron or owner and starts his creation.

There is limited historical data to inform on the rise of Balagargh as a boatbuilding centre. However, some speculation can be made about its later importance. After the decline of the ancient port of Tamralipta, in Bengal, Saptagram emerged as an important medieval inland port in eastern India on the banks of the Rivers Saraswati and Hugli. It could have been around this period that boat and ship builders settled around the port to build and repair boats and ships. Saptagram eventually declined as a port, but the boat builders who had settled there remained (author opinion; similar instances can be sought in the case of Jhum/Jhumi of East Medinipur district of West Bengal). Perhaps Balagarh can be associated with the ancient port of Saptagram, although there is limited evidence to support this hypothesis. However, the tradition of boat building continues in the area and families retain their family occupation and craft the *dingi* popularly known as *Balagarhi dingi*. There are also geographical reasons that may have had an impact on the growth of Balagarh as a boat building centre, its location close to the river promotes a riverine economy, and access to the raw materials used to construct the *dingi* e.g. bamboo-groves which also supply accessories (green bamboo sticks, bamboo pole etc) for the carpenters (Fig. 40.3).

Nimai Barik, the owner of a boatbuilding yard, can trace back his genealogy over six generations of boat builders. The Rajbanshis are the fisherfolk community (Risley 1981) that occupy a lower rung in the Hindu caste hierarchy. In Balagarh the Rajbanshis are believed to be the first boatbuilders and they claim to have been building for more than five generations. The few people who decide to become boatbuilders acquire their knowledge from their neighbouring Rajbanshi community. They approach the *mistiri* (in Portuguese, *mestre*; in Hindi, *misteri*; Marathi, *misteri/mistri*; Gujrati, *mistevi*; Bandyopadhyaya 1996; 1792) or carpenter (boatbuilding is considered to be a part of carpentry). The present author uses the term *mistir*, to refer to those who have inherited their knowledge and skill of making dugout and planked boats only. At present some of the important boatbuilding yards of Balagarh

Swarup Bhattacharyya

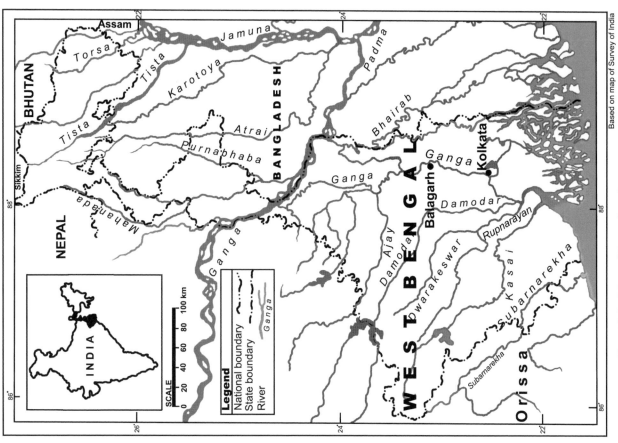

Fig. 40.1. Map of Bengal and its river systems.

include Tentulia, Chandra, Chandra colony and Sripur Bazar. The most important boat building centre at Rajbanshi Para has as many as sixteen different families that are *mistiris* who practice boat making as their livelihood. Balagarh produces a number of boat varieties predominantly used for transportation of sand from the dry riverbed.

Karkhana or Boatyards of Balagarh

Presently (2003) 47 *karkhanas* (boatyards) (Fig. 40.4) are spread in and around the Sripur Bazar region of Balagarh. In 1997, there were only 26 that operated throughout the year, the recent establishments being due

Fig. 40.2. Boats for sale. Note the shed.

to the massive floods in 2000. These yards or sheds are generally open sites scattered along the roadsides, under the shady bamboo-groves. The land is purchased or leased (for a maximum period three years). In 1994 an association, known as *Nouko Babosayee Samiti* (Boat Merchants Association), was formed with 42 individuals from different boat sheds.

Those employed in boat building are both Hindus as well as Muslims. Nimai Barik's shed is the only one which appoints workmen entirely from his own family. There are 26 workmen working in Nimai Barik's shed, and they enjoy the privileges of life insurance and a few national holidays. In other sheds workmen are frequently hired on a contractual basis. An expert (head *mistiri*) is

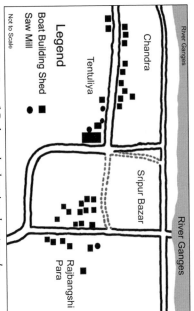

Fig. 40.4. *Map of Balagarh showing boatyards.*

Legend
■ Boat Building Shed
● Saw Mill

Not to Scale

River Ganges — Chandra — Tentuliya — Sripur Bazar — Rajbangshi Para — River Ganges

Fig. 40.3. Balagarhi dingi *under the shed of a bamboo grove.*

hired to undertake a specific contract and is given total charge of the supervision of the work. The selected head *mistiri* has the power of appointing other workers in his squad. The daily wage for skilled labour varies from Rs. 70/- to Rs. 80/- and for unskilled labour the range is between Rs. 40/- to Rs. 60/-. Apart from boats that are commissioned, some are made for ready sale at the boatyards or displayed in front of the builders' houses (Fig. 40.2).

Boatbuilding Materials

Wood

The preferred wood is *sal* (*Shorea robusta*) and *segun* (*Tectona grandis*) which were previously obtained from Burma and now from Raipur (Chhatisgarh). With the present policy in forestry it is possible to obtain sal from Mokam of Siliguri and teak from Rajabhatkhawa (North Bengal). If the client cannot afford the price of sal or teak, then cheaper wood is obtainable in the local market such as *gachhari kath* like *babla/babul* (*Acacia arabica*), *arjun* (*Terminalia arjuna*), *gilapi* (*Ingo dascis*), *khirish* (*Samania saman*), *sirish* (*Albizzia lebbek*), *subabul* (*Leucaena leacocephala*), and *chap* (*Michelia champaca*). Out of all those woods *babla* is the most popular one because of its easy availability, low price and relative hardness. Wood may be purchased either from local wood stockists or from middlemen. Five local sawmills also stock wood for ready sale.

Iron nails and staples

Iron nails, 23" to 83" in length, are obtained from local hardware shops. Those which are 23" to 33" in length, are called *tar kata* while those between 43" and 83" are called *perek*. The *tar kata* has a uniform circular cross section. In squarish *perek*, the circumference is maximum at the top, tapering down towards its point of termination. Staples used to join two planks edge-to-edge are called *jolui*. They are double-ended thin, flat pieces of galvanized or cast iron.

Tools and instruments

The tools employed in boat construction include the *Baga* or wooden clamp; the *Boa karan* which acts as a divider; the *Karan* which is effectively a modified iron nail with a bifurcation of 1/83" at lower end and that is used in rabbeting; the *Gharon* a wooden cylindrical block, used when fixing two planks as an aid to exerting inward pressure on the outer upper edge of the lower plank; and the Chekanta, a wooden block, 83x 35x 33, that is used as a ground support when making the rabbet in the plank.

Other items include the *gharon* (either iron blade of blunt chisel or stone chips), cylindrical wooden blocks called *bankata* which are used to align planks during the clamping procedure. Apart from these, the *raeda* (carpenter's plane), hammer, flat chisel, *tanga* (a blunt-edged chisel for stapling), rope (previously made of jute, *Corchorus olitorius*, now replaced by synthetic ropes), bamboo poles, iron nails of different sizes, *jolui*, sawdust, chalk (sometimes charcoal) and thread, thin bamboo sticks, planks of different sizes, pegs and galvanized wire, are also put to use.

Cognition of the boat

Uttorer (northern) *nouko* and *dokkhiner* (southern) *nouko* (*nouko* being the generic term of any non-motorised traditional wooden boat) are the two categories of boats built by the *mistiri* of Balagarh. The *uttorer nouko* (boat of the north) is predominantly used during the rainy season. The bow of these boats is made 33–43" lower than the stern, and they are used for transporting agricultural harvests like jute or paddy along the waterways and streams. The *dokkhiner nouko* (boat of the south) caters to the demand of the southern part of West Bengal. It has no seasonal use unlike that of its northern counterpart. The stem of this boat variety is always kept higher than its stern in order to combat the more turbulent and voluminous southern waters. Apart from these two types, there is another *dingi* called *khile* which is smaller than the common *dingi*, about 10 to 13 *haat* (1 *haat* = 1½, i.e., 183), equal to 152" to 195.2" in length. None of these boats have a prominent keel. As a corollary to the above, the *Balagarhi dingi* is a spoon-shaped, round-hulled, smooth-skinned, stapled and rabbetted wooden boat.

Boatbuilding Procedure

All planks are sawn at the mill to different breadths and thickness. Generally, the central plank ('plank keel' according to McGrail *et al* 2003: 302) is cut a little thicker than the other planks and the best quality wood is always used. *Sal* wood is the preferred variety. The current procedure for bending the central plank in many cases obviates the use of heat. Previously, however, this was not so in the case of the central plank. When it is necessary to lengthen the plank this is accomplished through a complex scarf joint called *dar saad* (Fig. 40.5). The central plank is 33" wide at its centre and tapers down to 23" at each end. At the same time the two attachments, *chhiya*, which, when attached to the *dara* will constitute the stem and stern ends of the boat, are also prepared. This *chhiya* (Fig. 40.6) is fashioned from a large block of wood. The dimension of the finished *chhiya* is 33" thick and 73" wide and 203" to 253" in length. Starting with a width of 73" at the top, the *chhiya* narrows down to 23" at the point at which the *dar sad* (scarf joint) attaches it to the central plank. The term *dara* is applied to the total length of the central plank, including the attachment of the two *chhiya*. As the boat is conceived as an animated concept with bodily parts, the term *dara* is used as a denominator

of *sirdara* (vertebral column), which forms the base of the structural aspect of the boat.

Marking on the central plank

A string is aligned from one end of the central plank to the other (that is from one *chhiya* to the other along the *dara*). Points are marked along the central plank with a chisel mark (+) (Fig. 40.7). The central mark is called

Fig. 40.5. Dar saad, *complex scarf joint.*

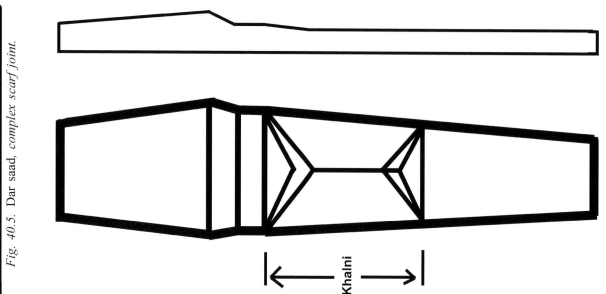

Khalni

Side view

Fig. 40.6. Chhiya, *the stem head.*

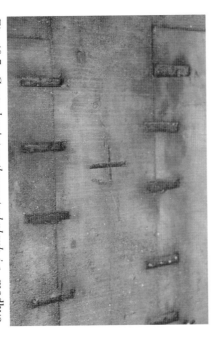

the *modhyo*, further marks are made that equally divide the central plank (see Fig. 40.8 for the appropriate terms). These marking points are called *fuli* and total seven in number, although currently boat makers restrict themselves to three *fuli* marks. This reduction from seven to three points of reference may have some relation to the increased pressures created in favour of quick production through increasing commercialization.

Heating and bending

The heating of planks is necessary for bending them into the desired shape. Earlier, all planks, including the central plank, were heated. In present times there is no application of cowdung or mud to the plank surface prior to firing. A shallow pit is made of sufficient length to accommodate the length of the planks. The fire is kept alight with sawdust, which provides slow and steady heat to prevent the wood from catching fire. Planks are placed above the glow on two sets of bricks placed at both ends and this singeing process continues between half to a full hour. After adequate heating the plank is positioned at the desired angle for insertion into the boat. If twisting is also required, a clamp, *baga*, is positioned at the desired angle. A wire tied to a peg maintains this angle. If only bending is required the plank can be left without clamping, positioned between bamboo supports. This is left in position for at least two hours or until the wood cools.

Fig. 40.7. *Central point on the central plank, i.e., modhyo, marked by + sign. Note also staples, are of two varieties sarong variety is on the left corner, others are banda variety.*

Fig. 40.8. *Erection of central plank and its different fuli.*

Fig. 40.9. *Support system of the central plank. Note placement of iron wire between two lower supports.*

Raising of central plank

The central plank is first rested on support planks 43" to 63" above the ground. The height of the support structure progressively increases towards either end. The two *chhiya* (stem and stern ends) can receive additional support by bamboo poles (Fig. 40.9). Additional holes are drilled at a distance of 183" apart along the *dara*. Wire is secured through these holes to pegs at ground level. This serves two purposes: the planks are bent to a curvilinear shape while the central plank is also kept in a steady position during carpentry. The bamboo support poles provide an upward thrust that acts as an alternate force to the wire and peg which constitute a graduated downward pull.

Assessing the depth

After making any necessary adjustments in alignment, the master carpenter suspends a plumb line and takes measurements at specific *fuli* (chisel marks) of his choice. The nodal depth is at *modhyo*. He adjusts depths at other *fuli* in order to create a point that facilitates the task of bailing. The term used for depth at any given point is *rag*. The *rag* of the boat is proportionate to the width of the hull planks measured at the *modhyo* point. An *aat-pad dingi* (*aat* is number eight and *pad* foot) would have eight rows of strakes on each side of the hull. Each *pad* measures about 63" in width (previously it was half of a *haat*, i.e., 93"). The ratio between circumference, stated in terms of *pad*, and the depth of a *dingi* that is intended to negotiate coastal water, is 4:1. Viewed from the top, the stern portion (*matha*), is narrower than the stern portion (*pachha*). The maximum width is not at *modhyo* but at the *fuli* or chisel mark known as *basok* (Fig. 40.8).

Placement of planks in the hull

Planking starts from the midships portion of the central plank. The garboard plank is called *char gala*. Before the placement of *char gala* all other planks for the first row on each side are selected. At first the planks are placed with various clamps and according to necessity they remove the strake and shape it accordingly with the help of an adze. The plank is aligned at the *dara*. An incised line is drawn on the upper face of the *dara* and the lower face of the garboard plank with the *karan*. The garboard plank is then taken off and a second line is incised along the thickness of the garboard plank and the central plank with the *kursud*. The lines incised by *karan* and *kursud* are chiseled out to form the inner faces of the rabbet joint, called *patam*. The rabbet joint (Fig. 40.10) is not perpendicular but is slightly cut inwards to ensure a better fit. After preparing the rabbet the two planks are put together again and tightly compressed. This procedure is repeated whenever a fresh plank is laid.

Stapling

When the alignment of the planks is complete, shallow slots about one-eighth of an inch wide, are cut across the seams of the inner hull of the boat at intervals of 23", 33" or 43". These intervals depend upon their position in different sections of the boat and the amount of money that is to be spent on the boat. The *Jolui*, a flat staple of galvanized iron pointed at either end, is first driven at an acute angle into the plank that lies ready in position to receive the next plank. The pointed end of the *Jolui* is driven at an angle of less than 75° into the newly added plank. The *char gala* (first row of planking, i.e., garboard strake) is first fixed at the central portion of the *dara*. As the planking progresses, the *char gala* is lengthened by means of a tongue and groove joint. Stapling is done both on the inner and outer skin of the boat but in the outer skin only above the waterline. In general, staples on the inner skin are more frequent than the outer one (Fig. 40.7).

Planking

After the *char gala* has been fitted, the *aat gala* or second row of planking is added alternately on either side of the boat. Thus, the boat increases on either side at a similar rate so that a constant watch can be kept on its shape. This is done by placing a green bamboo stick along the inner surface of the hull from the edge of the central strake to the outer edge of the filled plank. On both sides of the hull such processes are followed and the exact distance of the corresponding points will give the ultimate shape. Each row of planking has a different name.

Different names for the special position of each strake are well accepted in Balagarh boat construction.

One important aspect of the *Balagarhi dingi* is that all strakes placed in the hull are exactly straight and are of equal width. After positioning the strake the boat builder cuts it to size. Greenhill (2000) mentions, 'this is economical in the sense that all planks are sliced from a single block of wood in the saw mill.'

The fixing of each line of planks follows the same pattern as the first line. The planks are usually less wide at the stem than the centre. In order to provide for greater width of the hull, stealers (*chura*) are added. The *chura* does not extend along the whole length of the hull. Commencing from the stem the *chura* extends along two thirds of the length of the *dingi*. In *khile dingi* generally two *chura* are found, one on each side of the central plank. When the planking is complete to the penultimate row, the sheer strake, *dali*, is rabbetted to the lower row. The *dali* plank is stouter than the other planks. The thickness in the upper edge is double that of the lower edge. The *dali* covers all other strakes, even the stem head (Fig. 40.11).

Boat builders believe that their skill in boat building is to be assessed by accuracy of visual mapping, *chokher daekha*. Though they measure different angular measurements by bamboo strips, eye estimation is still the main tool of a boat builder. Building by eye is a trial and error method of application, whilst it is also a product of traditional wisdom that is transmitted as a part of creative excellence of the people and a continuity of knowledge.

Frames

After the hull has been fully planked frames are fitted in to the inner hull. Frames are of two types: *baak* and *gochha* (Fig. 40.3). *Baak* (floor timbers) are placed horizontally in on the floor of the *dingi*, while *gochha* (futtocks) are placed vertically along the rising surface of the hull. The *baak* and *gochha* are, in general, placed together at regular intervals of one *haat*. First the *gochha* and then the *baak* are laid before securing them in a permanent position. The *baak* is 43" thick and its shape varies in width according to the circumference of the boat at the place of fitting. A trial fitting identifies any changes that are required to be made on the *baak* to ensure a better fit on the hull. The adze is then used to provide the required shape. The *baak* is then fixed to the skin of boat by iron nails of 63" to 83" in length. Holes are drilled through the outer skin passing through the plank to the *baak*. The nail is hammered in through the outer skin. Drilling is never done on the central plank. In each *baak*, there are one or two holes on the lower edge called *bonal kata*. These are the water channels.

Gochha of various lengths with a thickness of 23" to 33" and width of 33" to 43" are fitted on to the inner hull after the final placement of *baak*. Builders usually keep a gap of 13" to 33" between each set of *baak* and *gochha*.

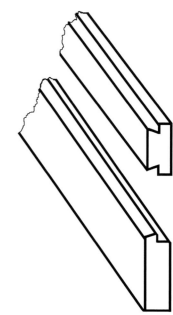

Fig. 40.10. Rabbet joint on the contact edge of two strakes. Note angular tongue.

Fig. 40.11. Placement of the dali, the sheer strake. Unfinished hull structure. Left sheer stake is already aligned but the right one is due. See also entire hull structure prior to the placement of ribs.

Thus, they are evenly spaced. The total number of *baak* in a *dingi* is half the number of *gochha*, the former being arranged centrally between two *gochha*, overlapping the latter. The *baak* supports the planks of the floor whereas the *gochha* supports the side of the hull. The top most section of the *gochha* reaches upwards to the upper edge of the *dali*.

Cross beams and ancillary construction members

Apart from these support timbers, the boats have cross-beams termed *guro*. They provide support for the temporary flooring of decks and strengthen the upper planks of the hull. Prior to the fitting of the *guro*, an inner stringer, the *daroga* 33" wide, 13" thick, is nailed 63" below the upper edge of the *dali* from stem to stem. The *daroga* is aligned alongside the *dali* being nailed to the *gochha* running up the surface of the *dali*. A second *daroga* is placed on the same alignment on the outer skin. Both are nailed transversally. If the *daroga* are to be lengthened the two connected edges are beveled and nailed by a 23" nail. The tongue-in-groove joint is not used here. The *guro* rests on a groove etched on the inner *daroga* called *kenko*. The number of *guro* employed match that of the *daroga*. The thickness and the width of the *guro*, however, vary. The *guro*, which supports the mast called *paal guro*, is relatively thick and wide and usually there is a hole in its centre. This *guro* is placed on the *fuli, anonto maja. The associated *baak* just below the *paal guro* has a round slot at its centre for supporting the bottom end of the mast, the *khorme* or mast step.

Sometimes, a stringer or *barbata* is placed on the inner skin and occasionally a second stringer is placed on the outer skin in alignment with the *malom*. This is called *malom* or *barbata*. The remaining accessories that are placed on the Balagarhi *dingi* include: *Darsoni*, a barrier plank which prevents the entrance of water from the stem region into the boat; *Godi kath* or *haal makri* a wooden plank nailed diagonally on the *dali* (sheer strake) towards the stern end with a small section projecting outwards. The steering oar or *haal*, is tied into position here. These are four in number, positioned close to the second inner stringer or *guro*, starting from the stem and stem ends respectively. The *haal*, steering oar, is made from a strong wood, preferably *sal*. The total length of the shaft is 103" to 123. The manipulating end is narrowed down, while the other end is 43" in width. Towards the dipping end, two planks, *pata*, of the dimensions 43" to 53" in length, 63" wide and 63" thick, are rabbeted and stapled onto the main shaft. After all the accessory activities have been completed the outer skin is smoothened by an adze or *raeda*. This procedure is called *pal sara*. This is an important finishing process as the smoother the outer skin the less friction in the water.

Caulking is not included in the budget for boat building, as owners like to inspect the hull on delivery. However, it can be done in the boat yard if required. Caulking (*kalapati/kalabati/gaoni*) is done by a specialist group of workers called *gaoni mistiri*. Cotton is pushed into spaces between planks by a blunt chisel, the *tanga*. After caulking from the outer skin *coal tar* is applied both on the outer as well as inner skin. In earlier times, *gab*, a gummy substance derived from the fruit of the *gab* tree, *Diospyros embryopteris* was used.

Distribution of the finished product

Boats are transported from the boat building yard to their desired location of use either by surface transport or through the waterways. Different means of transportation are used from rickshaw vans, on lorries, or on other boats along the waterways (Fig. 40.12).

Customary Practise

Boat building starts on an auspicious day with a short ceremony that is performed by either the owner of the boat or the head *mistiri*. This practice is very common except at the highly commercialized boat building centre of Balagarh. It is done only if a boat owner wishes to do so. If performed, the local priest or the chief carpenter conducts the ceremony. The priest smears vermilion to

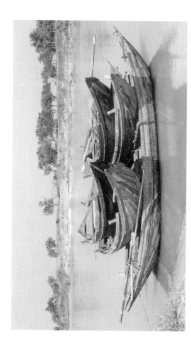

Fig. 40.12. Transport along the Ganga River. A specialised group assembling boats for delivery.

ritual accompanying the 'handing over' (Bhattacharya and Varadarajan 2000) of the boat involves presenting the 'bride' with the sixteen auspicious symbols of marriage. Among these sixteen wedding items are conch shell bangles (*sakha*), vermilion for the forehead (*sidur*), red colour to grace the bride's feet (*alta*), the bridal *saree* and a pot; all an integral parts of the Bengali bride's trousseau to mark her journey into a new life. The new owner receives the bride graciously for she is the commencer of wealth and munificence. Before embarking on her maiden voyage, or before setting sail after a long duration of idleness on shore, mango leaves are used to 'brush' her teeth, she is bathed in the sacred water of the Ganges and she is bedecked in vermilion paste to celebrate her 'married' status.

Thus, it is seen in West Bengal that the act of mere transaction of a boat, is embellished with various day to day scenes coated with ritualistic emblems to make it more meaningful. Therefore, each step starting from boat building to the maiden voyage, is elaborated with various rites.

From the data collected in religious contexts, it thus appears that Bramhanical influences have made little inroad into the traditional customs of the non-Brahminical boat builders and users. This was perhaps necessary because by not doing so the sanctity of the watercraft would have been lost and they would have failed in upholding a unified productive system of sacro-economic nature which the author attributes as the root cause of the continuity in technological tradition and the social system of production.

Conclusion

Thus, in conclusion, it can be said that the imagination of the boat builder is reflected in a practical sense, in the skill with which they execute the fashioning of a boat. Without formal training the boat builders have acquired an excellent knowledge of boat building, keeping pace with the changing environment and updated techniques and requirements. The knowledge of boat-making is acquired over generations and at the same time transmitted to future generations with the necessary modifications and adaptations. This is called continuity of knowledge. Thus, one comes across various types of watercraft of different regions (over forty traditionally built craft in the West Bengal region alone), all of which display different 'evolutionary changes'. Thus, to study and learn about watercrafts one probes into the different unique boat varieties which carry the traces of history, tradition, and 'evolutionary change', along with the excellent execution of the skilled boat-makers. In the manufacturing of the watercraft we find the unforgettable art of age-old traditional and modern culture, the creation of a grandiose fusion of skill and environment.

the *chhiya* of the *dingi* and then covers it with a red *shalu* (a piece of red cloth). Sometimes a garland of flowers is also placed on the *chhiya*. The *mangolik*, a diagrammatic representation of an anthropomorphic figure, is drawn on the *chhiya* with vermilion paste. During *Viswakarma puja* (*Viswakarma* is the deity of all artisans), festival day, no work is performed for two days. It should also be noted that no woman can participate in boat carpentry. They perform cleaning jobs but even this is prohibited for menstruating women. During the boat building period no person is allowed to mount the structure with shoes. At no time should the foot be placed on the *chhiya*.

Symbolism

The watercraft of West Bengal is not merely a 'boat' to the people who use and make boats, but it is something more to them as it is concerned with their main economic pursuit. Although the boat is essentially a means of transport, to the helmsman and oarsman the boat is a living entity that protects and steers them through troubled waters. To the boatman the boat is the mother in whose lap the sailor finds shelter and refuge from danger. The hull of the boat assumes the contours of the mother's sheltering lap and the sailor here is considered as the child whom the mother protects. By perceiving the boat as the compassionate mother, the sailor hopes to be protected against perils at sea. It is 'She' who like a patient mother eases her offspring's pains and worries and in her embrace the child is safe from danger. In the minds of the boatman and boat builder the boat always takes the form of a feminine personality, which can be Goddess, Mother or even Daughter. A host of Bengali legends and folksongs also subscribe to this view (Sen 1926, 1952).

The philosophical concept behind boat building is very unique as the boat is personified as the daughter of the builder who tries to build it with utmost care, sincerity and devotion. After the boat is made, the boat builder sells his boat to its new owner and this is tantamount to giving away his daughter in marriage to another. The

Acknowledgement

The author gratefully acknowledges the involvement of various organizations and academicians without whose support the present work would not have been completed, especially Dr. Lotika Varadarajan, who not only inspired the author but also coordinated the work that was funded by the National Institute of Science Technology and Developmental Studies, New Delhi. A note of acknowledgement is also due to the Anthropological Survey of India, Kolkata, where the author spent valuable academic years as a Senior Research Fellow, conducting this research work. The author is grateful to Mrs. Kaveri Dutta for her guidance and to Dr. Gautam Kumar Bera of the Anthropological Survey of India who has provided support in the pursuit of this research through to publication. The author especially owes sincere thanks to all informants specially the boat builders of Balagarh for their kind cooperation, help, and above all their warmth.

Note

1   Austric is a linguistic group used by the tribal of eastern India.

References

Bandyopadhyaya, H., 1996 [1966], *Bangiya Sabdakosh*. Sahitya Akademi. New Delhi.

Bhattacharyya, S. and Varadarajan, L., 2000, Patia of eastern India: Vestiges of a reverse clinker tradition. *Techniques and Culture*, 35–36: 440.

Bose, S.C., 1968, *Geography of West Bengal*. National Book Trust. New Delhi.

Census of India, 1991, *Census of India*. Registrar General of India, Ministry of Home Affairs, Government of India. Delhi.

Greenhill, B., 2000, The Mysterious Hulc. *The Mariner's Mirror* 86.1: 3–18.

McGrail S., Blue, L, Kentley, E. and Palmer, C., 2003 *Boats of South Asia*. RoutledgeCurzon. London.

Ray, N., 1993, *Bangalir Itihas: Adiparba*. Dey's Publishing. Calcutta.

Risley, H.H., 1981, *Tribes and Castes of Bengal*. Vol. II. Firma Mukhopadhyay. Calcutta.

Sen, D., 1926, *Purbobanga Gitika*. University of Calcutta. Calcutta.

Sen, D., 1952, *Maimansingha Gitika*. University of Calcutta. Calcutta.

41 The Roskilde ships

Morten Gøthche

During the construction of the Museum Island expansion of the Viking Ship Museum in Roskilde in 1996–97, no fewer than nine shipwrecks, dating from the late Viking Age to about 1350, were revealed (Figs 41.1 and 41.2). It is one of the largest ship finds in Northern Europe in the last sixty years. While the five Skuldelev ships, excavated only 20 km north of Roskilde, represent only a very short span of time, the Roskilde ships cover a period of 300 years. Among the nine ships was the longest Viking ship ever found. It was approximately 36 m long, which is 6 m longer than both the Skuldelev 2 and the Hedeby 1 finds (Crumlin-Pedersen 1997).

The first wreck, Roskilde 1, was found when dredging out the new Museum Harbour in 1996. Later that year, Roskilde 2 was discovered during the excavation of the canals surrounding the Museum Island. In the early months of 1997, keel ends of four more wrecks, Roskilde 3–6, were found in trenches dug along the sides of the canal, the keel of Roskilde 6 jutting out of the sediments in both sides of the canal! Later on, three more wrecks

were found, Roskilde 7, 8 and 9. Four of the ships had been brutally cut up by the contractor's sheet piling. The remaining ends of Roskilde 4, 5, 6 and 9 were excavated after the opening of the Museum Island in June 1997.

The nine ships can be divided into three groups (Fig. 41.3). Only one ship (no. 6) belongs to the first group; this is the long ship, which is preliminarily dated to the

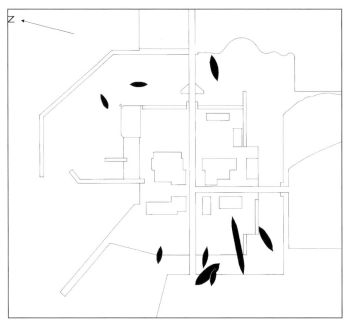

Fig. 41.2. *The find context of the ships from Roskilde. The nine wrecks lay at depths from 0.6 to 3 metres below the present sea level and give an idea of the level of the seabed in the Roskilde harbour area during the Viking Age and the Middle Ages. The investigation only concerned the finds made during the excavations for the canal and the harbour basin. No one knows how many ships still lie below the Museum Island. (author).*

Fig. 41.1. *The New Museum Island, located between the old Roskilde traffic harbour and the Viking Ship Museum. The picture was taken during the last phase of the archaeological investigation in the early autumn of 1997 while Roskilde 1 and Roskilde 6 were excavated. (Werner Karrasch, Viking Ship Museum).*

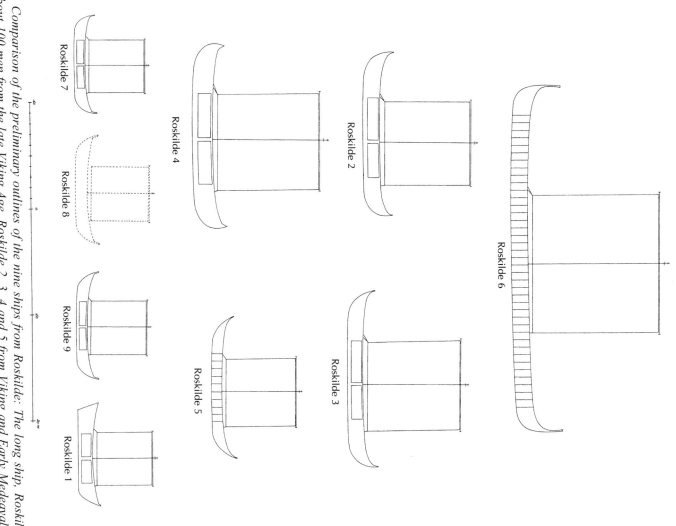

Fig. 41.3. *Comparison of the preliminary outlines of the nine ships from Roskilde: The long ship, Roskilde 6 with a crew of about 100 men from the late Viking Age. Roskilde 2, 3, 4 and 5 from Viking and Early Medieval Age with a cargo capacity from 5 to 50 tons and finally Roskilde 7, 8, 9 and 1 from the Medieval Age, all with a cargo capacity from 5 to 7 tons. (author).*

late Viking Age. The crew counted probably some 100 men, of whom 78 were oarsmen. The second group (Roskilde 2, 3, 4, and 5) consists of four different cargo ships dating from 1060 to around 1200. They were all of various sizes, with a cargo capacity ranging from 7 tons to 50 tons. To the last group belong Roskilde 1, 7, 8, and 9. They are all smaller cargo ships with a capacity of 5 – 7 tons. Moreover, they are also the youngest of the ships, dating from 1200 to 1350.

The nine ships from Roskilde are all built in the Nordic clinker tradition with a slender, double-ended hull and curved stems at both ends, except for Roskilde 1. They have all been rigged with a single mast and a single square sail. All of the ships have had a side rudder fixed to the starboard side of the hull, once again except for Roskilde 1, dating to c. 1350, which had a rudder hinged to the straight sternpost.

Fig. 41.5. Hammer-like object with a runic inscription found beneath Roskilde 6. The legible runes have been read as "Sakse carved these runes...." Unfortunately the rest of the sentence has been cut away. (Werner Karrasch, the Viking Ship Museum).

Fig. 41.4. Archaeologists excavating the 36 m long warship, Roskilde 6, which partly lay under the Museum Island, partly in the canal. (Werner Karrasch, The Viking Ship Museum).

The long warship

From Roskilde 6 (Fig. 41.4), the keel survives to almost its full length of about 30 m. It consists of three pieces, assembled in 2-meter-long, complicated scarfs. Of the planking, only the middle part of the bottom and the after part of the port side are preserved. A bit of the keelson and some of the keelson knees connected to it have survived as well. All the details are beautifully shaped, with a high standard of crafmanship.

A hammer-like object with a runic inscription was found underneath the planking of the long ship (Fig. 41.5). One end of the haft was stuck into a hole in the stone head, and an eagle head was carved in the other end. The runes were carved with a very pointed tool and are interpreted to be late Viking Age as well. The inscription says: "Sakse carved these runes...." The rest of the runes are unfortunately cut away. It cannot be said whether the rune-stick was tossed underneath the ship on purpose or it ended up there by accident.

The three largest long ships found up to now, Skuldelev 2, Hedeby 1 and Roskilde 6, all seem to have been built after the same concept. Although the three warships are

of various proportions, they all have the same features: a long slender shell of planks reinforced with a light frame system in the transverse direction and two or three stringers in the longitudinal direction. As an extra reinforcement, side frames have been inserted in between the floor timbers.

The sea-going traders

All the ships in this group are of various sizes and seem to come from far away places. Although the four cargo ships in this group were built in the Early Middle Ages, they all have the traditional *biti*-frame system, as we know it from the Viking Age. Roskilde 2 (Fig. 41.6) is a middle-sized cargo carrier, which has drifted ashore and wrecked. Many parts from the rigging, osiers, bast rope, etc., were found in and around the wreck during the excavation. The finds include a well-preserved shroud pin. It had been used to tighten up the rigging.

Roskilde 3 is also a medium-sized cargo ship, dated to shortly after 1060. In spite of its early date it has all the features of the early medieval ship, including the short distance between the frames. The ship seems to have been pulled half way up on the shore and thoroughly stripped. Only two pieces of frames remained when this was discovered. The removed wreck pieces have most likely ended up as firewood in the many fireplaces of the medieval town of Roskilde.

Roskilde 4 is the largest ship in its group, a heavy bulk carrier with a cargo capacity of about 50 tons. It has many similarities with the Lynæs ship (Englert, 2000), although it is a little bit shorter and a little wider. The wreck of Roskilde 4 is perhaps the best preserved of all the nine ships. Almost 12 strakes are preserved on the starboard side and 8 strakes on the port side. The characteristic, narrow frame spacing is also found in this ship. The *biti* system is situated very low in the ship, and horizontal knees indicate heavy beams higher up in the hull.

The smallest of the cargo ships in this group is Roskilde 5, from around 1130. It is built from planks of pine, while the frames are of different species. The distance between the frames was 0.8 m, and thus of Viking Age standard. The little ship is in its size and proportions very similar to the 100-year-older Skuldelev 3 (Crumlin-Pedersen, 2002).

Many different items were found around and underneath the wrecks; pottery, wooden needles, bone needles, leather shoes, etc. Among the finds was a ship model, which in its shape and proportion seems to represent the early medieval cargo ships in this group. These items do not have any connection to the wrecks. They seem to be dropped from ships visiting the harbour area.

The small, local trading vessels

To the last group of medieval ships belong Roskilde 1, 7, 8, and 9. They are all smaller cargo vessels of shallow draught, which enabled them to operate in shallow waters. The excavation of Roskilde 7 was carried out underwater, in great haste just before the opening of the Museum Island.

Roskilde 8 has actually not been excavated, but still remains under the pavement of the Museum Island. It has been estimated to be of the same size as the other small vessels in this group. Samples from some of the planks date the ship to after 1248.

The wreck of Roskilde 9 was found on top of Roskilde 4, the big cargo ship, with a layer of one meter of marine sediment between the two wrecks. Traces of what could have been the cargoes of the Roskilde ships were never found. Beech bark stuck to a thick layer of tar inside Roskilde 9 indicates the cargo of this vessel to have been firewood. Beech logs were found scattered all around the excavation area.

The last ship in this group, Roskilde 1 was, as said, discovered already in 1996 when the building contractors were dredging out the area for the new Museum Harbour. The excavation took place in 1997 and was carried out

The construction

All the four ships in middle group are provided with the *biti* system, as we know it from Viking ships. The big cargo ship, Roskilde 4, has its *bitis* placed very low, nearly built into the floor timbers. In addition, the ship has a layer of three or five heavier beams placed higher up in the ship. Apart from Roskilde 5, the cargo ships in this group have a distance between the frame units less than that of Vikings ships (75 – 100 cm). This indicates that the crew had relied on the sail as the main propulsion instead of oars. The ships in the last group are all smaller cargo vessels with a cargo capacity ranging from 5 to 7 tons and with a minimum of draft, which enabled them to operate in shallow waters. From around 1200, the *biti* system seems to disappear. Instead, three or five heavier beams were placed higher up in the vessel and connected to the planking with strong beam knees.

The history

The nine shipwrecks from Roskilde cover a period of 300 years from the late Viking Age to about the middle of the 14th century and supplement the existing, historical sources from the same period. In the late Viking Age,

under water. Here a semi-digital documentation system was used – the Web System, developed during the excavation of the *Mary Rose* (Marsden 2003). In the web system all tape measurements are loaded into the computer to calculate the positions of the measured positions in three dimensions.

With this little cargo trader, the Nordic shipbuilding tradition is broken: long scarfs, a rudder mounted on a straight sternpost, and the use of a saw on different parts, show a strong influence from the northern European shipbuilding tradition. Roskilde 1 has many features in common with the Gedesby ship, dated to the last quarter of the 13th century (Bill 1991).

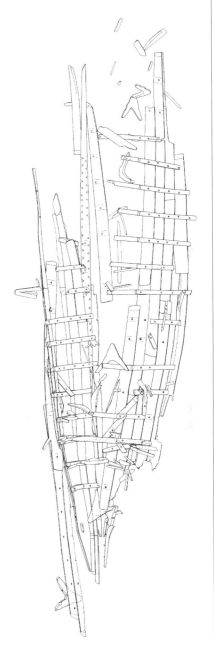

Fig. 41.6. Excavation plan of Roskilde 2. The state of the wreckage gives an impression of a dramatic shipwreck. (Werner Karrasch, The Viking Ship Museum).

Morten Gothche

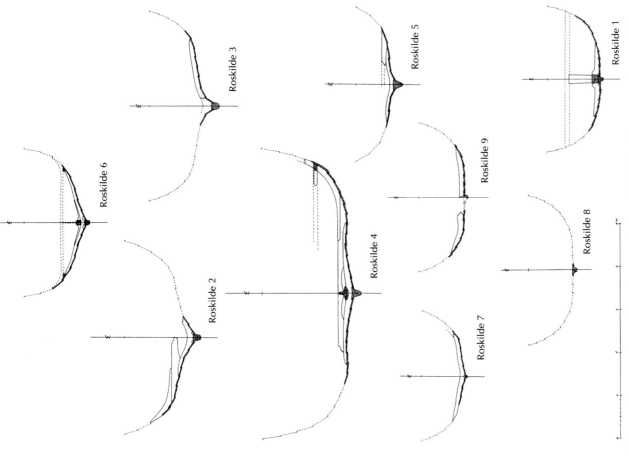

Roskilde 6

Roskilde 2

Roskilde 3

Roskilde 4

Roskilde 5

Roskilde 9

Roskilde 7

Roskilde 8

Roskilde 1

Fig. 41.7. Comparison of cross-section of the nine wrecks from Roskilde. The comparison, which only shows the parts actually found, illustrates the sections of the nine ships very well. (author).

Roskilde was the royal residence of the king. During the early Middle Ages, the capital of Roskilde was a flourishing trade city with a large number of trading vessels coming from near and far, as can be seen from the wrecks from Roskilde.

Around 1200, the city of Roskilde turned its back on the sea. As was the case for the rest of medieval Denmark, the Hanseatic east – west Baltic trade became dominant. Instead of relatively inaccessible places such as Roskilde, the Hanseatic traders used more suitable harbours such as Copenhagen, Køge or other coastal towns. The smaller vessels in the Roskilde find represent the period after

1200. They provided the medieval town of Roskilde with the necessaries of life: food, building materials, firewood, etc., from the hinterland around the Roskilde Fjord. But how did these nine ships end their days in the harbour of Roskilde? Have all nine vessels been abandoned in a ships' graveyard at the bottom of the fjord? No, this seems to be the case for just two of them. Roskilde 3 and 6 had been partly dragged on shore but were then abandoned in the shallow water. Roskilde 1, 7 and 8 seem to have sunk at the end of their anchor ropes in relatively deep water. Roskilde 2 obviously came adrift and wrecked in shallow water near the shore. Roskilde 4, 5, and 9 most likely

ship	type	date	length	beam	draft	cargo capacity	state of preservation
Roskilde 6	warship	aft. 1025	36.0	3.50	1.0	100 crewmemb.	25%
Roskilde 2	cargo ship	ca. 1185	16.5	4.50	1.1	15 t	60%
Roskilde 3	cargo ship	ca. 1060	18.0	4.40	1.0	11 t	20%
Roskilde 4	cargo ship	ca. 1108	20.5	6.60	1.5	50 t	50%
Roskilde 5	cargo ship	ca. 1130	14.0	3.60	0.7	5 t	30%
Roskilde 7	cargo ship	1270	10	3.00	0.8	5 t	35%
Roskilde 8	cargo ship	aft. 1248	0	0	0	0	1%
Roskilde 9	cargo ship	ca. 1175	11.0	3.40	0.8	5 t	30%
Roskilde 1	cargo ship	ca. 1336	10.0	3.25	0.6	7 t	65%

Fig. 41.8. Summary of the nine ships from Roskilde: type, date, dimension, cargo capacity and state of preservation in percentage. (Dendrochronological analysis by the Danish National Museum).

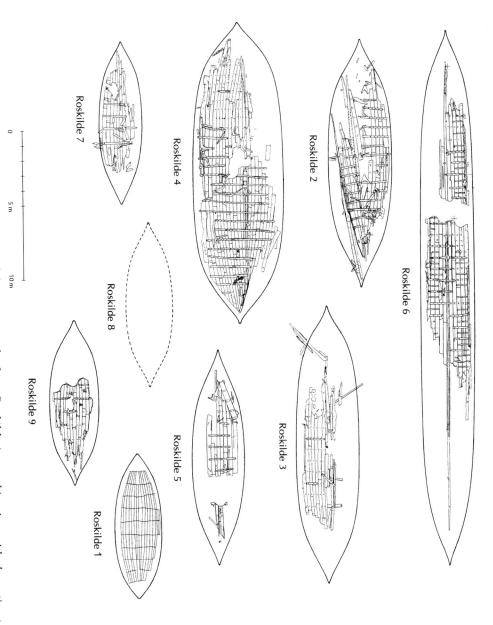

Roskilde 6

Roskilde 2

Roskilde 4

Roskilde 7

Roskilde 8

Roskilde 9

Roskilde 3

Roskilde 5

Roskilde 1

0   5 m   10 m

Fig. 41.9. Comparison of the excavation plans of the nine wrecks from Roskilde in combination with the estimated overall dimension and shape of the hulls. (author).

Status of the Roskilde Ships

Since the opening of the Museum Island in 1997, the National Museum (and after 2003, the Viking Ship Museum) has been working with the documentation of the many parts from the nine shipwrecks. The 1:1 documentation based on the experience from the documentation of the Skuldelev ships has been developed into perfection (Petersen, 1998). Digital photo document-

came adrift from their anchorage and may have sunk when they grounded (Figs 41.7–41.9).

ation has been introduced. The building of the replicas of the five Skuldelev Ships emphasizes the need of a thorough 1:1 documentation as well as professional photo documentation. The use of appropriate photo equipment and a proper setting of the light makes it possible to record even the smallest tool-mark.

In order to reduce the time consuming 1:1 document-ation a new medium for the documentation has been taken into use – the FaroArm – a three-dimensional coordinate measuring machine (CMM) writing data directly into the Rhinoceros™ computer programme. The use of the FaroArm system had been developed by the Centre for Maritime Archaeology during the documentation of the replica of the Hjortspring Boat *Telia Alsie* (Crumlin-Pedersen 2003) and the dismantled timbers of the Kolding cog (Hocker 2001).

At the moment we are more than halfway through the documentation of the nine ships. All the waterlogged wood, planks and frames that have already been doc-umented, are located in conservation tanks in the National Museum Conservation Department in Brede. Some of the wood has already been impregnated with PEG and is now ready for the freeze-drying process. The impregnation of heavier parts such as the keels from all the ships is ongoing and is estimated to be finished about the year 2012. The conservation of all the bast ropes from the Roskilde excavation is finished.

References

Bill, J., 1991, Gedesbyskibet. *Nationalmuseets Arbejdsmark*, 188 – 199. København.

Bill, J., Gothche, M. and Myrhøj, H.M.. 1998. Nordeuropas største skibsfund. Ni vrag fra vikingetid og middelalder under museumsøen i Roskilde. *Nationalmuseets Arbejds-mark*, 136 – 158. København

Bill, J. Gothche, M. and Myrhøj, H.M.. 2000, Roseskildeskibene. In T. Christensen and M. Andersen (ed): *Civitas Roscald –fra byens begyndelse*, 221 – 259. Roskilde Museum. Roskilde.

Crumlin-Pedersen, O., 1997. *Viking-Age ships and shipbuilding in Hedeby/haitabu and Schleswig*. Ships and Boats of the North 2. Schleswig and Roskilde.

Crumlin-Pedersen, O., and Olsen, O. (eds.). 2002, *The Skuldelev Ships I*. Ships and Boats of the North 4. Roskilde.

Crumlin-Pedersen, O., and Trakadas, A. (eds.). 2003, *Hjort-spring – A Pre-Roman Iron-Age Warship in context*. Ships and Boats of the North 5. Roskilde.

Englert, A., 2000, *Large Cargo Vessels in Danish Waters: AD 1000 – 1250*. Dissertation, Christian-Albrechts-Universität zu Kiel.

Hocker, F., 2001, Object documentation. *Maritime Archaeology Newsletter from Roskilde Denmark* 17: 21.

Marsden, P., 2003: *Sealed by the Time – The Loss and recovery of the Mary Rose. The archaeology of the Mary Rose*. Volume 1. Portsmouth.

Petersen, A.H., and Strætkvern, K., 1998, Arkæologisk Vaerk-sted på Museumsøen i Roskilde. *Nationalmuseets Arbejds-mark* 1998, 159–166. København.

42 Two double-planked wrecks from Poland

Waldemar Ossowski

Introduction

Towards the end of the Middle Ages, a new, large sailing ship was developed in Europe, with three or four masts, capable of carrying large cargoes and transporting them over long distances. The cornerstone was the development of a new skeleton-first technique which permitted the building of ships with capacities greater than before. The origin and development of this new building technique in the southern Baltic region is poorly understood.

A flush-laid hull could be built in several different ways. Olof Hasslöf hypothesises that this form of construction underwent a stage-by-stage development and shifted from a shell-first method to a combination of both shell and skeleton construction to the final stage, which was a strictly skeleton-first technique (1972). He presented examples of ship construction as evidence that the shell-first method was used to build a carvel hull, or that combinations of these two construction techniques were used with the end result being the so-called half-carvel.

These methods have been traced through archival sources all the way back to the 16th century (Hasslöf 1972: 59).

Since the year 2000, a research project supported by the State Committee for Scientific Research entitled *Pomeranian boat- and shipbuilding in the Middle Ages in light of tree-ring analysis* (grant No 1H01 H026 18) has been carried out at the Polish Maritime Museum in Gdańsk. Under this project, archaeological investigations were launched on two double-planked wrecks. The aim of this paper is to briefly present the results of recent research conducted on these finds.

Two double-planked wrecks from Poland

Wreck W-36

In the years 2001–2002 the remains of two ships, in which double-planked techniques were found, were uncovered on the Polish shore (Fig. 42.1). The first wreck was

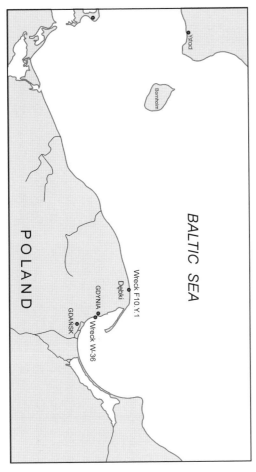

Fig. 42.1. Map of the southern Baltic Sea showing location of the two double-planked wrecks from Poland mentioned in text (drawing by author).

Waldemar Ossowski

first solution of this kind to be found in Poland, it was decided to extract all the elements in order to analyse them in a more detailed way.

Following suitable preparations, the whole wreck was dismantled, and all the elements were lifted and transported to the Conservation Workshop of the Polish Maritime Museum, where detailed documentation was carried out. The study of the extracted elements revealed a number of details, which allowed the construction process to be reconstructed.

From the longitudinal timbers, only an oak, T-shaped keel 5.3 m long survives. This was 18 cm high and with a maximum width of 21 cm. The after end was formed by a 28-cm-long, bevelled, flat scarf for the sternpost, with traces of six nails, 0.5 and 1 cm in size, which must have been used to fasten the sternpost.

There were two layers of planking. The first layer was made of overlapping, sawn, oak planks fastened by iron rivets. Luting material was animal hair. No remains of iron nails have survived, only traces of metal roves measuring 2.3 x 2.4 cm, spaced every 20 cm, could be seen underneath the floor timbers. The 3-cm-thick, oak planks were 3.5 to 3.7 m long and reached widths of 32 to 35 cm. The lands were 4–5 cm wide with a cove for plaited animal hair on the inner surface. The 30-cm-long, vertical planking scarfs were caulked with animal hair and tar and fastened by 5 nails driven in a vertical line along the edges.

Frames were fastened by means of oak treenails, 27 mm in diameter, and were placed into a hull made using the shell-first method (Fig. 42.3-1). Dendrochronological analysis showed that that stage of the ship's construction took place after 1596. At a later time, pine fillers with a triangular cross-section were fastened to the outer surface of the planking with small metal nails as a levelling layer (Fig. 42.3-2). Onto this surface another, complete layer of sawn pine planks, 3 cm thick and 23 to 31 cm wide, was laid. The planks were flush-laid and fastened at their edges by nails driven in every 35 cm (Fig. 42.3-3). These planks were also fastened to the floor timbers and futtocks (Fig. 42.3-4) by means of oak treenails 32 mm in diameter (Fig. 42.4). The oak treenails were dotted on the outside and wedged on the inside. Unfortunately, dendrochronological analysis of the pine planks has not been successful, and it is not possible to determine the period of time which elapsed between the building of the outer and inner planking.

Wreck from Dębki (F 10.Y.1.)

In the spring of 2002, following a storm, a large fragment of a wooden ship was washed ashore near the village of Dębki (Fig. 42.5). During the site inspection it turned out that we were dealing with the remains of a section of hull bottom built of two layers of planking, with a broken keel, resting on the shore upside-down. In order to secure the wreck, the hull was cut into three sections, lifted and

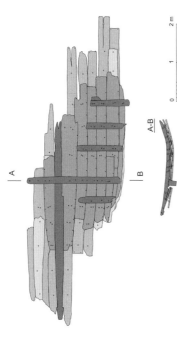

Fig. 42.2. Wreck W-36 – preserved parts of the hull (drawing by author).

Fig. 42.3. Wreck W-36 – stages of construction of the hull (drawing by author).

discovered by divers in 2001, approximately 250 meters from the shore in Gdynia-Orłowo, at a depth of 2.7 metres. It appeared under the water as a small mound of bricks constituting the vessel's main cargo. Inside the hull, beneath the evenly stowed bricks, 6.5 x 14 x 29 cm, a few fragments of dishes and Dutch pipes from the mid-17th century were found. On the basis of the size of the structural elements it is possible to estimate that the hull was originally 15–18 metres long, hence wreck W-36 is probably the remains of a small ship used in coastal or local navigation in the Bay of Gdańsk. The results of dendrochronological analysis show that the timber to build the sailing ship was cut in the area of the Vistula Bay; it was probably built in the area starting from the beginning of the 16th century, and this vessel may have been used for transporting bricks to coastal locations in the Bay of Gdańsk.

After the bricks were removed, the remains of a poorly preserved hull section were revealed (Fig. 42.2). Only its after, bottom section survives, measuring 8.8 m in length and inclined to starboard. Inside, the hull was reinforced by three floor timbers and the remains of three frames placed fairly regularly, with a spacing of 60 cm. Six overlapping strakes on the starboard side and two strakes on the port side were uncovered. Protruding from beneath were planks which formed a second layer of planking. As it was the

taken to the Conservation Workshop in Tczew for further investigations.

Closer inspection revealed that this was the bow end of a ship's bottom, with preserved dimensions of 9.2 m long and 3.5 m wide. The inner layer of planking was of clinker planks, 3–3.5 cm thick, up to 36 cm wide and caulked with animal hair. The land was 4 cm wide and the planks scarfs were 13 cm long, fastened with nails. The strakes were fastened with iron rivets and rectangular roves, spaced 14–15 cm apart.

The flush-laid outer strakes were of pine, 6 cm thick and only 17–22 cm wide. The keel and garoards were fastened to the floor timbers by means of metal bolts, 22 mm in diameter. The transverse scarfs of the carvel planking were each fastened with two oak treenails of rectangular cross-section, 18 mm square.

A characteristic feature of this ship is the frame elements, which were fastened to the planking very closely to one another. They are not interconnected, show great variability in scantlings and are of highly variable length; some are secondarily used (Fig. 42.6). There were 23 floor timbers, 11–18 cm sided, spaced approximately every 20 cm. The strakes were fastened to the frames by treenails, 34 mm in diameter, and by metal bolts. Ceiling

planks 45 mm thick and 16 cm wide were laid directly on the floor timbers.

Since the extracted sections are preserved intact and have not been dismantled, it has only been possible to study the building sequence at the five cross-sections which were made as a result of cutting the hull into pieces (Fig. 42.7). In all cases it has been observed that it is not possible to distinguish which treenails were used to join overlapping planks and which were used to fasten flush-laid ones. The oak treenails were dotted on the outside and wedged on the inside and were of the same length, so as to simultaneously join the ceiling, the frames and the

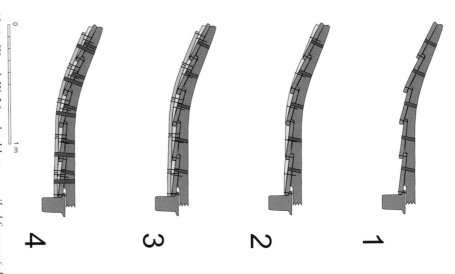

Fig. 42.4. Wreck W-36 – double-treenailed frames (photo by author).

Fig. 42.5. The Dębki wreck – a part of the ship washed ashore in 2002 (photo by author).

Fig. 42.6. The Dębki wreck – timbers have very variable scantlings and some are secondarily used (photo by author).

Waldemar Ossowski

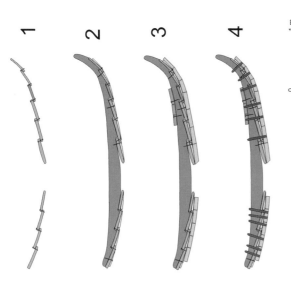

1

2

3

4

0   1 m

Fig. 42.7. The Dębki wreck – double layer of outer planking (photo by author).

Fig. 42.8. The Dębki wreck – stages of construction of the hull (drawing by author).

outer and inner planks. Hence, if we assume that the holes for treenails were not drilled twice, then the construction sequence differs from that of the former wreck. At first, the overlapping planks were fitted and fastened using the shell-first method (Fig. 42.8-1). Then, some or all of the frames must have been fastened in place with nails. The levelling planks and the carvel planks were nailed to this structure and caulked with moss (Fig. 42.8-2). Next, more floor timbers and futtocks (possibly all of them) were laid in and the ceiling was nailed from above (Fig. 42.8-3). It was only then that all of these elements were joined together using wooden treenails (Fig. 42.8-4). Hence, the double planking was not a result of repairs or rebuilding but rather it was part of the original construction.

In order to determine the age and place of origin of the wreck a number of samples were taken for tree-ring analysis and given to the dendrochronological laboratory of the Mining and Metallurgy University in Krakow. This analysis did not succeed in determining the age of any of the timbers on the basis of the dendrochronological curves available in Polish laboratories, but the set of 6 samples did show the highest similarity to the chronology from Hamburg (t=4.7) for the period 1508–1653 AD (Ossowski 2004).

The tree-ring curve generated for the ship did not match any of the master curves available in Polish laboratories. It seems to show that the ship was built from raw material originating from distant areas, perhaps from the northern Baltic. At the present time the results obtained from the samples are being tested in laboratories of other Baltic states, which may make it possible to determine the provenance of the wood used to build the vessel. In one case the tests confirmed that the clinker planks are of the same age as the flush-laid planks. This is confirmed by the observed fact that the inside and outside planking was built at the same time.

Finally, in order to determine the vessel's age, radio-carbon dating was conducted and the rendered result was

105±35BP. Unfortunately the ¹⁴C date is very close to the present, and with such a date the calibrated age fits in a very wide range, from the late 17th century through the whole 19th century.

Other double planked wrecks from the Baltic

In 1991, at the 6th ISBSA conference in Roskilde (1991), Vello Mäss presented the results of the investigation of an interesting wreck discovered near Maasilinn on the island of Ozylia in Estonia (1994). The remains represented a small single-masted sailing ship from the mid-14th century known as a *uisk*, which was used in navigation between the mainland and the islands of Dago, Ozylia and Muhu. A characteristic feature, which had not been encountered in the Baltic before, was that the ship's hull was built of two layers of planking –thin, overlapping inner planks were covered with thick, strong, flush-laid strakes. Although this may appear to be the result of repair or rebuilding, some structural features show that the hull was initially built with two layers of planking so as to be stronger. This is evidenced by the lack of any fastening of the keel to the floor timbers. They do not contact the keel, and the hull is joined to the keel by the outer planks only. The seemingly later carvel planking was thus necessary to support the keel and had to be laid simultaneously with the overlapping planks to reinforce the whole structure. This means that the keel section had to be moved forward ensuring better seaworthiness and to allow goods to be carried in a drier condition. This is evidenced by the slaked lime found inside the wreck, the likely remains of the main cargo. As it was difficult to haul such a ship onto the beach, the reinforced hull may have been suitable for wintering on the water in ice.

Double planking has been also found in the hull of a medieval ship from Gellen, which was discovered in 1996 near the old western entrance to Stralsund, currently at the Hiddensee island shore, west of Rügen. This sank with a cargo of Öland limestone slabs (Förster 2000). The ship was originally 28 m long and 8 m wide, and had been built primarily of pine. Unlike cogs, which were common in the 13th and 14th centuries and had flat, flush-laid bottoms and overlapping side planks, this craft is characterized by overlapping planks from the keel to the sheer. The overlapping planks were levelled by triangular-sectioned planks onto which another layer of flush-laid planks was set. Tree-ring analysis shows that the clinker construction was made about 1339 of timber originating in the south-eastern Baltic region. About the year 1364 the ship underwent a major repair, when the flush-laid planking layer was added.

Another double-planked wreck was found in 1981 at Nors Å in Denmark. The clinker-built vessel had flush laid planks which were nailed directly onto the outside, without levelling wedges. According to Morten Gøthche, the wreck could be of the *sandskude* type, ships used in Denmark so-called *skudehandel*, the trade between Norway and Denmark in the 17th–19th centuries (1985). Because such vessels were owned by local farmers and landed directly on the shore, this gave the name to the vessels in this particular trade. The remains of small craft of the 17th–19th century craft from Denmark often represent a special type or a combination of techniques employed during building (Gøthche 1991). The Nors Å ship was a typical example of giving an old vessel new life using a method popular in Scandinavia known as *putte det i konvolut* – "putting it into an envelope" – i.e. strengthening by laying new carvel planking on top of the original clinker sides (Gøthche 1985).

Discussion

The two wrecks from Poland presented here have revealed very interesting and rarely seen design solutions in the form of double planking and have shown that such planking can be joined in different ways with the framing. The analyses which have been conducted so far and the poor condition in which the watercraft have been preserved have not made it possible at this stage to explain clearly the reasons why such design solutions were employed. The use of double planking may be explained in the following way:

• an attempt to make repairs to extend the life of the vessel

• reinforcement of the hull as was necessary to drag the watercraft onto the flat and sandy shore of the southern Baltic, where there were no natural ports, or to protect the hull against ice

• an attempt to increase the hull's watertightness for the carriage of bulk cargos such as lime, salt or grain, which are readily spoiled by water

Hull repairs using double planking of the bottom are known from ancient times. With regard to the southern Baltic Sea, we know from written sources that repairs of this type were made in the 16th century in shipyards on the Vistula River estuary. For example, an item of information has been preserved in the books of an Elbląg carpentry workshop: In the year 1587, builder Claus made various repair works, including reinforcement of 24 oak hull planks by providing an additional outside layer and by caulking them with moss and oakum (Gierszewski 1961: 80). When comparing that note with the findings concerning the Gellen wreck, it may be noted that the use of double planking was a fairly popular way on the southern shores of the Baltic Sea of repairing a hull made of overlapping planks.

The wrecks discussed originate in a very interesting period in the history of shipbuilding, when the frame-first method started to be used in Baltic and North Sea shipyards. In the southern Baltic, this transition took place in the second half of the 15th century and in the first half of the 16th century, in the period when the Gdańsk shipbuilding industry had its heyday and when Gdańsk shipyards were building the largest seagoing ships in northern Europe. We know from written sources that in the second half of the 15th century, ships with a carrying capacity of up to 200 lasts were constructed in Gdańsk and that the works were conducted by foreigners — as we can, for instance, read in Caspera Weinreich's chronicle recording the death in 1473 of a certain Lombard, who was constructing a huge vessel with a keel that was 29 m long (Lienau 1943: 43). In the early 16th century, the demand for new ships was systematically growing. It was conducive to an increase in the number of specialists employed in a shipyard. According to the census of 1526 there were as many as 130 ship carpenters in Gdańsk. Such a workforce made it possible to build large ships for export at the end of the first half of the 16th century. It was in Gdańsk that three new warships for the navy of Henry VIII, King of England, were built (Litwin 1998: 31).

It is not definitely known when, to what extent and by whom the latest technological achievements in the form of the frame-first method were applied in Gdańsk. So far it has been believed that was connected to the arrival of the carrack *Pierre de la Rochelle* from France in 1462. The ship was damaged in Gdańsk as a result of being struck by lightning. Having been partially burnt, the ship was abandoned by the owner. In 1470 the vessel was taken over by the city, the hull was dragged to the shore, the ship was rebuilt and adapted for privateer purposes. The works having been completed, the warship began its service under the name of *Peter von Danzig*. It was described as a huge carvel, although it represented a type called a carrack in other places. It is known that soon afterwards, in the years 1475 and 1488, two new ships were built with flush-laid planking. In the opinion of some historians, the repair of the French carrack in Gdańsk caused a breakthrough in the local shipbuilding industry (Lienau 1943). It was allegedly from that time that changes in the technique of hull building were made: overlapping planking was replaced by flush-laid planking.

It seems that such argumentation cannot be accepted. Just inspecting, or even repairing a hull built using frame-first technology (which was new in the north of Europe) was not enough to learn how to build a new ship without having knowledge about the whole technological process. It was Hasslöf who first indicated in his works that flush-laid planking and the frame-first technology did not always go together (1972). As is proved by the results of investigations of Dutch and Danish wrecks from the turn of the 16th and 17th centuries, the new method of shipbuilding was adopted to a varied degree and mixed solutions were used (Maarleveld 1994, Lemée 2002). The case must have been similar in northern Baltic shipyards. An item of information has been preserved in written sources indicates that in 1488, Brosien Mellin, a citizen of Gdańsk, laid a keel for a carvel which was 39 m long and 12.5 m wide. The hull of that watercraft, above the water line, had carvel planking and the bottom section, the most difficult section to form, was built with the use of the traditional shell-first overlapping method (Litwin 1998: 30). The latest archaeological discoveries show that not only the bottoms of cogs but also the sides of large inland navigation watercraft were flush-laid as early as in the 14th century in Gdańsk, notwithstanding the fact that they were built with the use of the shell-first method (Ossowski in press).

The feature that the wrecks presented here have in common is that they were low-tonnage vessels, with regional features, that must have been built in local boatbuilding centres. The available results of the tests conducted on the double planking of the Dębki wreck show that the structure was made all at once and may illustrate an attempt to follow frame-first technology by using the shell-first method to obtain a hull bottom section made of flush-laid planks. This may reflect attempts to apply new achievements in the course of building or repairing small watercraft used in local navigation, in which rich farmers and peasants also participated at that time. Although no exhaustive studies are available on that subject, materials from the areas of Gdańsk and Elbląg show that some farmers not only indulged in navigation but organized shipbuilding on their own as well, and these were not isolated cases. More light is cast on this process in Western Pomerania in the 18th century, where 2–3 last *skuta* and 5-last yachts were used in navigation (Gierszewski 1961: 112).

When studying the wrecks presented here, one should also take into account the issues related to the organization of shipbuilding in the 16th–18th centuries. Like craftsmen in almost all other trades at that time, the craftsmen who were involved in shipbuilding were organized in a guild.

The Gdańsk shipbuilding industry, however, was based not only on guild craftsmanship but also on craftsmen and designers of foreign origin, who were not associated in guilds. As in other Baltic states, foreign boatbuilders, with their skill and new methods, were brought in to build large ships, mainly upon the king's orders at first (Adams and Rönnby 1996, Lemée 2002, Probst 1994). Local traditions could still be seen in ships built for private owners. Construction of smaller ships in smaller towns was limited mainly to river and shore watercraft and it usually did not require special and costly equipment or special knowledge. It is known from written sources that the ability to build ships of this type was covered by the scope of knowledge of village and small town master carpenter (Gierszewski 1961: 54). It was also as a result of conflicts with employers and the city council, as was for instance the case in Elbląg, that ship carpenters left their towns and settled in smaller towns, bringing their experience with them (Gierszewski 1961: 186–187; 1972: 170). It was in smaller towns located on the Bay of Gdańsk or the Vistula Lagoon that they continued local traditions and built ships still employing the shell-first method with overlapping planking into the mid-20th century (Form-acon and Salemke 1988).

Hence, the two newly discovered wrecks may show that the need to build larger, stronger and more watertight vessels led to attempts to reinforce the hull by using additional planking, which, while imitating the solution used on larger ships used in 16th–19th century navigation, was nonetheless still based on the old rules of constructing them.

References

Adams J. and Rönnby J., 1996, *Furstens fartyg*. Stockhom.

Fornacon S. and Salemke G., 1988, *Lommen und Buxer, Volkstümliche Schiffe in Ost- und Westpreussen*. Leer.

Förster T., 2000, Schiffbau und Handel an der südwestlichen Ostsee- Untersuchungen an Wrackfunden des 13–15. Jahrhunderts. In *IKUWA Schutz des Kulturerbes unter Wasser, Beiträge zur Ur-und Frühgeschichte Mecklemburg – Vorpommers*, Band 35, pp. 221–236.

Gierszewski S., 1961, *Elbląski przemyst okrętowy w latach 1570–1815*. Gdańsk.

Gierszewski S., 1972, Życie gospodarcze Tolkmicka jako królewszczyzny (1569–1772), *Rocznik Elbląski* 5: 159–174.

Gøthche M., 1985, "*Sandskuder*" – vessel for trade between Norway and Denmark in the 18th and 19 th centuries. In C.O. Cederlund (ed.) *Postmedieval Boat and Ship Archaeology*, BAR International Series 256, pp. 299–314. Oxford.

Gøthche M., 1991, Three Danish 17th–19th century wrecks as examples of clinker building techniques versus carvel building techniques in local shipwrightry. In R. Reinders and K. Paul (eds.), *Carvel Construction Technique*, Oxbow Monograph 12, pp. 85–88. Oxford.

Hasslöf O., 1972, Main principles in the technology of ship building. In O. Hasslöf, H. Henningsen, A. E. Christensen (eds.), *Ships and Shipyards, Sailors and Fishermen*, pp. 27–72, Copenhagen.

Lemée C.P.P., 2002, *Klamper, spigerpinde og skabeloner. Et bygningsarkaeologisk studium af 1500- og 1600-tallets skibsbygningsmetoder i Nordvesteuropa.* Unpublished PhD dissertation, Royal Academy of Architecture, Copenhagen.

Lienau O., 1943, *Das Grosse Kraweel der Peter von Danzig 1462–1475. Ein Beitrag zur Geschichte Deutscher Seegeltung.* Danzig.

Litwin J., 1996, *Morskie dziedzictwo Gdańska.* Gdańsk.

Maarleveld T., 1994, Double Dutch solution in flush-planked shipbuilding. In C.Westerdahl (ed.) *Crossroads in Ancient Shipbuilding.* Oxbow Monograph 40, pp. pp. 153–164. Oxford.

Mäss V., 1994, A unique 16th-century Estonian ship find. In C.Westerdahl (ed.) *Crossroads in Ancient Shipbuilding,* Oxbow Monograph 40, pp. 189–194. Oxford.

Ossowski W., 2004, Medieval large river craft from the Vistula River (Poland). In K. Brandt and H.J. Kühn (eds.), *Der Prahm aus dem Hafen von Haithabu. Beiträge zu antieken und mittelalterlishen Flachbodenschiffen.* Schriften des Archäologischen Landesmuseums 2, pp. 83–96. Schleswig.

Probst N. M., 1994, The Introduction of flush-planked skin in Northern Europe and the Elsinore wrecks. In C. Westerdahl (ed.) *Crossroads in Ancient Shipbuilding,* Oxbow Monograph 40, pp. 143–152. Oxford.

43 *Mynden.*
A small Danish frigate of the 18th century

Jens Auer

The discovery of the Arkona wreck

In the autumn of 1991, German navy divers discovered a small wooden shipwreck at a depth of 10m off Cape Arkona on the north coast of the island of Rügen, in the federal state of Mecklenburg-Vorpommern in north-eastern Germany (Fig. 43.1). They observed a number of guns on and around the wreck and salvaged four of them. The guns, three cast iron 'finbankers' and one bronze

cannon, were intitally put on display in front of the navy barracks, but were handed over to the *Landesamt für Vor-und Frühgeschichte* in Schleswig-Holstein (the cultural heritage authority in the federal state of Schleswig-Holstein) when heavy deterioration was noticed.

This led to the first archaeological survey of the site, conducted by Dr. W. Kramer of the *Landesamt für Vor-und Frühgeschichte Schleswig-Holstein.* Another two

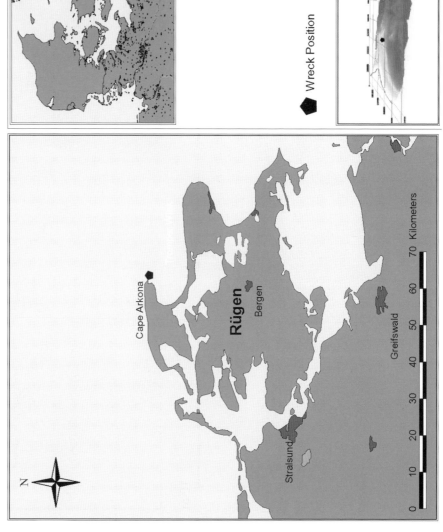

Fig. 43.1. Location of the wreck site (author 2003).

guns were lifted and handed over to the *Landesamt für Bodendenkmalpflege Mecklenburg-Vorpommern* (the cultural heritage authority in neighbouring Mecklenburg-Vorpommern). In August 1992, the Society for Underwater Archaeology of Mecklenburg-Vorpommern was commissioned to survey and manage the wreck site. Between 1993 and 1995, scattered artefacts were recovered and a preliminary sketch of the site was drawn. In 1995 two test trenches were dug in the presumed bow and stern area of the wreck (Förster 1994). Firewood from the ship's galley could be dendrochronologically dated to autumn 1718 (sapwood present). From 1999 to 2000, the wreck was studied as the

subject of an MA thesis (Auer 2000). All previously recovered artefacts were recorded, catalogued and identified. The remaining hull structure on the seabed was recorded in detail (Fig. 43.2). A basic plan of the trail of wreckage could be drawn. The information gathered during this project finally led to the identification of the wreck in the Danish National Archives in Copenhagen.

Description of the wreck site

The wreck site is composed of a large preserved part of the hull with surrounding artefact scatter and at least one trail of debris.

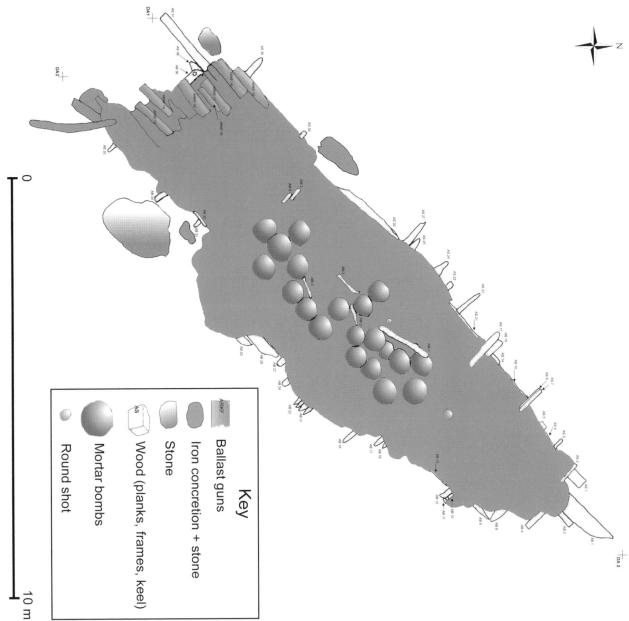

Fig. 43.2. Plan of the preserved hull remains (Ralf Bleile 1999).

Key

ARKF
AS — Wood (planks, frames, keel)
Stone
Iron concretion + stone
Ballast guns
Mortar bombs
Round shot

Fig. 43.3. Diver at the starboard side of the hull remains (author 1999).

The wreck is located in 10m of water just south of the main Arkona chalk reef. The seabed on the site consists of chalk with a thin cover of sand. A 15m-long and 5m-wide hull section from the stern to approximately amidships is preserved. It is oriented northeast-southwest and lies on its port side. A half-buried anchor and the partly excavated galley in the south-west indicate the ship's bow. No structural elements survive from forward of the amidships, where the keel is broken off. Stern cant frames are visible in the northeast. The sternpost and stern deadwood are missing.

The ship was carvel built from oak. Planking up to 8 cm thick and 20–34 cm wide is fastened to the frames with 3.5 cm treenails. 11 planks were observed on the partly buried port side, while only fragments are preserved to starboard (Fig. 43.3). Ceiling planks are 15–20 cm wide and up to 5 cm thick. The keel, measuring 35 cm square, is clearly visible due to the angle of the hull. Twenty-two floor timbers, between 20 cm and 30 cm square, are set across the keel on 39 cm centres. Only four 1st futtocks remain on the starboard side. The exact frame composition could not be determined due to *Teredo* damage and metal concretion.

The whole wreck is covered by a concreted layer of stones and iron ballast, including gun components, iron round shot and mortar bombs with diameters of up to 50 cm. The mortar bombs are filled with sand and scrap iron. Noteworthy among the ballast are seven cast iron 'finbanker' guns of different calibres. None of the ballast was removed during the surveys, as it was intended to preserve the wreck *in situ* as part of an underwater archaeological park.

An anchor, various parts of the rigging and a number of large wooden elements were discovered southwest of the main hull. In this area, part of the ship's galley was excavated in a test trench in 1995. The galley probably consisted of a wooden compartment with brick floor and coppered walls. A large copper kettle, discovered in 1995, was suspended over an open fire place on the brick hearth.

A trail of debris 190 m long leads from the wreck in a northwesterly direction towards the cape. This trail includes two anchors and at least three guns. Future surveys of this area might reveal more components.

Identification of the wreck

The archaeological information gathered during the various surveys and excavations proved to be crucial for the identification of the wreck.

The piece of firewood from the galley area, which could be dated to autumn 1718, suggested the loss occurred between autumn 1718 and spring 1719. Further to that, a lead seal inscribed with the year 1718 was found on the site. All artefacts recovered from the wreck date to the early 18th century. The dimensions of all preserved structural components indicated a smaller vessel, not longer than 30 m (Hoving 1994, van Yk 1697). 11 guns could be traced as definitely originating from the wreck site. This relatively high number of guns for the vessel's size pointed towards a small warship. As one of the guns from the site was Danish and the island of Rügen had been conquered by the Danes in 1715, research started in the Danish National Archives in Copenhagen.

A list of the Danish fleet for the year 1719 (Riksarkivet Copenhagen, *Søkrigskancelliet 930*) mentioned the loss of the small frigate *Mynden* (or *Windhund*) off the island of Rügen in 1718. Documentation of the incident, including letters of the ship's master to the admiralty, a full list of the crew, a list of all goods salvaged from the wreck, logbooks and the documentation of the trial following the loss of the frigate was found. In the logbook excerpts written by the ship's master after the loss, the exact location of the wreck, as well as the wrecking process were described. This information confirmed the identification of the Arkona wreck as the small Danish frigate *Mynden*.

A short history of the Royal Danish frigate Mynden

Mynden was built in 1679 by the Dutch master shipwright Thijs Hermansen van der Burgh at the naval dockyard in Copenhagen. She was classed as a small frigate, but often called *snau* in primary sources such as logbooks. In 1680–88 *Mynden* acted mainly as a convoy ship and took part in several longer voyages to Iceland and the Baltic States. Other tasks included guarding the naval harbour in Copenhagen and recruitment and transport of military personnel. During the Great Nordic War from 1709–1721, *Mynden* served as a convoy escort and cruiser, mainly on the routes between Denmark and Norway. In 1716 she took part in the battle of Dynekilen in a squadron under the command of the famous Tordenskjold. In 1718 first lieutenant Hans Friedrich Dreessen was given command of *Mynden*. The ship again accompanied convoys in the southern Baltic.

"...and she sank within seven minutes..." – the loss of Mynden

In a letter to the Danish admiralty in Copenhagen, first lieutenant Dreessen describes the circumstances of the loss of *Mynden* (Riksarkivet Copenhagen, *Admiralitetets indkomne sager* 603). Further accounts of the last journey of the frigate were found in the documentation of the subsequent courts martial.

In November 1718, *Mynden* was dispatched to the town of Lübeck to escort the *fluit Der Herbst* and five other vessels loaded with cargo for the Danish navy to Copenhagen (Fig. 43.4). The convoy left Travemünde on the evening of November 17th. Course was set for the island of Mon, but strong northwesterly winds forced the convoy to change course on the morning of November 18th. After a consultation with the first mate, an experienced pilot for the southern Baltic, it was decided to sail to the island of Rügen and seek shelter in the well known anchorage of Prorer Wiek. When at dusk the convoy had not yet reached Prorer Wiek, Dreessen decided to head for the closer Tromper Wiek and anchor to allow the slower merchantmen to catch up with the frigate.

At 15:30 on November 18th, the order was given to prepare to anchor, as the frigate sailed past Cape Arkona into the Tromper Wiek. About 800m off the cape, the frigate hit an underwater obstruction, presumably a big stone on the chalk reef that extends from the cape into the sea. Almost instantly water was noticed in the hold below the galley. The lieutenant attempted to keep the frigate on the obstruction to prevent the ship from sinking, but failed. A single shot was fired to signal emergency. The crew managed to launch the small yawl, but the pinnace could not be launched before the upper deck was submerged. The frigate sank within seven minutes in 12m of water. Thirteen sailors drowned, but 42 were rescued by local fishermen.

As the masts were still visible, first salvage attempts were made on the following day. A list of salvaged goods specifies everything that was recovered from the wreck (Riksarkivet Copenhagen, *Admiralitetets indkomne sager* 603). While most of the upper rigging could be saved, none of the guns or equipment in the ship were accessible. Guards were posted on all beaches in the area to collect drifting wreckage and prevent looting.

Lieutenant Dreessen kept a logbook of the events following the loss of the frigate and describes in great detail how the wreck was destroyed by natural forces such as storms and currents. According to his notes, the trail of wreckage was caused by the upper structure of the frigate which was separated from the rest of the wreck during a storm on the 9th of January 1719 and drifted northwestwards around the cape.

Associated finds

As *Mynden* was a warship, many of the finds recovered were part of the ordnance. A total of 11 cast iron three-pounder guns of the same type were found on the site (Fig. 43.5a). Their average length is 1.9m. They have double reinforcement rings, flat muzzle faces and trunnions marked with the letter "F". The guns can be classed as finbankers Type 2, Litra A and L of Dutch origin (Frantzen 1999, 151).

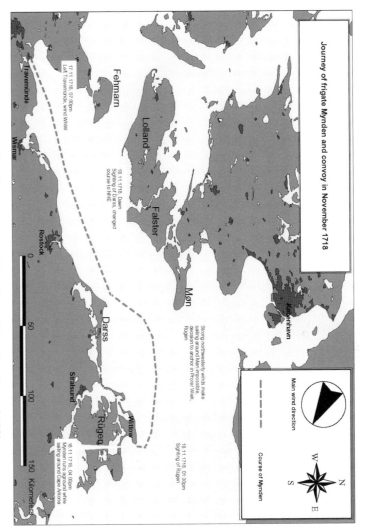

Fig. 43.4. The last passage of the frigate Mynden (Auer 2003).

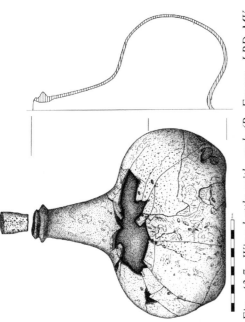

Fig. 43.7. Wine bottle with cork (B. Froese, LBD MV 1998).

The ammunition found on the wreck site included iron round shot, bar shot and grape shot for two-pounder and three-pounder guns. A number of iron hand grenades with well preserved wooden fuses and slow matches were found in the stern area of the wreck (Fig. 43.6). These grenades were designed to be thrown from the rigging onto the enemy's deck in boarding actions.

A number of other artefacts illustrate shipboard life on a small frigate in the 18th century. Finds include copper cooking pots from the ship's galley and wine bottles with corks preserved in the soft chalk sediment (Fig. 43.7). A wooden box, probably used to store a razor or pen, had been decorated with traditional Norwegian carvings (Fig. 43.8). A clay pipe of Dutch type was found in its wooden case (Fig. 43.9).

Some thoughts concerning a reconstruction of Mynden

The analysis of archaeological evidence combined with documentary sources makes it possible to make suggestions concerning the construction and appearance of the frigate.

The dimensions of *Mynden* according to the building contract were:

    Length between perpendiculars: 25.6 m
    Extreme breadth: 6.46 m
    Depth in hold: 3.13 m.

The frigate had three masts and a ship rig without topgallant sails. She had a spritsail under the bowsprit. *Mynden* carried 12 three-pounder guns and possibly two two-pounders. The quarterdeck was armed with six swivel guns. All guns were positioned on the upper deck. A structural lower deck did not exist. Galley, storage compartments and powder magazine were built into the hold. *Mynden* did not have a raised forecastle. A cabin

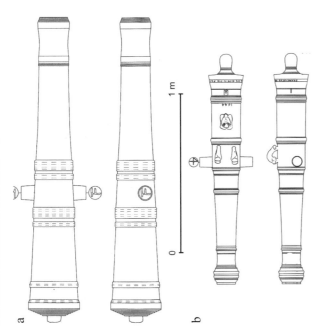

Fig. 43.5 a). Cast iron three-pounder finbanker from the wreck site (author 2000). b). Bronze two-pounder from the wreck site (author 2000).

Fig. 43.6. Concretion with hand grenade, priming iron (pricker) and powder horn (author 2000).

A single 1.54 m-long bronze two-pounder was also lifted off the site (Fig. 43.5b). The gun has dolphins and a profiled head. On the base ring it is inscribed: *Franciscus Roen me fecit Glückstadt* (I was made by Franciscus Roen in Glückstadt). The year 1644 and the nettle leaf arms are visible on the first reinforce. The right trunnion is marked with the number "4". Franciscus Roen was a gunfounder in the formerly Danish Neustadt from 1644 to 1677. The nettle leaf arms, the dolphins and the profiled head are all typical for the Danish naval ordnance system 1644 (Blom 1891, 73). The number "4" on the trunnion could stand for the Danish king Christian IV, the founder of the system 1644. The bronze gun is not mentioned in the official ordnance records for *Mynden* and might only have been taken aboard in 1718.

below the raised quarterdeck is mentioned in the building contract. The ship was equipped with a capstan and a windlass.

Evidence in surviving logbooks shows that the vessel could be rowed in calms and narrow waterways. The sweep ports were presumably situated between the gun ports on the upper deck.

The only known depiction of the frigate was found in the daybook of the Norwegian sailor Niels Trosner, who served in the Danish Navy from 1710 to 1714. Trosner made a sketch of *Mynden* at anchor off the island of Bornholm. Although the sketch is very simple, details of the rigging can be seen (Riksarkivet Oslo, *Manuskriptsamlingen*, quatro 48) (Fig. 43.10).

Mynden represents a typical small frigate of the late 17th and early 18th century. With the three-masted ship rig, the vessel resembled a "miniature warship". Such small warships were employed in all European navies of the time for cruising and convoy tasks or as dispatch and reconnaissance vessels. In the Danish navy these frigates were also called *snau* or, influenced by the French, *barque-longue*. A contemporary, but slightly larger Danish frigate, *Lossen*, was excavated off the Norwegian coast in the 1960s (Molaug and Scheen 1983).

Acknowledgements

I would like to thank all members of the Society for Underwater Archaeology Mecklenburg-Vorpommern and all other divers and "surface personnel" who helped with the survey of the frigate *Mynden* in the winter of 1999/

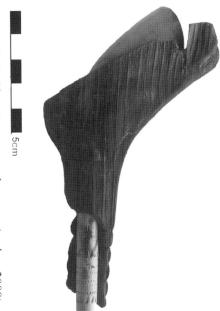

Fig. 43.9. Clay pipe in wooden case (author 2000).

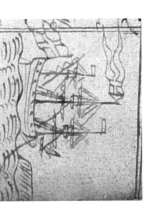

Fig. 43.10. Depiction of Mynden at anchor off Bornholm, in the daybook of Niels Trosner (Riksarkivet Oslo, Manuskriptsamlingen, quatro 48).

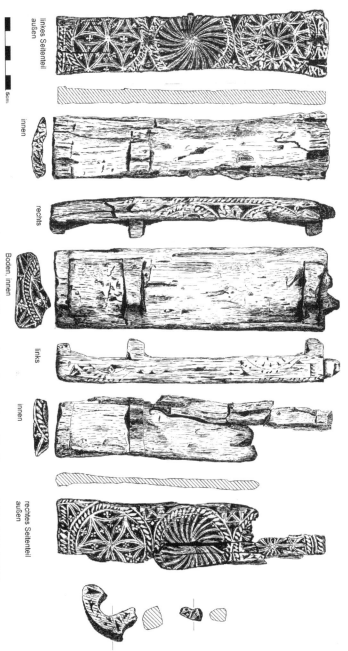

linkes Seitenteil
außen

innen

rechts

Boden, innen

links

innen

rechtes Seitenteil
außen

Fig. 43.8. Wooden box with traditional Norwegian decoration (B. Froese, LBD MV 1995).

Jens Auer

2000. I am also very grateful for the friendly assistance of the Riksarkiv Copenhagen and the Orlogsmuseet Copenhagen. The Tøjhusmuseet Copenhagen and especially the director, Mr. Ole Frantzen, greatly assisted with the identification of the ordnance.

References

Unpublished primary documents

Riksarkivet Copenhagen, *Admiralitetets indkomne sager* 603.
Riksarkivet Copenhagen, *Søkrigskancelliet* 930.
Riksarkivet Oslo, *Manuskriptsamlingen*, quatro 48.

Secondary works

Auer, J., 2000, Das Arkonawrack. Studien zu einem neuzeit-

lichen Schiffsfund vor der Küste Rügens. Unpublished MA Thesis. Greifswald University.

Blom, O., 1891, *Ældre Danske Metal og Jern Stykker. Et forarbejde til Artilleriets Historie.* Copenhagen.

Frantzen, O. L., 1999, Svenske Stöbejernskanoner i dansk tjenste 1660–1814. In *Athena och Ares*, 147–160. Stockholm.

Förster, T., 1994, Die Methodik der Prospektion und Dokumentation von Unterwasserfundstellen am Beispiel von sechs Wrackstellen des 16. bis 20. Jahrhunderts vor Rügen und Hiddensee. Unpublished MA Thesis. Hochschule für Technik, Wirtschaft und Kultur Leipzig.

Hoving, A. J., 1994, *Nicolaes Witsens Scheeps-Bouw-Konst Open Gestelt.* Franeker.

Molaug, S., and Scheen, R., 1983, *Fregatten "Lossen". Et kulturhistorisk skattkammer.* Oslo.

Van Yk, C., 1697, *De Nederlandsche Scheepsbouwkunst opengestellt.* Delft.

44 The wreck of a 16th/17th-century sailing ship near the Hel Peninsula, Poland

Tomasz Bednarz

In September 2002 the Department of Underwater Archaeology (DUA) of the Polish Maritime Museum in Gdańsk (PMM) conducted research on a newly discovered wreck near Swedish Hill on the Hel Peninsula (Figs 44.1–44.2). Initial information about the wreck appeared in 1992. A few years later, the DUA took a series of aerial

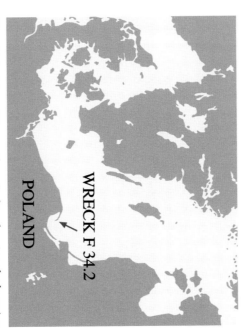

WRECK F 34.2

POLAND

Fig. 44.1. *Map of the southern Baltic showing the location of the Hel Peninsula on the Polish coast.*

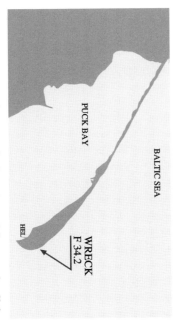

PUCK BAY

BALTIC SEA

HEL

WRECK F 34.2

Fig. 44.2. *Map showing the location of the wreck off the Hel Peninsula.*

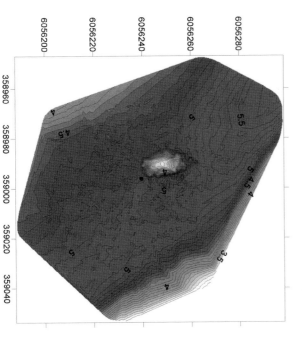

Fig. 44.3. *Plan view of site bathymetry (I. Pomian).*

photographs to document the coastline and shallow waters of Gdańsk Bay, Puck Bay and the Hel Peninsula. On this basis the search for the wreck began around Swedish Hill near Hel. Finally, the wreck was located in the autumn of 2001. In accordance with the Database of Underwater Archaeological Sites, introduced by DUA, the site was marked as F 34.2.

The wreck is situated at about 180 metres from the beach, between the first and the second submerged bars, at a depth of 5m (Figs 44.3 and 44.4). Prior to any research taking place it appeared as an oval heap of stones 1.5m in height, with wooden construction parts sticking out (Figs 44.5 and 44.6). The mound is 23 m long and 11 m wide. The wreck was covered with mussels and some algae. Amongst the stones there were some bricks and metal rings. The work on the site was carried out from the PMM research ship *Kaszubski Brzeg*. The PMM research team took part in the research along with volunteer divers from the whole of Poland.

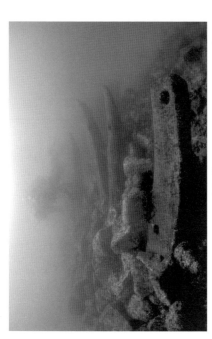

Fig. 44.4. Perspective, false-colour view of site bathymetry with exaggerated elevation (I. Pomian).

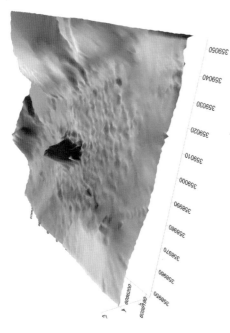

Fig. 44.5. Site plan of wreck F 34.2 before exploration in September 2002 (author).

stone ballast

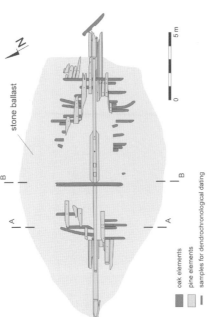

Fig. 44.6. Frames and ballast stones (J. Szymonik).

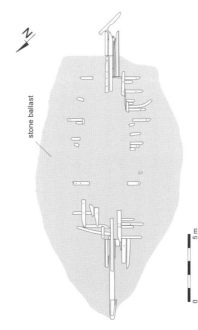

stone ballast

oak elements
pine elements
samples for dendrochronological dating

Fig. 44.7. Site plan of wreck F 34.2 at the end of the survey in September 2002 (author).

During the four weeks of research, a considerable part of the ship's structure was discovered underneath the ballast stones: keel, floor timbers, strakes, keelson together with mast step and its sisters and rider (Figs 44.7–44.10). Drawings and photographic documentation were also made and samples were taken for dendrochronological analysis. A number of smaller objects, mainly ceramics, were also found.

The keel and keelson are oriented southeast-northwest, parallel to the beach, with the bow to the northwest. The structure is composed of pine and oak. The beam keel, keelson and its sisters around the mast step, planking and ceiling were made of pine and the floor timbers and rider were made of oak. The vessel is constructed from carvel planking. Four to five strakes on each side of the keel were preserved. The planks are 20–30 cm wide and 6 cm thick. Animal hair, found in the garboard seam, was used for caulking. The planking is connected to the frames by pine treenails with pine wedges; the diameter of the treenails ranges from 3–4cm. In the garboard strake and on some other planks one can observe traces of iron nails. A characteristic element of the wreck is the mast step,

which consists of two rectangular mortises with the dimensions 32x28cm and 30x28cm, both 9cm deep, cut into the keelson 26cm apart from each other (Fig. 44.11). The mortises are strengthened by a pair of bolsters or sisters of similar scantling to the keelson, and an oak rider over the forward end of the maststep area.

Double mast steps, although of a different construction, may be found in some ships, for example a cog from Skanör dating from the end of the 14th century (Alopaeus 1996: 27) or the Cattewater wreck from the beginning of the 16th century (Redknap 1984: 99).

Altogether nine samples of wood were taken from the wreck for dendrochronological analysis, five from the oak frames and four pine samples from the keel, the two elements constituting the keelson and a ceiling plank. The dendrochronological study was carried out by T. Ważny (2002).

All of the pine samples could be dated and provenanced. The pine used in the construction of the ship comes from trees 150–200 years old, growing in an unconsolidated stand in the vicinity of Stockholm, Sweden, and felled in approximately the middle of the 16th

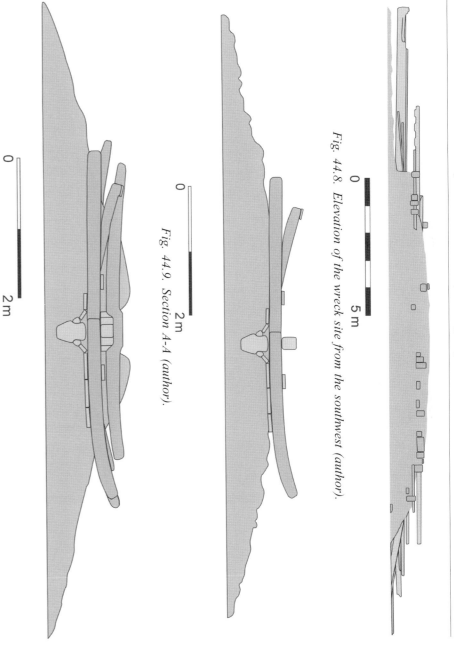

0 5 m

Fig. 44.8. Elevation of the wreck site from the southwest (author).

0 2 m

Fig. 44.9. Section A-A (author).

0 2 m

Fig. 44.10. Section B-B (author).

Fig. 44.11. The double mast step mortises (J. Szymonik).

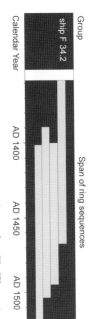

Group

ship F 34.2

Calendar Year

AD 1400   AD 1450   AD 1500

Span of ring sequences

Fig. 44.12. Dendrochronological results (T. Ważny).

century (no earlier than 1521, Fig. 44.12). The oak samples could not be dated or provenanced, as they contained too few annual rings.

The most interesting archaeological objects found at the wreck site are fragments of kitchen utensils, dishes and glass. About 40 fragments of ceramics probably come from the same bowl. The dish was made from light brown clay, painted inside: light yellow background with a yellow and brown ornament. This type is known as Werraware and dates to the first half of the 17th century (Stephan 1987: 85). Other artefacts include the bottom of a Westerwald stoneware mug with cobalt blue ornament. This type had been made since 1590 (Kilarska 1991: 24). A fragment of a three legged dish (a kind of clay saucepan used in the kitchen), two legs from such a dish as well as a fragment including the ornament, a few handles of dishes and three bricks with the dimensions 30x15x8cm were also found. Additionally, a few glass pipes with diameters from 20 to 35mm were found. The pipes were made of dark green glass, which flakes off as a result of corrosion.

The small number of archaeological finds at the wreck site is most probably the result of salvaging of the valuable objects and ship's equipment, as the ship foundered quite close to the shore at a relatively shallow depth. The

275

Thomasz Bednarz

destructive action of the sea and currents did the rest. A lot of contemporary elements were brought to the vessel from other wrecks in the vicinity, which causes additional problems with the site's interpretation. Its location near the shore and the influential dynamics of the seabed have adversely affected the state of preservation of the wreck. Summing up the course of the research so far, it may be stated that we are dealing with the wreck of a ship of carvel construction, which was probably built in the second half of 16th century and sank off the Hel Peninsula in the first half of the 17th century.

References

Alopaeus H., 1996, Koggen från Skanör, *Popular Arkeologi*, 14, s. 48–51.

Kilarska E., 1991, *Kamionka. Katalog zbioru Muzeum Narodowego w Gdańsku*. Gdańsk.

Redknap M., 1984, *Cattewater Wreck, The investigation of an armed vessel of the sixteenth century*, National Maritime Museum Archeological Series No 8. Greenwich.

Stephan H.-G., 1987, *Die Bemalte Irdenware der Renaissance in Mitteleuropa*. München.

Ważny T., 2002, *Analiza dendrochronologiczna wraka F34.2 z CMM w Gdańsku. Maszynopis w zbiorach CMM*.

45 Sewn boat timbers from the medieval Islamic port of Quseir al-Qadim on the Red Sea coast of Egypt

Lucy Blue

The sewn boat tradition of the Indian Ocean

The distinguishing feature of Arab craft of the Indian Ocean from antiquity through to the late 20th century, is generally agreed to be 'the use of fibre, rather than nails, to sew the planks of hulls together' (Said 1991: 107). Despite this, direct archaeological evidence for stitched vessels in the Red Sea and Indian Ocean in antiquity is limited.

Historical depth for sewn boat construction is provided by the finds from Ras al-Jinz in Oman where sewn planks dating to the third millennium BC were discovered (Cleuziou and Tosi 2000). Textual reference to 'small sewn boats' were first noted in the 1st century AD *Periplus Maris Erythraei* (Casson 1989: 141, 15.5.30). However, the majority of evidence relating to the traditional Arab practice of constructing sewn hulls is restricted to later textual references by travellers, historians and geographers, and to a few sketchy iconographic depictions.

The Byzantine historian Procopius writing in the 6th century AD states, in relation to the Persian Gulf, that 'all the boats which are found in India and on this sea... are bound together with a kind of cording' (Procopius *Bel. Pers.* 1.19.23). Abu-Zaid Hassan of Siraf, writing in the 10th century AD, describes how the people of Oman travelled to the islands (the Maldives and Laccadives) and having felled and prepared the timbers, stripped the bark of coconut trees to produce yarn 'wherewith they sew the planks together'. In the 12th century AD Ibn-Jubayr describes the sewn vessels built at Aydhab in more detail: 'For they are stitched with cords of coir, which is the husk of the coconut: this they thrash until it becomes stringy, then they twist from it cords with which they stitch the ship' (Hourani 1995: 92; McGrail 2001: 72).

Images of sewn boats may date from as early as the 2nd century BC (Mookerji 1912: 32). The painting that accompanies the 1237 AD manuscript of Al Hariri's *Maqamat* from Iraq, is a most convincing example. It shows a double-ended vessel with sewn planking (Hourani 1995: 92, plate 7). Beyond the Indian Ocean, a recent archaeological discovery of a 9th-century AD wreck of a

sewn constructed vessel in Indonesian waters provides detail of the stitching technique employed (Flecker 2000).

Marco Polo visited the Persian Gulf twice at the end of the 13th century AD and describes the ships as 'bad' and states how 'many get lost for they have no iron fastenings, being only stitched together with cord made from the husk of Indian nut' (Villiers 1952: 40; Johnstone and Muir 1962). In the 14th century, Friar Odoric described sailing from Bombay to Ormuz in a similar 'bark compact together only with hempe' (Johnstone 1988: 178). Vasco da Gamo noted Arab vessels along the coast of Mozambique in the 15th century AD built without nails, their planks being held together by cords, as did Lancaster a century later (Johnstone and Muir 1962; Stanley 1898: 26).

The implication therefore is that iron nails were not adopted in the construction of boats and ships in the region until the arrival of the Portuguese and that even then the practice of attaching planks by means of stitching was not abandoned altogether (Moreland 1939; Hornell 1942; Johnstone and Muir 1962). There are still a number of examples of stitched vessels in use around the shores of the Red Sea and Indian Ocean, including the *sambuk* of the Dhofari coast of Oman; the *huri* of the west coast of the Red Sea and East Africa; and the *masula* and the *vallam* of India (McGrail and Kentley 1985).

Evidence from the Red Sea

Quseir al-Qadim is the site of an ancient port located some 8 km north of the modern town of Quseir on the Red Sea coast of Egypt (Fig. 45.1). Excavation by the Oriental Institute of the University of Chicago between 1978 and 1982 (Whitcomb and Johnson 1979, 1982a, 1982b) and the University of Southampton between 1999–2003 (Peacock and Blue 2006), has revealed that the site was occupied from the late 1st century BC to the beginning of the 3rd century AD, and reoccupied again some one thousand years later between the late 12th to early 16th centuries AD.

Lucy Blue

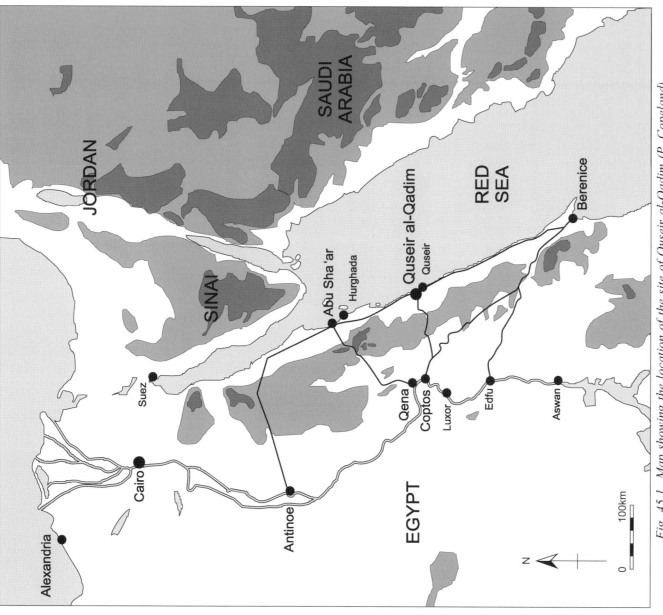

Fig. 45.1. Map showing the location of the site of Quseir al-Qadim (P. Copeland).

The Medieval Islamic settlement of Quseir al-Qadim is described by Arab geographers as the Red Sea port of Qus (Whitcomb and Johnson 1979: 3; Garcin 1976; Peacock and Blue 2006: 4) and operated alongside the chief port in this region, Aydhab, facilitating trade and overseeing the protection of pilgrimage to the Holy Cities, particularly Mecca. Yaqut describes it as 'a harbour of the Yemenite ships',[1] and Qalqashandi writing in the 14th century, recorded how ships frequented the port in order to transport merchandise the shortest distance across the mountains to Qus (Al-Qalqashandi 1913–1920: 465, cited by Whitcomb and Johnson 1979: 4).

Excavation of the site of Quseir al-Qadim[2]

The port of Quseir al-Qadim lies at the head of a now-silted lagoon or mersa, linked to the sea by a small inlet that cuts the coastal fringing reef. The site occupies an area of approximately ten hectares, the main area being located on the northern arm of the reef terrace approximately 8 m above the silted lagoon, over looking the entrance to the ancient harbour to the south (Blue 2002, 2006; Fig. 45.2).

The dry conditions of the region ensure excellent preservation of artefacts, particularly organic material, which has added greatly to our understanding of trade in the Red Sea region and beyond in both the Roman and later Medieval periods. Finds provide a wealth of evidence supporting extensive trade in exotic goods with the East. In the 2000 season alone over one thousand pieces of Medieval textiles were recovered, including one depicting an elephant, possibly from India (Handley 1999, 2000). These finds, in combination with the Medieval ceramic assemblage, paper documents, foodstuffs and other imported goods, are beginning to provide a vivid impression of life in the Medieval Islamic port of Quseir al-Qadim and the extensive trade network in which it operated (Peacock et al 1999, 2000, 2001, 2002, 2003).

Medieval Islamic necropolis

Although excavation of Medieval Quseir al-Qadim was

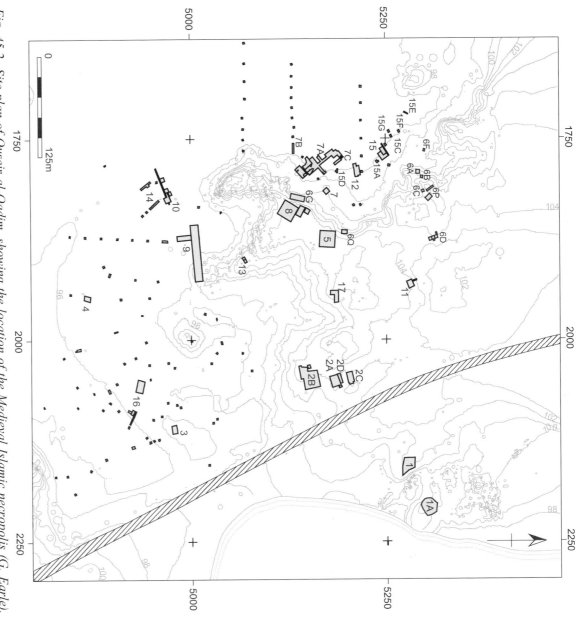

Fig. 45.2. Site plan of Quseir al-Qadim, showing the location of the Medieval Islamic necropolis (G. Earle).

more limited than the investigation of the Roman settlement of *Myos Hormos*, the eastern region of the site, particularly along the line of a proposed new road, proved to be quite fruitful (Fig. 45.2). This region appears to be predominately Medieval in date and on the shore to the east, a necropolis (Trench 1A) has revealed some one hundred inhumations, many, and unusually, of multiple burials.

The necropolis was first excavated by Whitcomb and Johnson (1979: 57–61, plate 18) and appeared to be associated with wall remains some 0.5 m in height, both above and adjacent to the burials. Subsequently, three seasons of excavation by the University of Southampton have revealed a total of over one hundred complete and numerous disturbed, often incomplete, disarticulated and dispersed inhumations (Macklin 1999, 2000, 2001, 2006: 157–158). Recent excavation also revealed additional

Lucy Blue

Fig. 45.3. Planks in situ (Tomb 1) Burial 61 (Photo A. Macklin).

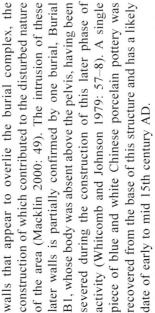

Fig. 45.4. Plank 6 in situ (Photo A. Macklin).

walls that appear to overlie the burial complex, the construction of which contributed to the disturbed nature of the area (Macklin 2000: 49). The intrusion of these later walls is partially confirmed by one burial, Burial B1, whose body was absent above the pelvis, having been severed during the construction of this later phase of activity (Whitcomb and Johnson 1979: 57–8). A single piece of blue and white Chinese porcelain pottery was recovered from the base of this structure and has a likely date of early to mid 15th century AD.

During the 2000 season one burial was excavated that is the only complete one of its type to have been found at the site. Burial 61 (Tomb 1) is a mudbrick-lined, cist-type grave that was located c. 1 m below the surface and was sealed with timber planks (Fig. 45.3). Within the grave the body of a woman was recorded, aged between 35–40 years and approximately 158 cm in height (Macklin 2000: 49). A second burial (Tomb 2) was located just to the south of Burial 61, again overlain with planks, but in this case the mudbrick grave was absent. The timber coverings to the two graves are so far unique to the site and the planks that covered Burial 61 are of particular interest.

Both graves exhibit reused planks. Tomb 2 was

covered with shorter, stockier and irregularly shaped timbers that had been originally fastened by iron nails. However, the timbers associated with Burial 61 (Tomb 1) were planked and more regular in shape, and had originally been fastened by fibres and sewn or lashed together through holes along their edges (Fig. 45.4). In their reused context, the planks were orientated roughly north-south and were not attached to each other, lying some 2–4 cm apart over the top of the grave. On closer inspection a number of characteristics of these timbers indicated that these could well be sewn boat timbers found reused in a terrestrial context in a region where wood was a rare commodity.

Tomb 1 (Burial 61) (summary description)

- Eight planks were excavated (between 70–98 cm in length; breadth 10–16 cm; average 3–3.5 cm thick; Table 45.1).

- Of those timbers whose species was identified, all were Indian teak (*Tectona grandis*) (Van der Veen, personal communication).

- All planks had traces of what is believed to be bitumen or pitch (not continuous) on at least one side (some

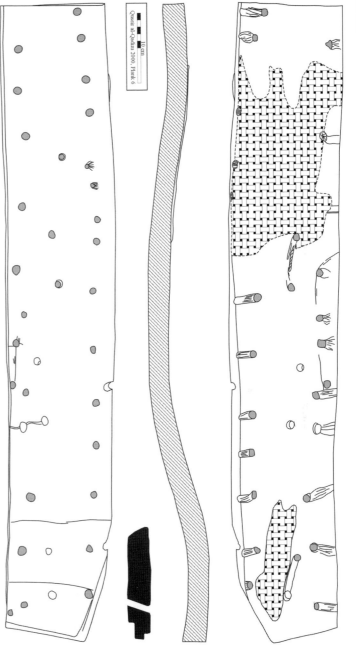

Quseir al-Qadim 2000, Plank 6

10 cm

Fig. 45.5. Plank 6 (P. Copeland and J. Whitewright).

Plank Number	Length	Breadth	Width
Plank 1	98	12.5	2
Plank 2	86	10	3.5
Plank 3	97.5	13.5	2
Plank 4 (bad condition)	c.44	c.13–16	c.3–3.5
Plank 5	76	15	3.5–4
Plank 6	90	16	3
Plank 7	77	11.5	3.5–4.5
Plank 8	70	11.5	4

Table 45.1. Tomb 1, Burial 61, Plank dimensions (in cms) (L.Blue).

had traces on both sides and/or along the plank edges).

- The majority of planks had matting on one side – invariably the same side as the bitumen, in some cases the matting adhered to the bitumen.
- Some planks also had traces of burning on one side.
- All but one plank (Plank 8) had holes (presumably drilled) located along the edges (generally but not always, along both edges).
- The holes were a maximum diameter of 1.5 cm, average diameter 1 cm.
- Four planks with holes had coconut coir and wooden (also teak) pegs still in situ that extended through the thickness of the planking.
- The majority of holes were located along the longitudinal edges of the planks and were generally driven at a slight angle through the plank thickness.
- The holes along the plank edges were located at a regular distance from the edge (this varied from plank to plank from 2–3.5 cm but tended to be similar on the same plank). The holes were positioned 2–6.5 cm apart (average 4–6.5 cm apart).
- A number of holes located along the plank edges were fed by a channel or groove recessed into the wood on one side of the timber. The recess extended at a right angle from the hole to the plank edge. Some of these recessed channels had coconut coir still in situ (Fig. 45.4 and Fig. 45.5).
- Some planks had additional holes drilled into the centre of the plank often identified in pairs. The pairs of holes also extended along the length of the plank and the majority (and average) distance between holes in a pair, was 7 cm.
- One of the eight planks (Plank 6) had what could be interpreted as a 'frame impression' on one side (Fig. 45.5). The impression or shadow of what may have been a frame was c. 6.5 cm wide and was located on the opposite side to the recessed stitching, the bitumen and the matting.
- Some planks had notches (Plank 2 and 3) on their edges, while others were scarfed at the ends (Plank 1, 8 and 3) or had bevelled edges (Plank 6; Fig. 45.5).

Interpretation of the timbers from Burial 61 (Tomb 1)

The characteristics of the timbers recovered from Burial 61 would appear to indicate that they were formerly used in the construction of a sewn plank-built vessel. The

Fig. 45.6 Detail of Plank 6 (Photo L. Blue).

timbers had been deliberately planed to an appropriate thickness and regular shape. The presence of holes along the plank edges, stitched with coir and subsequently pegged, is a common characteristic of sewn constructed vessels (McGrail and Kentley 1985), although at present there is no indication of the former sewing pattern, other than the association between the holes and recesses for stitches, described above. Future analysis of the relationship of holes within and between planks may help identify the sewing sequence and perhaps explain the presence of seemingly random holes in the planks – were they integral to the sewn vessel or associated with a later reuse/repair?

The fact that both the bitumen and the recesses for the coir stitches are uniformly located on the same side of the planks, would indicate that this particular side of the planks had originally been on the outside of the hull. The practice of cutting recessed channels from the stitch hole to the edge of the plank on the outside of the hull has been identified as a feature of sewn boat construction and is seen as a means of protecting the coir stitch. As Severin (1985: 283) observed in the construction of the Omani Boom *Sohar* 'a groove was cut between the pairs of holes, on the outside of the hull, so that the cord was recessed and protected from chafe'.

Plank 6 (Fig. 45.5) has a possible 'frame impression' on the alternate side from the bitumen and recesses for the coir stitching. The implication is that the 'frame impression' is all that remains of a frame that was formerly positioned inside the hull. A pair of holes have also been found in association with the possible 'frame impression', perhaps indicative of how the frame had originally been secured to the hull. It is possible that the frame was originally lashed, attached by coir to the plank through a pair of holes drilled in the middle of the plank. A number of additional, centrally-placed pairs of holes have been identified but no additional 'frame impressions' are discernible. However, a number of these central pairs of holes are associated with recesses for coir stitches on one side of the plank, again the same side as the bitumen, the side that is believed to be the exterior of the former hull of the vessel.

Dating of the burials

The evidence would indicate that the planks from Burial 61 were formerly used in the construction of sewn vessels. No grave goods were found in association with the burials, other than traces of cloth wrappings. However, the construction of the overlying walls would by association indicate that the burials antedate the buildings and thus date them to the early or pre-15th century AD. The earliest occupation of the Medieval Islamic site of Quseir al-Qadim recorded so far dates to the end of the 12th/beginning of the 13th centuries AD. This would indicate a date range for the burials of between the late 12th to early 15th centuries AD. However, the planks have obviously been reused and thus their original use as planks in a vessel of sewn construction could antedate the Medieval Islamic necropolis.

Conclusions

Recent discoveries at the Medieval Islamic site of Quseir al-Qadim thus afford further direct archaeological evidence for the construction of sewn plank-built vessels of the Indian Ocean. They provide a tentative date of between the end of the 12th to the beginning of the 15th centuries AD and more detail with regards to construction than most previous finds. They also give an indication of the origin of the materials used. The timber is Indian teak (*Tectona grandis*) (Van der Veen, personal communication), and we assume that the coir used to stitch the Quseir al-Qadim timbers may also have origins in India, as local coconut coir is still used to bind planks of sewn constructed vessels in southern India and nearby islands (personal observation; Hourani 1995: 91; Villiers 1952: 40; Johnstone and Muir 1962; Johnstone 1988: 178). Thus, despite the fact that the sewn timbers were finally deposited in the port of Quseir al-Qadim on the Red Sea coast of Egypt, they potentially provide insight into Medieval boatbuilding techniques throughout the Indian Ocean.

Notes

1   Yaqut was writing in 626/1228; translated D. Agius
2   All the unpublished reports detailing recent excavations at the site of Quseir al-Qadim by the University of Southampton, can be accessed on the Southampton website: http://www.arch.soton.ac.uk/Research/Quseir/

Acknowledgements

This work would not have been possible without the support of the AHRB who funded a two-year post-doctoral research project into the maritime aspects of the site of Quseir al-Qadim and overall funding of the project by the Peder Sager Wallenberg Charitable Trust. I would also like to thank Prof. D. Peacock and Dr. J. Dix, as well as Dr. D. Agius, Dr C. Ward and Dr A. Macklin for their help in writing this paper.

References

Blue, L.K., 2006. The sedimentary history of the harbour area. In Peacock, D.P.S. and Blue, L., (eds), 2006. *Myos Hormos – Quseir al-Qadim: Roman and Islamic Ports on the Red Sea. Volume 1: Survey and Excavations 1999–2003*, 43–61. Oxbow Books. Oxford.

Blue, L.K., 2000, Myos Hormos/ Quseir al-Qadim. A Roman and Islamic port on the Red Sea coast of Egypt – A maritime perspective. *Proceedings for the Seminar for Arabian Studies* 32: 139–150.

Casson, L., 1989, *The Periplus Maris Erythraei*. Princeton: Princeton University Press.

Cleuziou, S., and Tosi, M., 2000, Ra's al-Jinz and the pre-historic coastal cultures of the Ja'alan. *Journal Of Oman Studies* 11: 19–73.

Flecker, M., 2000, A 9th-century shipwreck in Indonesian waters. *International Journal of Nautical Archaeology* 29.2: 199–217.

Garcin, J.C., 1976, *Un Centre Musulman de al Haute-Egypt Médiévale*. Qus.

Handley, F., 1999, The Textiles. In Peacock et al (eds), In *Myos Hormos – Quseir al-Qadim: A Roman and Islamic Port Site. Interim Report 1999*, 46–48. University of Southampton [Unpublished circulated report].

Handley, F., 2000, The Textiles. In Peacock et al (eds), In *Myos Hormos – Quseir al-Qadim: A Roman and Islamic Port Site. Interim Report 2001*, 63–67. University of Southampton [Unpublished circulated report].

Hornell, J., 1942. A tentative classification of Arab sea-craft. *Mariner's Mirror* 28: 11–40.

Hourani, G., 1995, *Arab Seafaring*. New Jersey: Princeton University Press.

Johnstone, P., 1988. *The Sea-craft of Prehistory*. Routledge. London.

Johnstone, T.M. and Muir, J., 1962. Portuguese influences on shipbuilding in the Persian Gulf. *Mariner's Mirror* 48: 52–63.

Macklin, A., 1999, The Human Skeletal Remains. In Peacock et al (eds), *Myos Hormos – Quseir al-Qadim: A Roman and Islamic Port Site. Interim Report 1999*, 20. University of Southampton [Unpublished circulated report].

Macklin, A., 2000, The Human Remains. In Peacock et al (eds), *Myos Hormos – Quseir al-Qadim: A Roman and Islamic Port Site. Interim Report 2001*, 49. University of Southampton [Unpublished circulated report].

Macklin, A., 2001, Human Remains. In Peacock et al (eds), *Myos Hormos – Quseir al-Qadim: A Roman and Islamic Port Site. Interim Report 2001*, 41–42. University of Southampton [Unpublished circulated report].

Macklin, A., 2006, Trench 1A. In Peacock, D.P.S. and Blue, L., (eds), 2006, *Myos Hormos: Quseir al-Qadim: Roman and Islamic Ports on the Red Sea. Volume 1: Survey and Excavations 1999–2003*, 157–160. Oxbow Books. Oxford.

McGrail, S., and Kentley, E. (eds), 1985, *Sewn Plank Boats – Archaeological and Ethnographic papers based on those presented to a conference at Greenwich in November, 1984. National Maritime Museum, Greenwich, Archaeological Series No.10*. BAR International Series 276. Oxford.

McGrail, S., 2001, *Boats of the World: From the Stone Age to Medieval Times*. Oxford: Oxford University Press.

Mookerji, R.K., 1912. *A History of Indian Shipping*. London: Longmans.

Moreland, W.H., 1939, The ships of the Arabian Sea about A.D. 1500. *Journal of the Royal Asiatic Society of London* 1: 63–74.

Peacock, D.P.S. and Blue, L. (eds), 2006, *Myos Hormos – Quseir al-Qadim: Roman and Islamic Ports on the Red Sea. Volume 1: Survey and Excavations 1999–2003*. Oxbow Books. Oxford.

Peacock, D.P.S., Blue, L., Bradford, N., and Moser, S., (eds), 1999, *Myos Hormos – Quseir al-Qadim: A Roman and Islamic Port Site. Interim Report 1999*, University of Southampton [Unpublished circulated report].

Peacock, D.P.S., Blue, L., Bradford, N., and Moser, S., (eds), 2000, *Myos Hormos – Quseir al-Qadim: A Roman and Islamic Port Site. Interim Report 2000*. University of Southampton Unpublished circulated report].

Peacock, D.P.S., Blue, L., Bradford, N., and Moser, S., (eds), 2001, *Myos Hormos – Quseir al-Qadim: A Roman and Islamic Port Site. Interim Report 2001*. University of Southampton [Unpublished circulated report].

Peacock, D.P.S., Blue, L., and Moser, S., (eds), 2002, *Myos Hormos – Quseir al-Qadim: A Roman and Islamic Port Site. Interim Report 2002*. University of Southampton [Unpublished circulated report].

Peacock, D.P.S., Blue, L., and Moser, S., (eds), 2003, *Myos Hormos – Quseir al-Qadim: A Roman and Islamic Port Site. Interim Report 2003*. University of Southampton [Unpublished circulated report].

Procopius, *History of the Wars I*. Translated by H.B. Dewing, 183–184. Theloeb Classical Library: London.

Qalqashandi, Al, 1913–1920, *Subh al-A'sha*. Vol. 3.

Said, F. 1991, *Oman: A Seafaring Nation*. The Ministry of National Heritage and Culture, Sultanate of Oman. Second Edition.

Severin, T. 1985, Construction of the Omani Boom Sohar. In S. McGrail and E. Kentley (eds), *Sewn Plank Boats – Archaeological and Ethnographic papers based on those presented to a conference at Greenwich in November, 1984. National Maritime Museum, Greenwich, Archaeological Series No.10*, 279–288. BAR International Series 276. Oxford.

Stanley, H.E.J., (ed.), 1898, *The Three Voyages of Vasco da Gama* 1869. Hakluyt Society. London.

Villiers, A.1952, *The Indian Ocean*. London.

Whitcomb, D.S. and Johnson, J.H., 1979, *Quseir al-Qadim 1978. Preliminary Report*. Princeton: American Research Centre in Egypt. Cairo.

Whitcomb, D.S. and Johnson, J.H. 1982a, *Quseir al-Qadim 1980. Preliminary Report* (American Research Centre in Egypt, Volume 7, Cairo). Malibu: Undena Publications.

Whitcomb, D.S. and Johnson, J.H. 1982b, Season of Excavation at Quseir al-Qadim. *American Research Centre in Egypt. Newsletter* 120: 24–30.

Yaqut al-Hamawi Mujam al-Buldan, 1228, *Dar al-kutub al-almiyya, nd.* Vol. IV: 417. Beirut.

46 Roman river barge from Sisak (*Siscia*), Croatia

Andrej Gaspari, Miran Erič and Marija Šmalcelj

Introduction

Prehistoric *Segestica* and the subsequent Roman settlement of *Siscia* are located on the site of modern Sisak (100 m above sea-level), 57 km south of Zagreb, Croatia. They commanded a geographically strategic position on the intersection of waterways and roads between the Danube and the Adriatic, and between Italy and the Balkans, respectively, but also at a naturally defendable position on the confluence of the Kupa (*Colapis*) and the Sava (*Savus*) Rivers. Good waterways undoubtedly played a decisive role in the formation of the prehistoric settlement, as is discernible from the role of Segestica as a river port during Octavian's siege (Appian, *Illyr. 22–24*; Šašel Kos 2005: 437–442). Siscia, on the other hand, is rightly supposed to have been the base of the Pannonian fleet (*classis Pannonica*). The flourishing economy of the city, which received the status of a colony (*Colonia Flavia Siscia*) during the Flavian period, was also significantly influenced by the waterways since they provided a passage to the rich iron ore deposits in western Bosnia (Lolić 2003: 133–134).

The importance of the navigable waterways and the epigraphically attested river port (CIL III 11382) are best illustrated by the remains of loading platforms, a shipwreck, the focus of this paper, and a number of logboats, as well as numerous archaeological finds from the Kupa Riverbed. The latter represents one of the most extensive collections of objects obtained from European rivers. The majority of the several thousand finds, dating from the period between the Copper Age and the High Middle Ages, were initially discovered during dredging or amateur explorations, and only a small number through archaeological research, which took place during the 1980s and 1990s. The remains of three extensive groups of wooden piles from the Early and Late Iron Ages, as well as the Roman period, were detected and partially researched at several places along the eastern bank of the last meander of the River Kupa, in the region of Pogorelec, the site of the prehistoric settlement (Durman 1992).

This article discusses the wreck of a Roman river barge discovered in 1985 in the former swimming area of the city of Sisak, in a part of the riverbed long known among the locals as "the Mint", opposite the city centre. When water levels are low, the tops of wooden piles are visible in an extensive gravel sandbank, an area known to be rich in archaeological remains from the second half of the 19th century onwards (Fig. 46.1).

The ship's remains were documented during a rescue excavation conducted by the Department of Archaeology of the Faculty of Philosophy in Zagreb, headed by

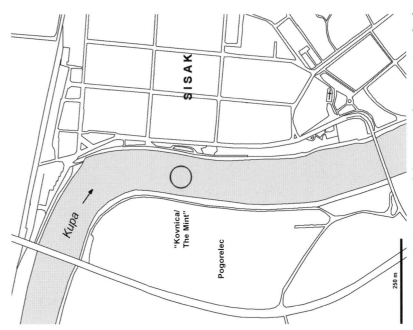

Fig. 46.1. The location of the site in the Kupa Riverbed next to the centre of modern Sisak (Executed by A. Gaspari).

Fig. 46.2. The view from the right bank of the Kupa River towards the site (Photo by K. Kiš).

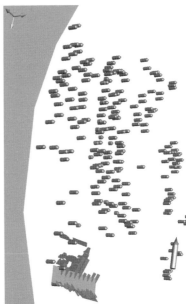

Fig. 46.3. The axonometric view of the piles and the remains of the barge (Executed by M. Erič).

Professor Marija Šmalcelj. The excavation took place from the 9th to the 17th October 1985 (Šarić 1986). They were enabled by the severe droughts of the summer of 1985 that dried out a large section of the Kupa Riverbed (Fig. 46.2), facilitating an almost dry land excavation of the site, including photographic documentation, a geodetic record of the piles, and several plans of the ship's remains. The latter were, unfortunately, not available during the preparation of this article. During the excavation, the piles and the ship parts were sampled by Aleksander Durman for subsequent dendrochronological and radiocarbon analyses. The excavation proceeded smoothly until unauthorised diggers also took advantage of the low water level, and, over one weekend in the absence of the archaeologists, they ransacked the site and the uncovered part of the ship was completely destroyed. Official excavation was subsequently suspended.

The site

The site lies on the eastern bank of the Kupa River in a region known as Pogorelec. The excavation covered an area of 20 x 15 m in total and comprised the easternmost part of the sandbank that extended from the right bank sloping gently down to the middle of the 100-m-wide riverbed. An alluvial layer covered the tops of innumerable wooden piles, vertically driven into the gravel bed. More or less densely positioned piles lay at least 2 m beneath the water (around 90 m above sea-level) during normal water levels and covered the entire width of the site (Fig. 46.1). Over 200 piles were documented during the 1985 excavations, made from round (20–45 cm in diameter) and square (10–20 cm in thickness) hewn oak trunks, with varying heights of up to 4 m. An extracted pile showed that the points of at least some of the piles were tipped with iron shoes and numerous pile tops still bore traces of rust patina left by iron pots. In some places there were also remains of wooden horizontal beams found, fastened with iron nails and positioned approximately 30–40 cm underneath the pile tops.

There were two large pile concentrations separated by a 2 m wide and 9 m long gap that extend along the direction of the river. The shipwreck discovered a few meters upstream from both groups of piles, might be related to the function of this gap (Fig. 46.3).

The excavation showed that the upper parts of the piles were covered by an alluvial layer with pieces of Roman brick, tegulae, as well as large limestone plates and worked stones. Approximately 50 cm underneath the pile tops there was a layer of fine sand with small sized stones mixed with archaeological material that dates, for the most part, from the 1st–4th centuries AD. Beneath was another alluvial layer that contained somewhat larger sized stones and numerous coins, mostly from the second half of the 4th century. Underneath, there was a layer of wooden shavings, interpreted as the possible surface of the foundation layer into which the piles were driven. Excavation did not extend to this layer. However, a coin of Gordianus III (238–244 AD) and a small, excellently preserved wooden chest with a metal lock, were found on top of this context. The natural colouring of the wood indicates that the material in this layer was not exposed to the river flow subsequent to its deposition. However, in contrast, the alluvial layers above were rather mixed. This is demonstrated by fragments of individual ceramic vessels found scattered at different ends of the groups of piles, as well as at different heights, even up to a meter apart (Wiewegh 2001: 92). Dendrochronological and radiocarbon analyses of over 100 samples, revealed episodes of repeated renovation of the wooden structure, with continual reuse of old piles that were gradually replaced by new ones. The precise data derived from the dendrochronological assessment of the boundary between the heartwood and sapwood, allowed us to infer that the piles were installed in series, approximately every seven years, over a period spanning two or three centuries i.e. between the 1st–3rd century (Durman 1992: 120). A good absolute chronological indicator is provided by the coin of Tiberius, found in a shoe of the extracted pile No. 153. The pile structure was only partially researched which

Fig. 46.4. The barge, not excavated in its entirety (Photo by K. Kiš).

Fig. 46.5. The joints and scarfs of the planks were joined by simple iron clamps (Photo by K. Kiš).

unfortunately hinders any interpretation of its function. However, the hypotheses that it represented the remains of a Roman pile dwelling (Brunšmid 1909: 24) or a bridge, that lead towards the western gate of *Siscia* (Koščević 1995: 10), seem less likely. The distribution and the number of piles lead most researchers to interpret the structure as a part of a platform, by way of which the gently sloping bank of the Pogorelec was extended, at an appropriate height towards the landing area, thereby bridging the silted flood area of the right bank (Šašel 1974: 722). Pile dimensions indicate a high load capacity and it is therefore possible that the above mentioned brick and stone building material actually represent the remains of a massive superstructure, most likely workshops or warehouses, that formed part of the port's infrastructure (Šarić 1986: 28; Wiewegh 2001: 90). The numerous finds of iron clamps, iron nails and wood working tools support this proposal.

The excavators believe that the gap between the two pile groups provided the waterpower to drive a metallurgic plant, which is suggested by the large amounts of blanks and it is therefore possible location of the different contexts and within different concentrations (for example, by products of fibulae and 600 keys, collective find of 19 axes, found together with coins from the 4th century). The location, however, was given its name by finds of blanks and even a coin die which indicated the possible location of the imperial mint, active in Siscia from the reign of Gallienus to the beginning of the 5th century (Lolić 2003: 144).

Geological research and the remains of Roman architecture on the left bank indicate that the navigable part of the river and the wooden construction were both located on the same side of the river as they are today (Durman 1992: 120). Due to considerable differences in water levels that extended up to 10 m, the Kupa River is nowadays navigable only in the port of Sisak. Nevertheless, the presumed elevation of the platform with wooden foundations allows us to suppose that these oscillations were much smaller in the Roman Period.

The remains of the barge

The remains of a large box-shaped vessel with a flat bottom and low sides were documented within a 7 m long and 4 m wide stretch of the riverbed (Fig. 46.4). The excavated remains included a steep side of the vessel and a substantial part of the width of the bottom of the craft with associated planking, floor timbers and frames. They were found positioned so that the bottom timbers jutted out at an oblique angle, and the side planking, on the other hand, was angled against the current. The opposite side of the vessel that protruded above the sediment was not discovered and was probably broken off by the river current. The eastern part of the vessel, that is the part that extended towards the deeper part of the river, was also missing. The western part of the ship, however, still lies underneath the sediment.

The barge lay on a layer of fine sand that begins about 50 cm under the pile tops and was covered by a 30–50 cm thick sediment. South of the vessel and partly within it, although not sitting directly on the planks, lay several large unworked stones. It is presumed that they did not represent cargo remains but rather ruins that originate from the topmost alluvial layer. Three wooden piles, driven through the bottom of the shipwreck, indicate that the vessel was probably intentionally sunk.

The planks of the vessel are 25 to 40 cm wide and around 6 cm thick. The planks on the inner side of the vessel, between which luting material of an undetermined plant species was preserved, were fastened with numerous iron clamps that were driven in perpendicular or slightly obliquely, across the joints every 4 to 7 cm (Fig. 46.5).

The clamps are simple crosspieces with perpendicularly bent ends that were driven up to a centimeter into adjoining planks. They do not vary greatly in size and do not exceed 5 cm in length. The clamps held together floor and side planks, but were also used to secure the scarfs of individual strakes. Identical clamps were found in great numbers throughout the area of the excavation. Only two planks (SIS-3, SIS-6) underwent a xylotomic analysis. They were radially cut out of the same oak trunk.

Ten transverse oak timbers and 14 knee-shaped oak frames were uncovered. Exceptionally massive floor timbers, rectangular in section (height 20–25 cm; thickness 10 cm), were positioned 55–60 cm apart, when measured from timber centre. Small, up to 2 cm high, triangular notches were cut in the lower faces of the timbers above the plank joints. The timbers were then fastened to the planks by one or two cylindrical treenails; no iron nails were detected within the vessel remains.

The knee-like frames extended from the top of the vessel's sides and across several floor planks. Naturally curved wood was used and was not always worked to a precise fit prior to installation. There were two knees, set slightly apart, positioned between two transverse timbers. The transition from the bottom to the sides was formed by chine-blocks with a near L-shaped cross-section, whose inner faces were hewn out in a semi-circle. The angle between the sides and the bottom of the vessel was estimated at 110 degrees.

Dendrochronological analysis of the planks revealed that they were made of wood contemporaneous with the piles from one of the renovations of the platform, dating most probably between the second half of the 2nd and the first half of the 3rd century AD. The Middle Imperial date of the ship was confirmed by radiocarbon analysis of the rib "K", performed at Leibniz AMS Laboratory in Kiel (sample KIA22918 K) which indicates the age of 1749 ± 36 BP or 241–264 cal AD at One Sigma Range. A bronze coin of Theodosius (388 AD) was found on one of the floor planks between timbers L and K. However, due to the disturbed stratigraphy any chronological relevance is not reliable.

The position of the vessel lying perpendicular to the gap in the wooden construction, the three piles driven through the floor planks and the ruins inside the vessel, all contribute to the opinion that we are dealing with an out-of-service vessel that was intentionally sunk during one of the platform renovations; in its secondary function it then served either to regulate the river flow in the gap or to relieve the pressure of water on the construction.

The analysis

The Roman barge from Sisak, despite the fact that some of its crucial characteristics, like the overall dimensions and the bow and stern sections, are not known, can nevertheless be compared to the Gallo-Roman barges from the northern provinces of the Empire dated between 1st – 3rd centuries AD. It can also be compared with some examples of Roman Age river vessels found in the area between the hinterland of the northern Adriatic and the lower Danube Basin. A geometric building concept, with a flat bottom and steeply inclined or vertical sides, the use of near L-shaped chine strakes, and the manner in which floor timbers and frames were fastened to the planks, all link this vessel to a group of barges from the Rhine and the Rhône region.

The relatively small spacing between the floor timbers that corresponds to two Roman feet (*dupondius*), usual for this type of cargo vessel, indicates a large vessel of the type described above. With the preserved width of the wreck exceeding 4 m, the original length of the ship should have surpassed 25 m (cf. Bockius 1998: 515).

The setting of the planks in parallel strakes with diagonal scarfs, represents an ancient technical solution, probably of Mediterranean origin. This method of hull assemblage occurs on Greek and Roman ships, both of sewn and mortise-and-tenon construction (Steffy 1994: 41, 48, 59 and 65). Floor planks with more or less parallel edges and diagonal scarfs are common also in the barges of Gallo-Roman type (for example the Zwammerdam 2 and 6 wrecks; Bockius 2000: Abb. 4, 6), as well as in river barges of later periods.

An exceptional constructional feature of the Sisak barge is the fastening of planks with tightly spaced iron clamps that held the joints between the floor and the side elements. The only known analogy for this type of fastening can be found in the wrecks of two other smaller vessels (possibly one vessel in two parts?) from the Danube near Kušjak in the Iron Gate area, of which the second is dated to the 2nd century AD (Bockius 2003). In the Kušjak 2 wreck, iron clamps were recorded on the inside along some of the joints between the floor and also between the side planks, spaced at 5 to 10 cm. In contrast to the Sisak barge, the sequence of clamps is broken in places and clamps in the Kušjak wreck were also used to secure the cracks. Elsewhere, Roman shipbuilders used typologically similar clamps only sporadically. In the barge from Yverdon-les-Bains they were used to repair cracks (Arnold 1992: 35), while in the Zwammerdam 2 wreck they reinforced the transition from the amidship section to the swim-heads (De Weerd 1988: 103, Figs. 51, 54, 59). In the vessels from Oberstimm, built using mortise-and-tenon technology, clamps were used during the construction itself and for repairing cracks (Bockius 2002: 53–54). Similar clamps were also used in medieval and later vessels, exclusively to reinforce the luting and not to fasten the planks (Bockius 2003). Bockius (2003) noticed that the tight distribution of metal clamps on the Kušjak wreck resembles the intervals between the stitch holes in planks of sewn ships, a similarity that is all the more obvious with the barge from Sisak. It seems that by using the metal clamps to fasten the planks they were looking to simplify a complex building process as well as to facilitate the expensive maintenance of sewn vessels.

Andrej Gaspari, Miran Erič and Marija Šmalcelj

The Sisak barge has another constructional feature in common with ancient ships of sewn construction, namely the limber holes that are cut into the lower parts of the floor timbers above the plank seams. These appear in the same places in wrecks from Mainz 1, Woerden 1, and Zwammerdam 2, while in Zwammerdam 4 and 6 they are cut above the centres of the planks (De Weerd 1988: 295–300). Both mortise-and-tenon joints and luting appear only sporadically in Gallo-Roman type barges. However, this arrangement was noted in addition to the Sisak and Kušjak vessels, in the vessels from Chalon-sur-Saône and Lyon, where a resin-soaked cloth was used for the purpose (Bockius 2000: 122). Another similarity with the sewn boats of the Roman period exists in the fact that treenails were used, almost exclusively, to fasten the frame to the shell (cfr. Beltrame 2000: 93 – 94).

This assumed technological link between the characteristics of the ships from Sisak and Kušjak and those of the Mediterranean shipbuilding construction technique, is further confirmed by floor timbers and pairs of knee-shaped frames that were installed in the same sequence as on Greek and Roman seagoing vessels (Steffy 1994: 49–50, 65 and 67).

Conclusion

The constructional features of the Sisak and the Kušjak vessels point to a Roman shipbuilding tradition of a probably southeastern European origin, heavily influenced by the technology of sewn ships from the area around the northern Adriatic Sea. The technology of sewing the entire planking was used along the coast of Central Dalmatia and the northern Adriatic during the late Republican Period and the first centuries of the Empire (Beltrame 2000; Marlier 2002). The early transfer and the subsequent adaptation of this technology from seagoing ships to cargo vessels for inland transport is attested by the approximately 30-metre long barge from Lipe at the Ljubljana Moor, dated to the early 1st century AD. The construction of a prototype of the later Gallo-Roman barges reveals a remarkable detail that is, with the exception of the Greek vessels, practically absent in the Roman sewn vessels with rounded hulls (Beltrame 2000: 93). The detail in question is the cylindrical wooden treenails that were used to hold some of the planks together (Gaspari 1998: 534, Taf. 72: 45, 100) by which the sewing process was facilitated and the longitudinal strength of the vessel increased; the latter being a very important characteristic in river transport. The barge from Sisak is much later in date than the Ljubljana barge and is the only recorded find of a high capacity vessel of the Roman Imperial Period in the mid- and lower Danube regions. Both the similarity of the Sisak barge with the contemporaneous Gallo-Roman barges and the rationalization of the building process by replacing the time-consuming sewing of the planks with the use of iron clamps, are clearly visible. The need for increased rigidity that probably originated from the increased transport

capacities dictated by the Roman military and the economy, is visible also in the massive construction and in the less precise execution of the constructional elements.

The vessel from Sisak was undoubtedly intended for the transport of heavy or bulk cargo, perhaps brick or iron from the ore deposits in western Bosnia, which is attested to this day by large quantities of slag. Down the Una, Sana and Japra rivers and further down the Sava and Kupa Rivers, iron was transported as ingots or shapeless pieces to Siscia where the general administration of *ferrariarum Delmaticarum et Pannonicarum* was stationed (Koščević 1995: 23 – 24; Lolić 2003: 134). The use of navigable waterways for the shipping of the goods is attested by the find of pieces of bronze statues in the riverbed of the Kupa near Karlovac, which are doubtlessly the remains of a cargo intended for the metallurgic workshops in Siscia (Šarić 1983).

References

Arnold, B., 1992, *Batellerie gallo-romaine sur le lac de Neuchâtel.* Éditions du Ruau, Archéologie Neuchâteloise 13. Saint-Blaise.

Beltrame, C., 2000, Sutiles naves of Roman Age. New Evidence and Technological Comparisons with Pre-Roman Sewn Boats. In V. J. Litwin (ed), *Down the River to the Sea. Proceedings of the Eight International Symposium on Boat and Ship Archaeology Gdansk 1997,* 91–96. Polish Maritime Museum. Gdansk.

Bockius, R., 1998, Zur rekonstruktion des römisches Plattbodenschiffes aus Woerden. *Jahrbuch Römisch-Germanischen Zentralmuseums, Mainz* 43.2: 511–533.

Bockius, R., 2000, Antike Schwergutfrachter – Zeugnisse römischer Schiffbaus und Gütertransports. In Steinbruch und Bergwerk (eds). Denkmäler Römischer Technikgeschichte zwischen Eifel und Rhein. Vulkanpark-Forschungen 2, 110–134. Mainz.

Bockius, R., 2002, *Die römerzeitlichen Shiffsfunde von Oberstimm in Bayern.* Monographien Römisch-Germanisches Zentralmuseums 30. Mainz.

Bockius, R., 2003, A Roman river barge (?) found in the Danube near Prahovo, Serbia. In C. Beltrame (ed), *Boats, Ships and Shipyards. Proceedings of the Ninth International Symposium on Boat and Ship Archaeology Venice 2000,* 169–176. Oxbow. Oxford.

Brunšmid, J., 1909, Rimski vojnički diplom iz Siska. *Vjesnik hrvatskog arheološkog društva* n. s. XI: 23–39. Zagreb.

Burkowsky, Z., 2000, *Pregled zaštitnih arheoloških istraživanja 1990–2000.* Gradski muzej Sisak. Sisak.

CII., *Corpus Inscriptionum Latinarum.*

De Weerd, M. D., 1988, *Shepen voor Zwammerdam.* Academisch Proefschrift. Universiteit van Amsterdam. Amsterdam.

Durman, A., 1992, O geostrateškom položaju Siska. *Opuscula Archaeologica* 16: 117–131.

Gaspari, A., 1998, Das Frachtschiff aus Lipe im Moor von Laibach (Ljubljana). *Jahrbuch Römisch-Germanischen Zentralmuseums Mainz* 45.2: 527–550.

Koščević, R., 1995, Finds and metalwork production. In R. Koščević and R. Makjanić (eds), *Siscia, Pannonia Superior,* 16–42. BAR Int. S621. Oxford.

Lolić, T., 2003. Colonia Flavia Siscia. In M. Šašel Kos, P. Scherrer (eds), *The Autonomous Towns of Noricum and Pannonia*. Situla 41: 131–152. Narodni Muzej Slovenije. Ljubljana.

Marlier, S., 2002. La question de la survivance des bateaux cousus de l'Adriatique. In L. Rivet and M. Scillano (eds), *Vivre, produire et échanger: Reflets Méditerranéens. Mélanges offerts à Bernard Lou*, 21–32. M. Mergoil. Montagnac.

Steffy, J. R., 1994, *Wooden Ship Building and the Interpretation of Shipwrecks*. Texas A & M University Press. College Station, Texas.

Šarić, I., 1983. Rimski brončani material izvaden iz rijeke Kupe kod Karlovca. *Obavijesti Hrvatskog arheološkog društva* 15.2: 17. Zagreb.

Šarić, I., 1986, Zaštitno arheološko istraživanje lokaliteta "Kovnica" u Sisku 1985. godine. *Obavijesti Hrvatskog arheološkog društva* 18.1: 28–29. Zagreb.

Šašel, J., 1974, RE suppl., XIV, s. v. Siscia, 702–741.

Šašel Kos, M., 2005, *Appian and Illyricum*. Situla 43. Narodni Muzej Slovenije. Ljubljana.

Vrbanović, S., 1981, Prilog proučavanju topografije Siscije. Arheološka istraživanja u Zagrebu i njegovoj okolici. *Izdanja Hrvatskog arheološkog društva* 6: 187–200. Zagreb.

Vuković, 1994, *Siscija*. Vizija rimskoga grada u Panoniji. Sisak.

Wiewegh, Z., 2001, *Siscija*. Rimska keramika iz Siska s lokaliteta "Kovnica". *Opuscula Archaeologica* 25: 89–92. Zagreb.

47 Contribution of maritime archaeology to the study of an Atlantic port: Bordeaux and its reused boat timbers

Patricia Sibella, John Atkin and Béatrice Szepertyski

N.B. – As of today, the results of the dendrochronological analysis are pending. Therefore, the following paper should be considered more as a presentation of the preliminary results rather than a synthesis of all the data.

The discovery of boat parts, either as isolated elements or fragments of larger structural assemblies, reused in a maritime or fluvio-maritime port context, provide an important contribution to our understanding of the life of a port. Earlier finds in Marseille, Toulon, Dublin, Bergen and particularly London, have already established the significance of port studies (McGrail 1993; Milne 2003; Tatton-Brown 1974). However, to date for numerous reasons, only a limited number of studies have been undertaken on reused boat and ship parts (Marsden 1996: 16–17).

In the context of the rescue excavations along the left bank of the Garonne River, Bordeaux, many boat parts were discovered, including a wreck, sections of other wrecks, and some dispersed elements.[1] The remains ranged in date from the Roman period to the beginning of modern times, and came from two sites: the *place Jean-Jaurès* – a Roman civic and religious centre and the northernmost point of the medieval port; and, further upstream, the *quai des Salinière*, a medieval harbour site that specialised in the manufacture and sale of salt and pottery.[2] While all of the finds were of interest, only those reused in waterfront revetments will be considered here.

A relatively large series of waterfront revetments were identified in the western part of the *place Jean-Jaurès* in Bordeaux.[3] Of various dimensions, the revetments on the far western side of the complex were composed of pieces of wood positioned vertically and held in place by nailed, horizontal lengths of wood. Other structures, situated towards the eastern side, were made up of large planks placed horizontally and supported by vertical posts (Fig. 47.1).

There were 49 reused boat parts distributed among a series of 13 waterfront revetments, each revetment being made up of two to eight parts. These reused boat parts were dated stratigraphically from the end of the 2nd

Fig. 47.1. *General view of the waterfront revetments. Place Jean-Jaurès, Bordeaux. (Photo by Patrick Ernaux/INRAP).*

Fig. 47.2. *Large section of a clinker vessel. Place Jean-Jaurès, Bordeaux. (Photo by Patrick Ernaux/INRAP).*

century to the 13th century AD.[4] Of the 49 parts inventoried, all were tentatively identified as oak, and grouped on the basis of their architectural technical characteristics as follows: firstly, 14 clinker fragments, consisting of isolated strakes, assembled strakes or a large section of a boat (Fig. 47.2); secondly, 15 isolated strakes with rabbeted dovetail joints; and finally, a third category of 20 fragments for which function has not yet been clearly identified. All bear traces of peg assemblage, some have rivets. A comparative study of these fragments with those found in other harbours would perhaps allow a better understanding of their function.

Preservation

The state of preservation of the clinker fragments and isolated strakes with rabbeted dovetail joints is relatively heterogeneous, the clinker strakes being often better preserved than the other fragments. Traces of wear, characterised by surface abrasions of the wood, are visible on both the internal and external faces. While some of this wear might date to the period when the boat was in use, other traces may relate to the position of the strakes in the various revetments.

Teredo marks

No signs were noted of woodborers such as the *Teredo* shipworm, which would indicate that any vessel had sailed in warm saltwater. The absence of holes, assuming they had existed, could be due either to erosion caused by long exposure of the outer surfaces facing the tide, or that the pieces studied were from the buried section of a boat and consequently, would have had little or no direct contact with the sea.

Size of the strakes

Most of the clinker strakes taper in section. This form, which is more pronounced on particular pieces, results from the radial splitting of a log, and has been found on examples discovered in Ireland, the Baltic and the Isle of Guernsey.[5] One of the strakes has a projecting lip on one end, which could indicate the place in the boat from which it came, perhaps situated in contact with the keel. Another peculiarity of this assembly is that none of the strakes seems to be scarfed. As for the strakes with the rabbeted dovetail joints, these seem to have been either radially split or tangentially cut.

Dimensions

A comparative study of strake lengths would have little meaning as most of the extremities are damaged and their dimensions are probably a product of their position in the revetment.

Clinker assembly

The clinker joining method, which is thought to have

been developed in Northwest Europe in the first centuries AD and widely employed by Atlantic shipwrights up to a comparatively recent date, is largely represented here (Rieth 2002: 88).

The examples studied contained numerous similarities and differences (Fig. 47.3). The upper strake always overlaps the external face of the lower strake; the overlapping of two strakes varies from 2.5 to 7 cm. There does not seem to be any relationship between the overlapping of the various pieces. Thus, two assembled fragments, which are situated in the same revetment and have similar overall dimensions, have strakes that overlap by 6 cm in one instance and by 2.5 cm in the other. This difference is far from negligible, and could perhaps be explained by relative strake movements over time or the specific position of a strake in the same vessel. Otherwise, these two pieces show all the appearances of having belonged to the same boat, and may have come from different areas of the same boat. The only exception to this non-specific arrangement appears to be the larger strakes where overlapping seems more uniform.

Strake assembly dovetails

The rabbeted dovetail joints, attested on 15 strakes, are characterised by thin planks (*circa* 1.5 cm thickness).

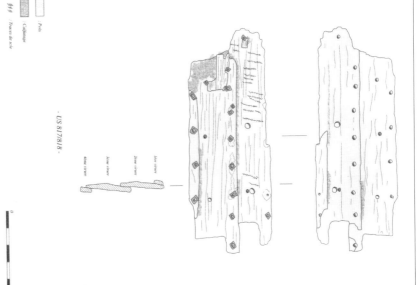

Fig. 47.3. *Series of four strakes (# 817/818), showing evidence of caulking, tar (?), as well as repairs. Place Jean-Jaurès, Bordeaux. (Drawn by P. Sibella).*

Partially preserved, they were cut in the direction of the wood grain and positioned perpendicular to the wood grain of the strakes to which they belonged. They are kept in place, inside the rebates, by nails generally placed on each side of the rabbeted dovetail joints, thus facing each other. Their heads are round and flat (circa 0.5 cm diameter). None of them have as yet been classified. A more extensive study of these elements could provide us with additional information on the method used to construct the boats from which these strakes came.

As for the rebates, their dimensions are similar, or slightly larger, than the rabbeted dovetail joints they cover. In the latter case, it could be that we are confronted with the use of different type of wood which would have deformed differently over time compared to the original wood. In this particular function, the rabbeted dovetail joints may also have contributed to the deformation of these thin pieces. The identification of the species of wood will be considered in a later study.

The layout of the rabbeted dovetail joints in the same strake corresponds to two distinct designs: either they face each other and are thus opposite from one edge to another, or they alternate. Their number per strake is variable and there does not seem to be a relationship between strake width and the number of dovetails. Spacing varies from one strake to another, being relatively homogeneous on one strake, and totally inconsistent on another.

Most of the strakes that belong to this assembly have grooves about 2 cm wide which are either along one, or both, of the edges, and are cut halfway up the strakes, level with the rebates. Their function is to allow two strakes to be fitted together. Nails that have round, flat heads, are inserted obliquely along certain grooves, and near the head of a dovetail. It seems that their function was also to ensure a better cohesion between two strakes.

Rivets

The clinker strakes are fastened in place with nails or rivets, probably of iron, with circular or domed heads, and with a square or rectangular shank cross-section, driven in from the outside of the boat (Fig. 47.2). Although the rove dimensions vary from one to another, they average 4 x 4 cm, with a thickness of 0.5 cm. One example reveals the forging technique used to make these roves. The latter were forged in the form of a long flat bar and then sectioned. Once the rove was in place, the extremity of the nail was then clenched, giving it a more or less rounded and bulged form (Bill 1994: 55–66).

Luting

Although watertightness of boats is a key construction factor, especially in the case of clinker strakes, no luting was observed in the case of the strakes with rabbeted dovetail joints. The diversity of the solutions found in the case of the Bordeaux clinker fragments is surprising as we are confronted not only with moss but also with vegetable (Fig. 47.2) and animal fibres (Fig. 47.3). These are either in the form of two or three strands of loosely twisted fibers placed parallel to the wood grain, or pads of fibres; both techniques could be observed in the same structure.

The use of vegetable fibre in clinker construction is attested sporadically in northern Europe before the 15th century, but appears more afterwards. On the other hand, the use of animal fibre is widely represented before the 15th century. An example is the Graveney boat (England), dated to the end of the 9th or beginning of the 10th centuries, in which caulking was made using sheep hair (Fenwick 1978). In Bergen, Norway, the caulking recovered from boat parts reused in harbour structures was composed of sheep fibres, for the fragments dating to the 12th century, and cattle and goat or sheep fibres for fragments dating to the 15th century (Walton 1988: 78–85).

In the absence of any systematic study of these materials, either from a chronological or geographical standpoint, we obviously cannot generalise this practice in relation to all the parts found at the Jean-Jaurès site. Consequently, since the study of the fibres on the clinker strakes from Bordeaux appears essential, initial research will focus on the identification of any remaining pollen present in the pitch or resin used with the luting. Pollen identification would allow us to determine the vegetable environment in which the boat was luted. Subsequently, it would be desirable to identify the fibres themselves.[6]

Finally, it should be noted that two of the strakes show traces of a yellowish colour, which belonged either to the luting itself or to an oxidation of the product used to protect and preserve the wood. No samples of this material were taken.

Treenails and treenail holes

Most of the strakes had treenail holes and, in some cases, the treenails were still in place. When found in situ, the treenails were removed for both typological study and wood species identification with the objective of creating a classification system.[7] The treenail heads either were flat, rounded and dome-shaped, or in the form of a "champagne cork" (Fig. 47.2). The average diameter at their extreme end varied, as a function of their form, between 2.5 and 2.7 cm; except in the case of a "champagne cork" where the diameter was closer to 6 cm. The shaft of the treenails was relatively consistent in diameter, tapering in section from head to end, and sometimes faceted, or with long flat surfaces, which obviously were caused by the way they had been cut. It is interesting to note that the treenails had not, at first sight, come from heartwood. Most of the treenails were not conserved to their original length, but it seems that their maximum length would be about 7 cm. The treenails or treenail holes were generally placed at the halfwidth of a strake. Treenail spacing along the same strake was in some cases regular and in others completely irregular.

Treenails usually indicated the framing pattern for the ship but, despite careful study, no indentations, dark marks on the wood or any other traces of framing were detected.

Although the second objective was to identify the wood species this could not be carried out due to lack of time.

Repairs

A limited number of clinker strakes had been repaired (Fig. 47.3). Appearing either on the interior or the exterior of the strakes, thin planks, luted and riveted, were used to fill depressions in the wood.

In other examples the repair related directly to a structural weakness in the wood (Fig. 47.4). In the case of US 1017–1018 a crack ran along the length of the widest strake and four dovetail-shaped repairs were placed in the grooves, spaced about 43 cm apart. They were held in place by small-diameter nails and other nails were placed on either side of the split in the wood. The fact that the split continued beyond the pieces used in the repairs suggests that the crack continued to grow despite the repair attempts.

The position of the reused boat parts in the waterfront revetments

It is clear that the revetments are concentrated around a centre of activity medieval in date, and are approximately contemporary with most of the boat parts reused in them. Not all the parts have been dated and some of those that have been dated need to have their dates verified. There does seem, however, to be a coherent chronology that begins at the end of the 2nd century (for one of the strakes) and continues to the 13th century for some clinker assemblies and the strakes with the rabbeted dovetail joints.

Four of the seven series of revetments in which the clinker assemblies were found are located in close proximity to each other. Ten of the 14 strakes belonged to this group and were all positioned perpendicular to the channel of the Garonne; the other four were distributed haphazardly. As for the 15 strakes with rabbeted dovetail joints, they were spread out among four series of revetments, positioned either perpendicular or parallel to the river. It is interesting to note the absence of boat parts among the revetments in the easternmost zone. These revetments were, at first sight, the last to be built and were in direct

contact with the Garonne and the standard of carpentry used seems to be higher than in the earlier revetments.

Overall, there seems to exist a concentration of strakes by type. Certain elements belonging to the same series of revetments show the same technical characteristics (form, dimensions, positions of the holes of treenails and of rivets, etc.), indicating that these could have belonged to the same boat. However, we must wait for the final publication by the excavators to confirm this hypothesis.

It is likely that certain strakes, especially those with the rabbeted dovetail joints, belonged to smaller, river craft. In the case of US 1017–1018, the dovetail-shaped repairs, together with the nails, also tend to indicate a type of river boat, which, by its dimensions, could well correspond to a barge of the Zwammerdam type (Rieth 1998: 81). Other parts and structural assemblages, however, display all the characteristics of seagoing vessels of medium, even large tonnage (strake dimensions, thickness, overlaps, distance between the rivets, luting, etc.). It is conceivable that these vessels were constructed elsewhere (for example in northern Europe) as there is no

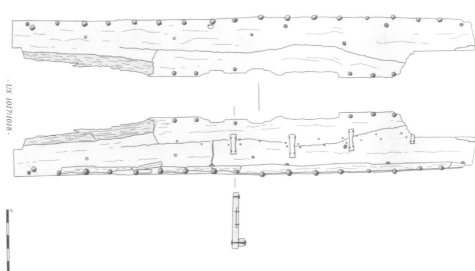

- US 1017/1018 -

Fig. 47.4. Clinker strakes (# 1017/1018), with dovetail-shaped repair. Place Jean-Jaurès, Bordeaux. (Drawn by P. Sibella).

historical evidence for the building of seagoing ships in Bordeaux before the 15th century. Can this be possibly true? Only the results of the dendrochronological analyses can provide fresh clues and would, without doubt, re-launch the debate concerning shipyards in Bordeaux (Bernard 1968). Additionally, once these results are available, we will be in a better position to discuss in detail the phenomenon of reused boat parts through the ages.

Finally, we can consider the type and number of boats represented by the parts that have been found. Certainly, at this stage of our study, and on the basis of the technical characteristics, we can propose that there would have been a minimum of six boats that came here to live a second life.

Notes

1   The excavations, related to the building of a tramway, were conducted from November 2001 to August 2003 by the *Institut National de Recherche en Archéologie Préventive* (INRAP), with F. Gerber as the field director and P. Sibella as the ship and boat specialist. I take this opportunity to thank F. Gerber, as well as the *Service régional de l'Archéologie* and its director, D. Barraud and engineer, P. Régaldo for their support.

2   These remains include: a flat-bottomed wreck dated to the end of the 17th- beginning of the 18th century (*quai des Salinières*); a monoxyle bottom of a plank boat archaeologically dated to the 14th century (*place Jean-Jaurès*); 11 isolated frames tentatively dated to the 16th century (*place Jean-Jaurès*); as well as 49 reused boat timbers (*place Jean-Jaurès*).

3   It must be pointed out that the exact number of revetments, as well as all the information relative to the disposition of the various elements in the revetment, the overlapping or not of these elements, their orientation, etc., are not actually available: the archaeological excavation report not yet having been officially completed. In consequence, we can only refer to field observations specific to boat and ship construction.

4   Due to the conditions specific to rescue excavations, it is most probable that other elements existed, but were not, or could not be identified.

5   I would like to thank D. Goodburn and J. Adams for introducing me to these sites.

6   The samples taken will be studied by M.-F. Diot from the *Centre National de Préhistoire*.

7   This work was essentially carried out by J. Atkin, contributor to this paper.

References

Atkin, J., 2003, *Une contribution de l'archéologie navale à l'étude des ports atlantiques européens de l'Antiquité au Moyen Age: le réemploi d'éléments de bateaux dans les structures portuaires*. Mémoire de Maîtrise. Université Michel de Montaigne – Bordeaux 3.

Bernard, J., 1968, *Navires et gens de mer à Bordeaux (vers 1400-vers 1550)*. Thèse de l'Université de Paris, Paris.

Bill, I., 1994, Iron Nails in Iron Age and Medieval Shipbuilding. In C. Westerdahl (ed). *Crossroads in ancient shipbuilding: proceedings of the sixth International Symposium on Boat and Ship Archaeology, Roskilde, 1991*, 55–66. Oxbow. Oxford.

Fenwick, V. (ed), 1978, *The Graveney Boat*. B.A.R. British Series 53. Oxford.

Hutchinson, G., 1994, *Medieval Ships and Shipping*. Leicester University Press. London.

McGrail, S. 1993. *Medieval Boat and Ship Timbers from Dublin*. Royal Irish Academy.

Marsden, P., 1996, *Ships of the Port of London: first to eleventh centuries AD*. English Heritage. London.

Milne, G., 1985, *The Port of Roman London*. Batsford. London.

Milne, G., 2003, *The Port of Medieval London*. Tempus Ltd. Stroud.

Rieth, E., 2002, Architecture navale à clin en France à la fin du XVIIe siècle. *Dossiers d'archéologie* 277: 88–94.

Sibella, P. 2003, *Rapport préliminaire rédigé dans le cadre des fouilles des bois de marine retrouvés à Bordeaux*. Service régional de l'Archéologie, AFAN/INRAP, Bordeaux (unpublished).

Tatton-Brown, T., 1974, *Excavations at the Custom House Site, City of London, 1973*. London and Middlesex Archaeology Society. London.

Walton, P. 1988. Caulking, Cordage and Textiles. In C. O'Brian, L. Brown, S. Nixon and R. Nicholson (eds), *The Origins of the Newcastle Quayside: excavations at Queen Street and Dog Bank*, 78–85. Society of Antiquaries of Newcastle upon Tyne. Newcastle.

48 A Roman barge with an artefactual inventory from De Meern (the Netherlands)

André F. L. van Holk

Introduction

In this paper I want to present some of the preliminary results of the excavation of the Roman barge "De Meern 1", carried out in the spring of 2003 by the Netherlands Institute for ship- and underwater Archaeology (NISA), which is part of the National Service for Archaeological Heritage (ROB).

As ships do more than floating alone, the central question I will try to answer here and now, is: what was this ship doing there and then? What was the function of this ship in her cultural and environmental context? In order to answer this question, we have to start with some archaeological basics: to what geographic, cultural and time frame does the ship belong?

The ship was found in 1997, totally unexpectedly, during building activities, west of the city of Utrecht, near the village of De Meern, in the central part of the Netherlands (Fig. 48.1). From the survey it became clear that we could be dealing with a complete ship and

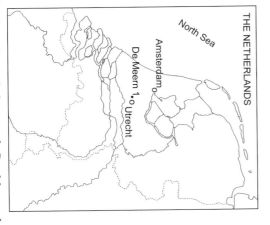

Fig. 48.1. Location of shipwreck De Meern 1 in the Netherlands.

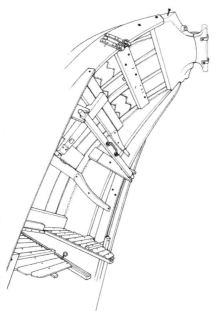

Fig. 48.2. Reconstruction drawing with view at the stern of the vessel De Meern 1 (J.-M.A.W. Morel, NISA/ROB).

artefactual inventory from the Roman period. So when analysis showed that the ship was threatened by oxygen-rich groundwater, it was decided to excavate the vessel.

Cultural and geographical context

During the excavation more and more evidence appeared that indicated we were dealing with a *Roman* barge. Let me start with the ship itself. What are the characteristic Roman (or more correctly Gallo-Roman) elements?

First of all, the outermost bottom-plank and the first strake of the side are made of one piece, a so-called transition strake, which is L-shaped in cross-section. Secondly, the frames are connected to the strakes only by iron nails. A third characteristic element is the T-shaped stern-board, as shown here on a reconstruction drawing (Fig. 48.2). One of the Roman ships excavated in Woerden (number 6) has a similar T-shaped stern-board. On top of this, a steering oar could be mounted. Yet another construction detail might have Roman roots (in this case Mediterranean roots): the way some of the strakes and scarfs are joined. Nails are hammered into the thin part of the planks, as you can see here in a scarf (Fig. 48.3).

along the *Limes* in *Germania Inferior*. One under Trajan (c 100 AD) and one under Hadrian (124/125 AD). From the date of the De Meern 1 ship it becomes clear that we can not link the presence of the ship to one of the two building programmes.

The next subject I want to address is the geographical context of the vessel. Quite astonishing and really not expected was the source of the wood used for building the ship. The best dendrochronological correlations were obtained with the master chronology of East Frisia (northern Germany) and two Dutch chronologies.

The ship had sunk in a silted-up side-branch of the Rhine, the Heldammer Stroom. The spot where the ship had sunk lies in the middle of an elaborate military infrastructure, dating from the Roman period, which is known as the *Limes*. The *Limes* consisted of four main elements: a river, a road, watchtowers and *castella* or fortresses. The ship of De Meern was located only 6 m from the Roman road.

What could have been the function of the ship in this spatial context? The vessel is very narrow, with a length of 24.6 m and a width of 2.6 m. It has an extreme length-to-breadth ratio of 9 : 1. Most other Roman barges have a length-to-breadth ratio of 7 : 1, such as those at Zwammerdam, for example. These were probably used to transport heavy cargo, especially building materials for the fortresses, watchtowers and road along the *Limes*. It has been suggested that the Zwammerdam-type ships were built on the Middle or Upper Rhine to make one journey to the Lower Rhine, where they would serve out their careers (one way traffic). At the *castellum* of Zwammerdam, they were even re-used as footings for quays. For a narrow ship, like the De Meern 1 vessel, it must have been easier to sail *up* the river as well and to navigate locally on narrow water.

Another question is: did the ship have a sail or not? A mast has not been found, but a maststep was there; from the mast partner only traces of nails remained. Was the mast used for a sail or as a bitt to which a rope was fixed, so the ship could be towed? The grave-stone of Brussus from Mainz (dated around 40 AD) may hold the answer. On it a ship is depicted, with a mast, but without a sail. If the ship had a sail it surely would have been visible on the picture. So the mast was probably used for towing the ship. This makes sense for a ship that also had to sail upstream. The De Meern 1 ship is clearly a river-barge, adjusted to sailing on narrow waters, like small rivers and canals.

Function of the vessel

But what exactly could have been the function of the De Meern 1 ship? To answer that question we will turn to the inventory and the use of space on board. At an early stage of the excavation it became clear that in the stern of the ship three bulkheads were present (Fig. 48.4). This was an exciting discovery, because even in ships of post-

Fig. 48.3. Scarf in L-shaped bilge-strake at the port side of the ship De Meern 1, showing a nail in the thin part of the plank, connecting two planks (T. Penders, ROB).

This way of fastening could be a mental template ("how a joint should look") of the use of mortise and tenon, as this is also a joint which connects the thin parts of two adjoining strakes.

Next to the construction of the ship itself, objects from the inventory could also be recognised as belonging to the Roman period. To mention just two examples: a black coated beaker, type Stuart 2, made in technique C/D with sand sprinkling, which can be dated between AD 180 and 220; and shoe, one of which is of a type which could be dated even more precisely: AD 180–200. The foundering of the ship thus probably took place in the last quarter of the 2nd century AD.

As part of the post-excavation research, dendrochronological samples were taken. The resulting felling date is AD 148 ± 6 AD (Hanraets 2003). So the time-frame during which the ship operated is well established, between 150 and 180–200. The ship must have been in use for 30–50 years. It is not unlikely for an inland vessel to have been in use for that long. This long life is also suggested by the investigation of the construction. It seems that the strakes of the bottom in the stern and bow have been subject to repairs to a certain extent. Hessing (1999: 151–155) mentions two phases of intensified building

medieval date it is a rare phenomenon to find panelling like this.

The after compartment, the cabin, where most of the artefacts were found, could be entered by two doors in the back, which were also still in place. In the foremost compartment the galley was situated. The floor of the galley (ceiling) and a roof tile were partially blackened by fire (Fig. 48.5). An interesting detail to be mentioned is the accessibility of the galley: it could only be entered through the forward bulkhead, which consists of two parts and could be taken out. So both rooms were completely separated. This might be a reflection of a social separation, or stratification of the crew abaft and before the cabin.

What about the artefacts? Almost all of them were found in the cabin. One explanation for this is the site-formation process: high in the cabin, a cupboard and two boxes, one large and one small, were found (Fig. 48.6). It appears that they started floating after the ship had sunk and got stuck against the roof of the cabin. So the roof of the cabin had been in place for at least some time after the ship had sunk.

To give an idea of the design of the cabin I should start by discussing the furniture. The cupboard is decorated with mouldings, as is the piece fixed at the top-front. The

cupboard still contained several objects, including scissors, a *stylus* (writing pen), a knife, a piece of chalk and a coin. The box was also worked with a decorative moulding. Except for a piece of rope, the box was empty. It might have been a tool-box, as some tools and a turned baluster were found loose next to the box. They had probably floated out of it.

Against the forward bulkhead of the cabin stood a fixed bed or bench. Above the bed, a rack with one shelf was located. The balusters of the rack were also decorated, this time with black diamond-shaped figures burnt into the wood. The bed was decorated too, with turned legs and a moulded rail.

The inside of the gangway, which was visible in the cabin, was also moulded. All in all, the cabin must have looked quite well tended, with the abundant decorations. Is this a clue to the status of the person who stayed in the cabin? The problem with answering this question is that comparative material on board ships from this period does not exist. On the other hand, it is clear that the decorations of the bed-bench were not in sight, but covered by (a secondary?) layer of planking. Besides that the turned legs of the bed-bench had been attacked by woodworm. So they could have been re-used. The cup-

Fig. 48.4. Partitions (bulkheads) dividing De Meern 1 into hold, galley, cabin and stern (J. Koch, Blaricum)

Fig. 48.5. Galley with blackened roof-tiles from the De Meern 1 wreck (T. Penders, ROB).

Fig. 48.6. Cupboard and box high up in the cabin of De Meern 1, stuck against the former roof of the cabin, which was lost during wreck formation (J. Koch, Blaricum).

Fig. 48.7. Plane from Roman wreck De Meern 1 (T. Penders, ROB).

Fig. 48.8. Handsaw, adze and terra sigillata cup and sherd in situ, on board of De Meern 1 (J. Koch, Blaricum).

Fig. 48.9. Second handsaw from de Meern 1 (T. Penders, ROB).

board is made of many different kinds of wood; re-use may also be the case.

Besides this, an amazing number of tools came to light during the excavation. Amongst others we have found three complete planes; one of them is shown in Fig. 48.7. The planes were not meant for shipbuilding, but rather for fine carpentry, such as furniture making. Next have been found, and these are the most spectacular: two complete frame saws, one of which could not be tightened and a second one of another type, which could be tightened by wire (Figs 48.8 and 48.9). These two saws seem to be the only complete ones known from the Roman period so far. It is possible that the saws also had started drifting after the ship had sunk and initially were kept in the tool-box. Two adzes also came to light, with short handles. One of them has what seems to be textile around the shaft. It may have been wrapped in a textile sack (Fig. 48.10).

From the make-up of this tool set it could be concluded that a travelling carpenter, specialising in fine wood-working, was on board. So one of the functions of the crew of this vessel might be the production, maintenance and repair of furniture, in use in the *castella* and watch-towers along the *Limes*.

There was also some heavier equipment present in the cabin. For example, a crowbar, of which the iron, like the

other metal artefacts, was in an extremely good condition. It is possible that the maintenance of other wooden structures, like buildings, was also handled. So a whole set of tools was present and these were probably not meant for shipbuilding or maintenance of the ship.

Several artefacts have been found, which could be related to the military. First of all, there are a pair of sandal soles with pointed nails at the outside (Fig. 48.11). The soles were size 41 and well made, which tells us something about their owner (van Driel-Murray 2004). A sole from a shoe, size 40–42, is probably from the same adult male. The location of the soles in the cabin suggests they could belong to the skipper. It is interesting to note that the skipper had two different pairs of shoes for different events. He seems to have been used to dressing according to Mediterranean customs. So he was relatively well-to-do and used to moving in the circles of the Mediterranean elite.

Furthermore, a so-called *dolabra* was found, a kind of pick-axe, which is considered to be standard equipment of Roman soldiers. In the galley a spearhead appeared. The location of this artefact and the fact that it does not have a haft (in contrast to the other artefacts) could mean it was re-used as a knife for cutting meat (pers. comm. J.-M.A.W. Morel). So this might point to a former (?) military occupation of the owner of the vessel.

The same could go for the *fibula*, a brooch, found during the survey. It is a simple one, of the kind used by soldiers. It is not clear how and if the simple *fibula* is related to the owner of the more luxurious shoes. Or did the fibula belong to another crew member? Whatever the case may be, there are several indications to be found in the artefactual assemblage which point to the shipper being a former (?) member of the military. At the least,

there are indications of the ship acting in a military context, due to the find spot along the *Limes* and artefact assemblage. Whether we are dealing with a purely military vessel with a military crew, or with a skipper (and crew), who is a civilian (maybe an ex-soldier) and had or started a business of his own and remained in regular contact with the Roman army, is the question.

Fig. 48.11. Sole of military sandal in situ, on board of De Meern 1 (T. Penders, ROB).

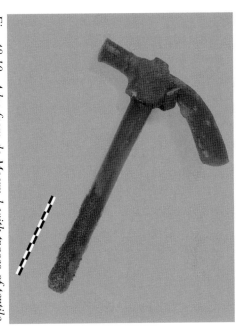

Fig. 48.10. Adze from de Meern 1 with traces of textile, in which it probably had been wrapped (T. Penders, ROB).

Conclusion

The narrowness of the vessel could be understood in the light of the operational environment. The ship was by its slender design, narrower than other Roman barges, suitable to sail up and down small rivers and canals. Moreover, she was able to enter narrow 'harbours' or landing places. The extreme length-breath ratio of the vessel must have to do with the desire to carry as much cargo as possible. The length of the vessel may also be an indication of the kind of cargo, in this case tree-trunks, the raw material of a carpenter either for building activities or other purposes. This does not, of course, rule out a general supply function for the vessel.

The military objects on board could either indicate we are dealing with a Roman military vessel or with a civilian (whether or not a former member of the Roman army) as skipper. The elaborate decoration of the cabin might be a result of the occupation of the owner, a travelling carpenter, rather than a reflection of status. On closer examination, the decorations are not very subtle; the different kinds of wood used for the cupboard point to reuse of the wood. The turned legs of the bed-bench were covered (in a later stage?) by panelling. Besides that most of the furniture was attacked by woodworms. So the elaborate decorations seem to be more the result of the occupation of the owner than a sign of any (military) rank.

So the abundance of tools makes it plausible that the ship functioned in the context of this huge military infrastructure, called the *Limes*, as a kind of maintenance ship, servicing the watchtowers and forts. Since the hold was empty, we don't have a clue to the cargo, but the maintenance function could have been coupled to a function as supply ship for wood and other raw material, as well as food.

References

Hanraets, A.E.M., 2003, *Rapportage daterend onderzoek de Meern 1*. RING Intern Rapport 2003 (083) Amersfoort.

Hessing, W.A.M., 1999, Building Programmes for the Lower Rhine *Limes*. The impact of the Visits of Trajan and Hadrian to the Lower Rhine. In H.Sarfatij, W.J.H. Verwers and P.J. Woldering (eds.), *In discussion with the past. Archaeological studies presented to W.A. van Es*, Zwolle/Amersfoort.

van Driel-Murray, C., 2004, *Vleuten-De Meern schip 1, DMN1 Ledervondsten: de schoenen van de schipper*. Internal report on file at ROB.

49 The Arade 1 shipwreck. A small ship at the mouth of the Arade river, Portugal

Filipe Castro

Introduction

The mouth of the Arade River has been inhabited since at least the Iron Age. Some scholars believe that Portus Hanibalis, an important harbour built by the Carthaginian general Amilcar in the 6th century BC, was located nearby (Carrapiço et al. 1974: 40). Later, after a predominantly rural Roman occupation of this area, North African Muslims colonized the territory from AD 715 to 1250, developing the village of Silves, a few miles upstream, and increasing the traffic on the Arade River. In AD 966 a fleet of 28 Viking ships attacked the region and was engaged and beaten on the Arade River by an Arab naval force sent from Seville (Coelho 1989, 2: 133; Marques 1993: 129).

In the 13th century the Portuguese conquest of this area brought new settlements and new settlers to the area around the mouth of the Arade River. The modern city of Portimão was a small settlement in the mid-13th century and had around 40 households in 1463, when it was named São Lourenço da Barroza. These 40 families are thought to have been dedicated predominantly to the fishing of tuna, an ancient activity in the region. Exposed to frequent pirate incursions, the village was fortified during the second half of the 15th century (Loureiro 1909, 4:189). Due to its growing economic importance during the following centuries, two fortresses were built in the first decades of the 17th century in order to protect the river from pirate incursions. By 1615 there were 1802 inhabitants in Portimão (Carrapiço et al. 1974: 28).

The population increased steadily in this area during the following three centuries and in 1926, as the development of the preserves industry in Portimão called for larger fishing vessels, dredging operations were carried out in the mouth of the Arade River. Then, in the 1940s, two jetties were built to protect the river mouth, and in 1970 major dredging works were carried out. After this the port authorities implemented maintenance dredging works approximately every decade.

The Arade River Shipwrecks

During the summer of 1970 the captain of the dredge *Mark*, working at the mouth of the Arade River, reported having struck five shipwrecks, which were said to have been either totally or partially destroyed.

Two of these shipwrecks – named Arade 1 and Arade 2 – were inspected by two rival groups of sport divers. Rumours of further destruction of shipwrecks hit the local press in the early 1980s, when a new dredging campaign was launched by the harbour authority. At least one other shipwreck was destroyed. In the 1990s further dredging works and the construction of a marina brought more news of possible shipwreck troves and destructions.

In 2001, following a public outcry against the potential destruction of yet more ship remains during a newly planned campaign of dredging operations, Centro Nacional de Arqueologia Náutica e Subaquática (CNANS) – the Portuguese National Agency for Nautical Archaeology created in 1997 – sponsored a survey at the mouth of the Arade River, with the help of Grupo de Estudos Oceânicos (GEO) a very active local group of amateur divers.

CNANS's team identified four sites of potential archaeological interest, to which were added another ten sites by the GEO divers. One of the CNANS sites, known as A1, proved to be the Arade 1 shipwreck of 1970. The surrounding area was surveyed, and a preliminary plan of the shipwreck was produced. In the summer of 2002 the excavation of this shipwreck was entrusted to a team from Texas A&M University/Institute of Nautical Archaeology under my direction.

Part of my job was to identify and organize all shipwreck sites reported intact or destroyed during the last three decades (Fig. 49.1). After consulting archives and talking to witnesses it became clear that the shipwrecks visited by sport divers in 1970 were not two, but three. The first shipwreck, Arade 1, had been surveyed and photographed by both groups of sport divers. Two good sketches and a short report were produced. The second shipwreck identification was less clear: according to the

49 The Arade 1 shipwreck. A small ship at the mouth of the Arade river, Portugal

301

first group it was located near one of the jetties, close to the place where a bronze gun had been found in the late 1950s. Moreover, it had more bronze guns in it, and was completely covered by silt before anybody could see it. For the other group the second shipwreck was located near the Arade 1 site, was totally exposed, and was clinker built. I have called these two vessels Arade 2 and Arade 6 respectively.

To this list of six shipwrecks another eight sites were added. Two with iron guns, located next to each other near the entrance of the jetties, were designated Arade 7 and 8. The site of the ship that had been destroyed in 1980 was located and called Arade 9, and three recent derelicts, either removed or covered during the construction of Portimão's marina, were marked as Arade 10, 11 and 12. The last two sites added to this list were identified in 2001 by the local group GEO. The first, Arade 13, was a large copper-fastened ship lying in the middle of river. The second, optimistically named Arade 14, was a plank showing pegged mortise-and-tenon joints, the first found so far on the Portuguese coast.

Arade 1 Shipwreck

Following the promising results of the 2001 survey, CNANS sponsored a large field season at the mouth of the Arade River in the summer of 2002. The team of this field season comprised GEO divers, a group of archaeologists from the University of S. Paulo (Brazil), and another from the Nautical Archaeology Program at Texas A&M University (USA).

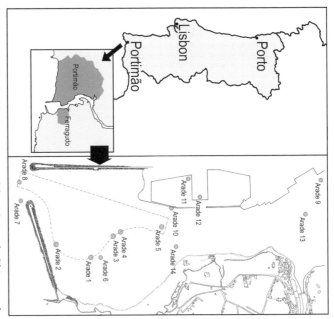

Fig. 49.1. Probable locations of the 12 Arade Shipwrecks (author).

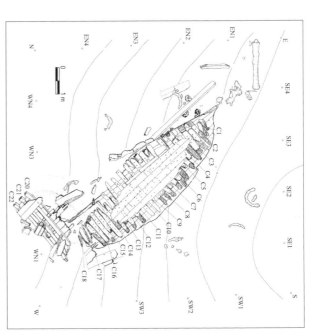

Fig. 49.2. Site plan (author).

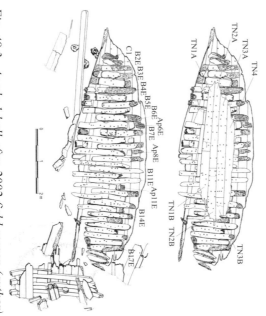

Fig. 49.3. Arade 1 hull after 2002 field season (author).

Under my direction, the Texas A&M team was entrusted with the excavation of the Arade 1 shipwreck. During that field season the remains of the Arade 1 ship were fully recorded, and the ceiling planking subsequently recovered. Four trenches were dug around the shipwreck, and a second portion of this hull, previously hidden in the sediments, was discovered and exposed (Fig. 49.2).

During the summer of 2003 a team from CNANS under the direction of Dr. Eric Rieth disassembled the upper portion of the shipwreck and transported the timbers to the CNANS warehouse, in Lisbon, for further study.

The upper section of the ship seems to correspond to the bow, and was preserved over an area of 7 x 3 m. It was composed of a keel, stem, apron, 18 partial frames, four strakes of ceiling planking, and six strakes of the

Keel – one section, as far as it could be observed @ C10/C11 level.
Sided – 15.5 cm (top); 11cm (bottom).
Moulded – 13.5 cm.
Preserved length – 6.05 m.
Scarfs – Not observed.

Stem – one section.
Sided – 14.5 cm (top); 9.5 cm (bottom).
Moulded – 13.5 cm.
Preserved length – 1.49 m.
Scarfs – Not observed.

Apron – Not fully measured.
Sided – 14.5 cm (top).

Floor timbers – fairly well shaped.
Sided – Average 17.6 cm.
Moulded – 16 to 17 cm.

Futtocks – roughly shaped. First and second futtocks were preserved.
Sided – Average 18 cm.
Moulded – 16 to 17 cm.

Room and space – irregular.
Around 42 cm between C1 and C8.
Around 29 cm between C9 and C18.

Ceiling planking (fixed) – Carefully shaped and laid. Linked through flat horizontal scarves.
Thickness – 6 cm.
Width – 23 to 27 cm.
Max length preserved – 3.28 m (TN3A).
Scarfs – Flat horizontal, 50 to 60 cm long.

Ceiling planking (loose) – Carefully shaped and laid.
Thickness – 5 cm.
Width – Variable. Min. 7 cm; Max. 29 cm.

Filler pieces – Carefully shaped and laid.
Thickness – 5 cm.
Width – Variable (=space between floors).
Length – Around 18 cm.

Hull planking – Carefully shaped and hung.
Thickness – 5 cm.
Width – Consistently 28 cm.
Max preserved length – Not recorded.

Fastenings – Both treenails and iron nails; remains of two bolts.
Keel/Stem – Not recorded;
Floors/Keel – Treenails, Ø = 3 cm;
Floors/Futtocks – Treenails, Ø = 3 cm;
Keel/Keelson (?) – Iron bolts, Ø = 3.2 cm;
Planking/Frames – Iron nails, side = 8 mm; treenails, Ø = 3 cm.
Ceiling/Frames – Iron nails, side = 8 mm; treenails, Ø = 3 cm.

Table 49.1. Scantling List.

outer planking (Fig. 49.3). A scantling list is presented above, in Table 49.1.

The keel was preserved to a length of 6.05 m on the upper portion of the shipwreck, and at least 1 m on its lower portion. Its section was observed both at the fracture between the two portions and between floor timbers C10 and C11. Much eroded, it seemed to have a T-shaped section with a trapezoidal body. Later, after the 2003 field season, it was found to have a trapezoidal section with the rabbet opened below its upper surface, leaving about 3 cm of rising wood on the keel above the back rabbet line.

The stem also presented a trapezoidal section with rectangular rabbets, but without rising wood. It was connected to the keel with a flat, vertical scarf. The remains of what seemed to be an apron were attached to the upper face of the keel at its forward end. It was much eroded and no details could be recorded.

There was no keelson towards the bow, where a group of loose ceiling planks covered the area above the keel. The remains of a large mast step were recorded in 1970. The keelson was preserved over a length of 5.13 m, tapered in the direction

of the stern, and showing shallow notches on some of the floor timbers. The 1970 sketch shows the mast step with a square section 20 cm sided and 20 cm moulded at the level of mortise. This mortise was 40 cm long, 8 cm wide and 5 cm deep.

The remains of 18 frames were partially preserved, with floor timbers, first and second futtocks. The position of a 19th frame was clearly indicated on the planking towards the bow.

The floor timbers could be divided into two main groups. The first, lighter and better shaped, comprised timbers C9 to C18 on the upper section of the hull, and C20 to C22 on its lower section. These central floor timbers were placed with 20 cm of clear space between them and presented almost square sections 15 cm sided and 16 cm moulded. Their lower surfaces appeared smoother and showed better adherence to the hull planking. The second group of floor timbers comprised the frames localized before floor C9. These floor timbers were placed over the keel at less regular intervals, although the average distance between them, 20 cm, did not vary much from the average distance between central frames.

However, since these bow frames presented heavier scantlings, the average value of the room and space varied greatly between the first and second group, with 35 cm for the central frames, and 42.1 cm for the bow frames.

All floor timbers were fastened to the keel with one, two or three treenails, with the exception of floor C1, which sat on the stem and was fastened to it with a single iron nail. All floor timbers showed trapezoidal limber holes 5 cm high, 6 to 8 cm on their tops. All floor timbers were cut from oak trees with diameters smaller than 20 cm, leaving sapwood and bark on the edges. Three of the bow floor timbers – numbers C3, C4, and C5 – presented a fore and aft groove of unknown function in their upper surfaces, approximately over the keel.

A total of 23 first futtocks were preserved in the upper portion of the hull, and another five were exposed on the lower portion of the hull. Futtocks were 15 to 22.5 cm sided, and about 16 cm moulded. They were generally roughly shaped, some – such as B5E, for instance – with bark still attached. No futtock was accurately recorded in this first phase of the excavation.

Several first futtocks were fastened to the floor timbers. However, since no futtocks were disassembled during the 2002 field season, the fastening pattern is not yet known. One feature raised interesting questions: it seems that, at least in four places, fore and aft treenails fastened three timbers at the same time.

Only four, badly eroded, second futtocks – probably top timbers – were preserved on the starboard side of the Arade 1 shipwreck. These were between 14 and 17 cm sided. It is impossible to know their moulded dimensions, since none was preserved over a length more than 25 cm or to its original thickness. The best-preserved – Ap6 – was preserved to a maximum of 9 cm high, surely less than its full original maximum moulded dimension.

Four strakes of ceiling planking were preserved on the port side. In the centre, between the four ceiling strakes and the keel axis, there were four, small loose ceiling planks, levelled by means of wedges, also not fastened, between the ceiling and the floor timbers. All ceiling planks were 6 cm thick and had a maximum width of 28 to 29 cm. Their average lengths cannot be estimated, because none was preserved in its entirety. The longest – TN4 – was preserved for 3.60 m. composed of two planks each, scarfed together with flat, horizontal scarfs originally around 40 cm long.

There was no apparent fastening pattern. Some planks were fastened to the frames with small nails whose heads had long eroded away. This may suggest either some kind of provisional fastening, or the nailing of some kind of matting over the ceiling planking. This matting was photographed in 1970 and was still preserved in an iron concretion of one of the nail heads.

The ceiling planking was sealed above the upper strake by a number of small independent filler pieces wedged between the first futtocks. A small and well carved piece

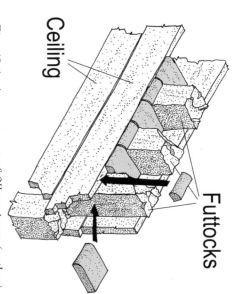

Fig. 49.4. Arrangement of filler pieces (author).

of wood was nailed to the inner face of these futtocks, lending continuity to this line of fillers (Fig. 49.4). In some of the 1970 pictures it looked like there was a continuous strake notched over the futtocks instead of these small timbers.

The hull planking was 4.5 cm thick and extended over a width of over two meters to the north (starboard side), forming seven continuous strakes with one stealer between strakes 5 and 6. To port, only two strakes were preserved. It is not possible to reconstruct the hull planking from the data collected in the 2002 summer season alone. Too many doubts remain. It looks, however, like there were seven fair runs of planking, all showing a maximum width of 37 or 38 cm, tapering gently towards the presumed bow. On each strake the planks were connected through flat scarves.

At this phase of the work there is very little information on the nature of the fastenings and fastening patterns. Both small iron nails, with square shanks about 4 x 4 mm in section, and treenails about 2.5 to 3 cm in diameter were found, as well as iron bolts around 2.8 cm in diameter. The keel scarves may have been fastened with iron nails, since remains of iron concretions were spotted on the lateral surfaces of the keel, in the supposed connection of the keel to the stem post. As mentioned above, floor timbers were fastened to the keel with one, two, or three treenails. The keel was fastened to the keelson or mast step with iron bolts in at least two places, between floor timbers C10 and C11, and floor timbers C14 and C15. The planking was fastened to the frames with one or two treenails per plank and per frame. The ceiling was also fastened to the frames with treenails, although it is not possible at this stage to say how many treenails were inserted from the outside, through the outer planking and frames, and how many – if any – were inserted from the inside. As mentioned before, it seems that some fore-and-aft treenails went through more than two timbers.

No traces of caulking were found in 2002. Some

timbers showed a white coating on the inside. Its nature is so far unknown.

Hull shape

Although there are enough data to attempt a reconstruction of the hull shape from the profiles taken during the 2002 field season, the effort seems premature at this stage of the project, in view of the amount of data that can still be retrieved after the recovery of the timbers in the 2003 field season.

As it is, the existing data shows that the shipwreck has suffered some deformation probably due to the impact of the dredge that broke its hull in two in 1970. The planking at the bow has fallen out slightly – frame C2 was tilted towards starboard – and the keel must have been severely hit in 1970. In fact, the first striking feature looking at this vessel is that the frames are not perpendicular to the keel.

The sketch made in 1970 could correspond to a section very close to amidships since it shows a fairly flat floor. The data retrieved during the summer of 2002 show a hull shape that is compatible with the sketch but ending – at floor timber C10 – well before the midships frame.

After ignoring stations C1 and C2, which were tilted outwards as a result of damage, the lines drawing of this portion of the hull showed it to be quite fair and compatible with a flat floor amidships of about 1.60 to 2.00 m, as suggested in the 1970 sketch. This suggests that Arade 1's overall dimensions could be around 4 m to 5 m in beam, around 12 to 15 m long, and 2 to 2.5 m of depth in hold. The scantlings seem heavy for a vessel at the lower end of this limit, but fairly normal for a vessel at the other extreme.

Dating the Arade 1 Shipwreck

A sample from the Arade 1 shipwreck was analyzed in the Centro de Investigação em Paleoecologia Humana of the Instituto Português de Arqueologia, and found to be oak (*Quercus faginea* Lam.), known in Portuguese as *carvalho cerquinho*, common in the centre and south of Portugal and Spain, Balearic Islands, Algeria and Morocco.

Three samples were dated with the radiocarbon method at Beta Analytic Inc. and yielded calendar dates of 1530 ±50, 1630 ±40, and 1600 ±40, placing the shipwreck in the second half of the 16th or the first half of the 17th century. These dates are consistent with the presumed dates of the few artefacts found on and around the shipwreck.

Artefacts

The artefact collection found within the 10 x 10 m area defined around the Arade 1 ship is small and quite poor. A cast iron gun, a pewter plate and a copper cauldron were found during the 2001 field season. An olive jar and

three dead-eyes were found during the 2002 field season. A total of 114 artefacts were raised and catalogued, mostly ceramic shards.

One of the most interesting artefacts recovered in 2002 is a concretion containing what is thought to be the bottom of the ship's pump. This concretion is asymmetrical and its lower sides show the imprint of wood grain. Given the fact that the pump sump was uncovered in 2002, carved on the lower portion of the hull, between floor timbers C21 and C22 (Fig. 49.3), it seems that the pump shaft was displaced and its lead bottom involved in an iron concretion. This concretion was formed on the bottom of the hull after the collapse of some of its inner structure, such as a bulkhead or the walls of the pump well.

Three heart blocks and a few pieces of rope were found on the port side of the shipwreck, in Trench 4. This particular type of block – in Portuguese *sapatas trincadas* – is documented in the second half of the 16th century, used for tensioning either the forestay or the shrouds (Nelson 2001: 107).

The gun was not recovered and it is therefore difficult to date. For the time being we can only state that it does not contradict the time frame established through carbon dating (Caruana 1994).

The same thing can be said about the pewter plate. There was a mark although it seemed completely eroded away. Only after conservation will it be possible to say whether or not it can help date this shipwreck more precisely.

The Spanish olive jar is a typical type B, Middle Period (1570–1800), after the classification by Gogin (Gogin 1964, James, Jr. 1988, Marken 1994). It bears a painted inscription on the rim, perhaps "MM," and a mark scratched on the shoulder in the shape of a crescent moon.

A number of round concretions were found around the shipwreck and tentatively identified as barrel hoops that were either part of the ship's cargo, or the crew's victuals (Fig. 49.2). One of the concretions was raised, but it is impossible to know for certain what it is until it is analyzed and X-rayed.

The study of the artefact collection will undoubtedly yield information that can help to identify and date the shipwreck. For now only basic conservation is being undertaken.

Conclusion

It is too early to draw conclusions about the vessel type, where was it coming from, or where it was going. At this stage there is no doubt that shipwreck A1 found in 2001 by the CNANS team is the Arade 1 shipwreck exposed by a dredge in 1970. The species of timber used in its construction – Iberian oak – suggests an Iberian origin for the ship, a suspicion that is reinforced by the individual filler pieces inserted between the futtocks, as well as the presence of a complete Spanish olive jar and many shards of this type of vase.

The few artefacts found in clear association with this shipwreck confirm the period established by radiocarbon dating for the loss of the Arade 1 ship; sometime during the second half of the 16th century and the first half of the 17th century.

The extent of the hull remains and the measure of the flat amidships, around 1.6 m, suggest a maximum beam of around 4 m, an overall length between 12 and 15 m, and a depth in hold around 2.5–3 m.

Should these dimensions, date and origin be confirmed, the Arade 1 vessel would be a rare example of a small 16th- or 17th-century Iberian ship, member of a family of watercraft types virtually unknown to us. In his 1580 *Livro da Fabrica das Naus*, Fernando Oliveira wrote that during his lifetime small ships had changed so much that some types unknown forty years before were common by 1580, and others, common forty years before, were gone and forgotten (Oliveira 1580: 76).

In spite of its probably humble origins and the lack of rare artefacts I have no doubts that its further excavation is well justified in terms of its scientific importance.

References

Alves, F., 1999, Acerca dos destrocos de dois navios descobertos durante as dragagens de 1970 na foz do Rio Arade (Ferragudo, Lagoa). In *As rotas oceanicas, Secs. XV–XVII*. Lisboa.

Alves, F., Machado, C., and Castro, F., 2001, Resultados preliminares da campanha de trabalhos arqueológicos Arade 2001 realizada no âmbito do projecto ProArade. In *Actas do Encontro de Arqueologia do Algarve*, Silves 27–29 September 2001 (in press).

Carrapiço, F. J., Palhinha, J. A., and Brazio, J. M., 1974, *As Muralhas de Portimão. Subsídeos para o Estudo da Historia Local*. Portimão.

Caruana, Adrian B., 1994, *The History of English Sea Ordnance 1523–1875*. Ashley Lodge.

Castro, F., 2002a, *The Arade 1 Ship – 2002 Field Season – Vol. 1 – The Site – ShipLab Report 3*. Unpublished report on file in IPA/CNANS library and in Nautical Archaeological Program Library, Texas A&M University.

Castro, F., 2002b, *The Arade 1 Ship – 2002 Field Season – Vol. 2 – The Hull – ShipLab Report 5*. Unpublished report on file in IPA/CNANS library and in Nautical Archaeological Program Library, Texas A&M University.

Castro, F., 2002c, *The Arade 1 Ship – 2002 Field Season – Vol. 3 – The Artifacts – ShipLab Report 6*. Unpublished report on file in IPA/CNANS library and in Nautical Archaeological Program Library, Texas A&M University.

Coelho, Antonio Borges, 1989, *Portugal na Espanha arabe*. Lisboa.

Gogin, John M., 1964, *Indian and Spanish Selected Writings*. Coral Gables.

James, Jr., Stephen R., 1988, A reassessment of the chronological and typological framework of the Spanish olive jar, *Historical Archaeology* 22.1: 43–66.

Loureiro, A., 1909, *Os Portos Marítimos de Portugal e Ilhas Adjacentes*. Lisboa.

Marken, Mitchell W., 1994, *Pottery from Spanish Shipwrecks 1500–1800*. Miami.

Marques, A. H. de Oliveira, 1993, *Portugal, das invasões romanas à "reconquista"*. Lisboa.

Nelson, A., 2001, *The Tudor Navy 1485–1603*. London.

Oliveira, Fernando, 1580, *O Livro da Fabrica das Naos* (Facsimile, transcription and translation into English published 1991 by Academia de Marinha). Lisboa.

50 A Black Sea merchantman

Kroum N. Batchvarov

Introduction

In the early 1980s Bulgarian archaeologists of the newly-established Centre for Underwater Archaeology at Sozopol discovered the remains of a post-medieval ship in the southern Bay of Kitten, below Cape Urdoviza near the Turkish border. In 1982, 1984 and 1986, Dr. Kalin Porozhanov directed a limited excavation of the site, until the excavation came to an abrupt halt when an Early Bronze Age settlement was discovered beneath the ship. Moreover, the Bronze Age settlement was threatened by the building of a marina on top of it and required immediate archaeological attention. The construction of the marina and the lack of ship specialists in Bulgaria led the excavators to rebury the ship and concentrate their efforts on the settlement. (Porozhanov, 2000: 92–96). The three seasons of excavation, however, yielded some interesting clues to the importance of the ship. Artefacts suggested the wreck dated to the Ottoman Period in Bulgaria (1396–1878). The presence of clay smoking pipes (mostly lost now) pointed to the 17th century or later. Two bronze inkpots implied that there were literate

people aboard the vessel, not a common occurrence among the population in the Ottoman Empire in those days. A piece of pig's hide and a small plaque with St. Andrew crosses incised in it suggested that the ship was in Orthodox Christian hands at the time of its loss.

In 2000 a joint Institute of Nautical Archaeology-Centre for Underwater Archaeology team returned to the wreck to inaugurate a full excavation and recording. Originally it was believed that no more than the bottom of the hull was still extant. Four seasons of excavation proved the initial assumption wrong. Rough bottom sediments covering the wreck and its surroundings, which resembled mortar in its consistency, caused additional problems for the archaeologists and slowed progress significantly, but nearly the entire surviving hull was eventually exposed and documented in detail.

It was believed that during previous work on the site, all notable artefacts had been raised. Again, the assumption proved incorrect. An extensive collection of copper vessels – plates, bowls, cups, pots, a candlestick, and teapot – were found in the stern area. Similarly, the team

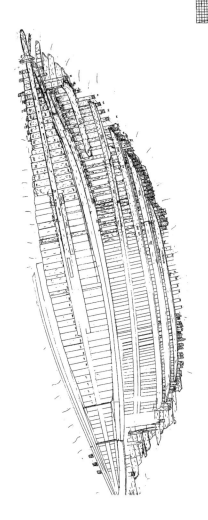

Fig. 50.1. Site sketch of remains of the hull (author).

recorded and raised ceramic jugs with pinched necks, plates and a large quantity of pottery sherds (plates, bowls, jugs, candlesticks). More than a dozen smoking pipes and pieces thereof, wooden spoons, nine brooms, two combs and two inkpots figured among the personal belongings recovered. Two lenses with thin wooden frames may have been part of a navigational instrument. A sounding lead was also retrieved. The finding of a glass incense burner, typical for Eastern Orthodox Christians, strengthens the hypothesis for Christian ownership.

No secure date for the wreck may yet be offered, but based upon the artefact assemblage, a late 18th or even early 19th century date is most probable. This excavation is the first extensive recording of a post-medieval merchantman from the Black Sea.

Description

The extant remains of the ship have a length of 19 m, a width of approximately 5 m and a depth in hold of 2.5 m (Fig. 50.1). The vessel lies heeled 12 degrees to starboard. The port side of the ship is almost completely missing, with only the bottom of the hull approximately up to the wrongheads preserved. The starboard side is much better preserved, nearly up to the height of breadth amidships. The vessel has settled down by the stern. The bow is eroded, but not broken up, while the stern is practically torn to pieces, especially on the port side. Frames are either completely missing, or heavily split and twisted.

Regrettably, the consistency of the bottom sediment prevented us from reaching and recording the keel in detail. It was partially recorded only in the bow, but even there the still extant garboard hid important and interesting details, including the connection with the stem. Nevertheless, indirect evidence suggests that the keel tapered in width from amidships to both ends and had a moulded dimension of more than 30 cm. On the starboard side, two planks from the keel, was found a longitudinal timber, parallel to the keel, with a thickness of 9.6 cm and 14.5 cm in width. The timber is notched to fit over the outer faces of the frames, to which it was fastened with spikes and possibly treenails (one treenail hole was recorded in the extreme forward edge of the timber). The length of the notches averages 21 cm. Remains of an identical timber were also found to port. That timber, however, was badly eroded. These timbers may have supported the lower end of the stem.

The stem is eroded almost down to the level of the keelson, but the remaining part is sufficient to suggest that it was strongly raked forward and had scantlings of 17 cm sided by 27 cm moulded. The rabbet of the stem is 10.5 cm wide by 2.5 cm deep. Interestingly, the stem is simply butted into the keel without a scarf. No trace survives of a knee or apron. Any strengthening of the joint must have come from breasthooks and the above-mentioned timbers on the exterior of the keel. Numerous wales probably added support higher up the side.

The sternpost, a naturally grown knee, survives in better condition than the stem. It has a length of over 2 m and includes the lower part of the post with the lower pintle. It was found torn off the hull and buried under the starboard quarter. The upper part of the sternpost demonstrates damage similar to that suffered by the frames in the stern, but the lower part is in remarkably good condition, affording us the opportunity to record it in some detail. It is certain that the sternpost was not scarfed but simply butted to the keel. The surface of the butt is original and clearly shows the half-round notch left by drilling for a stopwater. The thickness of the timber is almost uniform, varying between 16 and 16.7 cm. The width at the butt end is 15 cm, which implies that the keel tapered in thickness toward the stern (most probably from amidships aft). The depth of throat is 48 cm. The rabbet is cut to 3 cm width and about 2 cm depth. The pintle is now bent out of shape as result of the ripping away of the rudder, but extends to its original length of 2.27 meters. It tapers throughout its length. Two metal cheeks support the pintle on the sides of the sternpost and are held in place by forelock bolts driven from opposite directions. The plates are 3 cm thick by 9 cm wide and are 59 cm long. The two plates are connected with an integral strap of the same material and thickness, which supported the base of the pintle. The pintle lies on top of a long bolt that penetrates the sternpost and extends over 50 cm from the inner edge. Although the end is now broken, it is likely that this too was a forelock bolt. The long pintle proves something of the general shape of the wreck: the ship had a sharp round stern, similar to that of the sixteenth-century Ottoman wreck from Yassiada (Steffy 1994: 137).

On the Kitten shipwreck a bend of timbers consists of a floor, two futtocks and two toptimbers. The scantlings of the timbers vary, but most are 12 cm sided by 11.5 cm moulded at the turn of the bilge and taper slightly up the side. Extremes of the range of scantlings extend from 8 cm to 14 cm for sided, and from 10 cm to 13 cm for moulded dimensions. The floor timbers, including the midships frame, have sharp deadrise and are fairly short – the midships floor timber has a length of around 2.5 meters. There is no deadwood in the bow or in the stern. Instead, the floors are deep, grown Y-shaped timbers. There is evidence that the Y-shaped floor timbers continued on to the stem, thus obviating the need for cant frames. The lower faces of these timbers were cut at an angle and nailed to the stem, so that the futtocks would have been vertical. The few floor timbers that could be observed in detail do not show any limber holes. All timbers within a bend are longitudinally fastened. In the bow, the futtocks simply overlap the floor timbers and are fastened with a single nail. In the central part of the hull, beginning abaft the butt between the stem and the keel, the floor timbers and the futtocks are hook-scarfed in a manner similar to that found on Iberian vessels (Steffy 1994:129–133). The

Fig. 50.4. Keelson, with ends of sister keelsons at top of frame (author).

Fig. 50.2. Foothook scarfs in the wronghead of the floor timbers (author).

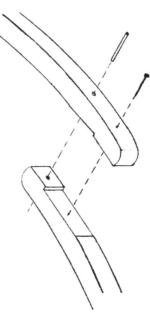

Fig. 50.3. Schematic sketch of foothook scarfs (author).

The fastening system could not have contributed much to the integrity of the hull in this area. The strength must have come from the attachment of the frame to the planking, stringers and wales. As it was impossible to disassemble the keelson, we were unable to determine how the rest of the floor timbers were attached.

The midships frame consists of a floor timber and a pair of futtocks on each side. The floor timber, 20 cm sided, is almost twice the sided dimension of the other floor timbers. The moulded is consistent with the other floor timbers at 13 cm. Futtocks are attached to both the fore and aft sides with foothook scarfs. The futtocks themselves are average in dimensions: 10.5 cm sided by 12.5 cm moulded cm and 9 cm sided by 12 cm moulded. A filler timber is fitted between the futtocks. It does not seem to be longitudinally attached to the futtocks.

Forward of amidships, the toptimbers and floor timbers are in line, with the futtocks on the fore edge of the floor timbers; abaft amidships, the sequence changes, with the futtocks being on the after side of the floor timbers. The toptimbers overlap the futtocks and are nailed to them. In a number of places, the futtocks of the adjacent bends had to be notched deeply to provide a clear path for driving the nails. This suggests that the toptimbers were installed

closest parallel for the scarfs, however, are those found on the sixteenth-century vessel from Yassiada (Cemal Pulak, pers. comm.; Steffy 1994:137). The hook scarfs are about 20–30 cm long with a depth of the hook of 2 cm. Each joint is fastened with a nail and a treenail, with no observable pattern to their distribution (Figs 50.2 and 50.3). Towards the stern the scarfing of futtocks and floors changes again. In the stern the futtocks are slightly notched for the floors, but no longer hook-scarfed. It was possible to determine that the bow floor timbers were toe-nailed to the keel with a single nail in the middle, driven through a triangular countersink cut into the floor timber.

after the floor timbers and futtocks were raised on the keel.

The keelson is a single timber, slightly longer than 16 m and tapering in section from 46 cm sided by 19 cm moulded amidships, to 19 cm by 15 cm in the bow (Fig. 50.4). It is even narrower in the stern. It is notched over every floor timber to a depth of about 3 cm and is spiked to the floors with giant staples and occasional bolts. No fastening pattern is identifiable. In comparison with Western shipbuilding traditions, the keelson is less heavily bolted. Amidships, two longitudinal timbers, sister-keelsons, run parallel and adjacent to the keelson to which they are spiked. The timbers are 5.17 m. long (about 1/3 the length of the keelson), 34 cm moulded and 17 cm sided. They, too, like the keelson itself, are notched over the floors to the same depth of 3 cm. The sister-keelsons protrude 16 cm above the upper edge of the keelson. The timbers are supported athwartships by two sets of butt-resses, which lie on top of floor timbers. Their length is 65 cm, thickness of 12–13 cm and width conformable to the shape of the floor timbers. The upper edge is tapered from the sister-keelsons towards the bilge stringers into which they butt.

The bilge stringers consist of three pieces, with the two shorter pieces forming the bow and the stern risings. The third and longest piece extends along the central part of the hull. The three pieces are fitted to each other with long, diagonal scarfs, but we found no evidence of fastenings. The timbers are heavy, 15 cm thick, and are notched over the frames, to which they are spiked. At 15 cm, the stringer is wide enough to cover most of the scarfs of the frames and is heavily enough attached to have successfully defied our attempts to disassemble it. The bilge stringer is partially covered by two thinner, but still massive strakes of footwaling(c. 10 cm thick) extending from about the middle of the stringer outboard.

The surviving part of the starboard side of the vessel has four more stringers fastened to it. They differ in scantlings and form two groups – narrow and thick, or wide and thin. The scantlings of the first group average in dimensions 15 by 8 cm and those of the second 20 by 4 cm. The heavier pieces are occasionally notched over the frames to which they are attached. The stringers are nailed to every frame timber they cross, thus causing serious headache to any archaeologist brave enough to try to disassemble them. The uppermost surviving stringer is thin and as its location coincides with the overlap between the toptimbers and the futtocks; it is likely that another stringer existed, higher up the side, and that this may have been the beam shelf.

In the bow, there is a timber, similar in scantlings to the heavier stringers, which butts into the outer strake of the footwaling and curves towards the stem, which it apparently reached. It is therefore likely to have been a breasthook. The timber is in very poor condition. Another longitudinal timber of 3.5 m length that almost certainly was a breasthook is located halfway between the foot-waling and the first stringer. To the outside of the bilge stringer, in the bow, there is a similarly notched timber of 15 cm thickness or nearly four times the thickness of the planking around it. In the stern, two timbers, sharply angled upwards, were fastened to the frames with spikes, staples and one treenail. Their upper ends are eroded, but likely formed sternhooks or transom timbers. Their lower ends butt into the bilge stringers, but are distinctly separate entities. They, too, are notched over the frames and are spiked to them. Most probably these timbers strengthened the attachment of the stem and sternpost to the hull.

Transverse ceiling, well preserved for the entire length of the ship, covers the bottom up to the turn of the bilge. The sides are covered only by the four sets of stringers. The ceiling planks are the same thickness as the exterior planks (3.5 cm). Notably they are nailed in place, and have their inner edges level with the *upper* edge of the keelson. The inner edges are fastened with nails to ledges nailed to the sides of the keelson. The ledges are 7.5 cm wide and 14 cm thick, resting on top of the floor timbers without being notched for them. The outer edges of the planks are butted into a batten, nailed on the bilge stringer. The inner footwaling edge butts against this batten. Thus the bilge stringer was completely covered by the ceiling and the footwaling planks. The ceiling planks themselves are nailed to the stringer, too. In one of the planks, located between the buttresses, there is a round opening of c 20 cm diameter that most likely housed the foot of a pump. The nailing of the ceiling planks in place makes it impossible to reach the bilges and clean the water route to the pump. Between the futtocks at the turn of the bilge are short boards, which cover the wrongheads and are dovetailed into the outermost strake of the footwaling, thus completely sealing off the bottom of the vessel from the hold. This arrangement is very similar to the one recorded on the Cattewater wreck (Redknap 1984: fig. 54, Steffy 1994:133).

Between the sister-keelsons is located the only sur-viving maststep. Taking into account its position and the length of the vessel remains, it is almost certain that the ship had only one mast. The maststep mortise is cut through the keelson, spans three floors and has a length of 70 cm and width of 20 cm. No traces of wear associated with the loads that the mast must have carried were found on the keelson around the opening. The excessive length of the opening suggests there must have been a wedging system to hold the mast in position that has not survived. This would explain the lack of wear on the keelson around the maststep. A very close parallel for this maststep is the one found on the Boccalama galley in the Venetian Lagoon (Mauro Bondioli, 2003: pers. com.). Similar maststep arrangements appear to have been used on the Sheikh-al-Sharim wreck and wreck DW2 from Israel (Cheryl Ward 2003: pers. comm.; Yaakov Kahanov 2003: pers. comm.)

Only one, nearly complete deck beam was found. That sole example proved to be very interesting and useful. The extant length is 6.23 m, but it was evidently about a meter longer. One face of the beam is very heavily eroded and no original detail is preserved, but the other side is in much better condition. The better-preserved face at the peak of the camber has a shallow indentation approximately 50 cm wide and less than 2 cm deep. The indentation is better visible at the upper part of the beam than at the lower, which suggests that the pressure causing it was applied at an angle. On both sides of the indentation are preserved deeply cut notches, which probably supported carlings. The notches were observed only on the side of the indentation, but this may be due to poor preservation of the opposite face of the beam. Another notch is cut into the lower face of the beam, in the middle of the indentation. It appears to have been the mortise for the tenon of a stanchion. One end of the beam is still preserved completely, although with damage from erosion. The end itself shows remains of a dovetail cut into it. It appears that the beam was secured to a beam clamp through dovetail joints. On the same arm, 1.1 m from the dovetail there is another notch cut into the upper edge of the beam. Likely, it was the bed for another carling, which also was dovetail-jointed. The other arm is broken precisely at the notch. Based on the symmetry of the beam, it can be estimated that the original length was around 7.25 m. The location of the beam and its purpose can also be reconstructed from the position of the stanchion notch on the keelson. As only one such notch was found on the keelson, it is likely that the corresponding notch on the beam was directly above it. The indentation is most likely to have been caused by pressure from the mast, and the two carlings around it would have formed the sides of the mast partners.

Thanks to this find, it is possible to come up with a very accurate estimate of the beam for the vessel – about 7.5 m. The recorded hull section at the notch in the keelson and the length of the beam permit us to estimate the hull depth as 3–3.5 m at this point. The position of the maststep and the reconstructed depth in hold at this location will also allow us to measure the rake of the mast and may help us to identify the rig and type of the vessel.

Within the time and funding constraints under which the archaeological team operated, it was impossible to uncover the preserved exterior of the wreck. Yet, it was possible to obtain some information about the external planking. Planks vary in width between 19 and 21.5 cm, with most being 21 cm wide. Thickness is almost uniform at 3.5 cm It was possible to identify at least three sets of wales. The wale strakes consist of two heavier, outward protruding strakes separated by a single thinner strake the thickness of a normal plank. Their dimensions from the lower to upper ones are as follows: 6 cm thick by 13 cm wide, followed by a normal plank and a 7 cm by 15 cm wale; 5.5 cm by 11.5 cm wale followed by an almost normal plank, which is narrower than average (16 cm) and then a 5.5 by 13 cm wale. The third set consists of two 6.5 cm by 13 cm wales, separated by a normal thickness, but narrow plank.

All planks are fastened with two nails per frame. No treenails were observed. Under the starboard quarter and below the waterline of the ship, we found a repair to one of the planks: a piece was cut out and replaced with a dutchman/graving piece.

Preliminary Conclusions

For the region, the vessel is large and likely displaced over 100 tons. The quality of the workmanship evident in the carefully finished timbers and tight joinery imply the ship was built in a professional shipyard that followed longstanding traditions. The regular framing, nearly uniform scantlings (especially of the planking) and clear fastening pattern of most timbers suggest the work of a master shipwright who had experience building similar vessels. The pre-assembly of floors and futtocks is evidence for a system of controlling the shape of the hull through some form of whole moulding, rather than building by eye.

The ship is built almost completely of oak. Some remains of softwoods were also uncovered in the first two seasons, but they were so poorly preserved that it was impossible to gather samples suitable for identification. It is probable that they were remains of a deck. Among the well-preserved oak parts of the hull it is possible to establish that timbers were carefully worked. None show any bark or even much sapwood. This confirms that they were cut from large baulks. The large grown Y-shaped floors in the bow and stern, the massive breasthooks (?) and the overall quality of the timber are evidence that the shipwright did not suffer from any shortage of quality material. As the vessel is almost entirely iron-fastened, it is natural to conclude that iron was plentiful and cheap. In the Ottoman period, these conditions – availability of timber and iron – existed in the territories of present-day Bulgaria. The Bulgarian town Samokov, located in the southwestern part of the country, was the principle supplier of iron within the Ottoman Empire. The Strandja Mountain chain, which reaches the southern coast of Bulgaria in the vicinity of Kitten was known for its export of timber and charcoal. At this stage of the research, it is too early to conclude that the ship was locally built, but it is at least very likely.

During the four seasons of work in the southern bay of Kitten, it was possible to confirm the reports of Bulgarian colleagues that at least five more ships lie around the wreck that was excavated. Usually the ships are almost completely covered by bottom sediment, but in 2001 a storm uncovered a double-ended ship of apparently identical construction to the one under study. This vessel was significantly better preserved with some decking still in place. Its extant overall length was found to be more than 27 m. The other wrecks have suffered more damage, but the scantlings of the visible timbers are generally heavier than those of the ship under study. This implies that despite popular belief to the contrary (for example,

Shterionov 2001), large ships were probably built and certainly operated along the coast. The carefully planned construction of the ship and the quality workmanship suggest that larger ships were not all that rare. The number of large shipwrecks found in the small bay of Kitten already supports that. The main exports of the Bulgarian territories were destined for the capital of the Ottoman Empire, Istanbul, and primarily consisted of bulky, low-value commodities like grain, hides, honey, timber, bulk iron, charcoal. This type of low-paying, but bulky cargoes requires large ships. The obvious implication is that economic conditions on the western Black Sea coast necessitated the existence of large cargo carriers. If the capital for their building was made available, the importance of seafaring for the local population must have been significant which points towards the existence of a vigorous maritime economy. The excavation of this wreck is thus poised to change some notions (see for example Tonev 1995) about the existing conditions on the Bulgarian Black Sea coast in the later centuries of the Ottoman Empire.

Acknowledgements

The excavation was made possible by the generous support of RPM Nautical Foundation, the National Geographic Council for Exploration, the late Mr. Harry Kahn II, Mr. and Mrs. Ron Factor and other private individuals. Our sincerest gratitude goes to them.

The support, advice and help of Dr. Kevin Crisman, Dr. Fred Hocker and Dr. John McMannamon were essential. Without them there would not have been a project. I would like to recognize the help of Mr. Mark E. Polzer and Mr. Troy Nowak for their work during the first two seasons. Bulgarian graduate students – too many to be listed here – from New Bulgarian University worked hard and had to learn fast: both diving and work under water. I thank them.

Last, but not least I would like to thank my colleague Dr Kalin Porozhanov of the Institute of Thracology for his great contribution to Bulgarian Nautical Archaeology, his steady support during the excavation seasons and generosity of heart.

References

Porozhanov, Kalin, 2000, The Sunken Ship Near Urdoviza: Preliminary Notes. *Archaeologia Bulgarica* 4.3:92–95.

Redknap, M. 1984, *The Cattewater Wreck*. Bar 131. Oxford.

Shterionov, Shteliyan, 1999, *The Southern (Bulgarian) Black Sea Coast during the National Revival*. Sofia. In Bulgarian.

Steffy, J. Richard, 1994, *Wooden Shipbuilding and the Interpretation of Shipwrecks*. Texas A&M University Press. College Station.

Tonev, Velko, 1995, *The Bulgarian Black Sea Coast during the National Revival*. Sofia. In Bulgarian.

51 Medieval boats from the port of Olbia, Sardinia, Italy

Edoardo Riccardi

During the excavation of a tunnel at the ancient port of Olbia, on the northeast coast of Sardinia, remains of twenty-four ancient boats were found in 1999 and recovered in 2000–2001. The excavation was directed by Dr Rubens D'Oriano, Dr Giovanna Pietra and Dr Giuseppe Pisanu and the author.

The wrecks belong to three different periods: 1st century AD, 5th century AD and 11th–14th century AD. An area in which were found many tools and only partially worked beams, was identified as a shipyard.

Ten of the 5th century wrecks belong to a fleet of cargo boats sunk as a result of human action, probably a Vandal raid. The remains of the sinking of the fleet of the 5th century were not removed after the disaster and this obstruction substantially reduced access to the port area. The archaeological evidence testifies to the subsequent decline and decay into which Olbia fell for several centuries, until Sardinia was divided into four realms – the Giudicati. The Giudicato of Gallura had strong ties with Pisa and in a later document it is reported that "Terranova (the ancient name of Olbia), has the port

towards the west that was filled in by the Pisani". In the tunnel area, very few ceramic fragments dating from the 6th to the 10th century have been found, thus showing only a sporadic use of the port during this period. Subsequently, as a result of an act of reclamation undertaken by the Pisans to make the stretch of water in front of the town operational again, a square was created that filled in the shallows obstructed by the old shipwrecks until a sufficient depth was reached. This was used as a framework for piers, and some old boats were fixed to the bottom with stakes and filled with gravel and stones to form a base. Of the remains of six medieval wrecks discovered, three were most certainly sunk for this purpose.

Given the urgency of the excavation, the wrecks were dismantled and recovered before final cleaning. Recording will be undertaken in the laboratory before the conservation process begins. This report therefore is limited to a simple description of the data gathered in the excavation phase.

WRECK C (Fig. 51.1)

Wreck C discovered during the July 1999 season, is believed to be a fragment of a sewn vessel. The only plank visible had unusual indentations on the visible plank face and a hole passing from the head of the indentation to the centre of the thickness of the same plank. During the excavation it was ascertained that the plank in question was broken and no corresponding part has subsequently been found. It is possible that the sewn plank or seam was a repair or belonged to the upper part of the hull. The possible association of the wreck with ceramics dating from the 12th and 14th century, the radiocarbon dating of the keel to 1020–1155, and the position of the plank lying outside the row of pales, permits us to suppose that it was sunk independently of the reclamation of the port. The boat fragment may have been lost in a fire, as inside the hull, fragments of burnt rope were found and there were also traces of fire on the planks. Remains of the cargo, apparently pyrite and sulphur (analysis still being conducted), whose oxides, set free by time, have partially

Fig. 51.1. Wreck RC (1020 – 1155AD), a skeleton construction associated with 12th – 14th century Pisan and Genoese pottery.

impregnated the wood determining a process of self conservation.

The wreck is conserved for a length of about 6 m and is 1.4 m wide at its maximum point. It is constructed frame-first and fastened with thin iron nails. The frames are 6 x 7 cm, the planking is 15–20 cm wide and 2.5 cm thick, the keel is on average 9.5 cm wide and about 7 cm thick. Wood species have been identified as follows: Keel – *Quercus suber*, Plank 4 – *Alnus* sp., Plank 7 – *Pinus pinaster*.

WRECK 4 (Fig. 51.2)

Wreck 4 probably sank after the reclamation of the port, not far from the end of the pier. There are some traces of fire on the timbers. Radiocarbon analysis of the keel dates it to between 1165 and 1265; a few ceramic fragments of dubious association are datable to the 12th to 14th centuries.

The keel is preserved with a large piece of side and many disconnected disarticulated frames; the whole vessel is in a very bad state of preservation. The keel has a shallow rabbet and the frames are almost entirely disjointed; some have a trapezoidal dovetail joint between the floor timbers and half floors.

Under the wreck lay a stone ball, probably from a catapult. It cannot be discounted that the reason for the sinking could be associated to the siege of Olbia by the Aragonesi, that began in 1323.

Wood species investigation revealed the following: Planks 13, 5, 8, 10, 11 and Frames 12, 17 – *Quercus robur*.

WRECK 5 (Fig. 51.3)

Wreck 5 represents part of the hull of a boat with a flat bottom. The plank-keel is made up of two planks (t.22–t.29). The attachments of the keel and the posts are not preserved. The frames are very thin and placed quite high up in the hull and there are no traces of limber holes.

The wreck was secured to the bottom of the seabed by four pales and flattened by the weight of the stones with which it has been sunk. However, the floor timbers are straight with their ends angled to take the frame and half-floor attachments, further confirming the flat-bottomed nature of the vessel.

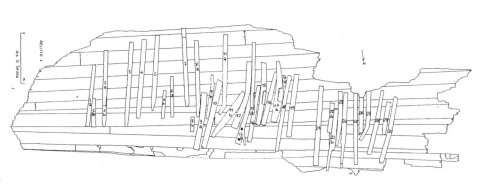

Fig. 51.2. Wreck R4 (1165 – 1265AD), skeleton construction, possibly sunk during the siege of Olbia by the Aragonesi, starting from 1323 AD.

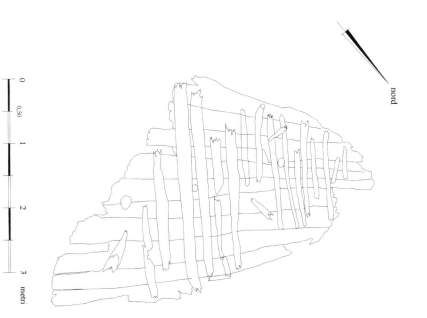

Fig. 51.3. Wreck R5, a flat bottomed boat, as with wrecks R8 and R9, it was reused as part of the base of the piers.

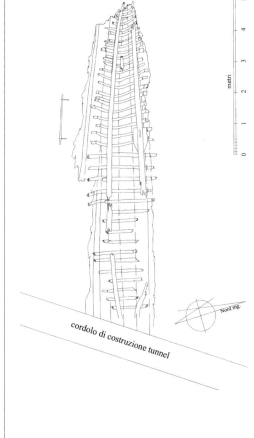

cordolo di costruzione tunnel

Nord mg.

metri

0 1 2 3 4 5

Fig. 51.4. Wreck R8 (895 – 995AD), a long boat, estimated to be 12 m long and 2.5 wide, with a flat bottom.

Wood species investigation results are as follows: Keelson – *Quercus robur*, Plank 18 – *Quercus sp.*

WRECK 8 (Fig. 51.4)

Wreck 8 appears to be the wreck of a boat without a keel but with a plank-keel and a length/beam ratio (about 6:1). The internal longitudinal structure is made up of a keelson with a step for the mast, reinforced by two lateral keelsons. A small piece of the cap with a peg is preserved. The plank-keel is the same thickness as the planking and alongside there are two external reinforcements of 6 x 6 cm, that extend along the entire length of the boat. The sternpost is missing, although a few fragments of the stem remains attached to the plank-keel. The vessel is fastened with iron nails 5 x 5 mm in section. A sample of a frame has been radiocarbon dated to 895–995 AD.

Wreck 8 appears to have been a long, fast vessel, propelled by sails and oars, about 12 m long and 2.5 m wide. The absence of a keel, the presence of two external reinforcements that functioned as anti-roll wings, and the scanty draught, leads us to believe that it may have been a fast vessel used only for journeys within the Gulf of Olbia.

The boat was used as a base for the construction of the pier, as indicated by a thick layer of gravel under the blocks of stone.

Wood species results indicate that: Frame 10 and 30 – *Ulmus*, Frame 31 and the lateral keelson – *Quercus sp.* Sez *Cerris*, Planks 2, 4 and 10 – *Alnus*.

WRECK 9 (Fig. 51.5)

Wreck 9 is the wreck of a small boat without a keel, divided into two parts. The two large pieces were intentionally separated as the traces of a saw indicate. They were lying perpendicular to each other, in the lee of the

paling, with the specific intention of forming a right-angle. They were subsequently filled with stones and evidently used to form the corner of the pier. The vessel was almost flat bottomed with a keel-board/plank-keel which was attached to the posts. A small piece of the stern with a rabbet is preserved. The sternpost has a rabbet and is flanked by two beams of the same section, which curve upward in order to form a round stern.

Radiocarbon analysis provides a date between 985–1030 AD. No wood species have yet been determined.

WRECK 10

Wreck 10 is a small vessel of light skeleton construction and a keel, but with no cargo extant. It has only been possible to observe a small section embedded in the concrete of the wall of the tunnel, which has obviously restricted any further investigation. It was abandoned or it sank at the end of the Middle Ages; radiocarbon analysis suggests a date between 1405–1440.

The measurements that could be taken indicate that the keel is 11 cm wide and 6 cm thick, and rounded on the lower face. It is made of Mediterranean pine. It was joined to a floor timber by a thin, iron nail and a wooden peg. Four frames were visible with a width of 5.5 cm to 7.5 cm and a thickness of 6–7 cm; all were made of *Quercus robur*. There were traces of three planks to the right and two to the left of the keel. The only two detectable ones are 16 cm and 18 cm wide and with a thickness of 2.5 cm. They are also made of *Quercus robur*.

Conclusions

Wrecks 5, 8, and 9 appear to have been used in association with the construction of the base of the reclamation installations. They appear to already have been old and unusable when they were reused in the port reclamation. They have a number of similar construction characteristics

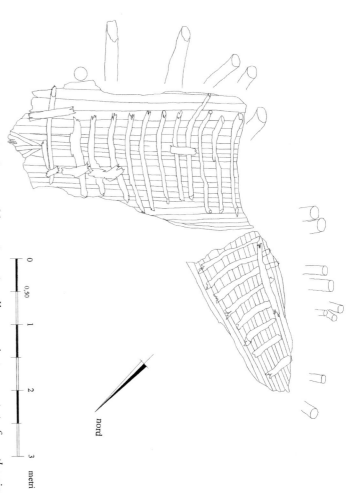

0   0.50   1   2   3

metri

nord

Fig. 51.5. Wreck R9 (985 – 1030AD), a flat bottomed boat, intentionally sawn in two parts to form the right angle base of a pier.

– although of different functions (a long boat and two round boats), the three boats are without a keel and the iron nails used as fastenings are similar. Thus, the nature of their construction and of the seas in the region of northeastern Sardinia, leads us to believe that they were vessels destined for traffic only in the internal Gulf of Olbia. Given the characteristics of this shallow sea, only boats with a minimum draught could (and can) navigate safety. The wood species investigation of samples of the three boats indicates a predominant use of *Quercus* and other woods that were present in the landscape of Olbia

in antiquity (the analysis of all the wood has not yet been completed). Thus, it is likely that the vessels were constructed in the vicinity of Olbia.

Acknowledgements

Translated by Shirley Baker. Botanical analysis: Dendrodata – Verona, Dr. Martinelli and Dr. Pignatelli. Drawings by Virgilio Gavini and Giovanni Sedda. All figures compiled by Virgilio Gavini, Giovanni Sedda and Edoardo Riccardi.